WILLA CATHER

a reference guide

WILLA CATHER

a reference guide

MARILYN ARNOLD

G.K.HALL&CO.

70 LINCOLN STREET, BOSTON, MASS.

Library of Congress Cataloging-in-Publication Data

Arnold, Marilyn, 1935–
  Willa Cather : a reference guide.

  (A Reference guide to literature)
  Includes index.
  1. Cather, Willa, 1873–1947—Bibliography.
I. Title. II. Series.
Z8155.65.A76 1986   016.813'52   86-14277
[PS3505.A87]
ISBN 0-8161-8654-5

This publication is printed on permanent / durable acid-free paper
MANUFACTURED IN THE UNITED STATES OF AMERICA.

To Mildred R. Bennett,
colleague and friend,
for her leadership in
Cather studies and her great generosity of spirit.

Contents

The Author

Marilyn Arnold is professor of English and dean of graduate studies at Brigham Young University. She received a Ph.D. in American literature from the University of Wisconsin at Madison where she was an E.B. Fred Fellow. She has also served as assistant to the president and director of the Center for the Study of Christian Values in Literature at Brigham Young University. The recent recipient of a Karl G. Maeser Research Award, she has published numerous articles on Willa Cather in scholarly journals, and a book titled Willa Cather's Short Fiction (Ohio University Press, 1984). She has also lectured at national Cather seminars in Nebraska and Massachusetts, and presented papers on Cather at many professional conferences. Her publications include articles on a variety of other American writers, notably Eudora Welty and Flannery O'Connor.

Preface

There will probably never be a truly comprehensive bibliography of the secondary materials relating to Willa Cather and her work. This book was begun in an effort to find as many of the existing pieces as was humanly possible. Three years into the work, however, made it clear that there are indeed limitations to human possibilities. There is simply an immense amount of material about Cather, and there is probably no way of discovering all of it. Even as late as the days of final manuscript editing, heretofore unknown items were still turning up. Thus, it became clear that the best that could be hoped for would be the identification in one volume of nearly all of the major pieces of published Cather criticism and a healthy representation of the rest.

Every known bibliography listing Cather criticism was consulted. She appears in virtually all of the standard bibliographies of twentieth-century American writers, and in a number of "specialty" bibliographies as well--such works as those treating only women writers or feminist issues, or those listing western (or even southern) writers or regional writers, or those taking psychological approaches to literature. Of particular help were the bibliographies prepared by Phyllis Hutchinson in 1954, published in the Bulletin of the New York Public Library, and by Bernice Slote in 1974, published as an essay in Sixteen Modern American Authors. The latter has been recently updated by James Woodress and was expected to be issued soon after the time of this writing. This guide, however, is the first attempt at something approaching a comprehensive survey of secondary materials on Cather. As such, it addresses what has been a major gap in Cather studies, providing a tool for students and scholars that has long been needed.

In addition to consulting bibliographical reference works, the writer searched bibliographies in academic journals and traced numerous citations in critical texts and documentary notes. Further, the large holdings of materials and bibliographical listings at the Willa Cather Historical Center in Red Cloud, Nebraska, were examined almost item by item. There, in multitudes of scrapbooks and file folders, are hundreds of periodical reviews and other clippings--many of them from personal family papers. Some even bear marginal notes in Cather's handwriting, obviously sent by her back to interested parties in Nebraska. The Center also owns a growing collection of scholarly criticism, including books, dissertations, and articles discussing Cather and her work. Thanks to the efforts of Mildred R. Bennett, founder of the Willa Cather Pioneer Memorial and Educational Foundation, and of what is now the Historical Center operated by the Nebraska State Historical Society, the process was begun of collecting and preserving materials that might have been lost or remained in attics, storage rooms, and private holdings. Archivists there assisted this writer tirelessly, not only on her several visits to Red Cloud, but on countless occasions by telephone and mail.

Still another rich source of materials and bibliography is the special collection of the papers of Virginia Faulkner, who was for many years editor of the University of Nebraska Press, and of Bernice Slote, who was regarded by many as the foremost Cather scholar in the world. The work of these two women in getting Cather's uncollected and early writings into print and promoting scholarly study of the whole Cather canon can scarcely be overpraised. Their untimely deaths left much work still in process. This writer, through the gracious generosity of archivists at Love Library on the University of Nebraska campus in Lincoln, was allowed to search through upwards of twenty large cartons of papers left to the library by Faulkner and Slote. There again were found many bibliographical notations, including a number of references to reviews in foreign periodicals, as well as many articles and reviews not listed elsewhere.

One other source of material deserves special mention. Margaret O'Connor, who is currently preparing a book that will reprint hundreds of reviews of Cather's books, generously made available to me manuscript copies of many of the reviews she had collected to date.

In addition to consulting sources mentioned above, the writer scanned the indexes of countless books whose subjects suggested that Cather might be discussed in them. Books on everything from southwestern American fiction to the fictional treatment of war yielded interpretive commentary on Cather. What became clear was that everything that mentioned Cather could not be included in this guide. The following things, therefore, were routinely eliminated: obvious sources of bibliography such as the annual listings in the MLA International Bibliography, American Literary Scholarship, and Western American Literature; entries in standard Who's Who publications; entries in standard reference works such as Encyclopedia Britannica; brief minor entries in biographical reference books; passing mentions of Cather in books and articles, even though these were sometimes included in various listings of Cather bibliography; reviews of secondary materials such as biographies, unless, as was the case with a few, they also offered interpretive commentary on Cather's work; most brief reviews, except those of Cather's earliest books; short, routine newspaper articles, especially those in rather obscure publications or unobtainable through interlibrary loan (unless they had some particular interest, such as an item by George Swetnam in 1960 that was included mainly for its headline, "Bill Cather's Buddy"; portraits of Cather (with one exception) in periodicals that carried only short captions and no discussion; most reviews of special broadcast programs about Cather; most articles reporting activities surrounding Cather observances; items from college newspapers, unless they had special value, such as the report of the Cather address at Bryn Mawr; Cather-inspired poetry, unless it had some topical interest or critical angle; and most textbook anthologies carrying Cather stories. Also missing are foreign articles that the repeated efforts of interlibrary loan staffs could not locate.

Particular effort was made to find Japanese and Swedish criticism of Cather's work, since interest has been higher in those countries than in other foreign countries. Research confirmed the existence of a good many items in those languages, and scattered pieces in other languages as well. When copies could be obtained, they were included. Surprisingly, the French, in spite of Cather's fondness for France, have not written a great deal about her.

The goal here is to represent the range as well as the depth of Cather criticism. Thus a few articles in national sorority and college alumni organs are included, along with pieces from physicians' and architects' journals. Furthermore, it was found that the length of an item was not always an indication of its value. Sometimes a few sentences or paragraphs provided a useful insight and were included in spite of their brevity.

As might be expected, a number of clippings in the scrapbooks and files of the Willa Cather Historical Center and in the Faulkner-Slote collection lack full publication data. Sometimes only page numbers are missing, but often dates and occasionally periodical names are missing as well. Where such data were typed or handwritten on the clippings and there was no reason to question their accuracy, items were entered with no notation; where missing dates could be determined from internal evidence within the articles, those dates were entered in brackets in the listing. At any rate, these items, when judged significant, were included with as much information as could be determined. If publication data could not be ascertained, items were entered with a notation as to where the original clippings, or copies of them, could be found—usually Red Cloud or Lincoln. (Materials in the Faulkner-Slote collection, however, had not been cataloged at the time of this writing; thus, individual items will be very difficult to find until that work is completed.) In some instances, items that could be obtained on microfilm were acquired and the missing data supplied. It was not felt worth the time and expense, however, to order a microfilm copy of a newspaper merely to obtain a page number.

An asterisk (*) next to an entry indicates an unseen item, something listed by a bibliographical source that could not be located through interlibrary loan or other means. In place of the missing annotation, one reliable source for the listing is provided. It should be noted, too, that some journals, such as Bookman and Vogue, have British as well as American publications. When the listing is for the British journal, that fact is noted parenthetically. The absence of a parenthetical notation means the American publication is being cited.

Doctoral dissertations presented a special problem. A number of them are not listed in Dissertation Abstracts International, and some owning university libraries do not circulate their copies. Photocopies or microfilms of dissertations can be purchased, but on a large project such as this cost became prohibitive. When abstracts or other indications of content could be procured, these were included. There are also quite a number of dissertations whose titles suggest that they might include discussion on Cather, but whose descriptions in Dissertation Abstracts International do not mention her specifically. These were not listed unless the presence of Cather material could be verified. A reference to Dissertation Abstracts International at the end of an annotation usually means that the annotation is a condensation of an entry there.

This guide is organized chronologically, beginning with the first entry in 1895 and ending with the last in 1984. Items are entered alphabetically under the year in which they appeared in print. Each entry is numbered according to its alphabetical order in the year of its publication. References to a particular item identify it by a number composed of its year of publication and its assigned number in that year's alphabetical ordering. Thus, the third item listed for 1926 would be identified in a later reference, or in a cross-reference, or in the index, as 1926.3. There are a few items for which dates could not be determined or even estimated. These appear at the end of the listings, after 1984.

Cut-off date for items in this reference guide is the end of 1984. Even then, it is likely that some things published late in 1984 (or dated 1984 but not appearing until 1985) might have been missed, particularly dissertations. Furthermore, a number of significant articles have appeared in the first half of 1985 which are not included here, but will be picked up when at some future time this Cather bibliography is updated. Additionally, at the time of this writing a number of books were forthcoming on Cather. Margaret O'Connor's book collecting Cather reviews has been mentioned; Susan J. Rosowski's book on the romantic elements in Cather's fiction as they vindicate the value of imaginative thought was at press; L. Brent Bohlke was preparing a collection of the published interviews with Cather; Sharon O'Brien was finishing a manuscript that takes a feminist approach to Cather's work; Roger Welsch, a folklorist, was preparing a manuscript called Cather's Kitchens, based on Cather cookbooks he found; Doris Grumbach's biography of Cather was about to be issued; and James Woodress was preparing what the academic world expects to be the definitive biography of Cather.

And now a word about procedural matters. Since the intent of this reference guide was simply to abstract the content of materials included, the annotations are nonevaluative. That is, they do not try to assess the worth or soundness of arguments and interpretations. The index lists all of the names of authors whose critical writing on Cather appears in this volume. It also lists the titles of works by Cather that are discussed and the names of other writers who are mentioned in connection with Cather. In addition, the index contains a variety of subject headings that direct the reader to sources of discussion on such things as theme or character. As was mentioned above, the identifying number for items in the index is the same as that used for cross-referencing. It refers not to the page in this volume, but to the year, and the number within that year, assigned to each item. Thus, the index reference number 1973.14 directs the reader to the fourteenth item listed for the year 1973.

These same identification numbers are used for all cross-referencing. A notation at the end of the eighth item in 1937 that reads "Reprinted: 1972.5" refers the reader to the fifth item listed under 1972, where the notation reads "Reprint of 1937.8." If only part of the item is reprinted, a note at the end of its annotation will read "Reprinted in part: 1972.5." Then item 1972.5 will bear the annotation "Reprinted from 1937.8." Items known to have been revised or reprinted in other publications appear under all pertinent dates and are cross-referenced to each other. Since, however, most annotations for doctoral dissertations were made from abstracts appearing in Dissertation Abstracts International, it was not possible to tell whether or not subsequent articles by the same author were revised from portions of theses. Books produced as revisions of theses, however, are identified as such.

It should be noted also that there are a number of apparent inconsistencies in these entries. For example, over the years publishers' names change, and the names of newspapers and their magazine supplements change. What one writer calls the Middle West, another calls the Midwest or the Middlewest. What one writes as Vergil, another writes as Virgil. These annotations use the form that is consistent with each individual source.

One additional matter. There have been several special Cather issues of journals. In such cases, all articles have been listed separately, with no entry for the issue itself. If a special issue editor is named and provides the introduction for that issue, however, the introduction is listed as a separate entry under the name of the special issue editor.

A few further acknowledgments are in order here. The services of people connected with Love Library at the University of Nebraska have been mentioned already, as have those of the Willa Cather Historical Center in Red Cloud. Specific tribute must be paid, however, to several Red Cloud people. Anne Billesbach, Center archivist, and her associate, Sue Fintel, gave unstintingly of their time and energy in tracking and procuring materials for me. They also made working space for me whenever I went to Red Cloud. Viola Borton, president of the Willa Cather Pioneer Memorial and Educational Foundation, and her staff supported this project in a multitude of ways. Mildred Bennett, who established the Cather Foundation and is now president of its Board of Governors, gave much personal as well as professional help. Brigham Young University administration, College of Humanities, and English Department, provided research time, funds, graduate assistants, and typists. And had it not been for the support of Sterling Albrecht, director of BYU's Lee Library, where staff, research facilities, and interlibrary loan services were at my disposal, the research necessary for this project could not have been done. There are others, too numerous to mention--my colleagues in Cather studies all across the country, who gladly and swiftly responded to requests for article copies and help of various kinds. Special thanks go to Helen Cather Southwick who went the extra many miles in tracking difficult to find Pittsburgh sources for me, and to John Murphy, who gave counsel and material support in a multitude of ways. Deserving mention, too, though they are not named individually, are the several people who provided translations of foreign language items. Jennifer Winnerborn merits particular thanks for the hours she spent in Sweden doing research and translating her findings. Finally, and perhaps most deserving of recognition for their contribution, are the four graduate students and the typist, who, over the course of three years, gave immeasurable assistance on successive phases of the task: Pauline Mortensen and Bonnie Quesada worked on the project in its earlier phases; Miriam Pierce brought it along through the year of "burial in the material," and Marianne Sorensen very nearly devoted her life to it in the closing months. Others gave dedicated labor to preparation and checking of the indexes-- Denise Wood, Debra Thornton, and Chris Tolman. And laboring endlessly and cheerfully at computer and printer, Lynda Schaelling, supervisor of the BYU English Department's word-processing center, typed the manuscript and saw it through many sets of additions and revisions.

Introduction

The purpose of such an introduction as this is generally to discuss the evolution over the years of critical responses to the writer
under consideration. In the case of Cather, however, that task has
already been admirably accomplished by John J. Murphy in his recent
collection, Critical Essays on Willa Cather (G.K. Hall, 1984).
Murphy's introduction, written with Kevin Synnott, traces the evolution of Cather criticism so carefully and in such detail that to do
more than sketch broad outlines here would create unnecessary redun-
dancy. What is said by way of introduction, therefore, will be more
in the manner of informal observations about various aspects of the
criticism.

To begin with, there is much to be gleaned from the annotations
in this volume in addition to conventional critical responses to
Cather's work. For instance, these materials offer much in the way
of indirect biography, noting as they do various newspaper accounts
of Cather's activities, including awards received and speeches delivered. They also provide insights into Cather's personality and
opinions in accounts of her interviews and public addresses. Furthermore, the entries in this guide reveal that there are a number of
Cather's letters in print, even though her will forbids such publication. Some of them, of course, appeared before her death, but some
have been printed since, most likely in ignorance of that stipulation.

Like almost any writer of stature, Cather has her admirers and
her detractors. For Fanny Butcher of the Chicago Tribune, who wrote
frequent reviews and articles about Cather, Cather could do no wrong;
for others she could do no right. All in all, however, Cather has
many more admirers than detractors. Her reputation during the 1920s
and well into the 1930s was almost surprisingly secure. Her name
appears at or near the top of several lists of favorite authors,
voted there by both the general public and selected teams of established literary critics. In 1929, for example, a survey of thirty of
America's most prominent critics ranked her as America's best novelist. Edith Wharton was second. Clearly Cather's reputation during
her lifetime was at its peak in the late twenties and early thirties.
Swedish criticism of that period indicates a strong base of support
for her selection as a Nobel Prize winner.

It is also clear that the Cather of legend--wild country girl on
bareback pony dashing about the prairie, rebellious teenager who
adopted a male identity, hard-nosed magazine editor, humorless recluse who loved only the past and shut out everyone but a few close
friends--is not the Cather seen by a great many of her peers. In
fact, judging from the number of interviews she granted and lectures
and speeches she delivered, Cather was a very public person in the
1920s. Furthermore, the content of those lectures and interviews
hardly sustains an image of the serene traditionalist she has often
been characterized to be. She would be better described as a radical
in the profession, speaking energetically against restrictive conventions in the writing of fiction. Freedom was her watchcry.

While many standard biographical accounts of Cather perpetuate
the legends, the dominant picture that emerges from reports of those
who knew her, interviewed her, met her casually, listened to her
speak--through the 1920s and into the 1930s, when Cather was approaching sixty--is of a warm, intelligent, approachable woman with
penetrating eyes and generous nature. She is characterized as a
person who knew her own mind, and who had no interest in literary
circles, luncheons, and recognitions. She was an artist who had a
gift and wanted the time and the privacy to practice it, and then to
be known only for what that gift produced when it was working well.

In addition to Cather's legion of admirers, there are critics
like John H. Randall, III, who, while offering sometimes stimulating
insights into Cather's work, cannot get past his distress over what
he sees to be her serious personality quirks and defects. That distress, and distaste, color his reading of her work, and it takes the
quiet sanity of Brooks Atkinson to remind Randall that creative artists have ever been and forever will be different from the rest of
us--fanatical, eccentric, difficult to understand. Atkinson points
out that both F. Scott Fitzgerald and Sinclair Lewis, contemporaries
of Cather, had more destructive flaws than Cather had. Her supposed
rejection of the world would not have mattered at all to anyone if
she had not had talent.

What is more surprising than the critical disagreement over the
value of Cather's work and the personality that created that work is
the fact that a writer who was held in so much esteem by critics and
peers in the middle part of her career--and whose reputation has
soared in the last decade and a half--could be virtually ignored by
the writers of some important studies in twentieth-century American
literature. For example, Henry Nash Smith does not even mention
Cather in Virgin Land, a study of the sort for which Cather's work
seems especially suited. The same is true for Leo Marx's The Machine
in the Garden. Although most books after 1970 that treat the modern
American novel discuss Cather's work, even as late as 1983 Britisher
Malcolm Bradbury could write a book on The Modern American Novel and
say nothing about Cather. But then, Edith Wharton is granted only
one paragraph in the book and Ellen Glasgow a few scattered mentions.
Later women writers like Carson McCullers, Flannery O'Connor, and
Eudora Welty are named only in a few odd listings, and Katherine Anne
Porter, Joyce Carol Oates, and Anne Tyler are not referred to at all.

Clearly, Bradbury is still seeing the American novel as a masculine phenomenon. Cather's name does not even appear in the index of a book like Joseph Warren Beach's American Fiction 1920-1940. Beach selects eight men for discussion.

A perusal of the contents of this reference guide will reveal an undercurrent of what perhaps every woman writer, like Cather, faces. While many readers and commentators give her the same consideration they give to male writers, a significant number seem to assume that women are not really serious about their writing--at least not the way men are. That women write at all is regarded as remarkable; that their work could ever equal that of men is out of the question. A certain condescension is apparent in the language of criticism in the earlier decades, as if the critic were saying, "Yes, she is very good --for a girl." She is frequently called the best woman novelist of the time, or one of the best women novelists of any time.

It is popularly believed, too, that once Cather left McClure's magazine she had little or no contact with other writers, that she worked in a kind of vacuum, unknown to most of them and unknowing of them as well. But it is obvious from materials cataloged here that Cather was well known among other writers, and highly regarded by some. In a letter to Louis Untermeyer, Robert Frost calls Cather our best novelist, and Wallace Stevens spoke of her as the "best we have." F. Scott Fitzgerald was known to admire her, and his biographers credit Cather with an important influence on his literary technique. Correspondence between Cather and Fitzgerald indicates mutual admiration. Cather also exchanged appreciative letters with Thornton Wilder, and Sinclair Lewis said that she was America's greatest living novelist and should have received the Nobel Prize awarded to him. John Galsworthy liked her work, and the young Truman Capote regarded Cather with something like awe. Still later writers like Eudora Welty and Wallace Stegner have expressed almost unqualified appreciation of her artistry and achievement. There are negative comments by her peers, too, however, such as Hemingway's famous dismissal of One of Ours and its "Catherized" treatment of the war.

Cather's best-known literary attachment was to Sarah Orne Jewett, who became acquainted with Cather when the younger writer was at McClure's. Most biographical entries in reference works echo the conclusions of biographers who take seriously Cather's own statements about Jewett's impact on her writing. In the last months of her life Jewett became an important influence in redirecting Cather's career to the use of materials from her own personal background. Further, Cather was influenced by Jewett's simplicity of manner and the suggestive qualities of her narrative. Before she met Jewett, Cather had admittedly been influenced by Henry James, and tried some fiction patterned after his in its urbanity and psychological thrust.

In the criticism represented here, however, Cather is compared to a wide variety of writers. Critics have seen influences and cross-influences from as diverse a group as Chaucer, Euripides, Defoe, Hawthorne, Twain, Flaubert, Turgenev, Longfellow, Emerson, Poe, Carlyle, D.H. Lawrence, Conrad Richter, Katherine Mansfield, John

Neihardt, Scott Momaday, Ole Rölvaag, and Vardis Fisher, and Canadians Gabrielle Roy, Ethel Wilson, and W.O. Mitchell. Throughout the criticism, though, regardless of to whom Cather is compared, or whether she is attacked or praised, she is considered an accomplished stylist. Occasionally someone sounds a negative note and criticizes her style, but those comments seem oddly out of tune with the general chorus of approval. Sometimes her style is the only thing a critic can find to praise, but praise it he or she does. Cather may be regarded as one who cannot structure a book effectively, or create living characters, or write dialogue, but nearly always she is credited with writing classically pure prose.

It should become apparent to a reader sampling frequently from this guide that, as David Stineback has suggested, the reviews offer some of the most interesting criticism on Cather's work, showing at times a keener understanding than later interpretations that have the benefit (or disadvantage) of much preceding analysis. Nearly all of the early entries here are reviews, of April Twilights and The Troll Garden. Not surprisingly, when the 1923 edition of April Twilights and Other Poems was published, it received much more attention than the first volume; by then Cather was an established writer.

Although Cather received some notice for her achievement in O Pioneers! and The Song of the Lark, it was My Ántonia and the accolades of such influential critics as H.L. Mencken that directed increasing attention her way. In the 1920s, Cather's most productive decade, she was written about a great deal. She published five novels in the six years from 1922 through 1927, and all of them were reviewed widely. In addition to reviews, however, the 1920s produced some isolated instances of very solid criticism of Cather's work as a whole. T.K. Whipple's essay on Cather, for example, appearing first in 1923 and reprinted in 1928 in Spokesmen, remains a hallmark in the field.

In the 1930s Cather still received a great deal of critical attention, though the ripening social conscience of increasingly influential reviewers looked at Death Comes for the Archbishop, Shadows on the Rock, Obscure Destinies, and Lucy Gayheart and pronounced Cather a hopeless nostalgic who could not, or would not, deal with contemporary issues. Clifton Fadiman even dismissed Death Comes for the Archbishop, saying it would not last. There are other unusual assessments in the thirties too. For example, in 1936 Arthur Hobson Quinn writes that he likes Alexander's Bridge, but not O Pioneers! and My Ántonia. W.D. Cobley writes in 1937 that Shadows on the Rock and Lucy Gayheart are his favorites in the Cather canon. The twenties and thirties also produced criticism in the form of parody and fantasy. Christopher Ward created a Claude Wheeler whose chief problem is that while other men are blessed with two collar buttons, he has only one. Later Joseph Reilly imagines that the Japanese have captured Manhattan and are appeased only by America's turning over to them one by one its greatest writers. Cather is saved until last, as America's least dispensable artist, more valuable even than Manhattan. Some criticism of the thirties, mentioning Cather's skill in drawing minor characters, also suggests possibilities for future study.

The volume of criticism diminishes considerably in the 1940s as Cather's writing virtually ceased. The swell of reviews and other criticism that reached 58 items in this guide for 1931, dwindled to nothing in 1945. Numbers pick up again in 1947 as reassessments of her contribution are generated by her death. Cather was seen as a traditionalist in a rapidly changing world who had little to offer a newer generation. Nevertheless, there was in the forties a group of critics who came to her defense, taking issue with those who argued her irrelevance. She was praised by these few faithful for not succumbing to popular trends or to the negativism of her contemporaries, and for her enduring artistry and values.

After the critical slump of the 1940s, interest in Cather began picking up in the 1950s, spurred undoubtedly by the publication of four full-length biographies/remembrances of Cather in the first half of the decade and by the establishment of the Willa Cather Pioneer Memorial and Educational Foundation in Red Cloud, Nebraska, in the second half. Interest continued to grow through the 1960s, and by the time Cather centennial observances began in 1973, it was clear that Cather had achieved a permanent place in the front rank of American letters. As more and more people have written more and more about Cather, however, criticism has turned from the review or the biographical sketch and broad general assessment of earlier years to a narrower and more complex analysis of fewer works. Critics have searched for angles of comparison with other writers, they have traced allusions, they have followed themes through intricate patterns of imagery, they have analyzed structure, and more recently they have done what Leon Edel began doing in the 1950s, explored Cather's own psychology and applied it to her works. In terms of sheer bulk, there are nearly as many items of Cather criticism in the 1970s as in the preceding three decades combined. And the first four years of the 1980s indicate a continuation of that pattern, with 1984 topping all the years that preceded it. There may well be more book-length treatments of Cather published in the 1980s than in all previous years combined.

Many things could be remarked upon in connection with the materials annotated here--the very little criticism on My Mortal Enemy, the singling out of "Coming, Aphrodite!" as Cather's best story up to that time, the use of A Lost Lady as a touchstone against which Cather's other works are judged, and the realization that as far back as the 1930s a few commentators were urging the resurrection of Cather's early journalistic writings. There are other less significant, but no less interesting, things to be learned from a perusal of these listings. For instance, at least a third of Cather's critics who comment on The Song of the Lark misspell Cather's heroine's name, writing Kronberg instead of Kronborg. Further, the confusion over Cather's birthdate, which she herself created by giving it out as 1876 instead of 1873, persists even into reference works in the 1960s, long after biographers had established the correct date. Cather was inconsistent in other matters too. Charles Poore reports that when Cather was asked what work by another she wished she herself had written, she replied, Rudyard Kipling's ballad, "The Mary

Gloster." But Fanny Butcher indicates that Cather's reply when Butcher put a similar question to her was <u>War and Peace</u>.

But, of course, much that is to be learned from the materials annotated here cannot be learned from the annotations, but must be gleaned from the materials themselves. What is hoped is that the annotations here suggest something of what can be obtained by searching out original sources.

Writings by Willa Cather

April Twilights. Boston: Richard G. Badger, 1903.

The Troll Garden. New York: McClure, Phillips & Co., 1905.

Alexander's Bridge. Boston: Houghton Mifflin Co., 1912.

O Pioneers! Boston: Houghton Mifflin Co., 1913.

My Autobiography. Attributed to S.S. McClure. New York: Frederick A. Stokes Co., 1914.

The Song of the Lark. Boston: Houghton Mifflin Co., 1915.

My Ántonia. Boston: Houghton Mifflin Co., 1918.

Youth and Bright Medusa. New York: Alfred A. Knopf, 1920.

One of Ours. New York: Alfred A. Knopf, 1922.

A Lost Lady. New York: Alfred A. Knopf, 1923.

April Twilights and Other Poems. New York: Alfred A. Knopf, 1923.

The Professor's House. New York: Alfred A. Knopf, 1925.

My Mortal Enemy. New York: Alfred A. Knopf, 1926.

Death Comes for the Archbishop. New York: Alfred A. Knopf, 1927.

Shadows on the Rock. New York: Alfred A. Knopf, 1931.

Obscure Destinies. New York: Alfred A. Knopf, 1932.

Lucy Gayheart. New York: Alfred A. Knopf, 1935.

Not Under Forty. New York: Alfred A. Knopf, 1936.

Sapphira and the Slave Girl. Alfred A. Knopf, 1940.

Posthumous Collections

The Old Beauty and Others. New York: Alfred A. Knopf, 1948.

Willa Cather on Writing. New York: Alfred A. Knopf, 1949.

Writings from Willa Cather's Campus Years. Edited by James R.
    Shively. Lincoln: University of Nebraska Press, 1950.

Five Stories. New York: Random House, Vintage Books, 1956.

Willa Cather in Europe. New York: Alfred A. Knopf, 1956.

Early Stories of Willa Cather. Edited by Mildred R. Bennett. New
    York: Dodd, Mead & Co., 1957.

Willa Cather's Collected Short Fiction, 1892-1912. Edited by
    Virginia Faulkner. Lincoln: University of Nebraska Press,
    1965. Rev. ed., 1970.

The Kingdom of Art: Willa Cather's First Principles and Critical
    Statements, 1893-1896. Edited by Bernice Slote. Lincoln:
    University of Nebraska Press, 1966.

The World and the Parish: Willa Cather's Articles and Reviews, 1893-
    1902. Edited by William M. Curtin. Lincoln: University of
    Nebraska Press, 1970.

Uncle Valentine and Other Stories: Willa Cather's Uncollected Short
    Fiction, 1915-1929. Edited by Bernice Slote. Lincoln:
    University of Nebraska Press, 1973.

Writings about Willa Cather, 1895–1984

1895

1   PEATTIE, ELIA [W.]. "Newspaperwomen of Nebraska." In
    Nebraska Editor.
       Explanatory note attached to a reprint of this article
    says it was "written for the Nebraska Editor by Mrs. Ella [sic]
    W. Peattie, Omaha. 1895." No other publication information is
    given. Claims that Cather's work as "associate editor" of the
    weekly Lincoln Courier has made it literarily the "brightest
    paper in Nebraska." Finds Cather's literary and dramatic criti-
    cisms "clever, original, and generally just," and her style
    elegant and full of "honest workmanship." She is the woman in
    Nebraska newspaper work who is destined to achieve a real repu-
    tation. Reprinted: 1923.39.

1896

1   PEATTIE, ELIA [W]. "A Word with the Women." Omaha World-
    Herald, 14 January, p. 8.
       Observes that in the tradition of Hamlin Garland most
    literature about plains life presents its discouraging aspects,
    and Cather's story "On the Divide" is no exception. The story
    is "saga-like," but Cather skillfully refines it.

1901

1   "Changes in the Faculty." Central High School Journal
    (Pittsburgh), [March-April 1901], p. 194.
       Indicates that a Miss Heard, who had taken Belle Wiedman's
    room (see 1959.11), had to be replaced because of ill health,
    and that Cather has been moved into Miss Heard's room where she,
    "an accomplished linguist," would teach "Latin, Algebra and
    Composition."

2   Review of "El Dorado: A Kansas Recessional." Lincoln
    Courier, 22 June.
        Quotes from an article attributed to the Kansas City
    Journal that takes Cather to task for her uncomplimentary
    depiction of the Solomon Valley in the story "El Dorado: A
    Kansas Recessional." She is said to be totally wrong about the
    area. The quoted article concludes with the regret that Cather
    is a woman and, therefore, by the "chivalrous code of western
    Kansas, cannot be killed and scalped."

1902

1   "Changes in Faculty." Central High School Journal (Pitts-
    burgh), [October 1902], p. 13.
        Notes that because Cather had not yet returned from an
    "extended European trip," a fellow teacher from the "Normal
    Department" would fill in for her.

1903

1   "Glimpses of Present Day Poets." Poet Lore 14 (Winter):
    113–15.
        Review of April Twilights refers to Cather's verse as
    "incidental and usually accidental" in contrast to her prose,
    and regards "Grandmither, Think not I Forget" as the best poem
    in the collection.

2   "Minor Verse from Boston." Academy and Literature 65
    (18 July):57–58.
        Review of April Twilights is appreciative of its tender
    and musical qualities. It is not exceptional verse, but neither
    is it silly; and it has moments of originality.

3   "New Books." Nebraska State Journal, 18 May, p. 6.
        Review of April Twilights finds Cather's poems to be dis-
    tinguished by their "quiet charm." They promise a future of
    creative achievement for their author.

4   PAYNE, WILLIAM MORTON. Review of April Twilights. Dial 35
    (16 July):40–41.
        Quotes "Prairie Dawn" as a poem "pretty enough" to merit
    quoting, and notes the quiet tone of Cather's "musings" and her
    "exquisite description."

5   "Recent Poetry: Various Publications of Mr. Richard Badger
    of Boston." New York Times Book Review, 20 June, p. 434.
        Review of April Twilights questions Cather's use of
    "lilting measures" to portray darker themes, but acclaims the
    musical and suggestive qualities of her phrasing. Reprinted:
    1982.60.

6   Review of April Twilights. Bookman 17 (July):542.
    Simply notes publication of a volume of poems by a young
Virginian who has spent considerable time in Nebraska and who
has done newspaper work.

7   Review of April Twilights. Book News 22 (December):541.
    Concludes that Cather's poems run smoothly but have no
distinctive qualities.

8   Review of April Twilights. Boston Evening Transcript,
    12 August, p. 16.
    Claims that the pieces in April Twilights have limited
interest, but singles out "The Night Express" and "The Namesake"
as verses that contain "genuine sentiment."

9   Review of April Twilights. Criterion 4 (October):53.
    Likes "The Tavern" best in the collection, finding in it
"a quaint beauty" reminiscent of some minor but well-known poems
of the seventeenth and eighteenth centuries.

10 SEIBEL, GEORGE. "A Pittsburgh Poet's Volume of Verse."
    Pittsburgh Gazette, 26 April, sec. 2, p. 4.
    Praises April Twilights for its originality and generally
flawless form. Notes a few imperfect rhymes, awkward rhythms,
harsh syllable combinations, and artificial conceits, but finds
that the work as a whole is simple and sensuous. Quotes at
length from the poems and comments on their strengths--restraint,
temperance, feeling for nature, and "haunting melancholy."

11 THOMAS, EDITH M. "Recent Books of Poetry." Critic 43 (July):
    81.
    Review of April Twilights calls Cather a "shy, wistful, and
winsome singer" who puts forth her "maiden effort" with considerable skill.

                              1904

1   PIKE, RAFFORD. Review of April Twilights. Bookman 19
    (April):196.
    Quotes "Prairie Dawn" as an example of Cather's writing
skill, but criticizes her alleged confusion of meanings and her
needless use of an explanatory footnote.

                              1905

1   "By a Pittsburgh Author." Pittsburgh Gazette, 16 April,
    pp. 1-2.
    Review of The Troll Garden. Lauds the collection and sees
in it the influence of Henry James, Paul Bourget, and Guy de
Maupassant, although its style is Cather's own. The stories
have little plot or moral, for their main concern is with character analysis. "Flavia and Her Artists" is the best story; next

is "A Death in the Desert." Identifies the volume's epigraph as being from Charles Kingsley.

2   DuBOIS, BESSIE. "Miss Cather's The Troll Garden." Bookman 21 (August):612–14.
     Attacks The Troll Garden as a collection of "freak stories that are either lurid, hysterical, or unwholesome," and of the Sunday supplement variety. Cather's characters are "mere dummies," except possibly Jim Laird and Paul. Any striking passages are there for their own sake. Cather knows thoroughly the world she writes about in a story like "A Death in the Desert"-- the "selfish, sensual world of song." Further, she defrauds the reader in "Paul's Case" by failing to tell what happens next. If her aim was to say unusual things, she has succeeded.

3   MacARTHUR, JAMES. "Books and Bookmen." Harper's Weekly 49 (May):757.
     Offers high praise for the memorable stories in The Troll Garden. They are "out of the beaten track," revealing truths about persons separated and estranged from their own kind. Moreover, they are written with "dramatic power" and "a distinctive style." Also identifies Charles Kingsley as Cather's title allusion. See 1954.11, for a note about reprints of this review.

4   "Notes on New Novels." Dial 38 (1 June):394.
     Review of The Troll Garden finds the stories both entertaining and thought-provoking, revealing a talent for contrastive design and "close delineation."

5   "Promising Stories." New York Times Book Review, 6 May, p. 303.
     Posits that The Troll Garden shows Cather's talent in embryo. Laments her overly ambitious psychological attitude, but views her as an author of feeling and promise. Sees "Flavia and Her Artists" as probably the best story in the collection.

6   Review of The Troll Garden. Bookman 21 (July):456–57.
     Comments favorably on Cather's use of actual incidents to create fiction.

7   Review of The Troll Garden. Critic 47 (November):476.
     Praises Cather's sincerity, realism, and insight; finds her work promising and eagerly awaits her first novel. "Flavia and Her Artists" is undoubtedly the best story in the collection.

8   Review of The Troll Garden. Independent 58 (29 June):1482–83.
     Finds Cather's style comparable to that of Guy de Maupassant and the Russian writers, but claims that her view of the prairies is one-sided. Like Hamlin Garland, she downplays the hopeful spirit of the pioneers.

9   Review of The Troll Garden. Reader Magazine 6 (September):
      477.
          Calls The Troll Garden a "collection of mood pictures"
    vivified by event and setting. A fine imagination has trans-
    formed life into art in writing that is strong and original.

1906

1   MOSS, MARY. Review of The Troll Garden. Atlantic Monthly 97
      (January):48.
          Compares Cather's style to Edith Wharton's, but finds that
    Cather has deeper feeling and simplicity. Every story is "reason-
    able, probable," yet still fresh. These short, unpretentious
    stories rank at the top of recent American fiction.

1908

1   FORD, MARY K. "Some Recent Women Short-Story Writers."
      Bookman 27 (April):152–53.
          Review of The Troll Garden commends Cather's ability to
    portray a character or a life from the description of a single
    incident. Cather has a "keen perception of emotional value."

1911

1   FIELDS, ANNIE, ed. Letters of Sarah Orne Jewett. Boston:
      Houghton Mifflin Co., Riverside Press, pp. 234–50.
          Contains several Jewett letters written to Cather, includ-
    ing one long and important one in which Jewett urges Cather to
    find her "own quiet centre of life" outside the bustle of office
    work at McClure's magazine. Only that way will her "gifts
    mature."

1912

1   Editorial announcement about "The Bohemian Girl." McClure's
      Magazine 39 (August):54.
          Claims that Cather has "hit upon a great American theme"
    in "The Bohemian Girl," that of racial conflict between foreign
    immigrants in the West who are striving to make their own stan-
    dards and ideals paramount. With extraordinary force Cather has
    presented this intense struggle between races in the heart of
    America.

2   "Explaining Her Novel." New York Evening Sun, [1912]. Un-
      dated periodical clipping in Faulkner-Slote Collection, Uni-
      versity of Nebraska Library, Lincoln.
          Indicates that Cather said of Alexander's Bridge that it
    was not the story of the building of a bridge, but the story of
    a man who "began life as a pagan, a crude force, with little
    respect for anything but youth and work and power." Cather said

she had no particular man in mind in writing the novel. She
simply gave Bartley Alexander characteristics she had seen in
engineers, architects, and inventors.

3   MENCKEN, H.L. "A Visit to a Short Story Factory." Smart Set
      38 (December):156-57.
      Review of Alexander's Bridge finds it imitative of Edith
Wharton, but still a well-crafted novel with believable portraits
of the main characters. Reprinted: 1968.24; 1984.51.

4   "Novels Worth Reading." Outlook 100 (20 April):849.
      Review of Alexander's Bridge prophesies Cather's success
and praises her writing ability.

5   Review of Alexander's Bridge. Athenaeum 12 (31 August):217.
      Calls Alexander's Bridge "psychological" and notes the
force of Cather's writing.

6   Review of Alexander's Bridge. Current Literature 53
      (September):337-38.
      Rehearses some of the critical responses to Alexander's
Bridge and argues for it as a lengthy short story rather than a
novel. Cather is "a realist and a psychologist" with an impressive facility in language. She intended to focus her novel on
character rather than to make it "an industrial exposure."

7   Review of Alexander's Bridge. Independent 73 (4 July):47.
      Finds some feeling in the story, psychologically, and some
effective writing, but regards the novel as somewhat "futile."

8   Review of Alexander's Bridge. Living Age 274 (20 July):192.
      In Alexander's Bridge, Cather exercises restraint while
creating photographic descriptions, and unfolds her powerful
theme subtly.

9   Review of Alexander's Bridge. New York Times Book Review,
      12 May, p. 295.
      Comments on Cather's ability to capture the essence of her
characters with precise prose, and observes descriptive and
dramatic qualities of the novel.

10 Review of Alexander's Bridge. Outlook 101 (8 June):317.
      Depicts the novel as tragic--one man pitted against a
careless fate--and commends Cather for her perception, artistry,
form, and diction. Reprinted: 1982.61.

11 SHERWOOD, MARGARET. "Some Recent Fiction." Atlantic Monthly
      110 (November):683.
      Review of Alexander's Bridge praises its development of
character, clean style, and austere tone.

<u>1913</u>

1   "Books and Authors." <u>Living Age</u> 278 (30 August):576.
    Review of <u>O Pioneers!</u> admires Cather's charity toward
humankind, and her appreciation for unconscious fineness in her
quiet, unpretentious characters. Sarah Orne Jewett's high regard
for Cather is justified.

2   COOPER, FREDERICK TABER. Review of <u>O Pioneers!</u> <u>Bookman</u> 37
    (August):666.
    Enjoys the novel's empathy and its perceptive use of de-
tail, but laments its lack of continuity and its loose organization. Cather fails to develop the one story worth telling, that
of Alexandra's battle to succeed on the land. Reprinted:
1984.18.

3   DELL, FLOYD. "A Good Novel." <u>Chicago Evening Post Literary</u>
    <u>Review</u>, 25 July.
    Speaks of <u>O Pioneers!</u> in highly complimentary terms as a
work of genius, and one of which the American Academy of Arts and
Letters should take notice. It is the most "subtle and artistic"
work of fiction produced in the past year. The narrative is not
unusual, but it strikes one as being somehow true at the very
core, as having a large and simple honesty, a nobleness. Reprinted in part: 1982.21.

4   H., F. "Willa Cather Talks of Work." <u>Philadelphia Record</u>,
    10 August.
    Interview with Cather in New York. Observes that the re-
cently published <u>O Pioneers!</u> shows a strong Whitman influence,
then reports Cather's comments about the necessity for honesty
and simplicity in art. Cather also speaks of what she learned
about honesty from Sarah Orne Jewett and describes her introduction to the prairie, stressing what the old women immigrants
there taught her about life. Reprinted: 1966.8; 1982.29.

5   HARRIS, CELIA. Review of <u>O Pioneers!</u> <u>Lincoln Sunday State</u>
    <u>Journal</u>, 3 August, sec. a, p. 7.
    Moving from "The Bohemian Girl," which is a transition
story dealing with elements from both East and West, Cather wrote
<u>O Pioneers!</u>, a book wholly about immigrants but written in a dis-
tinctly American manner. The character of Alexandra is a refreshing change in an age overly conscious of sex. <u>O Pioneers!</u>
is "at once homely and beautiful and strange." Reprinted:
1972.9.

6   KING, RICHARD. Review of <u>O Pioneers!</u> <u>Tatler</u> (London),
    no. 636 (3 September):284, 286.
    Singles out the book's scenic descriptions for particular
praise, and points to the reality of the characters and their
world. Reprinted in part: 1972.13.

7   "A Novel without a Hero." New York Times Book Review,
     14 September, p. 466.
          Lauds Cather's feel for the land in O Pioneers! The book
     is "American in the best sense of the word," and its central
     female characters symbolize the very essence of femininity.

8   Review of O Pioneers! Athenaeum 2 (September):252.
          Judges Cather's treatment of Emil to be the best aspect of
     the novel, but admires her characterization of Alexandra as well.

9   Review of O Pioneers! Chautauquan 11 (2 August):203.
          Cather's skill and insight in presenting character render
     O Pioneers! valuable in spite of its "slender" plot.

10   Review of O Pioneers! Nation 97 (4 September):210–11.
          Commends Cather's adroit handling of the book's tragedy and
     her ability to treat a large American subject without forcing
     emotion.

11   Review of O Pioneers! New York Herald Tribune, 18 July, p. 8.
          Claims that the drama and substance of O Pioneers!, and its
     realistic interpretation of the middlewestern immigrant pioneers,
     make it an honest account of the world it portrays.

12   Review of O Pioneers! New York Times Book Review, 30 Novem-
     ber, p. 664.
          Asserts that Cather's feeling for the land as a "patient
     and bountiful source of all things," and her use of symbolism,
     give American literature a new direction.

13   Review of O Pioneers! Outlook 104 (2 August):767.
          Regards O Pioneers! as an honest picture of immigrant life
     in the Middle West.

14   Review of O Pioneers! Sewanee Review 21 (October):509–10.
          Calls O Pioneers! a "romance of the modern West," and
     applauds Cather for breaking new ground with considerable skill,
     power, and insight as well as stylistic charm and artistic re-
     serve. The characters are individuals, not just types, and
     Cather presents her feminist theme with subtlety.

15   S., E.U. "O Pioneers! A New Heroine and a New Country
     Appear." Boston Evening Transcript, 16 July, p. 18.
          Applauds Cather's dramatic intensity and her broad, yet
     delicate touch, noting the stamina and courage of her characters
     and her understanding of the middlewestern immigrant.

16   "Trials of the Pioneers Recounted in Novel." Philadelphia
     Record, 9 August.
          Provides plot summary and sees in O Pioneers! a moving
     account of an important aspect of America's development.

17   WOOD, GARDNER W. "Books of the Day." <u>McClure's Magazine</u> 41
     (July):199.
          Review of <u>O Pioneers!</u> describes it as a romantic novel with
     Alexandra Bergson in the role of a "Nebraskan Valkyr."

                              1914

1   AKINS, ZOE. Review of <u>O Pioneers!</u> <u>Reedy's Mirror</u>, 11 Decem-
     ber, p. 6.
          Regards <u>O Pioneers!</u> as "the panorama of a great plain" with
     Alexandra's figure moving tall against the skyline, surrounded by
     lesser and leaning figures. Finds the "Under the Mulberry Tree"
     section exquisitely beautiful, and lying behind the tragedy of
     the young lovers is "the tragedy of the tragedy to Alexandra."
     <u>O Pioneers!</u> is less romantic and less picturesque than "The
     Bohemian Girl," but it is spiritually stronger.

                              1915

1   BOYNTON, H[ENRY] W[ALCOTT]. "The Great Novel Is Only a Dream
     but a Chapter in it is Willa Sibert Cather's <u>The Song of the</u>
     <u>Lark</u>." <u>New York Evening Post</u>, 13 November.
          Presents an overall view of Cather's first three novels.
     Finds <u>O Pioneers!</u> and <u>The Song of the Lark</u> superior to
     <u>Alexander's Bridge</u>, perhaps because their roots are in Cather's
     own life sources. Ranks <u>The Song of the Lark</u> with <u>The Rise of</u>
     <u>Silas Lapham</u> as one of America's important and truly indigenous
     works of fiction, and hence worthy to be included as a chapter
     in the Great American Novel.

2   _____. "Varieties of Realism." <u>Nation</u> 101 (14 October):
     461–62.
          Review of <u>The Song of the Lark</u> finds only positive quali-
     ties in the novel, asserting that its "creative realism" is even
     more penetrating than that of <u>O Pioneers!</u>.

3   COOPER, FREDERICK TABER. Review of <u>The Song of the Lark</u>.
     <u>Bookman</u> 42 (November):323.
          <u>The Song of the Lark</u> is rather casually narrated and lacks
     an imaginative plot, but in it Cather has created a group of very
     real people in a pleasant, observant manner.

4   "The Development of an American Novelist." Boston: Houghton
     Mifflin Co., 12 pp.
          Publisher's promotional pamphlet for Cather's first two
     novels as well as <u>The Song of the Lark</u>, and for Cather as a
     novelist. Provides biographical information and commends
     Cather's originality and penetrating restraint.

5   "Diminuendo." Review of The Song of the Lark. New Republic
      5 (11 December):153-54.
          Regards Cather as a highly gifted writer who does not
      measure up to her imaginative capabilities in The Song of the
      Lark. The story of Thea Kronborg's youthful struggle toward art
      is powerfully presented, but the story of her life as a success-
      ful opera singer is a dull and unfortunate falling off. Re-
      printed: 1984.72.

6   FORD, JAMES L. "Miss Cather's Story of a Prima Donna from the
      Western Desert." New York Herald Tribune, 9 October, p. 8.
          Values The Song of the Lark for its picture of an important
      period in the history of music in America. Although the book is
      overly long, and marred by the long conversations between Fred
      Ottenburg and Doctor Archie, it is full of good characterizations
      and scenes that make it worthwhile reading.

7   G., F.A. "A Woman's Climb from Nebraska to the Stage."
      Boston Evening Transcript, 13 October, p. 22.
          Lauds Cather's precise prose and realistic characteriza-
      tion, and her ability to awaken reader response in The Song of
      the Lark.

8   GUITERMAN, ARTHUR. "Rhymed Reviews: The Song of the Lark."
      Life 66 (28 October):822.
          Presents a lighthearted critique of The Song of the Lark in
      rhyme. Considers the second half of the book to be weaker than
      the first and the heroine less defined. The characterizations of
      Thea Kronborg's mentors are the central interest in the book.

9   HALE, EDWARD E[VERETT, Jr.]. "New Novels." Dial 59
      (25 November):496-97.
          Review of The Song of the Lark finds Cather's method puz-
      zling, for sometimes she explains too much, and sometimes she
      does not explain at all. Nevertheless, the book gives the reader
      something genuine, beautiful, and elusive--a rare kind of expe-
      rience.

10   HARVEY, MARGARET. "Willa Sibert Cather Thanks the West for
      Her Success as a Writer of Stories." Denver Times, 16 August.
          Reports an interview with Cather in which she indicated her
      indebtedness to the West for her materials and inspiration, and
      offered this advice to aspiring writers: write what you know,
      avoid descriptive overstatement, and do not try a subject that is
      beyond your power. Reprinted in part: 1915.12.

11   HOCKETT, ETHEL M. "The Vision of a Successful Fiction
      Writer." Lincoln Daily Star, 24 October.
          Interview with Cather. Focuses on Cather's advice to young
      writers, reporting that she urges them to experience life deeply,
      to be sensitive to language, to avoid imitating their favorite
      writers, and to write about things with which they are familiar.
      Reprinted in part: 1966.10.

12   "Lincoln Girls Who Have Been Successful in Literary Work:
      Willa Sibert Cather." Nebraska State Journal, 24 October,
      sec. b, p. 11.
          Reprinted from 1915.10.

13   "Lost in Colorado Cañon." New York Times, 26 August, p. 20.
          Reports on Cather's injuries and exhaustion after wandering
      through the night in a Colorado canyon because of an inexperienced
      guide.

14   MABIE, HAMILTON WRIGHT. "More New Novels." Outlook 111
      (27 October):525.
          Review of The Song of the Lark questions its excessive
      detail and length, but still regards Cather as a writer of
      ability.

15   Review of The Song of the Lark. Catholic World 102 (December):
      396-97.
          Maintains that the theme and the central character of the
      book are not significant enough, nor is the analysis thorough
      enough for someone of Cather's talent. Nevertheless, it is her
      best work to date and demonstrates her ability to vitalize the
      commonplace.

16   Review of The Song of the Lark. Living Age 287 (27 November):
      576.
          Laments the general weakening effect of the book's occa-
      sional vulgar diction, but finds The Song of the Lark extremely
      interesting.

17   Review of The Song of the Lark. New York Times Book Review,
      31 October, p. 420.
          Classifies the book as "a history rather than a story" and
      admires its clear style, colorful description, and realistic
      characterization. The Song of the Lark is narrated in a
      leisurely fashion, but it is an ambitious piece of fiction.

18   Review of The Song of the Lark. Wisconsin Library Bulletin 11
      (October):329.
          Appreciates the book's vivid detail and natural characters,
      calling it "more finished" than O Pioneers!.

19   "Stories to Taste." Independent 84 (15 November):272.
          Review of The Song of the Lark considers it to be a fine
      work written in an unusual style.

20   STRANATHAN, MAY. "Brilliant Literary Lecture Before Club-
      women." Pittsburgh Dispatch, 10 January.
          Reports mainly on Cather's description of the home of Mrs.
      James T. [Annie] Fields, and on her appreciative assessment of
      Sarah Orne Jewett's art.

21   "Willa Sibert Cather: A Novelist of Striking Powers and
      Author of The Song of the Lark." Unidentified periodical
      clipping [ca. 1915] at Willa Cather Historical Center, Red
      Cloud, Nebraska.
          Presents a biographical sketch, then quotes Cather's com-
      ments on Sarah Orne Jewett's influential advice to her. Praises
      Cather for writing artistic rather than conventional fiction of
      the West.

                              1916

1   GARNETT, EDWARD. "A Gossip on Criticism." Atlantic Monthly
      117 (February):184.
          Singles out Cather for her achievement in O Pioneers!,
      calling it a "delightful" exception to the generally unsatisfying
      products of contemporary American writing and criticism.

2   MENCKEN, H.L. "Cinderella the Nth." Smart Set 48 (January):
      306-7.
          Adjudges The Song of the Lark, a modern Cinderella story
      with no fewer than three Fairy Princes, to be intellectually
      stimulating and appreciates its occasional humor, exciting de-
      tail, and "gentle pity." Reprinted: 1967.34; 1982.43.

3   "New Novels." Times Literary Supplement (London), 20 April,
      p. 188.
          Review of The Song of the Lark considers it to be one of
      the better works in its genre, but feels that it deprives the
      reader of a full picture of Thea Kronborg.

                              1918

1   BOURNE, RANDOLPH. "Morals and Art from the West." Dial 65
      (14 December):557.
          Review of My Ántonia classifies Cather as a member of the
      "brevity school," and praises her candor and her poignantly
      beautiful interpretation of "the spirit of youth." The book has
      spontaneity, charm, and grace. Reprinted: 1984.10. Reprinted
      in part: 1973.8; 1982.13.

2   BOYNTON, HENRY WALCOTT. Review of My Ántonia. Bookman 48
      (December):495.
          Cather's artistry is that of "higher realism" and pure
      style as she creates a memorable and honest portrait of Ántonia.

3   BRUNIUS, AUGUST. "Utlandssvenken som romanfigur" [The Swede
      abroad as a character in a novel]. Idun (Stockholm),
      17 March, p. 2.
          In Swedish. Claims that Cather manages, especially in
      O Pioneers!, to paint very realistic portraits of Swedes. She
      captures both their strengths and their weaknesses. She is an
      artist, not a manufacturer of semireadable fiction.

                              12

4   H., C.L. "Struggles with the Soil." New York Call Magazine,
     3 November, p. 10.
        My Ántonia is a portrayal of the struggle of immigrant
pioneers to survive. Ántonia, an unconventional and stirring
heroine, is no more important than the physical background of the
story in that portrayal.

5   LINDER, OLIVER A. "Writers of Swedish Life in America."
     American Scandinavian Review 6 (May–June):158.
        Observes that Cather pictures her Swedish characters
realistically and does not exaggerate them. She is the only
American writer to have focused on Swedish-Americans.

6   "My Nebraska Ántonia." New York Sun, 6 October, sec. 5, p. 1.
        Commends the autobiographical nature of My Ántonia, the
"perfect portrayal" of pioneer life, and Cather's unconventional
method of storytelling. Cather deals in realities, not realism,
and she achieves believability through having Jim Burden narrate
her book. Reprinted: 1918.10. Reprinted in part: 1973.42.

7   OVERTON, GRANT. "Willa Cather." In The Women Who Make Our
     Novels. New York: Moffat, Yard & Co., pp. 254–66.
        Acclaims each successive novel of Cather's first four as
better than the previous one, though each is very good. Then, in
an effort to find the artist behind the books, Overton quotes at
length from a biographical sketch of Cather, but concludes that
it is from Cather herself--her essays, prefaces, and other published statements--that one learns the secret of her artistry.
She had to return to the West in her imagination, after time had
helped her to achieve emotional distance from it. Her books combine history, biography, and fiction, and are thus greater than
any one of these forms alone. Revised: 1928.12.

8   PEATTIE, ELIA [W]. "Miss Cather Writes Exceptional Novel in
     My Ántonia." Unidentified periodical clipping [Omaha World-
     Herald, 1918] in Faulkner-Slote Collection, University of
     Nebraska Library, Lincoln.
        Finds My Ántonia singularly beautiful and simple, a story
based in the only romance that endures, that of the human soul.

9   Review of My Ántonia. New York Times Book Review, 6 October,
     p. 429.
        Setting is the most important element in My Ántonia. Plow-
ing, planting, and harvesting are described in detail, making the
book a picture of Nebraskan farm life at the time of the earliest
foreign immigrants.

10   Review of My Ántonia. Red Cloud Chief, 10 October.
     Reprint of 1918.6.

11   Review of The Song of the Lark. Booklist 15 (December):107.
        Approves Cather's vivid description of the West, her real-
ism, and her musical feeling, but regrets the cumbersome length
of the novel and the overabundance of dialogue.

12   "Two Portraits." Nation 107 (2 November):523.
         Review of My Ántonia views the book as an unpretentious,
honest account of a part of America, the Middlewest, and the
struggle to survive and live with the land. The novel is not a
love story, but a "portrait of a woman."

1919

1   DAWSON, N.P. "Miss Cather's My Ántonia." Globe and Commer-
      cial Advertiser, 11 January.
         Finds My Ántonia alluring and original, effective in its
combination of realism and romanticism. Cather makes the reader
"see" the prairie through her vivid description.

2   "A Freedom in Her Book." Kansas City Times, 18 March.
         Speculates that the mental and physical freedom provided by
the raw landscape of western Nebraska is responsible for the
realism and vigor of Cather's writing. Quotes from positive
critical responses to My Ántonia and to Cather personally.

3   MENCKEN, H.L. "Mainly Fiction." Smart Set 58 (March):138-41.
         Assesses the state of current fiction and holds Cather up
as a wonderful exception to the general "balderdash." Praises
My Ántonia again as one of the best novels ever written by an
American. Cather perceives the fineness beneath the surface of
the peasant immigrant, and working by indirection and suggestion,
she writes a shapely, honest, intelligent, and moving book.

4   _____. "Sunrise on the Prairie." Smart Set 58 (February):
      143-44.
         Severely attacks William Allen White's latest novel and
praises My Ántonia for being everything that White's book is not.
Cather's work has shown remarkable improvement, and she has become so skilled as a craftsman that her techniques are subtly
unapparent. Her materials take on "an extraordinary reality,"
and her characters show genuine heroism of spirit as she portrays
humanity's "eternal tragedy." Similar to comments in 1920.8.
Reprinted: 1968.25. Reprinted in part: 1967.32.

5   "Paper Dolls or People." Daily News of Business 5, no. 4
      (12 April):1.
         Single sheet flyer published as part of the Chicago Daily
News vows that there is not a single paper doll in My Ántonia.
Cather achieves a "quality of realness" in this novel and its two
predecessors that is rare in literature of the frontier. She
captures the essence of a land and a place where communities are
composed of a working blend of a wide variety of ethnic peoples.
Reprinted: 1973.45.

6   Q., E.S. "En bok on svenskarna i Amerika" [A book about the
      Swedes in America]. Stockholms Dagblad, 20 December, p. 7.
         In Swedish. Praises O Pioneers! for its epic style and
avows that Cather's portrait of Alexandra is genuinely Swedish.

The first part of the novel is superior to the more dramatic last part.

7   Review of My Ántonia. Independent 97 (25 January):131.
     The novel's plot and action are weak, but Cather's excellent style makes the book well worth reading.

8   SELL, HENRY BLACKMAN. "Willa Sibert Cather: To Our Notion the Foremost Woman Novelist." Chicago Daily News, 12 March.
     Refers to Mencken's review of My Ántonia (1919.4), then describes a conversation with Cather about her life and career. Finds her work to have genuine charm.

1920

1   "An Artist in the Short Story." World Tomorrow 3 (November): 351.
     Admires Cather's artistic ability as she presents in Youth and the Bright Medusa the tragedy and disillusionment that often accompany youthful desires for art.

2   B., E.A. Review of Youth and the Bright Medusa. Freeman 2 (1 December):286.
     Asserts that Cather's overriding theme in Youth and the Bright Medusa is the same as that of many of her contemporaries. She insists that the artist cannot develop in an atmosphere of Americanism that is antagonistic or indifferent toward art. The later stories show the progress Cather has made in her fiction. "Coming, Aphrodite!," for example, is an exceptional piece of work. Cather is mistaken, however, in assuming that Europe offers a compatibility with art that America does not. The problem the artist faces is universal; it is not unique to America.

3   "Böcker och författare" [Books and authors]. Dagens nyheter (Stockholm), 18 October, p. 8.
     In Swedish. Centers on O Pioneers! and The Song of the Lark, because they have Swedish main characters. Cather has a true eye for national specifics, and she takes great joy in writing.

4   DOORLY, M.H. Review of Youth and the Bright Medusa. Undated [1920], unidentified periodical clipping in scrapbook II-19 at Willa Cather Historical Center, Red Cloud, Nebraska.
     Observes a brilliant style and sure touch in the stories collected in Youth and the Bright Medusa. Cather finds ways to put feelings into words, to offer insight into the artistic soul that is striving for expression in a sometimes difficult set of circumstances.

5   FLEISCHMAN, ELLA. "Willa Cather, Former Nebraska Girl, Puts
     Prairie in Literature." Omaha World-Herald, 1 February,
     sec. m, p. 1.
          Offers a personal glimpse at Cather, mainly through the
     eyes of three of her "Omaha friends and old schoolmates."
     Evaline Rolofson (Mrs. Harvey Newbranch) remembers vividly a
     "whack on the back greeting" from "Billy" Cather that almost sent
     her through the window, but she also recalls that Cather dressed
     formally to attend the theater. She would not review a drama
     without her white gloves. Dr. A.H. Senter remembers her as a
     popular, "high-spirited, brilliant student." Keene Abbott, then
     drama critic for the Omaha World-Herald, recalls Cather's admira-
     tion for Poe.

*6   G., A.L. "Willa (Sibert) Cather: Hell, Banbrytare!" [O
     Pioneers!]. Dagens Tidning (Stockholm), 3 February.
          In Swedish. Listed in Anderson 1957.1.

7   MENCKEN, H.L. "Chiefly Americans." Smart Set 63 (December):
     139-40.
          Praises Cather for presenting the artist in Youth and the
     Bright Medusa through his or her own perception. Every line of
     Cather's work reveals a "sure-footed and civilized culture," and
     the stories in this collection show her increased ability to draw
     characters and evoke feelings gracefully. Although "Paul's
     Case" and "A Death in the Desert" are a bit maudlin, "Coming,
     Aphrodite!" and "Scandal" are the wholly "competent" work of a
     writer of the "front rank." Reprinted: 1967.35; 1968.26.

8   ____. "Willa Cather." In The Borzoi 1920. Edited by
     Alfred A. Knopf. New York: Alfred A. Knopf, pp. 28-31.
          Similar to 1919.4. Attests that My Ántonia reveals Cather
     to be a novelist of extraordinary abilities. She portrays the
     grand human struggle in that novel, a struggle full of heroism
     and genuine pathos. My Ántonia is the best piece of fiction
     produced by a woman in America.

9   "New Novels." Times Literary Supplement (London), 14 October,
     p. 670.
          Review of Youth and the Bright Medusa describes Cather's
     writing as "picturesque" and "dramatic."

*10 O--DH. "Villa Sibert Cather: Lärksången." Svenska Morgonpost
     (Stockholm), 8 December.
          In Swedish. Review of The Song of the Lark. Listed in
     Anderson, 1957.1.

11   PEARSON, EDMUND LESTER. "Miss Cather's Stories." New York
     Times Book Review, 3 October, p. 24.
          "Coming, Aphrodite!" is the best story in Youth and the
     Bright Medusa, but all show Cather's sympathetic, realistic
     style.

12   ____. "New Books and Old." Weekly Review 3 (13 October):
      314.
          Review of Youth and the Bright Medusa cites Cather as one
      who handles a hackneyed subject--a story about artistic types
      living in the Washington Square vicinity of New York--with such
      skill that the usual generalizations about hackneyed subjects do
      not apply.

13   Review of Youth and the Bright Medusa. Booklist 17 (Decem-
      ber):115.
          Warns that the collection's realism might be distasteful to
      some, but finds Cather's writing skilled and honest.

14   Review of Youth and the Bright Medusa. New York Times Book
      Review, 3 October, p. 24.
          Offers unqualified praise to the collection in general and
      to "Coming, Aphrodite!" in particular. Cather provides imagina-
      tive yet realistic insights.

15   "Short Story Art and Artifice." Nation 111 (25 September):
      352-53.
          In Youth and the Bright Medusa Cather triumphs over pro-
      vincialism, though she occasionally lapses into "magazine
      English." Her stories are solidly structured, and her form is
      disciplined.

16   "Willa Cather, Former Nebraska Girl, Puts Prairie in Litera-
      ture." Omaha World-Herald, 1 February, feature sec., p. 1.
          Affirms that Cather's childhood is the background for her
      novels, and stresses her abilities as a drama and music critic.

17   WILLIAMS, BLANCHE COLTON. "A New Book of Stories." Bookman
      52 (October):169-70.
          The earlier stories in Youth and the Bright Medusa appeal
      to feeling, while the later stories, showing the skill of a
      novelist, stimulate the intellectual and artistic perceptions of
      the reader.

18   WILLIAMS, ORLO. "Paul's Case." Athenaeum (London), no. 4731
      (31 December):890.
          Recognizes in Cather a driving force and predicts that her
      depiction of western America as a stifling cultural desert will
      be the trend for future novelists. Attacks Cather, however, for
      her lack of style and her "dowdy" prose.

1921

1   ABBOTT, KEENE. "My Hymn of Shocking Hate." Omaha World-
     Herald, 23 October, p. 11.
         Notes Cather's upcoming lecture (see reports of it, 1921.6,
     11, 15-16) and says Abbott thinks he despises Cather because she
     wrote My Ántonia and he did not. The book is imperfect--out of

proportion in spots—but it is gloriously informal. It goes by
its own values, and it is fresh, sound, sympathetic, and true.

2   BECHOFER [ROBERTS], CARL ERIC. "Impressions of Recent American Literature." Times Literary Supplement (London), 23 June,
pp. 403-4.
        Identifies Cather as one of the writers of the Midwest who
focus successfully on the non-English elements in America.
Alexander's Bridge is dismissed and O Pioneers! and My Ántonia
are praised. In her work Cather reveals the incongruities of
America's "melting pot" society and its unusual resolution of
those incongruities. Reprinted: 1923.1.

3   CARROLL, LATROBE. "Willa Sibert Cather." Bookman 52 (May):
212-16.
        Reports an interview with Cather in which she tells of her
prairie experiences and her feelings about the midwestern landscape and its immigrant peoples. She also indicates that she
believes a writer acquires her basic materials before the age of
fifteen. She expresses dissatisfaction with most of her early
work, claiming that as a young writer she was too much absorbed
in how one writes. Her two principal interests are the immigrant
pioneer and the artist. This interview contains many of the
statements by Cather that have become bywords in Cather criticism. Reprinted in part: 1982.16.

4   FIELD, FLO. Review of Youth and the Bright Medusa. Double
Dealer 1 (February):73-74.
        Commends Cather's achievement in Youth and the Bright
Medusa, both her simplicity of manner and her capacity to awaken
as well as entertain her readers. Regards "Coming, Aphrodite!"
as the best story in the collection and finds irony, that is,
"tragic humor in the Every Day," in both "The Diamond Mine" and
"The Sculptor's Funeral." Also regards "A Gold Slipper" as a
"delicious fling."

5   [FISHER], DOROTHY CANFIELD. "Some Books of Short Stories."
Yale Review 10 (June):670-71.
        Review of Youth and the Bright Medusa praises Cather's
ability to refine her work over the years without losing any of
her early energy. "Coming, Aphrodite!" and "The Diamond Mine"
are the best stories in the collection. Reprinted: 1982.26.

6   "Flays Nebraska Laws That 'Regulate Personal Life.'" Omaha
World-Herald, 31 October, p. 1.
        Quotes from Cather's address to the Society of Fine Arts at
the Fontenelle Hotel in Omaha where she reportedly decried certain restrictive laws that regulate personal life in Nebraska.
She also suggested that cookery is an art when rightly practiced,
but neither it nor any other worthwhile things benefit from short
cuts. See Mason, 1921.11, and Newbranch, 1921.16, for other
accounts of this address. It was apparently also reported in the
New York Times (see 1921.15), but that account has not been found

and verified. (Issues were checked for 31 October and several
succeeding days.)

7   HACKETT, FRANCIS. "Miss Cather's Short Stories." New
    Republic 25 (19 January):233-34.
        The stories in Youth and the Bright Medusa are well-
    wrought, their essence being "the interplay of character and
    happiness" as Cather scrutinizes the ironies that mark the artis-
    tic temperament. The beginnings of the eight stories show her
    "remarkable magazinecraft" and the progressive skill she devel-
    oped in launching a story. Still, there is a deliberateness, a
    formality, about these stories that keeps them from being
    radiant. Cather seems to withhold something "intimate, essen-
    tial and ultimate."

8   HINMAN, ELEANOR. "Willa Cather, Famous Nebraska Novelist,
    Says Pioneer Mother Held Greatest Appreciation of Art--Raps
    Women Who Devote Themselves to Culture Clubs." Lincoln Sunday
    Star, 6 November, pp. 1, 2.
        Lengthy interview with Cather describes her as she takes a
    walk with her interviewer. Quotes extensively from Cather's
    conversation, stressing her love of life and her insistence on
    seeing the average life as fascinating. According to Cather, she
    does not collect material for writing, but finds it all in her
    childhood experiences. She admits, however, to going west for
    inspiration. Cather explains her methods and intentions in writ-
    ing My Ántonia and insists that art is not luxury but "springs
    out of the very stuff that life is made of." The farmer's wife
    who nourishes a farm and family "contributes more to art than all
    the culture clubs." Such a woman is of the same basic character
    stock as the prima donnas and other women artists Cather has
    known.

9   "Lure of Nebraska Irresistible, Says Noted Authoress." Omaha
    Daily Bee, 29 October, p. 2.
        Centers on Cather's unmitigated love for Nebraska, which
    has been "the happiness and curse" of her life. My Ántonia is
    her masterpiece.

10 MAHONEY, EVA. "How Willa Cather Found Herself." Omaha World-
    Herald Magazine, 27 November, pp. 7, 12.
        Praises Cather for her simplicity and strength, and regards
    her as the spokeswoman for prairie settlers. Relates in bio-
    graphical style Cather's growing realization of her need to write
    of things she knew and loved.

11 MASON, MYRTLE. "Nebraska Scored for Its Many Laws by Willa
    Cather." Omaha Sunday Bee, 30 October, sec. a, p. 5; Omaha
    Daily Bee, 31 October, p. 4.
        Reports an address by Cather to the Omaha Society of Fine
    Arts. Although Cather is reported as having lamented some of
    Nebraska's restrictive laws, such as those that prohibit the
    teaching of foreign languages below the eighth grade, her main
    concern was apparently with things that "retard art," particularly

standardization of thought and behavior. Furthermore, Cather
said, "Art cannot live in an atmosphere of manufactured cheer"
such as typifies the "'Pollyanna schools' of 'grape nuts' optimism.'" Art is best appreciated among "simple, earnest people
who love the natural things." (See also other accounts of this
lecture: 1921.6, 15–16.)

12   MENCKEN, H.L. Letter to "G____." In Letters on Contemporary
     American Authors. Edited by Martin MacCollough. Boston:
     Four Seas Co., pp. 93–97.
     Praises Cather for work that became progressively better
after Alexander's Bridge and reached a zenith with My Ántonia.
That book demonstrates masterfully the two elements contained in
all great fiction, characters that live and content that shows
the strivings of human beings against forces that rule them.
Cather is also a master of technique.

13   "Miss Cather in Lincoln." Interview in Lincoln State Journal,
     2 November, p. 7.
     Quotes statements attributed to Cather in which she speaks
in favor of preserving Nebraska's existing cottonwoods. Reprinted in part: 1972.8.

14   MOULT, THOMAS. "American Authors of To-Day and To-morrow."
     Bookman (London) 40 (August):200–202.
     Applauds the shift in American literature away from the
narrowness of simple optimism or raw brutality, and toward better
self-appraisal. Even though H.L. Mencken probably overpraises
My Ántonia, and "Coming, Aphrodite!" is too much like Katherine
Mansfield's stories, Cather is the most promising of the new
American writers.

15   "Nebraska Novelist Loyal." Unidentified periodical clipping
     [1921] at Willa Cather Historical Center, Red Cloud, Nebraska.
     Apparently a reprint, attributed to the Nebraska State
Journal. Reports on Cather's address to the Omaha Fine Arts
Society (see 1921.6, 11, and 16 for other accounts). Cites from
a New York Times account (unverified--see 1921.6) of the address,
which seems to have focused on Cather's censure of westerners who
try to imitate eastern ways, and of Americans who try to find
short cuts for everything, even cooking. Also notes Cather's
activities and her loyalty to Nebraska, and quotes from other
commentators on her work, including a bit of comical verse from
Preston's Splinters (1921.17).

16   NEWBRANCH, HARVEY. "Every Man a King." Omaha World-Herald,
     1 November.
     Summarizes Cather's Omaha lecture, stressing her argument
that people should be individualists. (See other accounts,
1921.6, 11, 15.) Having traveled through the Midwest, Cather had
observed the small cities trying to imitate New York, and she
condemns the practice. One should never imitate, not even a
great personality, for all imitations are counterfeit, and imi-
tators contribute nothing to progress. Praises Cather for

practicing what she preaches. She is "simply and frankly" herself, and this integrity of mind and soul enables her to produce work that will live.

17 PRESTON, KEITH. "Willa Sibert Cather." In Splinters. New York: George H. Doran, p. 29.
    A humorous bit of verse indicating that Cather has noisy boosters in H.L. Mencken and Sinclair Lewis, but that she is as good as they say she is. Reprinted: 1935.32.

18 "Readers and Writers." Nebraska State Journal, 9 October, sec. b, p. 6.
    Reprint of 1921.20.

19 Review of Youth and the Bright Medusa. Dial 70 (February): 230.
    Stories in the collection provide an excellent analysis of ambition, but the dearth of emotion in the characters will make them seem cold to a reader seeking a story rather than a theme.

20 "A Talk with Miss Cather." Webster County Argus (Red Cloud, Nebr.), 29 September.
    Reports a visit made by Cather to the Webster County Argus and the content of her conversation at the time. Stresses her regard for Red Cloud and her many friends there. Cather indicates that she believes ordinary people had "emotions and experiences" that were "just as interesting" as those of public persons. She also says that in My Ántonia she deliberately painted faithful representations of three Red Cloud people--her grandparents, who appear as the Burdens in the novel, and Mrs. J.L. Miner who appears as Mrs. Harling. Reprinted: 1921.18; 1980.16.

21 "To Live Intensely Is Creed of Willa S. Cather, Authoress." Omaha Daily News, 29 October.
    Quotes Cather as saying that "tremendous output" and "tremendous reserve" are what bring success in a vocation. She expresses gratitude that as a youngster she had no literary ambitions; thus, she was free to love the people and landscape where she grew up without thinking of them as "copy" for future writing enterprises.

22 "A Tribute to Willa Cather." Bladen (Nebr.) Enterprise, 15 April, p. 1.
    Reprints a report from the Nebraska State Journal (date unknown) on a tribute paid to Cather by Sinclair Lewis in an address before the Omaha Society of Fine Arts. He called Cather Nebraska's foremost citizen and predicted that she would be remembered long after William Jennings Bryan and General John J. Pershing are forgotten.

23   Van DOREN, CARL. "Contemporary American Novelists VII. Willa
     Cather." Nation 113 (27 July):92-93.
        Maintains that the characters most interesting to Cather
     are pioneers and artists, and that they are equals in her view.
     Her artists are athletes and have the same vitality as her
     pioneers. Furthermore, both groups are congenial to Cather's
     favorite theme--the struggle of a superior individual to overcome
     the restrictions of circumstance. Revised and expanded:
     1922.34; 1940.20.

24   "Willa Cather Will Speak to Fine Arts Society Today." Omaha
     World-Herald, 29 October.
        Announces Cather's address to be delivered at Omaha's
     Fontenelle Hotel on this date and quotes from her informal re-
     marks of the evening before. According to Cather, she had to
     work hard to pay for college. She says she was paid one dollar
     per night for her newspaper work, but on Sundays received four
     dollars for "four columns of trash." What could "a kid of 19"
     write but trash, she asks.

25   "Willa Siebert [sic] Cather Author of New Volume." Bladen
     (Nebr.) Enterprise, 28 January, p. 1.
        Review of Youth and the Bright Medusa. Attributed to the
     Omaha Bee (date unknown), this apparent reprint praises the work
     of Cather as one of Nebraska's own. Claims that one would expect
     this brilliant style and sure touch of a man, but not of a woman.
     Cather finds a way to express the inexpressible as she depicts
     the struggle of the poetic nature against the ugly aspects of an
     uncomprehending environment.

                                  1922

1   AKINS, ZOE. Review of One of Ours. New York World,
     14 September, p. 11.
        Declares that Cather's version of America's participation
     in World War I is unmatched in historic and artistic value.

2   "America's Literary Stars." Literary Digest, 22 July, p. 28.
        Presents the responses of twenty-nine editors and literary
     critics who were asked to name the writers whom they regarded as
     "the five leading American literary stars." Cather came in
     fourth, behind Joseph Hergesheimer, Eugene O'Neill, and Sherwood
     Anderson.

3   "Bidding the Eagles of the West Fly On." Greensboro (N.C.)
     Daily News, 8 October, sec. 2, p. 8.
        Laments the decline of greatness in America, a sad fact re-
     vealed warmly and simply through fiction in One of Ours.

4   BIRTWELL, LORNA R.F.   "'One of Ours' Again."   Literary Review
      of the New York Evening Post, 25 November, p. 254.
          Attacks the critics of One of Ours, claiming that those who
    do not like the book have their own preconceived notions of what
    it should be. Takes several schools of critics to task as spir-
    itually and emotionally dull, asserting that they completely miss
    the novel's "sustained noble movement" and "vibrant overtones."

5   BOYNTON, HENRY WALCOTT.   "Sweeping the Sky."   Independent 109
      (11 November):279-81.
          Questions the need for books 4 and 5 in One of Ours.
    Cather tells a story well, but she should have ended the novel
    with Claude's departure for France.

6   BRADFORD, GAMALIEL.   Review of One of Ours.   "Atlantic Book-
      shelf."   Atlantic Monthly 130 (November).
          Suggests that the "charm" of One of Ours, like that of
    April Twilights two decades ago, lies in its "sense of mystery
    and . . . beauty." Only now, in this "profound and powerful epic
    of the Great War," the mystery has become darker and deeper. Re-
    printed: 1923.6.

7   BROUN, HEYWOOD.   "It Seems to Me."   New York World, 13 Septem-
      ber, p. 13.
          Review of One of Ours declares that in this rather spirit-
    less novel Cather has taken an idealistic and sentimental view of
    war. She emphasizes the boredom of life in small-town America,
    but fails to show the dull routine also inherent in the conduct
    of war.

8   _____ .   "It Seems to Me."   New York World, 20 September,
      p. 11.
          Further review of One of Ours repeats opinions expressed in
    1922.7, finding Cather's account of war romantic and unrealistic.

9   BRYAN, GEORGE L.   "On One of Ours."   Literary Review of the
      New York Evening Post, 30 September, p. 78.
          Letter to the editor. Ventures to introduce an element of
    analysis in regard to One of Ours that Sinclair Lewis (1922.17)
    did not discuss in his review of the book. The war is presented
    not as Cather would have seen it, but as Claude sees it, and
    hence her account is neither secondhand nor second-rate. Further-
    more, Enid is merely an episode in the novel and was not intended
    to play a major role. Finally, Americans will idealize this war
    as many such things have been idealized, and Cather's picture of
    it will thus become the standard view.

10 "Fiction Recalls Violinist Lost in War."   New York Herald,
      24 December, sec. 8, pp. 4, 12.
          In an interview Cather identifies David Hochstein, a
    violinist killed in World War I, as her model for David Gerhardt
    in One of Ours. She describes her three meetings with him and
    her impressions of him in some detail, noting especially his
    feelings about the war. Reprinted: 1923.27.

11   [FISHER], DOROTHY CANFIELD. "Latest Works of Fiction." New
     York Times Book Review, 10 September, p. 14.
        Review of One of Ours praises Cather for completely losing
the mature, sophisticated writer in the consciousness of a struggling, simple-hearted, but great-souled boy. In One of Ours
Cather has accurately pictured what World War I was for thousands
of idealistic American boys, regardless of what it was for its
observers, its proponents, and its opponents. In Claude Wheeler
Cather has drawn a character who lives in a rich, glowing environment but can find little in that environment to meet the deep
needs of his soul. With the possible exception of David Gerhardt,
Cather's secondary characters are drawn with "savory gusto."
Reprinted: 1984.28.

12   FLEISHER, FLORENCE. "Prophets in Their Own Country: A New
     Tendency in American Fiction." Survey 49 (1 November):192,
     201 passim.
        Calls Cather "our most considerable woman novelist"; she
demonstrates real insight into what is troubling America.

13   G., P. "Story of Nebraska Boy's Revolt Told in Willa
     Cather's New Novel." Omaha Sunday Bee, 17 September.
        One of Ours is not a masterpiece, but it is realistic and
sympathetic. The book reveals Cather's tendency to value European culture over American.

14   HAWTHORNE, HILDEGARDE. "The Season's Books As Christmas
     Gifts." Literary Digest International Book Review, December,
     p. 70.
        Brief review of One of Ours sees "poignant beauty" in the
second half of the book, but regards the first half as stronger.

15   "Hero and Dreamer from Middle West." Springfield Republican,
     29 October, sec. a, p. 7.
        Questions the presence of the war chapters in One of Ours,
suggesting that they are alien to the real story of Claude's
development. Cather effectively combines imagination and realism
as she creates two sets of characters, the idealists and the
"prosaic" realists.

16   HOWARD, SIDNEY. "Miss Cather Goes to War." Bookman 56
     (October):217-18.
        Review of One of Ours. Cather is at her best when portray-
ing the Midwest, especially in My Ántonia, O Pioneers! and the
first part of One of Ours. Unfortunately, the war scenes in One
of Ours take her out of her element. She has a special talent
for choosing detail to show life's subtle shadings.

17   LEWIS, SINCLAIR. "A Hamlet of the Plains." Literary Review
     of the New York Evening Post, 16 September, p. 23.
        Declares that One of Ours is a book that is a must to read
and discuss. It is, however, inferior to Cather's previous
works. The second half of the novel is too contrived and in-
sincere. Reprinted: 1953.16; 1967.29.

18   L[EWISOHN], L[UDVIG]. "A Broken Epic." Nation 115
     (11 October):388.
         Attacks One of Ours for its incomplete and disjointed
     structure, for the fact that Cather lets "the Great War" take
     over and end her book. Nevertheless, applauds its stylistic
     execution.

19   LOVETT, ROBERT MORSS. "Americana." New Republic 32
     (11 October):177-78.
         Review of One of Ours compares it with Kathleen Norris's
     Certain People of Importance and finds that Cather uses the more
     conventional narrative scheme. Cather is perhaps a bit too ob-
     vious in this book, though she presents a true record of Claude
     Wheeler. Cather shows more skill and control in the first half
     of the book where she is dealing with familiar materials.

20   MANLY, JOHN MATTHEWS, and RICKERT, EDITH. Contemporary Ameri-
     can Literature: Bibliographies and Study Outlines. New York:
     Harcourt, Brace & Co., p. 30.
         Presents brief biographical data on Cather, study questions
     about her work, and a short listing of primary and secondary
     bibliography. Cather receives more attention in a revised edi-
     tion, 1929.12.

21   MAVITY, NANCY BARR. "One Soldier to Whom War Remained Bright
     Adventure." San Francisco Chronicle, 24 September, sec. d,
     p. 5.
         Claims that in One of Ours Cather maintains objectivity and
     an impersonal stance. Nevertheless, she identifies with her pro-
     tagonist, and thus allows no irony in depicting him.

22   MENCKEN, H.L. "Portrait of an American Citizen." Smart Set
     69 (October):140-42.
         Regrets that Cather's portrayal of war in the second half of
     One of Ours reads more like a Hollywood production than like the
     work of a novelist who can write beautifully and expertly when
     she deals with what she knows, the "soul of the American farmer-
     folk." The hard-hitting realism of John Dos Passos's Three
     Soldiers makes the second half of One of Ours look very bad in-
     deed, but the Nebraska part of Cather's novel is nearly as good
     as My Ántonia. Reprinted: 1967.33.

23   _____. Prejudices. Third Series. New York: Alfred A.
     Knopf, Borzoi Books, pp. 203-5 passim, 209-11.
         Claims that only in the writing of novels have women
     writers been as accomplished as men, and there they have ex-
     celled. Few American men equal Cather. In My Ántonia, an
     original, unconventional novel, Cather has proved that repre-
     sentation of the actual is not inimical to beauty. Cather does
     not suffer from the "lingering ladyism" that afflicts many women
     novelists.

24   "Minor Characters Well Done in One of Ours." Review of One of
      Ours. Unidentified periodical clipping [1922] in scrapbook
      II-22 at Willa Cather Historical Center, Red Cloud, Nebraska.
        Maintains that Cather is best when she is describing the
prairie folk that she knows well. Thus, her minor characters,
like Nat Wheeler, have more credibility than Claude. In spite of
its shortcomings, One of Ours is an "extraordinarily good book of
the day."

25   MURPHY, DONALD R. Review of One of Ours. Des Moines Register,
      [Autumn 1922].
        Criticizes what he sees as Cather's theme, that war is
justifiable because of what it does for its soldiers. It gets
them out of small towns and into the world. The novel is sentimental and simplistic.

26   PERTINAX. "Fine Work: But Willa Cather is Lacking in Archi-
      tectural Sense." Minneapolis Sun, 5 November, p. 3.
        Finds One of Ours to be of the highest quality in the
first half, but argues that the book is destroyed when Cather
takes Claude Wheeler to a war that is irrelevant to her purposes.

27   PONSONBY, MARION. "Across a Chasm." Literary Review of the
      New York Evening Post, 21 October, p. 138.
        Answers, in a letter to the editor, Sinclair Lewis's ob-
jections to One of Ours (see 1922.17), asserting that Lewis could
never fully comprehend Cather because she works intuitively and
her books are rich with the passion of caring. One of Ours is,
in fact, an epic of caring. Lewis, on the other hand, though he
writes appreciatively of Cather's "more obvious" qualities, lacks
the "intuitional equipment" required for fully understanding her.
He works mainly by clever mental and critical observation, she by
passion and intuition.

28   RASCOE, BURTON. "Mrs. Wharton and Some Others." Shadowland,
      October, pp. 35–36.
        Discusses Edith Wharton and Sinclair Lewis along with
others, but reserves highest praise for Cather who surpasses
Wharton in genius, intensity, and capacity for life. Claude
Wheeler in One of Ours expresses the spiritual concerns and the
aspirations of the American culture.

29   _____. "Prairie Dawn and Willa Cather." New York Tribune,
      10 September, p. 6.
        Views Cather as something of a rebel, but one of the great-
est writers of her time. One of Ours is an impressive novel that
presents the frustrations of a young man caught in a time and
place that allow no expression of his creative energies. His
perplexities are solved ironically by "a frightful miracle, war,"
but this is not a war novel. Claude is spiritual kin to Paul in
"Paul's Case," and is clearly Cather's "pet." Reprinted in
part: 1975.40.

30   SELDES, GILBERT. "Claude Bovary." Dial 73 (October):438-40.
        Attributes the dullness of One of Ours to Cather's absolute
   detachment, but regards the writing itself as honest, intelligent, and dignified. In the second half of the novel Cather is
   so impersonal that she fails to communicate.

31   STAGG, HUNTER. Review of One of Ours. Reviewer 3 (October):
        710-11.
        Admires the presence of Cather's personality in One of
   Ours, a presence that is most noticeable in the first two thirds
   of the book. The last part of the book is "not worthy" of the
   first part.

32   TOWNSEND, R.D. "Among the New Novels." Outlook 132
        (11 October):253.
        Review of One of Ours concludes that although the war
   scenes break the book in half and are not a fitting conclusion to
   Claude's problems, Cather is to be praised for her realism, her
   vivid descriptions of scenes and characters, and her capacity for
   emotion and understanding.

33   "Two Americans." Unidentified periodical clipping [1922] in
        scrapbook II-21 at Willa Cather Historical Center, Red Cloud,
        Nebraska.
        Notes the almost simultaneous appearance of One of Ours and
   Babbitt, and contends that although the two heroes are totally
   different in "mental fibre and temperament," one remembers them
   both, finally, for their "spiritual discontent."

34   Van DOREN, CARL. "Willa Cather." In Contemporary American
        Novelists 1900-1920. New York: Macmillan Co., pp. 113-22.
        A revised and expanded text of 1921.23. Repeats many
   things in the original article, but also notes that Cather
   transcends local colorists in presenting her immigrants locked in
   combat with nature. Further, her literary descent is from New
   England, and for her the chief interest of fiction is character.
   Revised and expanded: 1940.20. Reprinted: 1967.58.

35   WALPOLE, HUGH. "A British Advocate of American Literature."
        Literary Digest 74 (19 August):30-31.
        Reprints and offers comments upon an article published by
   Walpole in the London Daily Mail (date unknown). Walpole ranks
   Cather as second most important of America's new novelists--
   behind Joseph Hergesheimer--and calls My Ántonia one of America's
   greatest novels.

36   WILSON, EDMUND. "Mr. Bell, Miss Cather and Others." Vanity
        Fair 19 (October):26-27.
        Review of One of Ours finds the characters flat and life-
   less and asserts that Cather fails to show the effects of the
   novel's events on the soul of Claude Wheeler. Cather's writing
   is mechanically good, but it is dull. Reprinted: 1952.20;
   1967.62; 1982.85.

<u>1923</u>

1   BECHOFER [ROBERTS], CARL ERIC. <u>The Literary Renaissance in America</u>. London: William Heinemann, pp. 99–104.
      Reprint of 1921.2.

2   BENET, WILLIAM ROSE. "The Voice of the Thrush." <u>Literary Review</u> of the <u>New York Evening Post</u>, 28 July, p. 860.
      Review of <u>April Twilights and Other Poems</u>. Acclaims the lyricism of several poems, but contends that Cather is a better prose writer than a poet.

3   "Big Theme under Common Story in New Cather Book." Unidentified periodical (Autumn, p. 6) clipping in scrapbook II-7 at Willa Cather Historical Center, Red Cloud, Nebraska.
      Review of <u>A Lost Lady</u>. Claims that although Cather writes clear and simple prose, she is inconsistent in her characterization. Marian Forrester's sensitive nature cannot be reconciled with the pleasure she takes in the "gross advances" of Frank Ellinger and Ivy Peters. Furthermore, Cather's portrayal of "unwholesomeness" and adultery is unfortunate.

4   BOYNTON, HENRY WALCOTT. "The Pulitzer Prize Novel, <u>One of Ours</u>." <u>Providence Sunday Journal</u>, 20 May, sec. 5, p. 13.
      Commends the committee's choice of <u>One of Ours</u> for the Pulitzer Prize, but finds the novel to be weakened by its unimpressive hero. This fault stems from Cather's use of a male instead of a female as her main character. Predicts that the novel's heavy war theme will limit its future popularity. Cather is one who successfully combines old-fashioned optimism with modern concerns.

5   _____. Review of <u>A Lost Lady</u>. <u>Independent</u> 111 (27 October): 198–99.
      Points to the similarities between <u>A Lost Lady</u> and <u>My Ántonia</u>, in method of narration and scope of plot. Marian Forrester is a woman at the end of the pioneer era confused by the changes of modern times. <u>A Lost Lady</u> is elegaic, and Marian's character is paradoxical. She is a being both of her time and of all time. More than that, she is the essence of poised femininity and also of sexual abandon.

6   BRADFORD, GAMALIEL. Review of <u>One of Ours</u>. In <u>Fact, Fancy and Opinion: Examples of Present-Day Writing</u>. Edited by Robert M. Gay. Boston: Atlantic Monthly Press, pp. 349–51.
      Reprint of 1922.6.

7   BROUN, HEYWOOD. "It Seems to Me." <u>New York World</u>, 28 September, p. 9.
      <u>A Lost Lady</u> is Cather's best book, succeeding where <u>One of Ours</u> fails. Its length is workable, and it exhibits a sympathetic objectivity that effectively blends romance with realism.

8   BULLETT, GERALD. "America's War Novel." Spectator 131
     (3 November):661.
          Holds that One of Ours is destined to fade away because of
     its lack of literary merit. The book falls apart when it departs
     from Claude's psychological development and fastens instead on
     the war.

9   BUTCHER, FANNY. "Willa Cather's Story of a Lost Lady is
     Lovely, Fragile Work." Chicago Tribune, 15 September, p. 9.
          A Lost Lady combines all that Cather has done before. It
     is a delicate and artful miniature.

10   CANBY, HENRY SEIDEL. "Cytherea." Literary Review of the New
     York Evening Post, 22 September, p. 59.
          Praises A Lost Lady as Cather's "masterpiece," comparing
     Marian Forrester to Cytherea and to similar characters in John
     Galsworthy's Forsyte Saga and D.H. Lawrence's The Lost Girl.
     Like Cytherea, Marian is unexplained by moral laws. In her is
     the Hawthornian mystery in which evil lies at the heart of good
     and corruption feeds life. Sensuousness is at the core of her
     exquisite charm. Reprinted: 1924.3.

11   COLUM, MARY M. "Three Women Novelists." Freeman 7
     (18 April):138-40.
          Charges One of Ours with a scarcity of emotion and
     interest.

12   "Destiny of Miss Cather Prophesied in 1895." Unidentified
     periodical clipping [Omaha, 1923] in scrapbook I-25 at Willa
     Cather Historical Center, Red Cloud, Nebraska.
          Quotes from an early assessment (see Peattie, 1895.1) of
     Cather's potential and announces that a portrait of Cather to be
     hung in the Omaha public library is currently being prepared by
     artist Leon Bakst. Notes that Cather is abroad and that A Lost
     Lady will be off the press in September.

13   EDWARDS, JOHN B. Review of A Lost Lady. Sewanee Review 31
     (October-December):510-11.
          Criticizes Cather's lack of taste--in reporting such in-
     cidents as the blinding of the woodpecker--and lack of morality
     in A Lost Lady. Cather's superb talent deserves more elevating
     subject matter.

14   ELMORE, WILBUR THEODORE. "Criticizes Willa Cather." Nebraska
     State Journal, 19 February, p. 6.
          Prints the text of a Sunday sermon delivered by Elmore in
     which he acknowledges the charm but laments the dearth of imag-
     ination in One of Ours. Principally, however, he refutes
     Cather's negative picture of ministers and missionaries in One
     of Ours by citing numerous examples of illustrious church people
     who have served in and around Lincoln. Reprinted in part:
     1923.15.

15   ____. "The Religion of a Best Seller--One of Ours."
        Baptist, 17 March, pp. 219-20.
            Reprinted from 1923.14.

16   FARRAR, JOHN. "A Triumphant Character." Bookman 58
        (October):200.
            Perceives A Lost Lady to be an "allegorical presentation of
        love in all its phases." Cather's characterization is precise
        and illuminating, and her method can be favorably compared to
        that of Henry James.

17   ____. "Willa Cather: Long an Apprentice, She Is Now a
        Brilliant Technician." Time 2 (10 September):15.
            Links Cather's commendable writing technique in A Lost Lady
        to her reserved, yet positive and forceful, personality. She
        exercises precision of thought and character.

18   FIELD, LOUISE MAUNSELL. Review of One of Ours. Literary
        Digest International Book Review 1 (January):58-59.
            Judges One of Ours to be well-written, though not a great
        novel. It is a tragic book, but the tragedy is felt not so much
        for Claude's sake as for society's unacceptance of an idealistic
        manner of living.

19   FLETCHER, JOHN GOULD. "Three Women Poets." Freeman 7
        (18 July):452.
            Review of April Twilights and Other Poems dismisses the
        bulk of the collection as "simply pretty sentiment," but per-
        ceives honesty and clarity in one poem, "Macon Prairie."

20   ____. "Willa Cather's Poems." Boston Evening Transcript,
        20 June, p. 4.
            Finds some beauty and artistry in April Twilights and Other
        Poems.

21   [FORMAN, HENRY JAMES]. Review of A Lost Lady. New York Times
        Book Review, 30 September, p. 4.
            Classifies A Lost Lady as a romance, written with slow
        moving charm rather than the realism Cather is generally ac-
        claimed for. The characters of Captain and Marian Forrester are
        romantic figures. Reprinted: 1984.30.

22   GORDON, GEORGE. Review of A Lost Lady. Literary Digest
        International Book Review 2 (December):70.
            Describes A Lost Lady as "one of the fine novels of all
        time." With great skill Cather takes a tragic story and tells it
        with irony, sympathy, and beauty.

23   GORE, RUSSELL. Review of A Lost Lady. Detroit News,
        14 October, p. 12.
            A Lost Lady is the culmination, the "flowering," of
        Cather's talent. The book's great vitality makes Marian
        Forrester real and captivating.

24 GORMAN, HERBERT S. "Willa Cather, Novelist of the Middle
     Western Farm." New York Times Book Review, 24 June, p. 5.
        Observes that American writers no longer look through
English eyes, and few have captured the essence of a region, or
blended character with the land, better than Cather. Her books
of the prairie emit a strong sense of life that is absent from
her stories of the East. Although the latter are clever, they
are also psychologically superficial. It is Nebraska that makes
Ántonia Shimerda and Claude Wheeler what they are, and in their
narratives Cather happily weds the novel of the soul with the
novel of character. The land and the person are both of prime
importance; the result of their being linked as Cather links them
is high art.

25 HANEY, JOHN LOUIS. The Story of Our Literature: An Interpre-
     tation of the American Spirit. New York: Charles Scribner's
     Sons, p. 266.
        Commends Cather's style and imagination, calling O
Pioneers! a "thrilling story."

26 HUTCHISON, PERCY A. "Modern Verse Cut Loose from Literary
     Tradition." New York Times Book Review, 13 May, p. 7.
        Review of April Twilights and Other Poems. Analyzes
Cather's poetry, using the guidelines set forth in R.H.
Strachan's book, The Soul of Modern Poetry. Cather's verse in
April Twilights and Other Poems expresses a nostalgic quest for
beauty, which Cather finds in life's commonplaces, but does not
neglect the ugly and evil side of modern life. The harmony
Cather sees is a harmony of beauty.

27 "An Interview with Willa Sibert Cather." Commercial
     Advertiser (Red Cloud, Nebr.), 3 September.
        Reprint of 1922.10.

28 KRUTCH, JOSEPH WOOD. "The Lady As Artist." Nation 117
     (28 November):610.
        Argues that Marian Forrester in A Lost Lady is "lost"
because she has consciously created herself as a lady and then
been untrue to her art. Therefore, her failure is an artistic
one. She put her own happiness above her art instead of sacri-
ficing herself to it as artists must do. Cather is subtle in
this nearly perfect novel. Reprinted: 1967.25; 1982.36.

29 "The Lady Looks About Her." Unidentified periodical clipping
     [1923?], p. 60, in Faulkner-Slote collection at University of
     Nebraska Library, Lincoln.
        Review of A Lost Lady praises Cather's "finished artistry"
and describes an incidental meeting with a very charming and
gracious Cather. (Note: The clipping bears this inscription in
Cather's handwriting: "Isn't this funny!")

30   LITTELL, ROBERT. "Rich and Strange." New Republic 37
      (19 December):99.
           Review of A Lost Lady suggests that Marian Forrester is
real and vivid because the author does not intrude in her book.

31   "A Lost Lady: Miss Cather Reconstructs the West of the Rail-
      road Kings." Time 2 (1 October):14.
           Provides a plot summary of A Lost Lady, and quotes from two
critical responses to the book. Applauds Cather's creation of
three vitally alive characters and her evocation of a period gone
by.

32   "Modern Novel Is Praised by Willa Cather." Baltimore Sun.
      Undated [ca. 1923] clipping in scrapbook II-33 at Willa Cather
      Historical Center, Red Cloud, Nebraska.
           Reports Cather's comments upon receiving the Pulitzer
Prize. Quotes Cather as saying that she is optimistic about the
modern novel insofar as the novelist works for the pleasure of
creating characters and situations based on his or her knowledge.

33   MORTON, DAVID. "Poems Collected and Selected." Bookman 58
      (September):76.
           April Twilights and Other Poems shows Cather's interest in
both classical and western prairie themes, and her ability to
treat her subjects with delicacy of feeling. The poems are not
profound, but they are pleasing.

34   MURRY, J. MIDDLETON. "Miss Willa Cather." Nation and
      Athenaeum (England) 33 (14 April):54, 56.
           Review of Youth and the Bright Medusa and One of Ours.
Offers qualified praise for Cather, admitting that she writes
very well for one who has "the next best thing" to genius. Her
subject is the gap between the spiritual values of the artist and
the material values of most of America. The problem with One of
Ours is that Cather raises an issue but does not see it through.
Instead, she introduces a deus ex machina, the death of Claude
Wheeler, to get her out of it. Cather always writes with honesty
and integrity, however, and "Coming, Aphrodite!" in Youth and the
Bright Medusa is one of the best short stories America has produced in recent years.

35   "New Novels." Times Literary Supplement (London), 18 October,
      p. 688.
           Review of One of Ours sees in the work the same energy and
beauty that distinguish My Ántonia. For the most part, Cather is
ruthlessly complete in her descriptions, but the war scenes seem
rather stale.

36   "New Winners of the Pulitzer Prizes." Current Opinion 75
      (July):49–51.
           Reports on Cather's receiving the Pulitzer Prize for One of
Ours.

37 O'BRIEN, EDWARD J. The Advance of the American Short Story.
    New York: Dodd, Mead & Co. Reprint. Folcroft, Pa.: The
    Folcroft Press, 1969, pp. 208-9.
        The Troll Garden and Youth and the Bright Medusa show the
    aspirations of youth and the revolt that creates rather than
    destroys, the failure that points to success. The earlier sto-
    ries in these collections are less technically adept but more
    vitally real than the later ones.

38 OSBORN, E.W. "The Artistry of A Lost Lady." New York World,
    7 October, sec. e, p. 10.
        Commends A Lost Lady's completeness and Cather's ability to
    "write softly" and well. The character of Marian Forrester is
    totally developed and utterly unforgettable.

39 PEATTIE ELLA [ELIA] W. "Newspaper Women of Nebraska." In
    History of the Nebraska Press Association. Book 2. Edited by
    Henry Allen Brainerd. Lincoln, 1 July, pp. 31-32.
        Reprint of 1895.1. Reference is also made to the Brainerd
    volume in The Story of the Nebraska Press Association 1873-1973,
    comp. Arthur J. Riedesel (Lincoln: Nebraska Press Association,
    1973), pp. 37-38. A brief passage about Cather is quoted from
    the Peattie piece.

40 "Pulitzer Prizes for 1922 Awarded." New York Times, 14 May,
    p. 14.
        Cites Cather as recipient of the Pulitzer Prize for One of
    Ours, the 1922 novel that best represents "the wholesome atmo-
    sphere of American life."

41 RASCOE, BURTON. "The Lost Lady." New York Herald Tribune
    Books, 28 October, pp. 17-18.
        Accords high praise to Cather for the near perfection of
    A Lost Lady, her best novel, and one of the best in contemporary
    British and American literature. Marian Forrester's nature is
    conditioned by the way she is viewed by the men around her, and
    Niel Herbert hates her when he sees that other men's perceptions
    turn out to be different from his own. Only Cather's "superb
    adroitness" enables her to present Marian Forrester as she exists
    in others' minds.

42 Review of April Twilights and Other Poems. Book Review Digest
    19:88.
        Notes that the volume contains poems from the first edition
    as well as newer poems, some previously published, some not.

43 Review of April Twilights and Other Poems. Dial 75 (October):
    400.
        Criticizes the uniformity and cold perfection of the
    volume.

44 Review of A Lost Lady. Booklist 20 (November):55.
        Admires Cather's gentle artistry and the "finished" qual-
    ity of the book.

45   Review of A Lost Lady. Omaha World-Herald, 26 September,
     p. 10.
         Compares Cather's local color descriptions of the Midwest
     to Thomas Hardy's descriptions of Sussex. A Lost Lady depicts
     the end of the noble pioneer and the beginning of a new and
     decadent era, an era represented by Ivy Peters.

46   Review of One of Ours. Nation and Athenaeum (England) 34
     (10 November), supp., 258.
         Judges One of Ours to be a book not fully realized. The
     novel is smooth, but it lacks something vital at the core that
     would make it live as its own entity.

47   TIETJENS, EUNICE. "Poetry by a Novelist." Poetry: A Maga-
     zine of Verse 22 (July):221-23.
         Review of April Twilights and Other Poems. Expresses
     reservations about Cather's poetry, but calls her voice one of
     the most authentic in contemporary prose fiction. The poems have
     humanity, drama, sympathy, and directness of vision, but at heart
     Cather is not a poet. The nature of poetry cramps Cather rather
     than releases her.

48   Van DOREN, MARK. "Literature and the Land." Nation 116
     (27 June):753-54.
         Review of April Twilights and Other Poems contends that
     Cather is an epic poet who writes better fiction than verse.
     Anything she writes is good, but the artificialities of poetic
     convention hamper her natural sense of rhythm and pace.

49   W., C.R. "Miss Cather's Latest Novel." Christian Science
     Monitor, 19 September, p. 14.
         Praises A Lost Lady for its simplicity, realism, and per-
     ception, and also for its strong characterization and the quality
     of its background description.

50   WALPOLE, HUGH. "The Year's Best in American Fiction: An
     English Critic's View." Literary Digest International Book
     Review 1 (January):7, 70-71.
         Confesses to reversing his opinion of the second half of
     One of Ours after rereading it. Even though Cather's vision of
     the war is "borrowed," it is both grimly realistic and symbolic--
     and justifiable. Point of view is handled with subtlety and
     care.

51   WARD, CHRISTOPHER. "One of Hers: Long after Willa Cather."
     Literary Review of the New York Evening Post, 3 February,
     p. 435.
         Parodies One of Ours in the form of two chapters of a sup-
     posed novel titled The Young Hamlet of the Prairies. In the
     first chapter, Claude's chief problem is the fact that he has
     only one collar button while other men have two. In the second,
     Cather telephones Claude at his battle station and an argument
     ensues as to whether he has to do her bidding and mount the

parapet in the thick of battle. He pretends to accede to her
wishes, but fools both Cather and the enemy with a mannequin.
Reprinted: 1923.52.

52   _____. "One of Hers: Long After Willa Cather." In The
        Triumph of the Nut and Other Parodies. New York: Henry Holt
        & Co., pp. 94-104.
            Reprint of 1923.51.

53   WHIPPLE, T[HOMAS] K[ING]. "Willa Cather." Literary Review of
        the New York Evening Post 4 (8 December):331-32.
            Cather began as a realist, but even though she has become
        less and less one, she has an extraordinary capacity for absorb-
        ing experience. Her development away from snapshot recording of
        detail indicates the change in her concept of art and is evident
        in her shift in interest from the "local and accidental to the
        essential." She thus has become more objective. Her art is the
        art of conscious exclusion and of attaching significance to a
        single detail. This, plus the fact that she does not always con-
        vey to the reader the passion she apparently feels, may be a sign
        of her basic deficiency. Still, she is a writer who saw the
        world as tragic but not futile, who somehow found her way to art
        both in spite of and because of her experience of Nebraska. She
        writes with taste, tact, and imagination. Revised: 1928.20.

54   "Willa Cather's Nebraska." Commercial Advertiser (Red Cloud,
        Nebr.), 15 October.
            Apparently reprinted from the Omaha World-Herald, unknown
        date. Comments on the quality of the writing and the aptness of
        the observations made by Cather in her essay "Nebraska: The End
        of the First Cycle." Takes the essay as evidence that Cather
        still feels herself rooted in Nebraska, and that she sees in the
        foreign immigrant influx into America hope for spiritual re-
        generation.

55   WILLIAMSON, EDWARD. "Willa Cather's Latest Book Is Another
        Triumph." Clipping from unidentified Nebraska newspaper
        [Autumn], scrapbook II-5 at Willa Cather Historical Center,
        Red Cloud, Nebraska.
            Review of A Lost Lady. Observes Cather's meticulous abil-
        ity to conceal her literary technique. She works carefully to
        create "an impression of utter simplicity."

56   "Wrangling over the Pulitzer Awards." Literary Digest 77
        (9 June):29-31 passim.
            Observes disagreement among commentators over choices for
        the 1922 Pulitzer awards, including the one given to Cather for
        One of Ours. Cites Heywood Broun's preference for Babbitt, and
        notes a laudatory reaction to the Cather choice by the London
        Times.

1   BOYNTON, PERCY H. "Willa Cather." English Journal 13 (June):
    373–80.
        Cather arrived as a writer with O Pioneers! and The Song of
    the Lark, but that arrival was not recognized until My Ántonia.
    The fact that the stories in Youth and the Bright Medusa are not
    prairie stories indicates that Cather had not yet become estab-
    lished in her imaginative home. Her attachment to the prairie
    was perhaps mainly sentimental, like Jim Burden's. One of Ours
    shows her going off course, and A Lost Lady shows her losing her
    bearings entirely. Marian Forrester is drab and weak, not the
    kind of person with whom Cather works effectively. There is hope
    that Cather, unlike her male contemporaries, will find her way
    back on course. Reprinted: 1924.2. Modified: 1931.7; 1936.3;
    1940.4.

2   _____. "Willa Cather." In Some Contemporary Americans: The
    Personal Equation in Literature. Chicago: University of
    Chicago Press, pp. 162–77.
        Reprint of 1924.1.

3   CANBY, HENRY SEIDEL. "Miss Cather's A Lost Lady." In
    Definitions: Essays in Contemporary Criticism. Second
    series. New York: Harcourt, Brace & Co., pp. 233–36.
        Reprint of 1923.10.

4   COLLINS, JOSEPH. Taking the Literary Pulse: Psychological
    Studies of Life and Letters. New York: George H. Doran Co.,
    pp. 127–29.
        Assesses the relationship between Niel Herbert and Marian
    Forrester in A Lost Lady, noting his fear and lack of virility in
    the face of her feminine charm--and her adultery and alcoholism.
    Regrets that Cather subjected Marian to alcohol and would like
    very much for her to have written a sequel to the book which
    shows Niel growing to maturity.

5   FELD, ROSE C. "'Restlessness Such as Ours Does Not Make for
    Beauty.'" New York Times Book Review, 21 December, p. 11.
        Quotes Cather in an interview as saying that America's lack
    of cultural background allows for every mediocre artist to be
    called great. According to Cather, America's restlessness and
    success and striving "do not make for beauty." America is dif-
    ferent from France, which has such a purity of tradition that it
    simultaneously reverences and kills originality. Further, in
    this country we try to Americanize people even though they come
    here with sets of beautiful traditions from their homelands.
    Cather says that at its core My Ántonia is like a folk song that
    Grieg might have written. The same story could have been told in
    the city to express the quality of the people it portrays. Re-
    printed in part: 1982.25.

6   FISHER, DOROTHY CANFIELD. "Willa Cather." Scholastic,
      13 September, pp. 5, 32.
          Written for and to high school students to help them
    appreciate Cather's integrity. Asserts that her two outstanding
    qualities are her total honesty and her sympathy for things that
    make life vital and full of feeling.

7   MacAFEE, HELEN. "What They Are Reading in Books." Bookman 58
      (January):517-18.
          Refers, in a piece about what writers say about reading in
    their fiction, to the passage in A Lost Lady in which Niel
    Herbert's reading is described in some detail. Suggests, tongue-
    in-cheek, that in daring to have her character read at all, and
    then daring to describe the experience, Cather almost becomes a
    radical. It just is not done.

8   MENCKEN, H.L. "Three Volumes of Fiction." American Mercury
      1 (February):252-53.
          Review of A Lost Lady considers the novel to be more a
    sketch than a story, with several unexplained episodes and un-
    developed or stock characters. Cather, however, deliberately
    refuses to explain or specify because she wishes to emphasize
    relationships rather than plot or character.

9   MORRIS, LLOYD. "Willa Cather." North American Review 219
      (May):641-52.
          Cather is a mainstream American writer by virtue of her
    treatment of the West and the pioneer. She writes of the close
    of that epoch, but she expresses her dissatisfaction with con-
    formity and mechanism in a different way than her contemporaries
    do--by reviving the better and more heroic past. She uses the
    local and momentary to reveal the universal and the timeless, and
    she writes primarily of the individual's efforts to overcome
    obstacles of circumstance and environment. For Cather, the new
    frontier is an imaginative one, and yesterday's pioneers are
    today's artists in her work. In A Lost Lady Cather at last
    achieves harmony of form and content. Marian Forrester is re-
    lated to Cather's women who precede her in that she and they seem
    legendary, ruled by primitive passions and profound instincts.
    Ántonia Shimerda exemplifies that quality in its noblest form.

10 PRIESTLEY, J[OHN] B[OYNTON]. "Fiction." London Mercury 10
      (October):658-59.
          Review of A Lost Lady asserts that despite the novel's
    short length, Cather's exceptional narrative abilities bring it
    to life.

11 RASCOE, BURTON. "A Bookman's Daybook." New York Tribune,
      18 February.
          Offers a brief, anecdotal account of Rascoe's initial
    favorable impressions of Cather as a robust woman of easy manner
    and vital expression. Reprinted: 1929.19.

12   _____. "A Bookman's Daybook." New York Tribune, 22 February.
        Reports a second meeting with Cather, one in which she said
that the point of A Lost Lady was to portray Marian Forrester,
not the disillusionment of her young admirer. The butcher boy
and a number of others were as important as he; he just happened to be more closely associated with Marian than some
others were. Reprinted: 1929.18.

13   _____. "Contemporary Reminiscences: Willa Cather, Zoe
        Akins, Theodore Dreiser and Others." Arts and Decoration 20
        (April):28, 57, 62.
        Recalls initial impressions of Cather and conversations
with her, concentrating on her physical appearance and manner.
Her writing appeals to intellect and heart alike; her conversation is rapid-fire, decisive, and economical. Cather is the best
woman writer now writing in English. Reprinted: 1947.26.

14   Review of April Twilights and Other Poems. Times Literary
        Supplement (London), 18 September, p. 573.
        Finds Cather's earlier poems, with the exception of
"Prairie Dawn" and "Grandmither, Think Not I Forget," inferior
to her later verses, which have greater depth and realism.

15   SCOTT, C.A. DAWSON. "Some Interesting Novels." Bookman
        (London) 67 (October):50.
        Review of A Lost Lady regards it as an extraordinarily fine
rendition of "the Golden Helen," worthy to stand beside Edith
Wharton's The House of Mirth.

16   WILSON, EDMUND. "A Lost Lady." Dial 76 (January):79–80.
        Compares Cather to Henry James, claiming that she is at her
best when describing events "second hand." A Lost Lady shows
Cather's feeling for the land and her ability to create realistic
characters. The novel falters only when Cather shifts the narration from Niel Herbert. Reprinted: 1952.20; 1967.62.

17   WYMAN, MARJORIE. "Willa Cather, Novelist, Was Modern Flapper
        at Nebraska U 30 Years Ago." Lincoln Sunday Star, 29 June,
        p. 6.
        Provides an anecdotal account of Cather at the University
of Nebraska, stressing her talent as well as her independence in
matters of dress and hair style.

                                    1925

1   ASHLEY, SCHUYLER. "Willa Cather's Professor Is a Living
        Character." Kansas City Star, 3 October.
        Cather's technique of character creation is in the tradi-
tional rather than the psychological mode, and her characters
are individuals rather than types. The inclusion of Tom
Outland's story in The Professor's House is bold and effective,
but the book's ending is tired, as if Cather herself grew weary
of St. Peter's family. Reprinted: 1929.2.

2   BARTLETT, ALICE HUNT. "The Dynamics of American Poetry--IX:
     Emily Dickinson--Willa Cather--Robert Hillyer." Poetry Review
     (London) 16:405-14.
          Provides brief biographical details and quotes excerpts
     from several Cather poems, including the ones Cather indicated
     were her favorites.

3   BEER, THOMAS. "Miss Cather." In The Borzoi 1925. New York:
     Alfred A. Knopf, pp. 23-30.
          Reflects on Cather and her achievement, praising her for
     her "pictorial quality," expositional simplicity, and "literary
     tact," and for being literary America's "least sentimental stu-
     dent of sentiment."

4   BENÉT, LAURA. Review of The Professor's House. Commonweal 3
     (2 December):108-9.
          Explores Cather's portrayal of Godfrey St. Peter as a
     lonely, middle-aged man regretting the failure of what might have
     been. The novel's organization is faulty, but each character in
     the book serves to clarify another. Tom Outland is the control-
     ling factor.

5   BERG, RUBEN GUSTAVSON. "De nya invandrarna--Willa Cather"
     [The new immigrants--Willa Cather]. In Moderna Amerikaner.
     Stockholm: Hugo Gebers Forläg, pp. 81-99.
          In Swedish. Cather is one of five American writers dis-
     cussed in this book. She is praised for her creation of real-
     istic Swedish characters, and for her wisdom, her simplicity, and
     her knowledge of human nature. She is an outstanding artist, but
     A Lost Lady does not measure up to her abilities.

6   BRICKELL, HERSCHEL. "An Armful of Fiction." Bookman 62
     (November):339.
          Review of The Professor's House defends the interpolated
     story of Tom Outland as important to the book's theme and to the
     reader's understanding of Godfrey St. Peter. This is Cather's
     best novel. Its characters are realistic, and its symbolism is
     subtle.

7   BUTCHER, FANNY. "Willa Cather's Novel Wins Highest Praise."
     Chicago Daily Tribune, 19 September, p. 9.
          Considers The Professor's House to be about Tom Outland
     rather than about Godfrey St. Peter. This is not apparent until
     the end, however. Praises Cather for her subtlety, nobility,
     and lack of sentimentality.

8   CANBY, HENRY SEIDEL. "A Novel of the Soul." Saturday Review
     of Literature 2 (26 September):151.
          Cather, like Hawthorne, believes that there are profundi-
     ties in American life. She probes those profundities in The
     Professor's House, a novel about a man's "progress in self-
     realization," his decision to "follow his own soul." This novel
     is less poignant than A Lost Lady, but it is more subtle and
     sophisticated, with its real story running beneath the

narrative's "smooth flowing surface." The past is the most
important aspect of the story; hence, the narrative is told
backwards, with the future always pointing to the past. The
Professor's House is a bold, experimental novel, but it is not
always entirely successful in its experiment. Nevertheless, it
treats art's most important subject--the human soul--with moving
power. Reprinted: 1982.15; 1984.14.

9   CESTRE, C. Review of A Lost Lady. Revue anglo-américaine 2
    (April):375.
        Identifies Cather as a writer known for her use of realis-
    tic detail and her skill in characterization. She is not a part
    of the literature of revolt, nor does she follow the French
    naturalists. Rather, she writes in a genre between these groups.
    She exercises both reticence and prudence.

10 DICKINSON, ASA DON. One Thousand Best Books: The Household
    Guide to a Lifetime's Reading. Garden City, N.Y.: Doubleday,
    Page & Co., pp. 57-58, 382, 384.
        Presents a "variorum list" of authors, indicating the
    degree of their popularity. Cather is coming to be recognized as
    one of America's leading authors, but her reputation has been so
    newly won that she does not yet appear on many lists of best
    books. Nevertheless, contributors have commended O Pioneers!,
    The Song of the Lark, My Ántonia, and One of Ours.

11 "Empty House: Miss Cather's Clear Native Metaphor for Middle-
    Age." Time 6 (12 October):18.
        Finds in The Professor's House a portrait of the "secrets
    of human actions" and a psychological insight into circumstances
    close to home. The characters and situations are readily identi-
    fiable; the inevitable return to adolescence of the middle-aged
    is native to all.

12 FORD, JAMES L. "Willa Cather Visits the Cliff-Dwellers."
    Literary Digest International Book Review 3 (November):775.
        Regards The Professor's House as the best work Cather has
    produced, and Tom Outland's story as its most essential and
    memorable part. Reprinted: 1927.11.

13 "Galsworthy Here, But Not to Lecture." New York Times,
    12 November, p. 18.
        Contains John Galsworthy's comment that Cather's work had
    attracted his attention.

14 GIBBS, A. HAMILTON. "Contamination of Rewards: Willa
    Cather's Portrait of a Professor to Whom Success Was Extinc-
    tion." Literary Review of the New York Evening Post, 5 Sep-
    tember, p. 1.
        Claims that The Professor's House fulfills one's expecta-
    tions for a "queer, unusual book from Willa Cather." Suggests
    that the antagonisms in Godfrey St. Peter's family have nothing
    to do with money and everything to do with Tom Outland. The
    novel's action is "entirely spiritual" as it explores St. Peter's

reactions to his environment. Its subject is the change in a man whom life has actually treated very well, a change symbolized in the move from one house to another.

15   HAINES, HELEN E. "The House of the Professor Falls into Three Pieces." Unidentified periodical clipping [1925] in scrapbook II-4 at Willa Cather Historical Center, Red Cloud, Nebraska.
        Review of The Professor's House. Expresses disappointment, even amazement, that in this one instance "Cather's artistry should fail." The brilliant first book of the novel collapses into the interpolated story of Tom Outland that destroys the novel's unity. Book 3 is too weak to restore it.

16   HALL, MOURDANT. "An Indiscreet Woman." New York Times, Film Reviews sec., 19 January.
        Comments on the silent film adaptation of Cather's novel, A Lost Lady, calling Marian Forrester something of "a dolt" for not knowing "on which side her bread is buttered." She has a good, though elderly, husband, but she throws her affections about carelessly. The very nice Niel Herbert is well rid of her.

17   HANSEN, HARRY. "Rare, Beautiful Prose." [New York World, 1925]. Periodical clipping at Willa Cather Historical Center, Red Cloud, Nebraska.
        Appreciates Cather's prefaces to the Mayflower edition of The Best Short Stories of Sarah Orne Jewett and to the Knopf edition of Daniel Defoe's The Fortunate Mistress. In them Cather shows herself to be a polished writer who exemplifies in her own work the qualities of writing she commends in these prefaces.

18   HARPER, MOSES. "Americans All." New Republic 44 (16 September):105-6.
        Review of The Professor's House finds Cather sane and sensible, perhaps too much so. Her work is steady and clear, and Professor St. Peter is surely one of her best creations. The reader simply wishes sometimes for a hint of madness or irresponsibility to add zest to the novel.

19   HAWKINS, ETHEL WALLACE. Review of The Professor's House. "Atlantic Bookshelf." Atlantic Monthly 136 (December).
        Concludes that a draftsman could make a design of the novel's narrative course, at the center of which would stand Tom Outland's story. Calls it a thoughtful and penetrating study and notes that Louie Marsellus is particularly well drawn.

20   HERTZ, HENRI. French review of My Ántonia. Translated into French by M.V. Uona. Europe, 15 September, pp. 116-17.
        Sees in Cather's Ántonia Shimerda something of an American version of the Canadian Maria Chapdelaine, though they are very different in temperament. Maria is complacent and resigned while Ántonia rebels against social inequality.

21   KENNEDY, P.C. Review of The Professor's House. New Statesman
     26 (19 December):306.
          Notes Cather's ability to make ordinary people interesting
     and praises her sensitive and precise exploration of human emo-
     tion.

22   KRUTCH, JOSEPH WOOD. "Second Best." Nation 121 (23 Septem-
     ber):336.
          Attacks Cather's extensive treatise on Tom Outland, calling
     Tom "almost an abstraction," and definitely a distraction. The
     Professor's House is not one of Cather's better novels, but in it
     she shows marked ability to portray emotion nonanalytically.
     Reprinted: 1967.28.

23   LINN, JAMES WEBER. "Miss Cather's New Novel." San Francisco
     Examiner, 3 October, classified sec., p. 7.
          Questions the organization and substance of The Professor's
     House, and attacks its unrealistic characterization.

24   MANN, DOROTHEA L[AWRANCE]. "Willa Cather's Professor."
     Boston Evening Transcript, 16 September, sec. 2, p. 2.
          Review of The Professor's House. Examines Godfrey St.
     Peter as a man stifled, as so many men are, by the circumstances
     of his professional and family life. He is looking for an out-
     let. Cather bases her story on the symbol of the old house,
     particularly the study, which stands for the professor's sacri-
     fice for his family and his great productive act--the writing of
     his history.

25   "Menace to Culture in Cinema and Radio Seen by Miss Cather."
     Christian Science Monitor, 15 May, p. 5.
          Quotes rather extensively from Cather's address on literary
     technique at Bowdoin College. Cather wonders whether perhaps art
     has become too democratic. When it was inseparable from religion,
     there was appreciative ceremony attached to it. Plot is not al-
     ways essential to the novel, and characterization is "difficult
     because it is so simple." According to Cather, love is what
     produces great characters. Another important aspect of the novel
     is the writer's physical relation to it, the viewpoint he or she
     adopts. See 1926.33 for another report on this address.

26   MENCKEN, H.L. "Fiction Good and Bad." American Mercury 6
     (November):379-81.
          Review of The Professor's House applauds Cather for her
     sharp observation and freedom from artifice, but deplores her
     lack of form, contending that Tom Outland's story almost shatters
     the work. That story is powerful on its own and vital to the
     work as a whole, but it has a jarring effect on the novel.
     Cather can be forgiven for this structural flaw, however, because
     the book is gracefully textured.

27 MERRILL, FLORA. "A Short Story Course Can Only Delay, It Cannot Kill an Artist Says Willa Cather." New York World, 19 April, sec. 3, pp. 1–6.

   Interview. Quotes Cather's remarks on her journalistic career and its interference with her fiction. Also reports her observations about the beginning writer's tendency to imitate when learning the craft. Cather focuses on her own methods in A Lost Lady, where she claims not to have made a character of Niel Herbert but rather a "peephole" into the world she wanted to portray. Writing, Cather says, is the form an artist tries to give to an emotion, not to an idea. Reprinted: 1925.28.

28 _____. "Willa Cather Discusses Writing and Short Story Courses." Lincoln State Journal, 25 April, p. 11.
   Reprint of 1925.27.

29 MILLIS, WALTER. "Letters and Life." Edited by Leon Whipple. Survey 55 (1 December):310–12.

   Review of The Professor's House compares it to works by several other writers in order to draw a picture of the modern novel, a picture that shows its tendency to portray life as a series of minor incidents with no real focus. The book is "perfectly pointless," but as such reflects the lives of its characters. Whereas the nineteenth-century novel depicts external struggles, the modern novel focuses on futile internal struggles.

30 "Miss Cather's Professor." Springfield (Mass.) Sunday Republican, 13 September, sec. a, p. 5.

   Review of The Professor's House. Finds the novel "rather anemic" and lacking in form and coherence. The professor is interesting at times, but not totally realistic.

31 MORRIS, LLOYD. "Skimming the Cream from Six Months' Fiction." New York Times Book Review, 6 December, p. 2.

   Review of The Professor's House accuses it of leaving unresolved questions, unfulfilled promises, and an insufficiently developed main character.

32 MUIR, EDWIN. Review of The Professor's House. Nation and Athenaeum 38 (19 December):440.

   Admires Cather's style and method, but claims that her detachment and reserve result in cold characterization.

33 "New Novels." Times Literary Supplement (London), 19 November, p. 770.

   Review of The Professor's House finds the book to be unsatisfactory on the whole because Cather leaves too many loose ends. The characterizations are good—Godfrey St. Peter is compared to Anatole France's M. Bergeret—but the novel's lack of resolution at the end weakens it. Furthermore, the interpolation of Tom Outland's story damages its structure.

34   SERGEANT, ELIZABETH SHEPLEY. "Willa Cather." New Republic 43
      (17 June):91–94.
          Paints a personal and admiring portrait of Cather as a
      strong, determined woman whose basic impetus is her relation to
      the prairie and its people. Her second great passion was her
      feeling for the artist, especially the singer. There is a
      sparseness and an austerity about her work, and she had character
      and "certainty of aim." Reprinted in part: 1926.28. Abridged:
      1926.27. Revised: 1927.35.

35   SEWELL, C.S. "A Lost Lady: Irene Rich Does Remarkable Work
      in Warner's Dramatic Adaptation of Willa Cather's Novel."
      Moving Picture World, 7 February.
          Applauds the faithful transference of Cather's A Lost Lady
      to the silent screen. Calls the novel a "literary sensation," a
      deftly handled analysis of a woman of a certain type. Cather
      uses restraint in handling materials that have the potential for
      sensationalism.

36   SHERMAN, STUART P. "Willa Cather." New York Herald Tribune
      Books, 13 September, pp. 1–3.
          Written as a review of The Professor's House, but comes to
      that novel only at the end of a lengthy essay that provides sig-
      nificant commentary on all of Cather's major work to date. Finds
      her important for clarifying how the present age is like pre-1900
      society and how it departs from that society. Alexander's Bridge
      is highly significant to Cather's work. In that novel Bartley
      Alexander speaks about living out all of one's potentialities.
      This is the clue to the whole of Cather's work and to her pro-
      tagonists from Bartley through Alexandra Bergson, Thea Kronborg,
      Marian Forrester, Claude Wheeler, and Godfrey St. Peter, as well
      as to figures in her short stories. This concern circumscribes
      two basic themes, the struggle for existence (life-preservation)
      and art (life-expansion). Living out one's potential means some-
      thing different for different characters. While Marian
      Forrester has one talent, personal charm, Godfrey St. Peter is
      the "intellectual spirit" of America's Victorian era. Reprinted:
      1926.29.

37   TITTLE, WALTER. "Glimpses of Interesting Americans: Willa
      Sibert Cather." Century Magazine 110 (July):309–13.
          Cather is one of four writers treated in a series running
      in Century from June through September. Tittle recounts a visit
      with Cather in her Greenwich Village apartment where he chatted
      and took tea with her. Reports her "word-portrait" of Swinburne,
      her preference for French over British or American cuisine, her
      need to live in America rather than in France in order to stay in
      touch with the American idiom, her practice of writing in New
      York but going West regularly in order to find renewal "at the
      fountain-head" of her inspiration, and her regard for impres-
      sionistic painters like Manet.

38   Van DOREN, CARL, and Van DOREN, MARK. <u>American and British</u>
     <u>Literature Since 1890</u>. New York: Century Co., pp. 68–71.
         Cather is a writer of taste and intelligence who believed
     that in practicing the art of living it is best to be either a
     pioneer or an artist or both. Ántonia Shimerda is one who exem-
     plifies both of these qualities; Marian Forrester is one who
     fails in both. Expanded: 1939.7.

39   WALDMAN, MILTON. "Fiction." <u>London Mercury</u>, December,
     pp. 211–12.
         Review of <u>The Professor's House</u> sees its principal concern
     to be "time's chemistry" working in Godfrey St. Peter. Cather is
     an exceptional artist, but this book is rather "slight." Its
     parts are "slenderly linked," and Cather takes too many occasions
     to instruct the reader in matters of taste and manners.

40   "Willa Cather's <u>Professor's House</u> among New Novels." <u>New York</u>
     <u>Times Book Review</u>, 6 September, p. 8.
         Review of <u>The Professor's House</u> criticizes it for its gaps
     and digressions. Although the main characters are real and
     vital, the second section of the novel is "flat, stale and un-
     profitable" and the first and third sections are incomplete.

<u>1926</u>

*1   ARNS, KARL. "Willa Cather als Romanschriftstellerin." <u>Zs.</u>
     <u>für frauzosische und englische Unterricht</u> 25:494–98.
         Listed in <u>Bibliography of English Language and Literature</u>
     (1926).

2   ASHLEY, SCHUYLER. "Willa Cather Rigs up a Ship in a Bottle."
     <u>Kansas City Star</u>, 26 November.
         Classifies <u>My Mortal Enemy</u> as a "minute and tragic epic of
     egotism." Expresses high regard for Cather's abilities, but
     faults her for undercutting the book's potential impact by tell-
     ing its story through the nondescript Nellie Birdseye. Re-
     printed: 1929.1; 1931.2.

3   BEACH, JOSEPH WARREN. <u>The Outlook for American Prose</u>.
     Chicago: University of Chicago Press, pp. 172–73, 252–53.
         Regards Cather as a writer of taste, but claims that she
     lacks the force of some of her contemporaries who in turn lack
     taste. Compares a passage from "The Diamond Mine" with one from
     Sherwood Anderson to illustrate Cather's superiority as a
     stylist.

4   BUTCHER, FANNY. "<u>My Mortal Enemy</u> is a Masterpiece, by Willa
     Cather." <u>Chicago Daily Tribune</u>, 23 October, p. 15.
         Review of <u>My Mortal Enemy</u>. Notes Cather's ability to
     eliminate the inessential and to write with slow dignity. Her
     narrative is enhanced by her light but insightful treatment of
     human emotion.

45

5   "Culling the Sweet and Bitter Fruits of Six Months' Fiction."
     New York Times Book Review, 5 December, pp. 5, 34, 38.
          Review of My Mortal Enemy criticizes its meager structure.

6   DODD, LEE WILSON. "Alone, With Ourselves." Saturday Review
     of Literature 3 (23 October):234.
          In My Mortal Enemy Cather is trying to touch readers' minds
     rather than their emotions. Although the novel is sparse in
     characterization, its diction is precise and its outcome con-
     trolled.

7   DONDORE, DOROTHY ANNE. The Prairie and the Making of Middle
     America: Four Centuries of Description. Cedar Rapids, Iowa:
     Torch Press, pp. 328, 425–30 passim. Reprint. New York:
     Antiquarian Press, 1961.
          Contends that Cather's is the only notable fictional in-
     terpretation of the prairie conquest, yet her books try to carry
     too heavy a thematic burden.

8   DREW, ELIZABETH A. The Modern Novel: Some Aspects of Con-
     temporary Fiction. New York: Harcourt, Brace & Co.,
     pp. 149–51, 250–52.
          Regards Ántonia Shimerda as the incarnation of hope,
     beauty, and fruitfulness, and calls A Lost Lady an "exquisite
     study of a woman . . . who wanted life on any terms." In A Lost
     Lady character impressions are created as a series of pictures
     and dramatic passages; Cather makes no direct analysis, but works
     through Niel Herbert.

9   FIELD, LOUISE MAUNSELL. "What's Wrong with the Men?" Liter-
     ary Digest International Book Review 4 (November):761.
          Review of My Mortal Enemy contends that Cather is able to
     take ordinary life and portray it with a realism that is more
     tragic because of its lack of sentiment and extravagance.

10   GALE, ZONA. "My Favorite Character in Fiction." Bookman 63
     (May):322–23.
          Presents a sketch of Tom Outland by Anne Merriman Peck,
     then offers Gale's rationale for selecting Tom as currently her
     favorite fictional character. She likes him because he is
     possessed by one great idea unsullied by personal ambition.

11   HANSEN, HARRY. "My Ántonia Revised." New York World
     [October 1926]. Clipping in scrapbook II-14 at Willa Cather
     Historical Center, Red Cloud, Nebraska.
          Details the changes Cather made in the new edition of My
     Ántonia, particularly in the introduction, noting such things as
     the excisions of descriptions of Jim Burden and his wife.

12   HOMER, SIDNEY. "Willa Cather and My Mortal Enemy." Boston
     Evening Transcript, 11 December, p. 6.
          Refers to My Mortal Enemy as an incomplete "soul portrait."
     The narrator is ineffective; and the book, too short to do more
     than outline, skimps on the character of Myra Henshawe.

13 KRONENBERGER, LOUIS. "Willa Cather Fumbles for Another
    Lost Lady." New York Times Book Review, 24 October, p. 2.
       Compares My Mortal Enemy unfavorably with A Lost Lady,
    claiming that it suffers from weak characterization and sketchy
    content. Furthermore, its narrator, Nellie Birdseye, is color-
    less and seems to stand outside the story. The book is too
    spare; it "implies much, but connotes little." Reprinted:
    1984.48.

14 KRUTCH, JOSEPH WOOD. "The Modest Method of Willa Cather."
    Nation 123 (10 November):484.
       Comments appreciatively on Cather's modesty,. her way of
    distancing the reader from a story's events by focusing not on
    the events themselves but on the mind through which they are
    seen. Such a method has both its charm and its limitations. In
    My Mortal Enemy, it works to create an effectively brooding, even
    slightly melancholic, tone. The effect is Appollonian rather
    than dramatic. Reprinted: 1967.26. Reprinted in part:
    1982.37.

15 L[OVETT], R[OBERT MORSS]. "Thick and Thin." New Republic 49
    (24 November):22–23.
       Review of My Mortal Enemy disapproves of Cather's tendency
    to speak through her narrator, to overshadow and "extinguish,"
    and thus to blur, Myra Henshawe's character.

16 MICHAUD, RÉGIS. Le roman américain d'aujourd'hui: Critique
    d'une civilisation. Paris: Boivin et Cie.
       Published in English: 1928.9. See annotation there.

17 "Miss West Sails; Slaps Mencken." New York World,
    16 December.
       Reports remarks made by Rebecca West as she sailed for
    England. She allegedly declared that Cather is "America's great-
    est novelist" and attacked H.L. Mencken for exploiting his per-
    sonality rather than using his brain.

18 MOSHER, JOHN CHAPIN. "Willa Cather." Writer 38 (November):
    528–30.
       Speaks mainly of Cather's attachment to Nebraska, insisting
    that it is her true home and that she felt life and people were
    more real and wise there than in New York City. Part of a spe-
    cial section on Cather.

19 "Myra Henshawe, Another Great Portrait by Miss Cather." New
    York Sun, 22 October.
       Sees My Mortal Enemy to be distilled even more from the
    compactness that marks A Lost Lady. Cather's best work has
    focused on women's portraiture, and Myra Henshawe is in the tra-
    dition of Thea Kronborg, Ántonia Shimerda, and Marian Forrester.
    But while Marian seems to suffer little for her lapses of virtue,
    Myra is not rewarded for maintaining her virtue. She comes to
    despise the "soft bonds" by which Oswald holds her, but in his
    sentimentality he never understands that.

20   "New Books in Brief Review." Independent 117 (13 November):
     563, 568.
         Review of My Mortal Enemy acclaims Cather's grasp of the
American scene and her ability to develop character, but laments
her inclination to write shorter and shorter novels. She needs a
broader scope for her talent.

21   PATERSON, ISABEL. "When Desire Shall Fail." New York Herald
     Tribune, 24 October, p. 3.
         Cather's preoccupation has been with idealistic characters
who seek a nontemporal fulfillment. Life breaks Myra Henshawe in
My Mortal Enemy because of her grasping, hard, selfish nature.
Like Bartley Alexander in Alexander's Bridge, Myra is adumbrated
as a great nature, but she does not turn out to be so. In fact,
her "spiritual insignificance" falsifies the emotion generated in
her story.

22   PORTERFIELD, ALEXANDER. "Contemporary American Authors: V:
     Willa Cather." London Mercury 13 (March):516–24.
         Acclaims Cather's charm, style, and narrative ability, and
asserts that with One of Ours she comes into her own. There
Cather "lavishly" fulfills the promise of My Ántonia, surpassing
in quality the work of any of her contemporaries. A Lost Lady
shows still another advance and is Cather's masterpiece, but The
Professor's House is something of a decline. My Mortal Enemy is
better than any of the stories in Youth and the Bright Medusa.
Reprinted: [ca. 1927].29; 1928.15; [ca. 1929 or 1930].16; [ca.
1933].17; [ca. 1941].16.

23   PRESTON, KEITH. "Miss Cather's Prose Lyric." Chicago Daily
     News, [October], p. 14.
         Judges the characters in My Mortal Enemy to be overly con-
trived and the style too deliberate, but commends the writing for
its charm, poetry, and occasional "racy" crispness.

24   "Pride's Bed." Time 8 (18 October):38–39.
         Regards Cather as an artist in the tradition of Wordsworth
who thought art should convey "emotion recollected in tranquil-
ity." My Mortal Enemy is both subtle and intense, and its characters are treated with both delicacy and depth. Myra's mortal
enemy is her pride.

25   PRIESTLEY, JOHN BOYNTON. "Revolt and American Literature."
     Forum 75 (May):759–70.
         Notes that most current American literature is seething in
revolt, but generally is not advancing beyond merely turning current conventions upside down. Cather, however, is one of the few
in whom resides genuine artistic genius, in whom lies the promise
for American literature. A Lost Lady is "one of the best pieces
of fiction written in any country since the War."

26   RICHARDS, I.A. "Some Outstanding Novels." Forum 76 (August):
      318-19.
           Review of The Professor's House claims "invention" to be
      the only thing lacking in this book which actually contains two
      good novels, one inside the other. Suggests that Tom Outland's
      revolutionary scientific discovery is drawn from Rudyard
      Kipling's "With the Night Mail." Cather's work is rather static
      and lacks action, but it has impressive balance and perspective.

27   SERGEANT, ELIZABETH SHEPLEY. "A Novelist of Today: Willa
      Cather." World Review 3 (15 November):140-41.
           An abridged text of 1925.34.

28   _____. "Willa Cather: Her Books a Guide to Her Life Story."
      Writer 38 (November):530-31.
           Reprinted from 1925.34. Part of a special section on
      Cather.

29   SHERMAN, STUART. "Willa Cather and the Changing World." In
      Critical Woodcuts. New York: Charles Scribner's Sons,
      pp. 32-48.
           Reprint of 1925.36.

30   TITTLE, WALTER. "Four American Women: Portrait Drawings by
      Walter Tittle." Forum 76 (October):559.
           Pencil drawing of Cather. No text other than caption.

31   Van DOREN, CARL. "Desire under All Desires." Century Maga-
      zine 111 (January):379-81.
           Adjudges that Cather's artistry is not constant from novel
      to novel. The Professor's House marks a fall from A Lost Lady,
      dragging in places and failing to achieve the economy of which
      Cather's beautiful prose is capable. Nevertheless, the book is
      to be commended for the way its theme reaches inward to center in
      the professor's psyche, producing a gradual revelation of plot.

32   WHEELOCK, JOHN F. "Miss Cather Recounts an Endurance Test."
      Writer 38 (November):532-34.
           Focuses on three reasons why Myra and Oswald Henshawe re-
      main married throughout My Mortal Enemy, a circumstance necessary
      if Myra's asking why she must die alone with her mortal enemy is
      to be plausible. First, Myra's religious conviction would not
      allow divorce; second, Oswald's yielding, sentimental nature
      would not lean toward it; and third, their poverty holds them
      together. The article also contains one reprinted manuscript
      page from the novel with Cather's handwritten corrections. Part
      of a special section on Cather.

33   "Willa Catha [sic]--Novelist." An Institute of Modern Litera-
      ture. Brunswick, Maine: Bowdoin College, pp. 88-96.
           Reports and comments on Cather's 13 May 1925 lecture,
      titled "The Talk about Technique," at Bowdoin College. The
      account of her ninety-minute presentation is highly complimentary.
      She claims that she knows nothing at all about technique, for

technique is what actors and violinists develop from repeated
practice on one thing in a fixed way. But a writer cannot practice like that; a writer has to be always new, and so has no
technique. Further, the only plot in great literature is spiritual plot. According to Cather, characterization is not technique; it is love. Atmosphere is not technique either; one either
has a sense of it or one does not. For the writer technique is
really a minor consideration; a great novel can be full of technical faults and still breathe wonderfully with "force and
beauty." See 1925.25 for an earlier report on this address.

34   WILLIAMS, STANLEY [THOMAS]. Introduction to 1926 reissue of
     One of Ours. New York: Alfred A. Knopf, pp. vii-xx.
        Comments on all of Cather's novels from O Pioneers! through
     The Professor's House, observing especially Cather's increasing
     consciousness of her art and her increasingly subtle methods. It
     is obvious in her work that she experienced the prairie emotion-
     ally, that to her it meant life.

35   WILSON, EDMUND. "The All-Star Literary Vaudeville." In
     American Criticism. Edited by William A. Drake. New York:
     Harcourt, Brace & Co., pp. 340-42 passim. Also published
     anonymously in New Republic 47 (30 June):158-59.
        Concedes that Cather's work, although dull and unimagina-
     tive with the exception of a few stories, is well-crafted. Re-
     printed: 1952.19; 1956.24.

36   YUST, WALTER. "Rich Study of Woman Who Had Courage but Could
     Not Endure." Literary Review of the New York Evening Post,
     30 October, p. 3.
        Finds My Mortal Enemy a moving account of a courageous
     woman who meets defeat. Cather's elliptical manner is deliberate
     and effective.

                              1927

1   BALLOU, ROBERT O. "The Story of the West Which Willa Cather
     Sees." Chicago Daily News, 7 September, p. 14.
        Cather has written a western novel in beautiful, calm
     prose. Her pace in Death Comes for the Archbishop is unhurried,
     and her characters are vividly realistic.

2   BEATON, VERA. Review of Death Comes for the Archbishop.
     Chicago Journal of Commerce and LaSalle Street Journal,
     13 September.
        Calls Death Comes for the Archbishop a "prose poem," a
     story of love of country, church, and adventure, proving again
     Cather's immense versatility. The novel's only weakness is that
     those who have not experienced the desert landscape will not be
     able to relate to the book.

3   BRICKELL, HERSCHEL. "The Literary Landscape: Miss Cather in
    New Mexico." North American Review 224 (September–October),
    advertising sec.
        The sharp, clean outline of Death Comes for the Archbishop
    stays with the reader and stands as an example to younger writers
    who seem to prefer "murky, obscure" prose.

4   BUTCHER, FANNY. "Willa Cather's New Novel is Simply, Beauti-
    fully Told." Chicago Daily Tribune, 3 September, p. 8.
        Death Comes for the Archbishop contains some of Cather's
    finest prose—simple, unadorned, pure. The book is a portrait
    almost autobiographical in its knowledge of the character of one
    man, Jean Latour. The other characters, even Joseph Vaillant,
    serve mainly as vivid background for Latour.

5   CANBY, HENRY SEIDEL. Review of Death Comes for the Arch-
    bishop. Saturday Review of Literature 4 (10 December):421.
        In Death Comes for the Archbishop, Cather has succeeded in
    shaping a novel out of people and incidents rather than by means
    of plot and climax.

6   CHASE, MARY ELLEN. "Atlantic Bookshelf." Atlantic Monthly
    140 (November):67.
        Accords high praise to Cather's achievement in Death Comes
    for the Archbishop, conceding her right to ignore standard novel-
    istic conventions that would hamper her in presenting the life
    histories of her missionary priests. The style is simple and
    orderly, but unsurpassed in its abundant riches by anything else
    Cather has done.

7   "Congratulations from Willa Cather." Nebraska State Journal,
    24 July, sec. f, p. 6.
        Publishes a letter, dated in New York, 2 June, from Cather
    to the Nebraska State Journal on its sixtieth birthday observance.
    The letter was apparently written in response to a request for
    such from the current editor. In this letter Cather recalls that
    it was first seeing herself in print in the Journal (her college
    essay on Thomas Carlyle, published without her knowledge) that
    changed her career goal from science to writing. She expresses
    appreciation to Charles Gere, her first editor, for allowing her
    to "riot in fine writing," to get all the florid rhetoric out of
    her system in his pages, knowing that she would eventually "re-
    cover." Cather also describes Gere's hands in appreciative de-
    tail.

8   DOANE, GILBERT H. "Willa Cather, '95, Fictional Biographer."
    Nebraska Alumnus 23 (November):452.
        Terms Death Comes for the Archbishop "fictional biography"
    rather than a novel, and admires its great charm and beauty.

9   DODD, LEE WILSON. "A Hymn to Spiritual Beauty." <u>Saturday Review of Literature</u> 4 (10 September):101.
      Praises Cather for her quintessential distillation of the Southwest in <u>Death Comes for the Archbishop</u>, and for her break with the current trend that portrays man as soulless.

10   EDGETT, EDWIN FRANCIS. Review of <u>Death Comes for the Archbishop</u>. <u>Boston Evening Transcript</u>, 17 September, p. 6.
      Regards Cather as having been too much praised in the past, but feels <u>Death Comes for the Archbishop</u> is good because in it Cather is contented with being "a real storyteller" rather than "an apostle of modernist fiction." The novel's title, however, does not apply to its content.

11   FORD, JAMES L. "The Professor's House by Willa Cather." In <u>Modern Essays of Various Types</u>. Edited by Charles A. Cockayne. Merrill's English Texts. New York: Charles E. Merrill Co., pp. 275-79.
      Reprint of 1925.12.

12   FORD, LILLIAN C. Review of <u>Death Comes for the Archbishop</u>. <u>Santa Fe New Mexican</u>, 23 September, p. 4.
      Attributed to the <u>Los Angeles Times</u>, unknown date. Cather depicts the life of Bishop Latour so effectively that it "reads like a document left by a contemporary." It has simplicity and charm. One of the book's strengths is Cather's portrayal of the valiant and proud Pueblo Indians.

13   "Future of Art Demands Freedom, Says Willa Cather." <u>College News</u> (Bryn Mawr), 19 January, pp. 1-2.
      Reports in some detail on the Ann Elizabeth Sheble Memorial Lecture delivered by Cather at Bryn Mawr in mid-January, 1927. Cather's topic was "What is a novel?" but she preferred the term "imaginative prose" over the term "novel." Cather reportedly argues that fiction needs freedom in order to flourish, freedom from rules of technique taught in college classes, freedom to develop fresh forms. She says that the beginning of a genuine piece of imaginative prose is "personal emotional experience," an "explosion in the brain" that must not be tampered with very much.

14   GILMAN, DOROTHY FOSTER. "Willa Cather Writes a Fictional Biography." <u>Boston Evening Transcript</u>, 10 September, p. 2.
      Classifies <u>Death Comes for the Archbishop</u> as an historical biography rather than as a novel and applauds Cather's ability to deal with history, and the people involved in that history, sympathetically. Cather combines accuracy and imagination.

15   GREENBIE, SYDNEY. "Willa Cather in the Far Southwest." <u>Springfield</u> (Mass.) <u>Republican</u>, 13 November, sec. f, p. 7.
      Regards <u>Death Comes for the Archbishop</u> as puzzling because it cannot be unequivocally placed as either a novel or an historical text. Nevertheless, Cather renders noble and base actions alike into compelling human situations.

16 HAZARD, LUCY LOCKWOOD. The Frontier in American Literature. New York: Thomas Y. Crowell Co., pp. 269-74. Reprint. American Classics Series. New York: Frederick Ungar Publishing Co., 1961.
In Cather's work is the "supreme expression" of the pioneer's vital creativity and the vacuum left when the pioneer era disappeared. Love of the land dominates her work. O Pioneers! and My Ántonia portray the strong, if coarse, pioneer woman joining with the land in creative harmony, while One of Ours, A Lost Lady, and The Professor's House mourn the defeat of the pioneer spirit.

17 J., S.B. Review of Death Comes for the Archbishop. Catholic World 126 (November):275-76.
Subject and craftsmanship combine to make Death Comes for the Archbishop intensely interesting and important to the history of Catholicism. Cather exercises insight and restraint in treating a difficult subject.

18 KENNY, JOHN M., Jr. Review of My Mortal Enemy. Commonweal 5 (9 March):499-500.
Lauds Cather's subtlety, economy, and artistry in revealing the tragedy in a seemingly ordinary life story. Myra Henshawe's mortal enemy is her own warped soul.

19 KRUTCH, JOSEPH WOOD. "The Pathos of Distance." Nation 125 (12 October):390.
Likens Cather's treatment of the past in Death Comes for the Archbishop to the treatment of the past in the Celtic epic as described by Havelock Ellis. Cather writes in the elegaic mood rather than in the heroic mood of the Nordic epic, however, and her best effects are "static or picture-like." Death Comes for the Archbishop has no real plot, but holds the reader's interest through the "continuous presence of beauty." It is Cather's best work since A Lost Lady. Reprinted: 1967.27; 1982.38.

20 LASCH, ROBERT N. "Willa Cather." Prairie Schooner 1 (April): 166-69.
Presents a colorful account of Cather's youth, then focuses on A Lost Lady, judging it to be her best work and calling it the story of Anna Karenina and Madame Bovary both. It is a tragedy because Marian Forrester defines life in terms of pleasure and misses life itself.

21 "Literature Leads to High Place for Red Cloud Woman Nominated to Write Long Awaited Great American Novel." Hastings (Nebr.) Daily Tribune, 27 August.
Indicates that the casual visitor with Cather is not likely to elicit many comments from her on questions of current interest. Nevertheless, one discerns that literature has been good for Cather. It has sharpened her curiosity about the "causes of great movements," and it has "developed her interest in people and things."

22   LOVETT, ROBERT MORSS. "A Death in the Desert." New Republic
      52 (26 October):266-67.
         Calls Death Comes for the Archbishop "faultless art,"
      an accomplished narrative of life, told sensitively about a
      stranger to the desert by one who was also a stranger to it. The
      complementary figures of Jean Latour and Joseph Vaillant illus-
      trate the traditional contrast between idealist and realist.
      Reprinted: [ca. 1929 or 1930].11; [ca. 1933].11; [ca. 1941].11.

23   "Miss Cather Writes Inscription for Stone." Webster County
      Argus (Red Cloud, Nebr.), 20 October, p. 1.
         Prints Cather's letter of response to Mary Miner Creighton
      on being asked to write an inscription for the cornerstone of the
      new Brodstone Memorial Hospital in Superior, Nebraska. The let-
      ter was read at the exercises for the laying of the stone.

24   N., M. "En amerikansk familjefar" [An American father].
      Göteborgs Morgon Post, 14 November, p. 4.
         In Swedish. Asserts that the ideas in The Professor's
      House are only half-developed and that the section about Tom
      Outland's adventures on the mesa has nothing to do with the rest
      of the book. It is merely Cather being sentimental. The only
      complete portrait is of Godfrey St. Peter, who remains pleasantly
      memorable.

25   NEWMAN, FRANCES. "A Reservationist's Impressions of Willa
      Cather's New Mexican Catholic Missionaries of 1850." Literary
      Review of the New York Evening Post, 3 September, p. 8.
         Criticizes Cather's lack of wit and cleverness and declares
      that, with the exception of one sentence, Death Comes for the
      Archbishop has no literary merit at all. There is an unfortunate
      trend in society to find sentimental work such as this--work full
      of stock phrases and characters--appealing.

26   "New Novels." Times Literary Supplement (London), 1 December,
      p. 906.
         Review of Death Comes for the Archbishop calls it a "beau-
      tiful and unusual book" that conveys through its style a sense of
      holiness. Its religious imagery is subtle, but it lacks the
      tight construction of A Lost Lady.

27   PARRINGTON, VERNON LOUIS. Introduction to Giants in the
      Earth, by Ole Rölvaag. Harper's Modern Classics. New York:
      Harper & Brothers, pp. xvi-xvii.
         Makes reference to O Pioneers! and My Ántonia and the warm
      sympathy Cather displays in them. Cather sees the bleakness of
      the immigrants' lot, but backs away from final tragedy and
      futility. In her work, the prairie is finally subdued and the
      wounds it inflicted healed. Reprinted in part: 1930.9.

28 PELANTOVA, ARTEMIS. "Willa Cather and Her Conception of
    Creative Personality." Manuscript, possibly a thesis of some
    sort, prepared at the University of Chicago. Copy located at
    Willa Cather Historical Center, Red Cloud, Nebraska, 41 pp.
        Declares that Cather's interest is in the gifted, not the
    average. Her repeated theme is the "fate of a creative person-
    ality in an everyday world," and she tells the story of that
    personality. Pelantova moves chronologically through Cather's
    novels and collected stories discussing this theme. Reprinted in
    part: 1935.30.

29 PORTERFIELD, ALEXANDER. "An English Opinion: Willa Cather."
    In Willa Cather. See Knopf pamphlet [ca. 1927].42, pp. 4-14.
    Reprint of 1926.22.

30 RASCOE, BURTON. "Miss Cather and Others." Bookman 66
    (October):214.
        Review of Death Comes for the Archbishop avers that it
    lacks both form and theme.

31 Review of My Mortal Enemy. Dial 82 (January):73.
        Maintains that the book is excessively taut and lacks
    warmth. Cather needs to relax her severity and increase the
    emotional content of her work.

32 ROBBINS, FRANCES [C.] LAMONT. "Speaking of Books." Outlook
    147 (26 October):251.
        Review of Death Comes for the Archbishop judges it to be
    neither novel nor biography, but instead, a blending of truth and
    imagination. Cather demonstrates keen understanding and an
    ability to see beyond the actual.

33 RONNEBECK, ARNOLD. Review of Death Comes for the Archbishop.
    Rocky Mountain News (Denver), [Autumn 1927].
        Compares Cather's verbal artistry to the watercolor artistry
    of Santa Fe painter, Frank G. Applegate.

34 ROSS, MARY. "Bright Edges of the World." Survey 59
    (1 November):164.
        Review of Death Comes for the Archbishop. In the passing
    of Jean Latour, Cather beautifully portrays the passing of a
    "bright chapter" in his church's history and in the history of
    the United States.

35 SERGEANT, ELIZABETH SHEPLEY. "Willa Cather: Prairie Cliff."
    In Fire Under the Andes. New York: Alfred A. Knopf, pp. 4-7
    passim, 261-82.
        A revised text of 1925.34. Basically the same content as
    the previous essay, but notes also that Cather was impervious to
    the social and philosophical doctrines of her time. She lived by
    her own artistic creed, best stated in her preface to a collec-
    tion of stories by Sarah Orne Jewett. Abridged: 1931.43.

36   STUART, HENRY LONGAN. "A Vivid Page of History in Miss
      Cather's New Novel." New York Times Book Review, 4 September,
      p. 2.
         Expresses some reservations about a new type of fiction
      that uses historical materials extensively, thus blurring for the
      reader the distinction between fact and invention. Cather, how-
      ever, blends the two with remarkable skill, and at the same time
      "soaks" Death Comes for the Archbishop with the atmosphere of
      barrenness. Reprinted: 1984.89.

37   SWEET, WALDEN E. "In Old Santa Fe." Rocky Mountain News
      (Denver), 25 September, drama sec., p. 7.
         Praises Cather effusively in Death Comes for the Archbishop
      for her "dainty clarity" and her ability at characterization,
      regretting only some of her historical inaccuracies regarding
      particular gold mining sites and camps.

38   TALBOT, FRANCIS, S.J. "Willa Cather Eulogizes the Archbishop."
      America 37 (24 September):572–73.
         Commends Death Comes for the Archbishop as a beautiful
      Catholic novel, a love story in the highest sense of the term,
      but one that also suggests history and biography. There are only
      a few very minor mistakes in Cather's handling of the book's
      Catholic elements.

39   TAYLOR, RACHEL ANNAND. Review of Death Comes for the Arch-
      bishop. Spectator 139 (29 November):894.
         Finds the intention of Death Comes for the Archbishop
      "slightly perplexed" because the book is not really a novel. Its
      main character seems chiefly to provide a center for the presen-
      tation of "a series of impressions" of "strange inhuman land-
      scapes" that are not forcefully linked with the account of Bishop
      Latour's soul journey.

40   WEST, REBECCA. "Miss Cather's Business as an Artist." New
      York Herald Tribune Books, 11 September, pp. 1, 5–6.
         Review of Death Comes for the Archbishop. Offers almost
      unqualified praise for Cather's achievement, her portrayal of men
      of the Catholic Church who exemplify its recognition that human
      life is an experience of the senses as well as the spirit.
      Cather may not be as daring as D.H. Lawrence and some of the
      younger writers who in their politics decry the Puritan attitude
      that suffering is essential to salvation, but in their literature
      demand it. Perhaps what Cather does is better. She creates an
      aesthetically finer, more satisfying art than they, an art that
      has both sensitivity and "mountain pony sturdiness." In Death
      Comes for the Archbishop she makes "a composition out of the
      juxtaposition of different states of being." Reprinted: 1928.19.

41   WHITMAN, WILLIAM, III. "Eminence Comes for Miss Cather."
      Independent 119 (17 September):283.
         Considers Cather to be strong as a stylist and a writer of
      short stories, but weak in the narrative construction of a novel.

In Death Comes for the Archbishop she manages to avoid the structural pitfalls that had flawed her earlier novels.

42   Willa Cather: A Biographical Sketch, an English Opinion, and an Abridged Bibliography. New York: Alfred A. Knopf, 16 pp.
    This is the first of several undated pamphlets issued by the Knopf company, with each succeeding one containing some reprints from previous pamphlets. The biographical sketch that appears in each of them was apparently written by Cather herself and therefore is not listed here. On the basis of bibliographical listings in each pamphlet, it is possible to make an educated guess as to the approximate date of each. This issue contains a biographical sketch, a reprint of 1926.22, and a bibliography ending with My Mortal Enemy. Expanded: [ca. 1929 or 1930].27; [ca. 1933].21; [ca. 1941].20.

43   "Willa Cather in Somber Mood as She Writes Story of Taos and Santa Fe in Early Days." New Mexico State Tribune, 10 September, p. 6.
    Reviews Death Comes for the Archbishop in a report on books singled out in a National Education Association Book Survey. Death Comes for the Archbishop shows an exquisite sensitivity and a "poignant tenderness," but its plot is "negligible," and its primary illumination is derived from its religious content. It may at times seem oppressively somber.

44   WILLIAMS, MICHAEL. "Willa Cather's Masterpiece." Commonweal 6 (28 September):490–92.
    Urges that Catholics are duty-bound to read and to recommend Death Comes for the Archbishop, a true work of art that shows sensitive understanding of the purpose and spiritual nature of Catholicism. Reprinted: 1928.21.

1928

1   DICKINSON, ASA DON. The Best Books of Our Time 1901–1925. New York: Doubleday, Doran & Co., pp. 56–59, 341–42, 357.
    Publishes excerpts from critical praise for Cather and lists six of her novels among the quarter century's favorite books. Also prints rankings by number of endorsements received; Cather ranks fourteenth. Revised: 1931.16.

2   "4300 Graduates and Seven Distinguished Women and Men Get Degrees." New York Times, 6 June, p. 16.
    Reports that Cather received an honorary doctorate of letters from Columbia University where her work was described as accurate and profoundly insightful.

3   F[RISBIE], J[OSEPHINE]. "Willa Cather and Red Cloud." Present-Day American Literature 1 (July):30–31.
    Portrays Cather in Red Cloud, describing an afternoon tea which Frisbie attended as a youngster at the Cather home at Christmastime. Also tells local anecdotes about Cather.

4   GASS, SHERLOCK BRONSON. "Modernism and the Novel." Forum 79
     (May):757–64.
         Cites Cather as one who illustrates how modern art has
     gone awry in subscribing to a philosophy of literary effect. In
     such work the artist substitutes artifice for personal engage-
     ment. Cather begins The Professor's House as a real story, but
     midway through she steps back, inserts an irrelevant story, and
     then abruptly ends her novel before it is finished.

5   GRABO, CARL H. The Technique of the Novel. New York:
     Charles Scribner's Sons, pp. 74–77, 238–39.
         Adjudges Ántonia Shimerda to be a symbol, a personality
     rather than a character, and argues that point of view is effec-
     tive in My Ántonia, but not in A Lost Lady. Also cites passages
     from Henry James's The Wings of the Dove and A Lost Lady to show
     contrasting methods of character portrayal.

6   JESSUP, MARY E. "A Bibliography of the Writings of Willa
     Cather." American Collector 6 (May–June):67.
         Lists all of Cather's published books, with first edition
     publication data, from April Twilights in 1903 to Death Comes for
     the Archbishop in 1927.

7   MARBLE, ANNIE RUSSELL. A Study of the Modern Novel: British
     and American Since 1900. New York: D. Appleton & Co.,
     pp. 381–88.
         Presents a general estimate of Cather and some of her
     novels, including questions designed for students to ponder, and
     provides a short selected bibliography of books by and about
     Cather. Also points to influences on Cather's work, especially
     Sarah Orne Jewett. Regards The Professor's House as Cather's
     most complex novel, but insists that its two parts are not com-
     pletely linked.

8   MASTERS, HELEN GENEVA. "Nebraska Authors: Willa Cather."
     Nebraska Educational Journal 8 (March):127–28.
         As one in a series of sketches about Nebraska writers,
     presents a rather personal response to Red Cloud and the work of
     Cather, appreciating especially O Pioneers! and Death Comes for
     the Archbishop. To read Cather, one must free oneself from con-
     ventional expectations about fiction. She writes about the con-
     flicting aspects of a person's nature.

9   MICHAUD, RÉGIS. The American Novel To-day: A Social and
     Psychological Study. Boston: Little, Brown & Co., pp. 22,
     238–48.
         First published in French (see 1926.16). Treats Cather as
     one of many American writers obsessed with the problems created
     by the inhibitions of Puritanism. Through her sympathy for her
     characters, Cather softened the harsh social realism of some of
     her contemporaries. Nevertheless, there is in her work a strong
     strain of moral repression, evident in such novels as A Lost
     Lady (which depicts a modern-day King Lear). My Ántonia illus-

trates Cather's "static" but optimistic realism and shows her
sympathy. Style for Cather is always secondary to character.

10   "New Novels." Times Literary Supplement (London), 10 May,
       p. 354.
           Review of My Mortal Enemy calls it a "long short story," a
     work that fuses opposites with Myra Henshawe as its focal point.

11   OVERTON, GRANT. The Philosophy of Fiction. New York:
       D. Appleton & Co., pp. 136–37 passim, 184–96.
           Recommends A Lost Lady as a book to be studied by prospec-
     tive writers of fiction for its achievement as a novel of charac-
     ter. The shifting angle of vision in the novel is especially
     important, for it allows the reader to apprehend things about
     Marian Forrester that cushion the shock of revelations about her
     morality, revelations that strike Niel Herbert with full force.
     She is the instrument for Niel's emotional education. In other
     books, too, Cather's concern is less with a particular character
     than with the effect of that character on others.

12   _____. "Willa Cather." In The Women Who Make Our Novels.
       Rev. ed. New York: Dodd, Mead & Co., pp. 76–97. Reprint.
       Freeport, N.Y.: Books for Libraries, 1967.
           A revised text of 1918.7. After rehearsing biographical
     data, presents a more pointed, though still laudatory, critical
     discussion of Cather's first four novels. Then, launches into a
     discussion of the novels from One of Ours to Death Comes for the
     Archbishop. Claims My Ántonia, A Lost Lady, The Professor's
     House, and Death Comes for the Archbishop to be Cather's best
     four books. One of Ours may be her only failure, largely because
     she is sentimental over Claude. Restraint and understatement,
     plus lack of plot in the traditional sense, characterize her
     work.

*13 PHELPS, WILLIAM LYON. "Famous Women in Contemporary Litera-
       ture." World Review (London), 7 May, pp. 216–17.
           Listed in White (1977.37), item 195. Indicates that Cather
     is among the writers discussed.

14   PHILLIPS, R. LECLERC. "American Writers and English Readers."
       Bookman 68 (October):150–55.
           Speculates as to why the English reader has little interest
     in reading American novels. Considers Cather's A Lost Lady to be
     exceptionally well written, but even so, its background is thin
     and barren, and its characters seem slightly unreal.

15   PORTERFIELD, ALEXANDER. "Willa Cather." In Contemporary
       American Authors. Edited by J.C. Squire. New York: Henry
       Holt & Co., pp. 45–67.
           Reprint of 1926.22.

16   "Red Cloud Ladies Visit Hospital." Unidentified [Nebraska]
      periodical (reprint from the Superior Express [19 January
      1928]) in "Bookman" scrapbook, pp. 54-55, at Willa Cather
      Historical Center, Red Cloud, Nebraska.
           Recounts Cather's visit to the hospital in Superior,
      Nebraska, donated by two of her "old friends," "The Lady Evelyn
      Vestey and Lewis T. Brodstone." Cather wrote the inscription for
      the bronze dedicatory tablet (see 1927.23). Tells of Cather's
      conversation with a Dr. McMahon in which he suggests that she
      write a novel based on the experience of the American miner. She
      is said to have replied that one cannot write on something just
      because it interests her. The life must be lived first, without
      thought of turning it into fiction.

17   TAYLOR, JEAN ELSIE. "Main Currents of Regional Literature in
      the Lower Middle West from 1870 to 1927." Ph.D. dissertation,
      University of Missouri, 352 pp.
           Looks for a relationship between the regionalistic litera-
      ture of the Middle West and the period in which it was written,
      treating Cather only as a minor figure.

18   TREE, HESTER. "About the Novels of Willa Cather." Present-
      Day American Literature 1 (July):31-32.
           Relates Cather's work to Tree's theory of what constitutes
      art. In Tree's estimation Cather is one of the few novelists
      writing in English whose work qualifies as art. Her style is
      notable because it is nonexistent. My Mortal Enemy is the peak
      of Cather's achievement as over the years she improved her skill
      and lost her style. That novel has none of the "chunks of com-
      mon magazine writing" that mar Alexander's Bridge and appear in
      traces in Cather's other novels. Cather now works through over-
      tone: what cannot be stated about her fiction can nevertheless
      be understood.

19   WEST, REBECCA. "The Classic Artist." In The Strange Neces-
      sity. New York: Doubleday, Doran & Co., pp. 233-48; London:
      Jonathan Cape, pp. 215-28.
           Reprint of 1927.40. Reprinted: 1967.59.

20   WHIPPLE, T[HOMAS] K[ING]. "Willa Cather." In Spokesmen:
      Modern Writers and American Life. New York: D. Appleton &
      Co., 139-60. Reprint, without subtitle. Berkeley: Univer-
      sity of California Press, 1963.
           An expanded text of 1923.53. Uses the previous article as
      a core, but is even more laudatory, stressing Cather's develop-
      ment in artistic excellence in the novels between A Lost Lady and
      Death Comes for the Archbishop. Cather continually improves,
      eliminating weaknesses that flawed her earlier work while re-
      taining her strengths--her ability to delineate character and to
      charge a small detail with significance. This version of
      Whipple's text not only develops more fully the ideas introduced
      in the earlier article, and discusses the novels that appear in
      the interim, but it adds a discussion of Cather's style, noting
      its deliberate inconspicuousness and its power to evoke sensuous

and concrete imagery. Cather's favorite theme appears throughout her work: the superior person in conflict with an inferior society. Cather writes with perfect balance: she is sane and whole, poised and tactful. Reprinted: 1967.60.

21 WILLIAMS, MICHAEL. "Willa Cather's Masterpiece." In
    Catholicism and the Modern Mind. New York: Dial Press,
    pp. 270-79.
         Reprint of 1927.44.

22 "The Youth of Willa Cather." Present-Day American Literature
    1 (July):29-30.
         Places Cather in the context of the University of Nebraska
    where she studied under and with persons of extraordinary culture
    and ability. A principal concern of hers through the years has
    been the struggle of the artist or intellectual against the re-
    strictive conventionality of the small town.

1929

1 ASHLEY, SCHUYLER. Review of My Mortal Enemy. In Essay
    Reviews by Schuyler Ashley. Edited by Rose Adelaide Witham.
    Kansas City: Lowell Press, pp. 81-83.
         Reprint of 1926.2.

2 _____. Review of The Professor's House. In Essay Reviews by
    Schuyler Ashley. See Ashley 1929.1, pp. 78-80.
         Reprint of 1925.1.

3 CANBY, HENRY SEIDEL. American Estimates. New York:
    Harcourt, Brace & World. Reprint. Port Washington, N.Y.:
    Kennikat Press, 1968, pp. 9, 205-13 passim.
         A section titled "The Feminine Touch in Literature" asserts
    that women writers are in the ascendancy, and that since they
    tend to present men in their novels only in men's love relation-
    ships to women, the male image is bound to suffer serious fic-
    tional neglect and distortion. Although the male image suffers
    in A Lost Lady, in The Professor's House Cather proves to be one
    of the few women writers who can present a man whose central
    aspect lies outside feminine relationship.

4 FIEGENBAUM, MARTHA. "Midwestern Writers: Willa Cather As a
    Local Colorist." Prairie Schooner 3 (Winter):65-68.
         Praises My Ántonia and O Pioneers! for their realistic por-
    trayal of prairie life. In these books Cather treats local color
    as more than a device for setting; she sees it as something that
    depicts life and molds character.

5 FISCHER, WALTHER. Die englische Literatur der Vereingten
    Staaten von Nordamerika. Wildpark-Potsdam: Akademische Ver-
    lagsgesellschaft Athenaion M.B.H., pp. 112, 116.
         Primarily a biographical sketch of Cather.

6   [FISHER], DOROTHY CANFIELD. "An Outstanding Older Book."
Unidentified periodical clipping [1929] at Willa Cather
Historical Center, Red Cloud, Nebraska.
     Regards My Ántonia as a book that everyone should own, and
come to again and again, if not to read a whole section, then
just to enjoy a single page.

7   GLÖDE, O. Review of The Professor's House. Englische Studien
63 (January):323-24.
     Largely a plot summary of Tom Outland's story.

8   GRATTAN, C. HARTLEY. "Sarah Orne Jewett." Bookman 69 (May):
296-98.
     Speaks of Cather's discernment of Jewett's art and says
Jewett's influence on Cather was "profound." Cather's style
stems from Jewett.

9   LEISY, ERNEST ERWIN. American Literature: An Interpretive
Survey. New York: Thomas Y. Crowell Co., pp. 213-14.
     Provides a brief account of Cather and some of her novels
from O Pioneers! to Death Comes for the Archbishop. Cather is
both a poet and a realist, and her poetic powers are best seen
in A Lost Lady.

10   LEWIS, SINCLAIR. "The American Scene in Fiction." New York
Herald Tribune Books, 14 April, p. 1.
     Insists that there is much variety in American fiction and
points to Cather as an example, citing her treatment of many
subjects, from Bohemians in Nebraska to artists in Greenwich
Village. Her work is far above the standard fare of conventional
magazine fiction. Reprinted: 1953.15.

11   LOVETT, ROBERT MORSS. "An American Opinion." In Willa
Cather. See Knopf pamphlet [ca. 1929 or 1930].26, pp. 14-16.
     Reprint of 1927.22.

12   MANLY, JOHN MATTHEWS, and RICKERT, EDITH. Contemporary American Literature: Bibliographies and Study Outlines. Rev. ed.
Revisions and introduction by Fred B. Millett. New York:
Harcourt, Brace & Co., pp. 14-16, 39, 142-43.
     A revised version of 1922.20. Millett provides discussion
and an expanded bibliography for Cather. Suggests that even
though Cather is limited by her rather meager creative abilities,
she stands always for fineness and against shoddiness. Character,
not plot, is her interest, and she has a fresh, finished style.
She should be included among America's short story writers as
well as its novelists.

13   MATTHIESSEN, FRANCIS OTTO. Sarah Orne Jewett. Boston:
Houghton Mifflin Co. Reprint. Gloucester, Mass.: Peter
Smith, 1965, pp. 103, 105, 124-25, 129-32, 145-46.
     Contains several mentions of Cather, especially in regard
to Sarah Orne Jewett's interest in her and Jewett's remarks to
her in letters. Describes and quotes at length from Jewett's

famous letter of advice to Cather (see Fields, 1911.1) in which
she urges the magazine writer to get out of journalism and return
in her writing to her own background. Notes, too, Cather's lasting regard for Jewett and her work.

14   "Ohio College Honors Willa Cather." New York Times, 6 June,
     p. 17.
        Tells of Cather's being awarded the honorary degree of
Doctor of Literature at Mount St. Joseph College.

15   OVERTON, GRANT. "Willa Cather." An Hour of the American
     Novel. One Hour Series. Philadelphia: J.B. Lippincott Co.,
     pp. 148-52.
        Avows that Cather may be the country's top novelist, and
sketches brief plot outlines of her novels from O Pioneers! to
Death Comes for the Archbishop, excluding My Mortal Enemy.
Occasional interpretive remarks on the novels include the assertion that in A Lost Lady it is not Marian Forrester that matters,
but her effect on Niel Herbert.

16   PORTERFIELD, ALEXANDER. "An English Opinion: Willa Cather."
     In Willa Cather. See Knopf pamphlet [ca. 1929 or 1930].27,
     pp. 4-14.
        Reprint of 1926.22.

17   PRESTON, KEITH. Pot Shots from Pegasus. New York: Covici
     Friede Publishers, pp. 15, 233-38.
        Presents a little verse that plays on the name of Anita
Loos and the title of Cather's book, A Lost Lady. In a section
titled "The Professor and Modern Literature," Preston discusses
the professor as a type and then treats two books that feature
professors, Stanley Johnson's Professor and Cather's The Professor's House. The former is propaganda, the latter art. Still,
Cather succumbed to popular demand for happy endings in the book;
on artistic grounds, St. Peter should have died.

18   RASCOE, BURTON. "Another Glimpse of Willa Cather." In A
     Bookman's Daybook. Edited by C. Hartley Grattan. New York:
     Horace Liveright, pp. 210-11.
        Reprint of 1924.12.

19   _____. "First Meeting with Willa Cather." In A Bookman's
     Daybook. See Rascoe 1929.18, pp. 206-8.
        Reprint of 1924.11. Reprinted: 1952.14.

20   ROSICKY, ROSE. A History of Czechs (Bohemians) in Nebraska.
     Omaha: Czech Historical Society of Nebraska, p. 207.
        Lists Czechs who settled in Webster County and says that
they became famous there because Cather wrote about them with
such sympathy. She thoroughly grasped their psychology.

21 SMITH, R.D. HILTON. "The Novels of Willa Cather." Library
    Assistant (England), April, pp. 85-86.
         Declares that Cather deserves much more recognition than
    she has had. She "triumphantly achieves again and again" the
    novelist's highest art, the creation of a character who is highly
    individual but who at the same time embodies a country or a seg-
    ment of life.

22 STALNAKER, JOHN M., and EGGAN, FRED. "American Novelists
    Ranked: A Psychological Study." English Journal 18 (April):
    295-307.
         Presents, along with a lengthy justification and rationale,
    the results of a survey in which thirty-one eminent critics re-
    sponded with ratings of seventy-two American novelists on a scale
    of one to ten. Cather came out number one, Edith Wharton number
    two. They alone comprise the top group, with Dreiser, Cabell,
    Anderson, and Lewis in the second group.

23 "10,000,000 Given to Yale in a Year." New York Times,
    20 June, p. 16.
         Reports that Cather received an Honorary Doctor of Letters
    degree from Yale University, and that her work was praised for
    its penetration into the depths of human nature.

24 "Urges Appreciation of Cather by British." New York Times,
    30 November, p. 8.
         Reports a speech given by J[ohn] B[oynton] Priestley to the
    Oxford University English Club in which Priestley condemns Ameri-
    can writers for their rebellious attitude and praises Cather for
    avoiding this tendency. She is "one of the greatest living
    writers." Abridged: 1929.28.

25 Van DYKE, HENRY. "Death Comes for the Archbishop." In The
    Man Behind the Book: Essays in Understanding. New York:
    Charles Scribner's Sons, pp. 335-57.
         Expresses appreciation for Cather who has used her art to
    portray human goodness, then details the narrative line of Death
    Comes for the Archbishop, sometimes citing long passages from the
    book. The theme of the novel is "religion as adventure."

26 WAGENKNECHT, EDWARD. "Willa Cather." Sewanee Review 37
    (April-June):221-39.
         Defends Cather against her contemporary critics and
    society's attitudes toward art and artists generally by applaud-
    ing the affirmation of life and humanity found in her novels.
    Also draws a link between Cather's early life in Nebraska and her
    later artistic achievements. Discusses, too, Cather's technical
    failures—largely structural—and successes, as well as aspects
    of her artistic theory about the unfurnished novel. Cather is
    sound, genuine, and wholesome, and she passionately reveals the
    meaning and beauty in common things. Adapted: 1952.18.

27   Willa Cather: A Biographical Sketch, an English Opinion, an
     American Opinion, a Letter from Willa Cather, and an Abridged
     Bibliography. New York: Alfred A. Knopf, 23 pp.
          An expanded edition of [ca. 1927].42. Contains reprints of
     1926.22; 1927.22, and an updated primary and secondary bibliog-
     raphy that lists Death Comes for the Archbishop but not Shadows
     on the Rock. The bibliography also lists secondary works pub-
     lished in 1928. The letter Cather wrote to Commonweal regarding
     Death Comes for the Archbishop is reprinted here as well.

28   "Willa Cather in England." Des Moines Register, 29 December.
          An abridged text of 1929.24.

1930

1   BRUNS, FRIEDRICH. Die amerikanische Dichtung der Gegenwart.
     Leipzig: Verlag und Druck Von B.G. Teubner, pp. 62–67.
          Focuses on Cather's development as a literary realist,
     especially in her prairie novels.

2   CABELL, JAMES BRANCH. Some of Us: An Essay in Epitaphs.
     New York: Robert M. McBride & Co., p. 43.
          Confesses his ignorance of Cather's work and his admiration
     for her reputation, regretting that he is not qualified to dis-
     cuss her work in his essay.

3   "Crowd Hears Lewis Talk at Gothenburg." New York Times,
     20 December, p. 19.
          Indicates that when Sinclair Lewis accepted the Nobel Prize
     for literature, he agreed with Henry Van Dyke that Cather should
     have won the award.

*4   FEUILLERAT, A. "Romancières américaines: Miss Willa
     Cather." Figaro, 16 May.
          Listed in Bibliography of English Language and Literature,
     1930.

5   HARVEY, ALICE G. "Nebraska Writers: VI--Willa Cather."
     Nebraska's Own Magazine 1 (August):6.
          Cather's principal themes concern the foreign pioneer and
     his environment, the artist, and the American Southwest. Her
     works are not actually novels, but series of episodes, and her
     best works feature women. She excells at description.

6   LEONARD, WALLACE. "I Meet Willa Cather." Present-Day Ameri-
     can Literature, 4 (November):60–63.
          Tells of a longstanding desire to meet Cather, of a youth-
     ful enthrallment with O Pioneers!, and of a later captivation by
     A Lost Lady. Then describes an incident in which Leonard ob-
     served a young Swedish woman act with dignity in the way Cather's
     Alexandra Bergson might have. In this real life Alexandra he
     felt he had at last met Cather. (Note: article pages are

printed "December 1930" and hand corrected to read "November" in
the copy on file in the Faulkner-Slote collection, University of
Nebraska library, Lincoln.)

7   "Mr. Lewis's Nobel Prize." New York Times, 6 November, p. 26.
        Questions the selection of Sinclair Lewis as recipient of
the Nobel Prize for literature, and sees the award as affirming
popularity rather than quality. Points to the choice of Lewis as
a further example of the discrepancy between European and American literary values. Suggests Cather and others as more likely
choices.

8   The National Cyclopaedia of American Biography. Current
        vol. A. New York: James T. White & Co., pp. 537–38.
        Outlines biographical data and praises Cather for her in-
dividualistic style and her pure language, both of which are in
evidence in A Lost Lady, thought by some to be her masterpiece.

9   PARRINGTON, VERNON LEWIS. "Willa Cather: Epics and Women."
        In Main Currents in American Thought: An Interpretation of
        American Literature from the Beginnings to 1920. Vol. 3. New
        York: Harcourt, Brace & Co., pp. 382–84, 393–94.
        Appears in an "Addenda" section prepared and included
posthumously by the publisher from Parrington's syllabus notes,
apparently part of his design for volume 3. Contains notes on
Cather books up through A Lost Lady. These notes dismiss The
Troll Garden and Alexander's Bridge as inconsequential, but regard The Song of the Lark as American literature's "most convincing" story of artist life. Cather is an excellent craftsman
who developed slowly. She cannot be labeled as either romantic
or naturalistic, but she is unconcerned with contemporary problems. See also Cather discussion in the Rölvaag section of the
"Addenda" reprinted from 1927.27.

10   PATTEE, FRED LEWIS. The New American Literature 1890–1930.
        New York: Century Co. Reprint. Cooper Square Publishers,
        1968, pp. 181, 260–67.
        Places Cather with the "utter romantics" who in the new
urbanism are destined to lose their romanticism and become dis-
illusioned. Avers that Cather has never really been rooted or
totally at home anywhere and therefore lacks an emotional center.
Although she has mastered style and presented sharp-cut characters, there is little warmth in her work. The reader sees, but
cannot share feeling.

11   RAPIN, RENÉ. Willa Cather. Modern American Writers Series,
        edited by Ernest Boyd. New York: Robert M. McBride & Co.,
        119 pp.
        The first book-length assessment of Cather and her work.
Rapin gives biographical data and discusses each book in turn up
through Death Comes for the Archbishop, which may be "Cather's
greatest book." Alexander's Bridge is a failure, My Ántonia is
inferior to both O Pioneers! and The Song of the Lark, One of
Ours is her best book to date, A Lost Lady is "charming," but

still "minor art," The Professor's House has little story but is
"singularly moving," and My Mortal Enemy has "all the elements of
a great book" but is weak. Willa Cather's work is "classical."

12   ROBERTS, DENNIS. "Willa Cather and the Realistic School of
      Thought." Unidentified periodical clipping [ca. late 1920s
      or early 1930s] in scrapbook I-28 at Willa Cather Historical
      Center, Red Cloud, Nebraska.
            Claims that Cather, more than many of her contemporaries,
      is America's true realist because she sees the whole of America,
      without prejudice. She writes without cynicism of the funda-
      mentals, and she writes of noble men and women as well as of
      ignoble, and of victory as well as defeat.

13   "Social Meaning of Willa Cather." Present-Day American Lit-
      erature 4 (November):75-76.
            Uses Cather and her sensitive portrayal of the process of
      "Americanizing " immigrants to make a plea for tolerance and for
      appreciation of the cultural differences that have shaped America.
      (See note appended to 1930.6, regarding date of this publication.)

14   "Speech in America Defended by Arliss." New York Times,
      15 November, p. 15.
            Reports that Cather received the William Dean Howells Medal
      from the American Academy of Arts and Letters for her novel Death
      Comes for the Archbishop. Notes that the Academy praised the
      novel as the most distinguished work to come out of America in
      the last five years. (Most of the article is devoted to George
      Arliss's speech on the purity of language, delivered upon his re-
      ceiving a medal for his diction on stage.)

15   "Willa Cather Began Career As Journal Writer." Lincoln State
      Journal, 16 November, sec. c, p. 3.
            Reprints Cather's article on her trip to Brownville,
      Nebraska, and suggests that opening old newspaper files and read-
      ing in Cather's early journalistic pieces will reveal clear evi-
      dence of the style and spirit that mark her writing after that.

16   "Willa Cather Increases in Stature as Most Important and Most
      Interesting Figure Among Contemporary American Women Writers."
      San Francisco Chronicle, 10 August.
            Declares that Cather's intense interest in, and attraction
      to, immigrant farmers could have come about only through her
      introduction to them at an early age. If she had been born on
      the prairie, she would have taken the various life-styles for
      granted instead of contrasting them to the more staid life-style
      she had known in Virginia. Her work breaks away from the con-
      fining New England tradition of books about manners and presents
      fiction that is fresh, authentic, and original.

<u>1931</u>

1   ARVIN, NEWTON. "Quebec, Nebraska and Pittsburgh." <u>New</u>
      <u>Republic</u> 67 (12 August):345–46.
          Accuses Cather of failing to understand modern society.
    She is always an individual writing about individuals. Her
    writing style is good, but <u>Shadows on the Rock</u> is dull. Un-
    fortunately, Cather has written about something outside her
    experience, seventeenth-century Quebec.

2   ASHLEY, SCHUYLER. Review of <u>My Mortal Enemy</u>. In <u>Essays of</u>
      <u>Today: Informal and Formal</u>. Edited by Rose Adelaide Witham.
      Boston: Houghton Mifflin Co., Riverside Press, pp. 309–12.
          Reprint of 1926.2.

3   BATES, ARTHUR DYGERT. "History and Romance in Old Quebec."
      <u>Christian Century</u> 48 (9 September):1118–19.
          Accords high praise to <u>Shadows on the Rock</u> for its beauty,
    romance, and exquisite prose.

4   BLANKENSHIP, RUSSELL. "Beyond the Village: Willa Cather."
      In <u>American Literature As an Expression of The American Mind</u>.
      New York: Henry Holt & Co., pp. 435, 673–80, 718–20. Re-
      prints. 1949; Totowa, N.J.: Cooper Square Publishers, 1973.
          Refers to "The Novel Démeublé" and calls it the best criti-
    cism extant of Cather's work. Praises Cather for her restraint
    in treating reality, for achieving both objectivity and sympathy,
    and for daring to go against the critical grain. Her constant
    subject is the conflict between character and environment—often
    the village, and she explores that conflict effectively through
    an exceptional narrative style and a sense of design that does
    not require the usual expectations of plot. She will endure.

5   BOGAN, LOUISE. "American-Classic." <u>New Yorker</u> 7 (8 August):
      19–22.
          A highly complimentary overall assessment of Cather and
    her work, covering details of biography, personal appearance,
    manner, and artistry. Characterizes Cather as independent,
    natural, sound, and not given to bending with contemporary lit-
    erary winds. Her strength lies in her ability to portray in fine
    prose and solid narrative "the look of a place and the actions of
    people." <u>The Troll Garden</u> and <u>Alexander's Bridge</u> are missteps,
    but after them Cather found her own turf and has not faltered
    since. Reprinted: 1967.2.

6   BOOTH, ALICE. "Willa Cather." <u>Good Housekeeping</u> 93
      (September):34–35, 196–98.
          Ninth essay in a series titled "America's Twelve Greatest
    Women." Dramatizes Booth's first meeting with Cather, presents
    an account of Cather's life, and describes some of Cather's
    writing habits. Adjudges Cather to be a "direct" writer who does
    not adorn, who simply presents people as they are. Reports that
    Cather described her method in <u>The Professor's House</u> to be that

of "the <u>roman</u> in the <u>nouvelle</u>"; she also employed the "trick lighting and double <u>scene</u>" of Dutch painters.

7   BOYNTON, PERCY H. <u>The Rediscovery of the Frontier</u>. Chicago: University of Chicago Press, pp. 116–18, 124, 125.
        An abridged text of 1924.1. Focuses on Cather's treatment of the alien immigrant in her first three prairie novels about strong prairie women. Since Cather could know the immigrant only by "sympathetic observation," her work lacks hardihood and "scrupulous realism." Modified: 1936.3; 1940.4.

8   BUTCHER, FANNY. "Willa Cather Writes a Novel of Old Quebec." <u>Chicago Daily Tribune</u>, 15 August, p. 10.
        Finds the content of <u>Shadows on the Rock</u> less important than its beautiful, fluid style. It is one of the "most excitingly exquisite bits of prose in the English language."

9   CALVERTON, V.F. <u>American Literature at the Crossroads</u>. University of Washington Chapbooks, edited by Glenn Hughes, no. 48. Seattle: University of Washington Book Store, pp. 24–28 passim.
        Sees in Cather, as in others, a spirit of revolt against the lost values of rural life through the city's predatory gains.

10   C[ANBY], H[ENRY] S[EIDEL]. "A Letter by Willa Cather." <u>Saturday Review of Literature</u> 8 (17 October):216.
        Introduces a letter written by Cather, in response to Wilbur Cross's complimentary review of <u>Shadows on the Rock</u> (see 1931.15). The letter, which was later published in <u>Willa Cather on Writing</u>, sets forth what Cather was attempting to do in that novel. Canby indicates that the letter was not written for publication, but that Cather agreed to let it appear. Observes that ordinarily Cather is not one to explain or defend her work to the "dull" or "antagonistic," nor even to discuss it with admirers.

11   "Cather Pageant of Quebec in the Sixteen Hundreds." <u>Kansas City Star</u>, 1 August, p. 14.
        Regards <u>Shadows on the Rock</u> as less a novel than a combination of biography and history cast in the form of fiction. Its Catholic tones and imagery make it a companion piece to <u>Death Comes for the Archbishop</u>.

12   CHAMAILLARD, PIERRE. "Le cas de Marian Forrester." <u>Revue anglo-américaine</u>, 8, no. 5 (June):419–27.
        Cather's favorite subjects are the pioneer and the artist, and for her they are synonymous. This is apparent in her choices of Alexandra Bergson, Thea Kronborg, Tom Outland, Godfrey St. Peter, and Jean Latour as leading characters. Marian Forrester, however, is "une grande artiste"; she is both poet and poetry. But her kind of beauty is bound to bring trouble, and she becomes a tragic figure, one born at the wrong time, a middlewestern Emma Bovary. Niel Herbert in <u>A Lost Lady</u> evolves into representative

man, something of a universal observer, a "spectateur par excellence." He is the youthful idealist who is educated in the course of the novel.

13   CHAMBERLAIN, JOHN. "Willa Cather's Tale of Canada." New York
      Times Book Review, 2 August, p. 1.
          Compares Shadows on the Rock to a multipaneled fresco; it
      has a spiritual quality and is beautifully painted, but it has no
      plot or conflict or drama. Perhaps Cather, with her limited ex-
      perience, has lost her feel for realism.

14   COATES, ROBERT M. "The Art of Willa Cather." New Yorker 7
      (15 August):49-50.
          Review of Shadows on the Rock. Recognizes the relative
      unimportance of narrative to this novel, but nonetheless laments
      its lack of a rich story line. There is perhaps too much wist-
      fulness in the book; it seems fragile by comparison with A Lost
      Lady.

15   CROSS, WILBUR (GOVERNOR). "Men and Images." Saturday Review
      of Literature 8 (22 August):67-68.
          In Shadows on the Rock Cather undertakes a different sort
      of book, a difficult one likely to be misunderstood by many
      readers. Its title signals its method, which is to create a
      subdued poetic tone. Every touch is delicate, action is held to
      a minimum, political history is barely sketched in, characters
      are only glimpsed, quarrels are suggested rather than portrayed,
      hardships are downplayed. Cather's mind emits a "romantic glow,"
      and her prose has a lyrical quality. Reprinted: 1984.21.
      Cather's response to the governor's assessment appears in the
      17 October issue of Saturday Review of Literature, and is re-
      printed in Willa Cather on Writing.

16   DICKINSON, ASA DON. The Best Books of Our Time 1901-1925.
      Rev. ed. New York: H.W. Wilson Co., pp. 56-59.
          Essentially a reprint of 1928.1.

17   GRANT, ROBERT. Presentation of the Howells Medal of the
      American Academy of Arts and Letters to Willa Cather. Academy
      Notes and Monographs, no. 75, pp. 325-35.
          Prints the text of the presentation made by Robert Grant,
      a member of the Academy, to Cather for the writing of Death Comes
      for the Archbishop. Praises the book for its beauty and its
      inspired treatment of human values in a radiant landscape. In-
      cludes Cather's acceptance remarks.

18   GREGORY, HORACE. Review of Shadows on the Rock. Symposium 2
      (October):551-54.
          Maintains that Shadows on the Rock is unconvincing, that it
      distorts life in old Quebec by idealizing reality and failing to
      grasp the hardships experienced there.

19   HARRIS, WILLIAM E. "Willa Cather and Shadows on the Rock."
     Boston Evening Transcript, 1 August, p. 8.
         Studies Cather's transition from author of realistic biog-
     raphies to writer of mystical romance. What appears as romance,
     however, is really an understanding of all humankind. Cather is
     still an objective observer, but her vision has expanded. Shad-
     ows on the Rock is "a biography of a time and a place," not the
     biography of an individual.

20   HAWKINS, ETHEL WALLACE. Review of Shadows on the Rock.
     "Atlantic Bookshelf." Atlantic Monthly 148 (August):8, 10.
         Appreciates Cather's realistic portrayal of childhood, as
     well as her compassion and her sense of historical understanding
     in Shadows on the Rock. Notes also the book's harmonious struc-
     ture.

21   HICKS, GRANVILLE. "Bright Incidents." Forum 86 (September):
     vi, viii.
         Shadows on the Rock is mainly a series of incidents that
     deal with the conflict between solid faith and the changeable
     life of the frontier. This "incident" approach weakens the novel
     by robbing it of focus and giving it over to the author's passive
     observations.

22   "Home-Grown Parnassian." Time 18 (3 August):47–48.
         In addition to a cover picture, features a review of
     Shadows on the Rock and a biographical-personal sketch of Cather.
     Finds her work and her nature happily different from those of her
     contemporaries. Her style is simple and effective, but what best
     marks her work is something highly individual that shines through
     it, "like moonlight under water."

23   JONES, LLEWELYN. "Contemporary Fiction." In American Writers
     on American Literature. Edited by John Macy. New York:
     Horace Liveright, pp. 488–502 passim.
         Regards Cather as America's foremost novelist.

24   KAUFMAN, KENNETH C. Review of Shadows on the Rock. Southwest
     Review 16 (Summer):xi–xiii.
         Finds Shadows on the Rock disappointing in its inevitable
     comparison to Death Comes for the Archbishop. The earlier novel
     enjoys a major personality as protagonist, but the later one
     settles for a secondary character. Quebec itself is actually the
     main character, and Cather convincingly portrays life there.

25   KNIGHT, GRANT C. The Novel in English. New York: Richard R.
     Smith, pp. 350–51. Reprint. Totowa, N.J.: Cooper Square
     Publishers, 1972.
         Mentions several of Cather's novels and says her importance
     lies in her reminding writers that there is a story to be told in
     the relation of pioneers to the land.

26   KRONENBERGER, LOUIS.   "Willa Cather."   Bookman 74 (October):
     134–40.
         Divides Cather's novels into three periods: (1) O Pioneers!
through My Ántonia, (2) One of Ours through My Mortal Enemy, and
(3) Death Comes for the Archbishop and Shadows on the Rock.   The
best books are in the first period where Cather affirms life in
a world she knows well and produces a "tone of lyrical nostalgia."
The books of the second period are characterized by frustration
and unrest, and, with the exception of A Lost Lady, are not so
strong as the earlier novels.   Cather is better when she writes
about success than when she writes about failure.   The two books
of the third period partake of a genteel spirit and show Cather
to be going the wrong way.   Although the last books are "shape-
lier" than the earlier ones, they are paler and lacking in richness and earthiness.

27   KUNITZ, STANLEY J. [Dilly Tante], ed.   Living Authors: A
     Book of Biographies.   New York: H.W. Wilson Co., pp. 66–67.
     Reprint. 1935.
         Outlines Cather's biography and lists her works, noting
also such personal qualities as her vivid personality and the
"gentle frankness" of her speech.   Revised: 1942.6.

28   Le CRON, HELEN COWLES.   "Mrs. Le Cron Is Disappointed in Willa
     Cather's New Novel, Shadows on the Rock."   Des Moines Register,
     27 September, sec. 10-a, p. 4.
         Concludes that Shadows on the Rock, with its rather shallow
and dull approach, is readable, but not very important.

29   LEWIS, SINCLAIR.   "The American Fear of Literature."   In Why
     Sinclair Lewis Got the Nobel Prize.   Edited by Erik Axel
     Karlfeldt.   New York: Harcourt, Brace & Co.
         This small booklet contains the text of Lewis's Nobel
Prize acceptance address, delivered 12 December 1930.   Lewis says
in the address that if Cather had been given the award there
would have been criticism because A Lost Lady violates America's
patent idea of what constitutes virtue.   Karlfeldt was permanent
secretary of the Swedish Academy.   Revised: 1953.14.   This address is also published in vol. 15 of The Annals of America, by
Encyclopedia Britannica, Inc.

30   MacAFEE, HELEN.   "The Library of the Quarter: Outstanding
     Novels."   Yale Review, n.s. 21 (Autumn):viii.
         Review of Shadows on the Rock sees special importance in
its title, for Cather is dealing with the insubstantial shadows
cast by memories and by dreams that will go unfulfilled.   Even
though this book does not meet novelistic requirements of
"mounting event and emotion," it compensates through the cumula-
tive gathering of reflection on values, values that merit being
saved when civilization makes a transition from an old world to
a new, or from past to present.

31   McCOLE, CAMILLE. Review of Shadows on the Rock. Catholic
     World 133 (September):752-53.
          Cather is one of the few modern novelists to retain a
     simple yet noble vision, untouched by "sophistication." Of spe-
     cial note in Shadows on the Rock is her "perfect fusion of style
     and subject" through the creation of emotional undertones and
     shades of mood, her adherence to high ideals, her heroic and un-
     forgettable characters, and her evocation of a strong religious
     spirit.

32   MATTHIESSEN, F[RANCIS] O[TTO]. "New England Stories." In
     American Writers on American Literature. See Jones 1931.23,
     p. 413.
          Believes that much of Cather's style was inherited from
     Sarah Orne Jewett, but that in her later work Cather's style is
     too obvious in its classic and somewhat self-conscious restraint.

33   MEAGHER, CHARLOTTE M. Review of Shadows on the Rock.
     Quarterly Bulletin of the International Federation of Catholic
     Alumnae 14 (December):25.
          Discovers "added delights" for the Catholic reader of this
     "idyll of the North." There is no plot to Shadows on the Rock,
     for it is built out of episodes in a young girl's life that to-
     gether create "a richly colored pageant vibrant with the throb of
     the colony heart."

34   MURPHY, DONALD R. "Willa Cather's Admirers Defend Her Quebec
     Novel." Des Moines Register, 1 November, sec. 10-a, p. 5.
          Cites defenders of Shadows on the Rock who have come for-
     ward since several critics judged the novel to be second-rate
     among Cather's works. Perceives Cather's writing to be a "sub-
     dued oil painting of shadows" in contrast with the realistic
     style of her contemporaries. Shadows on the Rock is interesting
     to those who admire simple characters and basic strengths.

35   MURRAY, JOHN. Review of Shadows on the Rock. Canadian Book-
     man 13 (August):167-68.
          Believes Shadows on the Rock has been criticized unfairly
     by those who condemn it for lack of action. It is work of a dif-
     ferent sort, and it can go far in promoting religious tolerance
     and brotherhood among the various peoples that comprise Canada.

36   "Princeton Closes Its Academic Year with the Awarding of Many
     Degrees." New York Times, 17 June, p. 29.
          Comments that Cather's honorary Doctor of Letters degree
     attracted attention because it is the first time in Princeton's
     history that a woman has received such an award. Cather received
     an ovation and was praised for the truth and the "exquisite
     rightness" of her art.

37   PUGH, MARY. Review of A Lost Lady. Present-Day American
     Literature 4 (May):206-7.
         Perceives A Lost Lady to have nearly its total being in
     Marian Forrester. She is "the story, the language, . . . the
     whole." Frank Ellinger was the pivot of her life; her love for
     him was what sparked her dreams, her desire, and her daring.
     When he deserted her, she was lost, and she never completely re-
     covered from that setback.

38   REILLY, JOSEPH J. "A Singing Novelist." Commonweal 13
     (25 February):464-66.
         Quotes at length from some of the poems omitted from later
     editions of April Twilights and regrets their omission, contend-
     ing that the whole first volume of poems shows Cather to be a
     talented poet with a particular gift for discerning the loneli-
     ness of the human soul. In her poems Cather avoids the abstract
     and symbolic and presents the concrete and human.

39   Review of Shadows on the Rock. Catholic World 133 (September):
     752.
         Praises Cather's adherence to high ideals and her effective
     use of "undertone of feeling," and encourages Catholics espe-
     cially to read Shadows on the Rock for its strong religious
     spirit. Cather's characters are unforgettable, even heroic, in
     bringing their God to a new country, thereby making it richer.

40   "The Roamer." Baltimore Catholic Review, 11 September.
         Takes an almost reverential view of Shadows on the Rock,
     feeling that full appreciation of the novel requires understand-
     ing of the Catholic faith and culture. Cather exhibits honesty,
     simplicity, and faith as she captures the spirit of old Quebec.

41   ROBBINS, FRANCES [C.] LAMONT. "Three Novels by Women."
     Outlook 158 (5 August):440.
         Review of Shadows on the Rock appreciates Cather for her
     rich descriptions and restrained, yet alive, prose, but deplores
     her lack of plot and theme. Regrets, too, that her characters
     are mere "ghosts" without soul.

42   ROURKE, CONSTANCE. American Humor: A Study of the National
     Character. New York: Harcourt, Brace & Co., p. 281. Re-
     print. Doubleday & Co., Anchor Books, 1935.
         There is in Cather's books "the touch of distant music,"
     and they can be called romances even though their characters and
     circumstances convey a sense of the modern. Cather is more
     easily compared with poets than with novelists; she uses basic
     forms, and she enshrines the past. Reprinted in part: 1976.27.

43   SERGEANT, ELIZABETH SHEPLEY. "Willa Cather: Prairie Cliff."
     In Essays of Today: Informal and Formal. See Ashley 1931.2,
     pp. 273-80.
         An abridged text of 1927.35.

44   SMALL, HAROLD. "Willa Cather Tells 'Secret' Novel's Title."
      San Francisco Chronicle, 26 March, p. 19.
            Reports an interview with Cather on the occasion of her
      honorary doctorate from the University of California at Berkeley.
      She would not talk about her new book, soon to be released, ex-
      cept to give its title (Shadows on the Rock). But she talks at
      some length about Death Comes for the Archbishop, indicating that
      the reading of Father Machebeuf's letters to his sister stirred
      her deeply. By the next morning her book about the two priests
      had taken shape in her mind, had "projected" itself on the wall
      of her hotel room in Santa Fe "by a sort of magic lantern." She
      also describes the French painting that inspired the novel's
      opening scene.

45   SOSKIN, WILLIAM. "Willa Cather's Poetic Tale of Olden
      Quebec." Literary Review of the New York Evening Post,
      1 August, p. 10.
            Shadows on the Rock fails as a novel, for in it no story
      develops and no characters experience growth. It succeeds as a
      piece of impressive prose whose purpose is the creation of
      atmosphere.

46   TAYLOR, MARGARET RUTH. Review of Shadows on the Rock.
      Epsilon Sigma Alpha Sorority News, December, p. 5.
            Praises the "beautiful picture" Cather draws in Shadows on
      the Rock, but wishes the book offered more than that.

47   "That Final Sacrifice." New Mexico Quarterly 1 (November):
      419-21.
            Review of Shadows on the Rock. Cather's strength lies not
      in plot or action, but in description, characterization, and
      style.

48   "12 Women Declared Nation's 'Greatest.'" New York Times,
      24 February, p. 18.
            Reports that an all-male jury selected Cather as one of
      America's twelve greatest living women. Nominations were sent
      in by readers of Good Housekeeping magazine.

49   Van DOREN, CARL. "Willa Cather's New Chronicle of Virtue."
      New York Herald Tribune Books, 2 August, p. 1.
            Reviews most of Cather's novels prior to Shadows on the
      Rock and notes how effectively she portrays virtue and the
      heroic in her individual characters, especially the characters
      of the earlier novels. A Lost Lady is something of an "after-
      piece" to this group because Marian Forrester gives herself to a
      base, trivial, counterfeit lover. Cather then expands her
      imaginative conception of the pioneer experience to include the
      Catholic Church. In Shadows on the Rock, however, Cather re-
      verses her usual procedure. Instead of focusing on an heroic
      character set against a descriptive background, she focuses on
      details of setting and circumstance and introduces no powerful
      and virtuous central hero. The virtues Cather admires are attrib-
      uted to a whole community rather than an individual character.

50   Van DOREN, DOROTHY. "A Study in Comeliness." Nation 133
     (12 August):160.
          Review of Shadows on the Rock. Laments the novel's lack of
     flow and its "shadowy," lifeless characters. Nevertheless, the
     writing itself and the descriptions are beautiful, and Cather
     has a distinct ability to find virtue in life. She is neither a
     realist nor a romantic.

51   WHIPPLE, LEON. "Gold in What Hills." Survey 67 (1 November):
     151.
          Review of Shadows on the Rock calls it a "slight tale" with
     a pastoral quality. It is like a "gallery of old and mellow
     pictures," with beautifully drawn characters and sensitively
     rendered mood.

52   "Willa Cather a Classic." Omaha World-Herald, 13 September,
     p. 2.
          Announces a course to be taught, by Professor Charles C.
     Charvat at Creighton University, on Willa Cather's novels, short
     stories, and poetry. Claims that this is the first time such a
     course has been taught at any university.

53   "Willa Cather Raps 'Sincerity' Heresy." San Francisco
     Chronicle, 29 March, sec. d, p. 5.
          Reports an interview with Cather in which she talks about
     what true sincerity in art means. She believes that it has a
     great deal to do with form, and in fact demands form and fixes
     it. It has nothing to do with the impulse to formlessness, and
     grows through a natural process.

54   WILLIAMS, MICHAEL. Review of Shadows on the Rock. Commonweal
     14 (30 September):528.
          Examines the timeless quality of Shadows on the Rock, with
     people and events symbolizing the "shadows" and values of eter-
     nity. The novel combines simplicity and mysticism in the manner
     of folk-lore.

55   WILSON, JAMES SOUTHALL. Review of Shadows on the Rock.
     Virginia Quarterly Review 7 (October):585–90.
          Regards the book as compassionate, but notes that it is not
     based on "soft sentimentality." Shadows on the Rock will in-
     evitably be compared with Death Comes for the Archbishop, but it
     should not be. Although it deals with a smaller, more specific
     canvas, its selection of detail produces an image larger and more
     significant than the details themselves.

56   WOODSIDE, TILE[S]TON E. "Maine's Stake in Willa Cather."
     Journal (Lewiston, Maine), 21 November, sec. a, p. 8.
          Asserts the lasting importance of Sarah Orne Jewett's in-
     fluence in shaping the direction of Cather's work, quoting one of
     Jewett's letters that gives Cather advice about her work. Like
     Jewett, Cather writes in an episodic manner, with a quiet,
     simple, pure style.

57   WOOLLCOTT, ALEXANDER. "Miss Cather Speaks Again." McCall's
       59 (November):20, 101.
           Offers a highly personal response to Shadows on the Rock,
     finding in it an undaunted spirit captured by a serene art.

                                1932

1   A., C. Review of Obscure Destinies. Catholic World 136
       (November):246-47.
           Cather's main characters in Obscure Destinies have a
     sculptural and poetic quality about them. This is not Cather's
     best work, but it is honest and satisfying.

2   AUSTIN, MARY. Earth Horizons: Autobiography. Boston:
       Houghton Mifflin Co.; New York: Literary Guild, p. 359.
           Complains about Cather's allegiance to the French in Death
     Comes for the Archbishop and her sympathy with the Archbishop's
     desire to build a French cathedral in the midst of Spanish cul-
     ture, an event that Austin says was a terrible blow to that cul-
     ture. Also claims that Cather wrote part of the book while a
     guest in Austin's house.

3   ____. "Regionalism in American Fiction." English Journal 21
       (February):97-107.
           Asserts that Cather's Death Comes for the Archbishop is not
     an example of regionalism in writing, but rather of the skillful
     use of region as a backdrop for her story.

4   BEACH, JOSEPH WARREN. The Twentieth Century Novel: Studies
       in Technique. New York: Century Co., pp. 263-64, 275-76,
       367.
           Cites Cather as an example of American writers who lack the
     artistic strengths of John Galsworthy, and who assemble their
     units of narrative around one single effect. Cather is "narrow"
     and "easy" compared to Galsworthy, but she merits some praise.
     Tom Outland's story, for example, adds charm to The Professor's
     House and unifies it.

*5   BELFRAGE, SIXTEN. "En stor amerikansk författarinna" [A story
       by an American authoress]. Göteborgs-Posten, 21 May.
           In Swedish. Listed in Anderson 1957.1.

6   BUTCHER, FANNY. "Willa Cather Called Leading Woman Writer."
       Chicago Tribune [1932]. Undated clipping in scrapbook II-54
       at Willa Cather Historical Center, Red Cloud, Nebraska.
           Praises Cather as America's greatest living woman novelist,
     one who never compromises her standards. Cather writes from
     "inner urges," and in Obscure Destinies, again, she writes in her
     own way, not dictated to by tradition. "Two Friends" is less
     important than "Old Mrs. Harris" and "Neighbour Rosicky."

                                77

7   CALVERTON, V.F. The Liberation of American Literature. New
     York: Charles Scribner's Sons, pp. 350, 418, 424–25.
         Sees Cather as one of the writers who desolately lamented
     the loss of what the frontier and a relationship with the land
     meant. She did not partake of Jack London's positive vision that
     something could be done about it. Thus, novels like A Lost Lady
     and The Professor's House reveal that all the land devotion
     hailed in O Pioneers! and My Ántonia is devotion to a "lost
     cause."

8   CANBY, HENRY SEIDEL. "This is Humanism." Saturday Review of
     Literature 9 (6 August):29.
         Cather's achievement in Obscure Destinies, where she re-
     turns to the setting of her early novels, lies in her discovery
     and revelation of "great souls" inside the commonplace human
     beings called Grandma Harris and Neighbour Rosicky. With Mr.
     Dillon and Mr. Trueman in "Two Friends," it is the friendship
     that is great. Without resorting to tricks or stereotypes,
     without ignoring the ugly or the cruel, Cather provides a rich
     experience for the reader. Reprinted: 1984.13.

9   CHAMBERLAIN, JOHN. "The Return of Willa Cather." New York
     Times Book Review, 31 July, sec. 5, p. 1.
         Claims that Cather has two inspirational sources for the
     stories in Obscure Destinies, childhood and the artist's struggle
     in the pre-World War I West. Criticizes "Two Friends" for lack
     of development.

10   DAWSON, MARGARET CHENEY. "Miss Cather's New Portraits." New
     York Herald Tribune Books, 31 July, p. 3.
         Suspects, but is not certain because Cather's work is so
     elusive, that something may be lacking in the stories in Obscure
     Destinies that was present in Cather's earlier western fiction.
     Although less substantial than the other two stories, "Two
     Friends" may be the best in the collection. "Old Mrs. Harris"
     and "Neighbour Rosicky" make their impression and then "drop
     away from you" while "Two Friends" seems to be underpinned with
     qualities suggesting that even commonplace events imply some-
     thing more than themselves.

11   FADIMAN, CLIFTON. "Misted Memories." Nation 135 (3 August):
     107.
         Questions the realism of Cather's view of the West in
     Obscure Destinies, wondering whether or not Sarah Orne Jewett's
     influence is responsible. "Neighbour Rosicky," with its pure,
     excellent craftsmanship, is a good example of Cather at her best.

12   _____. "Willa Cather: The Past Recaptured." Nation 135
     (7 December):563–65.
         Regards Cather as a writer of essentially Vergilian tem-
     perament who has no power to change people's minds because she is
     steeped in the past. She recaptures the past effectively in her
     earlier novels, but Death Comes for the Archbishop and Shadows on

the <u>Rock</u> are merely "reworked legends," and will not last. They show Cather's diminishing capacity to deal with life in the present.

13   FORD, FORD MADOX. <u>Return to Yesterday</u>. New York: Horace
       Liveright, pp. 330-32.
          Relates the story, supposedly told to Ford by Cather, of
       the visit she and Isabelle McClung [and Dorothy Canfield] made to
       A.E. Housman. As Ford tells it, they were charged by the Pitts-
       burgh Shropshire Lad Club to deliver a gold laurel wreath to the
       poet. (Ford's account has been disputed by Cather and others.)

14   HALE, EDWARD E[VERETT, Jr.]. "Willa Cather." <u>Faculty Papers</u>
       <u>of Union College, Union College Bulletin</u> 26, no. 2:5-17.
          Prepared for posthumous publication by Raymond M. Herrick.
       Written originally for 1941.6, but permission granted for prior
       publication here. Makes the point while rehearsing Cather's life
       and career, and describing each of her novels in chronological
       order, that Cather's life is all of a piece. <u>Death Comes for the</u>
       <u>Archbishop</u> is something of a culmination of her best and most
       characteristic powers. Reprinted: 1941.6.

15   HAWTHORNE, HAZEL. "Willa Cather's Homeland." <u>New Republic</u>
       71 (10 August):350.
          Review of <u>Obscure Destinies</u>. Cather's genuine feeling
       makes "Old Mrs. Harris" the best story in the trilogy.

16   JONES, HOWARD MUMFORD. "Battalions of Women." <u>Virginia</u>
       <u>Quarterly Review</u> 8 (October):591-92.
          Review of <u>Obscure Destinies</u> questions Cather's character-
       ization, particularly that of Mrs. Rosen in "Old Mrs. Harris."
       The best of the three stories is "Neighbour Rosicky"; "Two
       Friends" is an "essay."

17   KENDON, FRANK. "The New Books at a Glance." <u>John O'London's</u>
       <u>Weekly</u> 28 (3 December).
          Makes general comments about Cather as a novelist and then
       observes that <u>Obscure Destinies</u> is a good example of her art.
       Cather is a conservative writer who focuses on character and
       effaces herself and her technique. Reprinted: [ca. 1933].9;
       [ca. 1941].8. Reprinted in part: 1974.31.

18   _____. Review of <u>Shadows on the Rock</u>. <u>John O'London's Weekly</u>
       26 (23 January):659.
          Appreciates Cather's clear, fundamental style and the
       "gentleness toward human nature" she shows in <u>Shadows on the</u>
       <u>Rock</u>. Her method is to make a stage of the apothecary's shop,
       introducing each character and then at the appropriate oppor-
       tunity stepping back into his or her history. Thus the reader
       meets those who people Quebec and gets a clear picture of the
       place.

19   KNIGHT, GRANT C. <u>American Literature and Culture</u>. New York:
     Ray Long & Richard R. Smith, pp. 421-25. Reprint. Totowa,
     N.J.: Cooper Square Publishers, 1972.
         Praises the realism, idealism, and taste of Cather's
     prairie novels, but claims that in her later attempts to un-
     furnish the novel and use no unnecessary words, she drained the
     lifeblood out of her work. To her reader's regret, the stylist
     replaced the storyteller.

20   LEVINSON, ANDRÉ. "Villa Cather et la Legende Dorée du nouveau
     monde." <u>Nouvelles littéraires</u>, 6 February, p. 6.
         Comments on several of Cather's books that deal with past
     experiences in the new world, including <u>My Ántonia</u> and <u>The Pro-
     fessor's House</u>, but describes <u>Death Comes for the Archbishop</u> and
     <u>Shadows on the Rock</u> in some detail, noting especially Cather's
     sympathetic achievement in <u>Shadows on the Rock</u>.

21   LEWISOHN, LUDWIG. <u>Expression in America</u>. New York: Harper &
     Brothers, pp. 538-43. Reprint under title <u>The Story of Ameri-
     can Literature</u>. New York: Random House, Modern Library, 1939.
         Praises Cather's style and suggests that she represents the
     flight to neo-Catholicism in American literature, the flight from
     the world's harsh realities. <u>Death Comes for the Archbishop</u> and
     <u>Shadows on the Rock</u> fit in this special category, but of her
     other works, <u>My Mortal Enemy</u> is her masterpiece.

22   MacAFEE, HELEN. "The Library of the Quarter: Outstanding
     Novels." <u>Yale Review</u>, n.s. 22 (Autumn):vi.
         Review of <u>Obscure Destinies</u> attests that activities such as
     creating and reading novels are not acts of escape from life's
     realities, but are simply types of expression of those realities.
     Cather's work largely inquires as to which of these expressions
     make "existence all the way up to death seem supportable or in-
     telligible." "Old Mrs. Harris," really a novel, is the best of
     the three stories. It exemplifies a satisfying completeness
     achieved through the simple observation of homely details.

23   MACC., M. "Willa Cather's Novel: Pioneer Days in North
     America." <u>Irish Press</u> (Dublin), 22 January, p. 5.
         Praises Cather's style in <u>Shadows on the Rock</u> and her stand
     for the simple and the beautiful as opposed to the shoddy and
     vulgar. Reprinted: [ca. 1933].12; [ca. 1941].12.

24   McNAMARA, ROBERT. "Phases of American Religion in Thornton
     Wilder and Willa Cather." <u>Catholic World</u> 135 (September):
     641-49.
         Argues that the bond between religion and art is essential
     to authentic American literature, and that Cather is greater than
     Wilder because she had all along "lived . . . in the light" and
     increasingly rejoiced in it. Cather has a "Catholic attitude,"
     and for her grace leads to truth. <u>Death Comes for the Archbishop</u>
     is the culmination of her conviction.

25   MANN, DOROTHEA LAWRANCE. "Willa Cather Returns to Her Beloved
      West." Boston Evening Transcript, Book sec., p. 2.
            Accords high praise to Cather generally, and to Obscure
      Destinies particularly, finding such a story as "Neighbour
      Rosicky" a welcome breath of fresh air from an earlier period
      that produced My Ántonia. Summarizes plots of the three stories
      in the collection, and applauds the realness of the characters
      and the "deceptive simplicity" of Cather's writing. Sees in "Two
      Friends" an echo of A Lost Lady, but regards "Old Mrs. Harris" as
      the "supreme story" of the group.

26   MOULT, THOMAS. "Miss Willa Cather." Manchester Guardian,
      16 December, p. 7.
            Appraises the stories in Obscure Destinies as lovely addi-
      tions to fiction, calling them noble "tributes" to the notion
      that human life is good and that humble people make worthy sub-
      jects for fiction. Reprinted: [ca. 1933].15; [ca. 1941].14.

*27   MURET, MAURICE. Review of Shadows on the Rock. Journal des
      débats, 24 January.
            Listed in Slote 1974.67.

28   MYERS, WALTER L. "The Novel Dedicate." Virginia Quarterly
      Review 8 (July):410-18.
            In Shadows on the Rock Cather approaches but does not quite
      achieve the novelistic ideal that Myers posits. A novel should
      reduce narrative artifice and release the reader into a realm of
      quiet, creative illumination that allows truth to be apprehended
      directly through the consciousness.

29   "New Novels." Times Literary Supplement (London), 21 January,
      p. 42.
            Review of Shadows on the Rock praises Cather for breathing
      life into a society two centuries gone and for her use of the
      first and last seasonal sailings between Europe and the new world
      as the high points of the novel. The characters are believable
      and interesting.

30   "New Novels." Times Literary Supplement (London), 1 December,
      p. 920.
            Review of Obscure Destinies focuses on Cather's attraction
      to common people, but in the main provides synopses of the sto-
      ries with particular emphasis on "Neighbour Rosicky."

31   PELANTOVA, ARTEMIS. "Willa Cather." Pts. 1-2. Rozpravy
      Aventina (Prague) 7, nos. 36-37:293-94, 300-301.
            In Czech. Contends that Cather exemplifies the strong
      pioneer spirit of America. Also observes that her work has great
      variety even though her theme is constant: the struggle of the
      creative personality to realize its potential in a mundane world.
      Traces Cather's fictional shifts in tone and mood from early
      pessimism, to optimism, to disillusionment, and finally to
      reconciled peace. In the end, Cather finds the spiritual values

modern America has lost in the faith depicted in her Catholic
novels, but her characters are less human and she is more
distant.

32   PHELPS, WILLIAM LYON. "A Literary Mystery." Delineator 120
      (January):12, 59.
         Argues that although in England today's liberated women
      writers are not the artists their Victorian counterparts were,
      the situation in the United States is just the reverse. Names
      Cather as one of America's six leading women writers. Her books
      immediately after One of Ours, which is her worst novel, show a
      satirical and ironic reaction against the sentimentality of that
      book. In Death Comes for the Archbishop and Shadows on the Rock,
      however, Cather once again demonstrates her capacity for sympathy
      and creates works of "serene beauty."

*33   PRIESTLEY, J[OHN] B[OYNTON]. "Coupon Controversy in the Book
      World." London Evening Standard, no. 33757, 1 December,
      p. 11.
         Review of Obscure Destinies listed in J.B. Priestley: An
      Annotated Bibliography, by Alan Edwin Day (New York: Garland
      Publishing, 1980); unverified.

*34   _____. "Rousseau--and a Slapdash Biography." London Evening
      Standard, no. 33524, 28 January, p. 9.
         Review of Shadows on the Rock listed in J.B. Priestley: An
      Annotated Bibliography. See Priestley 1932.33; unverified.

35   QUENNELL, PETER. Review of Obscure Destinies. New Statesman
      and Nation 4 (3 December):694.
         "Two Friends" is the best of the three stories in the
      rather uneven collection. "Neighbour Rosicky" leaves an indis-
      tinct impression.

36   REILLY, JOSEPH J. "When the Japs Beleagured Manhattan."
      Bookman 75 (April):1-5.
         Invents a little fiction wherein the Japanese have sur-
      rounded Manhattan and demanded that America surrender to Japan
      its five best novelists in exchange for the release of the
      island. The "Arbiter" who has to decide in which order to sur-
      render them--one each week, from least valuable to most valuable
      --relinquishes first Theodore Dreiser, then Sinclair Lewis, then
      Thornton Wilder. He has trouble deciding between Edith Wharton
      and Cather, for Wharton is the more skilled artist, but Cather
      is the greater genius. Wharton lacks Cather's heart and sympa-
      thy, so she is sent next. The Arbiter breaks under the strain of
      these decisions and dies before Cather's turn comes. But beside
      his body is a note saying that Cather cannot be given up to "the
      enemy." Manhattan should be sacrificed before Cather is. He had
      even secretly offered that choice to the foe, and they refused
      him, so he committed "hara-kiri."

37 Review of Obscure Destinies. Booklist 29 (September):17.
  Compares the characters in Obscure Destinies to those in
  My Ántonia, O Pioneers!, and A Lost Lady.

38 Review of The Song of the Lark. Commonweal 15 (24 February):
  475.
  This review of a supposed "new edition" maintains that the
  novel does not match My Ántonia artistically, but it does demonstrate rich feeling for the West and portray Cather's strongest
  heroine. There was no new edition of The Song of the Lark in
  1932, merely the sixteenth printing of the original plates. The
  revised Autograph edition appeared in 1937 (see Crane 1982.19,
  pp. 48–49).

39 STRONG, L.A.G. Review of Obscure Destinies. Spectator 149
  (9 December):844.
  Praises Cather for her ability to combine simplicity and
  serenity with a sound philosophical background. She avoids
  sentimentality in Obscure Destinies, and it is one of her best
  works.

40 SUCKOW, RUTH. "Middle Western Literature." English Journal
  21 (March):175–81.
  In this text of an informal address delivered at a creative
  writing conference at the University of Iowa, 30 October 1931,
  Suckow describes some of the qualities of middlewestern literature. She cites My Ántonia as an impressive example of that
  literature and calls it "the poem of the pioneers."

41 "Three Books Picked for the Prix Femina." New York Times,
  18 May, p. 19.
  Reports that Shadows on the Rock is one of three books
  nominated for the Prix Femina Américain award, calling it the
  most popular book of 1931.

42 "Three Stories of the West." Christian Science Monitor,
  17 September, p. 12.
  "Old Mrs. Harris," with its blend of realism and tenderness
  and its finely drawn characters, is the best of the three stories
  in Obscure Destinies. "Neighbour Rosicky" is delightful; "Two
  Friends" is less successful.

43 Van DOREN, IRITA. Review of April Twilights and Other Poems.
  New York Herald Tribune Books, 4 June, p. 4.
  The first group of poems in the collection are lyrical,
  written in traditional form with melodic language. The second
  group, dealing with the Midwest, are more personal, direct, and
  honest.

44   WARD, A[LFRED] C[HARLES]. American Literature 1880-1930.
      New York: MacVeagh, Dial Press; London: Methuen & Co.,
      pp. 146-49.
          Finds "a perfect clarity" in Cather's novels, a sense of
      form that subtracts nothing from their humanity, and a style that
      projects "austerity and emotional reticence." Singles out A Lost
      Lady as Cather's most ambitious character study.

45   WEEKS, EDWARD. Review of Obscure Destinies. "Atlantic Book-
      shelf." Atlantic Monthly 150 (September):16.
          Regards the stories in Obscure Destinies as "notable," full
      of the life that a reader can interpret through personal expe-
      rience. Rosicky, Old Mrs. Harris, and Dillon and Trueman, against
      their western background, are memorable people.

46   WILLIAMS, MICHAEL. "Willa Cather." Commonweal 16 (31 August):
      433-34.
          Uses Obscure Destinies to point to Cather's extraordinary
      artistic strengths. She is a writer who has an "almost magical
      power over words." It is pointless to argue, as critics have
      recently done, whether or not she erred in leaving more familiar
      territory to write of the early purveyors of Catholicism in the
      new world; she deals with spiritual beauty whether she writes
      about religion explicitly or not. Cather is uniquely gifted
      among contemporary writers, amply endowed with the creative
      writer's most important qualities, a "sympathetic imagination,
      and mastery of language." Reprinted: 1982.84.

47   WINSTEN, ARCHER. "A Defense of Willa Cather." Bookman 74
      (March):634-40.
          Takes issue with some of Cather's recent critics, insisting
      that her books lose no vitality by being set in the past. Her
      work is value centered and always engaged her deeper feelings.
      Shadows on the Rock is a triumphant achievement based on a founda-
      tion of cultural values that reviewers lack the imagination to
      appreciate.

48   _____. Review of Obscure Destinies. Bookman 75 (October):
      648-49.
          Grants that Cather is an excellent writer, but discovers
      nothing new in Obscure Destinies. Although "Neighbour Rosicky"
      is complete, the other two stories are more like unfinished novels
      and are therefore unsatisfactory.

                                  1933

1   BESSEY, MABEL A., and WILSON, J. HAROLD. "Willa Cather--
      Chronicler of the Western Pioneer." In Living Writers.
      Vol. 1. Columbus, Ohio: American Education Press, pp. 9-11.
          Acclaims Cather as one who made of a particular place--the
      windswept prairies--a preeminent literary setting. Her nature was
      especially suited to the prairie she wrote about with such purpose

and skill, though after One of Ours she left it and adopted a
more limited vision.

2   BOAS, RALPH PHILIP, and BURTON, KATHERINE. Social Backgrounds
     of American Literature. Boston: Little, Brown & Co.,
     pp. 265-70.
          Briefly traces Cather's literary output in terms of its
     social content--emphasizing its setting and its concern or non-
     concern with pioneer midwestern themes and characters.

3   ELGSTRÖM, ANNA LENAH. "Villa Cather." Svenska dagbladet
     (Stockholm), 5 November, pp. 5, 11.
          In Swedish. Observes that Cather sees dignity in humanity,
     even where no one else would. She portrays mostly the poor and
     hardworking, always with a fiery spirit and immense dignity.

4   FISHER, DOROTHY CANFIELD. "Daughter of the Frontier." New
     York Herald Tribune Books, 28 May, pp. 7, 9.
          Cather's abiding theme is uniquely American, and it is one
     about which she was uniquely qualified to write--by virtue of her
     transplantation from Virginia to Nebraska and her immense per-
     sonal drive and energy. It concerns the effects on personalities
     of leaving an old, established culture and moving to a new coun-
     try. Reprinted: 1933.5.

5   _____. "Willa Cather, Frontier Daughter." Omaha Sunday
     World-Herald Magazine, 4 June, p. 7.
          Reprint of 1933.4.

6   "Friends of the Library Dinner." Princeton Alumni Weekly 33
     (12 May):692.
          Quotes from Cather's address, as a former Pulitzer Prize
     winner, to the Friends of the Princeton Library dinner on 4 May.
     Cather reportedly said that the novel had to break loose from the
     notion that new work must fit into the frame of old stock forms.
     Rather, she said, a form should be made for every story.

7   HICKS, GRANVILLE. "The Case Against Willa Cather." English
     Journal 22 (November):703-10.
          An expanded text of 1933.8. Admits to a certain realism,
     as well as honesty and enthusiasm, in Cather's earlier pioneer
     novels, but for the most part sees a decline in her work after
     My Ántonia. She fails to participate in matters central to her
     age, something that has always engaged great writers. She turns
     to the romantic past when she should have thrown herself into the
     movement to tear down and reconstruct the industrial institu-
     tional structures she hated. Reprinted: 1967.16.

8   _____. "Two Roads: Mrs. Wharton, Hergesheimer, Cabell, Miss
     Cather." In The Great Tradition: An Interpretation of Ameri-
     can Literature since the Civil War. New York: Macmillan Co.,
     pp. 221-27. Reprint. 1935.
          An abridged text of 1933.7. Cather exemplifies the limi-
     tations of regionalism and the loss of vitality that mars the

work of those who ignore industrialism. In the end, all she
could do was paint pretty pictures.

9   KENDON, FRANK. "An Interesting Estimate of the Quality of
     Willa Cather's Novels." In Willa Cather. See Knopf pamphlet
     [ca. 1933].21, pp. 24-25.
         Reprint of 1932.17.

10   KIRKLAND, WINIFRED, and KIRKLAND, FRANCES. "Willa Cather, A
     Transplanted Writer." In Girls Who Became Writers. New York:
     Harper & Brothers, pp. 103-12.
         A highly laudatory appraisal of Cather and her work con-
     taining many of the common early biographical misconceptions
     about Cather's youth. Reprints in this volume are attributed to
     Good Housekeeping. What must be an earlier printing of this
     piece is on file at the Willa Cather Historical Center in Red
     Cloud, Nebraska. It bears no publication date. A check of Good
     Housekeeping issues through the early 1930s failed to turn up the
     article.

11   LOVETT, ROBERT MORSS. "An American Opinion." In Willa Cather.
     See Knopf pamphlet [ca. 1933].21, pp. 14-16.
         Review of Death Comes for the Archbishop. Reprint of
     1927.22.

12   MACC., M. "An Irish Review of Shadows on the Rock. In Willa
     Cather. See Knopf pamphlet [ca. 1933].21, p. 21.
         Reprint of 1932.23.

13   "Miss Cather Wins French Book Prize." New York Times,
     13 February, p. 15.
         Announces that Cather wins the first Prix Femina Américain
     for Shadows on the Rock. The award is designed to honor an
     American book that will increase the understanding of American
     life in France.

14   MORAN, HELEN. Review of Obscure Destinies. London Mercury
     17, no. 159 (January):272.
         Praises Obscure Destinies as a return from the "pastel"
     writing of her recent novels to the strength of books like My
     Ántonia and A Lost Lady. Here again Cather creates people rather
     than types.

15   MOULT, THOMAS. "An English Review of Obscure Destinies." In
     Willa Cather. See Knopf pamphlet [ca. 1933].21, pp. 23-24.
         Reprint of 1932.26.

16   "Perils of Control Stated at Smith." New York Times,
     20 June, p. 12.
         Notes that Cather received the honorary degree of Doctor of
     Humane Letters at the commencement exercises of Smith College.
     She was acclaimed for her language mastery and said to be "un-
     surpassed among contemporary authors."

17   PORTERFIELD, ALEXANDER. "An English Opinion: Willa Cather."
     In Willa Cather. See Knopf pamphlet [ca. 1933].21, pp. 4-14.
     Reprint of 1926.22.

18   Review of April Twilights and Other Poems. Book Review Digest
     29 (April):164.
         Reviews a 1933 printing of the 1923 edition of Cather's
     volume of poetry. Describes the earlier poems as emotional and
     romantic, the later ones as more realistic, in the tradition of
     her prose.

19   WALDMAN, MILTON. "Tendencies of the American Novel."
     Fortnightly Review 140 (December):717-25.
         Calls Cather the "most famous and talented" of the school
     of American novelists who chose to withdraw from the noisy,
     turbulent world that so fascinated another group of writers. She
     is an exquisite stylist, but she is uninterested in social anal-
     ysis. Her work has grown progressively more ethereal. Re-
     printed: 1934.15.

20   WALTON, EDA LOU. Review of April Twilights and Other Poems.
     New York Times, 11 June, p. 15.
         The early poems lack individuality and are subjective,
     romantic, and emotional. The later ones with midwestern themes,
     however, are detached and realistic. As poetic renditions of
     dramatic situations and character that work well in prose, they
     show the influence of Cather's fiction.

21   Willa Cather: A Biographical Sketch, an English Opinion,
     Reviews and Articles Concerning Her Later Books, and an
     Abridged Bibliography. New York: Alfred A. Knopf, 28 pp.
         An expanded edition of [ca. 1927].42. Contains reprints of
     1926.22; 1927.22; 1932.17, 23, 26. Also contains an updated
     bibliography and Cather's letter to Commonweal regarding Death
     Comes for the Archbishop, plus her letter to Governor Wilbur
     Cross regarding Shadows on the Rock (published in Saturday Review
     of Literature).

22   "Willa Cather Awarded First Prix Femina Américain."
     Publisher's Weekly 123 (11 February):623.
         Announces that Cather received the first Prix Femina
     Américain for Shadows on the Rock, and that the prize consists
     in translation of the novel into French and its publication in
     France under the auspices of the Prix Femina.

23   "Willa Cather's Poetry." Boston Evening Transcript, 14 June,
     p. 2.
         Makes note of the additions and deletions in Cather's later
     collection of poetry, April Twilights and Other Poems. Sees in
     "Poor Marty" a kinship with the western ballad, and appreciates
     the simplicity, and hence readability, of Cather's verse.

24   "Willa Cather Turns to Poetry." <u>Minneapolis Journal</u>, 18 June.
     Review of <u>April Twilights and Other Poems</u>. Insists that
Cather's late poems, the poems of her prairie experience, are
better and more authentic than the earlier poems in which she
adopted standard literary language and conventions to express
"lyrical feelings."

25   WILLIAMS, STANLEY T[HOMAS]. <u>American Literature</u>. Phila-
     delphia: J.B. Lippincott Co., pp. 143, 150–51. Reprint.
     Folcroft, Penn.: Folcroft Press, 1969.
     Maintains that Cather's real source of power is the con-
templative mood, the peace and calm, that permeate her work even
though she handles the same human problems treated by her neuro-
tic contemporaries.

<u>1934</u>

1   BREWSTER, DOROTHY, and BURRELL, ANGUS. <u>Modern Fiction</u>. New
     York: Columbia University Press, p. 399.
     Discusses <u>A Lost Lady</u> as a representative of the novelette
form. While Captain Forrester is presented in a full portrait,
Marian Forrester is presented retrospectively and indirectly--a
method that works in a novelette, but not a novel.

2   EDGAR, PELHAM. "Two Anti-Realists: Willa Cather and Cabell."
     In <u>The Art of the Novel: From 1700 to the Present Time</u>. New
     York: Macmillan Co., pp. 255–61.
     Claims that Cather does not follow the formula for writers
commonly called realists. Rather, she excells in the art of narration, with description at the heart of her method. In <u>Death
Comes for the Archbishop</u>, her most perfect book, the digressions
serve to develop additional narrative energy. This is not true
of the Tom Outland digression in the inferior novel, <u>The Professor's House</u>.

3   GAVIGAN, WALTER V. "Nuns in Novels." <u>Catholic World</u> 140
     (November):186–95.
     Concludes that Cather paints a positive picture of the nuns
in <u>Shadows on the Rock</u>, though her characterization of priests is
more successful. Her portrayal of the recluse lacks "much of the
warmth of true spirituality" associated with genuine Catholic
mystics.

4   HALLECK, REUBEN POST. "Willa Cather." In <u>The Romance of
     American Literature</u>. New York: American Book Co., pp. 315–20.
     Provides a brief biographical sketch and plot outlines of
several novels, indicating that generally Cather delineates character instead of creating plots. She is a "selective realist,"
choosing some details and omitting others, with a genuine capacity
for poetry.

5   HARTWICK, HARRY. "Simplicity with Glory." In <u>The Foreground</u>
    <u>of American Fiction</u>. New York: American Book Co., pp. 389–
    404.
         Outlines the substance of Cather's books through <u>Shadows on</u>
    <u>the Rock</u>, then, relying heavily on quotations from other commen-
    tators, discusses her themes and artistry. Cather's technique
    has steadily grown more selective and simple, and her particular
    ability lies in creating symbol through raising the actual into
    the figurative realm. She values the artist as she does the
    pioneer because the artist can discriminate and appreciate value
    and can link the past with the future.

6   HARVEY, ALICE G. "Willa Cather." In <u>Nebraska Writers</u>.
    Omaha: Citizen Publishing Co., pp. 13–14.
         Stresses the influence of Nebraska on Cather's work, but
    notes also the importance of the Southwest. Having strong con-
    victions and emotions herself, Cather is able to create vivid
    scenes and characters. Revised: 1964.10.

7   HOUGH, LYNN HAROLD. <u>Vital Control</u>. Forest Essays, first
    series. New York: Abingdon Press. Reprint. Freeport, N.Y.:
    Books for Libraries Press, Essay Index Reprint Series, 1970,
    pp. 168–70.
         Praises <u>Shadows on the Rock</u> for its gracious style and
    spiritual serenity.

8   LUCCOCK, HALFORD EDWARD. <u>Contemporary American Literature and</u>
    <u>Religion</u>. Chicago: Willett, Clark & Co., pp. 84–89.
         Commends Cather for blending frontier realism with an
    idealism that recognizes and appreciates the beautiful. She
    unapologetically espouses the values of morals and religion, yet
    at the same time indicts the sometimes provincial repressiveness
    of small town life.

9   NICHOLAS, Sister MARY. "Cather, Willa Sibert." In <u>Writers</u>
    <u>and Writings of New Mexico</u>. Edited by Lester Raines. Las
    Vegas, N.M.: Normal University, pp. 32–34.
         Tells something of how Cather came to write <u>Death Comes for</u>
    <u>the Archbishop</u> and outlines the facts of the narrative.

10 RANDALL, DAVID A. "American First Editions, 1900–1933." In
    <u>New Paths in Book Collecting: Essays by Various Hands</u>. Ed-
    ited by John Carter et al. London: Constable & Co.,
    pp. 208–9, 212.
         Claims that the real value of the very-hard-to-find
    sixteen-page advertising pamphlet issued by Knopf around 1924
    (see 1927.42) lies in the fact that Cather wrote the biographical
    sketch herself. Also traces some of the binding history of the
    first edition of <u>Alexander's Bridge</u> and indicates that it is very
    difficult for the collector to secure a copy with the "right"
    binding.

11   SCHWARZ, HEINO. Review of <u>Shadows on the Rock</u>. <u>Die neueren</u>
<u>Sprachen</u> 42 (November):521.
     Recommends <u>Shadows on the Rock</u> as a colorful, wonderfully
told story.

12   SENNWALD, ANDRE. Film Review of <u>A Lost Lady</u>. <u>New York Times</u>,
Film Review sec., 4 October.
     Finds the second film adaptation of Cather's novel, <u>A Lost</u>
<u>Lady</u>, to be vastly inferior to what is a real masterpiece in fic-
tion, a hauntingly beautiful book rendered through subtle indirection. The film, a "made-to-order" stereotype, is almost a
total stranger to the book.

13   SHUSTER, GEORGE N. "Willa Sibert Cather: Eine amerikanische
Erzählerin." <u>Hochland</u> 3 (September):573–76.
     Deals with Cather's development as a writer and the influ-
ences that affected her technique and subject matter, among them
Edith Wharton and Henry James.

14   VOCÁDLO, OTAKAR. <u>Současná literatura Spojených Států,</u>
<u>odzvolení presidenta Wilsona po velkou hospodářskou krisi</u>
[Contemporary literature of the United States, from the elec-
tion of president Wilson through the great economic crisis].
Prague: Jan Laichter, pp. 99–112.
     In Czech. Offers a general assessment of Cather, and then
traces her development as a writer by discussing in turn each of
her books from <u>The Troll Garden</u> to <u>Obscure Destinies</u>. Claims
that although she lacks artistic imagination, especially in the
matter of plot construction, she has two ingredients vital to the
artist--personality and material. She passes through several
phases in her work, beginning with melancholy fiction about the
present, moving through positive accounts of pioneering and
skeptical psychological novels, and returning in two Catholic
novels to a time when spiritual values were sustained.

15   WALDMAN, MILTON. "America." In <u>Tendencies of the Modern</u>
<u>Novel</u>. London: George Allen & Unwin, pp. 58–62.
     Reprint of 1933.19.

16   "Willa Cather Only Author with Four Books on White House
Library Shelves." <u>Kansas City Star</u>, 24 November, p. 12.
     Notes that President Roosevelt had recently received copies
of <u>Shadows on the Rock</u> and <u>Obscure Destinies</u> in a collection presented by the nation's booksellers. The president had received
<u>Death Comes for the Archbishop</u> and <u>My Ántonia</u> in 1930.

1935

1   ADAMS, J. DONALD. "A New Novel by Willa Cather." <u>New York</u>
<u>Times Book Review</u>, 4 August, p. 1.
     Provides a lengthy plot summary, observing that in <u>Lucy</u>
<u>Gayheart</u> Cather treats themes and materials she had used before.
Nevertheless, the book is sensitively written and demonstrates

Cather's ability to follow her own precept that art should sim-
plify, a precept that carries the requirement that art must then
also intensify.

2   ARVIN, NEWTON. "Fiction Mirrors America." Current History 42
     (September):610-16 passim.
     Identifies Cather as one whose preoccupation was with the
gifted individual "surrounded by incompetents" and thus bound up
in a "poetic solitude." Cather's work does not sustain its early
energy, but passes through periods of defeatism and finally the
loss of self in the "weak traditionalism" of Death Comes for the
Archbishop.

3   _____. "Sweet Story." New Republic 84 (11 September):138.
     Attacks Lucy Gayheart as banal, ordinary, and thin. Cather
allows sentimentality to blur her vision of the world.

4   BENET, STEPHEN VINCENT. "The Artistry and Grace of Willa
     Cather." New York Herald Tribune Books, 4 August, p. 3.
     Expresses immense appreciation for Cather, but feels that
Lucy Gayheart, in spite of its "perfections of observation" and
its fine rendering of landscape and mood, is one of Cather's
"rare failures." It is difficult to feel that Lucy is significant; hence, it is difficult to feel that her tragedy is significant. She symbolizes a passing phase of youth rather than youth
itself.

5   BRANDE, DOROTHEA. "Willa Cather and the Sense of Life."
     American Review 5 (October):625.
     The real hero or heroine of Lucy Gayheart is not one of its
characters, but rather "the sense of life." The book's ending is
no anticlimax, but embodies the very feeling of "continuing
life." The book has its problems--the ambiguous relation between
Lucy and Sebastian, and Lucy's sense of life that Cather talks of
but never makes convincing, for example--but Cather comes very
close to artistic perfection nonetheless. Reprinted: 1984.11.

6   BUTCHER, FANNY. "Willa Cather Writes Idyl of Spiritual
     Love." Chicago Daily Tribune, 3 August, p. 11.
     Admires Cather's ability to combine an experimental tech-
nique, in this case, the use of symphonic form, with a classic
prose style in Lucy Gayheart. The novel asserts that thought is
less easily erased than action. Lucy Gayheart is one of the few
real idyls in American literature.

7   CANTWELL, ROBERT. "A Season's Run." New Republic 85
     (11 December):149-53.
     Review of Lucy Gayheart laments Cather's failure to come
to terms with modern problems. Lucy Gayheart is a "maudlin"
novel by a wornout writer held up by outmoded critics.

8   CHAMBERLAIN, JOHN. "The World in Books." Current History 42
     (September):iv-v.
         Review of Lucy Gayheart adjudges that the vitality of
     Cather's depiction of the small town and some of its minor fig-
     ures does not compensate for the bloodless melancholy of Lucy
     and the feebleness of her portrayal.

9   CONNOLLY, CYRIL. Review of Lucy Gayheart. New Statesman and
     Nation 10 (3 August):166.
         Views Cather as the only modern American writer to break
     off all ties with Europe and concentrate on the American Middle-
     west. Lucy Gayheart is beautifully written, but its psychologi-
     cal development is incomplete.

10   [FISHER], DOROTHY CANFIELD. Review of Lucy Gayheart. Book-
     of-the-Month Club News.
         Listed in Faulkner-Slote notes, collection at University of
     Nebraska Library, Lincoln. Unverified.

11   GRIMES, GEORGE. "Willa Cather Returns to Nebraska to Write a
     Simple, Tragic Tale." Omaha Sunday World-Herald, 4 August.
         Believes that Lucy Gayheart shows Cather's expertise as an
     artist in this "fragile, tender, sympathetic story." Its chief
     preoccupation is with the tragedy of life.

12   HAAS, JAKOB. Versuch einer Darstellung der Heimatliteratur
     in den Vereinigten Staaten von Nordamerika. Bonn: Anton
     Brand, pp. 55-70.
         Published doctoral dissertation from Rheinischen Friedrich-
     Wilhelms-Universität zu Bonn regards Cather as a representative
     writer from the Midwest. Details Cather's interest in the re-
     newal of man's relationship to the land he lives on, and also
     includes commentary on Death Comes for the Archbishop.

13   HATCHER, HARLAND. "Willa Cather and the Shifting Moods." In
     Creating the Modern American Novel. New York: Farrar &
     Rinehart, pp. 58-71.
         Regards Cather as America's most talented escapist, con-
     cluding through a review of all of her novels to date that her
     central theme concerns the West's triumphant heroes and the
     sellout of later generations to materialistic vulgarity.

14   HAWKINS, ETHEL WALLACE. Review of Lucy Gayheart. "Atlantic
     Bookshelf." Atlantic Monthly 156 (September):10.
         The storyline of Lucy Gayheart is rapid and realistic; the
     narrative flows, and character development is complete.

15   HOWARD, JOHN TASKER. Ethelbert Nevin. New York: Thomas Y.
     Crowell Co., pp. 311-12.
         Cites from Cather's published description of the Nevin
     home, and mentions Cather in several other passing comments.

16   JACKSON, JOSEPH HENRY. "Youth's Valorous Way with Life Is
     Theme of Willa Cather's Latest. San Francisco Chronicle,
     4 August, sec. d, p. 4.
        Cather's writing style is delicate, yet direct, as she
creates in Lucy Gayheart another "lost lady."

17   JARRELL, RANDALL. "Ten Books." Southern Review 1 (Autumn):
     407-8.
        Review of Lucy Gayheart indicates that although it is not
an "important" book, it is worthwhile. Cather's style is the
sort that makes her faults obvious and her virtues apparent only
in careful rereading. Although Cather's style does not rank her
among first-rate writers, Lucy Gayheart is not false or roman-
tically sentimental. Cather is better at describing emotion than
sensation.

18   JONES, HOWARD MUMFORD. "Willa Cather Returns to the Middle
     West." Saturday Review of Literature 12 (3 August):7.
        Observes that Cather, with her insight and stylistic per-
fection, is one of the few modern novelists who sees the novel as
an art form. In Lucy Gayheart characterization and theme are
more important than plot.

19   JORDAN-SMITH, PAUL. Review of Lucy Gayheart. Los Angeles
     Times, 4 August.
        Lucy Gayheart demonstrates Cather's ability to find meaning
in everyday life. The characters are richly drawn.

20   KAUFMAN, K[ENNETH] C. "Truncated Destiny." Christian Science
     Monitor, 31 July, p. 12.
        Review of Lucy Gayheart. Complains that Cather exaggerates
the importance of Lucy Gayheart's love affair and cuts short
Lucy's life unnecessarily. Cather's prose is beautiful and her
minor characters are well-conceived, but she should have taken
more time to develop the novel. Lucy is more believable as an
artist than she is as a person.

21   KAZIN, ALFRED. "Symbolic Tragedy." Scribner's Magazine 98
     (September):2, 4.
        Behind Cather's apparent simplicity in Lucy Gayheart lies
great artistry and the ability to see clearly even when dealing
with things remembered.

22   LINN, JAMES WEBER, and TAYLOR, HOUGHTON WELLS. A Foreword to
     Fiction. New York: D. Appleton-Century Co., pp. 69, 73,
     75-77.
        Analyzes the three stages of action and the technique of
"delayed exposition" in "Paul's Case" to show how the story
exemplifies a well-made fictional plot.

23   MacAFEE, HELEN. Review of Lucy Gayheart. Yale Review,
     n.s. 25 (Autumn):viii.
        Lucy Gayheart is deliberately removed from the reader to
become "an airy rectilinear creation."

24 MAILLARD, DENYSE. L'Enfant américain dans le roman du Middle-
    West. Paris: Librairie Nizet & Bastard, pp. 55-234 passim.
        A published doctoral dissertation in French. Discusses the
    portrayal of youth in the middlewestern farm novel in relation to
    such things as family, education, nature, and psychological make-
    up. Of Cather's characters, Claude Wheeler receives the most
    frequent comment, followed by Thea Kronborg and Niel Herbert.

25 MANN, DOROTHEA LAWRANCE. "The Supreme Art of Willa Cather."
    Boston Evening Transcript, Book sec., 3 August, p. 3.
        Applauds the artistic unity of Lucy Gayheart and sees it as
    further evidence of Cather's greatness as an artist. Observes
    that Lucy's features receive very little attention in Cather's
    descriptions; Lucy is realized almost totally through motion.
    In Lucy's sister Pauline there is an echo of Cather's practical
    pioneer women.

26 MEAGHER, CHARLOTTE M. "Romance at Noonday." Commonweal 22
    (27 September):534.
        Praises Cather's understanding of human emotions and her
    sensitivity to setting. Lucy Gayheart has a forceful but subtly
    textured plot.

27 "Miss Cather's First Novel in Four Years." Kansas City Star,
    10 August, p. 14.
        Perceives the plot structure of Lucy Gayheart to be anti-
    climactic since both hero and heroine are drowned long before the
    end of the novel. Cather's development of Harry Gordon is un-
    balanced, for late in the novel he is thrust into the limelight
    without a suitable buildup.

28 "New Novels." Times Literary Supplement (London), 25 July,
    p. 476.
        Review of Lucy Gayheart remarks on the indelible impression
    left by Lucy, not only on the minds of the other characters, but
    on the reader as well. Lucy Gayheart compares favorably with My
    Ántonia in its structure and its portrayal of the main character.

29 P., R.H. "Willa Cather's Newest Effort." Omaha Sunday Bee-
    News, 4 August, p. 20.
        Claims Lucy Gayheart to be a composite of two character
    sketches rather than a novel. Even though the book fails to
    conclude, it is still "beautiful." It has that elusive quality
    that distinguishes most of Cather's writing.

30 PELANTOVA, ARTEMIS. "Willa Cather Now Writing in Canada."
    Nebraska Writers' Guild Bulletin, April, p. 23.
        Reprinted from 1927.28.

31 PLOMER, WILLIAM. Review of Lucy Gayheart. Spectator 155
    (2 August):200.
        Superficial and sentimental in its portrayal of both char-
    acters and place, Lucy Gayheart is innocuous at best.

32   PRESTON, KEITH. "Willa Sibert Cather." In <u>The New American
      Literature</u>, by Fred Lewis Pattee. New York: Cooper Square
      Publishers, p. 260. Reprint. 1968.
          Reprint of 1921.17.

33   Review of <u>Lucy Gayheart</u>. <u>Booklist</u> 32 (September):14.
          Cather's style of writing and her characterization are more
      powerful than her plot.

34   Review of <u>Lucy Gayheart</u>. <u>Catholic World</u> 141 (September):763.
          Lucy and Sebastian are both well drawn characters, but <u>Lucy
      Gayheart</u> suffers from weak structure and inconsistent plot.

35   RINEHART, MARY ROBERTS. "Women of the Year." <u>Pictorial
      Review</u> 36 (January):6.
          Chooses Cather as one of 1935's distinguished women, be-
      cause of her artistic integrity, her "vast indignation against
      evil and cruelty," and her commitment to rewriting.

36   ROBBINS, FRANCES C. LAMONT. "The New Fiction." <u>American
      Mercury</u> 36 (September):113-17.
          Review of <u>Lucy Gayheart</u> affirms that although it belongs
      with the Cather canon because of its retrospective tone, it is
      inferior to her earlier novels. Praises Cather for the emotional
      detail with which she portrays Lucy and for her restraint and
      clarity in style and structure. In the novel Cather delicately
      balances her two major themes, the zeal of youth and the resigna-
      tion of middle age, thus robbing the book of vitality.

37   SLOCUM, JOHN. Review of <u>Lucy Gayheart</u>. <u>North American Review</u>
      240 (December):549-50.
          Cather is effective in style, setting, and realistic char-
      acterization, but she fails to capture the essence of modern
      life and to develop completely the character of Lucy Gayheart.

38   TROY, WILLIAM. "Footprints in Cement." <u>Nation</u> 141
      (14 August):193.
          Sentimental and lacking in substance, <u>Lucy Gayheart</u> is
      "naively romantic" and disappointing.

39   WALTON, EDITH H. "The Book Parade." <u>Forum and Century</u> 94
      (October):v.
          Review of <u>Lucy Gayheart</u> describes it as "pathetic rather
      than tragic." Though flawlessly written, it does not measure up
      to predecessors like <u>My Ántonia</u>.

40   "Willa Cather's Tale." <u>Springfield (Mass.) Republican</u>,
      4 August, sec. e, p. 5.
          Provides a plot summary of <u>Lucy Gayheart</u> and acclaims it as
      Cather's loveliest book.

41   WILSON, JAMES SOUTHALL. "Two American Novels." Virginia
     Quarterly Review 11 (October):625-26.
          Review of Lucy Gayheart concludes that while the book is
     not Cather's most successful work, it contains her usual vivid
     description and firm prose.

                              1936

1   "American Essayist." Times Literary Supplement (London),
     5 December, p. 1007.
          Calls Cather an "older" novelist because her essays reflect
     her literary preferences for an older, more classical style. She
     is able to bring to life in her essays such minor characters in
     literary history as Gustave Flaubert's niece and Mrs. James T.
     Fields.

2   BARRON, Rev. MARK. "Communication: The Catholic Novel."
     Commonweal 23 (10 April):665.
          Suggests that Cather's Death Comes for the Archbishop could
     serve as a model for the Catholic novelist. Because she did not
     set out to write about Catholicism, her treatment of the New
     Mexico diocese is realistic and her novel is successful.

3   BOYNTON, PERCY H. Literature and American Life. Boston:
     Ginn & Co., pp. 787-89.
          Adapted from 1931.7. Also observes the cyclical nature of
     Cather's work.

4   BROWN, E[DWARD] K[ILLORAN]. "Willa Cather and the West."
     University of Toronto Quarterly 5 (July):544-66.
          Lucy Gayheart marks a return to the spirit of the West that
     had informed and vitalized several of Cather's earlier novels.
     There is a power emanating from the land in Cather's western
     writing that is absent from her other work. And like her, the
     characters in Cather's books who have a special relationship, an
     almost mysterious sense of union, with the land derive spiritual
     and creative energy--and largeness of spirit--through that rela-
     tionship. Generally, Cather found European peoples to be more
     receptive than Anglo-Saxon Americans to the West's spirit.

5   CANBY, HENRY SEIDEL. "Powerful Slightness." Saturday Review
     of Literature 15 (28 November):7.
          The essays in Not Under Forty appear to be on the personal
     level, but they actually deal with the qualities found in all
     great literature.

6   _____. Seven Years' Harvest: Notes on Contemporary Litera-
     ture. New York: Farrar & Rinehart, pp. 154, 257, 273, 278,
     287.
          Speaks complimentarily throughout of Cather as a tradi-
     tionalist whose chief interest lies in values and the search for
     them.

7   "Communications." Commonweal 23 (5 June):161–62.
       Letters to the editor department contains three letters of
    response to Cather's piece on escapism in art, published in the
    April 1936 issue of Commonweal. Albert J. Steiss takes issue
    with Cather's use of the term "escapism," and suggests that the
    word "freedom" would more appropriately be applied to true art.
    Joseph L. Richards disagrees with her contention that art and
    economics are "strangers." William Lyon Phelps admires Cather's
    essay and commends Commonweal for printing it. Steiss and
    Richards mainly use Cather's remarks as a springboard for the
    presentation of their own ideas about art. Phelps's letter is
    very brief.

8   GOTH, ELSIE. "Story by Willa Cather's Neighbors." Nebraska
       Alumnus 32 (April):6–7, 22.
       Reveals something of Cather's life and experiences in and
    around Red Cloud, Nebraska, ostensibly as told to Goth by people
    in Red Cloud who knew Cather. Some attention is given to a de-
    scription of the private "office" that was constructed for the
    young writer against the Cather barn.

9   KALTENBACHER, THERESE. "Willa Cather als Vertreterin des
       Westens." In Frauenfragen im amerikanischen Frauenroman.
       Kallmünz: Druckerei von Michael Lassleben, pp. 96–110.
       Published doctoral dissertation from Friedrich-Wilhelms-
    Universität zu Berlin deals with the problems of women in fron-
    tier settlements and the modernization of the West as seen
    through the works of Cather. Focuses primarily on O Pioneers!

10   KRONENBERGER, LOUIS. "In Dubious Battle." Nation 143
       (19 December):738–39.
       Review of Not Under Forty. Contends that Cather fails to
    deal with reality and escapes into the past. Her smugness,
    guilt, and "self-righteous loyalty" to the past have had a nega-
    tive effect on her art.

11   LAWRENCE, MARGARET. The School of Femininity: A Book for and
       about Women As They Are Interpreted Through Feminine Writers
       of Yesterday and Today. New York: Frederick A. Stokes Co.,
       pp. 355–64.
       Lauds Cather as the foremost woman writer of her time,
    pointing to her deep artistry, her "spiritual authenticity," and
    her romantic outlook. Discusses A Lost Lady, The Professor's
    House, Death Comes for the Archbishop, and Lucy Gayheart as they
    exemplify Cather's dignified, profound art. Abridged: 1937.8.

12   McCOLE, CAMILLE. "Willa Cather as a Critic." America 54
       (11 January):332–33.
       Finds Cather's essay "The Novel Démeublé" an accurate
    criticism of too much of today's fiction. Readers tend to con-
    sider that novel greatest that piles up, in reportorial fashion,
    the most physical detail, and to prefer sensory reaction over
    emotion. The essay should be required reading for all writers,
    critics, and students in writing courses.

13 PATERSON, ISABEL. "Remembering Happier Days." New York
    Herald Tribune, 22 November.
        In the main, describes the nature and contents of the
    essays in Not Under Forty, indicating that the book is full of
    pleasant nostalgia for the nineteenth century.

14 QUINN, ARTHUR HOBSON. "Willa Cather." In American Fiction:
    An Historical and Critical Survey. New York: D. Appleton-
    Century Co., pp. 683-97.
        Surveys Cather's work, including several of her short sto-
    ries, insisting that locale is much less important to her than
    character and the pursuit of beauty. Cather is not provincial,
    but has the universal quality that distinguishes art of high
    rank. Alexander's Bridge is a remarkably good book, but O
    Pioneers! and My Ántonia are not among her best; they are struc-
    turally weak and episodic. A Lost Lady, The Professor's House,
    Death Comes for the Archbishop, and Shadows on the Rock are
    especially strong because of their character studies. Cather's
    most enduring theme concerns the artist's contest with environ-
    mental limitations, especially in the West. Through her contact
    with, and appreciation for, a variety of races and cultures,
    Cather acquired a broad vision and a keen understanding of a
    multitude of differing points of view.

15 Review of Not Under Forty. Kansas City Star, 28 November.
        Comments on Cather's belief in the power of suggestion and
    her aversion to literalness in literature. Agrees with the title
    that the work is written for the older reader.

16 SOSKIN, WILLIAM. "Willa Cather's Excursions into the Literary
    Past." New York Times Book Review, 22 November, p. 2.
        Finds in the essays comprising Not Under Forty Cather's
    admiration for continental culture and velvety peace, and a
    "sentimental fondness" for writers who are inferior artistically
    but represent the social values Cather likes.

17 SWINNERTON, FRANK. Swinnerton: An Autobiography. New York:
    Doubleday, Doran & Co., pp. 317-19.
        Describes Swinnerton's association with Cather on the re-
    turn trip from England aboard the Berengaria in November 1923.
    He found her immensely intelligent, free from egotism, candid,
    wise, happily unruffled, and interested in life, people, and
    music.

18 TAYLOR, WALTER FULLER. "Willa Sibert Cather." In A History
    of American Letters. With bibliographies by Harry Hartwick.
    Boston: American Book Co., pp. 327-30 passim, 337, 357-64,
    573-74.
        Finds almost no fault with Cather's work, commending it as
    part of the central current of American literature. Cather's
    novels are humane, controlled, balanced admirably between romance
    and realism, rich with deft characterization and episode without
    being overly furnished, and imbued with an intangible personal
    quality all her own. She wrote novels of the prairie, novels of

the scholar and aristocrat, and novels of tradition and originality, but in all she is clearly attracted in equal measure to
vitality and cultivation. Shadows on the Rock is a nearly perfect novel. Hartwick provides both primary and secondary bibliography.

19   V., T. "Essays about the Art of Writing." Los Angeles Times,
     [29 November].
        Review of Not Under Forty. Adjudges that Cather's title
and preface are products of a "passing melancholy." Anything she
writes is art; and these essays, being no exception, will appeal
to all ages.

20   WALBRIDGE, EARLE F. Literary Characters Drawn from Life. New
     York: H.W. Wilson Co., p. 26.
        Identifies Olive Fremstad as Cather's model for her singer
in The Song of the Lark. Supplemented: 1953.24.

21   ZWART, ELIZABETH CLARKSON. "The Writings of Willa Cather 'Can
     Only Be Experienced.'" Des Moines Register, 22 November.
        Disagrees with the implications of Cather's title, arguing
that Not Under Forty has something for every reader. Cather's
style is so beautiful that it cannot be defined or analyzed; it
can only be experienced.

1937

1   BECKER, MAY LAMBERTON. "Read This One First." Scholastic 31
    (23 October):24-E.
       Suggests that a reader's initial experience with Cather
should be O Pioneers!, a book full of youth and the "human
beauty" created by a "born genius" who knew her materials firsthand and constructed an exceptional "almost . . . first novel."

2   BUTCHER, FANNY. "Willa Cather's Book Intended Not for Youth."
    Chicago Daily Tribune, 16 January, p. 15.
       Recommends Not Under Forty for its brilliant description,
critical insight, and refreshing clarity.

3   CLARK, JOHN ABBOT. "The Middle West--There It Lies."
    Southern Review 2 (Winter):462-73 passim.
       Regrets that most good writers of the Middle West, Cather
included, leave that area. They use it for a time as subject
matter and then leave it. Such writers should cast off the old
clichés about themselves and their subjects and present the experience of the Middle West with honesty and a sense of community.

4   CLEATON, IRENE, and CLEATON, ALLEN. Books & Battles: Ameri-
    can Literature, 1920-1930. Boston: Houghton Mifflin Co.,
    Riverside Press, pp. 8, 119, 159, 205, 248-49, 251.
       Mentions Cather many times throughout the book, but on
these pages praises her craftsmanship and "disciplined

imagination." Notes her taste, her avoidance of the spectacular, and her understanding of the immigrant, even though she herself had to leave Nebraska to enjoy the cultural advantages of metropolitan life.

5   COBLEY, W.D. "Willa Cather." In Papers of the Manchester Literary Club. Vol. 52. Manchester, England: Sherratt & Hughes, pp. 43–64.
      Discusses a number of Cather's novels as well as the story "The Diamond Mine" which is viewed as a "rough draft" for The Song of the Lark. In that novel Cather comes closer to the creation of genuine character than she does anywhere else. The painting of scenes, not the creation of character, is Cather's strength and her method. It is puzzling that some commentators rate the deeply flawed A Lost Lady and The Professor's House among Cather's best; much more beautiful are Shadows on the Rock and Lucy Gayheart. (This article contains many factual errors, especially in the names of characters in the novels.)

6   DICKINSON, ASA DON. The Best Books of the Decade 1926–1935. New York: H.W. Wilson Co., pp. 39–40, 170–74 passim, 184–86 passim.
      Provides a brief biography of Cather and lists among the decade's four hundred favorite books Death Comes for the Archbishop, Lucy Gayheart, Obscure Destinies, and Shadows on the Rock. Includes a brief note of description and praise for each.

7   JACK, PETER MONRO. "The Sense of the Past." New Republic 90 (10 February):25–26.
      Finds Not Under Forty "sad," a sentimental and nostalgic elegy for the "Victorian past."

8   LAWRENCE, MARGARET. We Write As Women. London: Michael Joseph, pp. 290–98.
      Abridged text of 1936.11.

9   LOGGINS, VERNON. I Hear America . . . Literature in the United States Since 1900. New York: Thomas Y. Crowell Co., pp. 197–98 passim, 207–16. Reprint. New York: Biblo & Tannen, 1967.
      Argues that Cather is a regional writer and writes well only when her work emphasizes a locality. Thus, O Pioneers!, The Song of the Lark, and My Ántonia are her greatest novels, while A Lost Lady, The Professor's House, and My Mortal Enemy have little importance.

10 MULLER, HERBERT J. "Virginia Woolf and Feminine Fiction." In Modern Fiction: A Study of Values. New York: Funk & Wagnalls Co., pp. 15, 325–26. Also in Saturday Review of Literature 15 (6 February):16.
      Avows that the later Cather moved away from her early robustness into a "wistful reminiscence" that produced "wispy" fiction.

11   Prospectus announcement of the forthcoming Autograph Edition
      of the Novels and Stories of Willa Cather. Boston: Houghton
      Mifflin Co., 14 pp.
          Outlines Cather's major creative achievements as they
      appear in the autograph edition of her works, calling One of Ours
      the first book of her second phase. Also describes the design of
      the edition and the achievement of the designer, Bruce Rogers.

12   REILLY, JOSEPH J. Review of Not Under Forty. Catholic World
      144 (March):754-55.
          Compares Cather with essayist Agnes Repplier, calling
      Cather an artist who is interested in other artists. Her
      nostalgia and love for beauty are to be savored, as are her depth
      and distinctive style.

13   SEDGEWICK, ELLERY. Review of Not Under Forty. "Atlantic
      Bookshelf." Atlantic Monthly 159 (February):1.
          Calls Not Under Forty a work that reverences the past.
      Such reverence is also observable in Cather's "oblique approach"
      to the famous people she presents in her essays. Flaubert is
      seen through his niece, for example, and James T. Fields through
      his wife.

14   SIMONS, W.J. "Willa Cather Addresses Herself to Mature
      Minds." San Francisco Chronicle, [31 January 1937].
          Review of Not Under Forty. Enjoys the sincerity, clarity,
      and subtlety of Cather's essays and applauds her ability to be
      modern without being superficial like many modern writers.

15   TRILLING, LIONEL. "Willa Cather." In After the Genteel
      Tradition: American Writers 1910-1930. Edited by Malcolm
      Cowley. New York: W.W. Norton & Co., pp. 52-63. Reprint.
      Crosscurrents Modern Critiques Series, edited by Harry T.
      Moore. Carbondale: Southern Illinois University Press, 1964,
      pp. 48-56.
          Reprint of 1937.16.

16   _____. "Willa Cather." New Republic 90 (10 February):10-13.
          Cather's entire work is an attempt to deal with what she
      perceived as the failure of the pioneer. And even if the pioneer
      succeeded, he "failed" because his ideal was not enough. Cather
      had to seek beyond the pioneer for a new spiritual ideal, in the
      mystery, culture, order, and permanence of religion. In the end
      Cather's work succumbs to a kind of domestic gentility that con-
      tains nothing of the western ideal. Even though Cather could
      never write successfully of the relationships between human be-
      ings, at least earlier books showed vital relationships between
      human beings and the land. Reprinted: 1937.15; 1967.56;
      1980.43-44.

17   W[ELLMAN], P[AUL] I. "The Home on the Nebraska Prairie Which
      Always Recalls Willa Cather." Kansas City Star, 10 July.
          Discourses on Cather and her continuing ties with Red
      Cloud, Nebraska, noting that she still retains her western accent
      and viewpoint.

18   WHITE, GEORGE LEROY, Jr. Scandinavian Themes in American
     Fiction. University of Pennsylvania, pp. 83-84, 114-19 pas-
     sim, 129, 134-35, 149, 168, 173-74, 193-208.
          Originally a doctoral dissertation. Examines Scandinavian
     themes in "Eric Hermannson's Soul," "The Bohemian Girl," O
     Pioneers!, The Song of the Lark, and My Ántonia, and notes that
     in Cather these themes are distinguished by being presented from
     an outsider's point of view. For the most part, the Scandinavian
     traits of Cather's characters are implicit rather than explicit,
     but they are there--in Alexandra Bergson's moral fortitude, in
     Nils Ericson's wanderlust, in Thea Kronborg's love for music.
     Cather often presents her Scandinavians in contrast with other
     races, and she is interested in the Americanization process that
     works on them.

                              1938

1   "Academy Elects Benet and Cather." New York Times, 11 Novem-
     ber, p. 24.
          Reports Cather's election to the American Academy of Arts
     and Letters.

2   BALLARD, DORIS. "Willa Cather, Novelist of America and
     Nebraska." Ph.D. dissertation, University of California at
     Los Angeles, 33 pp.
          Explores Cather's use of actual people and places in
     Webster County, Nebraska, as models and settings for some of her
     works. Information for this study was obtained from four sources:
     (1) Cather's early writings in a college publication, (2) news-
     paper clippings that quote Cather's statements about her use of
     actual places and people in her fiction, (3) interviews with Red
     Cloud people, and (4) visits to pertinent sites in the Red Cloud
     area.

3   FOOTMAN, ROBERT H. "The Genius of Willa Cather." American
     Literature 10 (May):123-41.
          Seeks to explain Cather's achievement by her own definition
     of genius in her preface to the stories of Sarah Orne Jewett.
     According to Cather, identifying a writer's limitations is one
     way to define her genius. Cather's limitations are (1) her way
     of relating to "symbols of authority," (2) her use of religious
     devotion, and (3) her aesthetic ideal or style. For Cather,
     mood is paramount; she depends on overtones to create an emo-
     tional quality in her work. She admired only one kind of char-
     acter, one set of qualities; she liked to write about people who
     had a sense of destiny, who wanted to live out their potential.

4   JONES, HOWARD MUMFORD. "The Novels of Willa Cather." Satur-
     day Review of Literature 18 (6 August):3-4, 16.
          On the occasion of the publication of a special edition of
     Cather's works in twelve volumes, Jones gives a general estimate
     of her fiction, praising her as a writer of classic bent whose
     transparent, flexible style and whose capacity to "command

pathos" rather than tragedy link her to writers like Hawthorne, Emerson, and Longfellow. Her strength lies in her ability to draw "a single curve of personalized experience" to create the atmosphere for the portrayal and development of a sympathetic personality.

5   LEWIS, SINCLAIR. "The Greatest American Novelist." Newsweek
    11 (3 January):29.
        Claims that Cather has preserved the American frontier in fiction as no one else has. Recommends her as one who has gone on writing vigorously for thirty-five years, producing beauty and avoiding literary dinners. He would vote for her as America's greatest living novelist.

6   MAJOR, MABEL; SMITH, REBECCA W.; and PEARCE, T[HOMAS]
    M[ATTHEWS]. Southwest Heritage: A Literary History with
    Bibliographies. Albuquerque: University of New Mexico Press,
    pp. 121-22. Revised. 1948, 1972.
        Acclaims Death Comes for the Archbishop as the finest novel ever written of the Southwest, and one of the finest novels written in America. The Cather material in 1948 and 1972 editions is essentially unchanged. The third edition, 1972, omits the name of Smith as an author.

7   ÖSTERLING, ANDERS. "Ormen och korset" [The snake and the
    cross]. Stockholms-Tidningen, 16 November, p. 6.
        In Swedish. Observes that in Death Comes for the Archbishop Cather captures in a very few words the look and feel of a landscape. The novel is like Bishop Latour's church--gray and Gothic against a red stone background. The people Cather creates are like the landscape.

8   "Willa Cather." Scholastic 32 (30 April):19-E.
        Accompanies a reprint of "A Wagner Matinee." Sketches Cather's life and stresses her love for music, asserting that she left her beloved Nebraska so that she could attend concerts regularly.

1939

1   ADAMS, FREDERICK B., Jr. "Willa Cather's Early Years: Trial
    and Error." Colophon, n.s. 1 (September):89-100.
        Outlines events in Cather's early life, noting particularly the contents and bibliographical details pertinent to the publishing history of a number of early stories and the various editions of her first three books. Also details information on binding and publication oddities. Mentions the book Cather wrote but never published, a book in the form of letters addressed to living actors, and refers to her role in the Milmine biography of Mary Baker Eddy and in S.S. McClure's autobiography. See 1940.1 for subsequent article.

2   ANGOFF, CHARLES. "Three Notes on American Literature." North
     American Review 247 (Spring):38-41.
         Observes that in American literature women have mainly
served as backdrops or props for male protagonists. Cather, however, presents a "special problem": her seemingly strong women
are merely shadows of their environments or complexities.

3   ATTIS. "Nybyggarbarn och pionjärkvinna" [Pioneer child and
     pioneer woman]. Svenska dagbladet (Stockholm), 22 October,
     Sunday sec., p. 2.
         In Swedish. Appreciates Cather's gentle portraits of
pioneers in My Ántonia and notes that even her evil characters
are depicted as human. She has qualities that endear her to the
reader, and there is justified support for her candidacy for the
Nobel Prize.

4   GIEROW, KARL RAGNER. "Pionjär" [Pioneer]. Nya dagligt
     allehanda (Stockholm), 6 November, p. 7.
         In Swedish. Argues that Cather is to the United States
what Selma Lagerlöf and Sigrid Undset are to the Scandinavians.
In her subject matter, Cather was a pioneer--none before her had
realistically portrayed pioneers. Her style is calm and cosmopolitan. She deserves the Nobel Prize.

5   HAMILTON, CLAYTON. The Art of Fiction: A Formulation of Its
     Fundamental Principles. New York: Doubleday, Doran & Co.,
     pp. 163-64, 188, 213, 255-56, 312.
         Quotes several passages from Cather's statements about the
writer's craft while making various points about the art of fiction.

6   HERRON, IMA HONAKER. The Small Town in American Literature.
     Durham, N.C.: Duke University Press. Reprint. New York:
     Pageant Books, 1959, pp. 394-402.
         Although in a number of stories and in many novels Cather
portrays the pettiness and strictures of small towns, and the
resulting conflict between character and environment, unlike her
contemporaries--Sinclair Lewis, Edgar Lee Masters, and Sherwood
Anderson--Cather shows that the small town is capable of producing noble characters who emerge from their environment and find
fulfillment.

7   Van DOREN, CARL, and Van DOREN, MARK. American and British
     Literature. Rev. ed. New York: D. Appleton-Century Co.,
     pp. 82-86.
         Reprints Cather section from 1925.38, and adds discussion
on the novels after A Lost Lady, indicating that in the later
fictions Cather's heroes and heroines become passive rather than
active. They lose something as Cather exchanges drama for
lyricism.

<u>1940</u>

1   ADAMS, FREDERICK B., Jr. "Willa Cather, Middle Years: The
    Right Road Taken." <u>Colophon</u>, n.s. 1 (February):103–8.
         Picks up where previous article (see 1939.1) left off,
    pursuing further Adams's attempts to distinguish among the early
    publishings of <u>Alexander's Bridge</u> and determine their priority.
    Describes the various bindings of the first edition of <u>O Pioneers!</u>
    and notes other features of the novel. Also discloses publish-
    ing, binding, and bibliographic details for <u>The Song of the Lark</u>
    and <u>My Ántonia</u>, then considers various critical estimates and
    autobiographical aspects of Cather's work. Maintains that
    Cather's strength is as an "historian of character."

2   ADAMS, J. DONALD. Review of <u>Sapphira and the Slave Girl</u>. <u>New</u>
    <u>York Times Book Review</u>, 8 December, p. 4.
         Although <u>Sapphira and the Slave Girl</u> is subtle, clear, and
    full of fine description, its conclusion is inconsistent. Fur-
    thermore, its Virginia setting lacks intensity by comparison with
    Nebraska or the Southwest.

3   BENET, STEPHEN VINCENT, and BENET, ROSEMARY. "Willa Cather:
    Civilized and Very American." <u>New York Herald Tribune Books</u>,
    15 December, p. 6.
         A highly complimentary general assessment of Cather.
    Stresses the importance of her link to both civilization and the
    frontier as the shaping forces in her life and work. Describes
    her as a woman of fortitude and warmth who brought together the
    two aspects of her background to produce true art in a euphonious
    and lucid style.

4   BOYNTON, PERCY H. "Willa Cather." <u>America in Contemporary</u>
    <u>Fiction</u>. Chicago: University of Chicago Press, pp. 150–63.
         A modified text of 1924.1; 1931.7; 1936.3, which includes
    an overall assessment of Cather's work. Faults her for her lack
    of hardihood, but praises her for finding the artistic mold that
    affirms the values of the past, rejects the material pressures of
    the present, and finds at last order in the tranquil tradition
    and authority of the Roman Church. Self-fulfillment is Cather's
    constant theme.

5   CANBY, HENRY SEIDEL. "Conversation Piece." <u>Saturday Review</u>
    <u>of Literature</u> 23 (14 December):5.
         Admires Cather's concise prose and her ability to capture
    a region and a life-style, and groups <u>Sapphira and the Slave Girl</u>
    with <u>Death Comes for the Archbishop</u> and <u>Shadows on the Rock</u> as
    examples of this ability. In <u>Sapphira and the Slave Girl</u> Cather
    subtly portrays a conflict of morals and philosophies, producing
    an increasing intensity which eventually takes over the story
    almost before the reader realizes it. Cather's photograph is
    also featured on the cover.

6   FADIMAN, CLIFTON. "Miss Cather." New Yorker 16 (7 December):
     103–4.
        Contends that Sapphira and the Slave Girl is a "minor"
     work, but praises Cather's self-control, her precise prose, and
     the narrative's reminiscent quality. The slaves in the novel are
     real people rather than teaching devices.

7   FISHER, DOROTHY CANFIELD. "Sapphira and the Slave Girl by
     Willa Cather." Book-of-the-Month Club News, December,
     pp. 2–3.
        Calls particular attention to the mellow mood of what was
     potentially an intense, exciting novel. Sapphira and the Slave
     Girl is based on a true story that Cather heard as a child, and
     she held it in her mind for many years before writing about it.
     Thus, the book's "golden human values" are rescued from "imme-
     diate, imitation-emotion" and made available to the reader in a
     spirit of tranquility. Reprinted: 1980.12; 1984.29.

8   GRIMES, GEORGE. "Willa Cather's Scene Her Native Virginia."
     Unidentified periodical clipping [Omaha World-Herald?]
     sec. c, p. 4, scrapbook II-65, at Willa Cather Historical
     Center, Red Cloud, Nebraska.
        Regards Sapphira and the Slave Girl as one of Cather's best
     novels, an intimate revelation of life in prewar Virginia told
     with a sure touch.

9   GUNSKY, FREDERIC R. "An Awaited Novel by Willa Cather." San
     Francisco Chronicle, 15 December, p. 14.
        Cather proves in Sapphira and the Slave Girl that she re-
     tains faith in common people and fine craftsmanship. Outwardly
     calm, Sapphira and the Slave Girl portrays an inward clash of
     will and personalities. Ranks Sapphira with Ántonia Shimerda
     and Marian Forrester as Cather's best portraits of women, and
     praises especially Cather's portrayal of minor characters.

10   HANDY, YVONNE. L'oeuvre de Willa Cather. Rennes:
     Imprimeries Oberthur, 222 pp.
        A published doctoral dissertation at Université de Rennes
     that, after introductory observations about Cather's life and the
     influence of the frontier upon her, traces the evolution of her
     work. Discusses, in turn, her philosophy, her psychology, and
     her art. Summarizes plots of the novels and several of the sto-
     ries and discusses the works as they represent Cather's values,
     especially pioneer values. Argues that Cather's psychology was
     "purely feminine" and her work universal rather than regional.
     Despite structural weaknesses in her work, Cather is an artist
     of the first rank.

11   KROCH, ADOLPH. Alfred A. Knopf Quarter Century. New York:
     Elmer Adler, pp. 44–45.
        Contains tributes to Alfred A. Knopf written by various
     associates, including Cather. In the tribute by a bookseller,
     Kroch also lauds Knopf's "greatest coup," Willa Cather. Claims

books would be better and fewer if others followed her practice
of averaging one book every three years.

12 LUCCOCK, HALFORD E. American Mirror: Social, Ethical and
    Religious Aspects of American Literature 1930-1940. New York:
    Macmillan Co., pp. 41, 88-89, 130, 152.
    Cather is now "dated," having done her most important work
before 1930, before she made her conspicuous retreat from contemporary life. In Obscure Destinies, however, she created some
strong characters.

13 M., S. "Skuggor från en annan tid" [Shadows from another
    time]. Nya dagligt allehanda (Stockholm), 29 September,
    pp. 8-9.
    In Swedish. Observes that in Shadows on the Rock Cather's
experience enables her to paint sympathetic and interesting portraits of people, while her economy with words enables her to
paint beautiful portraits of nature.

14 MILLETT, FRED B. Contemporary American Authors: A Critical
    Survey and 219 Bio-Bibliographies. New York: Harcourt,
    Brace & Co., pp. 25-27, 49, 63-64, 91, 289-92. Reprint. New
    York: AMS Press, 1970.
    Presents a general estimate of Cather's work, praising her
"chaste" style and the variety of her fictional approaches, but
regretting the waning vitality of her later novels. Also
sketches her biography and lists primary and secondary bibliography items.

15 PEARCE, T[HOMAS] M[ATTHEWS]. The Beloved House. Caldwell,
    Idaho: Caxton Printers, pp. 176-78, 183-84.
    Refers to Mary Austin's disappointment in Cather for sympa-
thizing with French rather than Spanish culture in Death Comes
for the Archbishop. Cather seems to have written some of the
novel while a guest at Austin's home. Cather actually does,
however, show genuine appreciation for native peoples in New
Mexico.

16 "Pre-War Tale." Time 36 (9 December):88.
    Finds Sapphira and the Slave Girl "dull" but pleasant. Its
strong points are its treatment of setting and character.

17 RAHV, PHILIP. "The Slump in American Writing." American
    Mercury 49 (February):185-91 passim.
    Asserts that no one currently publishing writes with the
vigor and significance of writers like Cather, F. Scott Fitzgerald, and others who between 1912 and 1929 transformed the
American literary scene. Unfortunately, those early writers have
now, for the most part, lost vitality. The once energetic Cather
has settled for the "serenity of pious meditation."

18   ROSS, MARY. "Willa Cather's First Novel in Five Years." New
     York Herald Tribune Books, 8 December, sec. k, p. 1.
        Credits Cather with characterizing the slaves in Sapphira
and the Slave Girl as "individuals who happen to be Negro." Although the book's conclusion is flawed and somewhat inconsistent,
its reminiscent mood throughout disallows excessive emotion.

19   SERGEANT, ELIZABETH SHEPLEY. "Willa Cather." Book-of-the-
     Month Club News, December, pp. [4–5].
        Stresses the importance of the Nebraska experience for
Cather, and the move from Virginia, noting that to date the only
biography available for this very private woman of simple tastes
lies in works like My Ántonia and Sapphira and the Slave Girl.
Her relationship to the earth and to people who live close to it
is instinctive, and she has never been wholly satisfied with city
life. See 1940.21, for a note about an alleged reprinting of
this item.

20   Van DOREN, CARL. "Willa Cather." In The American Novel 1789–
     1939. Rev. ed. New York: Macmillan Co., pp. 281–93.
        Indirectly classifies Cather as an instinctive biographer,
centering each of her novels around the life story of one person
who was always an individual and never a type. The mood of her
novels is epic, and her artists and pioneers resemble each other
in their single-mindedness and in their conflict with a threaten-
ing world. Cather wrote by no set formula, but found whatever
form best suited her purposes for each novel; thus, she is
fashionless and survives the passing of all fashions. In part
an expanded text of 1921.23, and 1922.34.

*21 Willa Cather: A Biographical Sketch, an English Opinion,
     Reviews and Articles Concerning Her Later Books, and an
     Abridged Bibliography. New York: Alfred A. Knopf [ca. 1940].
        A possible expanded edition of [ca. 1927.42]. According to
typewritten notes in the Faulkner-Slote Collection at the University of Nebraska Library, Lincoln, a 1940 edition of the Knopf
pamphlet contains, among other unidentified pieces, at least the
following: a reprint of the biographical sketch that appears in
all of the pamphlets, written by Cather herself; a reprint of
1926.22; and a reprint of 1940.19. The date and contents of the
pamphlet are unverified because the pamphlet was not located.
The 1940 date, however, may be erroneous since the 1940 Sergeant
essay supposedly reprinted here is dated December 1940. The two
printings may have been almost simultaneous, however, or the
alleged 1940 Knopf pamphlet may actually have been the issue
listed here in 1941. See 1941.20, for a description of contents.

22   "Willa Cather's Study of Virginia Woman." Springfield (Mass.)
     Republican, 22 December, sec. e, p. 7.
        Maintains that characterization rather than action forms
the center of Sapphira and the Slave Girl; compares Sapphira to
Marian Forrester.

23 W[ILLIAMS], M[ICHAEL]. "Miss Cather's New Novel." Christian
Science Monitor, 28 December, p. 11.
    Cather's ability to capture the essence of pre-Civil War
Virginia makes Sapphira and the Slave Girl melancholy and dis-
turbing.

24 ZABEL, MORTON DAUWEN. "The Tone of Time." Nation 151
(7 December):574–76.
    Even though Sapphira and the Slave Girl suffers from lack
of vigor, it is Cather's best book in thirteen years and ranks
with her top five books. At times there is a meagerness in
Cather's work, when her skill passes from "mastery to mere
formulation." At other times she is didactic and sentimental,
but her writing has integrity, and in her work our "spiritual
riches" are to some extent preserved. Reprinted: 1982.89.
Expanded and combined with 1947.38; 1957.24.

1941

1 BAKER, HOWARD. "An Essay on Fiction with Examples." Southern
Review 7 (Autumn):385–406.
    Points out Cather's ability to show realism through narra-
tion, and commends her for her lucid and simple prose.

2 BINSSE, HARRY LORIN. Review of Sapphira and the Slave Girl.
Commonweal 33 (10 January):306–7.
    Questions Cather's tendency to leave her secondary charac-
ters less than fully developed in Sapphira and the Slave Girl.
Admits, however, that the book demonstrates psychological and
Christian insights into the effects of slavery.

3 CHANG, L[OH-] C[HI]. "The Novels of Willa Cather." Ph.D.
dissertation, University of Shanghai, China, 44 pp.
    Provides something of an introduction to Cather and her
place in American literature, then offers plot summary and criticism on six novels--O Pioneers!, The Song of the Lark, The Professor's House, Death Comes for the Archbishop, and Sapphira and
the Slave Girl. Concludes with general commentary on Cather's
style, characterization, and philosophy.

4 ELGSTRÖM, ANNA LENAH. "Willa Cathers nya roman" [Willa
Cather's new novel]. Social-Demokraten (Stockholm),
25 October, p. 8.
    In Swedish. Argues that Sapphira and the Slave Girl is
about two kinds of people, those who believe in and respect human
worth, and those who merely use others. In her books Cather is
unmatched as one who portrays the importance of freedom of
conscience.

5 FAY, ELIOT G. "Borrowings from Anatole France by Willa Cather
and Robert Nathan." Modern Language Notes 56 (May):377.
    Notes Cather's allusion in The Professor's House to her
debt to Anatole France (in Le mannequin d'osier) for the dress-
maker forms in the professor's old study.

6   HALE, EDWARD EVERETT, Jr. "Willa Cather." In Famous Ameri-
     cans. Second Series. Edited by Warren Huff and Edna Lenore
     Webb Huff. Los Angeles: Charles Webb & Co., pp. 121-32.
          Reprint, lightly edited, of 1932.14.

*7   HAMADA, MASAJIRO. "Willa Cather as a Regionalist." Studies
     in English Literature (Tokyo) 21, January.
          Listed in American Literature in the 1940's (Tokyo: chapter
     of the American Literature Society of Japan, 1976).

8   KENDON, FRANK. "An Interesting Estimate of the Quality of
     Willa Cather's Novels." In Willa Cather. See Knopf pamphlet
     [ca. 1941].20.
          Reprint of 1932.17.

9   LITTELL, ROBERT. Review of Sapphira and the Slave Girl. Yale
     Review 30 (Winter):x.
          Comments on the contradictory qualities of Sapphira and the
     Slave Girl, noting particularly the book's blend of detachment
     and vitality.

10   LÖFSTEDT, ANNIE. "Fran Virginia" [From Virginia]. Review of
     Sapphira and the Slave Girl. Göteborgs Handels-och Sjöfarts-
     Tidning, 14 October, p. 3.
          In Swedish. Points out that in Sapphira and the Slave Girl
     Cather calls up her childhood memories using the perspective and
     judgment of age. Her writing cannot be aligned with any particu-
     lar literary school; she is incapable of banality.

11   LOVETT, ROBERT MORSS. "An American Opinion." In Willa
     Cather. See Knopf pamphlet [ca. 1941].20
          Reprint of 1927.22.

12   MACC., M. "An Irish Review of Shadows on the Rock." In Willa
     Cather. See Knopf pamphlet [ca. 1941].20.
          Reprint of 1932.23.

13   MONROE, N. ELIZABETH. "Trends of the Future in Willa Cather."
     In The Novel and Society: A Critical Study of the Modern
     Novel. Chapel Hill: University of North Carolina Press,
     pp. 225-45; see also pp. 167, 179, 254, 256. Reprint. Port
     Washington, N.Y.: Kennikat, 1965.
          Praises Cather highly for the spiritual quality of her work
     that produces a vision of America rather than merely a reproduc-
     tion of life's raw materials. This quality marks her as a writer
     and sets the pattern for future novelists. Cather transforms
     common humanity and humble virtues into art, but she has problems
     handling structure and point of view.

14   MOULT, THOMAS. "An English Review of Obscure Destinies." In
     Willa Cather. See Knopf pamphlet [ca. 1941].20.
          Reprint of 1932.26.

15 NARITA, SHIGEHISA. "Historical Novels in America." <u>Shincho</u>,
    May, pp. 50-55.
        In Japanese. Discusses <u>Death Comes for the Archbishop</u> and
    <u>Shadows on the Rock</u> in relation to their qualifications as his-
    torical novels. Observes that all of Cather's novels use mate-
    rials from the past--characters and atmosphere, not language--but
    they are not based on historical events. In that sense they dif-
    fer from the conventional historical novel.

16 PORTERFIELD, ALEXANDER. "An English Opinion: Willa Cather."
    In <u>Willa Cather</u>. See Knopf pamphlet [ca. 1941].20, pp. 4-14.
        Reprint of 1926.22.

17 Review of <u>Sapphira and the Slave Girl</u>. <u>Catholic World</u> 152
    (February):634.
        Claims the epilogue weakens <u>Sapphira and the Slave Girl</u>,
    but applauds Cather's excellent characterization and the direct-
    ness and smoothness of her narrative.

18 TARN, ALAIN. "Books of Southern Interest." <u>Southern Literary
    Messenger</u> 3 (March):146.
        Review of <u>Sapphira and the Slave Girl</u> finds little to
    praise in the novel except its delicate handling of theme.
    Otherwise, it is rather flat, pale, and unconvincing--below par
    for Cather.

19 WEEKS, EDWARD. Review of <u>Sapphira and the Slave Girl</u>.
    "Atlantic Bookshelf." <u>Atlantic Monthly</u> 167 (February):11.
        Acclaims Cather's beautiful prose style and attention to
    detail in <u>Sapphira and the Slave Girl</u>.

*20 <u>Willa Cather: A Biographical Sketch, an English Opinion, an
    American Opinion, Reviews and Articles and an Abridged Bib-
    liography</u>. New York: Alfred A. Knopf.
        An expanded text of [ca. 1927].42. Crane, 1982.19, p. 315,
    lists this edition and indicates that its contents are the same
    as for the [1933] edition. See <u>Willa Cather</u> [ca. 1933].21.
    Crane, however, lists only three instead of four editions (and
    possibly more) of this pamphlet, omitting the edition apparently
    published ca. 1929 or 1930. A note in the papers of the Faulkner-
    Slote collection, University of Nebraska Library, Lincoln, indi-
    cates that this pamphlet might also have contained a reprint of
    1940.19. See 1940.21.

21 WILLIAMS, MICHAEL. "Views and Reviews." <u>Commonweal</u> 33
    (7 February):399-400.
        Review of <u>Sapphira and the Slave Girl</u> refers to Cather as
    an "aristocratic genius," with exquisite technique and powerful
    control. She seeks quality, not mass production.

<u>1942</u>

1 BLANCK, JACOB. <u>Merle Johnson's First Editions</u>. 4th ed. New
   York: R.R. Bowker Co., pp. 103-5.
        The first edition of Johnson appeared in 1929, the second
   in 1932, and the third in 1936. The fourth edition, revised and
   enlarged by Jacob Blanck, lists and describes the first editions
   of Cather's works. It also lists other known first editions that
   contain Cather selections--stories, poetry, and essays--and two
   biographical sources.

2 FLANAGAN, JOHN T. "The Middle Western Farm Novel." <u>Minnesota
   History</u> 23 (June):113-25.
        In Cather's hands the farm novel reached a peak which had
   never been achieved before and has not been matched since. The
   romanticizing of her characters, however, makes them somewhat
   "unconvincing."

3 GEROULD, GORDON HALL. <u>The Patterns of English and American
   Fiction: A History</u>. Boston: Little, Brown & Co., p. 483.
        After turning to settings other than the Midwest, Cather
   had the odd experience of being praised for her handling of
   things from which she was trying to escape.

4 HAINES, HELEN E. <u>What's in a Novel</u>. Columbia University
   Studies in Library Service, no. 6. New York: Columbia University Press, pp. 52, 71-72, 111, 117, 250.
        Singles out <u>Lucy Gayheart</u>, <u>Shadows on the Rock</u>,
   and <u>Sapphira and the Slave Girl</u> as evidence of Cather's skill in
   capturing character and region.

5 KAZIN, ALFRED. "Elegy and Satire: Willa Cather and Ellen
   Glasgow." In <u>On Native Grounds: An Interpretation of Modern
   American Prose Literature</u>. New York: Harcourt, Brace & Co.;
   New York: Reynal & Hitchcock, pp. 247-64. Reprint. Toronto:
   McClelland & Steward, 1943; London: Jonathan Cape, 1943;
   Garden City, N.Y.: Doubleday & Co., Anchor Books, 1956; New
   York: Harcourt, Brace Jovanovich (fortieth anniversary edition), 1983.
        Emphasizes Cather's "philosophical nostalgia," her convic-
   tion that the world was turning away from primary values and the
   best one could do was endure to the end. In Captain Forrester
   and Godfrey St. Peter Cather created "the last of her great failures" and became "the elegist of the defeated." After that she
   withdrew and began writing novels of other times and places. She
   was, however, a remarkable artist. Reprinted: 1967.24.

6 KUNITZ, STANLEY J., and HAYCRAFT, HOWARD, eds. <u>Twentieth
   Century Authors: A Biographical Dictionary of Modern Litera-
   ture</u>. New York: H.W. Wilson Co., pp. 257-58.
        Supercedes 1931.27. Adds some biographical detail and
   critical commentary, claiming that the passionate, chaotic life
   of Cather's time passed her by and that a sense of timelessness
   is created in her "loose, plotless books." Her principal

weakness is the absence of a "tragic sense," an excessive emotional reserve that reduces the vitality of her later work.
Nevertheless, her work has a lasting, noble quality that out-
weighs its defects. Also provides a short bibliography of primary and secondary works. Revised: 1955.6.

7   LUNDKVIST, ARTUR. Diktare och avslöjare i Amerikas moderna
    litteratur [Poets and exposers in modern American literature].
    Stockholm: Kooperativa förbundets bokförlag, pp. 100-104.
        In Swedish. Regards Cather's Nebraska novels as her best,
    and focuses almost solely on her theme of the restrictiveness of
    the small town.

8   SMITH, REBECCA W. "The Southwest in Fiction." Saturday
    Review of Literature 25 (16 May):12-13, 37.
        Asserts that Death Comes for the Archbishop was the first
    book of southwestern fiction to be wholly successful. It was the
    first book to attract the attention of Americans in general to
    the literature of the Southwest. Reprinted: 1946.5.

9   WHITE, GEORGE L[EROY], Jr. "Willa Cather." Summaries of
    Eminent Living Novelists. Sewanee Review 50 (January-March):
    18-25.
        Praises Cather effusively as the "most permanent artist of
    our age." She has not gone the way of her contemporaries and has
    therefore, unfortunately, been labeled a precious classic and put
    on the shelf. Her work addresses the question of what the artist
    is and affirms the value of the artist as one who establishes a
    standard of perfection, who holds to principles.

1943

1   GREENSLET, FERRIS. Under the Bridge: An Autobiography.
    Boston: Houghton Mifflin, Riverside Press, pp. 77-78,
    116-21, 185.
        The editor of several of Cather's books before she switched
    to Alfred A. Knopf commends her for the poetic quality of her
    work and for her skilled use of the wise observer. Corrected
    drafts of Cather's manuscripts reveal her to be a creative re-
    viser, but her revisions always tone the style down rather than
    up. She trims words, phrases, and clauses, and deletes whole
    paragraphs.

2   STOVALL, FLOYD. American Idealism. Norman: University of
    Oklahoma Press, pp. 138-43, 147.
        Cather is one of the notable exceptions to the naturalistic
    tone and mood of twentieth-century fiction. Her work is not pes-
    simistic, for she creates characters of strength and moral forti-
    tude.

3   WHIPPLE, T[HOMAS] K[ING]. "Literature in the Doldrums." In
     Study Out the Land: Essays by T.K. Whipple. Berkeley:
     University of California Press, pp. 69–75 passim.
         Although American literature written between 1911 and 1929
     was mainly about a lost past, and has itself become history, at
     least it was based on traditions of strength and importance--
     principally the traditions of agrarianism and European culture.
     Today's literature has no such force behind it. This earlier
     literature, of which Cather is a prime example, is oriented to
     the strong individual rather than to a mechanized mass society.

                                   1944

1   ADAMS, J. DONALD. The Shape of Books to Come. New York:
     Viking Press, pp. 120–25.
         Defends Cather against the critics who think the novel's
     proper use is the exploration of contemporary social issues.
     Cather's books, like other great literature, speak of the human
     spirit and have relevance in any age, regardless of their subject
     matter. Her work is affirmative, informed by the belief that
     true success lies in the realization of one's potential.

2   CANBY, HENRY SEIDEL. Introduction to special issue celebrat-
     ing the twentieth anniversary of Saturday Review of Literature
     27 (5 August):11–13.
         Reviews and reflects upon the growth of American literature,
     particularly in its last twenty years. Considers Cather and
     other women writers to be ahead of their times in their sensitivity
     to the individual's responsibility for the future of the human
     race. Describes their prose as classical, a style in sharp con-
     trast to the brash, assertiveness of the young male writers who
     followed them.

3   DEVOTO, BERNARD. The Literary Fallacy. Lectures delivered as
     visiting professor for the Patten Foundation at Indiana Univer-
     sity, March 1943. Boston: Little, Brown & Co. Reprint.
     Port Washington, N.Y.: Kennikat Press, 1969, pp. 117–18.
         Includes Cather with the few writers in the 1920s who held
     themselves aloof from "the movement" of writers and critics whose
     work is finally trivial because it falsely denies the basic dig-
     nity of human beings. Cather's work is not sugary or aseptic,
     nor does it deny evil or life's indecencies; but it affirms that
     life has sanctity.

*4   LEWISON, NORA V. "The Achievement of Willa Cather." Ph.D.
     dissertation, State University of Iowa, 134 pp.
         Listed in McClure, 1975.29. Summary indicates that Lewison
     studies the nature of Cather's artistic unity, and thereby illus-
     trates the two main principles of her art. First, Cather allows
     her characters to tell their own stories with little explanation
     by the author; and second, she uses contrast and juxtaposition to
     present differences in character, setting, and idea.

                                   114

5   "Miss Cather Wins Institute Award." New York Times,
     28 January, p. 13.
         Announces that Cather received the gold medal of the
National Institute of Arts and Letters, an award given not for
any individual work, but for a lifetime of outstanding accom-
plishment. Provides brief biographical and bibliographical data
and mentions previous winners of the award.

6   NESTLBICHLER, PAUL. "Willa Cather als Darstellerin nord-
     amerikanischen Pionierlebens." Ph.D. dissertation, University
     of Vienna, 118 pp.
         Demonstrates that Cather's central theme is the portrayal
of the North American pioneer. Insists that with the exception
of "Paul's Case" and Lucy Gayheart, all of Cather's nonpioneer
fiction is of lesser quality than her pioneer fiction. Cites English and German critiques of Cather to show that this study
agrees with the literary experts on most points, but takes issue
with them on others. Concludes that Cather captures the spirit
and soul of the American folk.

7   "Willa Cather Receives Medal." Publisher's Weekly 145
     (5 February):688–89.
         Announces that Cather has been awarded the gold medal of
the National Institute of Arts and Letters.

                              1946

1   BROWN, E[DWARD] K[ILLORAN]. "Homage to Willa Cather." Yale
     Review 36 (September):77–92.
         Cather inherited the tradition of the increasingly burdened
journalistic novel, and her great contribution to her craft is "a
beautiful lightening of the novel form." Critics given to current vogue have failed to see what she was doing in her work.
For the most part, she was actually ahead of them in social and
economic matters--she perceived the role of the railroad and the
decay of the small town before others did, for example. Her
method resembles that of symbolist art, for she works with es-
sences and suggestions. Her vision is "never eccentric, dis-
proportional, or perverse." She will endure. Reprinted:
1967.3.

2   EDWARDS, VINCENT. "A Lesson in Democracy." Unidentified
     periodical clipping (3 February, p. 3) in scrapbook I-22 at
     Willa Cather Historical Center, Red Cloud, Nebraska.
         Summarizes Cather's background, suggesting that her lasting
distaste for sham, and her personal genuineness, may have come
partly from her early association with pioneering people who were
true lovers of freedom.

3　　GRAY, JAMES. "Aunts from Virginia: Willa Cather, Ellen
　　　Glasgow." In On Second Thought. Minneapolis: University of
　　　Minnesota Press, pp. 141-53.
　　　　　As novelists, Cather and Glasgow are classic traditionalists
　　who wrote in a very satisfying style, but their work lacks the
　　strenuous energy of some of their contemporaries. Cather's only
　　"out-and-out failure" is One of Ours. She is pleasing as a poet,
　　observer, and critic, but disappointing as a novelist. She never
　　really mastered the craft.

4　　JONSSON, THORSTEN. Sidor av Amerika: Intryck och resonemang
　　　[Pages of America: impressions and discussion]. Stockholm:
　　　Albert Bonniers Forlag, pp. 60, 119-21.
　　　　　In Swedish. Suggests that Cather's ideas about the value
　　of immigrant influx from Europe were similar to those of Jim
　　Burden in My Ántonia. She felt that American culture and artis-
　　try in the 1920s had disallowed originality and genius, and she
　　hoped that the immigrants could change this.

5　　SMITH, REBECCA W. "The Southwest in Fiction." In South-
　　　westerners Write. Edited by T[homas] M[atthews] Pearce and
　　　A.P. Thomason. Albuquerque: University of New Mexico Press,
　　　pp. 344-51.
　　　　　Reprint of 1942.8.

6　　WITTKE, CARL. "Melting-Pot Literature." College English 7
　　　(January):189-97.
　　　　　Calls Cather perhaps the best example of a native American
　　writer who used immigrants for her leading characters. Her back-
　　ground gave her firsthand knowledge of immigrants, and she wrote
　　of their struggles and hopes. The struggle made some vulgarly
　　conventional but ennobled others.

1947

1　　ADAMS, J. DONALD. "Speaking of Books." New York Times Book
　　　Review, 13 April, p. 2.
　　　　　Takes issue with Charles Angoff's (see 1939.2) assertion
　　that American literature is lacking in its presentation of mem-
　　orable women characters. Admits that Angoff may be correct in
　　stating that Cather's heroines are shadows of their environment,
　　but points out that these characters live in their own right and
　　that even living men and women are, in part, shadows of their
　　environment. Concludes that American literature's weakness lies
　　in its failure to present the internal life, which is the crux of
　　a good portrayal of a female character.

2　　_____. "Speaking of Books." New York Times Book Review,
　　　11 May, p. 2.
　　　　　Describes Cather as an artist who, like some of her
　　heroines, realized her potentialities, writing always with "a
　　burning affirmation" at the heart of her work. Death Comes for
　　the Archbishop shows, not her desire to escape from the world, as

some have charged, but her love for the Southwest and her interest in artistic form and method. Quotes from interviews with Cather.

3 ARMS, GEORGE W. "Cather's My Ántonia." Explicator, no. 5 (March), item 35.
    Argues that on the whole My Ántonia is integrated because its structure follows its main theme, which is concerned with the contrast between the pioneers and the townspeople. (See Scott response, 1947.27.)

4 ARVIN, NEWTON. "The New American Writers." Harper's Bazaar, March, p. 197.
    Describes the nature and course of American fiction in the twentieth century, observing that while a dominant strain of that fiction has been naturalistic, another group of writers like Cather, Edith Wharton, and F. Scott Fitzgerald have consistently produced work of a different sort. Their work has had a "real relation" to the work of the naturalists, but they have been "artists of a different mentality and a dissimilar character."

5 BUTCHER, FANNY. "The Literary Spotlight." Chicago Sunday Tribune, 4 May, sec. 4, p. 4.
    Comments on Cather's life and her recent death. She was a writer who implied rather than underlined, who experimented with technique and background, and who, unlike many of her contemporaries, found writing to be fulfilling and rejuvenative. Reprinted in part: 1947.6.

6 _____. "Willa Cather." Hobbies 52 (July):129, 133.
    In part, reprinted from 1947.5. Includes also an introductory paragraph lamenting Cather's death.

7 CANBY, HENRY SEIDEL. American Memoir. Boston: Houghton Mifflin Co., Riverside Press, pp. 286, 303-4.
    Reprinted from 1947.8.

8 _____. "Willa Cather (1876-1947)." Saturday Review of Literature 30 (10 May):22-24.
    Pays tribute to Cather as one whose mind was precise like a scholar's and at the same time warmly intellectual like a creative artist's. Her art was consistent and delusively simple; she worked with cadences rather than plot. She understood what it meant for this country to receive an influx of immigrants, and what it meant to those who came to confront a new country. Cather was "preservative, almost antiquarian," and the life of the emotions was what she sought to preserve. Reprinted in part: 1947.7. Revised: 1948.6.

9 Cather obituary. Newsweek 49 (5 May):54.
    Notes Cather's death, mentions her Pulitzer Prize, and names her best books as O Pioneers!, My Ántonia, and A Lost Lady.

10   Cather obituary. <u>Time</u> 49 (5 May):81.
        Gives notice of Cather's death and provides a brief biog-
raphy. Mentions her seclusion from public life in her later
years.

11   Cather obituary. <u>Wilson Library Bulletin</u> 21 (June):702.
        Announces Cather's death and lists her works. Claims that
many critics considered <u>A Lost Lady</u> to be her masterpiece.

12   CHAMBERLAIN, JOHN. "American Writers." <u>Life</u> 23 (1 Septem-
        ber):82–84, 86, 89–90, 92 passim.
        A lengthy article on the state of modern fiction contends
that the big novels of the 1920s, of which <u>A Lost Lady</u>--Cather's
best novel--is an example, had a more highly developed sense of
form and craftsmanship than has been achieved in novels of succeeding decades.

13   COLUM, MARY. <u>Life and the Dream</u>. Garden City, N.Y.:
        Doubleday & Co., p. 203.
        Tells of first meeting Cather in Pittsburgh, and of enjoy-
ing her exceptionally interesting conversations about New Mexico
Indian culture.

14   DRURY, JOHN. "In Red Cloud." In <u>Historic Midwest Houses</u>.
        New York: Crown Publishers, Bonanza Books, pp. 218–19.
        Pictures Cather's childhood home in Red Cloud, calling
attention to her background there and the part Nebraska plays in
her books.

15   FISHER, DOROTHY CANFIELD. "Novelist Recalls Christmas in
        Blue-and-Gold Pittsburgh." <u>New York Herald Tribune</u>,
        21 December, p. 42.
        Recalls Fisher's admiration for the slightly older Cather
who was a college freshman when they met, and tells of two visits
to Pittsburgh after Cather moved there. One in particular stands
out, a Christmas Eve spent with the George Seibels.

16   G[ARDNER], H[AROLD] C. "Willa Cather's Spirit." <u>America</u> 77
        (10 May):158.
        Pays tribute to Cather for her "sound and healthy spir-
ituality," calling her "truly modern, a truly Christian novelist."
Proves the point by quoting from a letter written to him by Cather
about the immense power of profound faith in influencing societies
for the better.

17   GEISMAR, MAXWELL. "Willa Cather: Lady in the Wilderness."
        In <u>The Last of the Provincials: The American Novel, 1915–
        1925</u>. Boston: Houghton Mifflin Co., pp. 153–220; London:
        Secker & Warburg. Reprint. American Century Series. New
        York: Hill & Wang, 1959.
        Treats Cather as a major American novelist, giving rather
full discussion to each of her books, including the stories she
collected and the essays in <u>Not Under Forty</u>. At the same time,
traces the course of Cather's psychological and spiritual

development which led her to back away from current social issues
and into a narrow psychological realm of her own making. Even
the earliest novels show the beginning of the despair that marks
the novels of the "middle" or crisis period of a writer who
valued life and splendor but saw the latter as almost unachieva-
ble. Her life and work are a record of an increasing disenchant-
ment that leads to a "final sense of complete spiritual defeat
and withdrawal." Reprinted: 1967.13.

18 GIERASCH, WALTER. "Thoreau and Willa Cather." Thoreau
    Society Bulletin, no. 20 (July):3.
        Points to brief echoes of Thoreau's philosophy regarding
luxuries and necessities in The Professor's House and Death Comes
for the Archbishop.

19 GURKO, LEO. The Angry Decade. New York: Dodd, Mead & Co.,
    pp. 53-54, 145-46. Reprint. New York: Harper & Row,
    Colophon Books, 1968.
        Labels Shadows on the Rock as the climax of Cather's re-
treat from an uncongenial world, and compares that retreat to
Hemingway's similar need to escape from an America that had become spiritually intolerable. Further compares Cather to Ellen
Glasgow, both of whom successfully blended their lives, careers,
and native regions, but never achieved the "front rank" in American literature.

20 KOHLER, DAYTON. "Willa Cather: 1876-1947." College English
    9 (October):8-18.
        Assesses Cather's career and work, paying tribute to her as
an artist of integrity who was sometimes thought old-fashioned
because she spoke quietly and followed her own bent. Her work
has three distinguishing qualities: (1) she characteristically
portrays nature and the relationship of human beings to it;
(2) she uses the past expertly; and (3) in her portrayal of the
small town, she engages in social criticism.

21 LEARY, LEWIS, comp. Articles on American Literature Appearing
    in Current Periodicals, 1920-1945. Durham, N.C.: Duke Uni-
    versity Press, pp. 190-91.
        Lists eighteen articles on Cather's work that appeared
between 1923 and 1943. Most listings are for the 1930s. Super-
ceded by 1954.7.

22 "Miss Willa Cather." Times (London), 26 April, pp. 4, 7.
        Obituary comments on Cather's work as distinctly American,
yet stemming from an older English tradition and being strongly
influenced by classic European models. Asserts, nevertheless,
that her studied style lacks power. Concludes, after providing
a biography and a literary chronology, that Sapphira and the
Slave Girl is Cather's most humane work.

23   MITCHELL, RONALD. "How to Write Dialogue." Writer's Digest
     27 (July):32.
         Argues that a detached narrative with little conversation
     is essential to the understanding of Paul's introverted, "exotic
     nature" in Cather's early story, "Paul's Case."

24   MORRIS, LLOYD. Postscript to Yesterday, America: The Last
     Fifty Years. New York: Random House, pp. 130–33.
         Cather produced her most impressive body of work after her
     true contemporaries had, for the most part, ceased writing.
     Thus, her work was contemporaneous with that of a younger genera-
     tion of writers with whom she seemed out of step. Her work is
     nostalgic, tracing her regret over the defeat of the pioneering
     ideal in the face of growing materialism.

25   PEYRE, HENRI. "American Literature through French Eyes."
     Virginia Quarterly Review 23 (Summer):421–38.
         Mentions Cather as one of the traditional or genteel
     writers, usually female, who, though "excellent craftsmen," are
     not writers who attract French readers.

26   RASCOE, BURTON. "Willa Cather." In We Were Interrupted.
     Garden City, N.Y.: Doubleday & Co., pp. 316–19.
         Reprint of 1924.13. Appears as one of the appendixes in
     this book, erroneously dated July 1924 instead of April 1924.

27   SCOTT, WILBUR S. "Cather's My Ántonia." Explicator, no. 5
     (June), item 58.
         Contends that Arms (1947.3) limits the theme of My Ántonia
     too much, and thus limits the book, especially by regarding as
     digressive all the incidents and episodes that do not fit his
     perception of theme and structural design. Actually, the struc-
     ture of the book entails the embracing of opposites.

28   SEIBEL, GEORGE. "Willa Cather from 'April Twilights' to
     April Midnight." Musical Forecast, June, pp. 5, 11.
         Pays tribute to the memory of Cather by recalling personal
     associations with her and by citing a letter from Dorothy
     Canfield Fisher recalling her own visit to the Seibel home with
     Cather one Christmas Eve. Also praises Cather's style, her
     appreciation for people, and her sense of humor.

*29 SHIGA, MASARU. Amerika gendai sakka [Contemporary American
     writers]. Osaka: Sogensha.
         In Japanese. Listed by Masao Shimura, "Books on American
     Literature: 1945–50," in The Traditional and the Anti-
     Traditional: Studies in Contemporary American Literature
     (Tokyo: Tokyo chapter of the American Literature Society of
     Japan, 1979). Indicates that Cather is discussed in Shiga.

30   SNELL, GEORGE. "Edith Wharton and Willa Cather: The James
     Influence." In The Shapers of American Fiction 1798–1947.
     New York: E.P. Dutton & Co., pp. 140–56.

Regards Wharton and Cather as America's most important women novelists, and Cather as the greater of the two because she was more concerned than Wharton with life's "eternal constants." A Lost Lady is Cather's best work, one of literature's best portraits of a femme fatale. Cather's subsequent novels, including Death Comes for the Archbishop, are somewhat disappointing.

31   WEBER, CARL J. "Willa Cather's Call on Housman." Colby Library Quarterly, 2d ser. (May):61-64.
     Quotes from letters written by Cather (housed at the Colby Library) to amend an erroneous account of her impromptu visit as a young woman to A.E. Housman, an account made current by Ford Maddox Ford in his Return to Yesterday, 1932.13.

32   "Willa Cather dead." Svenska dagbladet (Stockholm), 26 April, p. 7.
     In Swedish. Obituary compares Cather to Selma Lagerlöf and Sigrid Undset, praising her for capturing "the soul of the immigrant." Cather's deep perception and portrayal of people fascinated the reader and made of her works "living cultural history."

33   "Willa Cather Dies; Noted Novelist, 70." New York Times, 25 April, p. 21.
     Provides a brief biography and a list of Cather's awards and achievements. Characterizes her work as a "placid reminiscence," and credits A Lost Lady with being her most famous novel.

34   "Willa Cather, Novelist, Dies at Home Here." New York Herald Tribune, 25 April, p. 18.
     Obituary presents mainly biographical detail, calling Cather a "classic" writer and suggesting that her editorial experience benefited her writing career by leading her to decide that she did not want to write in the popular manner. That experience also gave her acquaintance with many of the day's leading literary figures. Only with Alexander's Bridge did Cather fumble. Reprinted: 1982.83.

35   "Willa Cather's Burial." New York Times, 27 April, p. 60.
     Notes that Cather was to be buried in Jaffrey, New Hampshire, a place she selected because she had vacationed and worked there for many seasons.

36   "Willa Cather." Washington Post, 26 April.
     Assesses Cather's contribution, suggesting that although by common judgment she was her generation's foremost novelist, her work, with its "beautiful serenity" and simplicity, somehow suffers from an inconclusiveness and incompleteness. Perhaps her desire to tell no more than was there leaves a strange unsatisfaction in the reader.

37   WITHAM, W. TASKER. Panorama of American Literature. [New York]: Stephen Daye Press, pp. 236-39.
     Links Cather with the ideals of New Humanism, commending her realism and its capacity to resist the negative impulses of naturalism. O Pioneers!, The Song of the Lark, My Ántonia, and

Death Comes for the Archbishop show the strength and capacity of
individual persons to triumph over circumstances. The merits of
Cather's style match those of her most heroic characters--sim-
plicity and directness.

38   ZABEL, MORTON DAUWEN. "Willa Cather." Nation 164 (14 June):
     713-16.
        Assesses Cather's career, placing her in a long line of
American romantic elegists of the heroic past. Cather's contribution to American letters is mostly minor, but in a few books
she left a valuable legacy. Her theory of the unfurnished novel
was too limiting, and her work lost vitality as she turned from
her early ideals of revolt and desire to veneration for the past.
Expanded and combined with 1940.24; 1957.24.

                                1948

1   BARDIN, JOHN FRANKLIN. "Turgenev and Cather." New Leader,
     Literary sec., 31 (11 September):10.
        Review of The Old Beauty and Others sees similarities in
Cather and Turgenev, both of whom subscribe to the basic values
of the European aristocracy. The strongest characters in the
work of both of these traditionalists are women, and their
"essential story is the fall of man." Both evoke moods through
the effects achieved by color, and both operate under the influence of Henry James's ghost, who towers above them.

2   BASSO, HAMILTON. "The Lost Lady." New Yorker 24 (25 Septem-
     ber):102, 105-6.
        Regards The Old Beauty and Others as a summation of
Cather's life and judges the title story, a work done with
economy and precision, to be the best of the three in the collection. Compares "The Old Beauty" to a portrait done in water-
colors rather than in oils. "Before Breakfast," however, is
placed on a par with Cather's earlier stories. The two basic
themes of Cather's work are present in this collection: the
inevitable crumbling of frontier values and the importance of
remaining a participant in life until the very end.

3   BIRTWELL, LORNA R.F. "Remembering Willa Cather." Woman's
     Press, November, pp. 8-10.
        Recalls the experience of being taught by Cather at the
Breadloaf School of English. In addition to presenting formal
lectures, Cather acted as informal critic in writing classes.
The novels of Cather's ripe maturity, beginning with Death Comes
for the Archbishop, are sure and masterful, but perhaps lack the
energy of the novels written by a woman struggling toward the
top. Her most vital book is The Song of the Lark; it fuses all
of Cather's themes into a "glowing whole."

4   BRENNAN, MARY ELIZABETH. Review of The Old Beauty and Others.
     Catholic World 168 (December):253.
        Cather's last stories show her capacity for restraint and

understanding, her ability to evoke sentiment without sentimentality.

5   BUTCHER, FANNY. "Three Long Short Stories by Willa Cather."
    Chicago Sunday Tribune, 12 September, sec. 4, p. 5.
        Review of The Old Beauty and Others. In "The Old Beauty"
    Cather captures in a few words the spirit of a bygone era. "The
    Best Years" and "Before Breakfast" are slighter pieces, the lat-
    ter exhibiting a faintly satirical tone. Cather always writes
    with beautiful artistic restraint.

6   CANBY, HENRY SEIDEL. "Willa Sibert Cather." In Literary
    History of the United States. Vol. 2. Edited by Robert E.
    Spiller, Willard Thorp, Thomas H. Johnson, and Henry Seidel
    Canby. New York: Macmillan Co., pp. 1212-16. Reprints.
    2d ed., incorporated into vol. 1, 1953; 3d ed., 1963; 4th ed.,
    edited also by Richard M. Ludwig and William M. Gibson, 1974.
        A slightly revised text of 1947.8.

7   COX, SIDNEY. "My Favorite Forgotten Book." Tomorrow 7
    (June):63-64.
        The favorite forgotten book is The Song of the Lark, a book
    with which one can find companionship, largely because it attests
    to the delight that is inherent in common, even rundown, things.
    What holds this reader's interest in The Song of the Lark is the
    succession of men who believe in Thea Kronborg and whose devotion
    helps her discover her greatness.

8   DEDMON, EMMETT. "Willa Cather's Last Three Stories." Chicago
    Sun-Times, 19 September, sec. 10, p. 7.
        The stories in The Old Beauty and Others show the restraint
    and detachment that distinguish Cather's genius.

9   DICKINSON, ASA D[ON], comp. The Best Books of the Decade,
    1936-1945. New York: H.W. Wilson Co., pp. 57, 255, 272.
        Lists Sapphira and the Slave Girl as one of the decade's
    four hundred favorite books and provides a brief biography of
    Cather. Sapphira and the Slave Girl ranks eighteenth on a list
    of forty titles of American fiction. Not Under Forty appears on
    the list of four hundred runners-up.

10 FARRELLY, JOHN. "Fiction Parade." New Republic 119
    (13 September):24-26.
        Review of The Old Beauty and Others comments on Cather's
    rise to fame and her relative obscurity at her death. Classifies
    Death Comes for the Archbishop and Shadows on the Rock as two of
    her "flimsier" novels and considers her latest work to give lit-
    tle reason for reviving her name. "The Old Beauty" is composed
    mainly of the "peevish memories of a faded demimondaine," and all
    three stories in the collection exude pessimism.

11 H[ASS], V[ICTOR] P. "Willa Cather's Last Stories are Flaw-
    less, Oddly Empty." Omaha World-Herald Sunday Magazine,
    12 September, p. 28.
        Review of The Old Beauty and Others. Regards "The Best

Years" as the only story in Cather's final trilogy that shows her at her best, as she once was. The other stories are beautifully written, but they lack substance and are without heart or emotion.

12   HELLMAN, GEOFFREY T. "Profiles." New Yorker 24 (27 November): 47–48.
      Profile of Cather portrays her as Alfred A. Knopf's perfect client because of her dependability, her agreeable personality, and her financial independence which made royalty advances unnecessary. Cather was attracted to Knopf as a publisher because he published "handsome" books.

13   JACKSON, JOSEPH HENRY. "Willa Cather's Last." San Francisco Chronicle, 21 September, p. 22.
      Recommends all three stories in The Old Beauty and Others, but indicates that the title story best shows the quality expected of Cather. There are aspects of A Lost Lady in "The Old Beauty" and similarities between My Ántonia and "The Best Years."

14   JESSUP, JOSEPHINE LURIE. "The Faith of Our Feminists: A Study in the Novels of Edith Wharton, Ellen Glasgow, and Willa Cather." Ph.D. dissertation, Vanderbilt University, pp. 51–76, 175–85, 192–93, 208–11.
      In a chapter titled "Willa Cather: Tutelary Patroness," takes up each of Cather's novels in turn, showing that all of them except Alexander's Bridge demonstrate that Cather's strength is apparent only when she exalts her own sex. Novels like One of Ours, The Professor's House, and Death Comes for the Archbishop flounder because they lack a strong female character who is either "a conservator of civilization" or a tutor/counselor/big sister to men. Cather is more subtle in her feminism than Wharton and Glasgow; she regards men as a warm-hearted older sister might. The feminism of these women does not argue for emancipation, but for disjunction, independent existence. Revised for publication: 1950.17.

15   JOHNSON, THOMAS H., ed. Bibliography volume of Literary History of the United States. Vol. 3. Edited by Robert E. Spiller, Willard Thorp, Thomas H. Johnson, and Henry Seidel Canby. New York: Macmillan Co., pp. 436–38. Reprints. 2d ed., incorporated into vol. 2, 1953; 3d ed., 1963; 4th ed., 1974.
      Lists Cather's works, both separate and collected, and edited reprints of them. Also provides selected bibliography of biography and criticism from 1924 to 1946. Supplemented by Ludwig: 1959.10; 1972.18.

16   "The Last Stories: Willa Cather's Genius Reaffirmed by Volume." Unidentified periodical clipping, 12 September 1948, at Willa Cather Historical Center, Red Cloud, Nebraska.
      Concludes that although Cather may have been losing some of her power by the time she wrote the stories in The Old Beauty and Others, she was still in full possession of her skill, percep-

tion, and "calm beauty." The title story is the best in the collection, while "The Best Years" is the closest Cather ever allowed herself to come to sentimentality.

17   MARSHALL, MARGARET. "Notes by the Way." Nation 167 (2 October):376.
       Views "Before Breakfast" as the most complete piece in The Old Beauty and Others. The title story has all the elements of an art form, but it lacks creative energy.

18   MORRIS, LLOYD. "Willa Cather's Valedictory to Lost Ideals." New York Herald Tribune Book Review, 12 September, p. 1.
       Finds The Old Beauty and Others worthy of respect, though not equal to Cather's best work. It is fitting that in the end Cather would return to Jamesian ideals and something of a Jamesian manner, for she had begun that way with Alexander's Bridge. More than anything, Cather inherited the "plight" of Henry James, feeling as he did, like an alien in America as she grew older. Her best books are elegaic, not history but "a kind of poetry with moral implications."

19   ORVIS, MARY BURCHARD. The Art of Writing Fiction. New York: Prentice-Hall, pp. 222–24.
       Discusses Ántonia Shimerda and Anton Rosicky as examples of the nondramatic, quiet heroes in literature who convey an affirmative feeling about life in their dignified, generous, unassuming way. Though Cather sees life's struggles and frustrations, she is not bitter. She is proof that one can write well and realistically and still demonstrate faith in humankind.

20   PEDEN, WILLIAM. "Willa Cather's Legacy." Saturday Review of Literature 31 (18 September):25.
       Review of The Old Beauty and Others. Gabrielle Longstreet in "The Old Beauty" exemplifies Cather's insight and her sympathetic treatment of a character. "The Best Years" is a "tone poem" that reflects quietly on the past in highly effective language. "Before Breakfast," on the other hand, is an inferior piece of work.

21   POORE, CHARLES. "The Last Stories of Willa Cather." New York Times Book Review, 12 September, p. 3.
       Review of The Old Beauty and Others. Reports that Cather, when asked what work of another's she might wish she had written, replied, Rudyard Kipling's "The Mary Gloster." A surprising choice, and yet that ballad contains elements inherent in Cather's work—conciseness, "a tragic sense of life," and a portrait of fortitude. Cather's last stories pick up again her old themes and values, and in "The Old Beauty" there is just "a faint ghost of absurdity." "The Best Years" shows Cather's response to modernity, but her actual commentary appears in "Before Breakfast." Cather rarely shouts, but she is always clear. Reprinted: 1984.69.

22   Review of The Old Beauty and Others. Unidentified periodical

clipping [Autumn, 1948] at Willa Cather Historical Center, Red
Cloud, Nebraska.
    Concludes that although Cather's last work reveals a loss
of narrative force, the stories in The Old Beauty and Others show
skill and insight. The irony Cather introduces in the title
story resembles that employed by Edith Wharton.

23   REYNOLDS, HORACE. "A Bit of the Old Gleam." Christian
      Science Monitor, 15 September, p. 22.
          Regrets that Cather's last work is not her best. The Old
Beauty and Others is rather vague and lacks power, but some parts
of each story provide insight. "The Old Beauty" is effective in
creating a mood.

24   SEIBEL, GEORGE. "Would We Had Kept a Log Book!" Pittsburgh
      Teachers Bulletin 42 (December):372-73, 379.
          Includes Cather in a reminiscence about various personali-
ties who visited the Seibel home in Pittsburgh. Tells a few
anecdotes about her, including one about her scheduled interview
with actress Anna Held that was aborted when Cather realized that
the interview was a publicity stunt.

25   SHIVELY, JAMES R. "Willa Cather Juvenilia." Prairie Schooner
      22 (Spring):97-111.
          Identifies poetry and fiction by Cather that appeared in
college publications, and reprints a few sample pieces. They are
important because Cather returned to these themes in her novels.

26   THURBER, JAMES. "A Call on Mrs. Forrester." In The Beast in
      Me and Other Animals. New York: Harcourt, Brace & Co.,
      pp. 120-27.
          Imagines himself, now in middle age, calling on Marian
Forrester, with whom he was once completely enamored. Thurber
realizes that at his age he is safer with Henry James's Madame
de Vionnet, but Mrs. Forrester's vibrantly careless charisma
could still almost make a man forget caution.

                                  1949

1   ADAMS, J. DONALD. "Women and Fiction." American Mercury 69
      (September):305.
          Notes in discussing women's fiction about men that Cather
does better in her memorable portraits of women. She seems to
portray men from a distance and does not get inside them. Reprinted: 1951.1.

2   BAUM, BERNARD. "Willa Cather's Waste Land." South Atlantic
      Quarterly 48 (October):589-601.
          Although Cather's work is bogged down in the genteel tra-
dition, at times she moves beyond it, encompassing the depth of
T.S. Eliot's Waste Land conception in her ability to integrate
the notions of both death and rebirth. The Professor's House
and Death Comes for the Archbishop provide particular opportunity
for observing these two thematic strands in Cather's work.

3   BENNETT, MILDRED R. "Catherton." Prairie Schooner 23 (Fall):
    279-87.
        Recounts Cather's girlhood experiences in Catherton, the
    Nebraska precinct named after her uncle George who had assisted
    with surveying the county. Catherton materials are plentiful in
    My Ántonia, but O Pioneers! gives an authentic picture of the
    Catherton of that time. Abridged: 1957.3.

4   BLOOM, EDWARD A., and BLOOM, LILLIAN D. "Willa Cather's
    Novels of the Frontier: A Study in Thematic Symbolism."
    American Literature 21 (March):71-93.
        Critics have separated content from form when studying
    Cather's fiction and have missed her overriding design, a design
    that coordinates moral meaning and structure. Her persistent
    theme is the struggle to find an aesthetic ideal, and her work
    tends to be allegorical because her characters often represent
    broad issues. In fact, her "moral realism" places her in the
    tradition of Hawthorne and James. Cather's chief symbol is the
    land, but its limitations turn her toward a more complex--and
    abstract--symbol, "the historical ideal." That ideal embodies
    mankind's spiritual quest, its reconciliation with, and subordi-
    nation to, divine will. Cather is, ultimately, a "philosopher of
    hope."

5   BREIT, HARVEY. "The Critical Cather." Atlantic Monthly 184
    (October):79-81.
        Complains of Cather's failure to confront time or change
    and points to her omission of Moby Dick from her list of three
    American books most likely to endure. Cather's critical pro-
    nouncements in Willa Cather on Writing indicate that she had
    taste but not discernment in her reaction against excessive
    realism.

6   BULLOCK, FLORA. "Willa Cather, Essayist and Dramatic Critic:
    1891-1895." Prairie Schooner 23 (Winter):393-400.
        Cather's first published essays from her student days fore-
    tell literary promise and predict the phase of her career when
    she would actively practice criticism. This important segment of
    her writing is little known, yet extremely important.

7   CADY, EDWIN HARRISON. The Gentleman in America: A Literary
    Study in American Culture. Syracuse, N.Y.: Syracuse Univer-
    sity Press, p. 208.
        With My Ántonia and A Lost Lady Cather became elegaic and
    tried to revive traditional cultural forms that had been lost.

8   COMMAGER, HENRY STEELE. "Traditionalism in American Litera-
    ture." Nineteenth Century 146 (November):311-26.
        Cather was the best representative among her contemporaries
    of tradition in twentieth-century America, particularly the tra-
    dition of the pioneer, the artist, and then the church. Her
    abiding theme is an assertion that spiritual and moral values are
    superior to social and commercial ones. She was attached to the
    land itself, as were other American romantics, and the passing of

the pioneer era meant to her the passing of the old virtues. A
Lost Lady is something of an allegory describing that passing,
and The Professor's House is a morality play with its characters
symbolizing virtues and vices. It portrays the defeat Cather
felt. Abridged: 1950.9.

9   DOUGHTY, HOWARD N., Jr. "Miss Cather as Critic." Nation 169
    (24 September):304.
         Respects Cather's belief in herself as a writer and a
    critic, finding her criticism as direct and concise as her fic-
    tion. The scope of Willa Cather on Writing is narrow, but its
    message is strong.

*10 FIGUEIRA, GASTON. Latin American article on Cather. Books
     Abroad. Winter.
         Reported in Slote 1974.67.

11 HANDLAN [CAMPBELL], BERTHA. "Suggestions for Reading and Dis-
    cussion." In textbook edition of My Ántonia. Boston:
    Houghton Mifflin Co., pp. 243-64. Reprint. Riverside Litera-
    ture Series. Edited by Kenneth S. Lynn and Arno Jewett, 1954.
         Discussion is divided into two parts, "The Novel as a
    Whole" and "Details of the Novel." The first section contains
    questions and discussion that relate elements of My Ántonia to
    the larger American experience--people being transplanted to a
    new land. Questions are designed to get at Cather's attitudes
    toward youth and the past, and her methods of character develop-
    ment and structure. The second section treats the novel in
    groups of chapters, raising questions and suggesting activities.
    The focus is chiefly on language and character.

12 H[ASS], V[ICTOR] P. "Willa Cather's On Writing." Unidenti-
    fied periodical clipping [Omaha World-Herald, 1949] at Willa
    Cather Historical Center, Red Cloud, Nebraska.
         Summarizes the contents of Willa Cather on Writing and
    stresses the book's importance in the Cather canon, citing it as
    proof that whatever Cather wrote "she brought to it genius and
    deep compassion."

13 HAVIGHURST, WALTER. "Prairie Life in My Ántonia." In text-
    book edition of My Ántonia. See Handlan, 1949.11, pp. v-xvi.
    Reprint. 1954.
         Focuses on elements of prairie life that find expression in
    Cather's prairie novels, giving special attention to My Ántonia.
    The dugouts and sod houses that many early pioneers lived in are
    described in some detail. The prairie gathered in people from a
    variety of European and American backgrounds, but it had little
    tradition of its own. It was criss-crossed, however, with the
    trails of travelers and finally of the railroad. Cather speaks
    in this novel through symbol and picture, and the memories that
    created My Ántonia stretched into her other works as well.

14   HINZ, JOHN P. "Willa Cather--Prairie Spring." <u>Prairie
      Schooner</u> 23 (Spring):82-88.
          Reevaluates the significance of Cather's prairie expe-
      rience to her work, indicating that all aspects of it had a
      lifelong effect on her consciousness.

15   _____. "Willa Cather, Undergraduate--Two Poems." <u>American
      Literature</u> 21 (March):111-16.
          Examines two of the twelve Cather pieces that appeared in
      University of Nebraska student publications, observing in both
      "Shakespeare: A Freshman Theme" and "Columbus" elements of
      Nebraska and classicism. These early efforts also blend the two
      themes that were to dominate her work, the artist and the
      pioneer.

16   JACKSON, JOSEPH HENRY. "Willa Cather's Last." <u>San Francisco
      Chronicle</u>, 20 September, p. 25.
          Considers Cather to have been a critic as well as a writer,
      and commends the sound advice and good examples contained in
      <u>Willa Cather on Writing</u>. In her critical essays and published
      statements about her own work, Cather reveals a "subtle, vigorous
      mind" that offers sound thinking in a day when the flashy and
      cheap often pass for art.

17   MERCIER, VIVIAN. Review of <u>Willa Cather on Writing</u>. <u>Common-
      weal</u> 51 (21 October):43-44.
          Notes Cather's concern with the "dilemma of detail" and the
      process of simplification, and praises Cather's ability to allow
      the reader to share her own learning experience in this process.
      Regards Stephen Tennant's preface (1949.29) to the collection as
      "turgid."

*18   NISHIKAWA, MASAMI. "My Antonia." <u>Amerika bengaku</u>, March.
          Listed in <u>Bibliography of English Language and Literature</u>,
      1949.

19   PEARSON, NORMAN HOLMES. "Learning to Write and Then Unlearn-
      ing." <u>Saturday Review of Literature</u> 32 (8 October):37.
          Comments on the brevity of <u>Willa Cather on Writing</u>, and
      doubts its potential as a textbook, but finds it an asset to
      understanding Cather's method. Cather's main emphasis in this
      work is on the imaginative powers, which explains the consterna-
      tion of critics who attempt to categorize Cather and her works.
      Compares Cather's theories to those of E.M. Forster in "Art for
      Art's Sake," and suggests that her explanations for Stephen
      Crane's reticence actually explain her own.

20   POORE, CHARLES. "Books of the Times." <u>New York Times</u>,
      22 September, p. 29.
          Review of <u>Willa Cather on Writing</u> greatly appreciates the
      attitudes toward writers and writing that Cather expresses, and
      maintains that not only does she have a gift for putting the
      right words in the right places, but she also has a "miraculous

genius for leaving all the wrong words out." Suggests that
someone ought to search out her newspaper writing.

21   PORTER, KATHERINE ANNE. "The Calm, Pure Art of Willa Cather."
     New York Times Book Review, 25 September, p. 1.
        Review of Willa Cather on Writing. Expresses appreciation
     for Cather's solid artistry, for her being one who did not sway
     with every gust of the popular wind. Cather stayed true to what
     she discovered was important for her own art. Her provincialism
     can be compared to that of Jane Austen, her morality to that of
     Leo Tolstoy, and her reserve to that of Melville. In some of the
     pieces in Willa Cather on Writing, Cather says the most interest-
     ing, profound things about writing and art that have been said in
     our time. Reprinted: 1954.8. A few of the ideas introduced
     here were to become part of a larger essay. See 1952.13.

22   Review of Willa Cather on Writing. American Mercury 49
     (November):628.
        Praises the essays in Willa Cather on Writing lavishly,
     asserting that Cather always writes brilliantly--"with great
     force, tremendous clarity, unimpeachable integrity, and dazzling
     insight."

23   Review of Willa Cather on Writing. New Republic 121
     (7 November):20.
        Finds Cather to be narrow-minded and overly strict in her
     critical appraisals.

24   Review of Willa Cather on Writing. New Yorker 25
     (22 October):115.
        Questions the limited scope of the collection as well as
     Cather's condemnation of naturalism and social criticism while
     defining fiction as "nuance and selection."

25   ROGERS, AGNES. Women Are Here to Stay: The Durable Sex in
     Its Infinite Variety Through Half a Century of American Life.
     New York: Harper & Brothers, p. 108.
        Features several women writers, including Cather, who were
     part of the literary flowering in the 1920s.

26   SEIBEL, GEORGE. "Miss Willa Cather from Nebraska." New
     Colophon 2, part 7 (September):195-208.
        Reminisces about personal experiences with Cather when
     Seibel knew her and she came regularly to his home in Pittsburgh.
     References to letters from Cather indicate that she modeled her
     protagonist in "Paul's Case" after two boys she knew in Pitts-
     burgh and regarded Oswald Henshawe as the person whom Myra
     Henshawe spoke accusingly of as her "mortal enemy" in the book
     My Mortal Enemy.

*27 SUZUKI, SACHIO. "Willa Cather's 'One of Ours.'" Eigokenkyo,
     July.
        Listed in Bibliography of English Language and Literature,
     1949.

28 TATSUNOKOCHI, JIKITAROH. Introduction to Japanese edition of
    Lucy Gayheart. Tokyo: Mikasa-Shobo.
        In Japanese. Compares Lucy Gayheart to musical composi-
    tions, especially Chopin's Nocturnes and Etudes, finding Cather's
    novel to be permeated with music and lyricism. In fact, the
    writer has avoided a literal translation of the novel, calling it
    Song of Farewell, instead of Lucy Gayheart, in an effort to con-
    vey its musical quality.

29 TENNANT, STEPHEN. "The Room Beyond." Foreword to Willa
    Cather on Writing: Critical Studies of Writing as an Art.
    New York: Alfred A. Knopf, pp. v-xxiv.
        Asserts Cather's superiority as a literary critic as evi-
    denced by the essays in this volume and in Not Under Forty. She
    was a shrewd judge of literary merit and saw beneath surfaces to
    the deeper significance of works she wrote about. She appre-
    ciated the common and ordinary, transforming them by the gift of
    her moral energy into something almost miraculous. Further, in
    her criticism Cather never lets her feelings override her judg-
    ment. Nevertheless, in her criticism she speaks like a poet.

30 TINGSTEN, HERBERT. "Willa Cathers sista bok" [Willa Cather's
    last book]. Dagens nyheter (Stockholm), 12 May, p. 4.
        In Swedish. Detects an undertone of bitterness in The Old
    Beauty and Others, and suggests that for Cather the only happi-
    ness to be found was in the Midwest of the 1890s.

                              1950

1   A-N, A. "Miniatrykonst" [Miniature arc]. Morgon-Tidningen
    (Stockholm), 24 October, pp. 4-5.
        In Swedish. Condenses Tingsten's argument (see 1949.30),
    noting also the undertone of bitterness in The Old Beauty and
    Others. Finds dialogue to be superbly executed in the book, and
    suggests that the stories are worthy of repeated readings.

2   BEECHER, GEORGE ALLEN. A Bishop of the Great Plains.
    Philadelphia: Church Historical Society, pp. 209-12.
        Contains the substance of the memorial eulogy Bishop
    Beecher delivered in Cather's honor in Red Cloud, Nebraska,
    2 November 1947, based on the text: "Blessed are the pure in
    heart, for they shall see God." Recalls confirming Cather and
    her parents as members of the Grace Episcopal Church, Red Cloud,
    on 27 December 1922.

3   BLACKBURN, WILLIAM. Review of Willa Cather on Writing. South
    Atlantic Quarterly 49 (April):260.
        Claims that the essays in Willa Cather on Writing offer in-
    direct insights into what Cather was attempting--and avoiding--in
    the creation of her own novels, and they provide a good clue as
    to where Cather fits in the "contemporary literary scene."
    Clearly, Cather restricts herself to the company of writers like
    Sarah Orne Jewett and others for whom art is basically escape.

4   BLOOM, EDWARD A., and BLOOM, LILLIAN D. "Willa Cather's
    Novels of the Frontier: The Symbolic Function of 'Machine-
    Made Materialism.'" University of Toronto Quarterly 20
    (October):45-60.
        In her frontier novels, Cather develops three groups of
    symbols to portray the progressive degeneration of the pioneer
    ideal into gross materialism--symbols of the land, of the his-
    torical ideal, and of "machine-made materialism." In Cather's
    work the small town is a clear manifestation of the materialistic
    drive, a negation of land idealism. Growing passivity allows the
    triumph of materialism.

5   BROWN, E[DWARD] K[ILLORAN]. Rhythm in the Novel. Alexander
    Lectures. Toronto: University of Toronto Press, pp. 34-35,
    71-78, 83-85 passim. Reprint. London: Oxford University
    Press, 1957.
        Cites Cather as one of several writers who use terms from
    arts other than literature to describe literary method. Cather's
    use of the various houses in The Professor's House illustrates
    the devices of "expanding symbol" and "interweaving themes." The
    houses in book 1 are set against the cliff dwellings in book 2,
    but not until book 3 are the two kinds of dwellings connected.
    There a link is made profoundly in a passage that describes the
    coffin and tomb as the final house of every person, the house for
    which the professor has been making unconscious preparation all
    along.

6   _____. "Willa Cather: The Benjamin D. Hitz Collection."
    Newberry Library Bulletin, 2d ser., no. 5 (December):158-60.
        Recounts Hitz's interest in Cather and the manner in which
    he amassed a collection of materials by and about her. The Hitz
    collection in the Newberry Library contains, among other things,
    copies of student publications for which Cather wrote, excerpts
    from her writings for Nebraska newspapers, books from her li-
    brary, and copies of April Twilights and The Troll Garden with
    her hand-made corrections.

7   BUTCHER, FANNY. "Willa Cather Wisdom Told Anew in Book."
    Unidentified periodical clipping [Chicago Tribune, 1950] in
    scrapbook III-11 at Willa Cather Historical Center, Red
    Cloud, Nebraska.
        Claims that publication of Willa Cather on Writing does a
    disservice to Cather's memory because it gives an inadequate
    representation of her work and her artistic ideas and ideals.
    She was a rich mine, but this book yields only shallow diggings.

8   CAHEN, JACQUES-FERNAND. "Ecrivains contemporains." In La
    littérature américaine. Paris: Presses universitaires de
    France, pp. 84-86.
        Regards Cather as one whose style and artistic disposition
    place her at opposite poles from the naturalistic violence and
    aesthetic indifference of some of her contemporaries. Comments
    particularly on A Lost Lady as a representation of Cather's con-
    cern over what the passing of the frontier era meant.

9   COMMAGER, HENRY STEELE. "The Traditionalists." In The Ameri-
      can Mind: An Interpretation of American Thought and Character
      Since the 1880s. New Haven: Yale University Press,
      pp. 150-55. Reprint. Clinton, Mass.: Colonial Press, 1959.
      An abridged text of 1949.8. Reprinted: 1967.6.

10   EVANS, ERNESTINE. "A Promising Student Named Cather." New
      York Herald Tribune Books, 6 August, p. 4.
          Writings from Willa Cather's Campus Years gives a good
      picture of a famous writer during her college years, but it pro-
      vides insufficient background on the cultural, social, and polit-
      ical climates of the 1890s. Cather's criticism and commentary
      reflect her ability to see her world and the world of artistic
      performance with succinctness and humor, and to describe them
      with an energetic style.

11   GANNETT, LEWIS. Review of Writings from Willa Cather's Campus
      Years. New York Herald Tribune, 6 March, p. 15.
          Comments on the recollections of Cather's college class-
      mates about her, and sees in Cather's own early writings a good
      deal of youth and self-consciousness. Bearing the "somewhat
      opulent" earmarks of the 1890s, her early stories nevertheless
      have her own special "quality of voice."

12   GERE, MARIEL. "Friends of Willa Cather's Campus Years." Un-
      identified Nebraska periodical clipping [1950] at Willa
      Cather Historical Center, Red Cloud, Nebraska.
          Attempts to correct false impressions about Cather that may
      have been created through the inclusion of certain letters by
      Cather's classmates in Writings from Willa Cather's Campus Years.
      Insists that Cather had many friends in Lincoln, that after her
      first two years at the university she wore feminine clothing and
      hair styles, and that those who knew her well found her surpris-
      ingly modest.

13   HAVIGHURST, WALTER. "Favorite Classics." Chicago Sunday
      Tribune, 10 September, pp. 3, 10.
          Reminisces about My Ántonia, the story of young people
      moving from old worlds to new and beginning life again. It is a
      "story of horizons," and it is also America's story and what is
      basic to it.

14   HINZ, JOHN P. "The Real Alexander's Bridge." American
      Literature 21 (January):473-76.
          Notes the influences on Cather in the writing of Alex-
      ander's Bridge, particularly the collapse of the Quebec Bridge
      over the St. Lawrence River. Many details and circumstances
      relating to the bridge in the novel parallel those of the actual
      bridge. One reason for the novel's inferiority is that it is too
      much like reporting and too little like art.

15   _____. "Willa Cather in Pittsburgh." New Colophon: A Book
      Collectors' Miscellany 3:198–207.
          Outlines Cather's professional experiences in Pittsburgh
      and gives an account of the pseudonyms she used in writing for
      various publications there. Several of these pseudonyms can be
      verified by duplicate articles and sections appearing under her
      full name in the Lincoln Courier. Hinz also provides a check-
      list, by pseudonym, of Cather's writings published in Pittsburgh
      periodicals and newspapers.

16   JACKSON, JOSEPH HENRY. "Cather on the Campus." San Francisco
      Chronicle, 22 March, p. 22.
          Writings from Willa Cather's Campus Years is significant in
      its discussion of Cather's college years and her classmates'
      recollections of her. The stories in the collection, such as
      "Peter" and "The Clemency of the Court," foreshadow future
      novels.

17   JESSUP, JOSEPHINE LURIE. "Willa Cather: Tutelary Patroness."
      In The Faith of Our Feminists: A Study in the Novels of Edith
      Wharton, Ellen Glasgow, Willa Cather. New York: Richard R.
      Smith. Reprint. Biblo & Tannen, 1965, pp. 54–75, 79–101 pas-
      sim, 112–17 passim.
          A revised text of 1948.14. Changes are mainly editorial.

18   LEISY, ERNEST E. The American Historical Novel. Norman:
      University of Oklahoma Press, pp. 8, 18, 53, 148, 193–96.
          Mentions several of Cather's novels, calling Shadows on the
      Rock thin, but pictorially rich, and praising Sapphira and the
      Slave Girl for its economy and "fine effect." My Ántonia is a
      "relaxed form of memoir," showing, along with other Cather novels,
      an aspect of national expansion.

19   MANDEL, SIEGFRIED. Review of Writings from Willa Cather's
      Campus Years. Saturday Review of Literature 33 (2 Septem-
      ber):33.
          Cather's college writings give little indication of her
      future ability and achievement. Comments by Cather's classmates
      included in the book are valuable for their insight into her
      personality.

20   MOORHEAD [VERMORCKEN], ELIZABETH. "The Novelist: Willa
      Cather." In These Too Were Here: Louise Homer and Willa
      Cather. Pittsburgh: University of Pittsburgh Press,
      pp. 40–41, 45–62. Reprint. Folcroft, Pa.: Folcroft Press,
      1969.
          Recalls Moorhead's first meeting with Cather in Pittsburgh
      and gives anecdotal accounts of subsequent associations over the
      years. Moorhead was struck by Cather's forthrightness initially
      and later came to value her artistic integrity as well. Re-
      printed in part: 1967.39.

21 PARIS, ROSEMARY. Review of Willa Cather on Writing.
    Furioso: A Magazine of Verse, Winter, pp. 75-77.
        Uses the occasion of the publication of Cather's "slender
    views" in the "slender volume," Willa Cather on Writing, to
    assess Cather's work generally. Regards Cather as an artistic
    failure at novel construction whose only virtue lies in her por-
    trayal of some large human truths in the early Nebraska novels.
    And even then, the shortcomings far outweigh the virtues. The
    essays in Willa Cather on Writing reveal her narrow prejudices
    and bigotry, and books like Death Comes for the Archbishop and
    Shadows on the Rock are formless and "lifeless as putty."
    Cather's work is afflicted by narrow vision, "gaucheries in
    style," stock characters, and romanticism that often turns into
    sentimentality.

22 RAPIN, RENÉ. "Willa Cather (1875-1947)." Études de lettres
    (Switzerland) 23 (September-October):39-50.
        Focuses on Cather's works of the Middlewest and the South-
    west, regarding these two areas as her most important sources of
    inspiration. Cather's treatment of the people of "obscure des-
    tinies" who live in these areas, like her treatment of the land-
    scape itself, is sensitive and realistic, presented with the
    unique simplicity of her classic style. She reveres the pioneer
    but dislikes the exploitive materialism of later generations.
    Her work stands as a salute to the life beautifully lived.

23 SCHLOSS, GEORGE. "A Writer's Art." Hudson Review 3 (Spring):
    151-56.
        Offers a general estimate of Cather's work as well as a
    review of Willa Cather on Writing. Finds Cather "refreshing"
    even in failure because she is so much more versatile than most
    of her fellow writers. She is balanced between groups of writers
    older and younger than she, but unlike many of them she knew
    where she wanted to go. Reprinted: 1967.46.

24 SHIVELY, JAMES R. Writings from Willa Cather's Campus Years.
    Lincoln: University of Nebraska Press, 142 pp.
        Presents stories, articles, and poems from Cather's college
    years, most of which have since been collected. Two juvenile
    dramatic sketches included, however, have not. They are "Daily
    Dialogues: or Cloak Room Conversation as Overheard by the Tired
    Listener" and "A Sentimental Thanksgiving Dinner: In Five
    Courses." Recollections of Cather by her classmates which appear
    in the final section of the book indicate varying responses to a
    bright, capable, and extremely independent young woman. A few
    details of Shively's brief biographical account of Cather in his
    introduction have been corrected by subsequent findings.

25 WAGENKNECHT, EDWARD. "Campus Days Writings of Willa Cather."
    Chicago Sunday Tribune, 23 April, sec. 4, p. 13.
        The style and themes of Cather's mature work are evidenced
    in Writings from Willa Cather's Campus Years. The poor and even
    "senseless" writing represented in her classmates' recorded
    recollections of her, however, detract from the book.

1951

1   ADAMS, J. DONALD. Literary Frontiers. New York: Duell,
    Sloan & Pearce, pp. 28, 36, 53, 57.
       Cather discussion on p. 57 is reprinted from 1949.1. Addi-
    tional commentary makes several mentions of Cather, stressing the
    point that only women writers, like her, present women realis-
    tically in their fiction.

2   BENNETT, MILDRED R. The World of Willa Cather. New York:
    Dodd, Mead & Co., 244 pp.
       Focuses mainly, but not exclusively, on Cather's Nebraska
    years, providing considerable history of the areas where Cather
    lived and the people who lived there. Emphasizes local lore,
    incidents and stories of human interest, things that provide in-
    sight into Cather, the person. Bennett interprets the Nebraska
    facts, asserting that the early years in Nebraska contain the
    seed for all Cather was to become. Events, people, and places
    were translated into art. Revised: 1961.6.

3   BROOKS, VAN WYCK. "Willa Cather." In Commemorative Tributes
    of the American Academy of Arts and Letters 1942-1951. New
    York: American Academy of Arts and Letters, pp. 65-69.
       After a brief biographical account, notes some of the
    things that mark Cather's work--her attraction to place, her
    feeling for imagery, her composure, her preference for suggestion
    over enumeration, her elegaic and often idyllic tone, and her
    humorous, buoyant style. Abridged: 1952.1.

4   CHAPMAN, JOHN. Review of Writings from Willa Cather's Campus
    Years. Nebraska History 32:335-38.
       Regards Cather's early writing collected in this volume to
    be an impressive indication of her talent in embryo. Some of it,
    in fact, is exceptional. Cather worked at her craft until she be-
    came one of America's finest artists--especially in her ability
    to draw character and background.

5   DAICHES, DAVID. Willa Cather: A Critical Introduction.
    Ithaca, N.Y.: Cornell University Press; London: Oxford
    University Press, 199 pp. Reprint. New York: Collier Books,
    1962.
       Presents a general estimate of Cather's work, beginning
    with some of the earliest stories. Takes up each of the novels
    in turn and then the three volumes of stories Cather herself col-
    lected, as well as the poetry and occasional prose. Believes the
    dominant theme in Cather's work to be the relation between old
    and new worlds. The Song of the Lark is a strong piece of work,
    One of Ours is difficult to assess, The Professor's House shows
    a delicate touch, My Mortal Enemy is contrived and melodramatic,
    and Death Comes for the Archbishop is "soft" and lacking in vi-
    tality. Cather's work shows an increasing nostalgia. Reprinted
    in part: 1967.9.

6   DEEGAN, DOROTHY YOST. The Stereotype of the Single Woman in
      American Novels: A Social Study with Implications for the
      Education of Women. New York: Columbia University, King's
      Crown Press, pp. 82, 86, 93, 105, 116, 154-63 passim.
         Introduces several of Cather's characters into a discussion
      of ways in which single women are represented in American novels.
      Among them are Lena Lingard, Tiny Soderball, Augusta, Thea
      Kronborg and her Aunt Tillie, Lucy Gayheart, and Alexandra
      Bergson.

7   HOFFMAN, FREDERICK J. "Willa Cather and Ellen Glasgow." In
      The Modern Novel in America: 1900-1950. Chicago: Henry
      Regnery Co., Gateway Edition, pp. 52-65. Reprint. 1956,
      1963.
         Argues that Cather's deliberate cultivation of drawing-room
      taste and sophistication caused her to reject the world closest
      to her and enervated her art. Cather's initial themes are the
      heroic tackling of the hard land and the creative drive of the
      artist for fulfillment, but in her next phase she rejects the
      modern world. Finally she moves into the static, two-dimensional
      purity of Death Comes for the Archbishop and Shadows on the Rock,
      losing the dramatic intensity that had vitalized her earlier
      work.

8   JACKS, L[EO] V[INCENT]. "The Vision of Willa Cather." Books
      on Trial 9 (April):285-86, 315.
         Though Cather may never be considered a "classic" writer,
      she is a remarkable one of considerable talent and immense devo-
      tion to her art. She is not strong on plot, but she writes with
      keen perception and intense feeling, creating books that do not
      overlap one another.

9   MIZENER, ARTHUR. The Far Side of Paradise: A Biography of
      F. Scott Fitzgerald. Boston: Houghton Mifflin Co., Riverside
      Press, pp. 183-84.
         Mentions Fitzgerald's delight over Cather's congratulatory
      letter to him about The Great Gatsby.

10   SCHERMAN, DAVID E. "Willa Cather Country." Life 30
      (19 March):112-23.
         Illustrates, through photographs and discourse, those geo-
      graphic areas of special importance to Cather's work--Nebraska,
      the Southwest, and Quebec. Cather's abiding theme, regardless
      of setting, is the confrontation between established European
      culture and the new world. Her work shows a kinship with the
      pioneer spirit.

11   SHERMAN, CAROLINE. "Willa Cather: Early Aftermath." In
      chapter or section titled "The Land" in chapter or section
      titled "Books and Papers." Unidentified book or journal clip-
      ping [ca. 1951], pp. 220, 223-24, at Willa Cather Historical
      Center, Red Cloud, Nebraska.
         Credits Cather with opening the door to America's rural
      areas for readers and publishers. Observes the recent or

forthcoming publication of several books about Cather and comments on their particular contribution to Cather studies. The
stories Cather told, in matchless prose, lie at the very roots of
American life. She had seen firsthand the "isolations and amal-
gamations" that characterize the immigrant pioneer experience.

12   STOVER, FRANCES. "A Town Willa Cather Never Forgot."
      Milwaukee Journal, 8 March.
        Uses Mildred R. Bennett's book, The World of Willa Cather,
1951.2, to compare Cather's characters in such novels as O
Pioneers!, My Ántonia, One of Ours, A Lost Lady, and Lucy
Gayheart with actual people who had lived in and near Red Cloud,
Nebraska.

13   STRAUMANN, HEINRICH. "Regionalism: The Example of Willa
      Cather." In American Literature in the Twentieth Century.
      Hutchinson University Library Literature series, edited by
      Basil Willey. London: Hutchinson House. Rev. ed. Grey
      Arrow paperback, 1962; Rev. ed. New York: Harper & Row,
      Publishers, Harper Torchbook, 1965; Rev. ed. Perennial
      Library (Harper), 1968, pp. 67-70.
        Cather text is the same in all editions, except for updated
bibliography. Affirms that Cather is concerned with values that
she quietly suggests by projecting them through characters whom
she makes lovable. These characters act consistently on principle, and they often respect the past. Cather's most lasting
books will probably prove to be My Ántonia, A Lost Lady, The
Professor's House, and Obscure Destinies.

14   WESTBROOK, PERRY D. Acres of Flint: Writers of Rural New
      England. Washington, D.C.: Scarecrow Press, pp. 45-49, 67,
      175. Rev. ed. Acres of Flint: Sarah Orne Jewett and Her
      Contemporaries. Metuchen, N.J.: Scarecrow Press, 1981,
      pp. 42-46, 61, 152.
        Cather text has only minor editorial changes in the revised
edition. Suggests that Sarah Orne Jewett is more accurately
termed a stimulus for Cather rather than an influence, and the
younger woman outstripped her mentor. Different though they are,
Cather and Jewett have many important things in common, among
them a reverence for what was valuable in the past. The whole of
Cather's work is a lament for the past, and she regarded the
Americanization of the immigrant to be a sad deterioration.

15   WHICHER, GEORGE F. The Twentieth Century. The Literature of
      the American People: An Historical and Critical Survey, ed-
      ited by Arthur Hobson Quinn, pt. 4. New York: Appleton-
      Century-Crofts, pp. 907-11.
        Follows Cather's perennial theme, a character's desire to
have life more abundantly, through each of her novels. Hope and
youth dominate the early novels while the power of a civilizing
force is paramount in the novels about the Southwest and Quebec.
A superior artist, Cather never relaxed her aesthetic standards.

16   WHITE, WILLIAM. "A Shropshire Lad in Shrewsbury." <u>Notes and</u>
      <u>Queries</u> 196 (June):281.
          Notes previously published errors in A.E. Housman scholar-
      ship and then cites another possible error in Cather's claim that
      she had seen some Housman poems in a newspaper where they were
      first published. See subsequent notes on this matter: 1957.23;
      1958.18; 1965.36.

<u>1952</u>

1   BROOKS, VAN WYCK. <u>The Confident Years: 1885-1915</u>. Vol. 5,
      <u>Makers and Finders: A History of the Writer in America</u>. New
      York: E.P. Dutton & Co., pp. 100-101, 165, 358-59, 367, 385,
      387, 500, 533-38.
          In part an abridged text of 1951.3. Makes several refer-
      ences to Cather in a variety of connections, then presents in
      modified form Brooks's American Academy tribute to her. Refers
      also to Cather's skill at rendering places and her innovative
      "sense of the teeming aesthetic resources of the multi-racial
      West." Abridged: 1956.4.

2   "Cather Novel Linked to Trip to Mesa Verde." <u>Rocky Mountain</u>
      <u>News</u> (Denver), 10 October, p. 44.
          Reports on Hugh W. Hetherington's findings that Cather pat-
      terned "Tom Outland's Story" in <u>The Professor's House</u> on the
      Wetherill brothers' discovery of the "cliff palace" at Mesa
      Verde, and on her own trip there in 1899.

3   CONNOLLY, FRANCIS X. "Willa Cather: Memory As Muse." In
      <u>Fifty Years of the American Novel: A Christian Appraisal</u>.
      Edited by Harold C. Gardiner. New York: Charles Scribner's
      Sons, pp. 69-87.
          Declares that Cather is more complex and ambiguous than she
      is generally credited with being, that she is full of contradic-
      tions and her books full of contrasts. Her critical period of
      development occurred between <u>My Ántonia</u> and <u>Shadows on the Rock</u>,
      and the novels of this period show her increasing maturity and
      disillusionment. She was moving toward a spiritual heroism in
      <u>Death Comes for the Archbishop</u>; but because she failed to per-
      ceive the potential for higher spiritual values than she pre-
      sented in that novel and in <u>Shadows on the Rock</u>, she was not as
      great an artist as she might have been.

4   COURNOS, JOHN, and NORTON, SYBIL. "Willa Cather: Exponent
      of Integrity." In <u>Famous Modern American Novelists</u>. New
      York: Dodd, Mead & Co., pp. 11-18.
          Offers a highly complimentary, sometimes factually in-
      accurate, account of Cather's life and work. Comments especially
      on <u>My Ántonia</u>, <u>A Lost Lady</u>, <u>The Professor's House</u>, and <u>Death</u>
      <u>Comes for the Archbishop</u>, praising the latter as her master-
      piece.

5   DOBIE, J. FRANK. Guide to Life and Literature of the South-
     west. Rev. ed. Dallas: Southern Methodist University Press,
     pp. 39, 76, 180.
        Lists Death Comes for the Archbishop under three categories
     of southwestern fiction, admitting that although Cather is not a
     southwesterner, Death Comes for the Archbishop is the best known
     novel about the Southwest, and one of America's finest fictional
     works.

*6   GERBER, PHILIP L. "Willa Cather: Novelist of Ideas." Ph.D.
     dissertation, State University of Iowa.
        Listed in McClure, 1975.29. Summary indicates that Gerber,
     while acknowledging that Cather's primary concern in her fiction
     is not with ideas, sees vital themes projected through her work.
     Cather writes about the corrupting influence of modern American
     materialism and about the passionate desires of youth. Behind
     these large themes are reinforcing themes of religion and art.
     Gerber further illustrates how Cather portrays her thematic ideas
     through images--especially images of music, birds, trains, and
     rock.

7   HEMINGWAY, ERNEST. Letter to Edmund Wilson. In The Shores of
     Light: A Literary Chronicle of the Twenties and Thirties, by
     Edmund Wilson. New York: Farrar, Straus & Young, p. 118.
        Criticizes Cather's version of the war in One of Ours as
     plagiarized and "Catherized."

8   JONES, HOWARD MUMFORD. The Bright Medusa. Urbana: Univer-
     sity of Illinois Press, pp. 12-34.
        In Cather's work, youth revolts against everyday culture
     and serves only art and the self in the company of other ini-
     tiates in the mysterious cult of art. To qualify for membership,
     one must have youth and a particular kind of temperament--and
     passion. Alexander's Bridge, "The Sculptor's Funeral," "Coming,
     Aphrodite!" and The Song of the Lark are discussed in connection
     with this idea. Cather and others make the perilous assumption
     that being a creator or an artist enhances one's dignity. While
     Henry James's exploration of the way art develops into truth is
     Apollonian, depicting an art based in wisdom, Cather's is
     Dionysian, depicting an art based in energy and radiance. She
     treats the fascination art holds for youth. Reprinted in part:
     1967.22.

9   KRAUS, JOE W. "Willa Cather's First Published Story."
     American Literature 23 (January):493-94.
        Notes that "Peter" appeared in the Boston weekly literary
     magazine, Mahogany Tree, before being published in the student
     journal, Hesperian, at the University of Nebraska.

10 LYNSKEY, WINIFRED, ed. Reading Modern Fiction: 30 Stories
     with Study Aids. New York: Charles Scribner's Sons,
     pp. 81-83.
        Reprints "Paul's Case" and then provides commentary and
     questions on what Paul's specific likes and dislikes reveal

about the nature of his maladjustment. Notes also the importance
of the fact that Paul is an adolescent with adolescent traits and
preoccupations. Furthermore, the story's action is "curiously
static," with the episodes serving more to establish Paul's
habitual life pattern (case history) than to advance plot.

11   PORTER, KATHERINE ANNE. "Critical Reflections on Willa
      Cather." Afterword to The Troll Garden, by Willa Cather.
      New York: New American Library, Signet Classic. Reprinted,
      with additional note, 1961, pp. 139-51; New American Library,
      Meridian Classic, 1984.
          Reprint of 1952.12. Reprinted: 1984.70.

12   _____. "Reflections on Willa Cather." In The Days Before.
      New York: Harcourt, Brace & Co., pp. 61-73.
          A minimally revised text of 1952.13. Reprinted: 1952.11;
      1962.15; 1970.20; 1980.36.

13   _____. "Reflections on Willa Cather." Mademoiselle, July,
      pp. 62-65, 102-4.
          Cather was attracted to the idea of nobility in people and
      fineness in art. Her natural reserve and lack of picturesqueness
      offered her good protection from the perversities prevalent in
      her time. Furthermore, she was unaffected by artistic movements;
      her moral and aesthetic qualities developed side by side. She is
      monumental, steadfast--a symbol of artistic virtue. Revised:
      1952.12.

14   RASCOE, BURTON. "First Meeting with Willa Cather." In The
      American Twenties: A Literary Panorama. Edited by John K.
      Hutchens. Philadelphia: J.B. Lippincott Co., pp. 341-42.
          Reprint of 1929.19.

15   SCHERMAN, DAVID EDWARD. America, the Land and Its Writers.
      New York: Dodd, Mead & Co., pp. 68-70.
          Illustrated text describes Cather as a woman of strong
      temperament whose strength conditions her pioneer heroines. She
      is virtually unequaled in her perception of the clash between old
      world immigrants and raw new world prairie. She adhered to no
      school of fiction, finding her own method best in the exclusion
      of the unessential.

16   SCHERMAN, DAVID E[DWARD], and REDLICH, ROSEMARIE. Literary
      America: A Chronicle of American Writers from 1607-1952 with
      173 Photographs of the American Scene That Inspired Them. New
      York: Dodd, Mead & Co., pp. 121-22.
          Cather's constant concern was the clash of old and new
      worlds when immigrants from Europe arrived on the inhospitable
      landscape of western America. She had her own theory about the
      unfurnished novel and adhered to neither romantic nor naturalis-
      tic school.

*17   TAKANO, FUMI. "The Relation between the Point of View and the
      Character in the Novels of Willa Cather." Eibungaku-kenkyu
      28:246-53.
         Listed in Bibliography of English Language and Literature
      (1952).

18   WAGENKNECHT, EDWARD. "Willa Cather and the Lovely Past." In
      Cavalcade of the American Novel. New York: Henry Holt & Co.,
      pp. 319-38.
         An adapted text of 1929.26.

19   WILSON, EDMUND. "The All-Star Literary Vaudeville." In The
      Shores of Light: A Literary Chronicle of the Twenties and
      Thirties. New York: Farrar, Straus & Young, pp. 232-33.
         Reprint of 1926.35.

20   ____. "Two Novels of Willa Cather." In The Shores of Light.
      See Wilson, 1952.19, pp. 39-43.
         Reprint of 1922.36; 1924.16. Reprinted: 1967.62.

                              1953

1   BROOKS, VAN WYCK. The Writer in America. New York: E.P.
      Dutton & Co., pp. 10, 27, 46, 58, 90, 145, 167.
         Frequently compares a character in Cather's fiction to
      Brooks or someone else. Commends her for having force enough to
      develop her own world in spite of her early attraction to the
      methods of Henry James and Sarah Orne Jewett.

2   BROWN, E[DWARD] K[ILLORAN]. Willa Cather: A Critical Biog-
      raphy. Completed by Leon Edel. New York: Alfred A. Knopf,
      373 pp.
         Blends biography with extensive interpretive commentary on
      Cather's works, describing how incidents and people and settings
      from Cather's Virginia and Nebraska experiences work their way
      into her fiction. The picture of Cather's developing personality
      and artistic growth comes through her newspaper columns. Her
      editing work was also very important in the development of her
      writing practices. Alexander's Bridge is a novel that must be
      taken seriously, and The Professor's House is a religious novel
      that, along with My Mortal Enemy, marks Cather's return to
      "primary realities" and "final issues." Cather's chief contri-
      bution to the art of fiction is "a beautiful lightening of the
      novel form" through symbol, picture, and style. Extracted in
      part: 1953.3.

3   ____. "Willa Cather's Canada." University of Toronto
      Quarterly 22 (January):184-96.
         Extracted from 1953.2. Points to the sources Cather used
      in gathering material for Shadows on the Rock, but concludes that
      the principal emotional drive behind the novel is in Cather's
      memories of Red Cloud, Nebraska. She was especially vulnerable
      to memory at this time because of the death of her father and the

extended illness of her mother. The connection of Shadows on the Rock with My Ántonia is also close. Pierre is an incarnation of Ántonia, and Auclair is very much like Ántonia's father.

4   BUCHAN, A.M. "Our Dear Sarah": An Essay on Sarah Orne Jewett. Washington University Studies--New Series Language and Literature, no. 24. St. Louis: Washington University, Committee on Publications, 50 pp.
         Deals with Cather as much as with Jewett, noting the simi-larities and relationships in the works of the two writers and using Cather's essays as a touchstone for exploring Jewett's methods. Cather's essay on Jewett is a statement of her own artistic creed; both writers suggest rather than describe. They agreed on the following principles: (1) writing is highly per-sonal and cannot be forced, (2) the writer must seek his or her own center, (3) the substance of the writer's work is the remem-bered impression of the past, and (4) the writer does not drama-tize, but presents common experience honestly and without embroidery.

5   BYNNER, WITTER. "A Willa Cather Triptych." New Mexico Quarterly 23 (Autumn):330-38.
         Compares the three Cather biographies published in 1953 with each other and with Bynner's own impressions of Cather, formed when he was associated with her at McClure's. Concen-trates on the breaking in two of Cather's world as discussed by her biographers and declares that even when he first met her she was old-seeming and overly authoritative. If she had looked at the world with some humor and maintained a more childlike re-sponse to life, her world need not have broken in two.

6   DICKINSON, ASA D[ON]. The World's Best Books, Homer to Hemingway. New York: H.W. Wilson Co., pp. 58-59.
         Lists and gives synopses of three thousand titles, ten of them by Cather.

7   FINESTONE, HARRY. "Willa Cather's Apprenticeship." Ph.D. dissertation, University of Chicago, 185 pp.
         Examines a great many of Cather's writings from her Pitts-burgh years--the stories collected in The Troll Garden, the pub-lished travel notes from her first trip to Europe, the uncol-lected stories from several periodicals, and the journalistic writings for Lincoln and Pittsburgh newspapers. Concludes that such an examination reveals the sharpening of a talent from im-maturity to mature art. It also reveals that the themes Cather was to use repeatedly in her later fiction began with her earliest publications. Cather was always concerned with the artistic ideal, whether expressed through immigrant pioneers or practicing artists.

8   GORDON, CAROLINE. "A Virginian in Prairie Country." New York Times Book Review, 8 March, pp. 1, 31.
         Reviews and quotes occasionally the Brown (1953.2) and Lewis (1953.13) biographies of Cather, but in the main presents

a critical assessment of the writer and her work. Speaks of
Cather's preoccupation with places and claims that she is both
like and unlike Henry James. Her purposes could not be served
with traditional Victorian novel forms, but she never found success with her attempts at fictional structure and narrative point
of view. She is "astonishingly ignorant of her craft."

9   HAVIGHURST, WALTER. "Willa Cather's High Mesa." Saturday
     Review 36 (11 April):49–50, 64.
         Provides an appreciative general estimate of Cather's life
and achievement. Stresses her concern with the solitary, individual human self and likens her fiction to a tall desert mesa--
something quiet and lasting.

10   HINZ, JOHN P. "A Lost Lady and The Professor's House."
     Virginia Quarterly Review 29 (Winter):70–85.
         Reviews Cather's diminished reputation in the 1930s when
Marxist critics both attacked and ignored her and genteel critics gave somewhat bewildered endorsements. Analyzes The Professor's House to show how wrong the critics were; in it Cather
perfected her theory of the unfurnished novel. The novel is
tightly structured, with connections skillfully drawn between the
mesa story and the professor's story. It is also foreshadowed in
Cather's earlier works and in her life, but it marks a shift in
Cather's fiction to the defensive. She now perceives that the
danger is within rather than without as a person ages and circumstances change. The psychology in the book is from Jung (his
collective unconscious), not Freud.

11   KAZIN, ALFRED. "Two Books Revealing the Intense and Private
     Vision of Willa Cather." New York Herald Tribune Books,
     15 March, pp. 1, 12.
         Reviews Brown (1953.2) and Lewis (1953.13) biographies, but
offers interpretive commentary on Cather also. Remarks especially on Cather's lack of association with the mainstream of
writers of her time, indicating that this was a function of her
intensely private creative vision. She was no more a recluse
than other artists who must protect their lives and energies in
order to work. There is in her work, however, a "curious echo
of heartbreak that invests all personal relationships." And her
"deep and compulsive" nostalgia comes out of a deep, incommuni-
cable, and inexplicable feeling.

12   LEARY, LEWIS. "The Art of Willa Cather." Progressive 17
     (June):32–33.
         Lauds Cather for her sensitivity and her ability to suggest
and to imbue her work with life, asserting that she came into
her own with A Lost Lady. The article concludes with brief reviews of the Lewis memoir (1953.13) and the Brown biography
(1953.2).

13 LEWIS, EDITH. Willa Cather Living: A Personal Record. New
York: Alfred A. Knopf, 215 pp.
Consists basically of a recollection of Cather as Lewis
knew her through many years of close association. An outgrowth
of Lewis's attempts to pull together materials for another biographer, the book recounts many stories told by Cather and creates
the personality of its subject, giving emphasis to the years
Cather spent at McClure's and to details about living accommoda-
tions and housekeeping. Lewis describes the genesis and production of some of Cather's books, but does not give critical
interpretation of them. Insists that Cather's efforts at seclusion in her later years were made in self-defense, to preserve
her energy. Her personality was marked by great vitality, but
throughout her life she had also been subject to a distinct
strain of melancholy.

14 LEWIS, SINCLAIR. "The American Fear of Literature." In The
Man from Main Street. See Lewis, 1953.17, pp. 3–17.
A revised text of 1931.29.

15 _____. "The American Scene in Fiction." In The Man from Main
Street. See Lewis, 1953.17, pp. 142–47.
Reprint of 1929.10.

16 _____. "A Hamlet of the Plains." Review of One of Ours. In
The Man from Main Street. See Lewis, 1953.17, pp. 171–75.
Reprint of 1922.17.

17 _____. The Man from Main Street: Selected Essays and Other
Writings, 1904–1950. Edited by Harry E. Maule and Melville H.
Cane. New York: Random House. Reprint. New York: Giant
Cardinal Edition, Pocket Books, 1963.
Contains many isolated mentions of Cather in a variety of
pieces by Lewis, including his Nobel Prize acceptance speech.
Also contains reprints of 1922.17; 1929.10; 1931.29. All Cather
mentions are listed in the index.

18 PEARSON, NORMAN HOLMES. "Witness Miss Cather." Yale Review
42 (June):595–98.
Mainly reviews three Cather biographies (1953.2; 1953.13;
1953.20), but also comments on her desire for privacy and her
distaste for critical formalities that tend to make rules for
novel writing. Claims that an official biography seems somewhat
superfluous because her books are so full of her life.

19 SERGEANT, ELIZABETH SHEPLEY. "The Roots of a Writer."
Saturday Review 36 (11 April):50, 72.
Consists of two prepublication fragments from Sergeant's
book (1953.20), one dealing with Cather's attendance at Robert
Frost's fiftieth birthday dinner and the likenesses and differ-
ences in the two writers. The other is a reflection on Cather's
burial at Jaffrey Center, New Ha ,shire.

20   ____. Willa Cather: A Memoir. Lincoln: University of
     Nebraska Press, 303 pp. Reprint. Bison Book edition, 1963.
        Offers personal observations and recollections of Willa
     Cather, the woman and artist, especially for the twenty years
     between 1910 and 1930. These were Cather's most prolific years
     as an artist and the years when Sergeant knew her best. The dif-
     ferences in the natures and attitudes of the two women are ap-
     parent in this memoir, with the clash over social issues and so-
     ciability a particularly sore spot. Cather's dress, appearance,
     and mood are noted frequently. As a younger woman, "Brim[ming]
     with physical life," she invariably conveyed the elemental energy
     of a midwesterner who knew the land. Sergeant reports many con-
     versations with Cather about work in progress and completed. Two
     prepublication fragments of this book appeared in 1953.19. Re-
     printed in part: 1967.52.

21   THOMAS, ELMER ALONZO. "Willa Cather As I Knew Her." Arti-
     cle 73 in 80 Years in Webster County. Hastings, Nebr.:
     Hastings Daily Tribune, pp. 111–14.
        Reprinted from undated articles published in the Red Cloud
     Commercial Advertiser and the Blue Hill Leader. Recalls Cather
     mainly for her masculine traits and complains that though she was
     a gifted writer, she was not a good citizen of Webster County.
     She never gave it her allegiance; she used it as material for her
     fiction, but chose to be buried elsewhere and never left money
     for a memorial in Nebraska. Some of Cather's high school news-
     paper pieces are reprinted here.

22   TINKLE, LON. "Willa Cather Remembered." Unidentified news-
     paper clipping [Denver? 1953] at Willa Cather Historical
     Center, Red Cloud, Nebraska.
        Reviews Brown (1953.2) and Lewis (1953.13) biographies, but
     also talks generally about Cather and her work. Admits Death
     Comes for the Archbishop is the best piece of fiction ever writ-
     ten about the Southwest, but confesses to a preference for im-
     pressive construction of a whole work rather than the precision
     in smaller things that is Cather's forte.

23   WAGENKNECHT, EDWARD. "Willa Cather's Radiance, Simplicity."
     Chicago Sunday Tribune Magazine of Books, 8 March, sec. 4,
     p. 3.
        Evaluates the Brown (1953.2) and Lewis (1953.13) biogra-
     phies of Cather. Also tells of Wagenknecht's correspondence with
     Cather and her misunderstanding his intentions, thinking he meant
     to reprint some of her early stories when in fact he did not.
     Basically, however, they disagreed over her desire to keep her
     uncollected stories from the public eye.

24   WALBRIDGE, EARLE F. Literary Characters Drawn from Life Sup-
     plement: 1936–1953. Offprint from Bibliographical Society of
     America 47 (2d quarter):5–6.
        Supplement to 1936.20. Under the heading "Key Novels,
     American and European," cites, in addition to The Song of the
     Lark, five other novels by Cather. Briefly notes her living

models for characters in The Song of the Lark, Alexander's
Bridge, A Lost Lady, Death Comes for the Archbishop, My Antonia,
and One of Ours.

25   WILLIAMS, STANLEY T[HOMAS]. "Some Spanish Influences on Amer-
     ican Fiction: Mark Twain to Willa Cather." Hispania (Ameri-
     can Association of Teachers of Spanish and Portuguese) 36
     (May):133-36.
         Praises Death Comes for the Archbishop and Cather's sensi-
     tivity in interpreting the blend of Spanish, French, and Indian
     cultures in the Southwest. Death Comes for the Archbishop is
     truly an "unfurnished" novel in which Cather creates her back-
     grounds in poetic outline rather than realistic detail. Abridged:
     1955.16.

                                1954

1   BASH, JAMES RICHARD. "Willa Cather: A Study in Primitivism."
    Ph.D. dissertation, University of Illinois, 247 pp.
        Cites internal evidence from Cather's works to show the
    presence of chronological and cultural primitivism in the form of
    admiration of one's own historical culture, recreation of the
    classical Golden Age, admiration of another's primitivistic so-
    ciety, and portrayal of the Noble Savage. See Dissertation Ab-
    stracts International 14 (1954):825. Abstracted: 1956.2.

2   BOLTON, SARAH K. "Willa Cather." In Famous American Authors.
    Revised by William A. Fahey. New York: Thomas Y. Crowell
    Co., pp. 175-90.
        Revision of 1905 edition which did not contain this chapter
    on Cather. The current edition presents largely an account of
    Cather's life and career that is designed for adolescent readers.
    It provides commentary on several Cather novels, and tells
    Cather's story partly through passages taken from her works.
    Notes that Cather often attaches significance to common things.

3   EDEL, LEON. "Willa Cather's The Professor's House: An
    Inquiry into the Use of Psychology in Literary Criticism."
    Literature and Psychology 4:66-79.
        Demonstrates three basic critical approaches to literature,
    using The Professor's House as a fictional model. The conven-
    tional approach might treat the symbolism of houses in the novel
    while the psychoanalytic approach would look at the novel's in-
    terior content, seeing psychological significance in such things
    as the professor's attachment to his attic room and the women's
    dress forms in it. The psychoanalytic approach, however, has
    little meaning unless it calls upon the resources of biography.
    Events and circumstances in Cather's life link her with the pro-
    fessor, particularly her feelings of displacement and rejection.
    The biographer must use the tools of both traditional criticism
    and psychoanalysis in order to understand the deep meanings of a
    work of art. Abridged: 1957.8; 1965.8.

4   JOHNSON, J[OHN] R. "Willa Sibert Cather: Writer Extraordi-
     nary." In Representative Nebraskans. Lincoln: Johnsen Pub-
     lishing Co., pp. 34–40.
          Provides biographical details, especially of Cather's life
     and activities in Nebraska. Emphasizes her resentment of change
     and its accompanying superficialities, and notes her use of
     acquaintances as models for her fictional characters. Cather saw
     the value of the influx of cultured immigrants from Europe, and
     in Lincoln she counted some of the highly cultivated families as
     her friends.

5   KING, MARION. Books and People: Five Decades of New York's
     Oldest Library. New York: Macmillan Co., pp. 142–43, 208–10.
          Reprinted in part from 1954.6. Contains an additional note
     praising the clean style and "immortal quality" of My Ántonia.

6   _____. "Willa Cather: The Sunlit Peak." Saturday Review 37
     (8 May):11.
          Reminisces about King's contacts and conversations with
     Cather who frequented the library where King worked throughout
     the writer's years in New York City. Their talk was mainly of
     books and everyday affairs. Cather came to the New York Public
     Library often to get background information on France when she
     was working on Shadows on the Rock. King regards Shadows on the
     Rock as "the first signal of diminishment" and "Old Mrs. Harris"
     as "the last splendid thrust" of Cather's pen. Reprinted:
     1954.5; 1959.9.

7   LEARY, LEWIS, comp. Articles on American Literature, 1900–
     1950. Durham, N.C.: Duke University Press, pp. 39–40.
          Lists seventy articles on Cather's work that appeared be-
     tween 1921 and 1950. Includes and supercedes items listed in
     1947.21.

8   PORTER, KATHERINE ANNE. "The Calm, Pure Art of Willa Cather."
     In Highlights of Modern Literature: A Permanent Collection of
     Memorable Essays from The New York Times Book Review. Edited
     by Francis Brown. New York: New American Library, Mentor
     Books, pp. 138–40.
          Reprint of 1949.21.

9   THORBERG, RAYMOND. "Willa Cather: A Critical Interpreta-
     tion." Ph.D. dissertation, Cornell University, 249 pp.
          Seeks to interpret Cather's life and art based on the
     theory that Cather wrote as an artist never quite satisfied with
     any one set of artistic principles. Uses this idea to explain
     the erratic changes in style apparent in her work, which is in-
     creasingly divided by twin principles of craft and material.
     Problems develop in Cather's work because of this dichotomy, but
     My Ántonia, The Professor's House, Death Comes for the Archbishop,
     and Shadows on the Rock are in part successful because in them
     Cather is able to resolve this conflict.

10   THROCKMORTON, JEAN LAVON. "Willa Cather: Artistic Theory and
         Practice." Ph.D. dissertation, University of Kansas, 314 pp.
            Evaluates Cather's major novels by her own organic theory
      of art and finds the prairie and southwest novels superior to the
      intellectual art novels. See Dissertation Abstracts Interna-
      tional 16 (1956):2170.

11   "Willa Sibert Cather." Red Cloud Commercial Advertiser,
         29 October.
            Reprints two notices about Cather, apparently introduced by
      E.A. Thomas, that are said to have appeared in the Webster County
      Argus (Red Cloud) 14 August 1903. The two are reprints (unveri-
      fied) attributed to the Omaha Sunday Bee and the Nebraska State
      Journal, and both refer to Cather's accomplishments and growing
      reputation. There is some question about the date, however, be-
      cause a third item, supposedly reprinted in the Argus of "June in
      the same year" from Harper's Weekly, is a review of The Troll
      Garden which first appeared in 1905 (see 1905.3).

                                1955

1   BLOOM, EDWARD A., and BLOOM, LILLIAN D. "The Genesis of Death
         Comes for the Archbishop." American Literature 26 (January):
         479-506.
            Explores in some detail Cather's use of sources in Death
      Comes for the Archbishop. Cather's greatest debt was to William
      Joseph Howlett's book, The Life of the Right Reverend Joseph P.
      Machebeuf, but Cather transformed everything she borrowed into
      art. She was less interested in fact than in incident and char-
      acter. Nevertheless, she rarely changed facts; rather, she
      manipulated them to her purposes. Death Comes for the Archbishop
      is a blend of history, Cather's own experiences, and her imagina-
      tion applied to what she encountered. Abridged for inclusion in
      1962.2.

2   BRADFORD, CURTIS. "Willa Cather's Uncollected Short Stories."
         American Literature 26 (January):537-51.
            Identifies three major themes in Cather's uncollected sto-
      ries, the pioneer, the artist's struggle and personality, and the
      passionate woman of a special type. Also speculates as to why
      Cather did not want a great many of her stories found and re-
      printed, and discusses her manipulation of the canon so as to
      determine the final impression her work would leave.

3   DAHL, CURTIS. "An American Georgic: Willa Cather's My
         Ántonia." Comparative Literature 7 (Winter):43-51.
            Observes how skillfully Cather weaves threads from Virgil's
      Georgics into My Ántonia, but contends that in some instances she
      distorts the poet's intent by adding a strong note of twentieth
      century realism to what were really more like farming textbooks
      than pastoral elegies or idyls. She has caught something of
      Virgil's artistry and spirit, but she projects her own ideas
      from them.

4   DuBOSE, LA ROCQUE. "American First Editions at Texas Univer-
     sity: IX. Willa Cather (1876-1947)." Library Chronicle
     (University of Texas at Austin) 5 (Spring):44-47.
         Lists the Cather first editions that have been acquired for
     the collection at Texas University and those, in order of prior-
     ity, Texas hopes to acquire.

5   HOFFMAN, FREDERICK J. The Twenties: American Writing in the
     Postwar Decade. New York: Viking Press, pp. 47-51 passim,
     60, 66-67, 153-62, 333.
         Like Edith Wharton and Dorothy Canfield [Fisher], Cather
     wrote in a more traditional way about war and its potential for
     heroism than did her other contemporaries. Cather attributed at
     least partial responsibility for changed and lost values in the
     twenties to World War I. In her prairie novels Cather developed
     an international theme that bore her particular stamp, the as-
     similation of the old world into the new. In those books also,
     she established a strong system of values that set the standard
     for the rest of her work. The Professor's House strongly re-
     flects those values. Like her central character, Cather was
     looking for a way to isolate herself in the past where modern
     complications have no force. Revised: 1962.11.

6   KUNITZ, STANLEY J., and COLBY, VINETA, eds. Twentieth Century
     Authors, First Supplement: A Biographical Dictionary of Mod-
     ern Literature. New York: H.W. Wilson Co., 180-81.
         Updates biographical and bibliographical material and
     abridges the text of 1942.6. Contains a brief estimate of
     Cather's achievement, citing several commentators who describe
     her place in American fiction.

7   MAGIDOFF, ROBERT. Yehudi Menuhin: The Story of the Man
     and the Musician. New York: Doubleday & Co. Reprint.
     Westport, Conn.: Greenwood Press, 1973, pp. 154-55, 181-96,
     208 and 250 passim.
         Describes the association of the Menuhin children with
     Cather and their great regard for her.

8   MEARS, LOUISE WILHELMINA. They Come and Go: Short Biogra-
     phies. Boston: Christopher Publishing House, pp. 87-89.
         Notes especially Cather's prairie novels, commends her
     narrative abilities, and lists her published works.

9   PFUND, HARRY W. "Willa Cather's German Characters."
     American-German Review 21 (June-July):9-11, 31.
         Points to the important roles played by characters of Ger-
     man extraction in The Song of the Lark, My Ántonia, and One of
     Ours, noting the sensitivity and understanding with which Cather
     portrays them in her melodious and disarmingly simple style.
     Although Cather's orientation was toward France, she loved German
     music, and her ability to blend character and landscape is remi-
     niscent of Germany's great realists of the nineteenth century.

10   POWELL, LAWRENCE CLARK. Heart of the Southwest. Great
     Southwest Travel series, no. 2. Los Angeles: Plantin Press,
     p. 8.
          Lists Cather's Death Comes for the Archbishop as one of
     119 books in this selected, annotated bibliography of a variety
     of fiction set in the area of Arizona-New Mexico. Notes its
     stylistic economy and understatement.

11   RAVITZ, ABE C. "Willa Cather under Fire: Hamlin Garland
     Misreads A Lost Lady." Western Humanities Review, Spring,
     pp. 182-84.
          Maintains that in his turnabout to political reactionism
     Hamlin Garland failed to perceive that A Lost Lady supported, not
     denied, his thesis that modernism was destroying the old values
     of honesty and integrity once held by western pioneers. Quotes
     from a Garland letter to demonstrate that he misunderstood
     Cather's intentions with the character of Marian Forrester.

12   RICHARDS, ROBERT FULTON, ed. Concise Dictionary of American
     Literature. New York: Philosophical Library, p. 26.
          After a brief biography, reviews several of Cather's works,
     indicating that her strength lies in the "manipulation of char-
     acters rather than events." Cather avoided exotic settings,
     gross realism, and unusual techniques, but still uncannily
     achieved "a quiet intensity of interest."

13   SMITH, THELMA M., and MINER, WARD L. The Contemporary Ameri-
     can Novel in France. Durham, N.C.: Duke University Press,
     pp. 16-17, 34 passim.
          Alleges that the French have not been much interested in
     Cather, probably because she is a realist without overtones of
     symbolism and naturalism. The lengthy bibliography in this book
     lists numerous French articles and books about Hemingway, Faulk-
     ner, Steinbeck, Caldwell, and Dos Passos, but Cather is scarcely
     ever mentioned.

14   SPECKNER, Rev. KILLIAN. "The Significance of the Artist in
     the Writings of Willa Cather." Ph.D. dissertation, University
     of Ottawa, Canada, 214 pp.
          Contends that Cather's one great concern in her fiction is
     with the art of living, and her writing focuses on the "creative
     personality." Cather's artists, pioneers, and missionary priests
     are all "artists" in living, by Cather's definition, and they
     have similar character traits as they pursue higher ideals in an
     unsympathetic world.

*15 WHITE, HAROLD N. "Willa Cather's Apprenticeship: A Collec-
     tion of Her Writings in the Nebraska State Journal, 1891-
     1895." Ph.D. dissertation, University of Texas at Austin,
     930 pp.
          Listed in McClure, 1975.29. Summary indicates that White's
     work, like that of Finestone (1953.7), is absorbed by Curtin's
     book (1970.6). White reprints thirteen of Cather's Nebraska
     State Journal columns, plus selections from her drama reviews,

and provides commentary on them. He sees in these writings the
basis of Cather's critical attitudes and fictional idealism as
well as strong evidence of her "complex intellectual makeup." A
glossary of actors' names is also included.

16   WILLIAMS, STANLEY T[HOMAS]. The Spanish Background of Ameri-
      can Literature. Vol. 1. New Haven: Yale University Press,
      pp. 211-14 passim, 244-46.
           In part an abridged text of 1953.25. Adds that Death Comes
      for the Archbishop is the culminating masterpiece of fiction cen-
      tering around Spanish-American themes. It shows fidelity to
      spiritual values that defined the Catholic Church in the American
      Southwest of the nineteenth century.

17   YATES, ELIZABETH. "Required Reading." New Hampshire Profiles
      4 (December):17-19.
           Recalls in memoir fashion conversations with Elizabeth
      Shattuck Austermann and Alice Edwards (like Cather, a guest at
      the Shattuck Inn) about Cather and her habitual activities during
      the twenty-odd years she spent summers in the Jaffrey, New
      Hampshire, area.

                                  1956

1   BALLOTTI, GENO. "The Southwest Indian in Fiction." In
      Studies in Literature of the West. See Hudson, 1956.12,
      pp. 140, 151-55.
           Reprint of sections of a master's thesis at the University
      of Wyoming titled "A Survey of Prose Literature about the South-
      west Indian." Classifies Cather with those writers who portray
      southwestern Indians and their culture artfully and with an
      understanding gained through actual experience inside Indian
      culture. Treats The Song of the Lark, The Professor's House, and
      Death Comes for the Archbishop, observing that in them Cather
      uses the Southwest Indian and his life symbolically.

2   BASH, JAMES R[ICHARD]. "Willa Cather: A Study in Primitiv-
      ism." Teachers College Journal (Indiana State Teachers Col-
      lege) 27 (January):59.
           Abstracted from 1954.1. Argues that Cather exemplifies the
      fusion of cultural primitivism--which is admiring the qualities
      of a level of society that is not one's own--with chronological
      primitivism, which is regarding the past with "nostalgic fond-
      ness." In Cather, the impulse toward cultural primitivism is
      more pronounced than that toward chronological primitivism.

3   BLOOM, EDWARD A., and BLOOM, LILLIAN D. "Shadows on the Rock:
      Notes on the Composition of a Novel." Twentieth Century Lit-
      erature 2 (July):70-85.
           Describes in some detail the various sources Cather con-
      sulted in the preparation of Shadows on the Rock, noting her
      particular debt to historian Frances Parkman. Still, it was
      through her own experiences in Quebec, Paris, and elsewhere that

Cather transformed historical materials into an innovative, "spiritualized account" of pioneer experience in Canada.

4   BROOKS, VAN WYCK, and BETTMAN, OTTO. <u>Our Literary Heritage:</u>
    <u>A Pictorial History of the Writer in America</u>. New York: E.P.
    Dutton & Co., pp. 208-9.
         An abridged text, with photographs, of 1952.1.

5   [EDEL, LEON]. Cather entry in <u>The Reader's Companion to World</u>
    <u>Literature</u>. Edited by Calvin S. Brown. New York: Dryden
    Press. Reprint. New York: New American Library, Mentor
    Books, pp. 80-81. 2d ed., 1973.
         Briefly traces the development of Cather's themes through
    her books, noting her focus on the pioneer virtues. Cather's
    published theories of fiction are largely a justification of her
    methods and her preference for nostalgic emotion over social
    consideration.

6   EDEL, LEON. "Nebraskan Abroad." <u>New York Times Book Review</u>,
    21 October, pp. 6, 50.
         Considers the travel sketches in <u>Willa Cather in Europe</u> to
    be part of a distinct American literary tradition and sees in
    them Cather's awareness of her Nebraska readers.

7   EDWARDS, OLIVER. "A Not-So-Lost Lady." <u>Times</u> (London),
    7 June, p. 13.
         Takes critics to task who say Cather's writing has had its
    day and cites several of her books to prove the point. Admits
    that Cather's style is traditional, that she was a regional
    writer, and that she, like her contemporaries, looked to Europe
    for her literary standard. <u>My Ántonia</u>, <u>A Lost Lady</u>, and <u>Lucy</u>
    <u>Gayheart</u> reveal Cather's stoicism, and they are unforgettable
    books.

8   FISHER, DOROTHY CANFIELD. "Young Writer in Old World." <u>New</u>
    <u>York Herald Tribune Books</u>, 21 October, p. 3.
         Enjoys the fresh perception and vivid description of the
    young Cather's articles in <u>Willa Cather in Europe</u>. They have
    both historical and literary value.

9   FLACK, FRANK M. "Willa Cather's Opera World." <u>Opera News</u> 20
    (9 April):7-9, 30.
         Describes Cather's great interest in opera and singers and
    her early experiences with them, noting many references to them
    in her novels and in stories collected before 1956. Gives par-
    ticular attention to Cather's admiration for Olive Fremstad and
    to her major use of the world of opera in <u>The Song of the Lark</u>.

10 GEISMAR, MAXWELL. "Formidable Farm Girl." <u>Saturday Review of</u>
    <u>Literature</u> 39 (20 October):19-20.
         Sees an honesty and innocence in the articles of the young
    Cather in <u>Willa Cather in Europe</u> that have unfortunately dis-
    appeared in her later work.

*11   GREENE, GEORGE WILLIAM. "Elements of Form in the Novels of
      Willa Cather." Ph.D. dissertation, Harvard University.
          Listed in McClure 1975.29. Summary indicates that Greene
      attempts to prove that Cather's values center around "her belief
      in the individual human personality." See 1957.11, for a recon-
      sideration and condensation of Greene's discussion here.

 12   HUDSON, RUTH, ed. "One Approach to Western Americana." In
      Studies in Literature of the West. University of Wyoming
      Publications (Laramie, University of Wyoming Graduate School)
      20 (15 July):3–14, passim.
          Describes the development of a course in western American
      literature, focusing on the significance of such literature and
      its principal concerns. Mentions Cather several times throughout
      the discussion, pointing to her works as they exemplify particu-
      lar themes and methods relevant to the study of western litera-
      ture.

 13   HUTCHINSON, PHYLLIS MARTIN. "Reminiscences of Willa Cather As
      a Teacher: With a Contribution toward a Bibliography of Her
      Writings." Pts. 1–3. Bulletin of the New York Public Library
      60 (June–August):263–88, 338–56, 378–400.
          Begins with a personal reminiscence about Pittsburgh's
      Central High School and recollections of Cather's insistence as
      a teacher on high standards. She knew the classics and Latin
      well, and frequently traced the meanings of words from their
      Latin roots. This essay, though appearing in three issues, is
      divided into two broad sections, the first of which contains
      Hutchinson's reminiscence and a bibliography of the various edi-
      tions and printings of all of Cather's works. The second sec-
      tion, divided into two parts, contains a bibliography, sometimes
      briefly annotated, of critical articles and reviews about Cather
      and her work published prior to 1956.

 14   JAY, KENNETH L. "Willa Cather Reconsidered." In Studies of
      Literature of the West. See Hudson, 1956.12, pp. 179–97.
          Reprint of portions of a master's thesis at the University
      of Wyoming titled "Willa Cather as Critic and Novelist." Surveys
      critical response to Cather and details some of Cather's artistic
      theories, discussing The Song of the Lark as the story of a
      developing artist.

 15   JONES, HOWARD MUMFORD. "Willa Cather." In The Frontier in
      American Fiction: Four Lectures on the Relation of Landscape
      to Literature. Jerusalem: Magness Press, pp. 75–95.
          Explores Cather's relationship to the agrarian frontier and
      the southwest desert, in both her life and her art, discussing
      her treatment in various works of two basic concerns, the two
      "modes of salvation": art and ancient history. My Ántonia is
      especially important, for in it Cather movingly captures an
      authentic moment in the development of America. Cather manages
      in her work to fuse soul with senses, and to triumph in her art
      as her priests in Death Comes for the Archbishop triumph in their
      lives--over time, principally through simplification.

16   KATES, GEORGE N. Introduction and notes for <u>Willa Cather in</u>
     <u>Europe: Her Own Story of the First Journey</u>. New York:
     Alfred A. Knopf, 178 pp.
          Emphasizes the importance of the fourteen travel articles,
     reprinted here, that Cather sent back to the <u>Nebraska State</u>
     <u>Journal</u> during her first trip abroad. They show youthful exu-
     berance and haste, but they also show the young writer finding
     her way to themes she would use and themes she would not use in
     her later work. In every case, however, they show her progress-
     ing from the conventional to her own individual modes of expres-
     sion. The old world was to be a continuing concern in her life
     and fiction.

17   _____. "Willa Cather's Unfinished Avignon Story, an Article."
     In <u>Five Stories by Willa Cather</u>. New York: Random House,
     Vintage Books, pp. 177–214.
          Declares that Cather's last story, the one interrupted by
     her death and destroyed at her request, is neither a shift from
     her old patterns and themes nor a total reversion and escape
     into the past. Many of her stories and novels show her interest
     in France and her juxtaposition of the old world with the new.
     Moreover, the projected title for the unfinished novelle, "Hard
     Punishments," and its subject matter, as remembered and sketched
     by Edith Lewis for Kates, clearly indicate that the story pre-
     sented no nostalgic escape from suffering. In fact, in this
     story suffering is literal and direct, for in the society that
     Cather depicts, physical mutilation was the common punishment for
     even such transgressions as blasphemy.

18   O'CONNOR, FRANK. "Prospectus for an Anthology." <u>Nation</u> 183
     (10 November):395–96.
          Concludes that Cather would probably be included, along
     with Sherwood Anderson and Ernest Hemingway, in an O'Connor
     anthology of American stories. But where Cather projects in
     <u>Youth and the Bright Medusa</u> the specialized "horror of the art-
     ist's loneliness" in an uncomprehending society, Anderson and
     Hemingway deal with "fundamental human loneliness."

19   REINO, VIRTANEN. "French Reactions to American Writers."
     <u>Prairie Schooner</u> 30 (Spring):76–85.
          Notes that Cather, along with such writers of the genteel
     tradition as Henry James, William Dean Howells, and Edith
     Wharton, have mainly been overlooked by the French.

20   RUSSELL, FRANCIS. "Miss Cather Travels in Europe." <u>Christian</u>
     <u>Science Monitor</u>, 21 November, p. 15.
          The articles in <u>Willa Cather in Europe</u> contain fresh in-
     sights and the seeds of greatness.

21   SAITŌ, HIKARU. Introduction to <u>Willa Cather: The Sculptor's</u>
     <u>Funeral and Paul's Case</u>. Tokyo: Nan'un-do, pp. i–iv.
          In Japanese. Sees Cather's work as stemming from her ex-
     periences. The rough intensity of these stories is evidence of
     the conflict Cather portrays between the artist and society. This

is Cather's own conflict as an artist; "The Sculptor's Funeral"
tells of her problem, and "Paul's Case" reveals her feelings
about it.

22   SMITH, ELEANOR M.   "The Literary Relationship of Sarah Orne
      Jewett and Willa Sibert Cather."   New England Quarterly 29
      (December):472–92.
          Lists the similarities and differences between Jewett and
      Cather and concludes that in spite of their differences there is
      a deep link between the two. Cather is by far the stronger
      writer, but both use regional materials and values in a way that
      goes beneath surface appearance and customs.

23   WALBRIDGE, EARLE F.   Review of Willa Cather in Europe.
      Library Journal 81 (15 October):2317.
          Calls Cather's articles "perfectly competent," but ques-
      tions the value of George Kates's annotations (1956.16).

24   WILSON, EDMUND.   "The All-Star Literary Vaudeville."   In A
      Literary Chronicle: 1920–1950. Garden City, N.Y.: Doubleday
      & Co., Anchor Books, pp. 78–80 passim.
          Reprint of 1926.35.

                                    1957

1   ANDERSON, CARL L.   The Swedish Acceptance of American Litera-
      ture. Uppsala: Almqvist S. Wiksell; Philadelphia: Univer-
      sity of Pennsylvania Press, pp. 66–70, passim.
          Although Cather had her champions in Sweden after
      O Pioneers! was translated in 1919, it was not until the 1930s
      that her work was treated as literature of real importance. Even
      so, she did not attract the attention accorded to Sinclair Lewis
      and Theodore Dreiser. She did not sustain her criticism of
      America as the Swedish critics expected her to.

2   BENNETT, MILDRED R.   Introduction and notes to Early Stories
      of Willa Cather. New York: Dodd, Mead & Co., 284 pp.
      Reprint. 1983.
          Contains a one-page introduction to the book and brief
      preludes to the stories, with comments on such things as theme,
      biographical relevance, possible genesis, and relation to other
      Cather works.

3   _____.   "Willa Cather of Red Cloud." In Roundup: A Nebraska
      Reader. Edited by Virginia Faulkner. Lincoln: University of
      Nebraska Press, pp. 124–30.
          An abridged text of 1949.3.

*4   CAMPAGNOL, MARCELLO.   "Willa Cather." Avvenire d'Italia
      (Bologna), 22 May, p. 4.
          Listed in MLA International Bibliography, 1957.

5   DAY, BESS EILEEN. "A Famous Nebraska Friendship." Omaha
    World-Herald Magazine, 28 July, sec. g, p. 4.
        Presents a character sketch of Anna Pavelka and compares
    her to her fictional counterpart in My Ántonia. Cather was drawn
    to Anna as a child and remained a close friend throughout her
    life.

6   DOOLEY, ROGER B. Review of Early Stories of Willa Cather.
    Catholic World 185 (May):158.
        Questions the significance of the volume except to the
    serious Cather scholar.

7   DURHAM, PHILIP. "A Comment on Willa Cather." Neuphilologische
    Mitteilungen 58:216-18.
        Notes the recent translation of Death Comes for the Arch-
    bishop into Finnish and calls it a book of extraordinary art and
    beauty, a book that is universal rather than regional, steeped in
    ancient tradition that predates recorded history.

8   EDEL, LEON. Literary Biography: The Alexander Lectures
    1955-56. Toronto: University of Toronto Press; London:
    R. Hart-Davis, pp. 60-80. Reprint. Garden City, N.Y.:
    Doubleday & Co., Anchor Books, 1959.
        An abridged text of 1954.3. Revised: 1982.23.

9   GREEN, NORMA KIDD. Review of Early Stories of Willa Cather.
    Nebraska History 38 (September):237-39.
        Concludes that this collection of Cather's early stories is
    useful only to the scholar, for the stories are uneven and
    awkward.

10 GREENE, GEORGE [WILLIAM]. "Death Comes for the Archbishop."
    New Mexico Quarterly 27 (Spring-Summer):69-82.
        Sees Death Comes for the Archbishop as a fine expression of
    the good life, the everyday life, that finds meaning and guidance
    in forms that have a spiritual basis. Bishop Latour, Cather's
    most fully developed character, is seeking personal equilibrium
    through a moral awareness that goes hand in hand with religious
    discipline, that aspires to higher levels of consciousness.

11 _____. "Willa Cather at Mid-Century." Thought 32 (Winter):
    577-92.
        Attests to Cather's enduring qualities and the limited
    vision of socially oriented critics and New Critics who have
    credited her with only minor significance. Numerous citations
    from her collected essays and references to works like Death
    Comes for the Archbishop demonstrate her "innate good sense" and
    her sound reliance in her fiction on the importance of moral
    choice and standards of value. Even though her last novel,
    Sapphira and the Slave Girl, shows a loss of feeling, her work as
    a whole confirms her belief that basically a human being rever-
    ences what is good.

12   INGERSOLL, L.K. "Shadows on the Rock: Willa Cather at Grand Manan." <u>Atlantic Advocate</u> 47 (April):13-17.

The rock referred to is Grand Manan Island where Cather spent a good many summers and where she eventually built a cottage and did a lot of writing. She was generally aloof from others on the island, but the more understanding of her neighbors attributed this to her need for isolation and quiet in order to concentrate on her work. A brief chronology of her life and novels is interspersed with comments about how Grand Manan figures in both, and with personal observations by and about people who knew her there. Reprinted: 1963.11.

13   JACKS, LEO VINCENT. "Music and Willa Cather." <u>Critic</u> 16 (August-September):5-6, 61-62.

Musical references, integral to the work, permeate Cather's fiction, reflecting her deeply subjective response to music. She did not care to play or perform herself, but she loved music passionately, especially opera. Music, like Cather's fiction, involves the creation and expression of moods.

14   _____. "Willa Cather and the Southwest." <u>New Mexico Quarterly</u> 27 (Spring-Summer):83-87.

Cather writes movingly and well about the Southwest because she loved it and was inspired by it--and because she herself shared common spiritual qualities with both the land and its people. She risks the unity of both <u>The Song of the Lark</u> and <u>The Professor's House</u> to include long sections set in the Southwest, an indication of her strong emotional attachment to the area. In Archbishop Jean Latour, Cather presents the southwestern ideal as she saw it.

15   McNITT, FRANK. <u>Richard Wetherill: Anasazi</u>. Albuquerque: University of New Mexico Press, pp. 27-29, 63. Rev. ed. 1966.

Cather section unchanged in the later edition. Asserts that Cather succeeded better than anyone else had done in describing the Cliff Palace of Mesa Verde. She herself saw it bathed in moonlight; and she based her fictional character, Tom Outland, on the experiences of Richard Wetherill who explored, and perhaps discovered, the Cliff Palace.

16   MILLER, JAMES E., [Jr.] <u>The Fictional Technique of F. Scott Fitzgerald</u>. The Hague: Martinus Nijhoff, pp. 12, 73-81. Rev. ed. <u>F. Scott Fitzgerald: His Art and Technique</u>. New York: New York University Press, 1964.

Stresses Fitzgerald's debt to Cather from whom he might have "learned the rudiments of form" and then excelled her in <u>The Great Gatsby</u>. He very likely saw and was influenced by her essay on "The Novel Démeublé." See 1964.15.

17   MOTT, FRANK LUTHER. <u>A History of American Magazines</u>. 5 vols. Cambridge, Mass.: Harvard University Press, Belknap Press, 3:40; 4:88-89; 5:26, 119.

Mentions Cather a number of times, telling which magazines published which of her stories and serialized novels. Also notes her connection with the Home Monthly, the Library, and McClure's.

18   ÖSTERLING, ANDERS. "Wilson och Willa Cather" [Wilson (Edmund) and Willa Cather]. Stockholms-Tidningen, 8 March, p. 4.
In Swedish. Maintains that when Cather was visiting Barbizon during her trip to Europe, she met just the kind of women she portrayed in her Nebraska novels--tan, strong, happy workers of the land. She also fell in love with the Provence region and was planning, until her death, to set a novel near the papal palace in Avignon.

19   POWELL, LAWRENCE CLARK. "Through the Burning Glass." Wilson Library Bulletin 32 (September):55-58.
Pays tribute to three writers, including Cather, who for him were burning glasses through whom he caught fire over the literature of the Southwest. He names the landmarks around Santa Fe that proved to be burning glasses for Cather and led to the creation of Death Comes for the Archbishop.

20   RANDALL, JOHN H., III. "Willa Cather's Search for Value: A Critical and Historical Study of Her Fiction." Ph.D. dissertation, University of Minnesota, 649 pp.
Divides Cather's search for value into her youthful search in the world of art, her middle-years search in the Nebraska of her childhood, and her later-years search in the historical frontier. Cather's mind was a product of the nineteenth century, for she saw value as being related to the realm of the ideal. Her rigidity of character did not permit her to make any concessions to changed circumstances; thus, when the view of life she developed on the Nebraska frontier failed to fit twentieth-century life, she simply rejected the twentieth century. Revised for publication: 1960.9. See Dissertation Abstracts International 20 (1960):4115.

21   THURBER, JAMES. "The Years with Ross." Atlantic 200 (December):45-50 passim.
Offers an anecdotal account of Thurber's recollections of his association with Harold Ross, former editor of the New Yorker. Recalls one incident when in conversation with H.L. Mencken and Thurber, Ross showed his ignorance of the American novel by taking "Willa Cather" for a man's name and then confusing Cather with John Erskine.

22   WAGENKNECHT, EDWARD. "Willa Cather Wouldn't Have Liked This Volume." Chicago Sunday Tribune, 10 March, sec. 4, p. 2.
Review of Early Stories of Willa Cather. Expresses pleasure in the publication of a group of early stories that Cather herself did not want republished. The stories foreshadow the themes in Cather's later art, and they are full of lovely material that the young writer had not yet learned to control.

23   WHITE, WILLIAM. "Willa Cather and A.E. Housman." <u>Notes and Queries</u> 202, n.s. 4 (July):313-14.
     Corrects the impression originally given by Cather, and repeated by others, that she saw some A.E. Housman poems in a Shrewsbury newspaper, printed there for the first time, and under the signature "A Shropshire Lad." See also White's comments on this matter in 1951.16; 1958.18; 1965.36.

24   ZABEL, MORTON DAUWEN. "Willa Cather: The Tone of Time." In <u>Craft and Character: Texts, Method, and Vocation in Modern Fiction</u>. New York: Viking Press, pp. 264-75.
     A combined version of 1940.24 and 1947.38. Reprinted: 1967.63.

1958

1   BASSETT, T.D. SEYMOUR. "The Dorothy Canfield Collection." <u>Vermont Historical Society News and Notes</u> 10 (December):27-29.
     Indicates that included in the Dorothy Canfield Fisher collection housed at the University of Vermont library are Cather's letters to her friend of many years (letters that may be read but not reproduced) and Cather's graduation gift to Canfield in 1899, a book of Horace's poems.

*2   BIANCHINI, ANGELA. "Willa Cather e l'Europa." <u>Letteratura</u> 6:117-23.
     Listed in <u>MLA International Bibliography</u> (1958).

3   BLOOM, EDWARD A., and BLOOM, LILLIAN D. "Willa Cather's Portrait of the Artist." <u>University of Toronto Quarterly</u> 27 (April):273-88.
     Identifies the nature and the role of the artist as one of Cather's major themes. In much of her fiction she explores the psychological development of the artist, seeing him as a spiritually superior, essentially tragic figure in an often hostile society. The artist is characterized by unconcern for social obligations in his struggle toward truth. Since he actually creates himself, his chief obligation is to himself. Cather is aware of the artist's failings, but forgives him his social amorality, his lack of caution, and his egotism, recognizing his disciplined commitment, his large, if impersonal, generosity, and his devotion to an ideal.

4   FRANCHERE, RUTH. <u>Willa</u>. New York: Thomas Y. Crowell Co., 169 pp.
     A fictional narrative for adolescent readers based on Cather's girlhood experiences in and around Red Cloud. Uses actual people, names, and places.

5   GALE, ROBERT L. "Willa Cather and the Past." <u>Studi Americani</u>
    4:209-22.
        Cather's fiction is informed by her use of the four most
    important circumstances in her past: (1) her family's move to
    Nebraska through which she encountered the immigrant experience
    firsthand, (2) her years in Lincoln where she discovered the
    world of performing artists, (3) her first trip to Europe, and
    (4) her discovery of the American Southwest. Her technique is
    characterized by the use of actual persons as models for charac-
    ters and by the transposition of the past into the present
    through flashbacks. Abridged: 1961.13.

6   GERBER, PHILIP L. "Willa Cather and the Big Red Rock."
    <u>College English</u> 19 (January):152-57.
        Although Cather could write of the wasteland that occupied
    her contemporaries, her dominant symbol became the rock that rose
    out of the wasteland to assert affirmative values such as fidel-
    ity, character, religion, and order. The symbolic possibilities
    of the rock expand from her introduction of it in an early story,
    "The Enchanted Bluff," through its connection with Thea Kronborg
    (who stood for artistic fidelity), Godfrey St. Peter (like the
    Biblical Peter, a rock of spiritual and ethical values), Tom
    Outland, and Father Latour ("the tower"). The symbolism cul-
    minates in <u>Shadows on the Rock</u> where the rock itself looks like
    a huge church.

7   HEINEY, DONALD. <u>Recent American Literature</u>. American Litera-
    ture series, vol. 4. Woodbury, N.Y.: Barron's Educational
    Series, pp. 189-201.
        Presents Cather in a standardized format, beginning with an
    overall estimate of her and her work. A biographical sketch is
    followed by a brief discussion of her "chief works." Insists
    that Cather is not an agrarian, but a psychologist whose main
    interest is in how the prairie affects the various personalities
    who inhabit it. Cather is basically romantic, and her overlying
    theme concerns the differences between the frontier and civiliza-
    tion. Her chief weakness is in construction, where she consist-
    ently tries to mesh disparate elements. She is, however, a good
    stylist, though her methods reveal her to be basically a writer
    of short stories and novelettes rather than novels.

8   HURST, FANNIE. <u>Anatomy of Me: A Wonderer in Search of Her-
    self</u>. Garden City, N.Y.: Doubleday & Co. Reprint without
    subtitle. New York: Arno Press, 1980, pp. 259-60.
        Recalls her impressions of Cather on first and subsequent
    meetings. Remembers feeling sure that this woman of vast surface
    serenity, but of complex intellect, did not like Hurst's own
    ebullient fictional style. Cather's work stood in "icy beauty"
    and "glacial splendor" aside from the uproar that some observed
    and lived in the 1920s.

9   LAVIN, J.A. Reply to William White's "Willa Cather and A.E.
     Housman." Notes and Queries 203, n.s. 5 (February):89.
        Reports having written to the present editor of the
     Shrewsbury Chronicle to ask if Housman had ever published poems
     in the Chronicle. The editor replied that although some Housman
     poems were reprinted in the Chronicle, there was no trace of
     first publication in the files. This information confirms
     White's supposition that Cather's report was inaccurate. See
     White items: 1951.16; 1957.23; 1958.18; 1965.36.

10   MacDOUGALL, CURTIS D. Hoaxes. Rev. ed. New York: Dover
     Publications, p. 12.
        Refers to the wolf-bridal story in My Ántonia as one of the
     earliest literary instances of the classic wolf story, citing as
     authority Viljahmur Stefansson who claims that wolves do not
     travel in packs or attack humans. The press and geography books
     have perpetuated such fictions.

11   MILLER, JAMES E., Jr. "My Ántonia: A Frontier Drama of
     Time." American Quarterly 10 (Winter):476-84.
        Contends that My Ántonia is unified structurally by its
     cyclic theme, a theme advanced through Cather's treatment of the
     cycling seasonal changes, the cycling stages of human life, and
     the cycling phases of civilization. These cyclical elements work
     together, through Jim Burden's growing awareness of them, to
     create an emotional structure for the book. Reprinted: 1967.36.

12   ODOŽILÍK, OTAKAR. "Kraj a díla Willy Catherové" [The coun-
     tries and the works of Willa Cather]. In Obrázky z dvou světů
     [Stories of two worlds]. Philadelphia: Skilzen Svobodne
     Tvorby, pp. 42-152.
        In Czech. Relates details of his own travels to geograph-
     ical areas important in Cather's work. Reminisces about New
     Mexico, Quebec, Nebraska, Virginia, Avignon, and Jaffrey, com-
     menting on Cather's methods and use of her materials. Shadows on
     the Rock is more loosely constructed than Death Comes for the
     Archbishop, for it has no central character around which it re-
     volves. My Ántonia is not a book to be taught in school as a
     good example of a well-structured novel, but it is useful as a
     portrayal of Czech immigrants on the American prairie. Cather is
     "miserly" with words, deft at dispensing information in a few
     words. (Typescript of English translation by the author can be
     seen at Willa Cather Historical Center, Red Cloud, Nebraska.)

13   REISCH, INGEBORG. Das Pionierideal in der Darstellung der
     amerikanischen Gesellschaft bei Willa Cather und Sinclair
     Lewis. Berlin, 97 pp.
        Published doctoral dissertation from the University of
     Berlin draws on the works of Cather and Sinclair Lewis to demon-
     strate the influence of pioneer ethics and ideals in the develop-
     ment of modern American society. Deals with the loss of inno-
     cence and the attempt to maintain the pioneer ethic in the face
     of increasing modernization.

14   STEVENSON, DAVID L. "Fiction's Unfamiliar Face." Nation 187
      (1 November):307-9.
          Speaks of Cather only to contrast her and other "pre-war
      giants" with contemporary writers who no longer care to convey
      solid values or to use standard literary forms.

15   STEWART, RANDALL. "The Old Cost of Human Redemption." In
      American Literature & Christian Doctrine. Baton Rouge:
      Louisiana State University Press, pp. 133-34.
          Claims that if T.S. Eliot's "Ash Wednesday" can be regarded
      as this century's most impressive Christian poem, then the same
      can be said for Cather's Death Comes for the Archbishop in the
      realm of fiction. It is an inspiring story, told with warmth and
      sympathy. Reprinted: 1968.33.

16   WEIGEL, JOHN A. "What Kind of Psychology for Students of
      Literature?" CEA Critic (College English Association) 20
      (April):1, 5.
          Describes the processes involved in applying truly scien-
      tific psychological methods--that is, laboratory as opposed to
      philosophical methods--to the study of literature. Tells of
      "administering" the Minnesota Multiphasic Inventory (MMPI) test
      to Cather's character Paul in "Paul's Case," answering the ques-
      tions for him on the basis of data contained in the story.
      Claims Cather was right in using the term "case," for a scien-
      tific analysis of Paul reveals him to be schizophrenic.

17   WERMUTH, PAUL C. "Willa Cather's Virginia Novel." Virginia
      Cavalcade 7 (Spring):4-7.
          In Sapphira and the Slave Girl, Cather's only work that
      deals significantly with her Virginia background, she examines
      southern social customs prior to the Civil War, analyzing the
      effects of slavery on people and treating her favorite theme:
      the individual in conflict with a hostile environment. The book
      conveys a tone of sadness in its nostalgic portrayal of a life
      long gone.

18   WHITE, WILLIAM. "A Note on Scholarship: Willa Cather on A.E.
      Housman." Victorian Newsletter, no. 13 (Spring):26-27.
          Reports that in spite of his calling attention to it
      earlier, the erroneous notion still persists in books about
      Cather that she saw old newspaper files containing some of A.E.
      Housman's poems before they appeared in book form. See other of
      White's comments on the matter in 1951.16; 1957.23; 1965.36.

1959

1   ANDERSON, JUNE. "Willa Cather's Sanctuary." Descant 3
     (Spring):22-30.
         Many of Cather's works prior to Death Comes for the Arch-
     bishop--including O Pioneers! and My Ántonia as well as the more
     obvious The Song of the Lark and The Professor's House--show her
     perennial interest in the Southwest, but Death Comes for the

Archbishop is the culminating work. There she not only idealizes
ancient southwestern cultures, but she treats them as sacred.

2   BELL, MARTHA S. "Special Women's Collections in United States
     Libraries." College and Research Libraries 20 (May):235-42.
         Offers brief descriptions of several library collections,
among them the Willa Cather Pioneer Memorial archives (later
named Willa Cather Historical Center) in Red Cloud, Nebraska.
Indicates that the organization was founded in 1955 and houses
material relating to Cather's work and her times.

3   BENNETT, MILDRED R. "Willa Cather in Pittsburgh." Prairie
     Schooner 33 (Spring):64-76.
         Describes Cather's activities in Pittsburgh and her asso-
ciation there with people like George Seibel, Ethelbert Nevin,
and Isabelle McClung who had a lasting influence on her life and
art. Quotes generously from Cather's journalistic writings of
that time and from the writings of Dorothy Canfield Fisher who
shared some experiences with her in Pittsburgh. Concludes that
the Pittsburgh years were important in Cather's growth and development, as a person and an artist, and that some of her stories reflect her experiences there.

4   BERTHOFF, WARNER. "The Art of Jewett's Pointed Firs." New
     England Quarterly 32 (March):31-53.
         Refers to Cather's classifying The Country of the Pointed
Firs with The Scarlet Letter and Huckleberry Finn and calling
them the three American books most likely to last. Suggests that
Cather's generosity perhaps came from her personal regard for
Sarah Orne Jewett and that later on she might not have "claimed
so much." All three books Cather named have regional flavor, but
at the same time, they transcend regionalism just as Cather's
work attempts to do. Reprinted: 1971.3.

5   CURTIN, WILLIAM MARTIN. "The Relation of Ideas and Structure
     in the Novels of Willa Cather." Ph.D. dissertation, Univer-
     sity of Wisconsin, 303 pp.
         Analyzes technique in Cather's novels in order to discover
its relation to her central themes. Cather is somewhere between
Henry James and Emile Zola in her use of internal psychology and
external documentation. See Dissertation Abstracts International
20 (1960):666-67.

6   FAVERTY, FREDERIC E. "An American Author's Masterpiece."
     Review of Death Comes for the Archbishop. Chicago Sunday
     Tribune, 22 February, sec. 4, p. 2.
         Regards Death Comes for the Archbishop as Cather's master-
piece, a work in which she follows her own principles for writing. Those principles insist on the writer's knowledge of and
sympathy for her subject, and on her capacity to create and leave
in the reader's mind a quality that is distinctively the writer's
own. Expanded: 1959.7.

7   _____. "Willa Cather's Death Comes for the Archbishop." In
     Your Literary Heritage. Philadelphia: J.B. Lippincott & Co.,
     pp. 188-90.
         An expanded text of 1959.6.

8   FLANAGAN, JOHN T. "A Half-Century of Middlewestern Fiction."
     Critique: Studies in Modern Fiction 2 (Winter):16-34.
         Discusses Cather in connection with other middlewestern
     fiction, calling attention to her sophisticated use of imagery
     for its vibrant pictorial quality.

9   KING, MARION. "Willa Cather: The Sunlit Peak." In The
     Saturday Review Gallery. Selected from the files of Jerome
     Beatty, Jr., and the editors of Saturday Review. New York:
     Simon & Schuster, pp. 351-52.
         Reprint of 1954.6.

10   LUDWIG, RICHARD M., ed. Supplement to Bibliography in
     Literary History of the United States. Edited by Thomas H.
     Johnson. New York: Macmillan Co., pp. 91-92. Reprints.
     With 3d ed. of Literary History of the United States, 1963;
     with 4th ed., 1974, pp. 885-86.
         Expands Cather bibliography of 1948.15 to include items
     published through 1958. Second supplement: 1972.18.

11   McCOY, WILLIAM DAVID. History of Pittsburgh Public Schools
     to 1942. Vols. 5-6. Pittsburgh, bound typescript, p. 120.
         Quotes from the minutes of the Central Board of Education
     for 11 June 1901 to the effect that Miss Willa Cather was recom-
     mended for election to the "Academic Department" at Pittsburgh's
     Central High School to fill the vacancy left upon the resignation
     of Belle Weidman.

12   MAY, HENRY F. The End of American Innocence: A Study of the
     First Years of Our Own Time 1912-1917. New York: Alfred A.
     Knopf, 89-90, 298.
         Cather may not have seemed part of the rebellion of young
     intellectuals in the teens, but her theme is theirs--the rebel-
     lious artist in America.

13   MEYER, ROY W. "The Scandinavian Immigrant in American Farm
     Fiction." American Scandinavian Review 47 (Autumn):243-49.
         Even though Cather was an outsider, she shows in her work
     a sensitivity toward, and an admiration for, the Scandinavian
     immigrant on the American prairie. In My Ántonia, but not in
     O Pioneers!, she treats the immigrants' social problems in deal-
     ing with the American community.

14   MUIR, JANE. Famous Modern American Women Writers. Famous
     Biographies for Young People. New York: Dodd, Mead & Co.,
     pp. 41-51.
         Sketches the outline of Cather's life and writing career
     in a style designed for the young reader. Regards Cather as a

"conservative and a classicist" who did not experiment with her fiction but preferred to use traditional forms.

15 RITENOUR, D.W. "Willa Cather, Authoress, Among Country's Distinguished Citizens." <u>Winchester</u> (Va.) <u>Evening Star</u>, 19 March, sec. 2, p. 17.
       Provides stories about Cather's ancestry and Virginia background.

*16 SCHROETER, JAMES. "Willa Cather's Literary Reputation." Ph.D. dissertation, University of Chicago.
       Listed in McClure 1975.29. Note indicates that Schroeter analyzes many critical writings on Cather's work from 1903 into the 1950s, and from them selects thirty-four representative pieces that he would eventually reprint in his book (see 1967.49).

17 ZUROSKY, ANN. "Author Still Lives in Vivid Memory." <u>Pittsburgh Press</u>, 22 April.
       Portrays Cather through the eyes of her niece, Helen Cather Southwick, who remembers Cather as being self-disciplined but kind, and one who liked order. Commemorates Cather as a "former Pittsburgher" on the anniversary of her death.

<u>1960</u>

1 <u>American Literary Manuscripts: A Checklist of Holdings in Academic, Historical and Public Libraries in the United States</u>. Austin: University of Texas Press, p. 68.
       Compiled and published under the auspices of the American Literature Group, Modern Language Association of America, by the Committee on Manuscript Holdings. Lists the figures for Cather manuscript, correspondence, and document holdings in thirty-seven United States libraries.

2 BENNETT, MILDRED R. "Willa Cather." <u>Seydell Quarterly</u> (Belgium) 12 (Winter):17–19.
       Illustrates Cather's skill at choosing the exact word and the right figure of speech, noting that she especially liked to borrow words from the animal kingdom for her descriptions of inanimate things.

3 COWLEY, MALCOLM. "The Ideas of an Artist." <u>New York Times Book Review</u>, 29 May, pp. 4, 16.
       Reviews the Randall book (1960.9) and then turns to Cather's own essays as the best door to her work, asserting that her own artistic principles were "vastly more important" than the social, political, and ethical ideals by which Randall judges her. Regards Cather's artistic integrity as "absolute"; each of her books, finding its own form, is an expression of that absolute integrity. Asserts that three of Cather's best books, <u>My Ántonia</u>, <u>A Lost Lady</u>, and <u>Death Comes for the Archbishop</u>, belong in the "small permanent body of American literature."

4   EDEL, LEON. <u>Willa Cather: The Paradox of Success</u>. Lecture
     delivered at the Library of Congress, 12 October 1959.
     Washington, D.C.: Library of Congress, 17 pp.
        Maintains that books of true artists like Cather have inner
     patterns that follow the designs of the writer's deepest life.
     Cather's books have two basic themes: conquest and death, be-
     cause for Cather, as well as for her heroine, Thea Kronborg, the
     struggle is everything. Success leads to disillusionment. After
     her books of despair, Cather saved herself by turning to <u>Death</u>
     <u>Comes for the Archbishop</u> and <u>Shadows on the Rock</u>. In them she
     found again the materials with which she had written her books of
     conquest—materials dealing with the old values of pioneer hardi-
     hood. <u>Death Comes for the Archbishop</u> has the word "death" in the
     title, but it is a novel of conquest. Cather's best books are
     success stories. Reprinted: 1967.12; 1973.21.

5   FLEISCHMANN, WOLFGANG BERNARD. "Willa Cather's <u>The Profes-</u>
     <u>sor's House</u> and Anatole France's <u>Le mannequin d'osier</u>."
     <u>Romance Notes</u> 1 (Spring):92–93.
        Suggests that Cather's "conscious literary model" for
     Godfrey St. Peter's old study was the converted sewing room used
     as a study by Monsieur Bergeret in <u>Le mannequin d'osier</u> (1897),
     a novel by Anatole France. Professor St. Peter alludes to
     Monsieur Bergeret in <u>The Professor's House</u>, but he remembers two
     forms in the Bergeret study instead of one, unconsciously making
     it conform to his.

6   FRANK, JOHN. "Cather and the Pursuit of Beauty. <u>Analects</u> 1
     (October):12–15.
        Cather rejected the machine-centered life and gave herself
     to her art, and through her art to the pursuit of beauty as she
     saw it. For her, beauty lies in moral values and goodness of
     character. Cather's one weakness may have been her tendency to
     see goodness/beauty mainly in those who are "physically or
     artistically superior." Her truth is not objective, but selec-
     tive, and the goodness she equates with beauty is also related
     to order.

7   HOWARD, LEON. <u>Literature and the American Tradition</u>. Garden
     City, N.Y.: Doubleday & Co., pp. 269–73.
        Observes that two of Cather's themes are the narrowness of
     village life and the ultimate value in linking past and present.
     For her the past meant life, not history. Ellen Glasgow's
     Dorinda Oakley in <u>Barren Ground</u> resembles Alexandra Bergson and
     Ántonia Shimerda.

8   MUGRIDGE, DONALD H., and McCRUM, BLANCHE P. <u>A Guide to the</u>
     <u>Study of the United States of America: Representative Books</u>
     <u>Reflecting the Development of American Life and Thought</u>. Ed-
     ited by Roy P. Basler. Washington, D.C.: Library of Congress,
     p. 108, items 1276–83.
        Devotes a column to Cather in the literature section, de-
     scribing the contents of the Library Edition of her works and

listing several book-length biographical studies of her. Identifies her principal theme as "the struggle between the spirit and
the world," and notes that she prefers the chronicle form over
traditional plot structure.

9   RANDALL, JOHN H., III. The Landscape and the Looking Glass:
    Willa Cather's Search for Value. Boston: Houghton Mifflin,
    435 pp.
        Revision of 1957.20. Still treats Cather's "search for
    value," but focuses more sharply on her rejection of twentieth-
    century life and her artistic weaknesses. Divides Cather's work
    into four basic periods with their corresponding themes, each of
    which is characterized by some sort of rejection. The first is a
    rejection of the West and a reaching out for the ideal which
    seems to reside in art. The second is an about-face rejection of
    the East and a return to nature as a focus of value. Cather's
    basic image in this period is the garden. The third period
    exemplifies a rejection of the postwar world, and the image of
    the garden is replaced by that of the wasteland. The fourth
    constitutes a rejection of the present in favor of the past.
    Throughout, Randall blames what he sees as deficiencies in
    Cather's art upon what he regards as deficiencies in her charac-
    ter and upon the influence of the art for art's sake movement.
    After a limited period of artistic success, between 1912 and
    1922, Cather suffered the "intellectual" and "emotional failure"
    that resulted in her artistic failure. Reprinted in part:
    1961.25; 1967.44; 1984.71.

10 ROSS, JANET. "Willa Cather and the Realistic Movement in
    American Fiction." Ph.D. dissertation, State University of
    Iowa, 200 pp.
        Evaluates Cather's work against objective criteria for lit-
    erary realism, arguing that although it contains a streak of
    romanticism she was indeed a realist who was selective in both
    material and technique. Like the realist, Cather writes ob-
    jectively of her own experiences and observations. Unlike the
    realist, however, she uses forms of allegory and often alters her
    narrative's chronological pattern. She remains an individual,
    and her style is a function of what is personal in her work. See
    Dissertation Abstracts International 21 (1960):1571-72.

11 SWETNAM, GEORGE. "Bill Cather's Buddy." Pittsburgh Press,
    3 July.
        Mentions Cather as a friend of Pennsylvanian Crawford A.
    Peffer.

12 TAKANO, FUMI. "Willa Cather--Her Interpretation of Life and
    Art." Tsuda Review, no. 5:1-21.
        Places Cather in her time and emphasizes her commitment to
    traditional values and order, but focuses mainly on the death,
    near-death, or deathlike experiences in O Pioneers!, The Pro-
    fessor's House, and Death Comes for the Archbishop. In the first
    two of these novels, an experience with death precedes a new
    commitment to life.

13   THORP, WILLARD. American Writing in the Twentieth Century.
      Library of Congress Series in American Civilization, edited
      by Ralph Henry Gabriel. Cambridge, Mass.: Harvard University
      Press, pp. 54–62.
          Traces Cather's career and summarizes several of her nov-
      els, noting turning points before One of Ours and The Professor's
      House in which she reveals her dismay at some aspects of the
      postwar world and looks to the heroic past for solace. Death
      Comes for the Archbishop and Shadows on the Rock are unique,
      perfect works of a particular kind. It is notable that Europe
      is present in all of Cather's novels.

14   THURSTON, JARVIS; EMERSON, O.B.; HARTMAN, CARL; and WRIGHT,
      ELIZABETH. Short Fiction Criticism: A Checklist of Inter-
      pretation Since 1925 of Stories and Novelettes (American,
      British, Continental), 1800–1958. Denver: Alan Swallow,
      pp. 25–27.
          Lists thirty-five of Cather's stories and names seven
      sources that offer commentary on them. Updated by Weixlmann
      1982.80.

15   "Writers of the Day." Writer 13 (June):90.
          Features several writers, including Cather. Describes her
      background and commends her sympathetic portrayal of immigrants
      in "Eric Hermannson's Soul."

                                    1961

1   ADAMS, THEODORE STANFORD. "Six Novels of Willa Cather: A
      Thematic Study." Ph.D. dissertation, Ohio State University,
      251 pp.
          Examines the dominating presence of pioneers, artists, and
      religious seekers in six of Cather's novels to see how they
      respond to society, nature, and the past. See Dissertation
      Abstracts International 22 (1961):570–71.

2   ATKINSON, BROOKS. "Cather's Novels Better Than Ever." New
      York Times News Service, 23 November; "Something Failed Willa
      Cather in 1922, But She Did Not Fail Her Craft." New York
      Times, 24 November, p. 28.
          Speaks of Cather's increasing stature and the durability of
      her writing as compared with that of less durable writers like
      Sinclair Lewis and Ernest Hemingway. It is true that after 1922
      the "ecstasy" that once marked her novels gives way to resigna-
      tion or tenacity, but her insight into character never falters.
      Reprinted: 1961.4; 1963.2.

3   _____. "Letter Written by Willa Cather Provokes Further
      Thoughts about Her Work." New York Times, 29 December, p. 20.
          Publishes a letter written by Cather to Katherine Foote
      [Raffy] in 1937, observing that it offers a "glimpse" into
      Cather's character because it shows both her "gloominess" of
      mood and her "sweetness" of feeling toward her friend. It also

                                   169

indicates Cather's nostalgia and her desire for privacy. Atkinson further reviews Randall's "doctoral dissertation" (1960.9) which had been sent to him by another critic/reviewer. Takes issue with Randall's unsympathetic treatment of Cather's idiosyncrasies, claiming that creative artists have always had what the rest of humanity regards as flaws and fanaticisms. No one would care about Cather's "spinsterish rejection of the world" if she had not had talent. But she was "inspired," and she left several works of "originality and beauty." Reprinted: 1963.1.

4   ____. "Willa Cather's Novels Show Gain in Stature." Omaha Sunday World-Herald Magazine, 31 December, p. 16.
      Reprint of 1961.2.

5   AUCHINCLOSS, LOUIS. "Willa Cather." In Pioneers and Caretakers: A Study of 9 American Women Novelists. Minneapolis: University of Minnesota Press, pp. 92-122.
      Sketches Cather's biography and treats each of her books in turn, including two of the story collections. Asserts that the love triangle of Emil, Marie, and Frank is irrelevant and destroys the unity of O Pioneers! The failure of The Song of the Lark is not that in the end the heroine loses herself in her art, but that Cather loses her, and the book becomes a book about opera and not about an opera singer. Sapphira Colbert, whose soul has been destroyed by the cancer of slavery, is Cather's most memorable character. Several of Cather's books show that for her the heart of the problem in the relationship between Europe and America was "the impact of the new world on the old in the new world."

6   BENNETT, MILDRED R. The World of Willa Cather. Lincoln: University of Nebraska Press. Also in Bison Book edition, 344 pp.
      Revised edition of 1951.2. Makes minor corrections and adds notes and index.

7   BOWDEN, EDWIN T. The Dungeon of the Heart: Human Isolation and the American Novel. New York: Macmillan Co., pp. 43-54.
      Places My Ántonia on a continuum with James Fenimore Cooper's The Deerslayer and Mark Twain's Huckleberry Finn as studies in frontier isolation. In her fruitfulness, in her participation in the family group, Ántonia finds a lasting value in the frontier's isolation. Cather's nostalgia indicates her concern that this value is being lost.

8   BRYDEN, RONALD. "The American Sublime." Spectator (London), no. 6935, 26 May, p. 767.
      Sees Cather as a writer out of step with her time in America, and yet finding appreciation in Europe. Her "gentility" alienated her from readers who were more excited by "the Sears Roebuck Catalogue-realism of Dos Passos and Lewis." Her central argument, however, is valid. Unless societies appreciate merit, they will perish, and civilization's power is transmitted through its rituals and forms.

9   CELLI, ALDO. "I romanzi di Willa Cather." Revista delle
     letterature moderne e comparate 14 (December):271-83.
          Cather's work is called the poetry of memory and nostalgia
     for the things that were. A major theme in her novels is the
     search for a happiness in which the individual feels himself a
     part of something larger that comprehends and gives purpose to
     life. Cather finds this ideal of fusion and unity by slipping
     into the past, which for her is not a means of evasion but a way
     of creating a poetical world that is estranged from the world in
     which she lived. A brief discussion of all ten of Cather's
     novels up through Shadows on the Rock indicates that Cather finds
     her most complete expression when the hope of union with the past
     is satisfied. But when she confuses memory as an artistic ex-
     pression with sentiment, she falls into sentimentality.

10   DAVENPORT, JOHN. "Neglected Genius." Observer (London),
     7 May, p. 51.
          Responds to the publication of British editions of A Lost
     Lady and The Professor's House by calling A Lost Lady "a marvel
     of lucidity" and The Professor's House a treatment of the con-
     flict Henry Adams described between the Dynamo and the Virgin.
     Cather may seem to be something of an archaic figure, but what is
     sometimes seen as nostalgia in her work is actually more a "re-
     gret for the loss of a continent, the failure of an idea."

11   FLANAGAN, JOHN T. "Middlewestern Regional Literature." In
     Research Opportunities in American Cultural History. Edited
     by John Francis McDermott. Lexington: University of Kentucky
     Press, pp. 134-38 passim.
          Mentions Cather's "quiet, sensitive portrait of the pro-
     fessional educator" in The Professor's House, her presentation of
     the second immigrant generation's triumph as prairie farmers, and
     her sympathetic interpretation of the prairie landscape.

12   FLOAN, HOWARD R. "El lugar de Europa en la vida americana:
     Tradición e invención en las novelas de Willa Cather." Trans-
     lated into Spanish by Francisco Yndurain. Arbor 48 (March):
     319-32.
          Many of Cather's novels are concerned with the transmission
     of culture from Europe to the new world. Her interest in tradi-
     tion, however, extends beyond European tradition to include other
     forms--Catholicism, Mexican and Indian culture, and railroad
     pioneering, for example. Cather's art is selective; she captures
     the small detail as well as the large landscape, and she knows
     how to communicate the quality of an experience.

13   GALE, ROBERT L. "Willa Cather and the Usable Past." Nebraska
     History 42 (September):181-90.
          An abridged text of 1958.5.

14   GERSTENBERGER, DONNA, and HENDRICK, GEORGE. The American
     Novel 1789-1959: A Checklist of Twentieth-Century Criticism.
     Denver: Alan Swallow, pp. 31-36.

Lists a few sources of criticism published before 1960 for
each of ten of Cather's twelve novels, then lists fifty-seven
sources of criticism on her work in general and one source of
bibliography.

15   HORGAN, PAUL. "In Search of the Archbishop." Catholic His-
      torical Review 46 (January):409-27.
      Describes Horgan's researches into the life of Jean
Bautista Lamy, the historical figure used by Cather in drawing
the character of Jean Latour in Death Comes for the Archbishop.
Also alludes to the day Horgan accidentally interrupted Cather at
work on the book on a hotel balcony in Santa Fe--the only time he
ever saw her.

16   JACKS, L[EO] V[INCENT]. "The Classics and Willa Cather."
      Prairie Schooner 34 (Winter):289-96.
      The classics are pervasive in Cather's fiction, organic
rather than simply allusory. Alexander's Bridge has the Paris-
Alexander myth at its core, O Pioneers! the Pyramus and Thisbe
story, and My Ántonia evokes the Aeneid. Cather was preoccupied
with Vergil, perhaps even identifying herself with him. Further,
The Professor's House and My Mortal Enemy recall Euripides, One
of Ours contains something of the Homeric epics, and Sapphira and
the Slave Girl suggests Terrence. It is the "logical quality" of
Cather's "reasoning" that aligns her with ancient writers of
tragedy.

17   JACOBSON, DAN. "An Old Kind of Gas." New Statesman 61
      (5 May):710.
      Dismisses A Lost Lady and The Professor's House as point-
less. The main characters are far less than they are touted to
be, and are therefore unbelievable. Any extensive review or
reading of the novels would be a waste of time.

18   KLEIN, MARCUS. Introduction to My Mortal Enemy. New York:
      Random House, Vintage Books, pp. v-xxii.
      Argues that My Mortal Enemy marks the crisis Cather's pre-
ceding novels were leading up to, especially from 1922 on, a
time when most major writers were observing the defeat of something in America. The new generation of writers were ironic and
the old were nostalgic, but Cather was neither; she was elegaic.
Her subject was not degeneration, but greatness. Time--mortal-
ity--that is the enemy, and mortal love is part of it. Her
novels all chart "the struggle to get beyond the necessity of
human relationships." Myra Henshawe's case is even more agoniz-
ing than Godfrey St. Peter's, for she would like to back away
from people as he does, but cannot. Her whole commitment is to
love, and that commitment ensnares her for life. She is defeated
by love, and she turns to the Church in order to grasp what
greatly endures. My Mortal Enemy is a strenuous, relentless
book.

19   "Listening to Our Heartbeats." <u>Times Literary Supplement</u>
     (London), 2 June, p. 344.
        Discovers in both <u>A Lost Lady</u> and <u>The Professor's House</u> a
     yearning for something lost that cannot be recovered. Commends
     Cather for her adherence to the truth, even at the expense of
     heightened drama. <u>A Lost Lady</u> is better written, but the main
     characters in both novels are so well drawn that they act as
     symbols without losing their individuality.

20   MARTIN, TERENCE. "The Drama of Memory in Willa Cather's Novel
     <u>My Ántonia</u>." In <u>The Frontier in American History and Litera-</u>
     <u>ture</u>. Edited by Hans Galinsky. Die Neuren Sprachen, Supp. 7.
     Frankfurt am Main: Verlag Moritz Diesterweg, ca. 1961,
     pp. 94–109.
        Based on a lecture delivered at the American Literature
     Seminar held in Bad Kreuznach in May 1960. Relates Frederick
     Jackson Turner's observations about the frontier to <u>My Ántonia</u>,
     and stresses the importance of Jim Burden's role as narrator.
     Everything valuable to Jim comes to be epitomized in Ántonia,
     while Lena Lingard, who is the antithesis of Ántonia, must be
     rejected. It is Ántonia who makes Jim's memories valuable in the
     present, who allows him, because of her vitality, to possess the
     past and make it meaningful in the present. Revised: 1969.12.

21   MENCKEN, H.L. <u>Letters of H.L. Mencken</u>. Edited by Guy J.
     Forgue. New York: Alfred A. Knopf, pp. 162, 183, 185, 186,
     207, 218, 245, 373, 377 passim.
        Contains a number of letters that mention Cather, including
     one that asserts that she is a better artist than she realizes.
     One letter written in 1921 says that all Cather's work is worth
     reading, but <u>My Ántonia</u> is her best. Mencken sometimes refers to
     her as "La Cather."

*22 OKITA, HAGIME. "From Henry James to Willa Cather." <u>Albion</u>
     (Kyoto University), no. 8, November, pp. 132–45.
        Listed in Leary, 1970.16.

23   PRIESTLEY, J[OHN] B[OYNTON]. Introduction to <u>A Lost Lady</u>.
     London: Hamish Hamilton, 5 pp.
        Praises the creation of Marian Forrester as both a charac-
     ter and a symbol. The novel is not allegorical, it is symbolic,
     and that is its triumph. It expresses the very essence of
     Cather.

24   _____. Introduction to <u>The Professor's House</u>. London:
     Hamish Hamilton, 5 pp.
        Asserts that although <u>The Professor's House</u> is a flawed
     book, it is profoundly close to contemporary experience. Godfrey
     St. Peter is only a sketch of a woman's idea of a particular kind
     of man, but his story is full of provoking perplexities.

25   RANDALL, JOHN H., III. "Willa Cather: The Middle West Re-
     visited." <u>New Mexico Quarterly</u> 31 (Spring):25–36.
        Extracted from 1960.9.

26   RUSSELL, LEONARD. "Dare I Read This Novel?" Sunday Times
     (London), 7 May.
        Notes the publication of British editions of A Lost Lady
and The Professor's House, recalling a youthful enthrallment with
Cather's charming sorceress in A Lost Lady, and postponing a
decision to reread the novel for fear of breaking the spell.

27   SATO, HIROKO. "In Quest of the Pioneer Spirit--Novels of
     Willa Cather." Pts. 1-2. Essays and Studies in British and
     American Literature (Tokyo) 9 (Winter 1961-Spring 1962):1-38,
     37-87.
        Provides a biographical introduction to Cather and her art,
then describes three phases of her work after Alexander's Bridge.
Phase one encompasses Cather's three pioneer heroines, Alexandra
Bergson, Thea Kronborg, and Ántonia Shimerda. They are striving
for a spiritual absolute that would lead to the establishment of
a new and distinctly American culture out of the same impulse
that established older cultures. Such an absolute would also
accomplish a sense of oneness with nature. Phase two chronicles
the struggle against the defeat of the pioneer spirit, with
Claude Wheeler returning to European origins for his inspiration,
the characters in A Lost Lady going down to defeat, and Godfrey
St. Peter and Myra Henshawe attempting to recapture the pioneer
spirit in history and Catholicism. Death Comes for the Archbishop, the only consequential book of Cather's third phase, is
the culmination of her themes. In it she retreats into the past
and religion in order to find what was permanent in the pioneer
spirit.

28   THORNTON, ELLA MAY. "The Mystery of Blind Tom." Georgia
     Review 15 (Winter):395-400.
        Sketches the life of the blind musician known first as
Thomas Green Bethune and then as Thomas Wiggins, claiming that
he is the model for Blind d'Arnault in My Ántonia.

                              1962

1   BENNETT, MILDRED R. "How Willa Cather Chose Her Names."
     Names 10 (March):29-37.
        Explores Cather's interest in names--where she got them and
how she transformed them into people and places in her fiction.

2   BLOOM, EDWARD A., and BLOOM, LILLIAN D. Willa Cather's Gift
     of Sympathy. Crosscurrents: Modern Critiques, edited by
     Harry T. Moore. Carbondale: Southern Illinois University
     Press, 272 pp.
        One section abridged from 1955.1. Focuses on Cather's
three major themes, the frontier spirit, the materialistic threat
to that spirit, and the artist. Behind these concerns is her
loftiest theme, the quest for the ideal, a quest undertaken by
both pioneer and artist. The Professor's House and Death Comes
for the Archbishop are given special attention, the first because
it is Cather's synthesis of what was happening to values in

modern society, the second because it expresses Cather's moral sensitivity toward the frontier, the quest, the past, and art. Cather's theories of composition are descriptive rather than prescriptive, and she is a classic American writer in the tradition of Cooper, Hawthorne, Melville, and James. She is thus naturally separated from most of her contemporaries, though she shares some similar concerns with writers like Steinbeck, Faulkner, Lewis, Wolfe, and especially poets like Robinson, Frost, and Eliot. Reprinted in part: 1967.1; 1984.7.

3   Cather entry in The National Cyclopedia of American Biography. Vol. 44. New York: James T. White & Co., pp. 138-39.
        A biographical sketch that mentions many of Cather's works and details her accomplishments and honors. Indicates that much of her mature work grew out of her understanding of her foreign immigrant neighbors.

4   CHASE, MARY ELLEN. "Five Literary Portraits." Massachusetts Review 3 (Spring):511-16.
        Provides personal insights into Cather and her work, based on Chase's acquaintance with her on Grand Manan Island in 1929. Quotes Cather as having said that she could not write plots because she saw "in terms of thought and imagery" rather than action. Cather intended Shadows on the Rock to be shaped by people and things, not by "movement or suspense."

5   FORMAN, HENRY JAMES. "Willa Cather: A Voice from the Prairie." Southwest Review 47 (Summer):248-58.
        Introduces Willa Cather, the writer, noting the various influences on her work and ascribing her greatness to her ability to portray happy people effectively. Calls her a classic American artist who is still on the ascent.

6   FURNESS, EDNA L. "Image of the School Teacher in Western Literature." Arizona Quarterly 18 (Winter):352.
        Mentions Gaston Cleric in My Ántonia, then describes Godfrey St. Peter in The Professor's House as a "high-minded, high principled character" who is disappointed in the materialistic shallowness of his family and colleagues.

7   [GRANT, DOUGLAS]. "The Frontier Dream." Times Literary Supplement (London), 27 July, p. 540.
        Virtue dominated the scene in the pioneering epoch as My Ántonia portrays it, but the interests of materialism and respectability, as seen in One of Ours and A Lost Lady, force the search for virtue into new frontiers, perhaps of the intellect. Cather's best novel, in terms of its "intellectual range and analytic power," is The Professor's House; but here the intellectual frontier is destroyed just as the civilization on Tom's mesa was destroyed. In Death Comes for the Archbishop and Shadows on the Rock, Cather completely rejects modern experience; and Lucy Gayheart, though it returns to Cather's persistent source of inspiration, the frontier dream, plunges helplessly into sentimentality. Abridged: 1965.15.

*8   HAMAYA, MIEKO. "Willa Cather." <u>Kamereon</u>, no. 4 (Spring), 88–97.
      Listed in Leary, 1970.16.

9   HERZBERG, MAX J., ed. <u>The Reader's Encyclopedia of American Literature</u>. New York: Thomas Y. Crowell Co., pp. 159–60.
      Provides a general overview of Cather's work, noting that her restrained classical style serves her subject matter well-- the portrayal of the "calm certitude" that follows a "hard struggle." Also cites several critics, and Cather herself, in an effort to describe her purposes and accomplishments.

10   HILLEGAS, C.K. <u>My Ántonia Notes</u>. Lincoln, Nebr.: Cliff's Notes, 83 pp.
      Summarizes each chapter of <u>My Ántonia</u> and gives commentary on it according to a standard format. Then presents critical analysis which treats structure, style, and technique--praising Cather for her use of language, symbolism (characters, moments, and seasons are often symbolic), and characters. Discusses each character in turn and ends with a section of questions.

11   HOFFMAN, FREDERICK J. <u>The Twenties: American Writing in the Postwar Decade</u>. Rev. ed. New York: Free Press, pp. 68–71 passim, 87–88, 181–90.
      Cather discussion is identical to that in 1955.5, with the exception of one deleted footnote in the later edition.

*12   KARCSEWSKA, IRENE (Sister M. PLACIDE). "Willa Cather: A Study in Values." Ph.D. dissertation, University of Ottawa.
      Listed in <u>Bibliography of English Language and Literature</u> (1962).

*13   KARITA, MOTOSHI. "'The Genteel Tradition' at Bay." <u>Sophia</u> (Sophia University, Japan) 2 (Winter):24–26.
      In Japanese. Listed in Schwartz, 1977.25.

*14   OMORI, MAMORU. "Some Problems in Cather's Works, Part II." <u>Studies in English Language and Literature</u> (Seinan Gakuin University, Japan) 3 (September):23–43.
      Listed in Leary, 1970.16. No information is given about part 1 of this article.

15   PORTER, KATHERINE ANNE. "Reflections on Willa Cather." In <u>Novelists on Novelists</u>. Edited by Louis Kronenberger. Garden City, N.Y.: Doubleday & Co., pp. 355–66.
      Reprint of 1952.12.

16 SCHMITTLEIN, ALBERT EDWARD. "Willa Cather's Novels: An Evolving Art." Ph.D. dissertation, University of Pittsburgh, 286 pp.

Traces the stylistic development of Cather's aestheticism, especially her control of emotion and thought through point of view. The ultimate ideal is "artistic ecstasy." See Dissertation Abstracts International 24 (1963):2041.

17 SCHOLES, ROBERT E. "Hope and Memory in My Ántonia." Shenandoah 14 (Autumn):24–29.

Relates My Ántonia to the Adamic myth, treating both Jim Burden and Ántonia as innocents who fall and learn from their fall. Although Ántonia triumphs, the book is pervaded by a feeling--enhanced by Jim's nostalgia--that the future looks dim. The time of the heroic "innocent" is past.

18 SLOTE, BERNICE, ed. "Willa Cather and Her First Book." Introduction to April Twilights (1903), by Willa Cather. Lincoln: University of Nebraska Press, Bison Books, pp. v–xxxxv. Rev. ed. 1968, pp. ix–xiv.

Sees Cather's work as having a single design, of which her poetry is an important part, and shows relationships between Cather's early journalistic writing and her poems. Furthermore, Cather's fiction is foreshadowed in the poems, which are, for the most part, quite conventional in form. For her themes and materials, Cather went largely to Arcadian and Appollonian myth, though the poems clearly demonstrate the influence of her admiration for Shakespeare and for the British artist, Sir Edward Burne-Jones. Only a few of the poems are rooted in the American West. Some themes and motifs in the poems are repeated in the fiction: a yearning for the old world; the metaphor of houses and rooms; a representation of the island, the river, and the rock; the expectancy of youth; and adventure and elegy. Reprinted in part: 1967.54; 1981.44.

19 THORBERG, RAYMOND. "Willa Cather: From Alexander's Bridge to My Ántonia." Twentieth Century Literature 7 (January):147–58.

Traces Cather's development from unsuccessful attempts at Jamesian moral complexity to solid achievements in portraying human possibility through the presentation of character. The technical decision in My Ántonia to set the stage in the consciousness of Jim Burden is immensely important, demonstrating Cather's increasing inclination to control, rather than be controlled by, her materials.

*20 TOKORO, ISAMU. "Willa Cather." Ritsumeikan bungaku [Ritsumeikan University literature], no. 210 (December):1–23.

Listed in Leary, 1970.11.

21   WILLIAMS, CECIL BROWN. <u>Regionalism in American Literature</u>.
     Heidelberg: Quelle & Meyer, p. 373.
          Surveys American literature by region, noting that Nebraska
     was literarily productive, especially in the works of Cather,
     John Neihardt, and Mari Sandoz. Cather wrote many good short
     stories and several novels, but the plains regional flavor is
     strongest in <u>O Pioneers!</u> and <u>My Ántonia</u>.

                                  1963

1   ATKINSON, BROOKS. "Letter by Willa Cather." In <u>Tuesdays and</u>
     <u>Fridays</u>. New York: Random House, pp. 155–58.
          Reprint of 1961.3.

2   _____. "Something Failed Willa Cather." In <u>Tuesdays and</u>
     <u>Fridays</u>. See Atkinson, 1963.1, pp. 140–42.
          Reprint of 1961.2.

3   BLISSETT, WILLIAM. "Wagnerian Fiction in English." <u>Criticism</u>
     5 (Summer):239–60.
          Explores the prominence of the Wagner motif in several
     writers, giving special attention to Cather. <u>The Song of the</u>
     <u>Lark</u>, the story of a singer and her rise to fame as a Wagnerian
     opera star, manifests "outward Wagnerism," while two short story
     collections, <u>The Troll Garden</u> and <u>Youth and the Bright Medusa</u>,
     are informed by "inner Wagnerism." "Paul's Case," in particular,
     may not be Freudian, but it is Wagnerian in its symbolic and
     searching method.

4   COOPERMAN, STANLEY. "Willa Cather and the Bright Face of
     Death." <u>Literature and Psychology</u> 13 (Summer):81–87. Entire
     issue reprinted. Amsterdam: Swets & Zeitlinger N.V., 1972.
          Compares Claude Wheeler in <u>One of Ours</u> to John Hershey's
     character in <u>The War Lover</u>. For Claude, the violence of war is
     translated into erotic fulfillment. He is always drawn to vio-
     lence, defined by it. He needs to strike and subdue, and he
     marries Enid Royce because he thinks her submissive. Passivity
     arouses him. But at the same time, war gives him the release he
     needs, and he is quickened by its violence. He wants violence
     and resents any delay in bloodshed. Peace comes to him after
     each bloody engagement, like the relaxation that follows orgasm.
     Reprinted: 1967.7.

5   EISINGER, CHESTER E. <u>Fiction of the Forties</u>. Chicago:
     University of Chicago Press, pp. 151, 174.
          Sees Cather as one in a line of descent from the
     "aristocratic-conservative tradition" in American letters—a
     tradition concerned both with manners and with the tensions
     introduced by a democratic system which fosters industrialization
     and immigration.

6   FOSTER, JOSEPH R. "Willa Cather." In <u>Contemporary Christian</u>
      <u>Writers</u>. Vol. 117, <u>The Twentieth Century Encyclopedia of</u>
      <u>Catholicism</u>. New York: Hawthorn Books, pp. 60–62.
         Identifies Cather as one who is sympathetic to Christian
themes and discusses <u>Death Comes for the Archbishop</u> as a quietly
told allegory of spiritual purpose in the face of life's daily
struggles.

7   FOX, CLYDE MAYNARD. "Revelation of Character in Five Cather
      Novels." Ph.D. dissertation, University of Colorado, 347 pp.
         Finds that while external reality may reveal character in
some Cather novels, it does not motivate or change people, for
they move by their own inner strength. See <u>Dissertation</u>
<u>Abstracts International</u> 24 (1964):4699–4700.

8   GALE, ROBERT L. "Cather's <u>Death Comes for the Archbishop</u>."
      <u>Explicator</u> 21 (May): item 75.
         The ringing of the Angelus bell, with its nine strokes
grouped in threes, suggests the nine-part (in thematic groups
of three) structure of <u>Death Comes for the Archbishop</u>. Further,
it is a reminder of the Virgin Mary, a motif appearing throughout
the novel, but very distinctly in three overt references to the
motto "Auspice Maria."

9   _____. "Manuel Lujon, Another Name by Willa Cather." <u>Names</u>
      11 (September):210–11.
         Prompted by Mildred Bennett's earlier article (1962.1) on
Cather's use of names, Gale submits that the name Manuel Lujon,
given to the generous rancher in <u>Death Comes for the Archbishop</u>,
is actually derived from Mabel Luhan who generously hosted Cather
at Taos.

10   HILFER, ANTHONY CHANNELL. "The Revolt from the Village in
      American Literature: 1915–1930." Ph.D. dissertation, Univer-
      sity of North Carolina at Chapel Hill, 442 pp.
         Studies social criticism in Willa Cather, Sinclair Lewis,
Thomas Wolfe, T.S. Stribling, and Zona Gale. Insists that although Cather projects strong emotion into her work, she lacks
power of characterization and power of intellect. Many of her
stories, as well as her novels from <u>O Pioneers!</u> through <u>The</u>
<u>Professor's House</u>, treat the theme of protest against herd
mediocrity. Nevertheless, they contain the repeated dilemma of
the creative rebel needing relationship with environment in order
to achieve self-realization. Cather's two characteristic moods
are celebration and invective. The problem with her projecting
her emotions into her characters and stories is that they remain
her emotions, and her characters do not justify them. <u>A Lost</u>
<u>Lady</u>, in spite of its faults, is Cather's one effective piece of
work. <u>Death Comes for the Archbishop</u> and <u>Shadows on the Rock</u>
suffer from pious pretense, from Cather's attraction to the
sentimentality that is sometimes substituted for religion. Revised for publication: 1969.10. See also <u>Dissertation Abstracts</u>
<u>International</u> 25 (1965):5258.

11   INGERSOLL, L.K. "Shadows on the Rock: Willa Cather at Grand
      Manan." In On This Rock: An Island Anthology. Grand Manan,
      N.B.: Gerrish House Society, pp. 55–66.
          Reprint of 1957.12.

12   KAROLIDES, NICHOLAS J. "The Image of the Pioneer in the
      American Novel." Ph.D. dissertation, New York University,
      427 pp.
          Analyzes the pioneer's role in shaping American society as
      seen through literature, including the work of Cather. Revised
      for publication: 1967.23. See Dissertation Abstracts Inter-
      national 24 (1963):745–46.

13   KNOPF, ALFRED A. "Random Recollections of a Publisher." In
      Proceedings of the Massachusetts Historical Society, vol. 73.
      Boston: Massachusetts Historical Society, pp. 99–101.
      (Listed as proceedings for January–December 1961.)
          Briefly describes Knopf's first meeting with Cather and the
      loyalty, yet the formality, that characterized their association.
      Cather knew that Death Comes for the Archbishop would make its
      mark; it was the only book she did with Knopf for which she re-
      quested an increased royalty. Enlarged: 1964.14.

14   LYON, PETER. Success Story: The Life and Times of S.S.
      McClure. New York: Charles Scribner's Sons, pp. 254, 299,
      342–43, 347, 398–99.
          Dramatizes Cather's first meeting with S.S. McClure. Also
      describes Cather's role in the preparation of a biography of Mary
      Baker Eddy and notes Cather's offer to write McClure's auto-
      biography as a favor to him as well. Remarks, too, on Cather's
      regular circumvention of McClure to keep the magazine going as
      she wanted it.

15   MORGAN, H. WAYNE. "Willa Cather: The Artist's Quest." In
      Writers in Transition: Seven Americans. American Century
      series. New York: Hill & Wang, pp. 60–81.
          Cather sought in her life and art that which endures. She
      celebrates individual effort and an aesthetic relationship with
      life and the land that sustains the human spirit. Increasingly,
      however, she looks to the past as the seat of stability and order.

*16   MUKOYAMA, YASUKO. "Cather's Love of Place." Thought Currents
      in English Literature (Aoyama Gakuin University, Japan) 35
      (February):71–82.
          Listed in Leary, 1970.16.

17   MURPHY, JOHN J. "Shadows on the Rock: Cather's Medieval
      Refuge." Renascence 15 (Winter):76–78.
          In writing Shadows on the Rock, Cather used Quebec as a
      substitute for France. It was really Avignon to which she was
      attached and which she invokes in Shadows on the Rock. As such,
      it is a sanctuary of order, almost medieval in spirit, through
      which she can forget that the genteel tradition has broken down
      in her own country.

18   ROBINSON, CECIL. <u>With the Ears of Strangers: The Mexican in</u>
      <u>American Literature</u>. Tucson: University of Arizona Press,
      pp. 172–74, 265–67.
         Uses Thea Kronborg's argument with her family--over her
      choosing to associate and sing with Mexicans in <u>The Song of the</u>
      <u>Lark</u>--to illustrate stereotypical attitudes toward Mexicans that
      are projected in literature. In <u>Death Comes for the Archbishop</u>
      Cather depicts Mediterranean Catholicism confronting Mexican
      Catholicism and the civilizing influence of the Church in a raw
      land. Reprinted with new title, but only minor changes in the
      Cather text: 1977.21.

19   WELLBORN, GRACE PLEASANT. "Willa Cather and the Southwest."
      <u>Forum</u> (University of Houston) 4 (Winter):38–41.
         Recounts in some detail the experiences of Cather's French
      Catholic priests in the American Southwest as she describes them
      in <u>Death Comes for the Archbishop</u>, and of Tom Outland and Godfrey
      St. Peter in <u>The Professor's House</u>. Notes their responses to the
      landscape and Cather's sensitive treatment of her early south-
      western materials, especially as she poses the values inherent
      there against an encroaching commercial attitude.

20   WEST, PAUL. <u>The United States and Other Countries</u>. Vol. 2,
      <u>The Modern Novel</u>. London: Anchor Press, Hutchinson Univer-
      sity Library, pp. 268–69, 273.
         Cather's sense of apathy is acute, as is her disdain for
      industrialism and democracy, but she cannot communicate tragedy.
      Naturally reticent, she is lacking in "animal vigor," and the
      substitute world she creates is rather aloof and wistful. In her
      brand of classicism, life is avoided rather than tamed. Her
      liveliest books are <u>Death Comes for the Archbishop</u> and <u>Shadows on</u>
      <u>the Rock</u>.

1964

1   ALLEN, WALTER. <u>The Modern Novel in Britain and the United</u>
      <u>States</u>. New York: E.P. Dutton & Co., pp. 65, 72–77, 86, 175.
         Treats <u>My Ántonia</u> and <u>A Lost Lady</u> as evidence of Cather's
      love for what she perceived as the American past and her hatred
      for the present. <u>Death Comes for the Archbishop</u> is the culmina-
      tion of this love. Cather's style and creation of character are
      commendable; she is a better artist and writer than Sinclair
      Lewis. Her move from Virginia to Nebraska is the experience that
      shaped her life and career. Discussion on <u>A Lost Lady</u> adapted in
      1969.1.

2   BAILEY, HELEN MILLER. <u>40 American Biographies</u>. Edited by
      Lewis Paul Todd. New York: Harcourt, Brace & World,
      pp. 189–94.
         Prepared as a supplement to seventh or eighth grade text-
      books in American history, this sometimes factually inaccurate
      biography of Cather focuses on her youthful experiences in
      Nebraska, especially those that led to the writing of her first

four novels about Nebraska--O Pioneers!, The Song of the Lark, My
Ántonia, and One of Ours.

3   BEEBE, MAURICE. Ivory Towers and Sacred Founts: The Artist
     as Hero in Fiction from Goethe to Joyce. New York: New York
     University Press, pp. 10-11, 99.
          Presents a brief discussion of The Song of the Lark in
     relation to Jung's theory about the creative person as someone
     divided into two selves, the human being who has a personal life
     and the artist who is simply a creative process.

4   BENNETT, J.Q. "Bibliographical Points on Cather and Fisher."
     American Notes and Queries 2 (February):85.
          Notes that a copy of S.S. McClure's My Autobiography
     (attributed to Cather) found in the properties of J.T. Chord
     lists the copyright date of that volume as May 1914 instead of
     the assumed date of September or later. See Duchnes response,
     1964.7.

5   BENNETT, MILDRED R. "Willa Cather's Ghost." Nebraska English
     Counselor 9 (January):3-4.
          Describes meeting an Indian chief who in Bennett's presence
     appeared to talk with his deceased father, a man who had some
     opinions about Cather. One of them was that she liked to hurt
     people; another was that some of her book manuscripts have sur-
     vived and are in the attic of a brick house somewhere.

6   CLOUGH, WILSON O. The Necessary Earth: Nature and Solitude
     in American Literature. Austin: University of Texas Press,
     pp. 157-60 passim.
          Cites Cather as one who writes of the West as a place of
     escape from anxiety and social complications. Cather's focus on
     escape is what prohibits her from achieving "true greatness" in
     her work.

7   DUCHNES, PHILIP C. "Cather Date Comment." American Notes and
     Queries 2 (April):121.
          Replies to the Bennett note (1964.4) that the May 1914 date
     for McClure's My Autobiography is erroneous. No part of the book
     was released before September 1914, and Chord's copy should read
     May 1915. He got one of the copies that contained the 1914 mis-
     print. Duschnes cites Frederick B. Adams, Jr., of the Pierpont
     Morgan Library as his authority.

8   GIANNONE, RICHARD [JOHN]. "Music in My Ántonia." Prairie
     Schooner 38 (Winter 1964-65):346-61.
          Music, one of three dominant dramatic patterns in My
     Ántonia, works in a variety of ways--in the metaphoric expres-
     sions of nature's rhythms and inner human experience as well as
     in actual expression through instruments, singing, and dance.
     Music provides human consolation, a bridge to a larger world, a
     symbol of value, and a means for identity. The center of My
     Ántonia, both structurally and symbolically, is the d'Arnault

episode that serves as a revelation and a realization of Ántonia's basic character. Adapted: 1968.18.

9   _____. "Music in Willa Cather's Fiction." Ph.D. dissertation, University of Notre Dame, 276 pp.
     Focuses on the musical components of Cather's individual works. Uses music in a broad sense, employing it not only in its formal aspects, but also in its aureal appeals that suggest life's harmonious qualities. Some of the stories that have not received much critical attention are discussed because music figures importantly in them. For Cather, music, as the soul's speech, gives expression to a mortal's spiritual self. While music often serves as a symbolic intensification in Cather's fiction, musical allusions also function as "counter-statement" on the novel's action. Giannone regularly traces Cather's allusions to operas as their plots and motifs follow or contrast with those of her novels. He concludes that Cather regards music as a bridge over obstacles to fulfillment. Through music she establishes the moral atmosphere of her fiction. Revised for publication: 1968.18.

10   HARVEY, ALICE G. "Willa Cather." In Nebraska Writers. Rev. ed. Omaha: Citizen Printing Co., pp. 22-23.
     Expanded from 1934.6. Makes only short additions to the original text. One addition asserts that Cather's attempts to write about artists and others she knew in the East were less than impressive. The other stresses her technical and stylistic independence.

11   HEARNE, LAURA GUTHRIE. "A Summer with F. Scott Fitzgerald." Esquire 62 (December):160.
     Mentions that Fitzgerald considered Cather to be the best woman novelist in the United States.

12   KNOPF, ALFRED A. "Publishing's Last 50 Years." Saturday Review 47 (21 November):21-23, 53-54.
     Adapted from 1964.14. Printed simultaneously with 1964.13.

13   _____. "Publishing Then and Now: 1912-1964." Bulletin of the New York Public Library 68 (November):560-64.
     Reprint of 1964.14. Printed simultaneously with 1964.12. Reprinted in part: 1982.35.

14   _____. Publishing Then and Now: 1912-1964. R.R. Bowker Memorial Lectures, no. 21. New York: New York Public Library, Astor, Lenox & Tilden foundations, pp. 10-14.
     Enlarged from 1963.13. Describes Knopf's working relationship with Cather, noting particularly her refusal to sacrifice principle for material gain. She allowed almost no motion pictures to be made from her books, no dramatizations, no cheap editions, no book club selections. She was very interested in the appearance of her books and in the marketing of them--she sometimes wrote advertising copy for them--but she was always modest. Reprinted: 1964.13. Adapted: 1964.12.

15   MILLER, JAMES E., Jr. F. Scott Fitzgerald: His Art and His
     Technique. New York: New York University Press, pp. 14–15,
     84, 86–92, 95.
          Revision of 1957.16. Contends that Fitzgerald was probably
     more influenced by Cather than has been realized, particularly by
     her essay on the unfurnished novel and her novels My Ántonia and
     A Lost Lady. From Cather Fitzgerald learned the importance of
     selection in the writing of fiction, and also something about
     mood, form, unity, and narrative point of view.

16   MILTON, JOHN R. "The Novel in the American West." South
     Dakota Review 2 (Autumn):56–76.
          Classifies western novelists into three groups, placing
     Cather in the group that includes a wide range of good writers
     who have dealt with the West, but are not necessarily westerners
     in the conventional sense. Her farm novels are "midwestern
     rather than western," and Mary Austin was probably right in sug-
     gesting that Cather did not know New Mexico well enough to be
     regarded as a westerner. Reprinted: 1974.43; 1980.27.

17   _____, comp. "The Western Novel--A Symposium." South Dakota
     Review 2 (Autumn):3–36.
          Reports responses of several writers to a set of questions
     about western writing in general and their own work in particu-
     lar. Forrester Blake mentions Death Comes for the Archbishop as
     an outstanding western novel, noting its "simplicity and beauty
     of line." Paul Horgan praises Cather's "quiet art" and her uni-
     versal quality. Michael Straight calls Cather one of the few
     novelists whose writing will endure. Other western novelists
     may not have measured up to her quality as yet.

18   NOLTE, WILLIAM H. H.L. Mencken: Literary Critic.
     Middletown, Conn.: Wesleyan University Press, pp. 231, 241.
          Claims Mencken especially admired Cather and her work be-
     cause she was clearly "American," and a pure artist with no
     causes to espouse. Mencken thought My Ántonia a remarkable book,
     but he disliked One of Ours.

19   NOURSE, JOAN T. Review Notes and Study Guide to Cather's "My
     Ántonia" and Other Major Novels. New York: Monarch Press,
     Thor Publications, 96 pp.
          Begins with a biographical sketch and a general assessment
     of Cather's work and contribution. Provides synopsis, commen-
     tary, and character analysis on each book in My Ántonia, and then
     presents general critical discussion on style, narrator, tone,
     and theme. Offers review questions and responses followed by
     summaries and brief comments on Cather's other major novels.

20   "Pulitzer Prize Winner in K-N Land." Flame 16 (September-
     October):6–9.
          Features the work of the Willa Cather Pioneer Memorial and
     Educational Foundation and identifies places in the Red Cloud,
     Nebraska area that appear in Cather's fiction.

21 SLOTE, BERNICE. "Willa Cather on Shakespeare." <u>Prairie Schooner</u> 38 (Spring):65–74.

Introduces four pieces on Shakespeare that Cather wrote for the <u>Nebraska State Journal</u> between April 1894 and April 1895, noting that even then Cather wrote nonacademic criticism that showed "good sense."

22 STROZIER, ROBERT. "Willa Cather, Story Teller." <u>Descant</u> 8 (Winter):41–48.

In Cather's novels narrative is the most important element; symbol, structure, and other such devices grow out of the narrative. Her method, her emphasis on narrative, is especially obvious in novels like <u>My Ántonia</u>, <u>Death Comes for the Archbishop</u>, <u>Shadows on the Rock</u>, and <u>O Pioneers!</u> which not only emphasize a central story line but also contain many short nårratives within the larger whole.

23 TAYLOR, J. GOLDEN. "The Western Short Story." <u>South Dakota Review</u> 2 (Autumn):37–55.

Lists forty short stories representing the American West and groups them into ten categories. Discusses "Neighbour Rosicky" briefly under the heading "The Farmers and the Townspeople" and calls Rosicky American Literature's "most charming immigrant," a fitting tribute to the Czech immigrants Cather knew in Nebraska. Reprinted: 1974.74.

24 TOLER, Sister COLETTE. "Willa Cather's Vision of the Artist." <u>Personalist</u> 45 (Autumn–October):503–23.

The themes running through all of Cather's works on artists reflect her vision of the artist as dedicated, uncompromising, and alive with creative genius deriving from God's "inscrutable wisdom." Cather is interested not only in the triumph of the artist and his or her genius, but also in the artist's self-discovery and struggle against philistinism and isolation. The artist's devotion gives meaning to others.

25 Van GHENT, DOROTHY. <u>Willa Cather</u>. Pamphlets on American Writers, no. 46. Minneapolis: University of Minnesota Press, 46 pp.

Provides an overview of Cather's life and works and discusses some stories and several novels in detail, bolstering plot summary with interpretive analysis. Points to Cather's repeated treatment of two basic themes, "the ancestors and the instinctive self." The two are related and are sometimes joined in one character as with Myra Henshawe. Most of Cather's work is concerned with the self's integration with the human past, and the search for self often involves a search for ancestors. Cather's weakest novels are <u>One of Ours</u> and <u>Lucy Gayheart</u>, though the interest of <u>Sapphira and the Slave Girl</u> is mainly historical and <u>The Old Beauty and Others</u> carries the marks of "querulous" old age. Reprinted: 1974.77; 1977.30.

26   "Willa Cather: A Portfolio." Prairie Schooner 38 (Winter
      1964–65):321–61.
         Features a "portfolio" section on Cather that contains the
      poem "Dedicatory" from April Twilights; two of Cather's early
      newspaper reviews, under the title "At the Concerts"; the story
      "The Treasure of Far Island"; and the article by Giannone listed
      above (1964.8).

                              1965

1   ANDERSON, QUENTIN. "Willa Cather: Her Masquerade." New
      Republic 153 (27 November):28–31.
         Makes a general assessment of Cather and her work. Like
      Walt Whitman, Cather tries to let the reader imaginatively
      possess a continent, but since the country has shrunk she has
      been reduced to masquerade. The masquerade is acted out in three
      phases of her work. In the first, the self seems capable of
      appropriating the world; in the second, the self discovers its
      own division and is limited by prescribed sexual roles; in the
      third, the self is willingly subordinated to Mary, the "great
      mother" who has succeeded Alexandra and Ántonia.

2   BENNETT, MILDRED R. Introduction to Willa Cather's Collected
      Short Fiction, 1892–1912. Edited by Virginia Faulkner.
      Lincoln: University of Nebraska Press, pp. xiii–xli. Re-
      print. 1970.
         Presents biographical data, largely in terms of Cather's
      journalistic experiences during the period covered by the stories
      collected in this volume. Points to numerous parallels among the
      stories and with the novels as well. The figure of the immigrant
      or alien is important, as is the artist, and the stories are full
      of Cather's early memories. Even the somewhat Jamesian stories
      of Cather's McClure's years show her advance in technical skill.
      "The Enchanted Bluff" marks a high point among this group of
      stories.

3   BERGAMO, RALPH. "The Polished Art of Willa Cather." Atlanta
      Journal and Constitution, 22 August.
         Review of Willa Cather's Collected Short Fiction, 1892–
      1912. Calls Cather a master of the short story, a fact sometimes
      overlooked because of her distinguished career as a novelist.
      Her early stories show the unfolding of the artist's mind and in
      a "pristine state" the motifs familiar in her other fiction––
      pioneering, the world of art, nature, and character.

4   BERTHOFF, WARNER. The Ferment of Realism: American Litera-
      ture, 1884–1919. Series on American literary history. Ed-
      ited by Quentin Anderson. New York: Free Press, pp. 255–63.
         Views Cather's work from a literary-historical perspective,
      praising O Pioneers!, The Song of the Lark, and My Ántonia for
      their authentic portrayal of a region's actual social history.
      Sees the novels following My Ántonia as indications of a decline

and a hardening, and the later novels as an effort to withdraw from life. Cather's work suffers from structural and narrative faults.

5   BRENNAN, JOSEPH X. "Willa Cather and Music," and "Music and Willa Cather." Pts. 1-2. University Review (Kansas City) 31 (Spring-Summer):175-83, 257-64.
     Part 1 describes Cather's great interest in music and musicians and the extent to which she uses music in her work. It is frequently through musicians that Cather presents the conflict between art and a commercial society. Music appears in her work in three distinct levels: music of nature, spontaneous music in humans, and the disciplined music of competent professionals. Cather uses music to shape character, advance plot, establish tone, and direct reader sympathies. Part 2 focuses on Cather's use of music in particular works to do the things detailed in part 1. In A Lost Lady music defines character, conveys meanings, and assists in giving the book form; in The Professor's House it defines the book's overall form; and in Death Comes for the Archbishop it works thematically.

6   CHARLES, Sister PETER DAMIAN. "Love and Death in the Novels of Willa Cather." Ph.D. dissertation, University of Notre Dame, 289 pp.
     Applauds Cather's understanding of the human condition through a chronological analysis of the love-death dichotomy as it develops in each of the novels and reaches a climax in Death Comes for the Archbishop. See Dissertation Abstracts International 26 (1965):2205-6.

7   _____. "Love and Death in Willa Cather's O Pioneers!." CLA Journal (College Language Association) 9 (December):140-50.
     Traces the dual thrusts of love/life and death in O Pioneers! and stresses the rightness of the linking of the impulses. Alexandra at varying times feels pulled toward both, and in the final scene between Emil and Marie the two are powerfully joined.

8   EDEL, LEON. "Willa Cather and The Professor's House." In Psychoanalysis and American Fiction. Edited by Irvin Malin. New York: E.P. Dutton & Co., pp. 199-221.
     An abridged text of 1954.3.

9   GASTON, EDWIN W., Jr. Conrad Richter. New York: Twayne Publishers, pp. 48, 83-84, 91-92.
     Quotes Richter who indicates that Cather influenced him because his own experience yields similar characters and background. There are similarities between the work of Richter and that of Cather, to some extent in his rendering of the southwestern landscape--though she manages to transcend it and he never does--but especially in his grieving over the passing of the frontier. Richter's The Lady is like A Lost Lady in its brevity and in its use of a young male narrator.

10   GIANNONE, RICHARD [JOHN]. "Music in The Professor's House."
     College English 26 (March):464-69.
         Discusses the function of music in the three-part structure
     of The Professor's House. Books 1 and 3 make specific reference
     to particular musical works, while book 2 introduces music only
     in nature's harmony and in the silence of the Blue Mesa. Musical
     references function in a variety of ways--to enhance structure,
     to intensify drama, to project theme, to enlarge meaning, to link
     past and present, to accompany action, to describe nature, and to
     underscore mood. Adapted: 1968.18.

11   _____. "One of Ours: Willa Cather's Suppressed, Bitter
     Melody." South Atlantic Quarterly 64 (Winter):72-86.
         Cather employs music and references to music to emphasize
     theme and movement in One of Ours. The suppression of, or lack
     of, music indicates the condition of a world insensitive to finer
     things of the spirit. The book itself moves from deafness to
     musical sensitivity through a series of "stirrings" in the
     natural world and in human beings, but it returns to silence in
     the end as the ultimate machine, war, destroys those who respond
     to music's appeals. Throughout, music is associated with life's
     true values, and Cather presents the conflict of values through
     posing the machine against music. Adapted: 1968.18.

12   _____. "O Pioneers!--Song of the Earth and Youth." South
     Dakota Review 2 (Spring):52-68.
         Explores Cather's use of music in O Pioneers! to assist in
     the development of her principal themes, the land and youth.
     Alexandra and Ivar are sensitive to earth rhythms and harmonies,
     though her response is naturalistic and active while his is
     sacramental and philosophical. Emil and Marie are also presented
     through musical themes, ironically opposing ones that underline
     Emil's misinterpretation of reckless passion as ideal love. As a
     whole, however, the book makes an optimistic statement in its use
     of music as a metaphor for the regenerative cycle. Cather
     counterpoints regeneration against the theme of the brevity of
     youth. Adapted: 1968.18.

13   _____. "The Professor's House: A Novel in Sonata-Form."
     Colby Library Quarterly 7 (June):53-60.
         Examines the relationship between The Professor's House and
     the sonata form, noting Cather's statement about her deliberate
     use of that form in the novel. The similarities are notable.
     Cather introduces a theme (material prosperity) and countertheme
     (devotion to an ideal) in book 1, picks them up and reverses them
     in book 2, and restates them in "personal terms" in book 3. But
     Cather is not bound to the form. She works within the order of
     the sonata structure to present the disorder of the professor's
     world. Adapted: 1968.18.

14   _____. "Willa Cather's My Mortal Enemy and Bellini's Norma."
     Die neueren Sprachen 14 (July):401-10.
         Argues that My Mortal Enemy is the culmination of the dark
     strain in Cather's fiction that began with One of Ours. It

becomes "an almost perverse attack on love." Nellie Birdseye, the narrator, makes musical allusions in relation to her memories of Myra, creating the character, but removing the audience from her. The reference to the Casta Diva aria provides the most penetrating insight into Myra, for she and Norma share the same temperament. Moreover, the novel and the opera treat the same theme, the opposition of sacred and profane love. Adapted: 1968.18.

15   GRANT, DOUGLAS. "Willa Cather: The Frontier Dream." In
      Purpose and Place: Essays on American Writers. New York:
      St. Martin's Press, pp. 142–47.
          An abridged text of 1962.7.

16   HART, JAMES D., ed. The Oxford Companion to American Litera-
      ture. 4th ed. New York: Oxford University Press. 5th ed.,
      1983, pp. 128–29.
          The Cather text is identical in the two editions. It pro-
      vides a brief biography and introductory commentary on each of
      Cather's books, maintaining that the books illustrate Cather's
      idealism and her attachment to the past.

17   HASKELL, HENRY C. "Scanning the Arts." Kansas City Star,
      14 March.
          Places Cather in the front rank of women novelists of this
      century, but sees an inexplicable dropping off after Death Comes
      for the Archbishop. Suggests that although she and Ernest
      Hemingway seem very different, they are "curiously alike," deep
      down, in the strange evocativeness of their styles, the sensory
      quality of their writing, and the simultaneous compassion and
      pessimism of their emotion. Cather may be less brutal in her
      manner, but she is probably "at bottom . . . more somberly
      despairing" than Hemingway.

18   HOWE, HELEN. The Gentle Americans 1864–1960: Biography of a
      Breed. New York: Harper & Row, pp. 74–77 passim, 85.
          Refers to Cather several times, using her description of
      the James T. Fields home to define the gentility of an era.

19   HUBBELL, JAY B. South and Southwest: Literary Essays and
      Reminiscences. Durham, N.C.: Duke University Press,
      pp. 299–302.
          Calls Cather fortunate in her move to Nebraska, though she
      did not get a proper perspective on that region until she moved
      east. Her discovery of the Southwest was also important, for
      there she found an historical past lacking in Nebraska.

20   JANEWAY, ELIZABETH. "An Epic Was Around Her." New York Times
      Book Review, 5 September, p. 1.
          Review of Willa Cather's Collected Short Fiction, 1892–
      1912. Traces Cather's progress as an author, from her poorly
      written short stories to her peak in The Professor's House, and
      then to her decline and return to the past in Death Comes for the
      Archbishop, Shadows on the Rock, and Sapphira and the Slave

<u>Girl</u>. Cather was one who created epic characters but was unable
to write an epic, though she developed "a simple flexible durable
American prose."

21   KEELER, CLINTON. "Narrative Without Accent: Willa Cather and
     Puvis de Chavannes." <u>American Quarterly</u> 17 (Spring):119–26.
         Shows the relationships between the style of Puvis de
     Chavannes' painting and Cather's method in <u>Death Comes for the</u>
     <u>Archbishop</u>. Answers some critical objections, especially those
     of John Randall (1960.9), to the unaccented nature of the book by
     insisting that the achievement of this effect is artistically
     justified. Stresses the stylized nature of both <u>Death Comes for</u>
     <u>the Archbishop</u> and the Ste. Genevieve frescoes that Cather said
     she used as models for her novel. Reprinted: 1984.46.

22   LAMBERT, MAUDE EUGÉNIE. "Theme and Craftsmanship in Willa
     Cather's Novels." Ph.D. dissertation, University of North
     Carolina at Chapel Hill, 326 pp.
         Reviews the criticism on Cather's novels and studies theme
     and craftsmanship in them to determine the cause for Cather's
     "unsatisfactory literary career." Her problem is inconsistency.
     Although she is strong in creation of character, she is incon-
     sistent in sustaining scenes, action, and point of view. See
     <u>Dissertation Abstracts International</u> 26 (1966):3925.

23   MATTHIESSEN, FRANCIS OTTO. <u>Sarah Orne Jewett</u>. Gloucester,
     Mass.: Peter Smith, pp. 103, 105, 124–25, 129–32, 145–46.
     Reprint of 1929.13.

24   MEYER, ROY W. <u>The Middle Western Farm Novel in the Twentieth</u>
     <u>Century</u>. Lincoln: University of Nebraska Press, pp. 38–47,
     59–60, 63, 75, 192–93 passim, 205.
         Avows that Cather is the first writer of American litera-
     ture to make art out of the immigrant experience and pioneering
     encounters with the land and suggests that perhaps her insights
     into the life of the European immigrant will surpass in impor-
     tance her treatment of pioneering. Contrasts Cather with Ole
     Rölvaag, noting that he emphasizes the external story and concen-
     trates on the tragic side of pioneer experience while she empha-
     sizes the internal story and moves past the tragic to the posi-
     tive aspects of pioneer experience. Both writers transcend the
     standard farm novel.

25   MOORE, HARRY T. Review of <u>Willa Cather's Collected Short</u>
     <u>Fiction, 1892–1912</u>. <u>Chicago Tribune</u>, 3 October.
         Observes the increase in Cather's reputation and believes
     that her prairie fiction contains her best work. Judges "The
     Sculptor's Funeral" and "Paul's Case" to be American classics.

26   MOTOYANAGI, FUMIKO. "W. Cather's <u>Death Comes for the Arch-</u>
     <u>bishop</u> and Its Epic Trend." <u>Kyusha American Literature</u>
     (Fukuoka), no. 8, pp. 36–40.
         Praises <u>Death Comes for the Archbishop</u> for its power to
     evoke "mysterious emotion," its simple style, and its creation

of two priests who bring God to a savage country in the manner of
ancient Greek and Roman epic heroes.

27   NYQUIST, EDNA. "The Significance of the Locale in the
     Nebraska Fiction of Willa Cather, Especially in My Ántonia."
     Wisconsin Studies in Literature, no. 2, pp. 81–89.
         Defends Cather against some of her critics and emphasizes
     the importance of her use of the Nebraska locale in the creation
     of works like My Ántonia.

28   PIPER, HENRY DAN. F. Scott Fitzgerald: A Critical Portrait.
     New York: Holt, Rinehart & Winston, pp. 132–35, 212.
         Considers Fitzgerald's debt to Cather, especially to the
     essay "The Novel Démeublé" and the novels My Ántonia and A Lost
     Lady for their form and narrative technique. Points also to
     letters the two writers exchanged, and Fitzgerald's almost ver-
     batim use in Tender Is the Night of one of Cather's comments to
     him about indirection in character presentation.

29   REEDER, ARMAND W. "Art and Simplicity in the Young Willa
     Cather." St. Louis Post-Dispatch, 19 September.
         Finds the stories in Willa Cather's Collected Short Fic-
     tion, 1892–1912 important in that they show Cather's growth in
     her craft and also illuminate her novels. Cather writes with
     "high seriousness," and with a "firm tone" and spontaneity. She
     writes beautifully and sympathetically of "faith and fortitude."

30   Review of Willa Cather's Collected Short Fiction, 1892–1912.
     New Yorker 41 (23 October):244.
         Praises the editing and several stories in the collection,
     particularly "On the Gulls' Road," but considers most of the
     stories dull.

31   SCHROETER, JAMES. "Willa Cather and The Professor's House."
     Yale Review 54 (Summer):494–512.
         Detects anti-Semitism in Cather's work, particularly in her
     portrayal of Louie Marsellus in The Professor's House. Cather
     clearly and repeatedly contrasts him with Tom Outland. She may
     have had personal reasons for her depiction of Marsellus, but in
     most of her portraits of Jews she simply reflects the stereotypes
     common in the fiction of nearly all of her consequential peers.
     American literature from the period prior to World War I and
     through the 1920s has a strong, stereotypical anti-Semitic
     strain. Reprinted: 1967.50.

32   SCHWEIDER, NANCY. "Stirrings of Growing Talent Captured in
     Early Stories." Lincoln Sunday Journal and Star, 5 September,
     sec. f, p. 11.
         Review of Willa Cather's Collected Short Fiction, 1892–
     1912. This collection of the stories that precede Cather's first
     novel is valuable in showing the development of her art. Even
     the early overly emotional and sometimes awkward pieces are full
     of life and energy. The stories show that Cather was not the

provincial she is often taken for, but in fact had cosmopolitan
interests.

33   STEGNER, WALLACE, ed. "Willa Cather: My Ántonia." In The
      American Novel from James Fenimore Cooper to William Faulkner.
      New York: Basic Books, pp. 144-53.
          My Ántonia is about the individual's struggle to reconcile
      the two aspects of experience--and hence of the self--represented
      by the old world and the new world. In exploring this theme,
      Cather presents the parallel lives of Jim Burden and Ántonia con-
      fronting the new but returning to the old. Reprinted: 1969.19.

34   TOLER, Sister COLETTE. "Man as Creator of Art and Civiliza-
      tion in the Works of Willa Cather." Ph.D. dissertation,
      University of Notre Dame, 233 pp.
          Traces the development of the creator theme in Cather from
      an early preoccupation with the artist as esthete, to the artist
      as creator of culture, to the pioneer as creator of civilization,
      and finally to the historical figure as creator of both culture
      and civilization. Cather's expanding vision draws increasingly
      on characters who intuit their place as creators. See Disserta-
      tion Abstracts International 26 (1965):2226.

35   WALTERS, RAYMOND, Jr. "Not Quite Lost Lady." New York Times
      Book Review, 5 September, p. 8.
          Comments that in spite of Cather's efforts to remain a
      private person, her work is widely read. Her fear of being an
      enemy to students forced to read her work (if it were to appear
      in paperback form) thus far appears to be groundless.

36   WHITE, WILLIAM. Note in "Letters" section. Prairie Schooner
      39 (Summer):187.
          Acknowledges his pleasure that Mildred R. Bennett in a long
      footnote to the Bison Book edition of The World of Willa Cather
      (1961.6) corrects the misconceptions about A.E. Housman that
      White had noted in 1951.16, 1957.23, and 1958.18.

37   WHITTINGTON, CURTIS [CALVIN], Jr. "'The Stream and the Broken
      Pottery': The Form of Willa Cather's Death Comes for the
      Archbishop." McNeese Review 16:16-24.
          Cather's basic method in Death Comes for the Archbishop is
      the organic accumulation of incidents and the generation of over-
      tones by means of juxtaposition--comparison and contrast. Through
      overtones Cather recreates in her readers the same emotional
      effects she felt in creating the novel. Death Comes for the
      Archbishop is the essence of this method that is basic to much of
      her work. The Archbishop may not be the center of the book, for
      he does not develop. The center may be time itself.

38   WILSON, BENJAMIN HARRISON, Jr. "Quiet Realism: Women Writers
      in the William Dean Howells' Tradition." Ph.D. dissertation,
      University of North Carolina at Chapel Hill, 436 pp.
          Analyzes the influence of Howells on several women writers
      in the early 1900s. Finds Cather's work most notably an example

of "quiet" realism, and contends that Howells's death in 1920 may
have been one cause for Cather's shift in literary style. See
Dissertation Abstracts International 27 (1966):218A.

1966

1   CHARLES, Sister PETER DAMIAN. "Death Comes for the Arch-
    bishop: A Novel of Love and Death." New Mexico Quarterly 36
    (Winter 1966–67):389–403.
        Jean Latour's intellectuality makes him vulnerable to the
    spirit of Thanatos, but it also helps him to accept the life (or
    love) and death conflict that troubles human experience by show-
    ing him the consumation of that conflict in the example of Jesus
    Christ. The basic conflict between Eros and Thanatos is por-
    trayed in the two priests, Vaillant and Latour, but it is left to
    Latour, who perceives its significance, to reconcile the apparent
    split through the fusing powers of Agape.

2   EARNEST, ERNEST. "The American Ariel." South Atlantic
    Quarterly 65 (Spring):192–200 passim.
        Discusses two of Cather's works, The Song of the Lark and
    "The Sculptor's Funeral," as examples of the American Ariel
    archetype as it appears in American fiction between 1915 and
    1930. Characteristically, this figure is an artist who lacks a
    capacity for lasting human affection and who longs for freedom.
    Thea Kronborg and Harvey Merrick, like many of their literary
    contemporaries, revolt against conventional hometown attitudes
    and mores, and seem uncompassionate toward their fellow humans.
    Significantly, Cather appears to accept Thea's values. Earnest
    treats this theme again in 1970.7.

3   EDEL, LEON. The Age of the Archive. Monday Evening Papers,
    no. 7. Middletown, Conn.: Wesleyan University, Center for
    Advanced Studies, pp. 17–18.
        In discussing the task of the biographer and the problem of
    the reliability of eyewitnesses, refers to Dorothy Canfield
    Fisher's recollections of Cather's Pittsburgh experience. Fisher
    painted a very rosy picture of Cather in Pittsburgh, but came to
    see, upon encountering other evidence, that her view could not be
    regarded as the full picture.

4   EDEL, LEON, and GEISMAR, MAXWELL. "Willa Cather." In
    Invitation to Learning: English and American Novels. Edited
    by George D. Crothers. New York: Basic Books, pp. 282–89.
        Based on interviews by Lyman Bryson on CBS Radio Network
    between 1950 and 1964. Mainly discusses The Professor's House as
    a revelation of Cather's distress over postwar America, her in-
    security over repeated losses of place, and her turn to the past
    and the rock in an effort to find stability.

5   FOLSOM, JAMES K. The American Western Novel. New Haven:
    College & University Press, pp. 189-93.
        The typical granger novel and western novel are pessimistic;
    but even though Cather is essentially a granger novelist, her
    world is a hopeful one, full of faith and optimism for the future.
    The faith projected in novels like Death Comes for the Archbishop
    and My Ántonia is based on belief in a benevolent historic
    process that will ultimately triumph over present ills.

6   FOX, [CLYDE] MAYNARD. "Two Primitives: Huck Finn and Tom
    Outland." Western American Literature 1 (Spring):26-33.
        Tom Outland and Huck Finn are alike in that they find their
    true selves, and something akin to the divine, in nature, in the
    freedom they experience away from the strictures of civilized
    society. Tom's story, set in the center of The Professor's
    House, serves as a precedent for St. Peter's finding his own
    primitive boy self. This is its important link to the rest of
    the novel.

7   GIANNONE, RICHARD [JOHN]. "The Southwest's Eternal Echo:
    Music in Death Comes for the Archbishop." Arizona Quarterly
    22 (Spring):5-18.
        Discusses the importance of music, in its broad sense, in
    Death Comes for the Archbishop. It is Father Latour who can per-
    ceive spiritual harmony in the Southwest, in spite of its diverse
    geography, and Father Vaillant for whom harmony is perceived in
    human terms. The Indian culture is in part defined by the bass
    human chant, the Mexican culture by the banjo. Adapted: 1968.18.

8   H., F. "Willa Cather Talks of Work." In The Kingdom of Art.
    See Slote, 1966.15, pp. 446-49.
        Reprint of 1913.4.

9   HARPER, MARION. "The West of Twain and Cather." Diliman
    Review 14 (January):60-80.
        Contrasts Cather's female-dominated West with Twain's male-
    dominated West, maintaining that Twain's West is characterized by
    transitoriness while Cather's is characterized by roots in the
    past, both European and American. Also considers the nature of
    the West as both Cather and Twain portray it--noting particularly
    its commitment to hospitality and its diversity of people.

10 HOCKETT, ETHEL M. "The Vision of a Successful Fiction
    Writer." In The Kingdom of Art. See Slote, 1966.15,
    pp. 450-52.
        Reprinted from 1915.11.

11 JONES, HOWARD MUMFORD. Jeffersonianism and the American
    Novel. New York: Columbia University, Teachers College
    Press, pp. 51-53.
        Groups Cather with Edith Wharton and Ellen Glasgow as
    writers of "aristocratic temperament and refined sensibility"
    whose work serves as a transition between the era of naturalism
    and local color and the fictional revolution that occurred in the

1920s. All three women became disenchanted with their materialistic societies and turned to the past. The dark side of their
work, however, attests that they found that it, too, was flawed.
Like Wharton, and Glasgow, Cather has gone out of fashion because
the assumptions about what constitutes American fiction have
changed drastically.

12   LEE, ROBERT EDSON. "The Westerners: Willa Cather." In From
      West to East: Studies in the Literature of the American West.
      Urbana: University of Illinois Press, pp. 112-35.
         Argues that Cather made a critical move when she became a
part of the McClung household. From that point on, her values
changed, her point of view became increasingly eastern. And even
when she turned again to the West for her subject matter, she no
longer treated those materials realistically as she had in her
earliest stories. Instead, she romanticized them and transformed
them into beautiful idylls of the West. She had voluntarily become an outsider, and that is what is wrong with her writing
after 1901. 0 Pioneers! is a case in point.

13   RABKIN, LESLIE Y., ed. Psychopathology and Literature. San
      Francisco: Chandler Publishing Co., pp. 7-8, 230.
         Reprints "Paul's Case" as an illustration of schizoid dis-
order, discussing it briefly as a story that could be used to set
up a case study for character analysis.

14   RANDALL, JOHN H., III. "Willa Cather and the Decline of
      Greatness." In The Twenties: Poetry and Prose. Edited by
      Richard E. Langford and William E. Taylor. Deland, Fla.:
      E. Edward Press, pp. 78-81.
         In her writings of the 1920s, Cather charts the decline of
greatness in the contemporary world, and hence her own alienation
from a world turned largely commercial. The pessimism of One of
Ours, A Lost Lady, and The Professor's House, plus Cather's turn
away from the present in Death Comes for the Archbishop, illustrate her conviction that a brutal, uncomprehending world is
bound to destroy the fine and the beautiful.

15   SLOTE, BERNICE, ed. Introduction and commentary for The
      Kingdom of Art: Willa Cather's First Principles and Critical
      Statements 1893-1896. Lincoln: University of Nebraska Press,
      503 pp.
         Reprints a large collection of Cather's early newspaper
writings that deal with art and provides commentary on individual
pieces. Introductory essays describe Lincoln, Nebraska, at the
time Cather attended the university there and detail her connections with the Nebraska State Journal and the Lincoln Courier.
Cather's early journalistic writings show "a constant concern
with literature and its craft" and "may be the most valuable of
all her critical writing." They reveal her to have been "primarily a romantic and a primitive." From those pieces of the
mid-nineties emerge certain governing principles: "life (or the
life force), degree, the ideal, and duality." There are also
three unifying principles that connect these writings with her

later work: "<u>continuity</u>" ("Willa Cather's first convictions and
principles of art were unchanged through the years, down to the
fundamental religious metaphor of art"); "<u>absorption</u>" (the early
work is absorbed into the later, and certain historical cycles
and myths are absorbed into the fiction); and "<u>memory</u>" (personal
and racial memory are blended together). Appendixes include
Cather's 1891 student essays, a heretofore uncollected short
story, a source for Cather's Troll Garden allusion, and some
early interviews with Cather. There are also a bibliographical
essay and a checklist of Cather's writings between 1891 and 1896.
Reprinted in part: 1981.44. Also contains a reprint of 1913.4,
and a partial reprint of 1915.11.

16 _____. "Willa Cather and Walt Whitman." <u>Walt Whitman Review</u>
   12 (March):3–5.
   Introduces a reprint of Cather's early essay on Whitman,
suggesting that it shows Cather working through the dual pulls
she felt, the mental one toward order, the emotional one toward
life's joy.

17 STEVENS, HOLLY, ed. Letter by Wallace Stevens to Leonard C.
   van Geyzel. In <u>Letters of Wallace Stevens</u>. New York:
   Alfred A. Knopf, p. 381.
   Recommends Cather as the best America has. Her quality is
easily missed because she works so hard to hide her sophistica-
tion.

18 STEWART, DAVID H. "Cather's Mortal Comedy." <u>Queen's</u>
   <u>Quarterly</u> 73 (Summer):244–59.
   Points to Cather's skill in combining the contradictory
styles of artists Puvis de Chavannes and Holbein in <u>Death Comes</u>
<u>for the Archbishop</u>, and then argues that she may have consciously
or unconsciously used the design and content of Dante's <u>Divine</u>
<u>Comedy</u> as a model for the book. The prominence of Mary, who
functions as a Beatrice for Fathers Vaillant and Latour, lends
credence to this reading.

19 STUCKEY, W[ILLIAM] J. <u>The Pulitzer Prize Novels: A Critical</u>
   <u>Backward Look</u>. Norman: University of Oklahoma Press, pp. 32,
   43–45.
   Claims that <u>My Ántonia</u> was far superior to the novel
awarded a Pulitzer prize in 1919, suggesting that it probably was
not even considered because it was too far outside the typical
Pulitzer pattern. Summarizes <u>One of Ours</u>, which did win the
prize later, and reports some diverse critical views of it, contending that it fails because Cather does not make her hero convincing and because her materials point in different directions
than she takes them.

20 TRESSIN, DEANNA. "Toward Understanding." <u>English Journal</u> 55
   (December):1170–74.
   Tells of using "Paul's Case" as a tool for beginning a unit
on understanding in her twelfth grade honors class. Paul does
not have the understanding of the people in his middle-class
environment, and it is important to realize that at some point

he moves from being simply a boy antagonistic toward his sur-
roundings to a boy who would commit suicide rather than return
to them.

21　WALKER, DON D. "The Western Humanism of Willa Cather."
　　Western American Literature 1 (Summer):75-90.
　　　　Although Cather has some kinship with the literary naturalists, and although she celebrates the primitive landscape, her
most typical stance emphasizes human beings in relation with the
landscape and with each other. It is the humanized West that
most engages her imagination.

22　WOLTEMATH, GLENDA. "Daughter of the Prairies." Electric
　　Farmer 20 (October):12-14.
　　　　Reprint of 1966.23.

23　　　　. "Daughter of the Prairies." Nebraskaland 44 (July):
　　44-45, 54-56, 58.
　　　　Throughout her life Cather drew memories and energy from
her Nebraska experiences and used them in her work. Reprinted:
1966.22.

24　WRIGHT, ROBERT C. "Hardy's Heath and Cather's Prairie as
　　Naturalistic Symbols." Mankato State College Studies 1 (May):
　　55-68.
　　　　Contends that in their treatment of heath and prairie both
Thomas Hardy and Cather exhibit a naturalistic view of the world.
Compares passages, characters, and situations in O Pioneers! and
The Return of the Native to demonstrate their similarity. Nature
as symbolically represented in these works has characteristics
that typify those prevalent in the work of literary naturalists.
The characteristics identified and compared are "(1) harsh
beauty, (2) permanence, (3) indifference, (4) paganism."

25　YASUHARA, SACHIKO. "Some Notes on Willa Cather's Works."
　　Collected Essays of Kyoritsu Women's Junior College, no. 10
　　(December):9-23.
　　　　Three-part essay, the first of which discusses the land in
O Pioneers! The second part of the essay describes My Ántonia as
a pastoral novel with no structural plot or central theme, a work
that achieves the "verbal mood" Cather describes in Not Under
Forty. The final section of the essay contrasts Cather's frontier novels with the work of Hamlin Garland, finding Cather's
outlook to be more bright and hopeful than Garland's, for it
shows fruitfulness following the struggle.

1967

1　BLOOM, EDWARD A., and BLOOM, LILLIAN D. "On the Composition
　　of a Novel." In Willa Cather and Her Critics. See Schroeter,
　　1967.49, pp. 323-55.
　　　　Reprinted from 1962.2.

2   BOGAN, LOUISE. "American-Classic." In Willa Cather and Her
    Critics. See Schroeter, 1967.49, pp. 126–33.
      Reprint of 1931.5.

3   BROWN, E[DWARD] K[ILLORAN]. "Willa Cather." In Willa Cather
    and Her Critics. See Schroeter, 1967.49, pp. 72–86.
      Reprint of 1946.1.

4   CAPOTE, TRUMAN. "Go Right Ahead and Ask Me Anything (and so
    she did)." McCall's 95 (November):76-77, 148-52, 154.
      Interview with Gloria Steinem. Capote tells Steinem of his
first meeting with Cather when he was eighteen, near the New York
Society Library in 1942 where he saw her occasionally. He was
impressed with her appearance and her conversational abilities,
and grateful for the friendship that sprang up between them.
Without knowing who she was, he praised her work and thus won her
interest. Capote tells essentially the same story in 1981.8.

5   CHARLES, Sister PETER DAMIAN. "My Ántonia: A Dark Dimension."
    Western American Literature 2 (Summer):91-108.
      Explores the spiritual kinship between Jim Burden and Mr.
Shimerda, asserting that it creates a dark dimension, a thanatos
element, in the narrative against which the brilliance of
Ántonia's eros nature is played. Jim is attracted to sunset
images, and his bond with Mr. Shimerda reinforces his mindset
toward death. In fact, Jim's unity with Ántonia comes largely
through the memory of her father. Even in book 3 where he is
absent, Mr. Shimerda is present in spirit because he would
applaud Jim's efforts at learning.

6   COMMAGER, HENRY STEELE. "Willa Cather." In Willa Cather and
    Her Critics. See Schroeter, 1967.49, pp. 209–15.
      Reprint of 1950.9.

7   COOPERMAN, STANLEY. "The War Lover: Claude." In World
    War I and the American Novel. See Cooperman, 1967.8,
    pp. 129–37.
      Reprint of 1963.4. Reprinted: 1984.19.

8   _____ . World War I and the American Novel. Baltimore:
    Johns Hopkins Press, pp. 29-33, 51-53.
      Contains commentary in addition to the reprinted essay
cited in 1967.7. Argues that although the midwestern sections of
One of Ours are effective, once the novel moves beyond a subject
Cather knows well it becomes laden with war rhetoric. Like other
sentimental fiction about World War I, it naively idealizes the
American boys in the fray and makes the action resemble a motion
picture production. The war-drive is shown in One of Ours to be
the means for young men to escape from a mundane existence and
become part of a larger destiny.

9   DAICHES, DAVID. "The Short Stories." In Willa Cather and Her
     Critics. See Schroeter, 1967.49, pp. 87–95.
          Reprinted from 1951.5.

10   DAUGHADAY, CHARLES H. "Willa Cather's 'Happy Experimenting':
     Artistic Fusion of Theme and Structure in the Novels of Willa
     Cather." Ph.D. dissertation, University of Kentucky, 303 pp.
          Maintains that stylistic devices remain relatively constant
     throughout the novels and that Cather's major recurring theme is
     "the individual's struggle for self-realization." See Disserta-
     tion Abstracts International 30 (1969):2017–18A.

11   DITSKY, JOHN MICHAEL. "Land-Nostalgia in the Novels of
     Faulkner, Cather, and Steinbeck." Ph.D. dissertation, New
     York University, 454 pp.
          Evaluates the dominating presence of land for three Ameri-
     can novelists, arguing that the land is a shaper of values in
     Cather's work. See Dissertation Abstracts International 28
     (1967):1072A.

12   EDEL, LEON. "Willa Cather: The Paradox of Success." In
     Willa Cather and Her Critics. See Schroeter, 1967.49,
     pp. 249–71.
          Reprint of 1960.4.

13   GEISMAR, MAXWELL. "Willa Cather: Lady in the Wilderness."
     In Willa Cather and Her Critics. See Schroeter, 1967.49,
     pp. 171–202.
          Reprint of 1947.17.

14   HARPER, HOWARD. "First Evidences of Willa Cather." Review
     of The Kingdom of Art and Early Stories of Willa Cather.
     Washington Sunday Star, 16 April, sec. a, p. 19.
          Observes that Cather has a secure place as a novelist of
     the rank just below America's top half dozen. Finds her news-
     paper columns reprinted in The Kingdom of Art to be important
     as revelations of the developing artist. Cather's criticism,
     "which rhapsodizes and moralizes" in Gilded Age fashion, shows
     the ambition and enthusiasm of a youthful writer with a breadth,
     though not a depth, of training and interests. The pieces in
     Early Stories of Willa Cather are interesting only as the be-
     ginning work of a gifted writer.

15   HASS, VICTOR P. "From a Bookman's Notebook." Omaha Sunday
     World-Herald Magazine, 3 March.
          Review of The Kingdom of Art finds the collection of some
     of Cather's early journalistic writings a notable achievement.
     Even as a student, Cather was an "amazingly good" writer.

16   HICKS, GRANVILLE. "The Case Against Willa Cather." In Willa
     Cather and Her Critics. See Schroeter, 1967.49, pp. 139–47.
          Reprint of 1933.7.

17   "H.L. Mencken's Short Story Selection." <u>Menckenian</u>, no. 21
     (Spring):1.
          Lists "Paul's Case" among the stories that Mencken intended
     to include in a collection of American short stories scheduled
     for release in 1923 through a German publisher. Postwar infla-
     tion thwarted the project.

18   ISHII, MOMOKO, ed. <u>Willa Cather</u>. 20th Century American-
     English Literature, no. 12. Edited by Rintaro Fukuhara and
     Masami Nishikawa. Tokyo: Kenkyusha, 210 pp.
          In Japanese. A collection of essays by several different
     writers and an overall evaluation by Hiroko Sato. There are
     essays on Cather's life and career, on Cather criticism, on some
     short stories, and on the following novels: <u>O Pioneers!</u>, <u>My</u>
     <u>Ántonia</u>, <u>A Lost Lady</u>, <u>The Professor's House</u>, <u>Death Comes for the</u>
     <u>Archbishop</u>, and <u>Shadows on the Rock</u>. A copy of this book, un-
     translated, is housed in the Faulkner-Slote collection at the
     University of Nebraska library, Lincoln.

19   JACKS, L[EO] V[INCENT]. "Nebraska" subsection of "The Writer
     in the Midwest." In a special supplement titled "Mid-America."
     Edited by Rex Burns. <u>Per/Se</u> 2 (Fall):58-59.
          Calls Cather the leading writer to have come out of and
     written about Nebraska. All the rest, in some sense, follow in
     her footsteps. She was well-grounded in the classics, and was
     rooted in the frontier. She has contributed significantly to the
     cause of education in Nebraska.

20   JOBES, LAVON MATTES. "Willa Cather's Last Novel." <u>University</u>
     <u>Review</u> (Kansas City) 34 (Autumn):77-80.
          Largely plot summary, but argues that <u>Sapphira and the</u>
     <u>Slave Girl</u> is a "masterpiece" of "historical perception."
     Sapphira is mistaken about Nancy and Henry, but her suspicions
     are well justified by custom. She, not Rachel, is the novel's
     central figure, and the novel as a whole is peaceful and serene.
     Its mood is acceptance.

21   _____. "Willa Cather's <u>The Professor's House</u>." <u>University</u>
     <u>Review</u> (Kansas City) 34 (Winter):154-60.
          Plot summary in the main, but addresses the thesis that
     the world of Hamilton portrayed in <u>The Professor's House</u> is
     wholly dead. Tom's mesa contrasts with the modern world, and
     the professor's sewing forms foreshadow the growing hardness and
     inhumanness of his wife and daughters. The professor is probably
     one of modern literature's most patient men.

22   JONES, HOWARD MUMFORD. "Excerpt from <u>The Bright Medusa</u>." In
     <u>Willa Cather and Her Critics</u>. See Schroeter, 1967.49,
     pp. 235-48.
          Reprinted from 1952.8.

23 KAROLIDES, NICHOLAS J. The Pioneer in the American Novel
      1900-1950. Norman: University of Oklahoma Press, pp. 113-14.
          Revision of 1963.12. Regards Cather as a pioneer writer
    of the highest rank. Unlike the standard pioneer novels of the
    time, Cather's books treat love realistically and avoid senti-
    mentality.

24 KAZIN, ALFRED. "Willa Cather." In Willa Cather and Her
      Critics. See Schroeter, 1967.49, pp. 161-70.
          Reprinted from 1942.5.

25 KRUTCH, JOSEPH WOOD. "The Lady as Artist." In Willa Cather
      and Her Critics. See Schroeter, 1967.49, pp. 52-54.
          Review of A Lost Lady. Reprint of 1923.28.

26 _____. "The Modest Method of Willa Cather." In Willa Cather
      and Her Critics. See Schroeter, 1967.49, pp. 57-59.
          Review of My Mortal Enemy. Reprint of 1926.14.

27 _____. "The Pathos of Distance." In Willa Cather and Her
      Critics. See Schroeter, 1967.49, pp. 59-61.
          Review of Death Comes for the Archbishop. Reprint of
    1927.19.

28 _____. "Second Best." In Willa Cather and Her Critics. See
      Schroeter, 1967.49, pp. 54-56.
          Review of The Professor's House. Reprint of 1925.22.

29 LEWIS, SINCLAIR. "A Hamlet of the Plains." In Willa Cather
      and Her Critics. See Schroeter, 1967.49, pp. 30-34.
          Reprint of 1922.17.

*30 MANE, ROBERT. "Willa Cather, romancière du Nebraska."
      Informations et documents, no. 253 (1 December):26-27.
          Listed in current bibliography section of American Litera-
    ture 40 (November 1968).

31 MENCKEN, H.L. "Modern American Short Stories." Menckenian,
      no. 22 (Summer):3.
          Prints the biographical sketch of Cather that Mencken in-
    tended should accompany a German anthology of the best American
    short stories (see 1967.17). Also lists Cather's published books
    through One of Ours, singling out My Ántonia for special praise.

32 _____. Review of My Ántonia. In Willa Cather and Her
      Critics. See Schroeter, 1967.49, pp. 8-9.
          Reprinted from 1919.4.

33 _____. Review of One of Ours. In Willa Cather and Her
      Critics. See Schroeter, 1967.49, pp. 10-12.
          Reprint of 1922.22.

34   _____. Review of The Song of the Lark. In Willa Cather and
        Her Critics. See Schroeter, 1967.49, pp. 7–8.
            Reprint of 1916.2.

35   _____. Review of Youth and the Bright Medusa. In Willa
        Cather and Her Critics. See Schroeter, 1967.49, pp. 9–10.
            Reprint of 1920.7.

36   MILLER, JAMES E., Jr. "My Ántonia: A Frontier Drama of
        Time." In Quests Surd and Absurd: Essays in American Litera-
        ture. Chicago: University of Chicago Press, pp. 66–75.
            Reprint of 1958.11.

37   _____. "The Nebraska Encounter: Willa Cather and Wright
        Morris." Prairie Schooner 41 (Summer):165–67.
            Between them Cather and Morris span the twentieth-century
        experience, providing a continuity from frontier to urban life.
        Both novelists deal with terror in the two Nebraska worlds they
        represent. The difference is that in Morris the violence and
        terror are man-made while in Cather they arise from human con-
        frontation with the elements.

38   _____. "Wharton and Cather: The Quest for Culture." In
        Quests Surd and Absurd. See Miller, 1967.36, pp. 76–92.
            Holds that the presumed "gap" in American literature be-
        tween 1900 and the end of World War I is not really a gap at all
        and could be called "the age of Wharton and Cather." Their
        landscapes and methods are different--Cather is poetic, Wharton
        is satiric--but together they exemplify the most basic character
        of American literature, the tension between east and west,
        civilization and frontier. Wharton is eastern in outlook, Cather
        western; Wharton is basically negative, Cather affirmative.
        Cather's most important books, O Pioneers!, My Ántonia, A Lost
        Lady, and The Professor's House, all depict superior individuals
        in conflict with their environments. Cather's closest spiritual
        literary kin is James Fenimore Cooper.

39   MOORHEAD [VERMORCKEN], ELIZABETH. "The Novelist." In Willa
        Cather and Her Critics. See Schroeter, 1967.49, pp. 101–13.
            Reprinted from 1950.20.

40   MURPHY, JOHN J. "Nebraska Romantic." New York Times Book
        Review, 19 November, pp. 12, 14, 16.
            Review of The Kingdom of Art. Finds in Cather's early
        critiques a devastating honesty as well as traces of the creative
        style that would distinguish her novels.

41   Nebraska Women Through the Years: 1867–1967. Prepared under
        the direction of the Governor's Commission on the Status of
        Women. Lincoln: Johnsen Publishing Co., pp. 42–43.
            Offers an account of Cather's Nebraska years and details
        some of her awards and accomplishments, noting her love for
        the classics and her accurate interpretation of the Red Cloud
        community.

42   PETERSON, GLENDA. "Catherland Tour: Stroll into Past with
     World-Famous Author." Nebraskaland 45 (August):35-37, 50.
         Describes Red Cloud and the inception and activities of the
     Willa Cather Pioneer Memorial and Educational Foundation. Points
     to places in Red Cloud and the surrounding countryside that are
     pertinent to Cather's work, declaring that her experiences there
     had a lasting effect on her.

43   QUINNETT, LOIS. "Willa Took 'Roads to Freedom.'" In Nebraska
     Centennial History. Depth Report no. 5 (March). Lincoln:
     University of Nebraska, School of Journalism, and Outstate
     Publishers Assoc., pp. 30-33.
         Details some of Cather's activities and experiences in
     Nebraska, insisting that Nebraska was Cather's "passion," the
     wellspring of her inspiration for numerous characters and events
     in her fiction.

44   RANDALL, JOHN H., III. "Interpretation of My Ántonia." In
     Willa Cather and Her Critics. See Schroeter, 1967.49,
     pp. 272-322.
         Reprinted from 1960.9.

45   SAVERY, GILBERT. "Willa Cather's 'Missing Years' Now Filled
     in." Lincoln Sunday Journal and Star, 26 March, sec. f,
     p. 11.
         Review of The Kingdom of Art. The early journalistic/
     critical writings of Cather reveal that she had written bril-
     liantly as a young reviewer and was already conscious that art
     demanded much discipline.

46   SCHLOSS, GEORGE. "A Writer's Art." In Willa Cather and Her
     Critics. See Schroeter, 1967.49, pp. 203-8.
         Reprint of 1950.23.

47   SCHNEIDER, Sister LUCY. "Willa Cather's Early Stories in the
     Light of Her 'Land-Philosophy.'" Midwest Quarterly 9
     (Autumn):75-94.
         Examines seven early Cather short stories and their rela-
     tionship to the "land philosophy" that emerges in her later fic-
     tion. When viewed collectively, the stories present—albeit in
     fragmented form—the ambiguities of thought and sentiment toward
     the role of the land in human life that would one day become a
     hallmark of Cather's work. Even in the darkest stories, however,
     there is the suggestion of the land as an enduring value, a view
     that would lie at the heart of most of Cather's writing.

48   _____. "Willa Cather's 'Land-Philosophy' in Her Novels and
     Short Stories." Ph.D. dissertation, University of Notre Dame,
     269 pp.
         Shows how land/rock formations on various cultural levels
     become symbolic of the human condition in Cather's work. See
     Dissertation Abstracts International 28 (1968):3683A-84A.

49   SCHROETER, JAMES, ed. Willa Cather and Her Critics. Ithaca,
     N.Y.: Cornell University Press, 405 pp.
        Provides a short introduction to a group of critical essays
     and reviews on Cather and to each of the sections into which the
     criticism and reviews are divided. The collection begins with
     what Schroeter calls "coming-of-age" criticism and advances
     through the various critical postures that have dominated Cather
     commentary through the decades. The collection ends with a
     bibliographical note. The following items are reprinted or
     partially reprinted in this volume: 1916.2; 1919.4; 1920.7;
     1922.17, 22, 34; 1923.28; 1925.22; 1926.14; 1927.19; 1928.19–20;
     1931.5; 1933.7; 1937.16; 1942.5; 1946.1; 1947.17; 1950.9, 20,
     23; 1951.5; 1952.8, 20; 1953.20; 1957.24; 1960.4, 9; 1962.2, 18;
     1965.31.

50   SCHROETER, JAMES. "Willa Cather and The Professor's House."
     In Willa Cather and Her Critics. See Schroeter, 1967.49,
     pp. 363–81.
        Reprint of 1965.31.

51   SEIBEL, GEORGE. "Willa Cather and the Village Atheist."
     Prairie Schooner 41 (Summer):168–71.
        Relates an anecdote about Cather's hearing the lecture of
     a certain Professor Seymour who was converted to whatever program
     or belief was the most lucrative for him. His listeners, Cather
     said, reminded her of "the traditional village atheist." This
     previously unpublished piece was given to Prairie Schooner by
     Seibel's widow.

52   SERGEANT, ELIZABETH. "Excerpts from Willa Cather: A Memoir."
     In Willa Cather and Her Critics. See Schroeter, 1967.49,
     pp. 114–25.
        Reprinted from 1953.20.

53   SHAW, JOHN MACKAY. Childhood in Poetry. Vol. 1. Detroit:
     Gale Research Co., p. 456.
        Basically an annotated catalog of poetry books containing
     poems about childhood. Indicates that Cather is best known for
     her fiction, the more lucrative field that "won her over and
     dulled the edge of her poetry." Lists April Twilights and Other
     Poems, and quotes "typical passages" from several of the poems.

54   SLOTE, BERNICE. "Willa Cather and Her First Book." In Willa
     Cather and Her Critics. See Schroeter, 1967.49, pp. 356–62.
        Reprinted from 1962.18.

55   SUTHERLAND, RAYMOND CARTER. "The Kentucky Girl in Two Liter-
     ary Classics." Register of the Kentucky Historical Society
     45 (April):134–43.
        Doña Isabella in Death Comes for the Archbishop is the
     stereotypical Kentucky girl, the northern-southern belle who
     charmingly exaggerates both her accent and her femininity.
     Nevertheless, the book as a whole has a depth that other books
     portraying such stereotypes often lack.

56 TRILLING, LIONEL. "Willa Cather." In <u>Willa Cather and Her</u>
<u>Critics</u>. See Schroeter, 1967.49, pp. 148–55.
Reprint of 1937.16.

57 UMLAND, RUDOLPH. Review of <u>The Kingdom of Art</u>. <u>Nebraska</u>
<u>History</u> 48 (Summer):193–95.
Judges from the quality of Cather's youthful writing collected in <u>The Kingdom of Art</u> that she knew a great deal about
art. The development of her credo is traced in the pieces collected here. In them she also shows great skill with language
and impressive critical acumen in assessing the performing arts.

58 Van DOREN, CARL. "Willa Cather." In <u>Willa Cather and Her</u>
<u>Critics</u>. See Schroeter, 1967.49, pp. 13–19.
Reprint of 1922.34.

59 WEST, REBECCA. "The Classic Artist." In <u>Willa Cather and Her</u>
<u>Critics</u>. See Schroeter, 1967.49, pp. 62–71.
Reprint of 1928.19.

60 WHIPPLE, T[HOMAS] K[ING]. "Willa Cather." In <u>Willa Cather</u>
<u>and Her Critics</u>. See Schroeter, 1967.49, pp. 35–51.
Reprint of 1928.20.

61 "Willa Cather, 'The Meatax Girl.'" <u>Horizon</u> 9 (Spring):116–19.
Reprints excerpts from some of Cather's early critical
columns in the <u>Nebraska State Journal</u> later published in <u>The</u>
<u>Kingdom of Art</u>. Introduction to the excerpts comments on
Cather's "devastating wit" in criticism that reads better than
a lot of novels. Cather unflinchingly took on anyone, often with
"delicious sarcasm."

62 WILSON, EDMUND. "Two Novels of Willa Cather." In <u>Willa</u>
<u>Cather and Her Critics</u>. See Schroeter, 1967.49, pp. 25–29.
Review of <u>One of Ours</u> and <u>A Lost Lady</u>. Reprint of 1952.20,
which combines 1922.36; 1924.16.

63 ZABEL, MORTON D[AUWEN]. "Willa Cather: The Tone of Time."
In <u>Willa Cather and Her Critics</u>. See Schroeter, 1967.49,
pp. 216–27.
Reprint of 1957.24.

64 ZEIGEL, JOHN STOUFER. "The Romanticism of Willa Cather."
Ph.D. dissertation, Claremont Graduate School and University
Center, 313 pp.
Labels Cather's agrarianism and elevation of the past as
"romantic excursions" from which characters must return and en-
gage the recognizable reality of the present. See <u>Dissertation</u>
<u>Abstracts International</u> 29 (1968):280A–81A.

1   ARNOLD, MARILYN. "Self-Division and Self-Unity in the Novels
      of Willa Cather." Ph.D. dissertation, University of Wiscon-
      sin, 318 pp.
         Discusses Cather's treatment of the divided self as a major
motif in most of her novels. A character is divided primarily
because his or her desires for self-fulfillment are thwarted,
usually through family and community. Integration may be
achieved through artistry, the discovery of an ideal, or an
expansive vision which enables the character to absorb the
dualities of life.

2   BAKER, BRUCE PAUL. "Image and Symbol in Selected Works of
      Willa Cather." Ph.D. dissertation, Texas Christian Univer-
      sity, 318 pp.
         Finds image and symbol not only basic to Cather's artistic
theory, but central to an interpretation of her works. See
Dissertation Abstracts International 29 (1969):3604A.

3   _____. "Nebraska Regionalism in Selected Works of Willa
      Cather." Western American Literature 3 (Spring):19-35.
         Examines Cather's changing and developing attitude toward
Nebraska as revealed in some of her earlier stories and novels.
In the earliest stories the land is seen as something that
destroys, but then Cather becomes ambivalent as she begins to
see the land also as something that nourishes. Her treatment of
a region thus takes on universal characteristics as she projects
through her work a system of enduring values.

4   BAKER, IRVING. "Willa's 'Easter Rabbit' a Welcome Lenten
      Visitor." Omaha Sunday World-Herald, 7 April.
         Reprints a Cather poem titled "The Easter Rabbit," dedi-
cated "on the Ides of March, 1896," to her younger sister Elsie.
The poem was first published, after its discovery among Cather
family papers, in the spring 1968 issue of the Willa Cather
Pioneer Memorial Newsletter. Baker praises the poem for its
fresh hopefulness and simplicity.

5   BENNETT, MILDRED R. Introduction to reprint of "The Incom-
      parable Opera House." Nebraska History 49 (Winter):373-78.
         Offers some background material on the Red Cloud Opera
House to accompany the reprinting of a 1929 Cather letter to
Harvey Newbranch, editor of the Omaha World-Herald. The letter
is about her fond recollections of the opera houses that graced
Red Cloud and other Nebraska towns. The original letter was
published in the Omaha Sunday World-Herald Magazine, 27 October
1929, p. 9, and reprinted in the Red Cloud Commercial Advertiser,
28 October 1929.

6   _____. "Two Cather Collections." <u>Prairie Schooner</u> 42
     (Summer):178-81.
         Maintains that the early Cather essays collected by Bernice
     Slote in <u>The Kingdom of Art</u> (1966.15) are valuable in revealing
     "the formation of an artist." Further, they show the young
     journalist to be "fearless," "impulsive," and inconsistent in her
     loves and hates. They also chart her attempt to close the rift
     between art and the world, between the artist and the person.
     The other "collection" being evaluated is the group of critical
     essays compiled by James Schroeter, 1967.49.

7   BUSH, SARGENT, Jr. "'The Best Years': Willa Cather's Last
     Story and Its Relation to Her Canon." <u>Studies in Short Fic-</u>
     <u>tion</u> 5 (Spring):269-74.
         Cather's chief accomplishment in this story is to affirm
     the value of youth, insisting at the same time that we must be
     reconciled to its loss. Lesley Ferguesson, a beloved sister and
     daughter in the first six sections of the story, takes on sym-
     bolic significance in the end as she comes to stand for the loss
     of youth.

8   BYRNE, KATHLEEN DERRIGAN. "Willa Cather's Pittsburgh Years
     1896-1906." <u>Western Pennsylvania Historical Magazine</u> 51
     (January):1-15.
         An address to the Western Pennsylvania Historical Society,
     17 October, 1967. Describes Cather's activities and friendships
     during the years she lived and worked in Pittsburgh, noting the
     nature of the work she did for various journals and her acquain-
     tance with the cultural opportunities Pittsburgh offered.
     Cather's journalistic writings reveal her to be an individual
     of strong opinion who was attracted to persons of superior in-
     tellect. Cather's work is all of a piece, and the writing she
     did in Pittsburgh--the articles, stories, and poems--is an im-
     portant part of the whole design.

9   CARY, RICHARD. "A Willa Cather Collection." <u>Colby Library</u>
     <u>Quarterly</u> 8 (June):82-95.
         Provides a representative listing of the Cather holdings at
     Colby Library, including Cather letters, books, and attributions
     as well as books, articles, and dissertations about her.

10   CHARLES, Sister PETER DAMIAN. "<u>The Professor's House</u>: An
     Abode of Love and Death." <u>Colby Library Quarterly</u> 8 (June):
     70-82.
         Sees Godfrey St. Peter pulled between life's two great
     forces, love and death. After he has completed his histories and
     become estranged from Lillian, he suffers the death of love. Tom
     Outland experiences the same conflict St. Peter does, a love of
     the heart vs. one of the imagination. The novel ends affirma-
     tively as St. Peter, through desiring death, comes to a more
     profound understanding of life. He realizes that life is com-
     posed not of love <u>or</u> death, but of life <u>and</u> death.

11 CREUTZ, KATHLEEN E. "The Genesis of Willa Cather's The Song
    of the Lark." Ph.D. dissertation, University of California at
    Los Angeles, 324 pp.
        Attributes the failure of The Song of the Lark to Cather's
    inability to fully assimilate the operatic world, which she ex-
    perienced only vicariously. See Dissertation Abstracts Inter-
    national 29 (1969):3130A.

12 CURTIN, WILLIAM M[ARTIN]. "Willa Cather: Individualism and
    Style." Colby Library Quarterly 8 (June):37-55.
        Traces the development of Cather's attitudes toward indi-
    vidualism, beginning early in her career with her complete sympa-
    thy for the creative individualist at odds with society. Later
    she developed a sense of the interdependence of human beings,
    and finally came to a realization that death is universal yet
    brings an individual to a sense of his uniqueness. Thus, the
    deepest individual feelings, subjective as they are, must be in
    accord with universal objective human experience in art. This
    realization is the measure of Cather's growth as an artist. Her
    style is delusively simple; she works through symbol to translate
    her subjective feelings into objective human impulses.

13 DANIELSON, JEANNETTE CRAIN. "A 'Sense of a Sense' of Place in
    the Works of Willa Cather." Ph.D. dissertation, Bowling Green
    State University, 247 pp.
        Maintains that the search for place in Cather's work
    evolves from the personal and geographical to the universal,
    unlimited by time and space. See Dissertation Abstracts Inter-
    national 30 (1969):718A-19A.

14 EICHORN, HARRY BERNARD. "Willa Cather: Stranger in Three
    Worlds." Ph.D. dissertation, Stanford University, 200 pp.
        Examines Cather's use of the outsider's point of view in
    relation to the settings of Red Cloud, Nebraska, the city, and
    the Southwest. See Dissertation Abstracts International 29
    (1969):4002A.

15 ELLMANN, MARY. Thinking about Women. New York: Harcourt,
    Brace & World, pp. 87-88, 113-14, 191-92. Reprint. London:
    Macmillan, 1969.
        Expresses misgivings over Cather's finding such "pictur-
    esque charm" in the sight of people, especially women, performing
    heavy labor. Further, in Marian Forrester Cather creates the
    stereotype of woman-as-balloon who drifts when cut off from the
    steadying, controlling hand of a strong man. Women writers are
    sometimes more offensive than men in applying stereotypes to
    women. And sometimes what they present as a virtue doubles back
    as a strike against women. Some of Cather's women, for example,
    are admired most for the manlike qualities in them.

16   FLOWER, D.S. Review of The Kingdom of Art. Personalist 49
      (Spring):276-78.
           Regards the effort involved in the production of this vol-
      ume of Cather's early journalistic writings to be perhaps more
      than is merited for a short period in the life of a "secondary
      writer." It is surprising that "the romantic and often reckless"
      Cather revealed here could actually emerge with the ordered set
      of principles about her own art that she did.

17   GARLAND, HAMLIN. Hamlin Garland's Diaries. Edited by Donald
      Pizer. San Marino, Calif.: Huntington Library, p. 117.
           Garland writes briefly about being present when Cather re-
      ceived the Gold Medal of the American Academy for Death Comes for
      the Archbishop in 1930. He claims that she was so changed and
      ungraceful that he did not recognize her, but asserts that in
      that novel "she did a noble book."

18   GIANNONE, RICHARD [JOHN]. Music in Willa Cather's Fiction.
      Lincoln: University of Nebraska Press, 263 pp.
           Revision of 1964.9, but essentially the same approach and
      content. Adapted in part from 1964.8; 1965.10-14; 1966.7. Re-
      printed in part: 1984.37.

19   HELMICK, EVELYN THOMAS. "Myth in the Works of Willa Cather."
      Midcontinent American Studies Journal 9 (Fall):63-69.
           In O Pioneers! and My Ántonia Cather has created a modern
      Aeneid, blending elements of classical and American frontier
      myth. She saw the opening of the American frontier as a brief
      heroic age.

20   JOHNSON, EDWARD R. "Evil, Vision, and Artistic Purity: The
      Existential Implications of Willa Cather." Willa Cather
      Pioneer Memorial Newsletter 12 (Fall):1-2.
           Explores parallels of viewpoint and technique between the
      existential approach to literature and the approach taken by
      Cather.

21   KENNEDY, Sister PATRICIA. "The Pioneer Woman in Middle
      Western Fiction." Ph.D. dissertation, University of Illinois,
      244 pp.
           Makes a survey of twentieth-century novels about nineteenth-
      century frontier life and determines that the female protagonist
      is not stereotypical, but rather is a combination of the real
      and ideal. The successful pioneer woman exhibits courage and
      resourcefulness; those who lack strength return to the East.
      Particularly memorable are Ántonia Shimerda in My Ántonia and
      Alexandra Bergson in O Pioneers! See Dissertation Abstracts
      International 29 (1968):606A.

22   LAVENDAR, DAVID. "The Petrified West and the Writer."
      American Scholar 37 (Spring):293-306.
           Observes in Cather the traditional view of the frontier as
      an "untrammeled place" where human ideals can flourish anew. In
      O Pioneers! and My Ántonia, for example, pioneer daughters can

find in the soil the stability lost in the upheaval of immigration. The subsequent taming of spirit and its accompanying disillusionment are also present in Cather, notably in A Lost Lady.
Marian Forrester is lost because she no longer has focus for her
energies or imaginative dreams. Reprinted: 1974.35.

23 MAYFIELD, SARA. The Constant Circle: H.L. Mencken and his
    Friends. New York: Delacorte Press, pp. 70–72.
        Describes Cather's appearance and her association with
    Mencken over the years, including his waning interest in her and
    her work from A Lost Lady on.

24 MENCKEN, H.L. "Willa Cather: Her First Novel." In H.L.
    Mencken's Smart Set Criticism. Edited by William H. Nolte.
    Ithaca, N.Y.: Cornell University Press, pp. 263–64.
        Reprint of 1912.3.

25 ____. "Willa Cather vs. William Allen White." In H.L.
    Mencken's Smart Set Criticism. See Mencken, 1968.24,
    pp. 264–66.
        Reprint of 1919.4.

26 ____. "Youth and the Bright Medusa." In H.L. Mencken's
    Smart Set Criticism. See Mencken, 1968.24, pp. 266–67.
        Reprint of 1920.7.

27 MIRANDA, JULIO E. "Edgar Allan Poe o la existencia
    amenazada." Cuadernos Hispanoamericanos (Madrid) 76
    (December):775–80.
        Mentions Cather as one of the major American literary fig-
    ures who had an affinity to Poe in regard to "la fragilidad de
    la existencia" and "la existencia amenazada."

28 REAVER, J. RUSSELL. "Mythic Motivation in Willa Cather's
    O Pioneers!" Western Folklore 27 (January):19–25.
        Contends that certain fertility rites and myths, especially
    those of the corn god, help the reader better understand O
    Pioneers! Initially, Alexandra, though encouraging fruitfulness
    in the land, fights it in herself when the corn-god vision first
    comes to her. Later, however, as evidence that Alexandra has
    matured, she acquiesces to the corn-god of her vision and also
    agrees to marry Carl Linstrum.

29 SCHNEIDER, Sister LUCY. "Artistry and Intuition: Willa
    Cather's 'Land-Philosophy.'" South Dakota Review 6 (Winter
    1968–69):53–64.
        Discusses Cather's lifelong compelling relationships with
    the Nebraska plains of her youth and the New Mexico desert of her
    later years and their impact upon her artistic vision. Briefly
    treats five cardinal points of Cather's "land-philosophy," out-
    lining its development from the early stories through her mature
    works.

30 _____. "'Land' Relevance in 'Neighbour Rosicky.'" Kansas
Quarterly 1 (Winter):105-10.
In "Neighbour Rosicky" Cather takes her land-philosophy a
step farther than she had done in her previous novels, moving
from a representation of the rock as the expression of tran-
scendent human need to the incarnation in the land of that need
through human living. Human need is fulfilled through human love
and goodness.

31 _____. "O Pioneers! in the Light of Willa Cather's 'Land-
Philosophy.'" Colby Library Quarterly 8 (June):55-70.
Considers and evaluates each character's response to the
land in O Pioneers! All of the characters provide a backdrop
for Alexandra.

32 STEENSMA, ROBERT C. "The Land of Desert Sweet: The Homesteader and His Literature." Rendezvous 3 (Winter):29-38.
Claims that most literature by and about American home-
steaders is weak and dull, but that Cather and Ole Rölvaag wrote
eloquently about them, speaking from firsthand experience. In
catching the homesteader's brief moment of greatness, Cather
turned America's eyes to the Great Plains.

33 STEWART, RANDALL. "The Old Cost of Human Redemption." In
Regionalism and Beyond: Essays of Randall Stewart. Edited by
George Core. Nashville: Vanderbilt University Press, 201-2.
Reprinted from 1958.15.

34 WAGER, WILLIS. American Literature: A World View. New York:
New York University Press, pp. 227-28.
Includes Cather in a discussion of the "quasi-dramatic
realistic novel" that continued into the twentieth century, noting that Cather's plots were not imposed on her material, but
were made to emerge organically from it.

35 WHITTINGTON, CURTIS [CALVIN], Jr. "The 'Burden' of Narration:
Democratic Perspective and First-Person Point of View in the
American Novel." Southern Humanities Review 2 (Spring):
236-45.
Compares and contrasts the narrators of Cather's My
Ántonia and Robert Penn Warren's All the King's Men. In both
novels the narrator tends to become more prominent than the
character whose story he started out to tell. The chief difference is that what Jack Burden learns leads him to look optimis-
tically toward the future, and what Jim Burden learns leads him
to look pessimistically toward the past. But both learn that
their own essential identity lies in discovering a sense of
relationship with others.

36 WOODRESS, JAMES, comp. Dissertations in American Literature,
1891-1966. Durham, N.C.: Duke University Press, nos. 272-95.
Lists twenty-four doctoral dissertations, some of them
outside the United States, written (or begun) on Cather between
1944 and 1965.

37   YOSHIKAWA, TOSHIKO. "Willa Cather: An Attempt to Interpret
      Her Ideals and Disillusionment." Keisen Onna Gakuen Tank
      Daigaku, Eibun Ka. Engei Seikatsu Ka Kenkyū Kiyō [Junior
      college English department bulletin, separate edition], no. 3,
      pp. 37–62.
           Traces the course of Cather's writing career, observing
      that her early prairie novels portray vigorous, strong pioneers
      or artists winning out over debilitating materialistic forces
      working against them. Cather, however, eventually saw these
      forces triumphing, and her reactionary aversion toward modern
      ways and people had a restrictive effect on her art. A further
      limitation was her belief that human affection often stood in the
      way of achievement or led to tragedy. Her value system was an
      aesthetic one, but in spite of its narrowness the beauty of her
      work enriches the lives of her readers.

                                1969

1   ALLEN, WALTER. The Urgent West: The American Dream and
      Modern Man. New York: E.P. Dutton & Co., pp. 101–3, 201–2.
           Posits My Ántonia as an example of an American novel that
      treats the seriousness of the cultural loss experienced by immi-
      grants to the United States. My Ántonia is a pastoral that
      subtly criticizes contemporary American life, and A Lost Lady
      depicts the loss of the western Edenic paradise. In A Lost Lady
      Cather created a myth and showed her preference for an ideal past
      over the present. Discussion on A Lost Lady adapted from 1964.1.

2   BALLARD, DORIS. "Literary Tour for Students: A Visit to
      Catherland." Bulletin of the Kansas Association of Teachers
      of English 55 (October):2–5.
           Highlights a tour of Catherland sites for high school stu-
      dents, making suggestions for planning such an excursion and re-
      counting positive responses to the event.

3   BRADLEY, VAN ALLEN. "Willa Cather's First Volume of Poetry."
      Chicago Daily News, 1 February, Panorama sec., p. 11.
           Describes the first edition of April Twilights and indi-
      cates that it is hard to locate. The poetry, though seeming old-
      fashioned today, "stands up very well against other work of the
      period." Cather had an "eye and ear for the telling phrase."

4   BUSH, SARGENT, Jr. "Shadows on the Rock and Willa Cather's
      View of the Past." Queen's Quarterly 76 (Summer):269–85.
           In Shadows on the Rock Cather fully reconciles past and
      present, something she had not quite achieved in her Nebraska
      novels. The book becomes a good index to Cather's true attitude
      toward the past, which is not elegaic. For her, the past is
      something memory uses constructively in the present.

5   CECIL, L. MOFFITT. "Anti-Intellectualism as Theme in Willa
    Cather's The Professor's House." Research Studies 37
    (September):235-41.
        Argues that Cather sees Godfrey St. Peter as a sympathetic
but flawed character, one who has given himself to intellect's
false god and "lost his sympathy for humanity." In this Cather
parable, Tom Outland is the Tempter, the Destroyer who enters the
St. Peter garden and draws St. Peter into the sterility of the
Blue Mesa ideal. But in the end, after St. Peter has exchanged
the life of human affection for increased intellectual powers, he
decides that the price one pays for remarkable intellectual or
artistic achievement is too great. Clearly, in examining the
choice St. Peter made for the Blue Mesa ideal, Cather is examining her own career. She understands St. Peter, but she does
not endorse his world view.

6   COOPER, CLARA BOMANJI. "Willa Cather: The Nature of Evil and
    Its Purgation." Ph.D. dissertation, Florida State University,
    149 pp.
        Sets forth Cather's notion that evil--a materialism that
leads to loss of values--can be purged only by submersion in the
land. Cather's optimistic belief that good overcomes evil is
naive. See Dissertation Abstracts International 32 (1972):6420A.

7   CURLEY, DOROTHY NYREN; KRAMER, MAURICE; and KRAMER, ELAINE
    FIALKA, eds. "Willa Cather." In Modern American Literature.
    4th ed. Library of Literary Criticism, vol. 1. New York:
    Frederick Ungar Publishing Co., pp. 202-8.
        Contains a cumulative sampling of excerpts from criticism
of Cather's work spanning the years from 1921 to 1965. Includes
listings from previous editions. Supplemented: 1976.4.

8   DAUGHADAY, C[HARLES] H. Review of April Twilights (1903).
    American Book Collector 19 (February):5.
        Rates the 1968 edition of Cather's poems as valuable and
informative, praising Slote's editorial work and her discussion
of Cather's use of the Arcadian theme. See 1962.19.

9   FOX, [CLYDE] MAYNARD. "Proponents of Order: Tom Outland and
    Bishop Latour." Western American Literature 4 (Summer):
    107-15.
        The lives of Tom Outland (The Professor's House) and Bishop
Latour (Death Comes for the Archbishop) follow a parallel pattern
of progression from a discovery of order bequeathed from the past
to the present, to a discovery of order in nature, and finally to
a discovery of order in human lives through living in the present. The chief symbol in both novels is the garden, suggestive
of paradise where the accepted norm is order and the present is
lovely and peaceful.

10   HILFER, ANTHONY CHANNELL. "Willa Cather: The Home Place,
      Stultification and Inspiration." In <u>The Revolt from the</u>
      <u>Village 1915-1930</u>. Chapel Hill: University of North Carolina
      Press, pp. 84-110, 230-32.
          Revision of 1963.10, with little change in approach.

11   McCORD, DAVID. "On Reading with a Pencil." <u>Harvard Today</u>,
      Spring, pp. 7-12.
          Advocates making notes in books when reading them, and
      indicates that McCord did so when reading <u>My Ántonia</u>. The heart
      of his own philosophy, as well as hers, he discovered, is in Jim
      Burden's observation that happiness is being "dissolved into
      something complete and great."

12   MARTIN, TERENCE. "The Drama of Memory in <u>My Ántonia</u>." <u>PMLA</u>
      84 (March):304-11.
          A revised text of 1961.20. Basically the same essay as
      before, though with some additions, deletions, and refinements.
      The original essay does more with setting the novel in the con-
      text of the American western frontier.

13   PETERSON, GLENDA. "Willa Cather: Daughter of Virginia."
      <u>Valleys of History</u> 5 (Spring):1-5.
          Sketches Cather's life, especially her early life in Red
      Cloud and Lincoln, noting the dual east-west pull she felt
      throughout her life and her personal unconventionality. An
      abiding theme of her fiction is the human being in conflict with
      himself and/or the universe.

14   Review of <u>April Twilights (1903)</u>. <u>Choice</u> 6 (July):642.
          Briefly describes the various editions of Cather's poetry,
      maintaining that although Cather's poems are conventionally
      Victorian and hence romantic and melancholy, a few of them show
      deep emotion and suggest a kinship with the work of a poet like
      Edward Arlington Robinson.

15   SLOTE, BERNICE. "Stephen Crane and Willa Cather." <u>Serif</u> 6
      (December):3-15.
          Traces Cather's obvious interest in Crane through articles
      and reviews she wrote about him and the presence of his work in
      journals with which she was associated. Suggests, too, that
      Cather seems to have identified with him in some respects. Pro-
      vides extensive bibliographical data on the Cather-Crane connec-
      tion.

16   _____. "Willa Cather Reports Chautauqua, 1894." <u>Prairie</u>
      <u>Schooner</u> 43 (Spring):117-28.
          Consists mainly of excerpts from Cather's newspaper reports
      of the Crete (Nebraska) chautauqua. These reports reveal
      Cather's responses to the weather, the lectures, the lecturers,
      and especially the singers. Cather was obviously interested in
      singers very early, and several passages are reminiscent of <u>The</u>
      <u>Song of the Lark</u>.

17 _____. "Willa Cather." In Fifteen Modern American Authors:
A Survey of Research and Criticism. Edited by Jackson R.
Bryer. Durham, N.C.: Duke University Press, pp. 23-62.
    A bibliographical essay providing a detailed overview of
research materials and criticism relating to Cather's work.
Materials are organized and evaluated in sections that describe
(1) available bibliographies, (2) editions of primary works,
(3) locations of some manuscripts and letter collections,
(4) books and articles that provide biographical treatments of
Cather, and (5) critical responses to Cather's work. Revised:
1974.67.

18 STEGNER, WALLACE. "History, Myth, and the Western Writer."
In The Sound of Mountain Water. Garden City, N.Y.: Doubleday
& Co., p. 194.
    Sees Captain Forrester in A Lost Lady as a figure "touched
with the tone of nostalgic regret," an example of sadness at what
American civilization can do to the noble, free, and self-
reliant. Mentions also Cather's portrayal of the ugliness and
vulgarity that sometimes surface in frontier towns.

19 _____. "The West Authentic: Willa Cather." In The Sound of
Mountain Water. See Stegner, 1969.18, pp. 237-49.
    Reprint of 1965.33.

20 STERN, GWYNNETH. Cather entry in Twentieth Century Writing:
A Reader's Guide to Contemporary Literature. Edited by
Kenneth Richardson and R. Clive Willis. London: Newnes
Books, p. 118.
    Summarizes Cather's achievement, describing her as a
"contemplative and symbolic writer" who turned from contemporary
disorder and "sought perfection of mind and spirit."

21 THRONE, MARILYN ELIZABETH. "The Two Selves: Duality in Willa
Cather's Protagonists and Themes." Ph.D. dissertation, Ohio
State University, 271 pp.
    Discusses the theme of mutability in terms of man's con-
flict with himself, dividing the novels into four groups: the
Heroic, the Bitter, the Religious, and the Novels of Resignation.
See Dissertation Abstracts International 30 (1970):3026A-27A.

1970

1 BALLOU, ELLEN B. The Building of the House: Houghton
Mifflin's Formative Years. Boston: Houghton Mifflin,
pp. 558-63, 565-74 passim.
    Traces the history of Cather's publishing relationship with
Houghton Mifflin and her apparent dissatisfaction with the way
that firm handled and publicized her books.

2   BONHAM, BARBARA. Willa Cather. Philadelphia: Chilton Book
    Co., 120 pp.
       A reduced and simplified compilation of materials from
    previous Cather biographies, especially Mildred R. Bennett's The
    World of Willa Cather (1951.2). Contains little analysis of
    Cather's work.

3   BROWN, MARION MARSH, and CRONE, RUTH. Willa Cather: The
    Woman and Her Works. New York: Charles Scribner's Sons,
    160 pp.
       Undocumented (except for general introductory attributions)
    anecdotal biography of Cather, produced from accumulated re-
    sponses of people who knew her and knew of her. Maintains that
    Cather's method is essentially portraiture and biography; she
    drew on real people for her materials. Her strengths are "her
    sensitivity, her originality, her pure--almost classical--style,
    her restraint, her careful elimination of extraneous material,
    her portrayal of character, and her integrity."

4   CALISHER, HORTENSE. "Women Re Women." Mademoiselle 70
    (February):188-89.
       In a discussion as to whether or not women write like men,
    claims that the gap between what men and women could write about
    was narrower in the early 1900s than in previous or later pe-
    riods. Cites Cather as an example of a woman who could write the
    same way men did (men at that time were still under the influence
    of William Dean Howells), particularly because the land was her
    subject, and it was not considered unfeminine to write about it.
    Thus she escaped the restrictions that have afflicted many other
    women writers. Reprinted: 1971.5.

5   CRANE, JOAN ST. C[LAIRE]. "Rare or Seldom-Seen Dust Jackets
    of American First Editions." Serif 7 (June):27-30.
       Describes the physical appearance of certain rare books
    found in the Clifton Waller Barrett collection at the Alderman
    Library, University of Virginia. Among them are Cather's The
    Troll Garden, Alexander's Bridge, O Pioneers!, and The Song of
    the Lark.

6   CURTIN, WILLIAM M[ARTIN], ed. The World and the Parish:
    Willa Cather's Articles and Reviews, 1893-1902. 2 vols.
    Lincoln: University of Nebraska Press, 1070 pp.
       Reprints a "representative collection" of articles and
    reviews from Cather's first decade of journalistic writing,
    dividing them into three chronological groupings and providing
    rather extensive editorial commentary. The first grouping covers
    the writing done while Cather was in Nebraska; the second begins
    with her move to Pittsburgh and draws from the writing done when
    she was with the Home Monthly and the Pittsburgh Leader and was
    sending her "Passing Show" column back to the Nebraska State
    Journal; the third includes the years Cather free-lanced in
    Pittsburgh and Washington, D.C., taught high school, and went to
    Europe for the first time.

7   EARNEST, ERNEST. The Single Vision: The Alienation of Ameri-
    can Intellectuals. New York: New York University Press,
    pp. 51-52, 137, 157-63, 216.
        Expands on the theme treated in 1966.2, the youthful Ameri-
    can Ariel in modern American fiction. Classifies Cather as a
    voice of the second American renaissance when it was popular for
    intellectuals to attack the philistinian attitudes of the city
    and elevate the simple country person as someone of superior
    moral and aesthetic sensibilities. Cather also regarded people
    of earlier, more primitive cultures as superior to contemporary
    Americans.

8   FEGER, LOIS. "The Dark Dimension of Willa Cather's My
    Ántonia." English Journal 59 (September):774-79.
        Observes a dark undertone dominating My Ántonia, conveyed
    primarily through dark imagery, through Jim's failure to learn
    what he should learn (the work is essentially a bildungsroman),
    and through the negative, often violent, interpolated stories
    and anecdotes.

9   FERGUSON, J.M., Jr. "'Vague Outlines': Willa Cather's En-
    chanted Bluffs." Western Review: A Journal of the Humanities
    7 (Spring):61-64.
        The uniting symbol or idea in Cather's work is the big
    rock, but Cather deliberately keeps its outline (or meaning)
    vague so that it can suggest rather than state outright the
    numerous elements of the value she affirms.

10 GERSTENBERGER, DONNA, and HENDRICK, GEORGE. The American
    Novel: A Checklist of Twentieth Century Criticism on Novels
    Written Since 1789. Vol. 2, Criticism Written 1960-1968.
    Chicago: Swallow Press, pp. 41-45.
        Lists sources of criticism published between 1960 and 1968
    for each of Cather's novels, then lists several items of general
    criticism on her work and three sources of bibliography.

11 IRELAND, NORMA OLIN. Index to Women of the World from Ancient
    to Modern Times: Biographies and Portraits. Westwood, Mass.:
    F.W. Faxon Co., p. 92.
        Indexes thirty published sources of Cather biography and
    portraits.

12 JAMES, STUART B. "Western American Space and the Human
    Imagination." Western Humanities Review 24 (Spring):
    147-55 passim.
        Treats O Pioneers! and My Ántonia, along with novels by
    other writers, as books that show the raw, untamed space of the
    prairie, a place where mortals are stripped bare and must rely
    on themselves. But the West is also a "waiting landscape" whose
    nothingness can be shaped by human beings.

13   KELLOGG, GENE. The Vital Tradition: The Catholic Novel in a
      Period of Convergence. Chicago: Loyola University Press,
      pp. 165–66.
         Terms Cather's novels regional rather than "Catholic," for
      their theology springs from universal rather than specifically
      Catholic religious impulses.

14   KLOTMAN, PHYLLIS R. "The Musical Soul of Willa Cather."
      Music Journal 28 (March):42–43, 80–81.
         Suggests that Cather's life could be called a "musical
      odyssey" on an ascending line which begins with a nadir of lim-
      ited exposure in Red Cloud and ends with an apogee of wide ex-
      posure in her mature years. Cather responded feelingly to
      music--especially to singers--and used music extensively in her
      fiction. She had a particular affinity for Wagner, probably
      because he brought music and drama together in a powerful blend.

15   La HOOD, MARVIN J. "Conrad Richter and Willa Cather: Some
      Similarities." Xavier University Studies 9 (Spring):33–44.
         Cather and Richter are alike in that they both mourned the
      passing of the frontier, preferred the "unfurnished" novel and a
      clear style, chose nostalgic narrators, and felt a strong attrac-
      tion to the Southwest. On the other hand, Cather was interested
      in the artistic temperament and Richter was not. In fact, her
      interest in the artist led her to emphasize the artistic aspects
      of the European immigrants she portrayed and to criticize the
      frontier in a way that Richter did not.

16   LEARY, LEWIS, comp. Articles on American Literature 1950–
      1967. Durham, N.C.: Duke University Press, pp. 49–52.
         Lists some ninety-five articles published on Cather, in-
      cluding a few in Japanese periodicals, that appeared between
      1950 and 1967.

17   McLAY, CATHERINE M. "Willa Cather: The Search for Order in
      Her Major Fiction." Ph.D. dissertation, University of
      Alberta.
         Explores Cather's search for order in nature, art, and
      religion through a consideration of her major novels as expres-
      sions of that search. In one group of novels, nature is seen as
      a form of salvation; in another group, art is seen first as
      accomplishment, but later as a measure of modern man's failure;
      and in a third group, religion is seen as a source of stability
      and permanence.

18   MILLER, WAYNE CHARLES. An Armed America, Its Face in Fiction:
      A History of the American War Novel. New York: New York
      University Press, pp. 108, 117.
         In One of Ours Cather is less concerned about the war than
      about the desolate cultural and moral condition of the Midwest.

19   NEVIUS, BLAKE, comp. <u>The American Novel: Sinclair Lewis to
     the Present</u>. Goldentree Bibliographies in Language and Lit-
     erature. Edited by O.B. Hardison, Jr. New York: Appleton-
     Century-Crofts, pp. 27-30.
         Selects Cather as one of forty-eight writers for whom this
     bibliographical survey is provided. Lists fifty-eight items,
     both articles and books, categorizing most of them as biography
     and criticism. Also lists Cather's writings collected by others
     than herself.

20   PORTER, KATHERINE ANNE. "Reflections on Willa Cather." In
     <u>The Collected Essays and Occasional Writings of Katherine Anne
     Porter</u>. New York: Delacorte Press, Seymour Lawrence Book.
     Reprint. New York: Dell Publishing Co., Delta Book, 1973,
     pp. 29-39.
         Reprint of 1952.12.

21   ROWSE, A.L. "Once More on the Campus Trek." <u>Spectator</u>
     (London), 5 December, p. 724.
         Speaks of visits to Nebraska and a regard for Cather, who
     will surely "achieve the status of a lesser classic." Praises
     Cather for her historical sense and her ability to evoke
     atmosphere. Loves her for her "courageous and strong" person-
     ality that is also "sensitive and tender."

22   SCHNEIDER, Sister LUCY. "Cather's 'Land-Philosophy' in
     <u>Death Comes for the Archbishop</u>." <u>Renascence</u> 22 (Winter):
     78-86.
         Emphasizes the religious aspects of <u>Death Comes for the
     Archbishop</u> as they are revealed in the affiliation between man
     and nature. But the book also suggests that through the redemp-
     tive incarnation of Christ, created essence is transcended and
     something of the divine is realized.

23   SIMONSON, HAROLD P. <u>The Closed Frontier: Studies in American
     Literary Tragedy</u>. New York: Holt, Rinehart & Winston,
     pp. 14, 82-83.
         Points to Jim Burden's name (in <u>My Ántonia</u>) as one that
     suggests the burden of history from which the frontier was sup-
     posed to offer escape but did not. Cather was able to idealize
     her immigrants; Ole Rölvaag, with his tragic vision, was not.

24   SLOTE, BERNICE. "Willa Cather As a Regional Writer." <u>Kansas
     Quarterly</u> 2 (Spring):7-15.
         Cather used her Nebraska experiences and materials to re-
     veal what is universal, whole, and unifying. The story of the
     early settlers in Nebraska is a universal human story of new
     beginnings, changing times, and humanization of the prairie.
     Even in the early stories Cather gives at least a double view of
     the prairie, and the strain of melancholy is countered by details
     that convey delight.

25   SMITH, DOROTHY J. "The Glamor of the Glittering Rails."
      Midwest Quarterly 11 (April):311-26 passim.
          Makes frequent reference to Cather's novels and stories,
      and to those of other writers, to demonstrate that American fic-
      tion reveals a wide variety of functions served by the railroads
      in American life. My Ántonia receives particular attention.

26   STINSON, ROBERT. "S.S. McClure's My Autobiography: The
      Progressive as Self-Made Man." American Quarterly 22
      (Summer):203-12.
          Indicates the nature of Cather's participation in the
      preparation of McClure's autobiography. The content is his, but
      the writing is essentially hers, shaped from what he told her.
      His "presentations" to her were in a form that closely resembled
      a series of lectures he had been doing.

27   STIRLING, NORA. "Willa Cather." In Who Wrote the Modern
      Classics? New York: John Day Co., pp. 83-113.
          Characterizes Cather, on the basis of published memoirs
      about her, as a strong-willed, private, and sometimes difficult
      person of great talent. Raises questions about her attachments
      to women and her desire for privacy. Cather had unusually strong
      feelings for places, and she feared love between men and women.

28   STODDARD, HOPE. "Willa Cather." In Famous American Women.
      New York: Thomas Y. Crowell Co., pp. 101-10.
          Presents Cather's biography, from her childhood move to
      Nebraska until her death, and a short bibliography.

29   STOUCK, DAVID. "The Country of the Pointed Firs: A Pastoral
      of Innocence." Colby Library Quarterly 9 (December):213-20.
          Suggests that when Cather states that The Country of the
      Pointed Firs, Huckleberry Finn, and The Scarlet Letter are three
      American books that will likely last a long time, she is not so
      much ranking Sarah Orne Jewett's novel with the other two as she
      is saying that they are its predecessors in the pastoral tradi-
      tion. Jewett's pastoral differs from a Cather pastoral, My
      Ántonia, in that the latter shows Cather's narrator circling back
      to the land and integrating that experience with the outside
      world he now lives in. Jewett's narrator, on the other hand,
      returns to the innocent simplicity of the pastoral retreat.

30   _____. "Perspective As Structure and Theme in My Ántonia."
      Texas Studies in Literature and Language 12 (Summer):285-94.
          The five physical divisions of My Ántonia help the narrator
      and the reader to come to know timeless values in the midst of
      change. Loss and estrangement are the book's primary emotions;
      what is established as somehow free and changeless in book 1 be-
      comes subject to time and restriction and change in books 2
      through 4. Cather and Jim Burden are both searching for some-
      thing permanent, and Jim's visit to Ántonia's farm gives his
      memories permanent value. Appears in altered form in 1975.49.

31   "Willa Cather's Nebraska." Nebraskaland, July, pp. 22-27.
       A photo-essay (photographs by Guy Beaumont) of Nebraska
scenes, each adorned with a passage from one of Cather's works.
Introductory text calls her books biographies of the land as well
as of characters. The West was established in literature as a
result of her writing.

32   WILSON, HAROLD S. McClure's Magazine and the Muckrakers.
       Princeton: Princeton University Press, pp. 119, 187, 205-7.
       Comments briefly on S.S. McClure's interest in Cather and
her role on the magazine. Quotes from Cather's letters to Will
Owen Jones about her first interview with McClure and her visit
to the office of controversial politician, Christopher Magee.

33   WOODRESS, JAMES. Willa Cather: Her Life and Art. Pegasus
       American Authors, edited by Richard M. Ludwig. New York:
       Pegasus, 288 pp. Reprint. Lincoln: University of Nebraska
       Press, Bison Books, 1975. Landmark edition, 1982.
       Regarded by Woodress as an interim, not a definitive,
biography that corrects some misinformation and gets in print
what is known about Cather to this point. Maintains that Cather
is a descendant of Emerson and Whitman in a direct line of American romanticism. Further, she enjoyed many happy accidents in
her life, such as the meeting of a great number of practicing
artists. The juxtaposition of opposites is a defining characteristic of her writing, and her work in the various genres treats
the same kinds of themes and characters. Some of her best work
came out of "inner explosions" such as the ones she experienced
when she met Olive Fremstad or saw Anna Pavelka with her children. One of Ours marks a crucial point in Cather's life.
Things changed for her after 1922, and it was not until the
writing of Death Comes for the Archbishop that she found the
redemptive peace she needed in order to face the rest of her
life.

1971

1   BECKMAN, DON. "The Song of the Lark." Opera News 35
       (27 February):6-7.
       Tells how Cather added to Beckman's appreciation for opera
and details his enjoyment of the musical scenes in "A Wagner
Matinee," The Song of the Lark, and My Ántonia.

2   BENNETT, MILDRED R. "Willa Cather: Is She Relevant Today?"
       Omaha Sunday World-Herald Magazine, 4 April, pp. 16-18.
       Describes Cather as a universal writer, one who writes for
all people of all times. Just as the individualistic Cather
struck out at a conformist society, so do her protagonists fight
for individuality. Cather also had a profound respect for those
who maintained their ties with their cultural backgrounds.

3   BERTHOFF, WARNER. "The Art of Jewett's Pointed Firs." In
     Fictions and Events: Essays in Criticism and Literary His-
     tory. New York: E.P. Dutton & Co., pp. 243–44.
          Reprint of 1959.4.

4   BRADLEY, VAN ALLEN. "In Defense of Cather." Chicago Daily
     News, 13–14 February, Panorama sec., p. 7.
          Describes correspondence and conversation with former
     Nebraskan Leonard Nathan, indicating Nathan's concurrence with
     Cather's desires to prevent her letters and early writings from
     being made public. Bradley disagrees with Nathan and has tried
     to persuade him to give the letters Cather wrote him to the
     Cather archives in Red Cloud.

5   CALISHER, HORTENSE. "No Important Woman Writer." In Women's
     Liberation and Literature. Edited by Elaine Showalter. New
     York: Harcourt Brace Jovanovich, pp. 224–25.
          Reprint of 1970.4.

6   CARLSON, CONSTANCE HEDIN. "Heroines in Certain American
     Novels." Ph.D. dissertation, Brown University, 188 pp.
          Uses Cather as an addendum to an analysis of Edith Wharton
     as a novelist of manners, noting Cather's definitive attitude
     toward her heroines. See Dissertation Abstracts International
     32 (1972):5175A.

7   CHURCHILL, ALLEN. The Literary Decade. Englewood Cliffs,
     N.J.: Prentice-Hall, pp. 20, 178, 276, 279, 281, 319–21
     passim.
          Speaks of Cather as a "girl reporter and lady magazine
     editor" who was one of "three ladies who in their fashion wrote
     realistic fiction." (Edith Wharton and Ellen Glasgow are the
     other two.) Contends that out of disillusionment with the pres-
     ent, Cather turned fondly to the past in her fiction, even using
     religion to evoke that past in Death Comes for the Archbishop.
     Mentions Cather also in connection with discussion about her
     publisher, Alfred A. Knopf, and refers to Sinclair Lewis's
     admiration for her.

8   DAVIS, ROBERT GORHAM. "A Lady for Whom Much Went Right and
     Something Went Wrong." New York Times Book Review, 21 March,
     pp. 4–5, 18.
          Review of The World and the Parish. Sees in Cather's early
     journalistic writing much that is honest and wise, but finds
     little that foretells her later achievement. Unlike her mature
     work, this writing, though characterized by wit and even elo-
     quence, lacks nuance and "personal evocation." Cather blends two
     opposing impulses, hearty pioneering romanticism, and nostalgic,
     ordered classicism.

9   EDEL, LEON. Cather entry in Notable American Women 1607–1950:
     A Biographical Dictionary. Edited by Edward T. James, Janet
     Wilson, and Paul S. Boyer. Cambridge, Mass.: Harvard Univer-
     sity Press, Belknap Press, pp. 305–8.

In addition to describing important events and circumstances in Cather's life, comments on many of her books, noting
that her recurrent theme is "the drive of strong-willed persons
to achievement and their discovery of how illusory success can
be." The lasting quality of her work is its "tone of pathos, its
commemoration of a recent past." She writes mainly about the
conquest of an environment or the rebellion against it. With
classic grace and deep sincerity she charts the struggle for success.

10 FOX, [CLYDE] MAYNARD. Review of The World and The Parish.
    Western American Literature 5 (Winter):311-13.
       Maintains that the Cather sketches reprinted in The World
    and the Parish are remarkably mature and form a Cather counter-
    part to the journals of a Hawthorne or Emerson. In them lies the
    raw material for her later fiction. The writings gathered here
    demonstrate unmistakably that Cather's work is all of a piece.

11 GELFANT, BLANCHE H. "The Forgotten Reaping-hook: Sex in My
    Ántonia." American Literature 43 (March):60-82.
       Argues that Jim Burden's role in the novel must be re-
    evaluated, for his turn to childhood memories is a turn that
    averts the threat of sexual love to the inviolate self. In
    Cather, sex is nearly always linked to destruction of self, even
    to death, and so must be repressed. The successful marriages are
    the nonthreatening ones between friends, not lovers. Even the
    inset tales and vignettes in My Ántonia, seen as digressions by
    some critics, "form a pattern of aversion" that pervades the
    novel. Jim has to renounce the sensual Lena and turn Ántonia
    into a safe memory of asexual independence, masculinity, and
    motherhood. Reprinted: 1983.14; 1984.31-32.

12 HASKELL, HENRY C. "A Character Willa Cather Made Human at
    Christmas." Kansas City Star, 19 December.
       Considers "December Night," from Death Comes for the Arch-
    bishop, on its own merit as a short story. It is as "heart-
    warming" as Charles Dickens' "Christmas Carol," but lacks the
    boisterous quality of the Victorian work. Even though it can be
    read in isolation, it is a vital part of Cather's novel since it
    reveals that Bishop Latour is subject to self-doubt and fear like
    any other person.

13 HUDSON, STEWART. Introduction to The Life of Mary Baker G.
    Eddy, by Georgine Milmine. 2d ed. Grand Rapids, Mich.:
    Baker Book House, pp. xv-xxxiv.
       Treats at length the parallels between Mrs. Eddy and a
    substantial number of characters in Cather's fiction, suggesting
    that Cather's extensive work on the Milmine biography of Mrs.
    Eddy, published serially in McClure's, called up philosophical
    notions regarding the reality of evil that were clearly troubling
    Cather. The central issue for Eddy was the denial of evil and
    the natural extension of that--denial of the physical. In "The
    Profile" Cather draws an Eddy-like figure and suggests that
    Virginia Dunlap's refusal to admit material imperfection results

in evil and moral deformity. Such denial cuts human beings off
from the sources of sympathy. There are other adaptations of
Christian Science in Cather's books, too, and even some of Eddy's
monism (evil is part of the whole, hence created by God), though
Cather celebrated rather than denied the material world.

14   McALPIN, Sister SARA. "Enlightening the Commonplace: The
     Work of Sarah Orne Jewett, Willa Cather, and Ruth Suckow."
     Ph.D. dissertation, University of Pennsylvania, 554 pp.
        Links Jewett, Cather, and Suckow by personal experience,
artistic convictions, thematic concerns, and narrative techniques. See Dissertation Abstracts International 32 (1971):
2061A.

15   MARTIN, TERENCE. Review of The World and the Parish.
     American Literature 43 (November):465-66.
        Commends the editorial work on the two volumes of Cather's
early journalistic writings and notes Cather's growth as an
"urbane" critic who still retained her own particularly outspoken
voice.

16   METRAK, KRZYSZTOF. "Z amerykánskiej klasyki XX wieku" [From
     an American classic of the twentieth century]. Nowe Ksiazki
     16 31-8:1087, 1091.
        In Polish. Comments on a number of Cather's short stories,
including "The Bohemian Girl," "A Wagner Matinee," "Coming,
Aphrodite!," "The Sculptor's Funeral," and "Paul's Case," noting
particularly their mutual concern with the struggle between the
idealistic desire for individuality and experience beyond the
narrow, materialistic commonplace that sometimes binds and re-
stricts the artistic temperament. Regards "Coming, Aphrodite!"
as the best story in Youth and the Bright Medusa.

17   MILTON, JOHN R., ed. Conversations with Frank Waters.
     Chicago: Swallow Press, Sage Books, p. 80.
        At one point Frederick Manfred joins Frank Waters and John
Milton in conversation. Milton records that Manfred alludes to
Cather as one who moved west from the city and as a result wrote
"depressing stories." Cather, he says, was reared in Virginia,
"and the contrast of the place of her formative years with what
she found in Nebraska led to those novels that were unhappy."

18   _____. "Conversation with Harvey Fergusson." In "Conversa-
     tions with Western American Novelists." South Dakota Review
     9 (Spring):39-45.
        Records a conversation with Harvey Fergusson in which the
novelist declares that Cather wrote no western novels at all.
Her appeal is "academic"; she was completely ignorant of the
West.

19   _____. "Conversation with Wallace Stegner." In "Conversa-
     tions with Western American Novelists." South Dakota Review
     9 (Spring):45-57.

Quotes Stegner as having said in an interview that he regards Cather as a western novelist and My Ántonia as possibly the best western novel ever written. Although Cather's area of Nebraska is a borderland between Midwest and West, it is at the point where the land begins to be West, and she has written authentic western novels.

20   O'CONNOR, MARGARET ANNE. "Willa Cather and the Short Story." Ph.D. dissertation, University of California at Davis, 300 pp.
     Traces Cather's artistic development in the novels through her parallel development in the short stories. See Dissertation Abstracts International 32 (1972):5240A.

21   OLDFIELD, BARNEY. "Cather, Theatre & Things." Nebraska Alumnus 67 (July):5-8.
     Speculates, in remarks first delivered at the annual Cather observance in Red Cloud, Nebraska, on how Cather would have responded as a young drama critic to some of the theater people Oldfield encountered during the days he served as a theater usher and as theater editor for the Nebraska State Journal in Lincoln.

22   PIPER, HENRY DAN. "Social Criticism in the American Novel of the Nineteen Twenties." In The American Novel and the Nineteen Twenties. Stratford-Upon-Avon Studies, no. 13. Edited by Malcolm Bradbury and David Palmer. London: Edward Arnold, pp. 60, 67, 71.
     Speaks of Cather principally in connection with her influence on a younger generation of writers like F. Scott Fitzgerald, William Faulkner, and Ernest Hemingway--an influence more pronounced than that of Henry James. Cather is also mentioned in another essay in this volume, "Sherwood Anderson," by Brian Way.

23   PRENDERGAST, ARLINE FRANCES. "One of Ours: Willa Cather's Successful Failure." Ph.D. dissertation, University of Pittsburgh, 257 pp.
     Through a biographical approach explains both the weaknesses of One of Ours and the artistic crisis suffered by Cather. See Dissertation Abstracts International 32 (1972):5242A.

24   QUANTIC, DIANE DUFVA. "Anticipations of the Revolt from the Village in Nineteenth-Century Middle Western Farm Fiction: A Study of the Small Town in the Works of Edward Eggleston, E.W. Howe, Joseph Kirkland, Hamlin Garland, William Allen White, Zona Gale, and Willa Cather." Ph.D. dissertation, Kansas State University, 146 pp.
     Explores literary expressions of restlessness in the works of several midwestern writers, including Cather. See Dissertation Abstracts International 32 (1972):5198A.

25   SAVERY, GILBERT. "Willa Cather: Life in the Parish." Lincoln Sunday Journal and Star, 4 April, sec. f, p. 15.
     Analyzes the unique contribution of The World and the Parish to Cather scholarship as a record of her journalistic

writings from 1893 to 1902. Even as a young woman Cather
observed with a keen eye and showed a particular interest in
immigrants and the arts.

26   SHELTON, FRANK WILSEY. "The Family in the Novels of Wharton,
      Faulkner, Cather, Lewis and Dreiser." Ph.D. dissertation,
      University of North Carolina, 384 pp.
            Finds agreement among the authors discussed, including
      Cather, that families are a source of stability and that urban
      breakdown of family leads to isolation and alienation. See
      Dissertation Abstracts International 32 (1972):5244A.

27   SMITH, ANNELIESE H. "The Persistent Hardness of Life in Willa
      Cather's Major Fiction: A Study of Her Dominant Stays Against
      the Hard Realities." Ph.D. dissertation, State University of
      New York at Albany, 305 pp.
            Shows that Cather's characters work to accommodate them-
      selves to the harsh realities of life rather than to escape or
      transcend them. See Dissertation Abstracts International 33
      (1972):2953A.

28   SUSSMAN, IRVING. As Others See Us: A Look at the Rabbi,
      Priest, and Minister through the Eyes of Literature. New
      York: Sheed & Ward, pp. 154-57.
            Tells the story of Jean Latour as Cather presents it,
      emphasizing his conflict with Padre Martinez, who exemplifies the
      stereotypical corrupt priest. In Death Comes for the Archbishop
      Cather prefigures the priest of the twentieth century, a man
      pulled between despair and hope, prayer and action, but he is not
      the priest of some other modern writers who is torn to the quick
      by his own unbelief.

29   THOMAS, CLARA. "Proud Lineage: Willa Cather and Margaret
      Laurence." Canadian Review of American Studies 2 (Spring):
      3-12.
            Compares and contrasts the Canadian prairie novels of
      Margaret Laurence with O Pioneers! and My Ántonia, suggesting
      that together the works of the two women "form a lineage and a
      cycle of their own in North American literature." The natural
      bonds between the two writers are deep; the differences between
      them lie mainly in tone of voice and the artistic path. While
      Cather relies on a few striking images which assume great power,
      Laurence prefers to create a sense of movement.

30   WOODRESS, JAMES. "Willa Cather Seen Clear." Papers on Lan-
      guage and Literature 7 (Winter):96-109.
            Reviews four collections of Cather's early writing--poetry,
      stories, and newspaper columns--and stresses the connections
      between Cather's early life and writing and the rest of her
      career. There is much more to Cather than most of her readers
      have suspected.

1972

1   ALLEN, DAVID ARTHUR. "Willa Cather: A Critical Study."
    Ph.D. dissertation, University of Denver, 180 pp.
         Discusses Cather's major ideas about the land, human rela-
    tions, and loss of the past, tracing her various stages of opti-
    mism. Cather is competent and consistent, but she is sentimental
    and occasionally dull. See Dissertation Abstracts International
    33 (1973):4397A-98A.

2   ANDERSON, DAVID D. "The World of Willa Cather: The Years
    That Shaped the Vision." Society for the Study of Midwestern
    Literature Newsletter 2 (Fall):4-5.
         Describes the various publications and projected publica-
    tions that include writings of Cather just coming to attention--
    the early columns and reviews and the short stories. Major
    attention must be given to the stories.

3   ANDES, CYNTHIA J. "The Bohemian Folk Practice in 'Neighbour
    Rosicky.'" Western American Literature 7 (Spring):63-64.
         Rosicky's optimism and good fortune even after his crop is
    scorched by the sun stem from an old Bohemian folk custom in
    which the burning in an orchard of crumbs from bread made on Good
    Friday was supposed to insure a bounteous fruit harvest.

4   BUTCHER, FANNY. "Willa Cather." In Many Lives--One Love.
    New York: Harper & Row, pp. 354-68.
         Recalls a long association with Cather that was both per-
    sonal and professional, and comments briefly on several of
    Cather's books. Cather was one of those fortunate few who found
    what she wanted to do in life and did it. Her artistic integrity
    was unwavering.

5   DINN, JAMES M. "A Novelist's Miracle: Structure and Myth in
    Death Comes for the Archbishop." Western American Literature
    7 (Spring):39-46.
         Death Comes for the Archbishop has a preternatural and a
    mythic dimension which give the book rich significance beyond
    that of ordinary historical fiction. Structurally Cather blends
    works of spirit with the literal world and presents Latour's life
    in images of the mythical questing knight. The priest's work is
    also linked with fertility myths as he brings to fruition God's
    creative purposes in New Mexico.

6   DURHAM, PHILIP. "Willa Cather's 'There-about.'" Neuphilo-
    logische Mitteilungen (Finland) 73:83-89.
         Cautions that creative artists often pass off fictions for
    facts, and mentions several instances when Cather does so. Thus,
    when she says that the world broke in two in 1922 "or thereabout,"
    it cannot be assumed that 1922 was indeed the year this happened
    for her. The word "thereabout" is very important. The sup-
    posedly factual utterances of writers should be approached with
    "scholarly skepticism."

7   ETULAIN, RICHARD W. Western American Literature: A Bibliog-
     raphy of Interpretive Books and Articles. Vermillion, S.D.:
     Dakota Press, pp. 43–46.
          Lists without commentary sixty-four articles and books con-
     taining Cather criticism from 1936 to 1970.

8   "Great Forking Trees." Willa Cather Pioneer Memorial News-
     letter 16 (Spring):2.
          Reprinted from 1921.13.

9   HARRIS, CELIA. Review of O Pioneers! Willa Cather Pioneer
     Memorial Newsletter 16 (Spring):2–3.
          Reprint of 1913.5.

10   HART, CLIVE. "The Professor's House: A Shapely Story."
     Modern Language Review 67 (April):271–81.
          The form of The Professor's House, with its intricate
     patterns and correspondences, reflects the moral relativism and
     ambiguity in the character of Godfrey St. Peter and shows the
     significant relationships within and among the three books of
     the novel. There are telling contradictions in St. Peter's
     character, and he wrongfully repudiates human relationships in
     favor of dead forms, represented by the dress forms in his attic
     and the mummies on Tom's mesa.

11   HINZ, EVELYN J. "Willa Cather's Technique and the Ideology of
     Populism." Western American Literature 7 (Spring):47–61.
          While Cather's techniques--her language, imagery, and
     symbolism, her use of humor, anecdote, poem, picture, and the
     like--suggest the methods and materials of populism, they achieve
     in her work a mythic universality that reaches beyond common
     meanings.

12   HUBBELL, JAY B. Who Are the Major American Writers? A Study
     of the Changing Literary Canon. Durham, N.C.: Duke Univer-
     sity Press, pp. 202–3, 209–27 passim, 280–83 passim, 294–302
     passim, 330–31 passim.
          Attempts to bring together various data collected in pre-
     vious decades of the twentieth century that show what people were
     selected by various groups and commentators as the most note-
     worthy American writers. Notes Cather's rankings on various
     polls and book lists as well as her inclusion in various antholo-
     gies and bibliographies.

13   KING, RICHARD. Review of O Pioneers! Willa Cather Pioneer
     Memorial Newsletter 16 (Summer):3–4.
          Reprinted from 1913.6.

14   KOBAYSHI, KENJI. Frontier Novels: A Study of Willa Cather.
     Tokyo: Kenkyusha, 203 pp.
          In Japanese. Analyzes in detail O Pioneers!, My Ántonia,
     A Lost Lady, The Professor's House, Death Comes for the Arch-
     bishop, and Shadows on the Rock, defending their structure in
     response to negative criticism. Views these novels primarily as

a chronicle of the rise and fall of the frontier and the frontier myth, noting Cather's harmony with American life and world view. Cather's later works are inferior--too sentimental, and lacking in frontier spirit and values.

15   KUEHAR, ROMAN V[OLODYMYR]. "The Homeland of Willa Cather."
      In Space and Freedom. London: Hays, pp. 81-86.
            In Ukranian. Presents a personal, lyrical response on a group visit to Cather's Nebraska, much of the time writing as if addressing Cather herself. Indicates that Cather's knowledge of the immigrant peoples about whom she wrote was severely limited by her experience. She both misnamed and misplaced them, but her intentions were good. For one thing, the immigrants came to the American prairie not to find land, but to find freedom.

16   LAUERMAN, DAVID ANTHONY. "The Garden and the City in the
      Fiction of Willa Cather." Ph.D. dissertation, Indiana University, 339 pp.
            Defends the validity of Cather's fiction on the basis of her integrated use of myth, which leads to a true and "richly textured vision of reality." See Dissertation Abstracts International 33 (1973):4421A-22A.

17   LOEBNER, HORST-DIETER. "Willa Cather: Paul's Case. Die
      Problematik der ästhetischen Existenz." Literatur in Wissenschaft und Unterricht 5:215-32.
            Discusses "Paul's Case" as an expression of Cather's concern for the plight of the modern artist in defining his role in a materialistic world.

18   LUDWIG, RICHARD M., ed. Second supplement to bibliography in
      Literary History of the United States. Edited by Thomas H. Johnson. New York: Macmillan Co., pp. 122-23. Reprint. With 4th ed. of Literary History of the United States, 1974, pp. 1160-61.
            Provides a second Cather bibliography supplement to Johnson, 1948.15. It includes items from 1958 to 1970, plus pre-1958 items not listed in the first supplement, 1959.10.

19   McFARLAND, DOROTHY TUCK. Willa Cather. New York: Frederick
      Ungar Publishing Co., 164 pp. Reprint. 1978.
            Offers some biographical details, mainly in connection with Cather's writing, but claims that criticism has generally read too much of Cather's life and personality into her work. Provides plot summaries and comment on most of the books, but mentions Alexander's Bridge only briefly in the introduction, and does not mention or discuss Sapphira and the Slave Girl at all.

20   MYERS, RAWLEY. "Willa Cather Espoused What Youth Tries to
      Tell Us." Unidentified Nebraska periodical clipping [1972?] at Willa Cather Historical Center, Red Cloud, Nebraska.
            Wishes to draw a lesson for the present day from Cather's example. She believed in excellence and loved the beautiful.

21   POLI, BERNARD. "Willa Cather, ou la nostalgie pure." In Le
      roman américain 1865-1917: Mythes de la frontière et de la
      ville. Paris: Librairie Armand Colin, pp. 37-42.
           Examines Cather's two prairie/pioneer novels, O Pioneers!
      and My Ántonia, and suggests that they are to Americans what
      Notre-Dame de Paris and Les misérables are to the French. They
      present an image of a time and place. Cather's concern is with
      the passing of the frontier, and in works like O Pioneers! and
      My Ántonia, she portrays the conflict of values between pioneer
      courage and aesthetic sensibility. Ántonia, representing the
      Jeffersonian matriarchal ideal, is the antithesis of Lena Lingard
      and Tiny Soderball who aspire to social and financial independ-
      ence.

22   POWELL, LAWRENCE CLARK. "Exploring Arizona's Literary
      Trails." Arizona Highways 48 (September):16-22.
           Identifies Cather as one of four writers of fiction who
      have particular significance for Arizona. It was Cather's
      lengthy visit to her brother in Winslow, Arizona in 1912 that
      changed her life and made a great writer out of her. While
      there she was struck with history, landscape, and love for a
      young Mexican musician and was changed forever.

23   _____. "Southwest Classics Reread: Willa Cather's Death
      Comes for the Archbishop." Westways 64 (February):22-25, 33.
           Recounts in memoir style the major events of Cather's
      life, emphasizing the importance of her New Mexico experiences
      to her development as an artist. Describes events and circum-
      stances surrounding the writing of Death Comes for the Arch-
      bishop. Abridged: 1974.53.

24   PRATT, ANNIS. "Women and Nature in Modern Fiction."
      Contemporary Literature 13 (Autumn):476-90.
           Discusses Cather's Genius of the Divide (who comes to
      Alexandra Bergson in her imagination in O Pioneers!) as the
      equivalent in women's fiction to the earth goddess who appears
      in other fiction based on the myth of the questing hero. This
      figure is an enabling one for Alexandra, leading her to a
      naturistic epiphany and ultimate sexual fulfillment through
      marriage to Carl Linstrum.

25   REYNARD, GRANT. "Willa Cather's Advice to a Young Artist."
      Prairie Schooner 46 (Summer):111-24.
           A memoir of gratitude to Cather who at the MacDowell Colony
      one summer told Reynard that her own work took an important turn
      when she stopped trying to write "fine" fiction and began looking
      for materials in her own memories. Reynard attributes his find-
      ing himself as an artist to the advice she subtly and indirectly
      gave him.

26   STALLINGS, FRANK L., Jr. "The West: Perpetual Mirage in
      Literature." In Myths and Realities: Conflicting Values in
      America. Edited by Berkley Kalin and Clayton Robinson.

Memphis: Memphis State University, John Willard Brister
Library, pp. 39-49 passim.
Refers to My Ántonia and Death Comes for the Archbishop on
several occasions to illustrate some of the qualities of the
western landscape that novelists like Cather have seen as con-
tributing to its illusory character. Among these qualities are
the immensely grand scale of it, the bigness and brilliance of
the sky, the fluidity of clouds and land, and the scarcity of
trees.

27 STOUCK, DAVID. "O Pioneers ! Willa Cather and the Epic
    Imagination." Prairie Schooner 46 (Spring):23-34.
    Discusses O Pioneers! in terms of its epic elements--its
nationalistic character, its hero (heroine) as representative of
the highest ideal of the group, its humble point of view, and its
traditional values. Carl Linstrum's view most closely approxi-
mates that of the author. Cather's love and sympathy for the
pioneers is very evident, and the reader tends to glorify what
Alexandra accomplishes. Reprinted: 1975.49.

28 _____. "Willa Cather and The Professor's House: 'Letting Go
    with the Heart.'" Western American Literature 7 (Spring):
    13-24.
    Postulates that The Professor's House shows Cather working
through the problem of power and possession. In her own life it
took the form of wanting to possess another person; in that of
others it took the form of desire for material possessions. Both
are corrupting. Cather concluded--as seen through the examples
of Tom Outland and the sewing woman Augusta--that one could
relinquish desires for power and possessions without relinquish-
ing human sympathy. Reprinted: 1975.49.

29 _____. "Willa Cather's Unfurnished Novel: Narrative in Per-
    spectives." Wascana Review 6, no. 2:41-51.
    Cather's "unfurnished" novelistic technique is accomplished
through her use of temporal and spatial perspectives rather than
customary methods of plot development. Movement in her novels
occurs through her narrator's growing awareness as time passes
rather than through a series of dramatic confrontations. A Lost
Lady and My Mortal Enemy are discussed as examples of this
method. Appears in altered form in 1975.49.

30 STOUCK, MARY-ANN. "Chaucer's Pilgrims and Cather's Priests."
    Colby Library Quarterly 9 (June):531-37.
    Points up elements in Death Comes for the Archbishop that
are reminiscent of Chaucer's pilgrims in the Canterbury Tales.
For example, in neither of the works are characters delineated by
a single virtue or vice, and some of Cather's characters seem
drawn from Chaucer's portraits, giving the two works at least a
similarity of effect. In both works it is the characters' moral
natures that are revealed.

31   STOUCK, MARY-ANN, and STOUCK, DAVID.   "Hagiographical Style in
      Death Comes for the Archbishop." University of Toronto
      Quarterly 41 (Summer):293-307.
           Death Comes for the Archbishop reflects Cather's reading
      about medieval Catholicism in which the religious significance of
      events was stressed rather than causal relationships. The form
      of Death Comes for the Archbishop is descriptive, not dramatic,
      and linear time is almost nonexistent, with events seemingly held
      in suspension in a continuum that is always present. The novel's
      form, its absence of plot, serves to detach the reader and force
      a response to the book's overall design. Cather does not present
      an allegorical landscape systematically, but rather isolates and
      concentrates on a particular feature of it in a way that gives it
      an aura of spiritual significance. Her priests become stereo-
      types of spirituality. Basically, the style is hagiographical,
      a style in which the individual is subordinated to "a spiritual
      and communal ideal." Appears in altered form in 1975.49.

32   STUCKEY, WILLIAM J. "My Ántonia: A Rose for Miss Cather."
      Studies in the Novel 4 (Fall):473-83.
           Jim Burden's necessity to idealize Ántonia is representa-
      tive of Cather's necessity to idealize experience through art.
      This is how she is different from--and inferior to--writers like
      Fitzgerald and Hemingway who do not have to beautify experience
      when they turn it into art. Neither Jim Burden nor Cather could
      accept reality as it is, but had to turn it into something of
      which they could approve.

33   SULLIVAN, PATRICK J. "Willa Cather's Southwest." Western
      American Literature 7 (Spring):25-37.
           The Southwest was important in the development of Cather's
      fiction, and her use of it underwent significant transformation.
      In "The Enchanted Bluff" it evokes remote mystery and its ir-
      reconciliation with human failure; in The Song of the Lark it is
      Thea Kronborg's ritualistic catalyst to artistic selfhood; in My
      Ántonia it is used briefly to harmonize the tensions of "The
      Enchanted Bluff"; in The Professor's House it presents those ten-
      sions again as it poses spiritual values against the diminishing
      of such values in the modern age; and finally, in Death Comes for
      the Archbishop, it provides, in spite of setbacks, a resolution
      of the old conflict. In Death Comes for the Archbishop the
      "Southwest has become the eighth sacrament."

34   WEALES, GERALD. "Willa Cather, Girl Reporter." Southern
      Review, n.s. 8 (Summer):681-88.
           Review of The World and the Parish. Criticizes Curtin for
      obscuring the content of Cather's early journalistic writings by
      focusing on their links with the novels, and then discusses the
      qualities of her early columns and reviews. Cather is most in-
      teresting as a drama critic, where she shows insight and "a
      robust popular taste." Her critical writing was mainly of the
      arts, and thus she worked right on the edge of the fictional
      world, using some of its methods, especially in delineating
      character and creating personae.

35 WHITTINGTON, CURTIS CALVIN, Jr. "The Use of Inset Narratives
    in the Novels of Willa Cather." Ph.D. dissertation, Vander-
    bilt University, 249 pp.
        Contends that not only are the inset narratives in Cather's
    work functional thematically and symbolically, but they also
    create ironic contrasts. Furthermore, they set time, locale,
    mood, and atmosphere. Cather's use of such techniques places her
    in the impressionistic tradition. See Dissertation Abstracts
    International 33 (1973):4440A.

36 "Willa Cather Circle Tour." Nebraskaland 50 (August):55–56.
        Outlines a tour of Cather sites around Red Cloud, Nebraska,
    identifying specific buildings and places and the people with
    whom they are associated, in Cather's life and in her works.

37 YONGUE, PATRICIA LEE. "The Immense Design: A Study of Willa
    Cather's Creative Process." Ph.D. dissertation, University of
    California at Los Angeles, 321 pp.
        Regards Cather's view of American history as a downward
    thrust away from order, stability, and motivation—a situation
    for which she blames Puritanism's emphasis on prosperity and
    industry. See Dissertation Abstracts International 33 (1973):
    5207A–8A.

38 _____. "A Lost Lady: The End of the First Cycle." Western
    American Literature 7 (Spring):3–12.
        A Lost Lady marks the end of a major imaginative cycle for
    Cather as it charts the decline of the pioneer West and of artis-
    tic sensibility, and hence of an ideal represented by Captain
    Forrester but never really understood by Marian Forrester.
    Marian does not absorb any values from the land. In the artistic
    sensibility of Niel Herbert Cather places her only hope for the
    future.

                                1973

1   ADAMS, THEODORE S. "Willa Cather's My Mortal Enemy: The
    Concise Presentation of Scene, Character, and Theme." Colby
    Library Quarterly 10 (September):138–48.
        Considers My Mortal Enemy's tightly restricted form, suc-
    cinct plot, and narrative voice in terms of the novel's dominant
    balancing themes—worldliness and the soul's poetry. Myra
    Henshawe is a paradoxical figure, and Nellie Birdseye never
    develops as a character. The reader wonders in the first part of
    the novel how a woman apparently so giving can also be so selfish
    and vengeful, and in the second part how such a cruel and dis-
    loyal person can also be a saint.

2   "American Woman: Willa Cather Centennial. Wee Winkie's
     Wanderings: A Just-Found Story." Vogue 161 (June):113, 162.
        Reprints for the first time, in commemoration of the cen-
tennial of Cather's birth, a copy of a very early children's
story identified by Bernice Slote as Cather's. It first appeared
in the young people's pages of a weekly called National Stockman
and Farmer, and is probably autobiographical. Introduction calls
Cather "heart-deeply American" and quotes Slote as to how she
discovered this sketch and determined it to be Cather's.

3   BARBA, SHARON ROSE. "Willa Cather: A Feminist Study." Ph.D.
     dissertation, University of New Mexico, 159 pp.
        Questions standard male point-of-view criticism, contending
that in presenting her heroines Cather breaks through male conventions. See Dissertation Abstracts International 34 (1973):
2605A.

4   BASH, JAMES R. "Willa Cather and the Anathema of Material-
     ism." Colby Library Quarterly 10 (September):157-68.
        Examines Cather's antimaterialism through references to
many of her works. She attacks these five manifestations of
materialism: (1) a fascination for man-made machinery, (2) a
misuse of the land, (3) a preoccupation with making money, (4) a
life that has become standardized, and, hence, (5) a life that
has been cheapened.

5   BENNETT, MILDRED R. "A Note on the White Bear Stories."
     Willa Cather Pioneer Memorial Newsletter 7 (Summer):4.
        Publishes a letter from Cather's sister, Elsie, in which
she recalls hearing Cather and her brother Roscoe tell stories
about the heroic White Bear featured in "The Strategy of the
Were-Wolf Dog."

6   ____. "What Happened to the Rest of the Charles Cather
     Family?" Nebraska History 54 (Winter):619-24.
        Presents, partly through letters by their children, brief
biographies of Cather's brothers and sisters.

7   BENSON, FREDERICK R. Cather entry in The McGraw-Hill
     Encyclopedia of World Biography. Vol. 2. New York: McGraw-
     Hill Book Co., pp. 419-20.
        Summarizes several of Cather's works, indicating that after
the frontier was lost Cather adopted the American Southwest as a
substitute for it. Her feelings for the land and the people who
live close to it give her work a mystical quality. Provides a
short bibliography of secondary sources.

8   BOURNE, RANDOLPH. "My Ántonia." Willa Cather Pioneer Memo-
     rial Newsletter 17 (Winter):3.
        A partial reprint of 1918.1.

9   BROWN, MARION MARSH, and CRONE, RUTH. "Famous Novelist Willa
    Cather Had Adventure at Mesa Verde." Pueblo Chieftain and
    Pueblo Star-Journal, Panorama sec., 26 November.
        Recounts Cather's adventure at Mesa Verde when an inexpe-
    rienced guide leading Cather and Edith Lewis on an expedition in
    Soda Canyon managed to lose his way.

10   _____. "It's a Good Year for Town Tour in Catherland."
    Omaha Sun, 26 July, sec. a, p. 9.
        Mentions the highlights of the Cather town and country
    tours in and around Red Cloud, Nebraska. Cather had a lasting
    affinity for that area and wrote most successfully on pioneer
    themes. She broke new ground in casting off the bonds of re-
    strictive Victorian conventions regarding the role of women.

11   BRUNK, CHARLOTTE. "Salute to Willa Cather." Des Moines
    Sunday Register, 26 August, sec. b, p. 31.
        Observes with pleasure the issue of a special edition of
    A Lost Lady, a refreshing reminder of Cather's artistry and
    honesty.

12   CAREY, GLENN O. Review of Uncle Valentine and Other Stories.
    Studies in Short Fiction 12:421-23.
        Pays tribute to Cather for her full and rewarding career
    and claims that in Uncle Valentine and Other Stories she follows
    her own dictum that "a good workman can't be a cheap workman."
    The stories in this collection are not her best, but they show
    her creative ability.

13   CARY, RICHARD. "The Sculptor and the Spinster: Jewett's
    'Influence' on Cather." Colby Library Quarterly 10
    (September):168-78.
        Considers some of Sarah Orne Jewett's advice to Cather and
    notes how it did or did not find its way into her fiction. It is
    puzzling that, though she had several opportunities to improve
    "The Sculptor's Funeral," Cather made only relatively minor
    changes in it over the years. It remains a much weaker story
    than Jewett's "Miss Tempy's Watchers," and one is left wondering
    why.

14   COLEMAN, MARION MOORE. "Books." Cheshire (Conn.) Herald,
    11 September.
        Tells of how a search for biographical materials pertaining
    to Polish actress Helena Modjeska led to Willa Cather and then to
    Red Cloud, Nebraska.

15   COOPER, RICHARD T. "Life in Cather Country, 100 Years Later."
    Unidentified periodical clipping [1973], pp. 1, 62, 66, at
    Willa Cather Historical Center, Red Cloud, Nebraska.
        Tells something of the character of Cather's home town of
    Red Cloud, Nebraska, as it was in Cather's day and as it is now,
    concluding that, really, not much has changed. The townspeople
    resented Cather's writing about them, and today most of them
    scarcely acknowledge the symbols of her remembered presence among
    them.

16   DINN, JAMES M. "'Only Two or Three Human Stories': Recur-
      rent Patterns of Action in the Major Fiction of Willa Cather."
      Ph.D. dissertation, University of Notre Dame, 255 pp.
          Sees three recurring patterns in Cather's fiction: the
      quest, the return to youth, and infatuation with music. See
      Dissertation Abstracts International 33 (1973):6351A-52A.

17   DODD, ORA. "Adventures in Print." NRTA Journal (National
      Retired Teachers Association) 24 (September-October,
      November-December):38-39, 46.
          Briefly outlines Cather's life and then the plot of My
      Ántonia, asserting that Cather's own past lies in the book, that
      the narrator is simply a male version of Cather herself. The
      November-December issue contains a fifteen-question quiz on My
      Ántonia.

18   DONOHUE, JOHN W. "Two Women: A Centennial." America 128
      (31 March):276-79.
          Pays tribute to Cather and St. Thérèse Martin in their
      centennial birth year, observing that while the circumstances of
      their lives were different, they had certain similarities of
      character and similar appreciations. Cather's most amazing
      achievement was to make "great literature out of good lives and
      great ideals" without becoming sentimental or pious.

19   DRAVES, [Rev.] CORNELIUS J. "Willa Cather Still Speaking As
      Loudly As Ever." Baltimore Sunday Sun, 9 December.
          Insists that Cather remains relevant because she was con-
      cerned with values and experiences that are basic to humanity,
      values that do not reside in immediate need gratification.

20   DUFFY, MARTHA. "The Old Sod." Time 102 (13 August):80.
          Review of the new centenary edition of A Lost Lady de-
      scribes Cather as a "minor writer" whose work, including A Lost
      Lady, is marred by her "moral nostalgia." In A Lost Lady, as
      elsewhere, Cather dispenses at the end "some sentimental benefi-
      cence" or exacts some "moral toll."

21   EDEL, LEON. "Willa Cather." In Literary Lectures Presented
      at the Library of Congress. Washington, D.C.: Library of
      Congress, pp. 350-67.
      Reprint of 1960.4.

22   EICHORN, HARRY B. "A Falling Out with Love: My Mortal
      Enemy." Colby Library Quarterly 10 (September):121-38.
          Explores the relationships between My Mortal Enemy and the
      works alluded to in the novel, including several Shakespearean
      plays--especially King Lear and King John--and also draws paral-
      lels with Bellini's opera, Norma. Cather uses the plays to let
      the reader know more than her narrator, Nellie Birdseye, can
      reveal. Myra sees parallels between herself and some of the
      plays, but Nellie does not. All Nellie knows and reports is
      what she sees and hears. She grows progressively more dis-
      illusioned until in the end she is left with an emotional poverty

as severe as Myra's financial poverty, for she comes to distrust
human love. As Nellie looks back after many years, she seems to
laugh at her romantic notions, producing the ironic tone in the
early descriptions that is seldom picked up by readers. Reprinted: 1984.27.

*23   ESCARTIN NUÑEZ, EMILIO. "La novela de Willa Cather." Ph.D.
      dissertation, University of Madrid, 857 pp.
         Listed in Bibliography of English Language and Literature
      (1973).

24   FETTY, AUDREY MAE SHELLEY. "Biblical Allusions in the Fiction
      of Willa Cather." Ph.D. dissertation, University of Nebraska,
      307 pp.
         Refers to Cather's biblical background and examines her
      works to discover the conscious and unconscious incorporation of
      biblical material, from direct allusion to informed syntactical
      speech patterns. Includes a tabulation of Cather's biblical
      allusions and a chronology of her life. See Dissertation
      Abstracts International 34:2621A-22A.

25   GOODWYN, LARRY. "The Frontier Myth and Southwestern Litera-
      ture." In Regional Perspectives: An Examination of America's
      Literary Heritage. Edited by John Gordon Burke. Chicago:
      American Library Association, pp. 196-98.
         In her early work Cather concentrated on the debilitating
      effects of the harsh land, but after she escaped from it to the
      cultured East, she was able to imprint it with a fashionable
      artificial literary sensibility. She could then write about the
      West romantically.

26   HASKELL, HENRY C. "Return as a Native Matured Willa Cather's
      Genius." New York Sun, 9 December.
         Uses the occasion of the issuance of a Cather commemorative
      postage stamp to reaffirm the importance of Cather's returning to
      Nebraska for her materials. Important as her experiences con-
      nected with the Southwest are, the migration of many Europeans
      to the prairie is at the heart of much of her work.

27   H[ASS], V[ICTOR] P. "7 Cather Stories Finish UN Task."
      Omaha Sunday World-Herald Magazine, 25 March.
         Review of Uncle Valentine and Other Stories. Offers brief
      plot summaries of the seven stories in the Uncle Valentine col-
      lection, and maintains that they are "jewels"--full of grace,
      irony, and wit.

28   HOWARD, PATSY C., comp. Theses in American Literature 1896-
      1971. Ann Arbor, Mich.: Pierian Press, pp. 20-25.
         Contains a listing of 125 unpublished baccalaureate and
      masters' theses, including some on Cather, collected by the
      compiler from "many southwestern, southern and eastern colleges
      and universities during the summer of 1970." Not intended to be
      comprehensive.

29   KENNEDY, P[ACIFICUS] J.A. "Ms. Willa Cather 1873-1973." Way:
      Catholic Viewpoints 29 (December):54-60.
         Emphasizes, in an account of Cather's youth and professional
      life, her personality and her decision to follow the life of a
      writer rather than pursue a more traditional role. One of her
      important themes is the struggle to maintain the individual self
      in spite of the demands inherent in a person's devotion to loved
      ones.

30   _____. "They Knew Willa Cather." Friar, July-August,
      pp. 78-84.
         Refers to a variety of incidents in Cather's life, quoting
      a number of statements made about Cather by her lifelong friend,
      Carrie Miner Sherwood, and raising questions about Cather's
      religiosity. Several of her novels show her Catholic sympathies,
      but she was also one who seemed to feel that blind chance operates
      freely in human experience.

31   KNOEPFLE, JOHN. "Crossing the Midwest." In Regional Per-
      spectives: An Examination of America's Literary Heritage.
      Edited by John Gordon Burke. Chicago: American Library
      Association, pp. 77-174 passim.
         Discusses many midwestern writers, especially contemporary
      writers, but calls Cather "the classical author of the plains."
      My Ántonia is a prose pastoral, a Virgilian eclogue of pioneer
      life. It is Cather's most affirmative piece of work.

32   McBRIDE, MARY ELLEN. "Willa Cather's Prose Captured Pitts-
      burgh." Pittsburgh Post-Gazette Daily Magazine, 18 July.
         Describes Cather's life in Pittsburgh and points to mate-
      rial and sources which she drew upon for her short fiction in
      Uncle Valentine and Other Stories. Also reports conversation
      with one of Cather's nieces now living in Pittsburgh.

33   McCARTHY, COLMAN. "Willa Cather and America's Past."
      Washington Post, 30 June, sec. a, p. 14.
         Suggests that Cather's works are studied and enjoyed by
      those who share her interest in and appreciation for the past.
      Comments on Cather's dislike of change and modernity. Reprinted:
      1973.34.

34   _____. "Willa Cather Is Not Being Ignored: Study of Cather
      Is Quiet, But It Runs Deep." Omaha World-Herald, 22 July.
      Reprint of 1973.33.

35   McCLURE, CHARLOTTE SWAIN. "The American Eve: A Tragedy of
      Innocence." Ph.D. dissertation, University of New Mexico,
      268 pp.
         Characterizes the American Eve as a woman kept from self-
      knowledge and full participation in society and therefore doubly
      innocent. As the American Eve is freed from her limitations,
      she achieves self-knowledge and then faces the crisis of estab-
      lishing a new identity. Cather's is an affective Eve as opposed
      to the intelligent or awakening Eve found in the work of other

writers of the same period. Cather's Eve is an affectionate one
who would join with man in building and maintaining a social
order. See Dissertation Abstracts International 35 (1974):
1663-64A.

36   MILLER, BRUCE E. "The Testing of Willa Cather's Humanism:
      A Lost Lady and Other Cather Novels." Kansas Quarterly 5
      (Fall):43-50.
         The three tenets of Cather's humanism, "the struggle to
      realize an ideal," "human effort," and "freedom," are tested
      through encounters with evil in the novels that follow My Ántonia.
      In Cather's earlier novels the protagonists struggle toward an
      ideal and toward freedom, and they prevail unscathed. In A Lost
      Lady and The Professor's House, and some later novels, the pro-
      tagonists survive only by compromising their desired ideals.

37   MOERS, ELLEN. "Willa Cather and Colette: Mothers of Us All."
      World 2 (27 March):51-53.
         Uses the occasion of the centennial birth year for both the
      French writer, Colette, and Cather to point out links between the
      two, in spite of their obvious differences. The major link they
      share is their mutual obsession with the mother figure. Most of
      Cather's mother figures bear no children, but they "run the
      world." Cather's treatment is not consciously feminist.

38   MORRILL, CLAIRE. A Taos Mosaic: Portrait of a New Mexico
      Village. Albuquerque: University of New Mexico Press, pp. 7,
      114, 154, 155.
         In addition to making brief mentions of Death Comes for the
      Archbishop, avers that Elliott Arnold's The Time of the Gringo
      gives a more balanced portrait of the notorious Padre Martinez
      than does Cather's novel.

39   MURPHY, JOHN J. "The Respectable Romantic and the Unwed
      Mother: Class Consciousness in My Ántonia." Colby Library
      Quarterly 10 (September):149-56.
         My Ántonia testifies sadly to the unfulfilled potential of
      the American West. The emergence of class consciousness out of
      what approached social equality during the years of struggle with
      nature, and the materialism that accompanied class consciousness,
      thwart the early promise of the frontier.

40   MURRAY, MICHELE. "Observance of Miss Willa Cather's Birth
      Date Prompts Reissuance of One of Her Finest Novels."
      Hastings (Nebr.) Daily Tribune, 12 September.
         Reprint of 1973.41.

41   ____. "Willa Cather: Her Artistry Endures in a Different
      Age." National Observer, 15 September, p. 24.
         Pays tribute to Cather in the centennial year of her birth
      (and on the issuance of A Lost Lady), judging that she will soon
      outrank such writers as Ernest Hemingway, F. Scott Fitzgerald,
      and John Steinbeck. Cather's great theme is the imprint of
      humanity on the wilderness, and the garden is her symbol for

that. Cather rightly sees the destructive capabilities of sexual
desire and knows that uncontrolled passion of any kind exacts a
high price. In the order of art she found the freedom to express
her gift. Reprinted: 1973.40

42   "My Ántonia." Willa Cather Pioneer Memorial Newsletter 17
      (Winter):1-2.
            Reprinted from 1918.6.

43   OLSON, LAWRENCE. "Reconsideration: Willa Cather's Song of
      the Lark." New Republic 169 (7-14 July):28-31.
            Maintains that The Song of the Lark fails because Cather
      was not able to write effectively about Thea Kronborg once she
      got beyond youth. Cather did not know how to write about mature
      artists, and her ideas of art were so overly romantic that she
      could not write meaningful literature about or for the modern
      age.

44   OVERING, ROBERT. "Willa Cather and Mari Sandoz." Mari Sandoz
      Heritage (Chadron, Nebr.) 2 (Spring):1-4.
            Compares and contrasts the purposes, methods, and outlook
      of Cather and Mari Sandoz, finding them complementary in their
      contrasting portrayals of western life. Cather looks through a
      telescope, Sandoz through a microscope; Cather sees symbolically
      and selectively, Sandoz inclusively; Cather lives in her
      heroines, Sandoz lives apart from her characters. Both writers,
      however, view Nebraska with a certain nostalgia.

45   "Paper Dolls or People." Willa Cather Pioneer Memorial News-
      letter 17 (Winter):2-3.
            Reprint of 1919.5.

46   PARKER, JERALDINE. "'Uneasy Survivors': Five Women Writers
      1896-1923." Ph.D. dissertation, University of Utah, 120 pp.
            Analyzes the fictional heroine's responses to change in the
      wake of Darwin, Freud, and the industrial revolution. Considers
      the work of Cather, Sarah Orne Jewett, Mary E. Wilkins Freeman,
      Ellen Glasgow, and Edith Wharton. Revised for publication:
      1975.38. See Dissertation Abstracts International 34 (1973):
      1927A.

47   POLK, NOEL. Review of The World and the Parish. American
      Literary Realism 6 (Spring):162-63.
            Enjoys the vigor and self-confidence of Cather's early
      journalistic writings and sees in them the "discriminating self-
      assurance" that later enabled her to experiment boldly with
      structure in her novels. The writings are sometimes authori-
      tarian and uneven, but they are always interesting.

48   POWELL, LAWRENCE CLARK. "Personalities of the West: A Nice
      Place to Visit." Westways 65 (September):37-39, 66.
            Reports a conversation with Cather's publisher and friend,
      Alfred A. Knopf, in which Knopf made a few comments on Cather.
      According to Knopf, Cather recognized that Death Comes for the

Archbishop was an exceptional book, but she never wanted any of
her books to be required college reading.

49   POWNALL, DAVID E. Articles on Twentieth Century Literature:
     An Annotated Bibliography, 1954 to 1970. New York: Kraus-
     Thomson Organization, pp. 426–38.
         "An expanded cumulation of 'Current Bibliography' in the
     journal Twentieth Century Literature. Volume One to Volume Six-
     teen. 1955–1970." Contains a rather extensive listing of arti-
     cles about Cather over a fifteen-year period, including annota-
     tions in the form of direct quotation or paraphrase. Items are
     categorized, with general articles and a few pieces by Cather
     herself preceding separate listings for each Cather book.

50   "Prairie Priestess: Fictional World of Willa Cather." MD 17
     (April):109–15.
         Offers a general account of Cather's life and a summary of
     most of her novels, mentioning briefly the physicians in Red
     Cloud who befriended her and noting her early inclinations toward
     medicine. Cather's use of a narrator-observer allowed her to
     move freely among her own emotions and memories in her novels.
     In 1933 she withdrew from contemporary life. Sapphira and the
     Slave Girl is a powerful novel in the vein of Cather's best work.

51   QUANTIC, DIANE DUFVA. "The Revolt from the Village and Middle
     Western Fiction 1870–1915." Kansas Quarterly 5 (Fall):5–16.
         Argues that middlewestern "revolt from the village" litera-
     ture actually began long before 1915. Some of Cather's earliest
     stories contain elements of it, but "The Sculptor's Funeral" and
     The Song of the Lark, where the artist is portrayed in conflict
     with hometown values and attitudes, represent her fullest expres-
     sion of that revolt. The essential conflict in this literature
     grows out of the tension created by the dual perception of the
     Middlewest as both desert and garden.

52   RICE, GINGER. "People Worth Knowing." Lincoln Sunday Journal
     and Star, 15 April, sec. h, p. 21.
         The fiction in Uncle Valentine and Other Stories makes a
     good introduction to Cather, displaying her strengths in charac-
     terization, plot, and theme, and her ability as both storyteller
     and intellectual.

53   RILEY, PAUL D., ed. "Cather Family Letters." Nebraska History
     54 (Winter):585–618.
         Publishes and comments upon a set of letters written to
     Willa Cather's grandmother, Emily Ann Caroline Cather, by various
     family members. Claims that these letters are interesting to
     Cather literary historians, and also to historians of the fron-
     tier, principally for what they reveal about how the extended
     family--all of the surviving Cathers of the immediate family
     finally lived in one area of Nebraska--functioned on the
     frontier.

54   ROTHOVIUS, ANDREW E. "Author Adopted Jaffrey As Home."
      Jaffrey (N.H.) Recorder and Monadnock Breeze, 20 September,
      pp. 9, 14.
           Reviews Cather's life, emphasizing her admiration for the
      openhearted and direct relationships enjoyed by the immigrant
      pioneers. She is buried in Jaffrey because she liked to do her
      writing there.

55   RUCKER, MARY E. "Prospective Focus in My Ántonia." Arizona
      Quarterly 29 (Winter):303–16.
           From the "prospective focus," My Ántonia is the story of
      Jim Burden's working out his destiny as he is pulled first toward
      the barren landscape and then toward the human aspects of agrarian
      life represented sexually in Lena Lingard and ideally in Ántonia.
      But at the same time he is drawn toward the god of his destiny,
      letters and learning. This is his essential mission, and it is
      a lonely one. The novel traces the working out of these con-
      flicting desires in Jim's life; and regardless of what Cather had
      at first intended in the novel, Ántonia represents only one of
      them.

56   SCHEIDEMAN, J.W. "H.L. Mencken and Willa Cather in Louis
      Auchincloss' Pioneers and Caretakers." Menckeniana, no. 47,
      pp. 24–25.
           Comments on Auchincloss's observation in Pioneers and Care-
      takers (1961.5) that Cather luckily created a mystical link be-
      tween ancient Indians and modern America, a link that "saved her
      from degenerating into a shrill and ineffective version of H.L.
      Mencken." Maintains that Mencken appreciated and encouraged
      Cather's sense of the past and, in fact, rejuvenated his own
      style through using it just as she did.

57   SCHNEIDER, Sister LUCY. "Artistry and Instinct: Willa
      Cather's 'Land-Philosophy.'" CLA Journal (College Language
      Association) 16 (June):485–504.
           Catalogs the "seven cardinal points" of Cather's "land-
      philosophy" and examines the function of the major "land details"
      found in her fiction. A general study with scattered references
      to specific works, this essay presents a varied complex of ideas
      and facts to illustrate Cather's multifaceted view of the land
      and man's relationship to it.

58   _____ . "Of Land and Light: Willa Cather's Lucy Gayheart."
      Kansas Quarterly 5 (Fall):51–62.
           Nebraska had ambivalent effects on Lucy Gayheart, but the
      values of Lucy and Harry Gordon are central to the book and are
      based on the land.

59   _____ . "Willa Cather's 'The Best Years': The Essence of her
      'Land-Philosophy.'" Midwest Quarterly 15 (October):61–69.
           In Cather the land represents reality and the rock tran-
      scendence, both of which are suggested in "The Best Years," as
      they are in "Neighbour Rosicky." "The Best Years" is a culminat-
      ing view of Cather's land-philosophy and the values one gains

from the land. Miss Knightly and Lesley Ferguesson, and even Mrs. Ferguesson, are associated with the land. Mr. Ferguesson is not, even though he is a farmer.

60   SELLARS, RICHARD WEST. "The Interrelationship of Literature, History, and Geography in Western Living." Western Historical Quarterly 4 (April):171-85.
       Western literature has been more closely associated with geography than with history, but the culmination of history and geography in the West has led to something like "ancestor worship" in the literature of the West. America thus applauds itself through its western literature. In My Ántonia farm literature becomes part of western literature; and geography, through Cather's imagination, gives Ántonia heroic dimensions. In Death Comes for the Archbishop, Cather achieves a unique mix of the West's geography, literature, and history.

61   SEYMOUR-SMITH, MARTIN. Funk & Wagnalls Guide to Modern World Literature. New York: Funk & Wagnalls, pp. 51-52. Originally published in London under the title Guide to Modern Literature.
       Regards Cather as "undoubtedly" the "most considerable woman novelist" of her time, though she developed late. My Ántonia is her best novel; in other works she tends to manipulate her characters in order to reveal the corrupting influences of urbanization. She was too intense in her hatred of urbanization, and she wrote best when dealing with things she loved. Death Comes for the Archbishop represents her greatest stylistic achievement.

62   SLOTE, BERNICE. Introduction to Uncle Valentine and Other Stories: Willa Cather's Uncollected Short Fiction, 1915-1929. Lincoln: University of Nebraska Press, pp. ix-xxx.
       Discusses each of the seven heretofore uncollected stories in Uncle Valentine and Other Stories, noting themes and relationships with Cather's other work. These are all urban stories, ironic tales mainly of little people who do not achieve fame, but who matter. The stories rely heavily on the motif of the double, or the other self, and on the problem of exile and alienation. Reprinted in part: 1981.44.

63   _____, ed. "My Ántonia: Early Reviews." Willa Cather Pioneer Memorial Newsletter 17 (Winter):1-3.
       Briefly summarizes initial critical reaction to My Ántonia, then reprints three early reviews listed above. See 1973.8, 42, 45.

64   _____. "Willa Cather: Storyteller for Children." Willa Cather Pioneer Memorial Newsletter 7 (Summer):1-2.
       Introduces reprints of two early sketches attributable to Cather that make reference to Cather family experiences. Both appeared in 1896 in the National Stockman and Farmer, a journal associated with the Home Monthly when Cather edited that magazine.

65   ____. "Willa Cather's Work Began with Terrible Scrawl."
        Lincoln Evening Journal, 25 October, pp. 1, 23.
            Describes Cather's early career as a journalist in Lincoln,
        observing that her early writing style was typified by "high
        stepping rhetoric" which soon developed into a supple form with-
        out excess. She achieved this as early as 1913 in her novel
        O Pioneers!.

66   SLOTE, BERNICE, and WOODS, LUCIA. Willa Cather: A Pictorial
        Memoir. Lincoln: University of Nebraska Press, 1973, 144 pp.
            Slote provides the text and Woods most of the photographs
        in an effort to suggest "Willa Cather's union of life and art."
        The book is divided into two parts, the first providing a some-
        what personal view of places and people in Cather's life, and the
        second emphasizing her "American quality" by portraying her
        special ability to capture the essence of the several physical
        regions of America described so realistically in her art.
        Cather's own encounter with the Nebraska frontier was "a micro-
        cosm of the American frontier experience" in which one first
        feels erased by its cosmic grandness, then awed by its destiny.
        Reprinted in part: 1981.44.

67   SMITH, DAVID. "Willa Cather of Back Creek." Winchester (Va.)
        Evening Star, 5 May, p. 30.
            Deals with Cather family history and briefly recounts
        Cather's Virginia experience at Back Creek near Winchester.
        Describes the Cathers' Willowshade house in connection with her
        account of Nancy's homecoming in Sapphira and the Slave Girl.

68   STAFFORD, JEAN. Review of A Lost Lady. Washington Post Book
        World, 26 August, pp. 1, 6-7.
            The unfortunate changes that have occurred in the plains
        since Cather wrote A Lost Lady can be better appreciated by
        today's reader than by the reader at the time the novel was first
        issued. Cather was never shrill and derisive in her criticism,
        but was instead serene and judicious, especially in her Nebraska
        novels.

69   STINEBACK, DAVID C. "Willa Cather's Ironic Masterpiece."
        Arizona Quarterly 29 (Winter):317-30.
            In The Professor's House Tom Outland functions for Godfrey
        St. Peter as the image of his younger, adventuresome self, but
        St. Peter is essentially a man of thought while Tom is a man of
        action who is too close to history to apprehend it. St. Peter
        sees Tom as one who has escaped the strain and mundanity of con-
        temporary society. St. Peter simply cannot accept the fact of
        inevitable change and disorder, so he longs for an ideal of order
        he perceives in ancient civilizations. But what he ultimately
        yearns for is extinction; the real war is between life and death.
        Cather saw that nostalgia was dangerous as well as appealing, and
        that one had to accept the fact of change. She was more a real-
        ist than a romantic. Abridged: 1976.31.

70 STOUCK, DAVID. Review of Uncle Valentine and Other Stories.
     Southern Humanities Review 9:329-30.
          Contends that the New York stories in the Uncle Valentine
     collection show the marks of magazine fiction written for income.
     As art, they have varying degrees of value. The Pittsburgh sto-
     ries, however, are "vintage Cather," suave, subtly modulated, and
     elegaic. Links James Mockford in Lucy Gayheart with the "figure
     of death" in the Jamesian story, "Consequences."

71   _____. "Willa Cather's Last Four Books." Novel: A Forum on
     Fiction 7 (Fall):41-53.
          Argues that Cather's last four books give evidence that as
     she grew older Cather realized that life and human relationship
     are more important than the art to which they are too often
     sacrificed. The last books, then, are in the paradoxical situa-
     tion of being art that devalues itself; thus, with the exception
     of "Old Mrs. Harris," they show a decline in artistic vigor.
     Expanded: 1975.49. Reprinted: 1984.88.

72 STOUCK, MARY-ANN, and STOUCK, DAVID. "Art and Religion in
     Death Comes for the Archbishop." Arizona Quarterly 29
     (Winter):293-302.
          In Death Comes for the Archbishop Cather takes up again the
     theme of relinquishment of power. The valued art objects are
     communal ones, and the individual creative act that produced them
     is downplayed. Personal ambition must give way to selflessness,
     and the novel's central motif, Latour's cathedral, resolves the
     conflict between desiring art for the personal pleasure it gives
     and desiring it for its social and moral significance. The
     cathedral is an art object whose function is communal and whose
     service is to an ideal. Appears in altered form: 1975.49.

73 STUCKERT, SHIRLEY. "She Turned Nebraska into Willa Cather
     Country." Milwaukee Journal, 27 May, sec. 5, p. 2.
          Notes Nebraska's pride in Cather, and describes sites and
     people in and around Red Cloud that appear in her fiction.

74 SUTHERLAND, DONALD. "Willa Cather, Novelist: The Best of
     Her Time?" Washington Star-News, 13 May.
          Regards Uncle Valentine and Other Stories as a "treasure"
     for scholars, a collection containing characteristic Cather
     themes and displaying her virtuosity. Even if the city stories
     are basically magazine fiction, they are not trivial. And behind
     the reticence of language in "Coming, Aphrodite!" is "a pressure
     of genuine sexuality," just as there is in A Lost Lady. "Uncle
     Valentine" and "Double Birthday" are from the "expansive period"
     in Cather's career that also produced Death Comes for the Arch-
     bishop; their eloquence is "more overt" than that of the other
     stories.

75   TIBBETTS, JOHN C. "Vital Geography: Victor Seastrom's The
     Wind." Literature/Film Quarterly 1 (July):251-55.
         Regards The Wind as Catheresque because, like My Ántonia,
     it treats nature as both terrible and beautiful. Cather saw the
     tragic element in the mutual relationship between nature and
     humanity.

76   TOWER, SAMUEL A. "Willa Cather, American Novelist." New York
     Times, 9 September.
         Written on the occasion of the issuance of the Cather com-
     memorative stamp. Applauds Cather's honest writing and her
     disciplined stylistic precision. Also rehearses details of her
     life and quotes her as having said that the principal end of
     education is "learning how to do something well."

77   VARGO, EDWARD P. Rainstorms and Fire: Ritual in the Novels
     of John Updike. Port Washington, N.Y.: Kennikat Press,
     pp. 16-17, 47.
         Cites My Ántonia as a novel built around overlapping cyclic
     patterns that take on the character of ritual.

78   VEST, MIRA M. "Willa Cather, You're Forgiven!" Omaha Sunday
     World-Herald Magazine, 22 April, pp. 13-14.
         Seeks to reconcile the fact that Cather preferred writing
     about Red Cloud to living there, and provides a brief history of
     the town, describing its innovations and improvements since
     Cather's rise to fame.

79   VOSS, ARTHUR. The American Short Story: A Critical Survey.
     Norman: University of Oklahoma Press, pp. 157-58, 174-78.
         Concludes, from a consideration of the stories in the three
     books of short stories that Cather collected--plus the posthumous
     collection, The Old Beauty and Others--that although Cather's
     achievement in short fiction has not matched her achievement in
     the novel, it is a significant accomplishment nevertheless.

80   WELLS, NANCY. "Women in American Literature." English
     Journal 62 (November):1159-61.
         Describes the use of My Ántonia as the initial book
     assigned in a course on "Women in American Literature" developed
     at San Pedro High School, San Pedro, California. It was chosen
     for its literary value and also because it provides for discus-
     sion of American women at a particular historical moment.

81   "Willa Cather's Tribute to Mark Twain." Mark Twain Journal 17
     (Winter 1973-74).
         Reproduces on the outside back cover of the journal a
     typewritten Cather letter, over her handwritten signature and
     containing her handwritten editorial changes. In the letter
     Cather tells of encountering in Paris a Russian violinist who
     had read Huckleberry Finn. Cather wonders how that book, with
     its several dialects, could possibly be translated into Russian.

82   WOODRESS, JAMES, ed. "The Pre-eminent Magazine Genius: S.S.
      McClure." In Essays Mostly on Periodical Publishing in Amer-
      ica. Durham, N.C.: Duke University Press, pp. 171–92
      passim.
           Mentions Cather a number of times in connection with her
      activities with S.S. McClure and his magazine, giving some detail
      about her first meeting with him when he made arrangements to
      publish several of her stories.

83   _____. "Sarah Orne Jewett and Willa Cather." In English
      Studies Today. Eighth Conference of the International Asso-
      ciation of University Professors of English, no. 5. Edited
      by Sencer Tonguc. Istanbul, pp. 447–88.
           Regards both Jewett and Cather as romantics in the tradi-
      tion of Wordsworth and Emerson even though their materials appear
      outwardly realistic. Cather was influenced by Jewett to get away
      from immediate concerns and let her materials mature. Then those
      materials could issue forth from a quiet center inside her.

84   WOODS, LUCIA. "Views from Willa Cather's World." Text and
      photographs. Sweet Briar College Alumnae Magazine 44 (Fall):
      2–15.
           Traces the photographer's steps to various settings of
      importance in Cather's life and works, pointing to connections
      with the works and stressing the visual quality of Cather's writ-
      ing. Cather simultaneously affirms life and accounts for its
      pain; she values the primitive and understands the aristocrat.
      Furthermore, she sees the essential relationship between humanity
      and nature, and, like the philosopher, she is especially con-
      scious of light.

                              1974

1   BEAN, MARGARET. "Willa Cather and Dr. Sweeney." New
      Hampshire Profiles, August, pp. 44–45.
           Tells the story of how Cather came to use Dr. Frederick
      Sweeney's diary--and Sweeney himself--in her account of the voy-
      age of the Anchises in One of Ours. Also tells of Cather's con-
      nections to Jaffrey, New Hampshire.

2   BENNETT, S.M. "Ornament and Environment: Uses of Folklore in
      Willa Cather's Fiction." Tennessee Folklore Society Bulletin
      40:95–102.
           Although Cather did not employ the materials of folklore
      extensively, in at least three novels these materials have ex-
      panding significance. They are used mainly as ornament in My
      Ántonia, and they disappear when the Burdens and Ántonia move
      from farm to town. In Death Comes for the Archbishop they create
      a whole cultural environment, especially as they are used in
      legends and miracles. And finally, in Shadows on the Rock, they
      become the fabric out of which the whole religious and domestic
      environments are woven.

3   BLOOM, LILLIAN D., with BLOOM, EDWARD A. "The Poetics of
    Willa Cather." In Five Essays on Willa Cather: The Merrimack
    Symposium. See Murphy, 1974.47, pp. 97–119.
        Based on the chapter titled "The Sympathetic Imagination"
    in 1962.2. Cather's criticism is intuitive, like her art, and
    based on feeling rather than logic. For Cather, feeling and in-
    telligence, or genius, make a perfect blend in the artist. Feel-
    ing and thought are the same. Cather's art is composed of series
    of scenes and of great moments of feeling and realization. Para-
    doxically, Cather depended on remembered events and details, yet
    she disliked literalism. Furthermore, she experimented while
    disliking conscious invention. Art's only justification is in
    the evocation of emotion that is valid, and the objective non-
    commitment of the naturalists was Cather's chief objection to
    them. Her ideal novelist was both compassionate and restrained.

4   BOHLKE, L. BRENT. "Beginnings: Willa Cather and 'The
    Clemency of the Court.'" In "Willa Cather: A Portfolio."
    Prairie Schooner 48 (Summer):133–44.
        This early piece shows the way Cather creates a story by
    blending memory--her experiences with immigrants and the land,
    and perhaps her acquaintance with Turgenev--with a current con-
    cern over conditions in penal institutions. The beginnings of
    her fictional technique are evident in "The Clemency of the
    Court."

5   BOWMAN, ANTHONY. "Willa Cather's Pioneer Country." Photo-
    graphs by Lucia Woods. America Illustrated 211 (May):2–6.
    Published for distribution in the Soviet Union by the Press
    and Publications Service, United States Information Agency.
        In Russian, with titles and summary in English. Presents
    Cather as one who extolled the virtues of an earlier age in non-
    urban America. She has found popularity among a new generation
    of readers who value the American spirit she portrayed, a spirit
    that they perceive has been lost.

6   BOYE, ALAN. "The Design of the Retablo in Death Comes for the
    Archbishop." Saltillo 37 [1974]:37–45.
        Suggests that Cather accomplishes in Death Comes for the
    Archbishop what the New Mexican Retablo--"a group of paintings
    which may be taken separately, each having its own meaning, or
    together, to form a story, a complete unit of thought"--does in
    art. Both signal the beginning of the Modern Age and effect the
    reconciliation of opposites involved in the transition between
    the frontier and civilization.

7   CELLI, ALDO. Excerpt from "Italian Perspectives." Willa
    Cather Pioneer Memorial Newsletter 18 (Summer):1.
        Prepublication reprint from 1974.8.

8   _____. "Italian Perspectives." In The Art of Willa Cather.
    See Slote and Faulkner, 1974.69, pp. 103–18.
        Cather's interest in classical Italy is apparent; her
    attitude toward contemporary Italy is harder to deduce. But the

Italian reader sees her work in the context of the larger myth of primitivism in which American literature is viewed in Italy. Cather is also seen as one writing in the European tradition, and in the mode of romantic evasion. Cather might be profitably approached, not through a thematic or symbolic search, but through her narrative and linguistic devices, especially "the movement of her narrative along the syntagmatic [horizontal] and paradigmatic [vertical] axes." There are many dimensions to Cather's complex art--her use of oppositions, archetypes, anticipation, and melodramatic patterns. Reprinted in part, prior to publication: 1974.7.

9   CLEMONS, WALTER. Review of The Professor's House. Newsweek 83 (18 February):95.
     Appreciates the novel's broad understanding and its clear, simple style.

10   COOK, DAVID M., and SWAUGER, CRAIG G., eds. "Artist on the Frontier," and "Midwest Pioneers." In The Small Town in American Literature. New York: Dodd, Mead & Co., pp. 89-99, 100-111.
     A casebook anthology, two chapters of which are devoted to the work of Cather. The first reprints "The Sculptor's Funeral" and provides introductory commentary to the effect that the story develops the themes of the gifted person in conflict with social prejudices and conventions. The second reprints excerpts from "The Hired Girls" chapter in My Ántonia and takes the position that My Ántonia, in spite of its nostalgic mood, is a realistic portrayal of the Middle West.

11   CROSS, LESLIE. "It's Willa Cather's Year--in Milwaukee, Too." Milwaukee Sunday Journal, 24 March.
     The fiction in Uncle Valentine and Other Stories shows clear vision and understanding.

12   CUNLIFFE, MARCUS. Excerpt from "The Two or More Worlds of Willa Cather." Willa Cather Pioneer Memorial Newsletter 18 (Summer):3.
     Prepublication reprint from 1974.13.

13   _____. "The Two or More Worlds of Willa Cather." In The Art of Willa Cather. See Slote and Faulkner, 1974.69, pp. 21-42.
     Explores the differences between the approaches of Frederick Jackson Turner and Cather to the meaning of the frontier, and suggests that Cather's imaginative approach adds a dimension not always properly appreciated by the historian. Cather, in fact, does a highly commendable job of creating fiction out of material that is difficult to define and understand. For example, was the West a place of new direction and promise, or a place of backwardness? Cather does not treat East and West as opposites but as coordinates. Other coordinates are time and space. Reprinted in part, prior to publication: 1974.12.

14   DITSKY, JOHN. "Nature and Character in the Novels of Willa
        Cather." Colby Library Quarterly 10 (December):391-412.
            Discusses each Cather novel in turn in relation to each of
    the three ways in which she uses the land in her novels--as an
    entity that embodies history, as a source for future dreams, and
    as a means for defining character.

15   DOUGLAS, ANN. "Willa Cather and Her Heroines." With photo-
        graphs by Lucia Woods. University: A Princeton Quarterly 61
        (Summer):6-11.
            A personal response to Cather, expressing some perplexity
    over a woman who seems, by her very nature, not to have had to
    pay the price often paid by gifted women to practice their art.
    Her calm, her "incipient complacency," her "lack of social con-
    science," make her unapproachable, for so many of her sisters
    have suffered fragmentation and self-destruction while she has
    bypassed rebellion. Cather has the manner of an owner--she
    possesses and she knows she possesses; thus, her books ultimately
    tell of recovery, of return, not loss. Cather writes for the
    dispossessed, but she herself is intact, unscarred. Abridged:
    1982.22.

16   EDEL, LEON. Excerpt from "Homage to Willa Cather." Willa
        Cather Pioneer Memorial Newsletter 18 (Summer):2.
            Prepublication reprint from 1974.17.

17   _____ . "Homage to Willa Cather." In The Art of Willa Cather.
        See Slote and Faulkner, 1974.69, pp. 185-204, 264.
            Relates personal anecdotes about the work of completing the
    Brown biography (1953.2) of Cather, giving particular attention
    to such details as her 1873 birthdate and her given name
    "Wilella." Although Cather was a writer of surfaces whose
    imagination and sense of experimentation were severely limited,
    she was a gifted storyteller, and she sought for permanence, for
    things that endured. She was a strong and proud woman whose
    artistic strength lay in her capacity for lyricism and artistic
    sympathy. Reprinted in part, prior to publication: 1974.16.

18   EIFRIG, GAIL M. "Willa Cather: An Introduction." Cresset
        37 (May-June):20-28.
            Approaches what are commonly regarded as Cather's most
    important novels one at a time, asking questions designed to
    enhance understanding of the books rather than to discover hidden
    techniques. Regards My Ántonia as "an almost perfect novel," but
    finds an "ambiguity of intention" in One of Ours and a deliberate,
    "off-centeredness" in A Lost Lady. In Cather's culminating work,
    Death Comes for the Archbishop, she wants to give the reader a
    "primary understanding about life, that it is faithfulness that
    redeems it," faithfulness that is detected in the quality of
    actions rather than in the actions themselves.

19   FLEMING, PATRICIA JEAN. "The Integrated Self: Sexuality and the Double in Willa Cather's Fiction." Ph.D. dissertation, Boston University Graduate School, 270 pp.
    Discovers in Cather's fiction the presence of dual characters whose two selves, in essence, represent the separate halves of a fragmented psyche in the process of sexual initiation. See Dissertation Abstracts International 35 (1974):1653A.

20   FOX, [CLYDE] MAYNARD. "Symbolic Representation in Willa Cather's O Pioneers!" Western American Literature 9 (Fall): 187-96.
    Demonstrates how, through the use of symbol and image in "symbolic representation," Cather establishes relationships among characters and creates links among narrative events in O Pioneers!

21   FREYDBERG, MARGARET HOWE. "Willa Cather: The Light Behind Her Books." American Scholar 43 (Spring):282-87.
    Cather's great accomplishment lies in the total fusion of the woman with her art. Her personal integrity, her idealism, her love of virtue, are assimilated into her art to produce monumental characters. Her best books are those in which she successfully fuses art and subject and creates characters about whom she cares personally. Her less impressive novels are those in which she is not totally engaged.

22   GERVAUD, MICHEL. Excerpt from "Willa Cather and France: Elective Affinities." Willa Cather Pioneer Memorial Newsletter 18 (Summer):2.
    Prepublication reprint from 1974.23.

23   ____. "Willa Cather and France: Elective Affinities." In The Art of Willa Cather. See Slote and Faulkner, 1974.69, pp. 65-81, 260-61.
    In her admiration for France and French culture, Cather exercised a "selective blindness," overlooking France's faults and idealizing its strengths. Cather's affinities with France were deep; they permeated her life and work. In French civilization she invariably found whatever it was she needed at any particular stage of her career, though she could write only as an American in America. Reprinted in part, prior to publication: 1974.22.

24   GIANNONE, RICHARD [JOHN]. "Willa Cather and the Human Voice." In Five Essays on Willa Cather: The Merrimack Symposium. See Murphy, 1974.47, pp. 21-49.
    Trained in the oral tradition of literature, and particularly aware of the vocal dimensions of language, Cather seeks to restore literature to itself as a function of voice. Hearing, more than any of the other senses, reaches into the deepest centers of being. Thus, Willa Cather brings a much needed quality into the literature of an age which favors sight. She uses sound thematically, but she also uses it to give form to her novels. More and more Cather saw her novels as oral performance,

looking first to literary oral models and then to her own
acoustical forms.

25   HARRIS, RICHARD CASEY. "Energy and Order in Willa Cather's
     Novels." Ph.D. dissertation, University of North Carolina,
     247 pp.
        Considers Cather's method of juxtaposition in terms of
energy and order. Finds her works competently written, but often
suffering from artistic and technical inadequacies. See Dissertation Abstracts International 35 (1974):3742A.

26   HENDERSON, HARRY B., III. Versions of the Past: The Histori-
     cal Imagination in American Fiction. New York: Oxford Uni-
     versity Press, pp. 233, 246–49 passim, 250–55, 267.
        Includes Cather among writers like Hart Crane and William
Faulkner who tried to reconstruct history in an ideal form, thus
converting it into myth. Cather is a holistic writer, yet she
also links that tradition with the catastrophic notion suggested
by Henry Adams. Death Comes for the Archbishop is praised for
its attractive characters and beautiful descriptions, but criti-
cized for its attempted marriage of the Protestant success story
with Catholic hagiography.

27   HERMAN, DICK. "Memories of Willa Cather Shared with New
     Hampshire." Lincoln Sunday Journal and Star, 29 December.
        Describes Jaffrey, the New Hampshire town near the place
where Cather did a great deal of writing for many years, and
where she is buried.

28   HORGAN, PAUL. "The Pleasures and Perils of Regionalism."
     Western American Literature 8 (Winter):167–71.
        Urges writers associated with a region to follow the exam-
ple of Cather who transcends the merely regional in her art,
allowing her experience of life in a particular place to take on
general human significance.

29   IKUTA, TOSHIKO. "A Lost Lady: The Problem of Point of View."
     An excerpt from Kyusha American Literature. Synopses of Re-
     ports at the Annual Seminar, 1973, no. 15. Roppon-matsu,
     Fukuoka, Japan: Kyusha University, School of General Educa-
     tion, Kyusha American Literature Society, pp. 85–87.
        Assesses the advantage of A Lost Lady's being told with an
omniscient authorial point of view behind Niel Herbert's romantic
perspective. Marian Forrester makes of Niel a kind of "Ancient
Mariner," and the Forrester house becomes for Niel like the
Mariner's "ship of death."

30   KAUFMAN, MARJORIE R. "Willa Cather and Her Aunt Franc."
     Mount Holyoke Alumnae Quarterly 58 (Fall):164–69.
        Suggests that in light of Cather's personal attachment to,
and fictional representations of, her Aunt Frances (Mrs.
George P.) Cather, an alumna of Mount Holyoke Seminary, Cather
may have had deep roots in New England that began earlier than

her readers and critics have realized. Reprints excerpts from
"A Wagner Matinee" and notes that Aunt Franc was the inspiration
for Aunt Georgiana in that story, and probably for Mrs. Wheeler
in One of Ours as well.

31   KENDON, FRANK. Review of Obscure Destinies. Willa Cather
     Pioneer Memorial Newsletter 18 (Winter):3-4.
          Reprinted from 1932.17.

32   KNOPF, ALFRED A. "Miss Cather." In The Art of Willa Cather.
     See Slote and Faulkner, 1974.69, pp. 205-24.
          Outlines a chronological history, book by book, of Knopf's
     twenty-seven-year professional association with Cather as her
     publisher. The account is interspersed with stories and personal
     reminiscences, relating particularly to Cather's consistent re-
     jection of requests to film, reprint, broadcast, dramatize, con-
     dense, and anthologize her works.

33   KUEHL, LINDA. "Talk with Mr. Knopf." New York Times Book
     Review, 24 February, pp. 3, 12.
          Details an interview with Alfred A. Knopf, Cather's pub-
     lisher, in which he discusses his good working relationship with
     Cather and her desire for privacy. He protected her privacy, but
     even though he was "close" to her, there was always a certain
     formality in their relationship.

34   LATHROP, JOANNA. "On the Title." Willa Cather Pioneer
     Memorial Newsletter 18 (Winter):3.
          In Obscure Destinies Cather features individuals whose
     lives seem commonplace, like the lives of those described in
     Thomas Gray's elegy. Yet Cather takes each major figure and,
     after giving him or her a particular name and role, universalizes
     that figure to represent all of humanity. Thus, she emphasizes
     the importance of the individual in the larger scheme.

35   LAVENDAR, DAVID. "The Petrified West and the Writer." In
     Western Writing. Edited by Gerald W. Haslam. Albuquerque:
     University of New Mexico Press, pp. 143-56.
          Reprint of 1968.22.

36   LEWIS, JACQUELYNN S. "The Expression of Loneliness." Willa
     Cather Pioneer Memorial Newsletter 18 (Winter):3.
          Discusses Cather's subtle use of opposition and contrast
     to surprise the reader and create an atmosphere of loneliness.
     Obscure Destinies is a good example of this technique, but the
     device is present in many of Cather's works.

37   McMORRIS, ROBERT. "Willa Cather's Hunt for Youth." Omaha
     World-Herald, 25 October.
          Tells of Cather's altering her birthdate in the family
     Bible, making it 1876 instead of 1873, and of her carrying on the
     ruse until her death--causing confusion in biographical reports
     and universal errors in her obituaries.

38   MAGILL, FRANK N.; KOHLER, DAYTON; and TILGHMAN, TENCH FRANCIS,
     eds. Cyclopedia of World Authors. Rev. ed. Vol. 1. Engle-
     wood Cliffs, N.J.: Salem Press, pp. 334-37.
         Assesses Cather's total career, stressing the importance of
     the frontier experience in establishing her center of value.
     With the corruption of pioneer values, Cather grew increasingly
     disillusioned, as her fiction of the early and middle 1920s at-
     tests. Finally, she took the course Godfrey St. Peter had taken
     in The Professor's House and turned back to history and imagina-
     tion. Death Comes for the Archbishop was the result, and later
     Shadows on the Rock. A bibliographical summary of secondary
     sources is also provided.

39   MATTERN, CLAIRE. "The Themes That Bind." Willa Cather
     Pioneer Memorial Newsletter 18 (Winter):1.
         Notes that in each of the stories in Obscure Destinies
     Cather studies "the dependence of the weak and trusting upon the
     strong."

40   MILLER, JAMES E., Jr. Excerpt from "Willa Cather and the Art
     of Fiction." Willa Cather Pioneer Memorial Newsletter 18
     (Summer):2.
         Prepublication reprint from 1974.42.

41   _____. "My Ántonia and the American Dream." In "Willa
     Cather: A Portfolio." Prairie Schooner 48 (Summer):112-23.
         My Ántonia is pervaded by a sense of melancholy and loss
     for a dream that is not fulfilled. The image of the plow that
     looms large against the setting sun and then fades essentially
     defines the national experience, and Jim Burden is trying to
     discover what went wrong with the dream. In his hope, Jim
     Burden resembles Jay Gatsby. Ántonia, with her many children
     and her sense of fulfillment, shows what Jim has missed.

42   _____. "Willa Cather and the Art of Fiction." In The Art of
     Willa Cather. See Slote and Faulkner, 1974.69, pp. 121-48,
     262-63.
         In spite of obvious surface differences, Cather's best work
     shows that her principles of fictional art were fundamentally
     very much like those of Henry James. Like him, she saw true
     fiction as art and enunciated and practiced theories he had
     urged--about foreshortening, about narrative "registors and
     reflectors" who are essential to a novel's meaning, about working
     from one's own experience, and about the importance of the inter-
     nal life or consciousness. The most vital of Cather's three
     periods of artistic capability extends from My Ántonia through
     My Mortal Enemy. One of Ours and The Professor's House are dis-
     tinguished works that concentrate on the expansion of the inner
     self. Reprinted in part, prior to publication: 1974.40.

43   MILTON, JOHN R. "The Novel in the American West." In Western
     Writing. See Lavendar, 1974.35, pp. 69-89.
         Reprint of 1964.16.

44 MIYAKE, TSUNO. "On Willa Cather's Pioneer Novels--Referring
    to O Pioneers! and My Ántonia." In Kyusha American Litera-
    ture. See Ikuta, 1974.29, pp. 83-84.
        Singles out for discussion three qualities in Cather's two
    pioneer novels: masculinity of both character and theme, a de-
    tached style which gives the works objectivity, and a religious
    feeling.

45 MONTEIRO, GEORGE. "McNaught's Monthly: Addenda to the
    Bibliographies of Cather, Dickinson, Fitzgerald, Ford,
    Hemingway, Hergesheimer and Machen." Papers of the Biblio-
    graphical Society of America 68:64-65.
        Lists two reviews of Cather's work and one reprinted poem
    that appeared in McNaught's Monthly, a journal subtitled An
    Independent, Informal Review that published forty-three issues
    beginning in January 1924 and running through July 1927.

46 MOSELEY, ANN. "The Voyage Perilous: Willa Cather's Mythic
    Quest." Ph.D. dissertation, University of Oklahoma, 415 pp.
        Cather's novels constitute an "archetypal quest for artis-
    tic and spiritual truth" wherein she confronts various dualities
    such as reason and passion, order and disorder. See Dissertation
    Abstracts International 35 (1975):6102A.

47 MURPHY, JOHN J., ed. Five Essays on Willa Cather: The
    Merrimack Symposium. North Andover, Mass.: Merrimack
    College, 151 pp.
        Publishes the major essays presented at the Cather centen-
    nial symposium held at Merrimack College in 1973. Contains
    1974.3, 24, 48, 56, 68.

48 _____. "Willa Cather: The Widening Gyre." In Five Essays
    on Willa Cather: The Merrimack Symposium. See Murphy,
    1974.47, pp. 51-74.
        Contrasts Cather's earlier males of the Carl Linstrum,
    Emil Bergson, Jim Burden, and Claude Wheeler type--sensitive,
    weak, idealistic--with her later mature missionaries, Fathers
    Latour, Vaillant, and Chabanel. The latter were realistic men
    who conquered both themselves and their environments. The
    development illustrated here from earlier to later characters,
    with Godfrey St. Peter as a transitional figure, shows Cather's
    movement from a conflict between the real and the ideal (largely
    played out in male responses toward women and sex) to a recon-
    ciliation between them.

49 MURPHY, JOHN J., and FRENCH, WARREN. "Directions: Additional
    Commentary." In The Art of Willa Cather. See Slote and
    Faulkner, 1974.69, pp. 236-47.
        Murphy comments on some of the papers printed in this vol-
    ume from the international Cather seminar and suggests that
    through the "filter" of France Cather came to know and use both
    Nebraska and the Southwest. Advises that future criticism could
    benefit from close attention to Cather's texts, and from search-
    ing out her complexities and her relationships with her American

literary predecessors. French suggests that Cather's work can be examined in its relation to the techniques of modern painters, particularly post-impressionists like Cézanne, Van Gogh, and Mondrian. French points to Cather's experiments with painterly methods, especially as they relate to distancing, in the novels from A Lost Lady through Lucy Gayheart.

50   MURPHY, MICHAEL WALTER. "The Complex Past in Willa Cather's Novels of the Twenties." Ph.D. dissertation, University of Texas at Austin, 132 pp.
      Claims that Cather's reputation should rest on her novels of the twenties wherein she negates the practice of clinging to a futile and sentimental past. See Dissertation Abstracts International 35 (1974):3001A.

51   O'CONNOR, MARGARET ANNE. "A Guide to the Letters of Willa Cather." Resources for American Literary Study 4 (Autumn): 145–72.
      Provides listing of libraries that have letters written by Cather in their collections, including dates where available, names of correspondents, restrictions and photocopying policies of the various libraries, and some brief content descriptions. Cather's will prohibits quoting from her letters, and policies about reading and note-taking vary from library to library. There are approximately nine hundred letters in forty-three collections, though many others were undoubtedly destroyed by Cather's correspondents at her request. A second section of the article provides an index of Cather's correspondents with brief notes of identification.

52   PERS, MONA. "Two Friends." Willa Cather Pioneer Memorial Newsletter 18 (Winter):2.
      Applauds the mood created in "Two Friends" by the narrator's detachment. The two men in the story are actors on a stage whose masks are stripped off at the end, revealing characters that are both real and imperfect.

53   POWELL, LAWRENCE CLARK. "Death Comes for the Archbishop." In Southwest Classics: The Creative Literature of the Arid Lands; Essays on the Books and Their Writers. Los Angeles: Ward Ritchie Press, pp. 121–35.
      An abridged text of 1972.23.

54   PRAKKEN, SARAH L. The Reader's Adviser: A Layman's Guide to Literature. 12th ed. The Best in American and British Fiction, Poetry, Essays, Literary Biography, Bibliography, and Reference, vol. 1. New York: R.R. Bowker Co., pp. 558–60.
      In addition to listing Cather's books in print and some books about her, claims that her work has "purity of style" and "artistic integrity." Her western novels show the "conflict between meanness and grandeur," and end in triumph, whereas novels like A Lost Lady and The Professor's House chart the failure of idealism.

55 QUINN, JAMES. "Cather's My Ántonia and the Critics: An
    Annotated Bibliography." Kansas English 59 (February):20-21.
        Lists and annotates twenty-two articles and books published
    between 1947 and 1973 that deal with My Ántonia.

56 RANDALL, JOHN H., III. "Willa Cather and the Pastoral Tradi-
    tion." In Five Essays on Willa Cather: The Merrimack Sym-
    posium. See Murphy, 1974.47, pp. 75-96.
        Suggests that Cather's course in Greek and Latin poetry at
    the University of Nebraska planted in her consciousness a feeling
    for the pastoral tradition that finds an outlet in her prairie
    novels, O Pioneers!, My Ántonia, and A Lost Lady. There are many
    points of comparison, especially with Virgil's Eclogues (and his
    Georgics in My Ántonia). The prairie novels are Cather's best
    works, but they falter in the few places where she departs from
    the pastoral form.

57 Review of Uncle Valentine and Other Stories. Virginia Quar-
    terly Review 50 (Winter):x.
        The stories in the collection show vitality, restraint, and
    variety.

58 RUBEL, WARREN G. "Willa Cather: The Fragile Web of Memory."
    Cresset 37 (May-June):7-12.
        Explores Cather's narrative technique which links "a nos-
    talgic, even archaic sense of distance in time" with Cather's
    own passionate feeling for her central characters. The resulting
    "opposition between distance and passion" generates a dynamic
    tension in Cather's work, enabling her to create a past that is
    a vital component to the present and future. She makes memory,
    with its selective eye functioning much like the artist's eye,
    an inextricable facet of immediate consciousness.

59 RUSHMORE, ROBERT. "To Bind the Whirlwind." Opera News 38
    (June):20-21.
        Notes Cather's love for the opera and her fictional treat-
    ment of singers, but concludes that she chose for her artistic
    expression the opposite of externalized emotion. Her method was
    to create art by binding and controlling emotions.

60 St. JOHNS, ADELA ROGERS. Some Are Born Great. Garden City,
    N.Y.: Doubleday & Co., pp. 129-30. Reprint. N.Y.: New
    American Library, Signet Books, 1975.
        Alleges that Cather was America's best woman novelist, but
    she was a terrible woman. She launched a viciously inaccurate
    but futile attack on the indomitable Mary Baker Eddy in a series
    of magazine articles that later appeared as a biography under the
    name of Georgine Milmine.

61 SATO, HIROKO. Excerpt from "Willa Cather in Japan." Willa
    Cather Pioneer Memorial Newsletter 18 (Summer):3-4.
        Prepublication reprint from 1974.62.

52   ____. "Willa Cather in Japan." In The Art of Willa Cather.
      See Slote and Faulkner, 1974.69, pp. 84-97, 261-62.
          Although Cather is a truly American writer, she has some
      qualities that separate her from her fellow Americans and explain
      the special affinity the Japanese feel for her. Cather's work
      has a basic European literary character, but she is compatible
      with the Japanese in at least three ways: in her view of the
      harmonious relationship possible between humanity and nature, in
      her regard for the importance of family roots, and in her belief
      that ideally the artist shapes a better social order. Reprinted
      in part, prior to publication: 1974.61.

63   SCHNEIDER, Sister LUCY. "Permanence and Promise: Cather's
      Shadows on the Rock." Renascence 26 (Winter):83-94.
          Summarizes the plot of Shadows on the Rock and then names
      the book's central symbols--the rock, the past, and religious
      beliefs--and lists their occurrences. The weaknesses of the book
      include its inclination to preach and give facts, its plot con-
      trivances, its unnecessary repetitions, and its character incon-
      sistencies. The book's strengths include the mystery of Blinker,
      the character of Saint-Vallier, and the relationship between
      Cécile and Pierre.

64   SHULTS, DONALD. "Willa Cather: Style in Death Comes for the
      Archbishop." In Kyusha American Literature. See Ikuta,
      1974.29, pp. 75-83.
          Enumerates the characteristics of Cather's style as re-
      vealed in Death Comes for the Archbishop, her greatest stylistic
      achievement. Her spelling is traditional, her punctuation con-
      ventional, her diction simple and exact, and her method economi-
      cal. Cather's dialogue is not dramatic, but she is "a master of
      sequence" and understatement. She uses figurative language
      sparingly, and employs scenes and incidents for their cumulative
      effect.

65   SLOTE, BERNICE. "A Gathering of Nations." In The Art of
      Willa Cather. See Slote and Faulkner, 1974.69, pp. 248-53.
          Serves as the summary piece for the International Seminar
      (see 1974.69), reviewing the variety of responses presented and
      stressing Cather's international qualities. Concludes that
      whether one views Cather as a conscious artist or an intuitive
      artist, there is a multicolored magic in her art that partakes of
      both the primitive and the civilized.

66   ____. "Willa Cather and the West." Persimmon Hill 4, no. 4:
      48-59.
          Rehearses some of Cather's connections with the West, which
      for her included the whole vast area between the Missouri River
      and the Rocky Mountains as well as the desert country of Arizona
      and New Mexico. The West often served as the wellspring of her
      imagination, and she regularly traveled there to gain inspiration
      for her work. She saw in the West the process of civilization
      and the blending of nationalities.

67   _____. "Willa Cather." In Sixteen Modern American Authors:
      A Survey of Research and Criticism. Edited by Jackson R.
      Bryer. Durham, N.C.: Duke University Press, pp. 29-73.
           An updated text of 1969.17. A further update of this
      bibliographical essay is being prepared by James Woodress for
      materials through 1983.

68   _____. "Willa Cather: The Secret Web." In Five Essays on
      Willa Cather: The Merrimack Symposium. See Murphy, 1974.47,
      pp. 1-19.
           Beneath the simple surface of Cather's work there is a hid-
      den level of complexity, a fact which echoes in her life as well
      as in her work. This secret web, which links the experiences of
      both life and art, can be seen operating in such a book as O
      Pioneers! where there is a secret web of connections to Walt
      Whitman. A Lost Lady and My Mortal Enemy operate through a
      beneath-the-surface system of allusions.

69   SLOTE, BERNICE, and FAULKNER, VIRGINIA, eds. The Art of Willa
      Cather. Lincoln: University of Nebraska Press, 279 pp.
           Includes lectures, commentary, and a panel discussion
      ("Definitions and Evaluations," pp. 227-35) presented at "The
      Art of Willa Cather: An International Seminar," held in Lincoln
      in October 1973 as a part of the Cather Centennial Festival.
      Contains 1974.8, 13, 17, 23, 32, 42, 49, 62, 65, 73, 79, 85.

70   STOUCK, DAVID. "The Works of Willa Cather." Audio-cassette
      discussion of My Ántonia. Deland, Fla.: Everett/Edwards.
           Describes My Ántonia as a pastoral novel--a portrayal of
      innocence. My Ántonia is Jim's story, and Jim, as the central
      conscience, seeks to retreat from society, age, and death and
      return to Eden. The book's chronological sequence, however,
      proves the futility of Jim's efforts as time moves inexorably
      onward. Jim is preoccupied with eliminating sexuality--espe-
      cially in Ántonia whom he sees as a mother figure--and its in-
      herent responsibilities. This preoccupation creates the artistic
      tension of the novel: the seeking of a past that cannot be re-
      captured. Jim's search and eventual satisfaction in recapturing
      his boyhood through Ántonia's boys leaves the reader with
      ambiguous feelings--which is part of the novel's greatness.

71   SUDERMAN, ELMER F. "Perceptions of the Prairie in My Ántonia."
      Iowa English Bulletin Yearbook 24 (November):49-56.
           The article is made up mostly of a group of poems in which
      Suderman tries to capture the feelings Cather conveys about the
      prairie in My Ántonia. He explains in his introduction to the
      poems that he relies heavily on Cather's own words as they appear
      in the novel, cutting and changing only to enhance the effect her
      language and feelings create. His poems become, at once, a
      translation--thus a simplification--of the novel's significant
      emotions and a critical commentary on them.

72   SUTHERLAND, DONALD. Excerpt from "Willa Cather: The Classic
      Voice." Willa Cather Pioneer Memorial Newsletter 18 (Summer):
      3.
          Prepublication reprint from 1974.73.

73   _____. "Willa Cather: The Classic Voice." In The Art of
      Willa Cather. See Slote and Faulkner, 1974.69, pp. 156–79,
      263.
          The very essence of Cather is Virgilian, especially in that
      she, like Virgil, sought to achieve the effects of energy and
      passion by the use of seemingly flat, pale statements of such
      concentrated realism that the very "behavior of living," the
      "quick of the process," is revealed instead of a philosophical
      sense of life. Cather dealt with essentials rather than with
      the kinds of social-psychological matters that occupied the re-
      puted novelists of her day. Reprinted in part, prior to publica-
      tion: 1974.72.

74   TAYLOR, J. GOLDEN. "The Western Short Story." In Western
      Writing. See Lavendar, 1974.35, pp. 90–108.
          Reprint of 1964.23.

75   THOMPSON, BERNITA LONETTE ARNOLD. "Continuity in the Work of
      Willa Cather." Ph.D. dissertation, University of Nebraska,
      221 pp.
          Perceives Cather's view to be tragic but not hopeless in
      her dominant concerns for the artist, the land, and the past.
      See Dissertation Abstracts International 35 (1974):3013A–14A.

*76   TRIER, MARILYN ROBB, ed. World Topics Year Book, 1974. Lake
      Bluff, Ill.: Tangley Oaks Educational Center.
          The Willa Cather Pioneer Memorial Newsletter for fall 1974
      indicates that this volume contains a feature on the events of
      the Cather centennial in its "pictorial survey of important news
      and cultural events of 1973." A computer search turned up a copy
      of this book at the Library of Congress, but not at regular
      interlibrary loan locations.

77   Van GHENT, DOROTHY. "Willa Cather." In American Writers: A
      Collection of Literary Biographies. Edited by Leonard Ungar.
      Vol. 1. New York: Charles Scribner's Sons, pp. 312–34.
          Reprint of 1964.25.

78   WELTY, EUDORA. Excerpt from "The House of Willa Cather."
      Willa Cather Pioneer Memorial Newsletter 18 (Summer):4.
          Prepublication reprint from 1974.79.

79   _____. "The House of Willa Cather." In The Art of Willa
      Cather. See Slote and Faulkner, 1974.69, pp. 3–20, 259.
          Cather's art depends on the creation of the essence of a
      physical world, but her landscapes stretch between present and
      distant past, with nothing in the middle distance. The conti-
      nuity is provided by the pioneer who lives it and the artist who
      perceives it. Passion is the key to Cather's art. It embodies

the artist's physical world, and the physical world in turn gives
each novel its form, for it is here that the emotions are rooted.
The house on the landscape is the evidence of human life lived
there. So it is with Cather's art. The "house" she constructs,
the physical form of her art, is the embodiment of her idea, the
form given her truth. She symbolizes this process in the "houses"
of Tom Outland and Godfrey St. Peter in The Professor's House.
Abridged: 1974.80. Reprinted: 1978.33; 1980.47; 1984.93. Reprinted in part, prior to publication: 1974.78.

80   ____. "The Physical World of Willa Cather." New York Times
        Book Review, 27 January, pp. 19-20, 22.
           An abridged text of 1974.79.

81   WHALEY, ELIZABETH GATES. "Cather's My Mortal Enemy." In
     "Willa Cather: A Portfolio." Prairie Schooner 48 (Summer):
     124-33.
        Explains My Mortal Enemy by focusing on the character of
     Myra Henshawe. She is a victim of her great uncle's need to
     dominate her life, and she in turn victimizes others the same
     way. She tries to program everyone to suit her will. Myra seems
     to be speaking for Cather at this stage of her life as she seeks
     in the end for what is immortal. Myra does not have art as
     Cather does, so she turns to religion. Myra's mortal enemy may
     well be her own mortality.

82   WINNER, VIOLA HOPKINS. Cather entry in Dictionary of American
     Biography. Supp. 4, 1946-1950. Edited by John A. Garraty and
     Edward T. James. New York: Charles Scribner's Sons,
     pp. 153-55.
        Provides a rather detailed biographical sketch, including
     some genealogical details, of Cather's life and offers evaluative
     commentary on several of her works. Sees relationships between
     Cather and such writers as Ernest Hemingway, F. Scott Fitzgerald,
     and Sherwood Anderson, and regards some of her writing in the
     1920s to be an expression of the "wasteland spirit of postwar
     writing." Cather's best work reflects her own personal involve-
     ment with her materials; her sensibility was derived from the
     nineteenth century. A bibliographical essay concludes the entry.

83   WOODRESS, JAMES. Cather entry in Encyclopedia of American
     Biography. Edited by John A. Garraty and Jerome L. Stern-
     stein. New York: Harper & Row, pp. 183-84.
        Provides a bio-bibliographical sketch and observes ways in
     which particular Cather novels express her themes, convictions,
     feelings, and theories of fiction. She blends romance and real-
     ism, using myth and symbol in such a way as to remove her work
     from temporal and geographical constraints.

84   ____. Excerpt from "Willa Cather: American Experience and
        European Tradition." Willa Cather Pioneer Memorial Newsletter
        18 (Summer):1.
           Prepublication reprint from 1974.85.

85   _____. "Willa Cather: American Experience and European Tra-
      dition." In The Art of Willa Cather. See Slote and Faulkner,
      1974.69, pp. 43–62, 260.
         Cather's appeal to both the inexperienced reader and the
      literary expert lies in the fact that her work is an effective
      blend of the life of the body and the life of the mind. She cap-
      tures the emotional excitement of life experienced in the new
      world of prairie and desert and fuses that with the intellectual
      excitement of the Old World tradition that she absorbed through
      opera, books, and trips to the continent. The complexity of myth,
      symbol, and allusion, in conjunction with the reality of American
      experience, are present in her work. Reprinted in part, prior
      to publication: 1974.84.

86   _____, comp. "Willa Cather." In American Fiction, 1900–1950:
      A Guide to Information Sources. American Literature, English
      Literature, and World Literatures in English: An Information
      Guide Series, vol. 1, edited by Theodore Griedor. Detroit:
      Gale Research Co., pp. 55–60.
         Ranks Cather among America's best stylists and craftsmen
      and notes her intense interest in the artist and in social and
      moral values and relationships. Takes the form of a bibliograph-
      ical essay describing and evaluating sources of Cather informa-
      tion, both primary and secondary, under each of the following
      headings: bibliography and manuscripts, works of fiction, edi-
      tions and reprints, biography, and criticism. Comments on trends
      in Cather criticism and recommends sources of additional criti-
      cism, including Cather's own writing about her craft.

87   YONGUE, PATRICIA [LEE]. "Neighbour Rosicky." Willa Cather
      Pioneer Memorial Newsletter 18 (Winter):2–3.
         "Neighbour Rosicky" is an appropriate epilogue to Death
      Comes for the Archbishop, and both stand out as moments of
      "splendid finish" in a time of national pessimism. Like Jean
      Latour, Rosicky lives a life fulfilled by his own creativity.

                                    1975

1   AICHINGER, PETER. The American Soldier in Fiction, 1880–1963:
      A History of Attitudes Toward Warfare and the Military Estab-
      lishment. Ames: Iowa University Press, pp. 4–5, 8–12 passim,
      19, 41, 47, 50.
         Cather and Edith Wharton treat war in their novels mainly
      as it affects the individual personality. Generally, their nov-
      els about war are prowar; they simplify war to a battle between
      the forces of right (the allies) and their enemies. There are
      Odyssean images in One of Ours that suggest a link between Ameri-
      can and Greek heroes. Furthermore, there is a crusading aspect
      in the resemblance between Claude's going off to save the sister
      state, France, and Enid's going off on a religious mission to
      save her sister in China.

2   ANDERSON, DAVID D. "Willa Cather's Second Century." Society
     for the Study of Midwestern Literature Newletter 5, no. 1:
     13-14.
          Expresses some misgivings over the international focus of
     the seminar held in Nebraska to commemorate the one hundredth
     anniversary of Cather's birth in 1973. Cather's best and most
     durable work is the work she produced as a regional writer, and
     future studies should recognize that Nebraska is her point of
     departure and the source of her most perceptive inspiration and
     insight.

3   ARNOLD, MARILYN. "Cather's Last Stand." Research Studies 43
     (December):245-52.
          The motif of escape is central to Sapphira and the Slave
     Girl, both in plot and in the habitual life patterns of the
     characters. What the characters want most is to live without
     disruption of peace, without threat to comfort, without having to
     deal openly with conflict or admit that conflict exists. The
     book becomes almost a fierce insistence that whatever else one
     has lost, one can still live with dignity and pride if one ad-
     heres to a construct of order and decorum and refuses to let that
     construct fall.

4   _____. "The Function of Structure in Cather's The Professor's
     House." Colby Library Quarterly 11 (September):169-78.
          Observes that the structural line of the novel is split,
     with chapters titled "The Family" and "The Professor" divided by
     "Tom Outland's Story" just as the professor is divided from his
     family by Tom Outland and the nonmaterialistic, solitary ideal he
     represents. Moreover, the basic movement of the book, and of
     Godfrey St. Peter's life, is from society to solitude. But in
     the end of the book, Cather works a dramatic reversal and swings
     St. Peter back to a rather grim acceptance of his role as a
     social being. Cather may be saying that the mesa ideal is not
     really one that modern man is able to embrace.

5   BENNETT, MILDRED R. "Willa Cather and the Prairie." Nature
     Conservancy News 25 (Winter):8-11.
          Illustrates Cather's lifelong regard for the prairie
     through citing passages from her novels and from her published
     interviews. Notes also the establishment of the Willa Cather
     Memorial Prairie. Reprinted: 1975.6.

6   _____. "Willa Cather and the Prairie." Nebraska History 56
     (Summer):231-35.
          Reprint of 1975.5.

7   BOHLKE, BEVERLY. "On Death Comes for the Archbishop." Willa
     Cather Pioneer Memorial Newsletter 19 (Summer):3-4.
          Death Comes for the Archbishop probes sensitively into
     human relationships--particularly those between different cul-
     tures. The friendships between Bishop Latour and the Indians
     Eusabio and Jacinto show respect, honesty, and trust toward one
     another and toward the land.

8   BOHLKE, L. BRENT. "The Ecstasy of Alexandra Bergson." <u>Colby Library Quarterly</u> 11 (September):139-49.

      Whether or not Cather made a conscious connection between Alexandra's mystical experience with the Genius of the Divide in <u>O Pioneers!</u> and St. Teresa of Avila's autobiographical descriptions of her "ecstasies" or "raptures," there are marked similarities between them. Both women experience the sensation of being carried off, by someone or something familiar and strong, after a prior sense of heaviness or anguish.

9   BORGMAN, PAUL. "The Dialectic of Willa Cather's Moral Vision." <u>Renascence</u> 27 (Spring):145-59.

      Cather's novels reveal the development of her moral vision--from the portrayal of longing or hope, to an assertion of faith, and, finally (in <u>Sapphira and the Slave Girl</u>) to a union of hope and faith that is embodied as love.

10   BRUNAUER, DALMA H[UNYADI]. "The Problem of Point of View in <u>A Lost Lady</u>." <u>Renascence</u> 28 (Autumn):47-52.

      Some criticism has mistakenly assumed that the views of Niel Herbert toward Marian Forrester are also those of Cather. Niel is, however, a prude, and Cather's sympathies are with Marian and Captain Forrester. Niel can be compared with John Marcher in Henry James's "The Beast in the Jungle." Both men fail to appreciate fully the woman before them.

11   BRUNAUER, DALMA HUNYADI, and KLAMECKI, JUNE DAVIS. "Myra Henshawe's Mortal Enemy." <u>Christianity and Literature</u> 25 (Fall):7-40.

      Reviews the somewhat limited and generally sketchy critical reaction to <u>My Mortal Enemy</u>, then launches into a discussion of the book's narrative angle. The novel has been misread because critics have often failed to perceive that Nellie Birdseye, like Jim Burden and Niel Herbert, is an unreliable narrator. With her monocular, "bird's eye" vision, Nellie fails to see that Myra's great disappointment is not that she married for love but that her lover, like Norma's lover in Bellini's opera, is unfaithful. Myra's mortal enemy could just as well be Nellie as Oswald, but it may also be Myra's mortal body--the thing that stands between her and immortality.

12   BUDZ, JUDITH KAUFMAN. "The Immigrant Experience on the Great Plains." <u>Illinois Schools Journal</u> 55 (Fall):21-27.

      That the American character is actually defined by the immigration experience can be seen in the novels of Ole Rölvaag and Willa Cather. The immigrant's life is one of contradiction, for an effort to make things better for the family is usually the motivation behind immigration, but the experience of the immigrant is usually one of increased isolation and corrupted vision, both within and between families.

13   CAHILL, SUSAN. Women and Fiction: Short Stories by and about
     Women. New York: New American Library, Mentor Books,
     pp. 27-28.
         Introduces "A Wagner Matinee," which appears in this
     anthology, with a brief biography. Adds that Cather's Nebraska
     fiction is her best, and cites comments by other writers--Eudora
     Welty, Louise Bogan, and Wallace Stevens--on Cather's work.

14   CURTIN, WILLIAM M[ARTIN]. "Willa Cather and The Varieties of
     Religious Experience." Renascence 27 (Spring):115-23.
         Cather's characters who have religious traits can be under-
     stood better through an applied reading of William James's The
     Varieties of Religious Experience, but so can other characters
     like Thea Kronborg for whom religious experience is a mystical
     realization that brings her two selves into union. Thea exempli-
     fies the specific marks of mystical experience as described by
     James, including transiency and ineffability.

15   DAVIDSON, COLLEEN TIGHE. "Beyond the Sentimental Heroine:
     The Feminist Character in American Novels, 1899-1937." Ph.D.
     dissertation, University of Minnesota, 201 pp.
         Devotes one chapter to analyzing Cather's The Song of the
     Lark along with works of other women writers whose heroines are
     career-minded. Combines this chapter with others to create a
     picture of the new standards for feminine behavior introduced by
     women authors through their heroines at the turn of the century.
     See Dissertation Abstracts International 37 (1976):306A.

16   DRAVES, Rev. CORNELIUS J. "Willa Cather Recalled."
     Evangelist, 9 January.
         Praises Cather for her ability to write about human needs
     and capabilities, and finds a "certain sacredness" in her art.
     Compares her statement from My Ántonia ("this is happiness: to
     be dissolved into something complete and great") to the Christian
     theme of merging with a greater purpose to achieve the ultimate.
     Cather's presentation of characters in the process of becoming is
     a comforting acceptance of all that is human.

17   FREEDMAN, RICHARD. The Novel. New York: Newsweek Books,
     pp. 106-7.
         Cather is a regionalist in the manner of Sarah Orne Jewett,
     but she is also like Edith Wharton in that for her too civiliza-
     tion spells the demise of a heroic past.

18   GERBER, PHILIP. Willa Cather. Twayne United States Authors
     Series. Boston: G.K. Hall & Co., 187 pp.
         Provides biographical data and links Cather's novels
     thematically to her life and to each other, indicating that
     Cather's central theme up to and including Youth and the Bright
     Medusa is the flight from modern values. One of Ours is her
     "pivotal novel" wherein the "theme of personal heroism gives way
     to the hitherto subordinated concern for an endangered society."
     The most important of Cather's artistic principles is "selectiv-
     ity," but her passwords are "passion, beauty, emotion." The

concluding chapter deals with Cather's achievement of fame and
the reception accorded her over the years by critics and lay
readers.

19   GOLDBERG, RAQUEL PRADO-TOTARO. "The Artist Fiction of James,
     Wharton, and Cather." Ph.D. dissertation, Northwestern Uni-
     versity, 368 pp.
         Concludes through general comparisons that Henry James,
     Edith Wharton, and Willa Cather are each unique in their own
     visions of the artist. See Dissertation Abstracts International
     36 (1976):4475A.

20   GOODMAN, CHARLOTTE. "Images of American Rural Women in the
     Novel." University of Michigan Papers in Women's Studies 1
     (June):57-70.
         Treats Cather's Alexandra Bergson in O Pioneers! as one of
     several portraits of strong rural women in American fiction,
     women who do not fit the sentimental or mythical stereotypes
     perpetuated in works like Earl Hamner's Spencer's Mountain and
     John Steinbeck's The Grapes of Wrath.

21   HAFER, JOHN WILLIAM. "The Sea of Grass: The Image of the
     Great Plains in the American Novel." Ph.D. dissertation,
     Northern Illinois University, 301 pp.
         Presents a chronological survey of the American novel and
     discusses its varying treatment of the Great Plains in both theme
     and setting. Devotes one chapter each to O Pioneers!, My
     Ántonia, and A Lost Lady, analyzing how their settings function
     to reflect a changed attitude from previous writers. See Disser-
     tation Abstracts International 36 (1976):6098A.

22   HASKELL, HENRY C. "Cather's Archbishop: Truth from Her
     Intuition." Kansas City Star, 21 September, sec. d, p. 1.
         Uses Paul Horgan's biography, Lamy of Santa Fe, to compare
     Cather's character, Jean Latour, with his real life counterpart.
     The two are similar in fact as well as spirit. In Death Comes
     for the Archbishop, Cather skillfully keeps Latour in the fore-
     ground despite the appealing human qualities of her second char-
     acter, Joseph Vaillant.

23   HELLER, SHIRLEY H. "Willa Cather (1873-1947)." In 20th Cen-
     tury American Women Authors: A Feminist Approach. Monarch
     Notes, edited by Walter James Miller. New York: Simon &
     Schuster, Monarch Press, pp. 27-32.
         Provides a brief Cather biography, underlining Cather's
     early interest in "mannish pursuits," and her feeling of repul-
     sion toward the present and attraction to the past. Then con-
     centrates on a feminist critique of My Ántonia, indicating that
     Ántonia's choice for motherhood--she is an archetypal earth
     mother with "only the positive side of the archetype showing"--is
     not in answer to conventional role expectations, but is in "ful-
     fillment of her deepest self." Lena Lingard and Tiny Soderball
     make different choices for their lives, but they, like Ántonia,

are allowed choice. "Willa Cather's women all succeed in a man's world."

24 HELMICK, EVELYN THOMAS. "The Broken World: Medievalism in A Lost Lady." Renascence 28 (Autumn):39-46.
Cather's treatment of the decline of the heroic West in A Lost Lady is an allegory patterned after the medieval courtly romance, with Captain Forrester resembling King Arthur and Marian Forrester imaging the lovely lady to whom the knight (Niel Herbert) dedicates his life. The feudalistic class-consciousness of Cather's idealized world is present, as is the stress on such qualities as loyalty and worship of a chivalric ideal. Reprinted: 1984.43.

25 LATHROP, JOANNA. "On One of Ours." Willa Cather Pioneer Memorial Newsletter 19 (Winter):1-2.
One of Ours is an ironic novel treating the defeat of the American ideal, for Claude Wheeler had only two choices. He could die holding onto an illusion, or he could live with disillusionment. Concludes that "war and dying are not practical solutions to the search for values."

26 _____. Response in "Symposium: Women and Tragedy." Prairie Schooner 49 (Fall):232-34.
Responds to the question: "Why is it that no woman has ever written great tragedy?" Answers that women have written in their particular genres what must be considered tragic sequences. For example, in Cather's My Mortal Enemy the narrator, Nellie Birdseye, functions like a Greek chorus. Furthermore, Myra Henshawe gives up position for love only to feel betrayed because she can accept nothing less than total "inter-involvement" in close human relationships. In tying her to a common life, as well as betraying her with a younger woman, Oswald becomes her enemy. But the ultimate mortal enemy is human frailty.

27 _____, comp. Willa Cather: A Checklist of Her Published Writing. Lincoln: University of Nebraska Press, 131 pp.
Contains a chronological listing of 776 known Cather writings, but does not attempt to be comprehensive. Includes printings and reprintings in English, but does not list publication in textbook anthologies. Lathrop regards this work as providing interim assistance to researchers until a more complete bibliography can be prepared.

28 LEE, HECTOR. "Tales and Legends in Western American Literature." Western American Literature 9 (February):239-54.
Refers to Death Comes for the Archbishop in connection with the observation that legends in western literature are sometimes borrowed from the old world or eastern United States and then inserted in western stories. Such a one is the story about Fathers Junipero Serra and Andrea being entertained in the desert by the Holy Family. This is actually "the old folk motif of the revenant hosts" and is not western at all.

29   McCLURE, CHARLOTTE S[WAIN].   "Willa Cather." In "Guide to
     Dissertations on American Literary Figures, 1879–1910; Part
     One." Compiled by Noel Polk. American Literary Realism 8
     (Summer):209–20.
        Assesses the nature and value of forty-eight doctoral dis-
     sertations done on Cather from the 1940s through the early 1970s,
     commenting on trends in dissertation criticism, subsequent publi-
     cation from dissertations, and the content, currency, and ade-
     quacy of the contribution made by the studies.

30   McLAY, CATHERINE M. "Religion in the Novels of Willa Cather."
     Renascence 27 (Spring):125–44.
        Cather's experience with the narrow aspects of religious
     practice is evident especially in her earlier novels. Later she
     sees religion as something of an aesthetic quest and a sanctuary.
     But always, her ideal saints closely resemble her ideal artists
     and pioneers--sensitive, brave, and dedicated. In the struggles
     and determination of her characters, Cather reveals her own per-
     sistent doubts and trials of faith.

31   MAGLIN, NAN BAUER. "Rebel Women Writers: 1894–1925." Ph.D.
     dissertation, Union for Experimenting Colleges and Universi-
     ties, 247 pp., passim.
        Discusses My Ántonia, along with twenty other works, as an
     example of a book that in terms of such sociological aspects as
     sexuality, marriage, family, and work, is a product of its time.
     Analysis is set against an American historical background. See
     Dissertation Abstracts International 36 (1976):8048A.

32   MAROTTA, CONNIE. "My Ántonia: Another Look." Unidentified
     periodical clipping [1975] at Willa Cather Historical Center,
     Red Cloud, Nebraska.
        Focuses on My Ántonia as, on one level, the account of a
     young girl's growth into maturity as she symbolizes the land and
     embodies the concept of love, thus forming the link between what
     is human and what is universal or eternal. My Ántonia offers
     woman a new sense of dignity and respect--in Lena Lingard and
     Tiny Soderball who choose the business world rather than mater-
     nity, and in Ántonia Shimerda who, at the same time that she
     falls within and accepts a woman's traditional role, transcends
     the boundaries generally drawn for women.

33   MURPHY, JOHN J. "Willa Cather and Hawthorne: Significant
     Resemblances." Renascence 27 (Spring):161–75.
        Explores likenesses between particular works of Hawthorne
     and Cather, and suggests a spiritual kinship between the two
     writers. Both use the Fall of Man as central myths, Hawthorne
     in "Rappaccini's Daughter" and The Scarlet Letter, Cather in A
     Lost Lady and other works. Points also to parallels such as
     those between Jim Burden (My Ántonia) and Miles Coverdale (The
     Blithedale Romance), and suggests that Death Comes for the Arch-
     bishop and The Marble Faun have a number of similarities.

34 NANCE, WILLIAM L. "Eden, Oedipus, and Rebirth in American
    Fiction." Arizona Quarterly 31 (Winter):353-65.
        Uses A Lost Lady as one of the works illustrative of the
    pattern of "Oedipal rebuff" which in some American fiction is
    linked to the "Nature-death Motif." The response of Cather and
    others to the loss of America's natural Eden is nostalgia.

35 O'BRIEN, SHARON. "The Limits of Passion: Willa Cather's
    Review of The Awakening." Women and Literature 3 (Fall):
    10-20.
        Regards Cather's youthful review of Kate Chopin's The
    Awakening as a forerunner for attitudes she would project in her
    fiction many years later. Cather denounces Chopin, not for de-
    picting an adulterous woman (as many of the book's critics did),
    but for creating a heroine who, like Emma Bovary and Anna
    Karenina, was self-limited because of her male-dependent sexual
    passion. The passion of Cather's strong heroines--Alexandra
    Bergson, Thea Kronborg, and Ántonia Shimerda--transcends the
    self, and their love relationships are the relationships of
    friends, not lovers. Her weaker heroines, on the other hand--
    Marian Forrester, Myra Henshawe, and Lucy Gayheart--like Marie
    Shabata, focus their passion on the men they love. These women
    either die or live to regret their choice. For Cather, sexual
    passion results in self-destruction.

36 _____. "Stronger Vessels: Willa Cather and Her Pioneer
    Heroines." Ph.D. dissertation, Harvard University, 272 pp.
        Focusing on O Pioneers!, The Song of the Lark, and My
    Ántonia, argues that Cather's heroines represent a significant
    revision of the representation of women in nineteenth-century
    American literature. Whereas the strong heroines of Cooper and
    Hawthorne are chastened or weakened by writers ultimately un-
    comfortable with their power and the heroines of sentimental/
    domestic fiction are confined by the traditional female plot,
    Cather's pioneer women achieve self-definition through connection
    to forces larger than the self--the land, art, the family.
    Places the fiction in the context of Cather's concerns with
    gender and sexuality as well as the American literary tradition.

37 PANNILL, LINDA SUSANNE. "The Artist-Heroine in American Fic-
    tion, 1890-1920." Ph.D. dissertation, University of North
    Carolina at Chapel Hill, 232 pp.
        Discusses the conflict between the woman artist and society
    as treated in the works of Ellen Glasgow, Cather, and Mary
    Austin. Cather and Glasgow portray their artist-heroines as
    driven by their genius and thus strong enough to flout society's
    perceptions of woman's duty, while Austin depicts the woman who
    is able to combine the roles of traditional woman and artist.
    See Dissertation Abstracts International 37 (1976):1551A-52A.

38 PARKER, JERI [Jeraldine]. "Willa Cather." In Uneasy Sur-
    vivors: Five Women Writers. Salt Lake City: Peregrine
    Smith, pp. 93-98, 115-16.
        Revision of 1973.46. Provides a critical anthology of
    works from five women writers. The section on Cather introduces
    reprinted excerpts from My Ántonia and O Pioneers! with bio-
    graphical data and brief commentary on the novels. In Cather's
    work, the landscape is a spiritual testing ground, and the
    changes it suffers show the changing face of America.

39 PERS, MONA. Willa Cather's Children. Stockholm, Sweden:
    Almqvist & Wiksell International, 124 pp.
        Published doctoral dissertation at Uppsala University sug-
    gests that Cather uses children extensively in her writings for
    two reasons: her "absorbing" lifelong interest in them and her
    desire to recover the self she was as a child. Generally, Cather
    uses children in her fiction to reveal the character of adults,
    to symbolize love and hope, and to present point of view. Dis-
    cussion is divided into three parts. Part 1 considers the "ex-
    tent and nature" of Cather's interest in children; part 2 deals
    with the effect of Cather's childhood self on her literature;
    and part 3 describes the consequences in her life and art of
    Cather's "child-centered attitude." Children who serve as point
    of view characters are alter egos for Cather herself, and she
    never changed her belief that childhood is the best part of life.

40 RASCOE, BURTON. "From an Early Review of One of Ours."
    Willa Cather Pioneer Memorial Newsletter 19 (Winter 1975-76):
    4.
        Reprinted from 1922.29.

41 REIGELMAN, MILTON M. The Midland: A Venture in Literary
    Regionalism. Iowa City: University of Iowa Press, pp. 65-66.
        Observes that although Cather's work did not appear in the
    influential "little magazine," The Midland, the editors praised
    her highly in its pages.

42 ROBERTS, BILL. "Willa Cather." Daily Nebraskan, 10 December,
    p. 12.
        Provides a biography of Cather to accompany prairie pic-
    tures that bear captions from three of her prairie novels.

43 RUBIN, LARRY. "The Homosexual Motif in Willa Cather's 'Paul's
    Case.'" Studies in Short Fiction 12 (Spring):127-31.
        Without violating the moral taboos of her time, Cather is
    able to portray Paul's alienation from his society in terms of a
    subtly suggested homosexual motif. Clues to this motif are
    present in Paul's clothing, physical appearance, manner, habits,
    thoughts, and relationships with males.

44 RULE, JANE. "Willa Cather." In Lesbian Images. Garden City,
    N.Y.: Doubleday & Co., pp. 74-87.
        Argues that critics have distorted the meaning of biograph-
    ical facts in order to read proof in Cather's fiction that she

had an emotional and erotic preference for women. This practice also distorts the fiction by suggesting that it invariably shows heterosexual relationships as destructive to women, and any close relationship as something to be avoided. In fact, Cather's fiction does not do this. Furthermore, her sensibility is not masculine at all; she is able to transcend sexual identity to see her characters' "more complex humanity." Cather is also preoccupied, as no other women writers have been, with the artist's nature and role. A genuinely gifted writer like Cather never writes simply veiled autobiography. Godfrey St. Peter may have been weary of life, but his story is told out of Cather's passion and vitality.

45   SCHNEIDER, Sister LUCY. "Something That Endures." Willa
      Cather Pioneer Memorial Newsletter 19 (Winter 1975-76):2-4.
         Discusses One of Ours as it exemplifies Cather's "land-
      philosophy." The land measures the value systems of Claude
      Wheeler and the other characters too, thus defining character and
      conveying theme at the same time.

46   SCHOLES, ROBERT. "The Fictional Heart of the Country: From
      Rølvaag to Gass." In Ole Rølvaag: Artist and Cultural
      Leader. Papers presented at the Rølvaag Symposium at St. Olaf
      College, October 1974. Edited by Gerald Thorson. Northfield,
      Minn.:   St. Olaf College Press, pp. 1-13.
         Examines images of the midwestern landscape in the work of
      Rølvaag, Cather, Sinclair Lewis, and William Gass, claiming that
      certain of their books provide a history of the Midwest. In My
      Ántonia the limitless frontier is gone; the cultivated fields
      present a poised moment in time between the wild frontier and the
      overly tame and selfish life of the town. The farm becomes "the
      ideal, the center of existence," and the jump from My Ántonia to
      Main Street is not so great as might be assumed. Gopher Prairie
      is just a larger Black Hawk.

47   SLOTE, BERNICE. "An Appointment with the Future: Willa
      Cather." In The Twenties: Fiction, Poetry, Drama. Edited
      by Warren French. Deland, Fla.: Everett/Edwards, pp. 39-49.
         Although some of Cather's work in the twenties portrays a
      wasteland in the spirit of T.S. Eliot's poem, it contains also a
      countermovement toward life. That Cather was forward-looking is
      evident in her experimentation with form, her implicit support of
      ethnic individuality, and her ecological awareness.

48   STONER, VIC. "Cather Accused of Distortion." Omaha Sun,
      6 March, sec. b, pp. 1-2.
         Cites from a paper titled "Willa Cather and Historical
      Reality: The Black Legend in New Mexico," delivered by Univer-
      sity of Nebraska history professor Ralph H. Vigil, at a session
      of the Eighteenth Annual Missouri Valley History Conference. In
      the paper Vigil insists that Cather is unfair and in error in her
      portrayal of Padre Martinez in Death Comes for the Archbishop.
      See 1975.50 for the published version of the paper.

49   STOUCK, DAVID. <u>Willa Cather's Imagination</u>. Lincoln:
      University of Nebraska Press, 261 pp.
         Cather's imagination shaped her work into various tradi-
      tional modes and forms and led her to choose art and life as her
      basic themes. Part 1 describes the characteristics of the epic,
      pastoral, and satirical modes and shows how some of Cather's work
      fits these modes. Part 2 describes the mortal comedy, the
      saint's legend, and the historical novel and suggests that <u>My
      Mortal Enemy</u>, <u>Death Comes for the Archbishop</u>, and <u>Shadows on the
      Rock</u> fit, at least loosely, the criteria for those respective
      forms. Part 3 argues that Cather's early books and stories
      generally affirm the artist's life and commitment to art, but
      that her last four books suggest that art may be less important
      than other things in life, especially human relationships. Parts
      of this book were published previously, sometimes in different
      form: 1970.30; 1972.27-29, 31; 1973.71-72.

50   VIGIL, RALPH H. "Willa Cather and Historical Reality." <u>New
      Mexico Historical Review</u> 50 (April):123-34.
         Asserts that Cather's portrayal of Father Martinez in <u>Death
      Comes for the Archbishop</u> seriously distorts the facts and life of
      the real Martinez. He worked for greater religious tolerance,
      but evidence suggests that he was not the immoral rebel Cather
      makes of him.

51   WHITNEY, BLAIR. "A Portrait of the Author as Midwesterner."
      <u>Great Lakes Review</u> 1 (Winter):30-42.
         One of the several characteristics of the midwestern writer
      discussed here is his or her belief in the mystery of sex. Al-
      though Cather has been criticized for so-called prudery, her work
      is full of sexuality expressed in indirect ways, especially
      through metaphor.

52   WOODRESS, JAMES. "Willa Cather: The World and the Parish."
      Photographs by Lucia Woods. <u>Architectural Association Quar-
      terly</u> (London) 7 (April/June):51-59.
         Based on a paper presented at a special lecture arranged
      for by the Architectural Association and the American Embassy in
      London in 1975 to coincide with the Lucia Woods photographic
      exhibition, "The World of Willa Cather." Takes the reader on a
      verbal journey over the route traveled by Cather from the parish
      to the world and back again. <u>Alexander's Bridge</u>, Cather's
      derivative and least typical novel, is the outermost point on
      her orbit. After that she turned to the materials that had been
      mellowing inside her over the years. With <u>O Pioneers!</u> Cather
      abandons derivative techniques, including realism and naturalism,
      and becomes mythic and romantic.

53   YACO, ROSEMARY MORRIS. "Suffering Women: Feminine Masochism
      in Novels by American Women." Ph.D. dissertation, University
      of Michigan, 357 pp.
         Cather is one of several women writers discussed whose
      heroines are explained by a theory advanced by Karen Horney, a
      theory postulating that masochism in women is a result of

demeaning and restricting factors in society. Cather creates
strong women, and she also creates men who have distinctly romantic perceptions of those women. See <u>Dissertation Abstracts
International</u> 36 (1975):3134B.

54   YAMAGUCHI, TETSUO, and SATO, HIROKO, eds. Introduction to
     <u>Willa Cather's Three Short Stories</u>. Tokyo: Bunri Co.,
     pp. i-iii.
         In Japanese. Judges that Cather's childhood had a strong
influence on the creation of these stories ("Coming, Aphrodite!,"
"Scandal," and "Paul's Case"). For Cather, the pioneer is an
artist who elicits order and beauty from nature, a nature which
can otherwise kill both art and passion. Cather is different
from her contemporaries in that many of her characters <u>are</u> able
to find harmony with nature and imbue it with European culture.

55   YONGUE, PATRICIA LEE. "Search and Research: Willa Cather in
     Quest of History." <u>Southwestern American Literature</u> 5:27-39.
         Compares Godfrey St. Peter and his uniquely imaginative
historical work, <u>Spanish Adventurers in North America</u>, to Cather
herself and her own creative efforts. Both historian and novelist are in search of an American past full of "color, passion,
strength, love of land, and even 'heroic savagery.'" Like
Cather's contemporary, historian Adolph Bandelier, St. Peter and
Cather see the American West with its Spanish explorers as the
repository of such a past. Narrative art becomes the vehicle for
transmitting the past to the present and thus for achieving an
integrated human consciousness.

1976

1   BENNETT, SANDRA MARGARET. "Structure in the Novels of Willa
     Cather." Ph.D. dissertation, University of Utah, 137 pp.
         Offers thematic explanation of Cather's novels through
analysis of her cyclical structural techniques which employ
alternation, juxtaposition, and flexible use of time. See
<u>Dissertation Abstracts International</u> 37 (1976):2857A.

2   BRIDGES, JEAN B. "The Actress in Cather's Novel <u>My Ántonia</u>."
     <u>Society for the Study of Midwestern Literature Newsletter</u> 6
     (Spring):10-11.
         Seeks to establish that Sarah Bernhardt was the actress who
deeply moved Jim Burden and Lena Lingard in the performance of
<u>Camille</u> that they attended in Lincoln.

3   COK, GEORGETTE WEBER. "The Allegorical Mode in American Fic-
     tion." Ph.D. dissertation, City University of New York,
     344 pp.
         Devotes a chapter to exploring Cather's use of allegorical
techniques in her fiction. Contends that the allegorical mode is
readily adaptable to people caught in a conflict between the real
and the ideal as Cather's characters often are. See <u>Dissertation
Abstracts International</u> 36 (1976):8056-57A.

4   [CURLEY], DOROTHY NYREN; KRAMER, MAURICE; and KRAMER, ELAINE
     FIALKA, eds. "Willa Cather." In Modern American Literature,
     supp. 4th ed. Library of Literary Criticism, vol. 1, edited
     by Leonard S. Klein. New York: Frederick Ungar Publishing
     Co., p. 91.
        Adds two excerpts from criticism of the 1970s to the
     entries in 1969.7.

5   DEMAREST, DAVID P., Jr., ed. From These Hills, From These
     Valleys: Selected Fiction about Western Pennsylvania.
     Pittsburgh: University of Pittsburgh Press, p. 144.
        Reprints "Double Birthday," and introduces Cather and the
     story, indicating that the story deals with typical Cather
     themes: the contrast between success-oriented values and
     culture-oriented values, and the unfortunate changes a city
     undergoes over a period of time.

6   EDMISTON, SUSAN, and CIRINO, LINDA D. Literary New York: A
     History and Guide. Boston: Houghton Mifflin, pp. 50–51,
     63–65.
        Treats Cather as one of many writers who lived and wrote
     in New York's Greenwich Village, describing her various resi-
     dences and her professional and social activities.

7   GEORGE, BENJAMIN. "The French-Canadian Connection: Willa
     Cather as a Canadian Writer." Western American Literature 11
     (November):249–61.
        In Shadows on the Rock Cather articulates the Canadian
     rather than the American attitude toward the wilderness and
     civilization. Unlike the typical American who sees the plunge
     into the wilderness as the breaking of European cultural shackles,
     Cather sees the wilderness as somewhat threatening to the cul-
     tural ideals represented by western Europe. Like other Canadian
     literature, Shadows on the Rock celebrates the preservation of
     western European civilization in Quebec. Reprinted: 1984.36.

8   GRAY, DOROTHY. "Willa Cather: Pioneer of Western Litera-
     ture." In Women of the West. Millbrae, Calif.: Les Femmes,
     pp. 147–58.
        Refers frequently to events in Cather's life and credits
     her with changing the course of American literature by transmut-
     ing for the first time "the American West" and the pioneer expe-
     rience into major literature. Before O Pioneers! the "Eastern
     establishment" had defined what constituted American literature,
     but "suddenly," American writing became "authentically American."
     Cather also pioneered in being the first to create substantial
     female protagonists.

9   HALAC, DENNIS. "Novel or Biography?" Commonwealth 103
     (26 March):210–11.
        Compares Bishop Lamy of Paul Horgan's biography with
     Cather's archbishop in Death Comes for the Archbishop and con-
     cludes that although Horgan is innovative in drawing his charac-
     ter--and thus adopts some of the novelist's methods--it is

Cather's character who is an imaginative product the reader recognizes through familiarity with her other works. She creates him and invests him with traits she admires, but her strongest link with him may be his famous garden, the garden being her favorite symbol.

10   HAMNER, EUGÉNIE LAMBERT. "Affirmations in Willa Cather's A Lost Lady." Midwest Quarterly 17 (Spring):245–51.
      Although A Lost Lady traces the decline of the pioneering spirit and its accompanying values, through shifting point of view into the maturing perceptions of Niel Herbert--who does grow and succeed in the present as a cultural realist--Cather assures a continuation of Captain Forrester's values. She thus gives a strong sense of affirmation to what has generally been viewed as a rather gloomy novel.

11   HELMICK, EVELYN [THOMAS]. "The Mysteries of Ántonia." Midwest Quarterly 17 (Winter):173–85.
      There is a good deal of myth in My Ántonia, but of particular interest is the book's final chapter, "Cuzak's Boys," which parallels the sequence of events enacted in Greek ritual celebration of the Eleusian Mysteries. These are feminine mysteries, associated with the earth and fertility, to which the male--in this instance, Jim Burden--must be initiated.

12   HORGAN, PAUL. "Preface to an Unwritten Book." Yale Review 65 (March):321–35.
      Treats the subject of the continual conflict between the cultural and aesthetic values of the East and the values of the raw, untamed landscape that characterize the earlier West, and also considers the erosion through technological enterprise of initial idealism about the frontier West and its potential. Cites examples of early Cather novels and stories in which she treats three important western themes, "the cultural exile, the all-powerful railroads, and the act of going west to get well, or die." "A Wagner Matinee" is Cather's most bitter story about cultural exile.

13   KULKIN, MARY-ELLEN. Her Way: Biographies of Women for Young People. Chicago: American Library Association, pp. 62–63.
      Provides a brief biography of Cather and evaluates the three Cather biographies (Bonham 1970.2; Franchere 1958.4; and Brown and Crone 1970.3) directed at the young reader. Identifies Cather's main theme as "the American drive to achieve and express individuality."

14   LANEGRAN, DAVID A., and TOTH, SUSAN ALLEN. "Geography Through Literature." Places 3 (March):5–12.
      Suggests ways by which the geographer can gain a greater understanding of place by reading and interpreting literature that deals with place. Analyzes passages from My Ántonia to show how Cather evokes the feeling of a landscape through a variety of techniques and thus adds an important dimension to what can be perceived through scientific objectivity.

15   MAGLIN, NAN BAUER. "Early Feminist Fiction: The Dilemma of
     Personal Life." Prospects 2:167-91.
          Discusses Cather along with other women writers of the time
     who were questioning the traditional role of woman as wife and
     mother. In Lena Lingard and Tiny Soderball, in My Ántonia,
     Cather quietly portrays an apparently workable alternative to
     marriage.

16   MARTIN, ROBERT A. "Primitivism in Stories by Willa Cather and
     Sherwood Anderson." Midamerica 3:39-45.
          Compares "Neighbour Rosicky" and Anderson's "A Death in the
     Woods," which were written at about the same time. They similarly
     "reflect the primitivistic credo" that a person at one with nature
     is superior to a person in a civilized state. In spite of their
     different approaches, Cather and Anderson project similar themes,
     points of view, and patterns of imagery. Nevertheless, Cather's
     primitivism is "cultural," while Anderson's is "psychological."

17   MELDRUM, BARBARA. "Images of Women in Western American Lit-
     erature." Midwest Quarterly 17 (Spring):252-57.
          In My Ántonia Cather presents several women of pioneer
     background who achieve success--Tiny Soderball, Lena Lingard,
     and Ántonia Shimerda. Although Ántonia is shown to be the most
     successful of the three--and she follows the conventional
     fulfillment-in-marriage-and-family stereotype--the others pursue
     independent careers and achieve perhaps greater self-realization
     than Jim Burden.

18   MOERS, ELLEN. Literary Women. Garden City, N.Y.: Doubleday
     & Co., pp. 163, 189-92, 207-8, 230-42 passim, 255-63 passim.
          Considers Cather along with other women writers who to-
     gether represent a peak in women's literary achievement. All of
     them raise questions about woman's role as a mother figure, and
     in combination they signal the "revival of a specifically female
     impetus to literature." Unfortunately, there is no appropriate
     language to describe the sexuality of the female landscape in
     literature as there is to describe that of the male. But certain
     kinds of landscapes appear in the writings of women as uncon-
     scious symbols for the mystery of femaleness and the expression
     of female independence. Cather's The Song of the Lark, in its
     description of Panther Canyon, for example, is almost overtly
     sexual in female terms. In Cather, the landscapes convey not
     only female sexuality, but female assertion as well. Abridged:
     1982.44.

19   MURPHY, JOHN J. "The Art of Shadows on the Rock." Prairie
     Schooner 50 (Spring):37-51.
          In Shadows on the Rock Cather achieves a blending of past
     and present, spiritual and physical, through artfully patterning
     the work after a musical composition in six movements. Each of
     the six books in the novel has a dominant theme, such as "order,"
     or "national identity," but the other themes appear too, over-
     lapping each other and thereby achieving a sense of simultaneity
     instead of progression. The deliberate disjunction forces "a

temporary suspension of completeness" and creates dramatic intensity, for none of the themes are concluded until the end of the
book.

20   MYERS, CAROL FAIRBANKS. Women in Literature: Criticism of
      the Seventies. Metuchen, N.J.: Scarecrow Press, pp. 35–36.
           Provides a selected bibliography of articles, books, dis-
      sertations, and parts of books published about Cather and her
      work between January 1970 and spring 1975. Lists particularly
      those items that focus on Cather or her characters as women.
      Supplemented: 1979.9.

21   O'BRIEN, SHARON. "Sentiment, Local Color, and the New Woman
      Writer: Kate Chopin and Willa Cather." Kate Chopin News-
      letter 2, no. 3:16–24.
           Contrasts the nineteenth-century sentimental and local
      color women writers with writers like Sarah Orne Jewett and Kate
      Chopin, who insisted that women could be artists without apology.
      Willa Cather, who in her early journalistic writing disparaged
      the supposedly limited gifts of women writers, closes in her own
      life and works the gap between woman and artist that had hampered
      women writers for a century.

*22   OMORI, MAMORU. Wira Kyasa no shosetsu: Hitotsu no ikikata no
      tankyu [Willa Cather's novels: Search for a way of living].
      Tokyo: Kaibunsha, 324 pp.
           Listed in MLA International Bibliography (1976).

23   PERS, MONA. "Repetition in Willa Cather's Early Writings:
      Clues to the Development of an Artist." American Studies in
      Scandinavia 8, no. 2:55–66.
           Cather not only repeated columns and parts of columns in
      the various periodicals for which she wrote, but she also in-
      corporated borrowings from them into some of her early stories.
      Even her novels reveal incidents and images she had used else-
      where. These repetitions nearly always contain revisions that
      show the developing stylistic consciousness of the maturing
      artist. In the revised versions, the language is tighter,
      clearer, simpler, more concrete, and more naturally rhythmic.

24   _____. "Through the Looking-glass with Willa Cather." Studia
      neophilologica (Sweden) 48, no. 1:90–96.
           Suggests that Cather's numerous window images convey a
      sense of her tragic vision in their portrayal of incompatible
      human needs. Those inside feel trapped and long for the freedom
      enjoyed by those outside, and those outside long for the feeling
      of belonging enjoyed by those inside. It was that way for Cather
      herself; she wanted acceptance at the same time that she insisted
      upon freedom to pursue her life and art.

25   ROHRBACH, Sister CHARLOTTE. "Willa Cather, an Historian of
      Western Webster County, Nebraska: An Inquiry." Ph.D. dis-
      sertation, Saint Louis University, 261 pp.

Classifies Cather as an historian on the supposition that history is interpretive as well as accurate. See Dissertation Abstracts International 37 (1977):7824A.

26   ROULSTON, ROBERT. "The Contrapuntal Complexity of Willa Cather's The Song of the Lark." Midwest Quarterly 17 (Spring):350-68.
      The Song of the Lark is structured around a vast complexity of dualities that pervade it, through character, situation, and theme. The major characters, especially Thea Kronborg, are ambiguous, as is Moonstone itself. Through the principal dualism, which is the tension between mediocrity and heroic striving, the other dualities and the book's basic design are made apparent. Appropriately for this novel, the contrapuntal pattern is Wagnerian.

27   ROURKE, CONSTANCE. "Round Up." In Critics of Culture. Edited by Alan Trachtenberg. New York: John Wiley & Sons, pp. 227-28.
      Reprinted from 1931.42.

28   SEYMOUR-SMITH, MARTIN. Who's Who in Twentieth Century Literature. London: Weidenfeld & Nicolson, pp. 73-74.
      Comments on several of Cather's novels, but always from the position that Cather's "bruised nature" led her to treat woman's vulnerability to masculine intrusion. In One of Ours she even explores "herself-as-man" through her main character.

29   SHELTON, FRANK W. "The Image of the Rock and the Family in the Novels of Willa Cather." Markham Review 6 (Fall):9-14.
      Cather's use of the rock as symbol is more complex than had been supposed. For Tom Outland and Thea Kronborg it came to represent the image and values of the extended family, but it was finally unsatisfying because it meant isolation from living, breathing mortals. Godfrey St. Peter, in the end, though he yearned toward the mesa ideal, opted for human association. In Death Comes for the Archbishop the rock (Ácoma) represents disorder and inhumanity, the enemies of family. It is only in Shadows on the Rock that the image of the rock is fully and effectively linked with the ideal of family and community.

30   _____. "The Wild Duck Image in Willa Cather and Henryk Ibsen." American Notes and Queries 15 (October):24-27.
      In O Pioneers! Cather uses Ibsen's wild duck image twice to show, not the "permanence of illusion" as Ibsen uses it, but the "permanence of truth." In so doing, she also reasserts the value of the romantic over the realistic in literature and life.

31   STINEBACK, DAVID C. "'Roving tribes' and 'brutal invaders': Willa Cather's The Professor's House." In Shifting World: Social Change and Nostalgia in the American Novel. Lewisburg, Penn.: Bucknell University Press, pp. 101-114; London: Associated University Press.
      A minimally revised text of 1973.69.

32   STOUCK, DAVID. "Willa Cather and the Indian Heritage."
     Twentieth Century Literature 22 (December):433–43.
          Although much of Cather's work is in the romantic tradi-
     tion, several of her novels break with it. Whereas the romantic
     tradition concentrates on selfhood, Cather sometimes adopts the
     mode of modern art which downplays the individual and emphasizes
     harmony and order in the natural universe. Cather clearly ad-
     mires the harmonious, unaccented relationship between the Indians
     of the American Southwest and their environment. In The Song of
     the Lark, The Professor's House, and Death Comes for the Arch-
     bishop (probably her best novel), Cather uses these Indians as
     models for her own artistic methods. In Death Comes for the
     Archbishop especially, she moves beyond the romantic ambiguity
     and subjectivity of some preceding novels and gives herself to
     the ordering influence of the landscape that is her setting.

33   WEAVER, DOROTHY. "Willa Cather: Novelist of the Frontier."
     English Teaching Forum: A Journal for the Teachers of English
     Outside the United States 14 (April):32–39.
          Provides an account of Cather's life and career in addition
     to plot summaries and commentary for several of her novels.
     Stresses her insistence on a system of values in which vulgarity,
     materialism, and mass-mindedness are rejected. Also contains
     "Selections from Willa Cather," pp. 40–41.

                              1977

1   BENNETT, MILDRED R. "Water Imagery in Death Comes for the
     Archbishop." Willa Cather Pioneer Memorial Newsletter 29
     (Spring):3–4.
          Explores Cather's use of water imagery in Death Comes for
     the Archbishop, observing that Jean Latour's life can be aptly
     described in terms of a voyage. Water suggests both the light
     and the dark aspects of Latour's experience.

2   BERKEBILE, JOHN W. "Willa Cather . . . Nebraska Newspaper-
     woman, Novelist." Nebraska Newspaper 29 (September):2–5.
          Praises Cather's achievement as an artist, noting espe-
     cially the extensive journalistic undergirding of that achieve-
     ment. Before she was anything else, Cather was a newspaperwoman.

3   BLOOM, LILLIAN D. "On Daring to Look Back with Wharton and
     Cather." Novel: A Forum on Fiction 10 (Winter):167–78.
          Compares and contrasts Cather and Wharton in terms of
     background, critical reception, outlook, and method, and then
     gives a detailed evaluation of recent books about the two
     writers. Regrets that Wharton and Cather generally have not
     received the attention they deserve.

4   BOHLKE, L. BRENT. "On Cather's Death Comes for the Arch-
     bishop." Willa Cather Pioneer Memorial Newsletter 29
     (Spring):1-2.
         Observes Cather's continuing interest in religion and her
     early expression of the doubter's yearning envy of those who have
     faith. Jean Latour in Death Comes for the Archbishop resembles
     St. Paul in that he, too, was called to minister outside his
     homeland and to provide leadership over a wide geographical area.

5   CALLOW, JAMES T., and REILLY, ROBERT J. Guide to American
     Literature from Emily Dickinson to the Present. New York:
     Harper & Row, Barnes & Noble, pp. 114-15, 234-36.
         Sketches details of Cather's life, then discusses her as a
     traditionalist with literary ties to Henry James. Summarizes
     three "representative works"--"The Sculptor's Funeral," My
     Ántonia, and "Neighbour Rosicky"--claiming that Cather will be
     best remembered for her writings based on her girlhood expe-
     riences. A separate section provides a list of Cather's works
     and a descriptive bibliography of a variety of works about her,
     including sources of biography, bibliography, and criticism.

6   FOLSOM, JAMES K. Cather entry in The Reader's Encyclopedia of
     the American West. Edited by Howard R. Lamar. New York:
     Thomas Y. Crowell Co., pp. 170-71.
         Observes that Cather's treatment of western themes has been
     criticized by those who insist that she make a social statement
     in her work, a statement either praising or condemning the hard-
     ships of pioneer life. Some say she idealizes that life; others
     say she pictures it too harshly. She, however, consistently pre-
     sents pioneer hardships as trials that can be overcome by those
     who exercise faith in the future.

7   FOMINES, MARJORIE ANN. "House, Procession, River: Domestic
     Ritual in the Fiction of Seven American Women, 1877-1972."
     Ph.D. dissertation, George Washington University, 488 pp.
         Finds the symbols of house, procession, and river to be
     dominant in American literature, with the house symbolizing
     domestic shelter, the procession domestic ritual, and the river
     the undomestic world. The conflict among the images is central
     to Cather's work and a principal contributor to its ambiguity.
     Her characters continue to strive for domestic ritual even though
     it belongs to a previous age. See Dissertation Abstracts Inter-
     national 38 (1978):5467A.

8   GROSS, BARRY. "In Another Country: The Revolt from the
     Village." Midamerica 4:101-11.
         Cather is the Midwest's most complicated writer, for her
     quarrel is not with rural life or town, but with progress itself,
     with the "citification" of the rural world.

9   GROVER, DORYS CROW. "The Pioneer Women in Fact and Fiction."
     Heritage of Kansas: A Journal of the Great Plains 10
     (Spring):35-44 passim.
         Cather is one whose depiction of pioneer women contrasts
     with the more romantic portraits of such women in popular

fiction. Ántonia Shimerda has the same freedom and the same
responsibility as a frontier man.

10   HINZ, JOHN. "The Hand of the Artist in Shadows on the Rock."
     Studies in American Fiction 5 (Autumn):263-68.
        Examines sentence by sentence the revisions Cather made in
     one brief manuscript passage, the passage used as a frontispiece
     for the Library edition of Shadows on the Rock. The revisions
     show Cather to be a ruthless self-critic who readily excised
     descriptive language that her critical eye later showed her
     should have suggested and evoked.

11   HOWARD, MAUREEN, ed. Introduction to Seven American Women
     Writers of the Twentieth Century. Minneapolis: University of
     Minnesota Press, pp. 3-27 passim, 10-13, 79-121.
        Reprints the Van Ghent essay (see 1964.25) and others in
     the Minnesota pamphlet series. Also points to some of the dis-
     tortions of Cather's work perpetuated by critics who misunder-
     stand her intelligence and subtlety. One misconception holds
     that her women are not lovers; another insists that Ántonia
     Shimerda is an earth-mother and cannot engage our imaginations as
     a real woman; another misses the ironies in A Lost Lady that
     undercut the lamentations for the past; and still another claims
     that Cather's technique was traditional rather than innovative.

*12 INAZAWA, HIDEO. American joryu sakka ron: Cather, Buck,
     McCullers no sekai [American women writers: The world of
     Cather, Buck, and McCullers]. Tokyo: Shimbisha, 126 pp.
        Listed in MLA International Bibliography (1977).

*13 KOBAYASHI, KENJI. "Willa Cather: Koyano tankyusha" [Willa
     Cather: Seeker of the wilderness]. In American Shosetsu no
     Tenkai [Development of American novels]. Edited by Katsuji
     Takamura and Iwao Iwamoto. Tokyo: Shohakusha, pp. 154-66.
        Listed in MLA International Bibliography (1977).

14   LATHROP, JOANNA. "On the Title." Willa Cather Pioneer
     Memorial Newsletter 29 (Spring):2-3.
        Cather's choice of words in the title of Death Comes for
     the Archbishop indicates that the one who dies is an extraordinary
     being, not just one of the masses. He does not simply die, he is
     sent for; death makes a special journey just for him.

15   McCLURE, CHARLOTTE S[WAIN]. "Studies of Willa Cather." Willa
     Cather Pioneer Memorial Newsletter 29 (Spring):4.
        Lists the eighteen dissertations on Cather in the current
     holdings of the Georgia State University Library and indicates
     that they are available for borrowing through interlibrary loan.

16   McREYNOLDS, DOUGLAS J. "American Literature, American Fron-
      tier, All American Girl." Heritage of Kansas: A Journal of
      the Great Plains 10 (Spring):25-33.
         Identifies the characteristics that have been associated
      with ideal American womanhood historically, and thus literarily,
      and points to Ántonia Shimerda as one who falls outside the
      ideal. She is not desired as wife or lover by a major character,
      and she has "mannish" qualities.

17   MENUHIN, YEHUDI. Unfinished Journey. London: MacDonald &
      Jane's, pp. 128-31, 144-45.
         Characterizes Cather and describes Menuhin's association
      with her, calling her an embodiment of America, one who had a
      special appreciation for nature and wrote about people who were
      part of their environment. Cather stressed the importance for
      the artist of knowing two worlds--American and European. She
      represented America, but she also gave the Menuhin children the
      values of Europe. In addition Cather advised Menuhin about
      choosing a wife.

18   MURPHY, JOHN J. "Sources and 'Tom Outland's Story.'" Willa
      Cather Pioneer Memorial Newsletter 21 (Fall):4.
         Indicates that Cather's account of her source of the Tom
      Outland story in The Professor's House raises some questions that
      need answering. Her account varies from the actual known facts
      in several important ways, all of which reveal something about
      her artistic purposes.

19   POGEL, NANCY H. "Images of the Midwest: Cornfields in
      Poetry, Fiction, and Film." Heritage of Kansas: A Journal of
      the Great Plains 10, no. 4:17-28.
         Discusses corn imagery as it distinguishes literature deal-
      ing with the Midwest, noting Cather's balanced portrayal of
      realistic and romantic aspects of the land. Refers particularly
      to "Neighbour Rosicky" and Rosicky's attachment to his cornfields
      despite the hardships associated with them.

20   POPA, ECATERINA. "Willa Cather si experienta americana a
      frontierei" [Willa Cather and the American frontier expe-
      rience]. In Cuceritorii preeriei [Conquerors of the prairie].
      Cluj-Napoca: Dacia, pp. 5-17.
         In Romanian. Provides an overview of Cather's life and
      career and then discusses her pioneer novels in connection with
      the ambivalent nature of the American frontier. The frontier
      symbolizes vitality and opportunity for the idealist, but it has
      also been fraught with violence. Focuses on O Pioneers! for more
      detailed discussion, noting that Alexandra Bergson, who repre-
      sents the ideal of the farmer-pioneer, is basically a romantic.
      Therefore, she is bound to experience conflict with people like
      her brothers Lou and Oscar.

21   ROBINSON, CECIL. Mexico and the Hispanic Southwest in Ameri-
      can Literature. Tucson: University of Arizona Press,
      pp. 174-76, 281-83.

Reprint with only minor changes, including the title, of 1963.18.

22 ROBINSON, FORREST G., and ROBINSON, MARGARET G. Wallace
    Stegner. Twayne United States Authors Series. Boston:
    G.K. Hall & Co., pp. 161, 166-68.
        Sees in Stegner's admiration for Cather an affirmation of
    his own methods and themes. His essay on My Ántonia (1965.33)
    could almost be seen as self-analysis, especially in its praise
    for Cather's use of the narrative mask to write about regions
    dear to her. In both writers, life and work are unified.

23 ROSOWSKI, SUSAN J. "Willa Cather's A Lost Lady: The Para-
    doxes of Change." Novel: A Forum on Fiction 11 (Fall):51-62.
        A multifaceted essay that deals with the complexities of A
    Lost Lady by focusing on its broad theme of the ability of human
    beings to adapt to change or to transform commonplace things into
    universal truth. Ironically, it is the seemingly unstable Marian
    Forrester who, in her capacity for adaptation and transformation
    of experience, becomes the constant and enduring factor in the
    novel, and not the inflexible Captain Forrester. In the end,
    Niel Herbert finally matures to the point where he no longer
    judges Marian against inflexible standards of value and is able
    to pay tribute to "the essential constancy of Marian Forrester's
    effect upon others."

24 SALTER, CHRISTOPHER L., and LLOYD, WILLIAM J. Landscape in
    Literature. Resource Papers for College Geography, no. 76-3.
    Washington, D.C.: Association of American Geographers,
    pp. 8-10, 24.
        Uses a passage from the opening pages of O Pioneers! to
    make the point that Cather is describing a typical prairie set-
    tlement whose hold is tenuous at best. Mark Twain and Sherwood
    Anderson also capture this feeling of the impermanence of such
    places that were left stranded when the railroad systems con-
    solidated.

25 SCHWARTZ, NARDA LACEY. Articles on Women Writers: A Bibliog-
    raphy. Santa Barbara: Clio Press, American Bibliographical
    Center, pp. 44-49.
        Presents a rather extensive alphabetical listing of arti-
    cles and doctoral dissertations on Cather, including some foreign
    items, under the heading of bibliography, general works, and
    individual works. Covers publications from 1961 through 1975.

26 SLOTE, BERNICE. Introduction to Alexander's Bridge. Lincoln:
    University of Nebraska Press, Bison Books, pp. v-xxvi.
        Rehearses the critical reception of Alexander's Bridge,
    Cather's views of the book, and the sources she used--both con-
    temporary and mythological. Explores the similarities between
    Alexander's Bridge and The Professor's House, suggesting that the
    book is not an aberration in the Cather canon, despite what
    Cather said about it, but is instead a treatment of themes always
    central to her work. A major theme that is pertinent to Cather

herself as well as to Bartley Alexander is the conflict of a self
divided between urges toward order and civilization and urges
toward pagan freedom. Reprinted in part: 1981.44; reprinted:
1984.82.

27 STEVENSON, ANNE. "Draughts of Old Romance." Times Literary
    Supplement (London), 24 June.
        Review of April Twilights (1903). Suggests that the imita-
    tive, romantic idealism of Cather's early verse might better have
    been left in the archives for scholars. It is fortunate that in
    her fiction Cather turned from a make-believe Arcadia to the
    realities of frontier life.

28 TUTTLETON, JAMES W. "'Combat in the Erogenous Zone': Women
    in the American Novel Between the Two World Wars." In What
    Manner of Woman: Essays on English and American Life and
    Literature. Edited by Marlene Springer. New York: New York
    University Press, p. 276.
        Notes the social ostracism experienced by both Ántonia
    Shimerda and Marian Forrester over their extramarital adventures.
    Cather's tough women survive by linking themselves to some
    "suprapersonal, suprasocial conception," like nature.

29 TYLER, RALPH. "Willa Cather." In "Classic Corner: The Works
    of Great Writers Available Today." Bookviews, December,
    pp. 34–35.
        Observes that Cather is regarded as underrated by the
    literati; she is read but scarcely talked about, perhaps because
    she is not easily labeled. Reports responses of Leon Edel, Ellen
    Moers, and Alfred A. Knopf to questions about Cather. Also
    sketches a biography and offers brief summary and evaluative
    comment on each of Cather's novels and some of her collected
    stories and essays.

30 Van GHENT, DOROTHY. "Willa Cather." In Seven American Women
    Writers of the Twentieth Century. See Howard, 1977.11,
    pp. 79–121.
        Reprint of 1964.25.

*31 VIERNEISEL, KAREN HELENE. "Fugitive Matriarchy: Willa
    Cather's Life and Art." Ph.D. dissertation, University of
    Chicago.
        Listed in Western Historical Quarterly, July 1980.

32 WAGNER, LINDA W. "Tension and Technique: The Years of
    Greatness." In American Fiction: Historical and Critical
    Essays. Edited by James Nagel. Boston: Northeastern Uni-
    versity Press, pp. 70–71 passim.
        Reprinted from 1977.33.

33 _____. "Tension and Technique: The Years of Greatness."
    Studies in American Fiction 5 (Spring):65–67 passim.
        Like other moderns, Cather is a master of characterization,
    but like them she seems to today's readers to oversimplify the

issues. Cather is essentially a somewhat nostalgic storyteller
who has the reputation of holding interest mainly for prairie-
dwellers. Reprinted: 1977.32.

34   WATKINS, FLOYD C. "Death Comes for the Archbishop: Worlds
      Old and New." In In Time and Place: Some Origins of American
      Fiction. Athens: University of Georgia Press, pp. 105-30.
         Discusses the ways in which Cather uses and alters history,
      anthropology, and legend to create her narrative, which is more
      in the form of legend than of standard fiction. She did not know
      as much about the Indians of the New Mexico territory as she did
      about the Mexicans, so her treatment of the former is more gen-
      eral and idealized. Typically, her picture of the Anglo-Americans
      in Death Comes for the Archbishop is less flattering than that of
      either the Mexicans or Indians. In fact, her "stick figure"
      portrayal of Anglo-Americans slightly flaws the book.

35   _____. "My Ántonia: 'Still, All Day Long, Nebraska.'" In
      In Time and Place: Some Origins of American Fiction. See
      Watkins, 1977.34, pp. 73-101.
         Considers My Ántonia to be a novel shaped by geographical
      experience, primarily the experience of people whose lives were
      disrupted by a severe cultural and geographical change when they
      immigrated to the prairie. In immigrating, they exchanged
      variety for a great amount of the same thing, for quantity, at
      least in terms of landscape. The book is Cather's "most intense
      study of the relationship between person and place." The land
      has something of a naturalistic control over the humans who in-
      habit it, but those who leave it are doomed to personal (though
      not financial) failure.

36   WATTS, EMILY STIPES. The Poetry of American Women from 1632
      to 1945. Austin: University of Texas Press, pp. 151-52.
         Cather may have had forefathers in British verse, but she
      also had foremothers in American, and she used imagist methods
      and mythology in her poetry without any coaching from writers
      like T.S. Eliot and Ezra Pound.

37   WHITE, BARBARA A. American Women Writers: An Annotated
      Bibliography of Criticism. New York: Garland Publishing,
      pp. 1, 20, 28, 47, 51-53, 58, 78-79, 85, passim.
         Provides listings and annotations for general sources of
      bibliography, both books and articles, on American women
      writers--some of which treat Cather. Cather sources are some-
      times, but not always, identified in the annotations. Items
      span more than a century, beginning in the 1800s and ending in
      the 1970s.

38   WOODS, LUCIA. "Lucia Woods' Visit with Irene Rich." Willa
      Cather Pioneer Memorial Newsletter 21 (Fall):2-3.
         Describes a visit to the star of the 1925 silent film
      version of A Lost Lady.

39   ZEMAN, ANTHEA. <u>Presumptuous Girls: Women and Their World in</u>
     <u>the Serious Woman's Novel</u>. London: Weidenfeld & Nicolson,
     pp. 8, 101.
        Observes that Cather and other women writers conscien-
     tiously bestowed accolades on each other and that she and others
     showed in their writing an interest in intellectual concerns.

40   ZLOTNIK, JAN. "The Virgin and the Dynamo: A Study of the
     Woman as Hero in the Novels of Edith Wharton, Ellen Glasgow
     and Willa Cather." Ph.D. dissertation, Syracuse University,
     378 pp.
        Uses Henry Adams's vision of modern mechanization and free
     will to show how Wharton, Glasgow, and Cather create female pro-
     tagonists who assert individual will in the face of determinis-
     tic forces. See <u>Dissertation Abstracts International</u> 39 (1978):
     878A-79A.

                                    1978

1   ARNOLD, MARILYN. "<u>One of Ours</u>: Willa Cather's Losing Battle."
     <u>Western American Literature</u> 13 (November):259-66.
        Argues that the chief problem with <u>One of Ours</u> is that
     Cather tries to make a hero out of the kind of character who by
     nature and inclination plays a supporting role in her other
     novels. Thus, for the idealistic Claude Wheeler, war becomes
     the center of value. But since Cather herself hated war, a false
     value is seated in the principal character, leaving the novel
     without a genuine center of value. Cather's personal affection
     for Claude is not enough to save the book.

2   BASS, EBEN. "The Sculptor of the Beautiful." <u>Colby Library</u>
     <u>Quarterly</u> 14 (March):28-35.
        Sees correspondences between Hawthorne's allegorical "The
     Artist of the Beautiful" and Cather's satirical "The Sculptor's
     Funeral," and suggests that in writing her story about the con-
     flict between the practical and the ideal, Cather may have used
     Hawthorne's story as a model.

3   BRUCCOLI, MATTHEW J. "'An Instance of Apparent Plagiarism':
     F. Scott Fitzgerald, Willa Cather, and the first <u>Gatsby</u>
     Manuscript." <u>Princeton University Library Chronicle</u> 39
     (Spring):171-78.
        Cites a letter from Fitzgerald to Cather in which he ex-
     presses concern that in one particular description of Daisy
     Buchanan he might appear to have plagiarized a passage from the
     newly released <u>A Lost Lady</u>. He encloses copies of pages from
     his manuscript draft as evidence that he wrote his description
     before he read <u>A Lost Lady</u>. Cather apparently replied that she
     saw no sign of plagiarism. This letter also appears in Matthew
     J. Bruccoli and Margaret M. Dugan, eds., <u>Correspondence of</u>
     <u>F. Scott Fitzgerald</u> (New York: Random House, 1980), pp. 155-56.

4   BRYFONSKI, DEDRIA, and MENDELSON, PHYLLIS CARMEL, eds.
    Twentieth-Century Literary Criticism. Vol. 1. Detroit:
    Gale Research Co., pp. 150-67.
        Presents a brief biographical sketch and a list of Cather's
    works, then provides often lengthy excerpts from published criti-
    cism on Cather's work ranging from rather early evaluations in
    the 1920s through 1974. Criticism from the 1920s, 1950s, and
    1960s predominates the selection.

5   CASSAI, MARY ANN. "Symbolic Techniques in Selected Novels of
    Willa Cather." Ph.D. dissertation, New York University,
    226 pp.
        Describes four types of symbolism--adumbrative, character,
    landscape, and juxtapositional--and Cather's use of them in O
    Pioneers!, My Ántonia, One of Ours, Shadows on the Rock, and
    Death Comes for the Archbishop. See Dissertation Abstracts
    International 39 (1978):2269A-70A.

6   CHADBOURNE, RICHARD. "Two Visions of the Prairies: Willa
    Cather and Gabrielle Roy." In The New Land: Studies in a
    Literary Theme. Edited by Richard Chadbourne and Hallvard
    Dahlie. Waterloo, Ontario: Wilfrid Laurier University Press
    for Calgary Institute for the Humanities, pp. 93-120.
        Investigates the affinities and the differences between two
    prairie-minded writers. Cather's prairie vision is one that
    synthesizes historical insights with poetry, while Roy's perspec-
    tive, though broad like Cather's, interweaves pioneer memories
    (her mother's) with "the personal drama of a child's coming of
    age." The note Roy strikes is not elegaic like Cather's, but it
    is more openly autobiographical.

7   CHALIFF, CYNTHIA. "The Art of Willa Cather's Craft." Papers
    on Language & Literature 14 (Winter):61-73.
        Cather's habitual narrative structure yokes two stories
    together but shows no overt links between them. This indicates
    her subconsciousness operating in their creation, working out her
    notion that childhood's innocence is the best time of life. She
    sets ancient primitive myth against stories of prematuration
    innocence and suggests that sexual maturation is what causes
    trouble for the human race. "The Enchanted Bluff" and The
    Professor's House are important expressions of these concerns,
    and so, to a lesser degree, are "Coming, Aphrodite!" and
    O Pioneers! In Death Comes for the Archbishop Cather avoids the
    problem of intimate human relationship by making her protagonist
    a celibate priest.

8   "The Complete Willa Cather." Bancroftiana, no. 69 (February),
    2-3.
        Sketches a brief account of Cather's life and career, not-
    ing that the Bancroft Library of the University of California,
    Berkeley, now has a full collection of Cather first editions.
    It also has a memoir of Cather's visit to the University in 1931
    when she was awarded an honorary doctorate.

9   COWLEY, MALCOLM. --And I Worked at the Writer's Trade:
     Chapters of Literary History, 1918-78. New York: Viking
     Press, pp. 188-89.
         Reports that Cather told him that she got herself started
     at the daily writing task by reading a passage from the Bible,
     not from a pious urge, but from a desire to "get in touch with
     fine prose," even though the Bible's prose rhythms were not the
     ones she was seeking. Cowley suspects, however, that there was
     a touch of piety in the practice because authors sense that their
     success comes partly from powers beyond themselves.

10   DONALD, MILES. The American Novel in the Twentieth Century.
     Newton Abbot, England: David & Charles; New York: Harper &
     Row, Barnes & Noble Import Division, pp. 7-8, 43, 57, 71.
         Indicates that Cather does not receive major treatment here
     because in spirit she predates the era of F. Scott Fitzgerald,
     and she was best as an historical novelist. Cather, like Sinclair
     Lewis and Sherwood Anderson, exalts some of the same aspects of
     American life that she also attacks as crippling. Furthermore,
     these three writers, like Hawthorne and Thoreau before them, do
     not see the connection between the land and the repressive,
     hypocritical attitudes they attack in rural communities. Also
     regards My Ántonia as one of America's "classic" cries against
     the ill-treatment of the immigrant.

11   DONALDSON, SCOTT, and MASSA, ANN. American Literature:
     Nineteenth and Early Twentieth Centuries. Comparative Litera-
     ture Series. London: David & Charles, pp. 36-37, 189; New
     York: Harper & Row, Barnes & Noble Import Division; North
     Vancouver, British Columbia: Douglas David & Charles.
         Speaks of the success of the Scandinavian and Bohemian
     families in establishing themselves in America, as revealed in
     O Pioneers! and My Ántonia. Cather was America's only major
     writer who was optimistic about a person's ability to change.
     Her work "constitutes a fine humanistic statement of mind over
     matter." The creative Alexandra Bergson is an example of this.

12   DRIFTMIER, DAVID. "David Driftmier Writes about Nebraska's
     Famous Author." Kitchen-Klatter Magazine, July, pp. 15, 20.
         Recommends, in the form of a personal letter, Cather's
     novels to readers. Cather's happiest book, O Pioneers!, projects
     America's basic ideals. Death Comes for the Archbishop is
     forward-looking, voicing ideas far ahead of its time.

13   GIANNONE, RICHARD [JOHN]. "Willa Cather and the Unfinished
     Drama of Deliverance." Prairie Schooner 52 (Spring):25-46.
         Cather's large subject, in the unity of all her work, is
     the yearning of the human spirit for freedom and fulfillment.
     Basing her final novel, Sapphira and the Slave Girl, on the
     Biblical paradigm of wilderness enslavement and deliverance
     through divine mercy, Cather culminates the yearning expressed
     through all her work. It is a spiritual yearning and will con-
     tinue; but in the human counterpart of divine mercy, which is

human love, she finds at least a momentary answer and fulfillment. In art, too, in the creation of such a book as Sapphira
and the Slave Girl, is at least a human means for satisfying the
spirit's "infinite longing."

14　HALLER, EVELYN. "The Iconography of Vice in Willa Cather's
　　My Ántonia." Colby Library Quarterly 14 (June):93-102.
　　　　Uses Chaucer's "Parson's Tale" as it illustrates the Seven
Deadly Sins of the medieval taxonomy of sin to show parallels
between characters in My Ántonia and allegorical representations
of the sins in Chaucer. Wick Cutter is guilty of both lust and
avarice, Larry Donovan pride, Mrs. Shimerda and Lazy Mary envy,
Pavel and Mrs. Cutter anger, Russian Peter gluttony, and Mr.
Shimerda "accidia." By contrast, Ántonia represents charity.

15　HARRIS, RICHARD C. "Renaissance Pastoral Conventions and the
　　Ending of My Ántonia." Markham Review 8 (Fall):8-11.
　　　　O Pioneers! and A Lost Lady, like My Ántonia, have obvious
pastoral elements in the classical mode, but My Ántonia also
manifests four major Renaissance pastoral elements: (1) simplicity and beauty of location, (2) evidence of "erotic idealism," (3) a harmonious relationship between humanity and nature,
and (4) evidence of regenerative powers in both nature and the
pastoral goddess who is at home there. Seeing My Ántonia this
way adds importance to the book's final scene wherein Jim Burden
is transformed by his return to Ántonia and the landscape she
inhabits.

16　KRAUSE, JANET BOETTCHER. "Self-actualizing Women in Willa
　　Cather's Prairie Novels." Ph.D. dissertation, University of
　　Nebraska, 188 pp.
　　　　Applies theories of self-actualization to Cather's work and
argues that her women characters are forced to contend with traditional role expectations which are difficult, but not impos-
sible, to overcome. See Dissertation Abstracts International 39
(1979):6132A.

17　LINGEMAN, RICHARD R. "Home Town, U.S.A.: In the Footsteps
　　of Four Novelists." New York Times Travel sec., 29 January,
　　pp. 1, 14.
　　　　Recounts a visit to Red Cloud, Nebraska, the home of
Cather's youth, as well as to the home towns of Sinclair Lewis,
Sherwood Anderson, and Edgar Lee Masters. Calls Cather less a
rebel than an artist who maintained a "love-hate tie" with Red
Cloud throughout her life.

18　McGILL, ROBERT ALAN. "Heartbreak: Western Enchantment and
　　Western Fact in Willa Cather's The Professor's House." South
　　Dakota Review 16 (Autumn):56-79.
　　　　Observes particularly the western content of The Professor's House, the landscape and values that Cather characteristically uses in her fiction. The two focal points of the novel
are Tom Outland and Augusta, the one projecting the potential for
enchantment but also betrayal, the other projecting the potential

for an enduring civilization. Together, in juxtaposition, they
in their western outlook absorb and counter the heartbreak and
distress generated in the novel.

19   MURPHY, JOHN J. "Willa Cather's Archbishop: A Western and
     Classical Perspective." Western American Literature 13
     (August):141-50.
        In the character of her archbishop, Cather combines the
traditions of the western American frontier hero and the classical hero. Parallels with the Virginian and Natty Bumppo are
evident--celibacy, male friendship, and concern over land ex-
ploitation. Also evident are parallels with Aeneas--the calling
to a special mission, otherworldly "intrusions," and qualities of
character. Through combining these two perspectives, Cather
achieves a sense of timelessness. Reprinted: 1984.58.

20   MURPHY, MICHAEL W[ALTER]. "Willa Cather's Mortal Affirma-
     tion." Greyfriar 19:40-48.
        In Myra Henshawe (My Mortal Enemy) Cather has created a
character who stands as a corrective to Oswald's nostalgic
sentimentality and Nellie Birdseye's simplistic and provincial
modernism. Myra sees that the past has shaped the present, and
she refuses to live in it as Oswald does. She seems cruel because she will not allow Nellie her romantic and comfortable
illusions. Myra is proof that Cather understood both the lure of
the past and the necessity to live in the present.

21   NICHOLS, KATHLEEN L. "The Celibate Male in A Lost Lady: The
     Unreliable Center of Consciousness." Regionalism and the
     Female Imagination 4, no. 1:13-23.
        Suggests a Freudian interpretation of A Lost Lady that
bases Niel Herbert's repulsion toward Marian Forrester's sexuality in Oedipal feelings reaching back to the mother he lost
and is searching for. His readings--of Don Juan, Tom Jones,
Wilhelm Meister, and the Heroides--provide an important clue to
Niel's repressed sexual desires for Marian Forrester. It is the
Captain, not Niel, who is the ideal celibate, who has the proper
appreciation for the woman Marian is. Niel is not a reliable
narrator. Reprinted: 1984.61.

22   O'BRIEN, SHARON. "The Unity of Willa Cather's 'Two-part
     Pastoral': Passion in O Pioneers!" Studies in American
     Fiction 6 (Autumn):157-71.
        Demonstrates the tight unity, conscious or not, achieved
in O Pioneers! through the contrasting juxtaposition of Marie's
sexual passion against Alexandra's submergence of her sexual
self and her expression of passion through an ordered, creative
union with the land. In Cather, sexual passion nearly always
leads to destruction.

23   O'FLAHERTY, TERRENCE. "From a Schoolroom Past." San
     Francisco Chronicle, 9 May, p. 40.
        Comments on the Public Broadcasting System film portrait
of Cather titled "Into the Morning: Willa Cather's America,"

but also speaks of her craftsmanship and her desire for privacy. Quotes some parts of the broadcast script.

24   OLSEN, TILLIE. "Willa Cather." In Silences. New York: Delacorte Press, Seymour Lawrence, pp. 137–39.
       Treats Cather in these pages and in passing mentions throughout the book as one of those who experienced periods of silence when her artistic work was denied or deferred. For Cather the critical time of silence was when she was doing other work full-time and writing only an occasional "Jamesian" story on the side, the years between The Troll Garden and Alexander's Bridge. Cather admired James at this time, but he failed to offer interest or encouragement. Fortunately, Sarah Orne Jewett came along and advised Cather to get out of the workaday world and allow her gift to flower.

25   PIECHOWSKE, MARJORIE PAULINE. "Social Classes and Upward Mobility in American Urban Fiction from Howells to Cather." Ph.D. dissertation, University of Wisconsin, 220 pp.
       Describes Cather, along with seven others, as a writer of the "urban frontier." Concentrates on the social groupings which these writers establish for their characters according to those characters' capacity to adjust to urban development. See Dissertation Abstracts International 39 (1979):5515A.

26   POPKEN, RANDALL L. "From Innocence to Experience in My Ántonia and Boy Life on the Prairie." North Dakota Quarterly 46 (Spring):73–81.
       Perceives many similarities between My Ántonia and Hamlin Garland's Boy Life on the Prairie, comparing the experiences of Jim Burden and Lincoln Stewart as they first confront the prairie's primitivism in innocence, then become aware of the presence of evil, and finally attempt a reconciliation with both the benign and malignant forces in the universe. In the end, Cather turns from reality and allows Jim to escape into memory, while Garland refuses his character that retreat into "false optimism."

27   ROSOWSKI, SUSAN J. "Narrative Technique in Cather's My Mortal Enemy." Journal of Narrative Technique 8 (Spring):141–49.
       Far from being the rather sparsely conceived narrator of typical critical commentary on My Mortal Enemy, Nellie Birdseye becomes one of Cather's most fully realized narrators. It is through Nellie's gradual but emphatic development from romantic to realist that Cather projects her principal theme: the limitations in human terms of the myth-making process. Myra Henshawe as the romantic heroine of legend is transformed in Nellie's understanding to the real woman of bitter old age. The child Nellie begins in myth, goes through adolescent disillusionment when she perceives reality, and arrives at an adult understanding and sympathy for Myra as she is at the end of the novel, a perspective Oswald Henshawe refuses to embrace.

28   _____ . "Willa Cather's Pioneer Women: A Feminist Interpre-
        tation." In Where the West Begins: Essays on Middle Border
        and Siouxland Writing. Edited by Arthur H. Huseboe and William
        Geyer. Sioux Falls, S.D.: Augustan College, Center for West-
        ern Studies, pp. 135–42.
            In her pioneer women characters, Alexandra Bergson and
        Ántonia Shimerda, Cather portrays women transcending their tradi-
        tional female roles--Alexandra by synthesizing the dual urges
        toward expansion and value maintenance, and Ántonia by providing
        the impulse for expansion in others.

*29   SATO, HIROKO. Kyazā: Bi no saishi [Cather: A priestess of
        beauty]. Tokyo: Tōju-sha, 351 pp.
            Listed in Bibliography of English Language and Literature
        (1978).

30   SEIDEL, ALISON P. Literary Criticism and Authors' Biographies:
        An Annotated Index. Metuchen, N.J.: Scarecrow Press,
        pp. 31–32.
            Lists sixteen books that contain chapters about Cather and
        her work, all of them published between 1940 and 1970.

31   SMITH, ANNELIESE H. "Finding Marian Forrester: A Restorative
        Reading of Cather's A Lost Lady." Colby Library Quarterly 14
        (December):221–25.
            Argues that Marian Forrester, not Niel Herbert, is central
        to A Lost Lady, and that it is she who is betrayed by each of the
        men in her life, not she who does the betraying. Even Captain
        Forrester is the lord of this feudal society, and he puts his
        "honor" above any consideration for her. Cather may have chosen
        an epigraph from Hamlet deliberately to show that in her novel as
        in the play, "women are victims of masculine heroics, self-
        interest, and ignorance."

32   STOUCK, DAVID. "Women Writers in the Mainstream: A Review
        Essay." Texas Studies in Literature and Language 20 (Winter):
        660–70.
            Notes the curious omission of Cather from some major criti-
        cal works on American literature, and comments on the renewed in-
        terest in her work in the last decade, triggered both by the
        Women's Movement and by the efforts of the University of Nebraska
        Press to make her work accessible to readers. Summarizes the
        content of the major published papers from the international
        seminar marking her centenary in 1973 (see Slote and Faulkner,
        1974.69).

33   WELTY, EUDORA. "The House of Willa Cather." In The Eye of
        the Story: Selected Essays and Reviews. New York: Random
        House, pp. 41–60.
            Reprint of 1974.79.

34   WILD, BARBARA. "'The Thing Not Named' in The Professor's
        House." Western American Literature 12 (February):263–74.

Reasons that "the thing not named," but rather suggested and subtly revealed in The Professor's House, is the deep friendship between Godfrey St. Peter and Tom Outland. This friendship is very important to the book, and it is the loss of Tom and all he means that is most responsible for the professor's melancholy. There is a profusion of religious suggestion and imagery in the book, and the friendship between Tom and the professor can be compared to the biblical friendship between the apostle Peter and Jesus Christ.

35 "Willa Cather's America." Choice, May, p. 7.
Comments on the television production, "Into the Morning: Willa Cather's America," and notes Cather's espousal of traditional values. Claims her three goals were "to make it in a man's world, to create art, and to be a Virginia lady like her mother."

36 WOODRESS, JAMES. "The Genesis of the Prologue of Death Comes for the Archbishop." American Literature 50 (November): 473-78.
Contends that Cather's prologue to Death Comes for the Archbishop "invites comparison" with a painting by French artist Jehan George Vibert. Cather indicated in an interview that the painting--which she called "The Missionary's Return," but which Vibert referred to as "The Missionary's Story"--supplied the inspiration for the scene in her prologue. It is somewhat surprising that Cather would have been moved by what was not a very appealing painting.

37 _____. "Willa Cather and History." Arizona Quarterly 34 (Autumn):239-54.
Cather found the present very painful in the aftermath of World War I, and her novels from One of Ours through My Mortal Enemy reflect that. She turned from the historical idea of progress to fiction that allowed her to treat history as a series of separate eras. In such eras she could find characters who earned her empathy. Her greatest novel, Death Comes for the Archbishop, is a reflection of that turn, and also of the fact that Cather's interest was in historical romance, not history. Though the book is based on actual figures, it is largely fiction. Shadows on the Rock is another of her historical romances, and like Death Comes for the Archbishop uses "Representative Men" of the period. Sapphira and the Slave Girl, on the other hand, is based on family history and personal memory.

38 YONGUE, PATRICIA LEE. "Willa Cather on Heroes and Hero-Worship." Neuphilologische Mitteilungen (Finland) 79, no. 1: 59-66.
Fathers Latour and Vaillant in Death Comes for the Archbishop are fashioned in the manner of Thomas Carlyle's Hero and Ordinary Man in On Heroes, but they go beyond Carlyle's limits in that both are heroes in their own right. Latour is the quintessence of the artist's nature, perfect in his spiritual disembodiment from daily concerns--complete, finished in immortal

permanence. Though a worshiper in Latour's church, Vaillant is
not only Ordinary Man, but a hero too. The two men come together
in Death Comes for the Archbishop as complementary principles--
lord and servant, ideal and real, Bishop and Vicar--in Cather's
realization of her "immense design."

*39   YOSHIDA, MICHIKO. "Jonetsu to soz: Willa Cather ni kansuru
      ichi kosatsu" [Passion and creation: A study on Willa Cather].
      Oberon: Magazine for the Study of English and American Lit-
      erature (Tokyo) 17, no. 2:15-35.
          Listed in MLA International Bibliography, 1978.

                              1979

1   ALBERTINI, VIRGIL. "Willa Cather's Early Short Stories: A
     Link to the Agrarian Realists." Markham Review 8 (Summer):
     69-72.
         In four of her earliest stories, three written while she
     was in college, Cather portrays the immigrant experience on the
     western prairies with the same pessimism evident in agrarian
     realists like Edgar Watson Howe, Joseph Kirkland, and Hamlin
     Garland. Not only is the land hard, as many farmers on the
     prairie when Cather was in college would have attested, but it
     often destroys rather than ennobles those who try to live upon
     it.

2   BENIDT, BRUCE. "Willa Cather and the Prairie." Minneapolis
     Star Saturday Magazine, 28 July, pp. 10-11.
         Focuses mainly on Cather's Nebraska environment--the
     prairie and the town of Red Cloud--but includes material from an
     interview with Mildred Bennett. With only occasional sentimen-
     tality, Cather presents both the harshness and the beauty of the
     land.

3   BENNETT, MILDRED R. "Willa Cather's Virginia 1873-1883."
     Pts. 1-2. Willa Cather Pioneer Memorial Newsletter 23,
     no. 4:25, nos. 2-3 (Makeup issue 1979; Literary issue 1981):
     1-4, 5-10.
         In these special issues of the Newsletter, Bennett recon-
     structs Cather's Virginia family background from a multitude of
     stories and recollections gathered from letters and interviews
     with the family. Two family letters are printed here, and a
     number of anecdotes are reported.

4   BLAKE, NELSON MANFRED. "How to Learn History from Sinclair
     Lewis and Other Uncommon Sources." In American Character and
     Culture in a Changing World: Some Twentieth-Century Perspec-
     tives. Edited by John A. Hague. Contributions in American
     Studies, no. 42, edited by Robert H. Walker. Westport, Conn.:
     Greenwood Press, pp. 113-14.
         Contrasts Cather's O Pioneers! with the work of Hamlin
     Garland, noting that the frontier Cather portrays focuses on
     times of prosperity after the early struggle.

5   BORDNER, MARSHA STANFIELD. "The Woman as Artist in Twentieth-
    Century Fiction." Ph.D. dissertation, Ohio State University,
    187 pp.
        Refers to Thea Kronborg in The Song of the Lark as the
    "archetypal artist-heroine" of the period from 1920 through 1929.
    Characters like Thea are strong protagonists whose success
    parallels the success of the women's movement of the time. These
    heroines, however, are performers rather than creators; the
    creative heroine emerges in the novels from the second women's
    movement. See Dissertation Abstracts International 40 (1980):
    5438A.

6   COOPER, CLARA B[OMANJI]. "The Central Androgynous Characters
    in My Ántonia." Indian Journal of American Studies 9 (July):
    65–67.
        In her writing Cather was able to project the same androgy-
    nous ideal she achieved in her life, a healthy combination of the
    masculine and feminine. Throughout his life, Jim Burden exempli-
    fies both active and passive traits. Ántonia, however, moves
    from an essentially feminine role into a more assertive, mascu-
    line one, and then in the end becomes the epitome of the androg-
    ynous ideal in her role as the mother figure who embodies mascu-
    line strength.

7   DUNBAR-ODOM, DONNA. "The Ordered Home: The Secondary Charac-
    ters' Purpose in Shadows on the Rock." Willa Cather Pioneer
    Memorial Newsletter 22, nos. 3–4:3–4.
        Even though Shadows on the Rock may appear to portray char-
    acters and situations that stand in opposition to the ideals of
    order and permanence that Cather espouses in the novel, these
    characters actually either reflect the values of the Auclairs, or
    they show the consequences if those values are absent.

8   DYRUD, DAVID LYNN. "Varieties of Marginality: The Treatment
    of the European Immigrant in the Middlewestern Frontier
    Novel." Ph.D. dissertation, Purdue University, 258 pp.
        Examines seventy-seven novels, including Cather's work,
    about frontier immigrant experience published between 1890 and
    1970. Finds in the novelists a common impulse toward nostalgia
    and didacticism, and a "fascination for historical detail." Sees
    a similar theme of conflict for the immigrant, conflict within
    himself or with family, with nature, with earlier immigrants, and
    with the established "Yankee" society. See Dissertation
    Abstracts International 41 (1980):249A.

9   FAIRBANKS [MYERS], CAROL. More Women in Literature: Criti-
    cism of the Seventies. Metuchen, N.J.: Scarecrow Press,
    pp. 67–69.
        Extends coverage of 1976.20, to include critical and bio-
    graphical books, articles, and dissertations from 1970 through
    1977. Supplements earlier volume and does not repeat entries.

10   FAULKNER, VIRGINIA. "The Cather Bookshelf." Willa Cather
      Pioneer Memorial Newsletter 23, no. 2:3–4.
         Combines descriptive commentary about recent books that
      treat Cather's work with notations about various collections,
      both foreign and domestic, that contain Cather stories. "The
      Sentimentality of William Tavener" has recently been in great
      demand by editors of anthologies.

*11   FRIEDL, BETTINA. "Frauen in der Literatur: Amerikanische
      Autorinnen des 20. Jahrhunderts." In Einfuhrung in die
      amerikanische Literaturgeschichte. Edited by Jakob J.
      Kollhofer. Heidelberg: Deutsch-Amerikanisches Institut,
      pp. 246–78.
         Referred to in the section of American Literary Scholarship
      for 1979 prepared by Hans Galinsky. He indicates that the
      writers discussed are Cather, Edith Wharton, Ellen Glasgow,
      Carson McCullers, Katherine Anne Porter, and Lillian Hellman.
      (Unverified.)

12   FUKUI, GOICHI. "Introduction to Willa Cather and Her Novel,
      One of Ours." General Education Review (Toho University)
      11:55–66.
         Presents a general estimate of Cather's life and work,
      stressing her dedication to her art and suggesting that beauty is
      a noble pursuit. Her hatred of materialism is apparent generally
      in her work, and One of Ours is no exception. The central pas-
      sion of One of Ours is Claude's suffering. The subtitle (and one
      chapter title) of the book, "Bidding the Eagles of the West Fly
      on . . . ," comes from Vachel Lindsay's poem about William
      Jennings Bryan, and Claude's defeat may well represent Bryan's.

13   FUNK, RUTH CHRISTY. "Order and Chaos: A Study of Cultural
      Dialectic in Adams, James, Cather, Glasgow, Warren, and
      Fitzgerald." Ph.D. dissertation, Syracuse University,
      179 pp.
         Analyzes Cather's My Ántonia using Henry Adams's symbols
      of order and chaos—the Virgin and the Dynamo. Although the
      other authors are shown to deal with the reality of the Dynamo,
      or chaos, in human life, or with the futility of seeking the
      Virgin, Cather effectively presents the fabled unity that man
      yearns for but never can achieve in reality. See Dissertation
      Abstracts International 40 (1979):2679A.

14   GERVAUD, J. MICHEL. "A Note on Willa Cather and Flaubert."
      Willa Cather Pioneer Memorial Newsletter 23 (Fall):2, 6.
         Observes some similarities between statements about the
      nature of fictional art made by Gustave Flaubert and Cather.
      Both regard the truest reality as that which has been passed
      through the artist's imagination and has thereby taken on a
      quality beyond the strictly literal.

15 HEILBRUN, CAROLYN G. Reinventing Womanhood. New York: W.W. Norton & Co., pp. 79-81.
    Discusses Cather as one of a number of female novelists who work through their own female identity crises in their novels and end up denying females a creative destiny--even though they themselves achieve it. Cather begins with a male protagonist, Bartley Alexander, then moves to two successive creative female protagonists. After The Song of the Lark, however, Cather uses mainly male heroes and male viewpoints.

16 HEYECK, ROBIN, and WOODRESS, JAMES. "Willa Cather's Cuts and Revisions in The Song of the Lark." Modern Fiction Studies 25 (Winter):651-58.
    In revising The Song of the Lark for the 1937 Library edition of her work, Cather cut the novel, but did not change it basically. Cather makes six kinds of alterations: (1) removal of outdated topical references, (2) removal of a young writer's indiscretions (such as references to smoking and drinking), (3) removal of youthful extravagances (including foreign expressions), (4) removal of lapses of taste (such as a sexually suggestive passage and an anti-Semitic reference), (5) removal of excessive detail (the most extensive deletions), and (6) modification of character portrayal (such as effusive passages about Thea Kronborg's beauty).

17 HOFFMAN, C., and HOFFMAN, A.C. "Re-Echoes of the Jazz Age: Archetypal Women in the Novels of 1922." Journal of Modern Literature 7 (February):62-86.
    Discusses Cather and One of Ours along with several other modern novelists, male and female, whose novels of the "watershed" year 1922 portray woman as archetypal "love goddess" or "mother imago." In One of Ours Claude Wheeler's wife, Enid Royce, is "a vestal virgin, an untouchable love-goddess," and his mother is "the ultimate archetypal mother as love-goddess." She prefers that he die for a beautiful cause rather than live in disillusionment.

18 HOLMAN, C. HUGH. Windows on the World: Essays on American Social Fiction. Knoxville: University of Tennessee Press, pp. 183-88, 189-93 passim.
    Cites My Ántonia and A Lost Lady as examples of the American bildungsroman. Jim Burden is not simply a narrative device, but a vital element in My Ántonia's theme. Ántonia represents the spirit that opened and built the frontier, and Jim represents the diminishing vitality of the succeeding era (suggested in the plow image that shrinks as he and the others watch it). In both novels the once young observers learn that they have witnessed the decline of the West's Golden Age. A Lost Lady is linked with The Great Gatsby in this common concern with historical change.

19 HSU, PEI-TZU. "The Love of the Land in Pearl Buck's The Good
    Earth and Willa Cather's O Pioneers!" Fu Jen Studies:
    Literature and Linguistics, Republic of China (Taipei) 12:
    71–82.
        Compares and contrasts Pearl Buck's Wang Lung with Cather's
    Alexandra Bergson, finding the two to be similar in their tough-
    ness and their devotion to land values. Nevertheless, Wang
    Lung's relationship with the land is closer and more personal
    than Alexandra's.

20 KEOUGH, JAMES. "Willa Cather's Pastoral Vision: Going Home
    to Rural America." Sierra 64 (January–February):62–66.
        Cather's work is informed by a tension created through her
    pulls to both the land and art. Cather is a preservationist,
    paradoxically ahead of her time though sometimes regarded as too
    deeply tied to the past. She was attracted to the elemental,
    which has an unbreakable bond with the aesthetic, and she often
    valued her fictional characters according to their response to
    and appreciation for the land.

21 KHARE, A.K. "A Study of the Themes in the Novels and Short
    Stories of Willa Cather: As a Clue to Understanding Her Mind
    and Artistic Preoccupations." Ph.D. dissertation, Ravishankar
    University, Raipur (Madhya Pradesh), 330 pp.
        Contends that although Cather is no longer "fashionable,"
    her themes are always relevant. Her work has a lasting freshness
    and an ultimate hopefulness. Treats Cather's developing concerns
    as in her mature work she deals first with the land and then with
    the artist. She became sensitive to the "shadow of Europe," and
    she went through a period of doubt; but she was finally to affirm
    that fulfillment is possible through religious devotion.

22 KRAFT, STEPHANIE. "Willa Cather, the Prairie, and Red Cloud."
    In No Castles on Main Street: American Authors and Their
    Homes. Chicago: Rand McNally & Co., pp. 11, 94–104.
        Observes Cather's use of Nebraska people and materials in
    her writing, but praises her for lifting the regional to the
    universal and making art of it. Her achievement should rid
    readers of the habit of regarding "regionalism" in literature as
    pejorative.

23 KROETSCH, ROBERT. "The Fear of Women in Prairie Fiction: An
    Erotics of Space." In Crossing Frontiers: Papers in American
    and Canadian Western Literature. Papers delivered at a con-
    ference in Banff, Alberta, April 1978. Edited by Dick
    Harrison. Edmonton: University of Alberta Press, pp. 73–83.
    Response by Sandra Djwa, pp. 84–88.
        Illustrates through My Ántonia and Sinclair Ross's As For
    Me and My House a preponderant theme and problem in prairie fic-
    tion. No close human relationship, no meaningful sexual union,
    is possible in a landscape of great space. Fear and isolation
    preclude that union. Djwa avers that the novels are more complex
    than Kroetsch's formula allows for, and that in My Ántonia Jim is
    actually in the end uniting with his muse and the Nebraska

landscape. Ántonia comes out of a long literary tradition, that of mythic woman as muse, and in that tradition Jim and Ántonia can be close, but they cannot be lovers.

24 LEARY, LEWIS, and AUCHARD, JOHN, comps. Articles on American Literature, 1968-1975. Durham, N.C.: Duke University Press, pp. 64-67.
    Lists a large number of articles on Cather's work, including a few in foreign periodicals, that appeared between 1968 and 1975.

25 MAGILL, FRANK N., ed. Magill's Bibliography of Literary Criticism. Vol. 1. Englewood Cliffs, N.J.: Salem Press, pp. 322-29.
    Provides separate listings of a large number of articles and books, published mainly between 1951 and 1977, that deal with seven of Cather's twelve novels.

26 MAINERO, LINA. "Willa Sibert Cather." In American Women Writers: A Critical Reference Guide from Colonial Times to the Present. Vol. 1. Edited by Lina Mainero and Langdon Lynne Faust. New York: Frederick Ungar Publishing Co., pp. 315-21.
    Cather's "highwater period" produced the great novels The Professor's House, My Mortal Enemy, Death Comes for the Archbishop, and Shadows on the Rock, all of which affirm the importance of religion. All of Cather's books are about herself; in spite of her insistence on privacy, some need drove her to reveal her inmost self. From these simultaneous contradictory impulses to reveal and conceal comes the tension that produces some of the power in her work--"the romantic confessional temperament writing in the classical restrained mode." A Lost Lady is one of America's finest novels, and The Professor's House is "double autobiography." Tom Outland embodies Cather's younger self, Godfrey St. Peter her middle-aged self.

27 MASON, ELIZABETH B., and STAR, LOUIS M. The Oral History Collection of Columbia University. New York: Oral History Research Office, p. 157.
    Indicates that among the holdings at Columbia is an oral history of Alfred A. Knopf, Cather's publisher. That history, which can be read only with permission of the Knopf estate, contains a vignette about Cather.

28 MASSEY, DAVID G. "Simplicity with Suggestiveness in Willa Cather's Revised and Republished Fiction." Ph.D. dissertation, Drew University, 191 pp.
    Examines Cather's revising process, observing that almost invariably she deletes material, thereby achieving greater brevity, objectivity, and suggestiveness. See Dissertation Abstracts International 40 (1979):2063A.

29   MEDOFF, JESLYN. "An Anglo-American Author Creates Anglo-
     American Villains." Heritage of Kansas: A Journal of the
     Great Plains 12 (Spring):31–39.
         Through the eyes of good Anglo narrators, Cather creates
     stereotypical Anglo-villains who are a threat to certain good
     ethnic women, but are not victorious over them. Cather's three
     prominent Anglo-villains are Buck Scales in Death Comes for the
     Archbishop, Wick Cutter in My Ántonia, and Martin Colbert in
     Sapphira and the Slave Girl.

30   MONTEIRO, GEORGE. "Addenda to the Bibliographies of Cather,
     Conrad, De Forest, Dreiser, Forster, Hardy, Hawthorne, London,
     Norris, Poe, Wharton, and Whitman." Papers of the Biblio-
     graphical Society of America 73 (October-December):478–81.
         Adds a review of One of Ours to Hutchinson's (1956.13)
     listing. Addenda to some other writers also contain mentions of
     Cather.

31   MOSELEY, ANN. "The Dual Nature of Art in The Song of the
     Lark." Western American Literature 14 (May):19–32.
         In The Song of the Lark Cather delineates the Dionysian and
     Appollonian aspects of art and nature through the character of
     Thea Kronborg. The novel is divided into three parts, two books
     in each. The first illustrates the Dionysian urge for desire
     and freedom; the second illustrates the Appollonian urge for
     reason and order; the third shows the linking of the two urges
     in the passion and discipline equally important in the production
     of great art.

32   O'BRIEN, SHARON. "Tomboyism and Adolescent Conflict: Three
     Nineteenth-Century Case Studies." In Woman's Being, Woman's
     Place: Female Identity and Vocation in American History.
     Edited by Mary Kelley. Boston: G.K. Hall & Co., pp. 351–72.
         Uses Frances Willard, Louisa May Alcott, and Cather as case
     studies in investigating the consequences of contradictions
     created when Victorian society encouraged Tomboyism (because it
     was healthy) in girls, but expected a quick reversal to sub-
     servient femininity once a girl reached puberty. The young
     Cather apparently identified creative ability and achievement
     with maleness, and for a period of four years adopted a mascu-
     line identity. Later on, however, she encountered strong, able,
     artistic women who had kept their female identity--but who had
     not assumed the feminine role outlined for them in Victorian
     advice books--and they became role models for her. She thus
     satisfactorily resolved her adolescent conflict.

33   PARKS, B.K. "A Dedication to the Memory of Willa Cather."
     Arizona and the West 21 (Autumn):211–24.
         A biographical essay that concludes with the assertion that
     Cather's best books were those that dealt with the West. Through
     them the western experience is made more complete.

34 PEARCE T[HOMAS] M[ATTHEWS], ed. Literary America 1903-1934: The Mary Austin Letters. Contributions in Women's Studies, no. 5. Westport, Conn.: Greenwood Press, pp. xiii, 139, 202-5.

Briefly describes the nature of Cather's letters to Austin, and paraphrases one written while Austin was in St. Louis and Cather was a guest in Austin's home in Santa Fe.

35 PIACENTINO, EDWARD J. "The Agrarian Mode in Cather's 'Neighbour Rosicky.'" Markham Review 8 (Spring):52-54.

In "Neighbour Rosicky" Cather not only stresses simple rural values over those of the city, but she also employs imagery, poetic figures, and other kinds of referents that emphasize the story's agrarian characteristics.

36 ROSOWSKI, SUSAN J. "The Novel of Awakening." Genre 12 (Fall):313-32.

Includes discussion on My Mortal Enemy as one of several novels by women that develop the theme of woman's awakening to the limitations of her traditional role as prescribed by society, bildungsromans with a female slant. Cather's version of the novel of awakening corrects what she saw as problematic with heroines like Edna Pontellier (Kate Chopin's The Awakening) and Emma Bovary (Gustave Flaubert's Madame Bovary). Each of them, and hence the contextual narrative, moves inward toward an unrealizable dream of romantic love. Cather's account, however, through Nellie Birdseye's narrative voice and developing consciousness, moves by stages from an inward romantic dream to reality and an insistence on permanent values that lie in universals outside the self--religion, nature, and art.

37 SLOTE, BERNICE. "Willa Cather and the Sense of History." In Women, Women Writers, and the West. Edited by L.L. Lee and Lewis Merrill. Troy, N.Y.: Whitston Publishing Co., pp. 161-71.

Cather did not try to write history, but she wrote out of a "sense of history." Her writing was an attempt at the realization of a lengthened past, on both an individual scale and a social scale, a past that would allow individuals and cultures to acquire a sense of identity.

38 STEWART, G[RACE] B. "Mother, Daughter and the Birth of the Female Artist." Women's Studies 6, no. 2:137.

An abridged text of 1979.39. Notes, too, Thea Kronborg's fear of returning to her mother and being absorbed by her.

39 _____. A New Mythos: The Novel of the Artist as Heroine 1877-1977. Monographs in Women's Studies, edited by Sherri Clarkson. St. Alban's, Vt.: Eden Press Women's Publications, pp. 17-21, 67-69, 121-23.

Discusses Cather's The Song of the Lark as one of several books by women that are based on the struggles and realizations of the artist-as-heroine. Like the other books treated, The Song of the Lark shows the woman artist in conflict with the

patriarchal Faustian myth that tends to see woman in traditional
mythic ways. It also contains strains of the Demeter/Persephone
myth with its implications for the pull between mothers and
daughters. Finally, in The Song of the Lark Thea Kronborg becomes an artist only by making a journey to the center of herself, casting off all but the essence of her, which is her artist
self. A new mythos is needed that will provide a base and foster
the growth of the female artist. Abridged: 1979.38.

40 STOUCK, DAVID. "Mary Austin and Willa Cather." Willa Cather
    Pioneer Memorial Newsletter 23, no. 2:2-3.
        Notes the similarities and differences between Cather's
    early story, "The Conversion of Sum Loo" (1900), and Mary
    Austin's slightly earlier story, "The Conversion of Ah Lew Sing,"
    and speculates about Cather's reasons for choosing a title so
    nearly like Austin's. Cather's story has a more "tragic caste"
    and is generally less successful than Austin's. Cather's
    strength is not in making plots.

*41 SUDA, MINORU. "A Note on Willa Cather's Art in Death Comes
    for the Archbishop." Journal of the English Institute (Japan)
    9-10:108-28.
        Listed in MLA International Bibliography (1981).

42 WESTBROOK, PERRY D. Free Will and Determinism in American
    Literature. Cranbury, N.J.: Associated University Presses,
    pp. 213, 241-44.
        Cather, along with writers like Frost and Faulkner, demon-
    strates that the deterministic philosophy did not wholly pre-
    dominate in early twentieth-century American literature. Al-
    though her early story, "Paul's Case," is wholly deterministic,
    works like The Song of the Lark and My Ántonia show that charac-
    ter can win out over circumstance. Thea Kronborg proves that
    "art is a supreme exertion of the will," and artistic achievement
    is a manifestation of the artist's having liberated her will from
    circumstance.

43 WOODRESS, JAMES. Cather entry in Great Writers of the English
    Language: Novelists and Prose Writers. Edited by James
    Vinson and D.L. Kirkpatrick. New York: St. Martin's Press,
    pp. 237-40.
        Provides, in accord with an established format, a brief
    biography, a bibliography of Cather's books, a short reading list
    of books about her, and an essay about her and her work. Charac-
    terizes Cather as a careful, dedicated craftsman who had a rare
    gift for capturing place. Comments on several of Cather's works,
    noting the particular artistic method employed in each. For
    example, My Ántonia and Death Comes for the Archbishop are
    organically episodic while A Lost Lady is "unfurnished." Cather
    successfully treats realistic materials with a romantic sensi-
    bility and is thus closer to William Wordsworth than to the
    realists and naturalists of her own time. Reprinted: 1983.34.

44   WRIGHT, WALTER F.   "Captured Shadows."   Willa Cather Pioneer
      Memorial Newsletter 22, nos. 3-4:1-3.
          Finds Shadows on the Rock very appealing visually, but
      finds in it also the limitations described in Jane Austen's ad-
      vice to her aspiring-writer niece, Anna.   Austen warns Anna
      against writing about places and times she does not know first-
      hand, and against writing about girls before they are grown up.
      She suggests further that amiability is not usually enough to
      carry a character.   By these criteria, Shadows on the Rock lacks
      the "authentic precision of detail" found in My Ántonia and Death
      Comes for the Archbishop.   Furthermore, its characters are too
      amiable and simple, like characters in a fairytale.

45   YONGUE, PATRICIA LEE.   "Willa Cather's The Professor's House
      and Dutch Genre Painting."   Renascence 31 (Spring):155-67.
          In The Professor's House Cather appropriates not only the
      pictorial effect of the open windows in Dutch genre paintings,
      but also the lesson they teach about the necessity for balancing
      the real and the ideal, a lesson Godfrey St. Peter has to learn.
      So caught up is he in what he regards as the ideal of the past
      that he needs the corrective suggested by Dutch genre paintings;
      he needs to throw over his pessimism about the present and seek
      to live creatively, using the past to inform and enrich, but
      never to replace, the present and the future.

                                1980

1   BROWN, MARION MARSH, and CRONE, RUTH.   Only One Point of the
     Compass: Willa Cather in the Northeast.   Danbury, Conn.:
     Archer Editions Press, 141 pp.
         Describes in journalistic narrative style the northeastern
     settings where Willa Cather spent thirty summers in retreat from
     the city, and gives fictionalized accounts of Cather's expe-
     riences there.   She spent several summers near Jaffrey, New
     Hampshire (where she chose also to be buried), a great many sum-
     mers at Grand Manan Island (where she eventually built a summer
     home), and a final few at Northeast Harbor, Maine.   A woman of
     "difficult" temperament whose primary concern was achieving
     privacy, she found in these settings the peace and the natural
     inspiration to do some of her best writing.

2   BYATT, A.S.   Introduction to A Lost Lady.   London: Virago,
     pp. v-xiv.
         Suggests that over the years critics have judged Cather by
     their various biases, but have by and large missed the crux of
     her work, which is "to describe the nature and movement of human
     vitality, and its failure, accurately and memorably."   Cather's
     portrayal of Marian Forrester is indeed a portrait, and she sets
     Marian's vitality and passion against Niel's lack of them.
     Cather had the great novelist's gift, the ability "to show human
     beings almost as forms of energy."

3   BYRNE, KATHLEEN D[ERRIGAN], and SNYDER, RICHARD C. Chrysalis:
    Willa Cather in Pittsburgh, 1896–1906. Pittsburgh: Histori-
    cal Society of Western Pennsylvania, 1980, 132 pp.
        Contends that the years Cather spent in Pittsburgh were
    very important in providing the atmosphere and experiences that
    allowed her genius to "sprout" and "flourish." The book is the
    culmination of twenty years of somewhat sporadic collecting of
    materials. It recounts Cather's personal and professional
    activities and shows parallels between these events and Cather's
    literary works. The first half of the book concentrates on
    Cather's friendships with such people as George and Helen Seibel,
    Ethelbert Nevin, and Isabelle McClung, and at the same time
    quotes from a number of Cather's journalistic pieces of the
    period. The second half quotes from many of Cather's high school
    students and colleagues who responded to the authors' requests by
    mail or through interviews.

4   "The Cather Museum." In The American Literary West. See
    Etulain, 1980.11, pp. 78–79.
        Reprint of 1980.41, there attributed to Henry Sweets, III.

5   CLINE, EMILY J. "Inside The Professor's House." Cobblestone
    1 (December):30–31.
        Highly recommends "Tom Outland's Story" to young readers,
    suggesting that they read section ten in book one of the novel as
    an introduction to Tom's narrative that makes up book two.

6   CRANE, JOAN [ST. CLAIRE], ed. Miracles of Perception: The
    Art of Willa Cather. Charlottesville: University of Virginia,
    Alderman Library, 35 pp.
        Publishes tributes to Cather by Alfred A. Knopf (1980.21)
    and Yehudi Menuhin (1980.26) and reprints a lecture/essay on
    Cather by Eudora Welty (1980.47). This pamphlet was prepared to
    accompany a special exhibition of the Clifton Waller Barrett
    Library of American Literature which houses the Cather collection
    at the Alderman Library. Exhibition dates were 18 October 1980
    to 15 January 1981.

7   _____. "The Non-Sectarian Bull: A Willa-the-Wisp?" American
    Book Collector 1 (September–October):6–7.
        Correspondence between Ferris Greenslet (at Houghton
    Mifflin) and Cather, beginning in February 1940, reveals a re-
    quest from a Utah bookseller for one thousand copies of My
    Ántonia if Cather would agree to change the name of one of the
    bulls mentioned in the book from Brigham Young to something
    else. After a bit of bantering, Cather agreed, but there is no
    further correspondence to indicate whether or not the transaction
    ever went through.

8   _____. "Willa Cather's Corrections in the Text of Death Comes
    for the Archbishop, 1927 to 1945." Papers of the Bibliograph-
    ical Society of America 74 (2d Quarter):117–31.
        Follows the publishing history of Death Comes for the
    Archbishop, noting changes and corrections Cather made over the

years in subsequent editions. Lists the approximately one hundred "significant" textual changes (of a total of two hundred) from the book's serial printing in Forum (January to June 1927) to its issue as a book. Three sections in the book did not appear in the serial version. When the Knopf 1945 edition was printed (and this is the edition used for the Random House Vintage paperback), apparently a stand-in supervisor returned to the 1927 first edition for the setting copy instead of the meticulously corrected 1940 fifth printing of the illustrated edition.

9   ERISMAN, FRED. "Western Regional Writers and the Uses of Place." In The American Literary West. See Etulain, 1980.11, pp. 36-44.
     Reprint of 1980.10.

10   _____. "Western Regional Writers and the Uses of Place." Journal of the West 19 (January):36-44.
     Major western regionalists, including Cather, in a manner suggested by Emerson, have developed and projected a sense of place that goes deeper than the surface particulars treated by local colorists. The regionalists have seen a continuity that is emotional, cultural, and intellectual--a link with basic human currents. The West feeds ambition, but emphasizes the workings of tradition and creates a sense of unity with nature and life processes. The Song of the Lark, My Ántonia, and Death Comes for the Archbishop are discussed in connection with these concerns. Reprinted: 1980.9.

11   ETULAIN, RICHARD W., ed. The American Literary West. Manhattan, Kan.: Sunflower University Press, 81 pp.
     Contains reprints of 1980.10, 41; plus an introduction by Etulain that argues that Cather is indeed a western writer although some contend that she is not. She is, in fact, a "major western writer."

12   FISHER, DOROTHY CANFIELD. Review of Sapphira and the Slave Girl. Willa Cather Pioneer Memorial Newsletter 24 (Winter): 3-4.
     Reprint of 1940.7.

13   GELLÉN, JÓZSEF. "Willa Cather and O.E. Rölvaag: Two Ways of Looking at the Immigrant in Fiction." Paper presented at the International Seminar of English and American Studies, in Debrecen, September 1978. Hungarian Studies in English 13: 117-23.
     Cather, speaking as an outsider, is interested in the immigrant as an individual, while Rölvaag is interested in the immigrant as a member of his or her cultural group. The immigrant gives Cather a device for escaping into an earlier, unspoiled time, and Rölvaag a means to picture the present.

14   GIANNONE, RICHARD [JOHN]. "Willa Cather as Psalmist." Notre
     Dame English Journal 13 (Fall):1-15.
          In "Old Mrs. Harris," Grandmother Harris regularly contem-
     plates the Twenty-third Psalm before retiring, and it becomes an
     informing presence in the story--in theme, mood, and method.
     Mrs. Harris's life follows the pattern of the Psalm, which de-
     scribes the Lord as a good shepherd and host. In unconsciously
     living her life in accord with this pattern, Mrs. Harris plays
     that role in the family that she lives with and serves.

15   GLENN, ELLEN WALKER. "The Androgynous Woman Character in the
     American Novel." Ph.D. dissertation, University of Colorado,
     143 pp.
          Defines Cather's O Pioneers! as an apologue and shows how
     such a novel can allow for the presence and workability of an
     androgynous woman character. A nonrealistic form frees the
     author to re-create the role of woman and redefine the social
     structure in which she moves. See Dissertation Abstracts Inter-
     national 41 (1981):4713A.

16   HIERS, JOHN T., and WATKINS, FLOYD C. "A Chat with Willa
     Cather." Resources for American Literary Study 9 (Spring):
     35-38.
          In part, a reprint of 1921.20. Reprints the account of
     Cather's 1921 visit to a local paper in Red Cloud and speculates
     that this informal appearance was Cather's attempt at reconcilia-
     tion with her home town. In her youth she felt some hostility
     toward the area and its people.

17   HUMES, DAVID BRYANT. "The Importance of the Solitary Indi-
     vidual: A Study of Solipsism in Willa Cather's Protagonists."
     Ph.D. dissertation, Columbia University, 242 pp.
          Examines Cather's depiction of human relationships in her
     works written before 1927, but includes Lucy Gayheart because of
     its stylistic similarities with the earlier fiction. These
     novels focus on two kinds of situations: the young person break-
     ing away from the family and community in order to achieve self-
     fulfillment, and the middle-aged person seeking the same freedom
     from emotional ties. In both cases, the family and community are
     stifling to the individual. See Dissertation Abstracts Inter-
     national 43 (1982):1545A.

18   JACOBS, JOHAN UYS. "The Alter Ego: A Study of the Dual
     Persona of the Artist in the Late Nineteenth and Early
     Twentieth Century Novel." Ph.D. dissertation, Columbia
     University, 457 pp.
          Asserts that the rise of the alter-ego character in Ameri-
     can literature reflects the split of the American creative
     imagination between outmoded European tastes and an emerging form
     unique to America. This aesthetic conflict in Cather's O
     Pioneers! is internalized in Alexandra Bergson and cannot be
     resolved. See Dissertation Abstracts International 41 (1981):
     3107A.

19   JENSEN, MARVIN D., and SCHMIDT, OTIS RHEA. "Social Studies
     and Literature: The Discovery Approach." Iowa Curriculum
     Bulletin 5 (Fall):17-20.
          Illustrates, through Cather's work, the value of taking the
     artist's approach, the inductive approach, to the study of human
     behavior rather than always taking the traditional deductive
     approach of the social scientist. The former approach, Cather's,
     focuses on individuals, exceptional individuals, rather than on
     averages and norms. Teachers can draw helpful illustrations and
     insights from many of Cather's works about individuals struggling
     with external conditions and internal conflicts.

20   KIMBEL, ELLEN. "Chopin, Wharton, Cather and the New American
     Fictional Heroine." Ph.D. dissertation, Temple University,
     208 pp.
          Observes in the work of these authors a heroine increas-
     ingly free from traditional (Puritanical) role models and laments
     the disappearance of such heroines in more recent male-dominated
     fiction. See Dissertation Abstracts International 42 (1981):
     703A-4A.

21   KNOPF, ALFRED A. "Publishing Willa Cather." In Miracles of
     Perception. See Crane, 1980.6, pp. 1-4.
          Recalls Knopf's first reading of Cather's work and quotes
     from her own description of their first meeting. Cather's asso-
     ciation with the Knopfs is characterized as warm and understand-
     ing--they shared many of the same feelings and prejudices--but
     also as retaining a note of respectful formality.

22   LILIENFELD, JANE. "Reentering Paradise: Cather, Colette,
     Woolf and Their Mothers." In The Lost Tradition: Mothers
     and Daughters in Literature. Edited by Cathy N. Davidson and
     E.M. Broner. New York: Frederick Ungar Publishing Co.,
     pp. 160-75.
          In "Old Mrs. Harris" and Sapphira and the Slave Girl,
     Cather works through and rediscovers her feelings for her mother.
     The complexity of her feelings for other women relates to her
     feelings for her mother, and the power struggle that had sepa-
     rated Cather from her mother is the central issue in Cather's
     last novel.

23   LOVERING, JOSEPH P. "The Friendship of Willa Cather and
     Dorothy Canfield." Vermont History 48 (Summer):144-54.
          Refers frequently to the correspondence between Dorothy
     Canfield (Fisher) and Cather (correspondence now housed in the
     Guy W. Bailey Library at the University of Vermont) in appraising
     the lifelong friendship of the two women who became acquainted
     when Cather was attending the University of Nebraska. Although
     Canfield was seven years younger, and came from a rather genteel
     academic family, the two found much in common.

24   MACHEN, MEREDITH R. "Carlyle's Presence in The Professor's
      House." Western American Literature 14 (February):273–86.
          Points to many parallels, particularly in structure and
      character, between Cather's The Professor's House and Thomas
      Carlyle's Sartor Resartus. In writing The Professor's House,
      Cather returned to her early feelings about Carlyle as revealed
      in her college essay on him.

25   McHENRY, ROBERT, ed. Liberty's Women. Springfield, Mass.:
      G. & C. Merriam Co., p. 67.
          Recounts Cather's career as a writer of fiction, noting
      that some of her works reveal her distaste for the "stifling
      conventionality of small town life" while others express her
      growing disillusionment with the modern age.

26   MENUHIN, YEHUDI. "An Appreciation." In Miracles of Percep-
      tion. See Crane, 1980.6, pp. 5–7.
          Pays tribute to Cather and his memory of her, stressing her
      dual attachment to the earth and its rhythms and to the city and
      its creative opportunities. Through her "buoyant and totally
      affirmative presence" she called up the most basic human feelings
      of loyalty, stability, and purpose.

27   MILTON, JOHN R. "The Novel in the American West." In
      Critical Essays on the Western American Novel. Edited by
      William T. Pilkington. Critical Essays on American Litera-
      ture, edited by James Nagel. Boston: G.K. Hall & Co.,
      pp. 3–19.
          Reprint of 1964.16.

28   _____. The Novel of the American West. Lincoln: University
      of Nebraska Press, pp. 316–19.
          Compares Death Comes for the Archbishop with Conrad
      Richter's The Sea of Grass, suggesting reasons why Cather's novel
      seems to be set in a much earlier time than it actually is. It
      is not the land, but the church, and the humanizing influences of
      personality, that provide the standard of value in the novel.

29   MUNRO, ALICE. "Dulse." New Yorker 56 (21 July):30–32,
      39 passim.
          Fancies a meeting between the narrator and an elderly man
      on an island off the coast of New Brunswick. This man is a
      long-time admirer of Cather, but he never fully convinces the
      narrator that Cather, who could be a difficult woman, is worthy
      of his unconditional admiration.

30   MURPHY, JOHN J. "'Lucy's Case': An Interpretation of Lucy
      Gayheart." Markham Review 9 (Winter):26–29.
          Suggests that Lucy Gayheart is perhaps best read in con-
      nection with "Paul's Case," for Lucy is really more like Paul
      than she is like Thea Kronborg. Her worlds, Haverford and
      Chicago, take the form her perceptions give them, just as Paul's
      do. She regards Haverford as banal, and Chicago--when she is on
      a high in her feeling for Sebastian--as full of splendor. It is

only in retrospect that Harry Gordon, and thus the reader, transforms Lucy into a symbol of youthful energy and verve.

31 _____. A Teacher's Guide to Willa Cather's "O Pioneers!" and "My Ántonia." Boston: Houghton Mifflin Co., 14 pp.
Provides plot summaries of O Pioneers! and My Ántonia and discussion of the narrative methods of both novels, with special emphasis on the way in which Jim Burden performs as narrator of My Ántonia. Cather's principal themes center around Nebraska and civilization and the cultural uprooting that Cather and some of her characters experienced. Her subordinate themes include the function of memory and the glorification of childhood and pioneer days. The characters of Alexandra Bergson, Ántonia Shimerda, and Jim Burden are described; Cather's relationship to American literature in general is commented upon; and discussion questions and bibliography are provided.

32 NANKIN, FRANCES. "Willa Cather: 1873–1947, America's Novelist, Nebraska's Pioneer." Cobblestone 1 (December): 6–11.
Provides a brief history of Nebraska's pioneering movement, noting that Cather's family went to Nebraska as pioneers and that she knew personally a lot of European immigrants. Those people and their experiences give her fiction a strong historical base.

33 O'FLAHERTY, TERRENCE. "Candle-Lit Rooms Full of Flowers." San Francisco Chronicle, 11 February.
Reviews the television adaptation of "Paul's Case," describing the story as a sensitive account of an artistic nature smothered and defeated by a narrow-minded society. To Cather, this was a great loss. Reprinted: 1980.34.

34 _____. "Candle-Lit Rooms Full of Flowers." Willa Cather Pioneer Memorial Newsletter 24 (Spring):3.
Reprint of 1980.33.

35 OHASHI, KENSABURO, ed. The Traditional and the Anti-Traditional: Studies in Contemporary American Literature. Tokyo: Tokyo chapter of the American Literature Society of Japan, pp. 223, 240, 263–64, 309.
Various essays by various writers in this volume provide bibliographical information about Japanese critical interest in American writers. Cather is mentioned in four of the essays.

36 PORTER, KATHERINE ANNE. "Reflections on Willa Cather." In Women Writers of the Short Story: A Collection of Critical Essays. Edited by Heather McClave. Twentieth-Century Views Series, edited by Maynard Mack. Englewood Cliffs, N.J.: Prentice-Hall, pp. 50–60.
Reprint of 1952.12.

37   PRAMPOLINI, GAETANO. "On N. Scott Momaday's House Made of
      Dawn." Dismisura, 39-50:58-75.
           Compares House Made of Dawn with My Ántonia, using as a
      springboard for discussion two central and in some ways similar
      images in the two novels--Cather's plow magnified against the
      sun and Momaday's cricket magnified against the moon. Cather's
      plow is a symbol that celebrates colonization and the conquest
      of the West, and Momaday may have intentionally inverted her
      meaning. What to Cather and her pioneers was a wilderness to be
      tamed, was to the Indian not a wilderness at all, but a cosmos.
      The Indian's story, unlike that of the standard frontier American
      story, is not the tale of a new culture's birth.

38   ROWSE, A.L. "On the Track of Willa Cather in Nebraska."
      Pts. 1-2. Blackwood's 328 (August-September):84-92, 164-71.
           Weaves back and forth between memory and literary criti-
      cism, recalling a first visit to Cather country and a conversa-
      tion at that time with Cather's sister, Elsie, as recorded in
      Rowse's journal in October 1957. Cather's great strength as a
      novelist is the same as Hawthorne's--a special ability to link
      poetry and the past. The greatest writers have all been nos-
      talgic. Cather's sympathy was intense but not sentimental; she
      was a fearless, independent woman. Recalls also, through journal
      citations, a conversation with the then 85-year-old and irascible
      Louise Pound, who spoke in sometimes uncomplimentary terms about
      Cather. Finally, eulogizes both Cather and Red Cloud in response
      to a recent visit there. The Silas Garber home triggers comments
      on A Lost Lady, and the observation that Cather was born with a
      strong streak of gentility.

39   SALO, ALICE BELL. "The Professor's House and Le mannequin
      d'osier: A Note on Willa Cather's Narrative Technique."
      Studies in American Fiction 8 (Autumn):229-31.
           Godfrey St. Peter's misleading allusion to the dress forms
      in a novel by Anatole France serves as a warning to the reader
      that the professor's statements cannot be accepted without ques-
      tion. Cather communicates more than she writes.

40   SCOTT, JOHN CHARLES. "Between Fiction and History: An Ex-
      ploration into Willa Cather's Death Comes for the Archbishop."
      Ph.D. dissertation, University of New Mexico, 272 pp.
           Contends that Death Comes for the Archbishop has been taken
      by the populace to be a kind of history; it has therefore
      strongly influenced the general perception of what territorial
      New Mexico was like. Further, how Bishop Lamy is perceived has
      been irrevocably influenced by Cather's literary creation of
      Bishop Latour. A combined study of history and Cather's novel
      provides a more faithful picture of nineteenth century New
      Mexico than a single study of either source. See Dissertation
      Abstracts International 41 (1981):3111A.

41 SWEETS, HENRY H., III [anonymous?]. "Cather--Museum."
   Journal of the West 19 (January):78-79.
   Briefly describes the nature, work, and goals of the Willa
Cather Pioneer Memorial and Educational Foundation. Includes
several photographs of Red Cloud sites. Reprinted as an anony-
mous piece in 1980.11. Richard Etulain edited both sources for
this article, and he may have discovered an error in originally
attributing it to Sweets.

42 TAWARADA, HARUE. "From a Japanese Viewpoint." Willa Cather
   Pioneer Memorial Newsletter 24 (Summer):2-3.
   Suggests several reasons for Cather's popularity in Japan:
her sentence structure is uncomplicated; her diction and style
are crisp and clear; she opens up the worlds of prairie and
desert unknown in Japan; she is sensitive, like the Japanese, to
nature and seasonal changes; and she values tradition.

43 TRILLING, LIONEL. "Willa Cather." In Speaking of Literature
   and Society. Edited by Diana Trilling. New York: Harcourt
   Brace Jovanovich, pp. 92-99.
   Reprint of 1937.16.

44 _____. "Willa Cather." In Women Writers of the Short Story:
   A Collection of Critical Essays. See Porter, 1980.36,
   pp. 61-68.
   Reprint of 1937.16.

45 TUCKER, JEAN M. "The American Mother in Three Stories--
   Freeman, Cather, and Gates." Doshisha Literature: A Journal
   of English Literature and Philology 29:116-33.
   Compares the portrayal of women in traditional roles in
"The Revolt of Mother," "Old Mrs. Harris," and "Accomplished
Desires," concluding that those roles have evolved from woman as
mother, sister, and daughter of male patriots to woman seriously
questioning traditional roles. The women who figure in these
stories, however, are basically very much alike, wanting more
for themselves than their inherited roles allow.

46 Van VLECK, CHARLOTTE. "Willa Cather: Nebraska's Pioneer."
   Cobblestone 1 (December):12-19.
   Introduces Cather to young readers by highlighting the
story of her move to Nebraska and her experiences there, especially those of her first years.

47 WELTY, EUDORA. "The House of Willa Cather." In Miracles of
   Perception. See Crane, 1980.6, pp. 8-30.
   Reprint of 1974.79.

48 WESTBROOK, MAX. "The Western Esthetic." In Critical Essays
   on the Western American Novel. See Milton, 1980.27, pp. 73-85.
   Treats O Pioneers! briefly in a discussion of "variant
versions" in the tradition of western romantic fiction.

49   YONGUE, PATRICIA LEE. "Willa Cather's Aristocrats." Pts. 1-2. Southern Humanities Review 14 (Winter-Spring):43-56, 111-25.
      Cather was pulled between her admiration for the pioneer spirit and the Virginia side of her nature that gave her aristocratic tastes. Her distinctly aesthetic taste for the things money could buy can be seen especially in her relationship with the charming young British nobleman, Stephen Tennant. Yongue's personal conversations and correspondence with Tennant, and her reading of Cather's letters to him, convince her that Cather sought out the young man because he seemed to represent a way of life that was scarce in an ever more vulgar America. The image of "the lady" in several Cather novels points up Cather's ambivalence in valuing both the aristocratic and democratic ideal. This is especially prevalent in A Lost Lady, where Niel Herbert's aesthetic/aristocratic motives lead him to be rather inhumane, and in My Mortal Enemy; but it is also present in such novels as Alexander's Bridge and even O Pioneers!

1981

1   ARNOLD, MARILYN. "Willa Cather." In Critical Survey of Short Fiction. Edited by Frank N. Magill. Vol. 3. Englewood Cliffs, N.J.: Salem Press, pp. 1075-81.
      After encyclopedic information, explores the major themes in Cather's principal short fiction--art and the land--and demonstrates that in them Cather found her primary values. In her stories both the artist and the person who loves the land are in conflict with the exploitive materialism that threatens them.

2   _____. "Willa Cather's Nostalgia: A Study in Ambivalence." Research Studies 49 (March):23-34.
      Suggests that Cather's work has both a nostalgic and an antinostalgic counterthrust and that her nostalgic characters cannot invariably be taken as spokespersons for their creator. In fact, in some of her stories--notably "Eleanor's House," "On the Gulls' Road," and "The Old Beauty"--Cather shows her nostalgic characters to be pathetic, even ridiculous. That she herself, in spite of her nostalgic impulses, preferred forward-looking people who live with gusto in the present over those who languish in the past is apparent from the corrective characters she provides in her novels and stories and from certain people like Madame Grout whom she features in her essays.

3   BENSON, PETER. "Willa Cather at Home Monthly." Biography 4 (Summer):227-48.
      Appraises the owners (establishing that one was probably James Wickliffe Axtell, not Charles Axtell), the general contents, and the editorial policies of the Home Monthly, as well as Cather's role and duties there, and the stories she published in the magazine. Her experience at the Home Monthly was important in the germination and development of her art, and in her arriving at a sense of what an audience demands of a writer.

4   BETTS, GLYNNE ROBINSON. <u>Writers in Residence: American</u>
     <u>Authors at Home</u>. New York: Viking Press, Studio Books,
     pp. 124-29.
          Features in photographs and essays Cather and others by
     geographical region. Pictures of scenes in and around Red Cloud
     are captioned mainly by passages from Cather's works, and a short
     essay describes the Red Cloud of Cather's experience.

5   BONGARTZ, ROY. "Willa Cather's Red Cloud." <u>Ford Times</u> 74
     (January):2-6.
          Describes Red Cloud and the sites there that Cather used,
     without sentimentality, in her works.

6   BRENNER, SIDNEY H. "Lost Continuities: Alternative Urban
     Visions in Chicago Novels, 1895-1915." <u>Soundings</u> 64 (Spring):
     29-51.
          Observes the different perceptions of male and female
     novelists in their portrayal of Chicago, suggesting that male
     writers have generally treated issues rather than people and have
     not seen the possibilities for human community that women writers
     have. Cather is like other women writers when in <u>The Song of the</u>
     <u>Lark</u> she blends nature--Lake Michigan, that is--with the city.
     Unlike them, but like their male counterparts, Cather describes
     a character who experiences Chicago as an outsider. Furthermore,
     Thea Kronborg is one who, in order to achieve her professional
     goals, has to leave Chicago for a still broader world.

7   BURCH, BETH. "Willa Cather's <u>A Lost Lady</u>: The Woodpecker and
     Marian Forrester." <u>Notes on Contemporary Literature</u> 11
     (September):7-10.
          Considers the scene of the woodpecker's blinding to be a
     prefiguration of later events in <u>A Lost Lady</u>. In its entrapment
     and blindness, the bird symbolizes Marian Forrester as she is
     contained and restricted by circumstances and blinded to the
     threat presented by Ivy Peters. Nevertheless, she triumphs in
     the end, and the novel concludes optimistically.

8   CAPOTE, TRUMAN. <u>Music for Chameleons</u>. New York: New
     American Library, Signet Books, pp. 256-59.
          Essentially repeats what Capote had said in 1967.4.

9   CHANG, L[OH-] C[HI]. "A Chinese Reader's View on <u>Sapphira</u>
     <u>and the Slave Girl</u>." <u>Willa Cather Pioneer Memorial Newsletter</u>
     25 (Summer):14.
          Believes Henry Colbert to be Cather's spokesperson on the
     matter of slavery, though human value, not slave-holding, is the
     principal issue in the novel.

10   COMEAU, PAUL. "The Fool Figure in Willa Cather's Fiction."
     <u>Western American Literature</u> 15 (February):265-78.
          The fool figures in Cather's novels of the West--Crazy Ivar
     in <u>O Pioneers!</u>, Tillie in <u>The Song of the Lark</u>, and Mahailey in
     <u>One of Ours</u>--provide a symbolic representation of her shift from
     the epic mode of the early frontier novels to the satirical mode

of One of Ours. This shift, in which Claude Wheeler becomes the
quixotic fool-hero, dramatizes Cather's confusion and despair
over the decline of values in the chaos of western modernism.

11   ____. "The Importance of Hamlet to Cather's A Lost Lady."
        Markham Review 11 (Fall):1-5.
        Explores parallels between Hamlet and A Lost Lady. Niel
Herbert, like Hamlet, is a sensitive idealist; and Marian
Forrester, like Ophelia, suffers the death of a father figure and
the failure of a lover. Cather's very early critical pronounce-
ments on Hamlet suggest the similarities also. Further, both
works embrace times of cultural and economic transition, the
decline of an old order. The epigraph from Hamlet that Cather
chose for her novel captures the emotional and psychological
impact of such a transition.

12   ____. "Willa Cather's Lucy Gayheart: A Long Perspective."
        Prairie Schooner 55 (Spring-Summer):199-209.
        Cather boldly risks sentimentality in Lucy Gayheart,
choosing a sentimental heroine and presenting a conventional love
story, in order to show the very thing she depicts in the aging
soprano's ability to invest the trite, sentimental songs of The
Bohemian Girl with freshness and vitality. Through the long
perspective of memory Cather does in her art what Clement
Sebastian does in his song and the opera singer does in her role.
Thus, what she achieves in Lucy Gayheart, "possibly her most
daring and certainly her most profound novel," is an important
commentary on "the artistic process and its relationship to life,
death, and immortality."

13   COOPER, BEVERLY J. "What the 1981 Conference Meant to Me."
        Willa Cather Pioneer Memorial Newsletter 25 (Summer):12-14.
        Presents more than a personal report of the annual spring
Cather conference events in Red Cloud, Nebraska. Responds to
guest speaker Maya Angelou's assessment of Sapphira and the Slave
Girl by suggesting that Cather treats the relationship between
Till and Nancy with more understanding than Angelou gives her
credit for.

14   CORSE, LARRY B., and CORSE, SANDRA, comps. Articles on Ameri-
        can and British Literature: An Index to Selected Periodicals,
        1950-1977. Chicago: Swallow Press, pp. 93-94.
        Lists thirty-five articles on Cather published between 1950
and 1977.

*15   DOLININ, ALEKSANDR. "Vospominanie o 'poteriannom rae'" [On
        the Russian language translation of My Ántonia]. Literaturnoe
        obozrenie 1:62-63.
        Listed in MLA International Bibliography (1981).

16   ELIASSON, TORSTEN. "Rik livskälla" [A rich life source].
        Arbetet (Stockholm), 1 July, sec. 1, p. 3.
        In Swedish. Review of My Ántonia. Commends Cather's por-
trait of Ántonia as that of a woman who is genuine, strong, totally alive, and warm.

17   FRYER, JUDITH. "Cather's Felicitous Space." <u>Prairie Schooner</u>
     55 (Spring-Summer):185-98.
         Applies Gaston Bachelard's notion of the "felicitous space"
     (<u>The Poetics of Space</u>, 1969) to Cather's work, especially <u>The</u>
     <u>Song of the Lark</u>, <u>The Professor's House</u>, and <u>Death Comes for the</u>
     <u>Archbishop</u>. In each of these novels, characters find certain
     places that are, or can be transformed into, places of intimate,
     protective repose or soul expansion.

18   GEHRKI, BARBARA ANN. "Willa Cather's Families: Fictions and
     Facts in Her Plains' Writings." Ph.D. dissertation, Univer-
     sity of Nebraska, 276 pp.
         Claims that recognizing the dominant role of the family in
     Cather's plains' writings is the key to understanding her work.
     Examines marital, parent-child, and surrogate parent relation-
     ships in Cather's fiction in conjunction with her own familial
     experiences. Cather's creative response to human relations
     results in a variety of family portraits in her writings. See
     <u>Dissertation Abstracts International</u> 42 (1982):3999A.

19   GERBER, PHILIP L. "Willa Cather." In <u>A Bibliographical Guide</u>
     <u>to Midwestern Literature</u>. Iowa City: University of Iowa
     Press, pp. 160-64.
         Comments briefly on critical response to Cather's work over
     the years, noting the general admiration accorded it in the
     1920s, the turn against it led by Marxist critics in the 1930s,
     and the renewed interest in it after her death. Recent criticism
     has opened two new areas of study, feminist and mythic aspects of
     her writing. Cather's major works are listed along with a check-
     list of criticism.

20   GERVAUD, MICHEL. "Un regard autre: L'immigrant vu par Willa
     Cather dans ses romans de la prairie." In <u>Les Américains et</u>
     <u>les autres</u>. Actes du Grena Groupe de Recherche et d'Études
     Nord Américaines. Aix-en-Provence Cedex: Université de
     Provence, 1981-82, pp. 65-81.
         Explores the contribution of both the Anglo-Saxon and non-
     Anglo-Saxon pioneer immigrant to the prairies of the Midwest as
     revealed in the work of Willa Cather, noting the difficulties
     that often accompany efforts at assimilation. Jim Burden's
     grandparents in <u>My Ántonia</u> represent the dignity of the estab-
     lished Anglo-Saxon order, while Ántonia, through her father,
     becomes the embodiment of the finest traits inherent in the non-
     Anglo-Saxon immigrant. Cather took special interest in the
     habits of cuisine that separate foreign immigrants from more
     established Americans, and admired the authenticity and natural
     superiority she saw in many non-Americans.

21   GISH, ROBERT F. "Paul Horgan and the Biography of Place."
     <u>Prairie Schooner</u> 55 (Spring-Summer):226-32.
         In "biography of place," aspects of place go beyond ordinary
     traits of setting to take on qualities of character. Paul
     Horgan's biography of Archbishop Lamy and Cather's fictional
     portrayal of him as Jean Latour show similar "sensibilities,

themes, and techniques." Horgan knew of Cather, even experienced
a brief encounter with her, and spoke appreciatively of her work.

22   GRAY, PATRICE K. "The Lure of Romance and the Temptation of
     Feminine Sensibility: Literary Heroines in Selected Popular
     and 'Serious' American Novels, 1895–1915." Ph.D. disserta-
     tion, Emory University, 322 pp.
        Applies the traditional romance formula to popular and
     serious fiction, in Cather's case to The Song of the Lark. See
     Dissertation Abstracts International 42 (1981):2130A.

23   GREENE, GEORGE [WILLIAM]. "Willa Cather's Grand Manan."
     Prairie Schooner 55 (Spring–Summer):233–40.
        Personal sketch of Greene's own boat trip to Grand Manan,
     with commentary on Cather and Shadows on the Rock, a copy of
     which he took with him. Cather teaches us how to approach place,
     and how to understand the relationship between person and setting.

24   GROSS, BARRY. "Willa Cather and the 'American Metaphysic.'"
     Midamerica 8:68–78.
        Defends Cather and her outlook, especially against de-
     tractors such as those who attack One of Ours for its unrealistic
     portrayal of war. Such an attack shows a misguided effort to
     devalue the humanistic, reflective ideal in favor of overt ex-
     perience. Cather is in the tradition of Hawthorne and James, an
     artist superior to male worshipers of action as life's highest
     value.

25   GUBAR, SUSAN. "Blessings in Disguise: Cross-Dressing As
     Re-Dressing for Female Modernists." Massachusetts Review 22
     (Autumn):477–508.
        Discusses Cather as one of the women artists who, at the
     turn of the century, dressed like a man as a way of "ad-dressing
     and re-dressing the inequities of culturally-defined categories
     of masculinity and femininity." Cather realized that in wearing
     male clothing, she was alienating herself from roles and activi-
     ties conventionally female, and in her fiction she often writes
     from the point of view of a male admiring a female character.
     She thus achieves for herself a kind of male authority at the
     same time that she partially identifies with her female protago-
     nist.

26   HUF, LINDA. "Portrait of the Artist as a Young Woman: The
     Female Kunstlerromane in America." Ph.D. dissertation,
     University of Maryland, 236 pp.
        Finds that the kunstlerromane written by women has its own
     set of characteristics distinct from those present in similar
     works written by men. Devotes one chapter to discussion of
     Cather's The Song of the Lark as an example of the genre. See
     Dissertation Abstracts International 42 (1982):3600A. Revised
     for publication. See 1983.16 for more specific summary of Cather
     discussion.

27 INOUE, KAZUKO. "Willa Cather: The Development of Her Art."
    Essays in Foreign Languages and Literature (Sapporo) 28:
    77–137.
        In Japanese with summary in English. Avows that Cather
    constructed her art around her life's central theme: the search
    for order. Outlines the stages in Cather's literary career,
    identifying her forties as the time of "flowering" of her art.
    In her fifties she began to doubt her choice for art, and The
    Professor's House and My Mortal Enemy show her anguish. Still
    later, she came to feel that a life dedicated to art was selfishly
    limiting. The dominant theme of her last two novels, Lucy Gay-
    heart and Sapphira and the Slave Girl, is regret and reconcilia-
    tion.

28 KLEMANS, PATRICIA A. "The Courageous Soul: Woman as Artist
    in American Literature." CEA Critic (College English Asso-
    ciation) 43 (May):39–43.
        Regards Cather's The Song of the Lark as the first major
    treatment in American literature of the woman artist. Typically,
    this woman struggles against difficult odds in a society that
    has restrictive ideas about women's roles and their artistic
    opportunities.

29 KLUG, MICHAEL A. "Willa Cather: Between Red Cloud and
    Byzantium." Canadian Review of American Studies 12 (Winter):
    287–99.
        Cather is representative of a whole group of modern writers
    who suffered serious internal division, pulled on the one hand
    toward realization of the individual self and on the other toward
    participation in ordinary humanity. Cather's own personal strug-
    gle she transformed into "her one great work," My Ántonia, which
    presents powerfully this division of the American soul. There is
    no solution; each choice leaves a gap in the other direction.

30 LOVE, GLEN A. "Willa Cather's Code Hero: Tom Outland as
    Shane." Heritage of the Great Plains 14 (Winter):3–12.
        Tom Outland in many ways functions, like Shane, as the code
    hero of a classic American western. But while Shane operates
    simply and clearly in a nonambiguous context, Tom Outland is
    caught in the complexities and ambiguities faced by a man like
    Godfrey St. Peter, middle-aged and disillusioned with the way the
    world has gone. Thus Cather simultaneously affirms and questions
    the myth of the code hero.

31 McFARLAND, DOROTHY TUCK. In Encyclopedia of World Literature
    in the 20th Century. Rev. ed. Vol. 1. Edited by Leonard S.
    Klein. New York: Frederick Ungar Publishing Co., pp. 423–25.
        Comments, after a brief biography, on several of Cather's
    books, observing "mythic undertones" in O Pioneers! and seeing in
    Ántonia Shimerda "an image of the life-force itself." Some of
    Cather's novels in the 1920s are discussed as examples of
    Cather's distress over the decline of spiritual values in an
    increasingly acquisitive society. Imaginatively Cather is a
    romantic, but stylistically she is a classicist.

32   McLAY, CATHERINE [M.]. "Ethel Wilson's Lost Lady: <u>Hetty</u>
     <u>Dorval</u> and Willa Cather." <u>Journal of Canadian Fiction</u> 33:
     <u>94–106.</u>
          Compares <u>Hetty Dorval</u> with <u>A Lost Lady</u>, and at times with
     <u>My Ántonia</u>, on several points: the leanness of the narrative,
     the character and importance of the narrator, the passivity and
     sensual attractiveness of the central character, and the signifi-
     cance of that person to the narrator. In spite of these similar-
     ities, however, the philosophies of Cather and Wilson are quite
     different, and the difference is reflected in the endings of the
     novels. Cather's narrators typically look backward; the narrator
     in <u>Hetty Dorval</u> looks ahead.

33   MAYES, DENNIS. "Willa Cather's Lonely Road." <u>Desert:</u>
     <u>Magazine of the Southwest</u> 44 (December):42–45.
          Claims that Cather's first long visit to the Southwest
     changed the course of her career and gave shape to her personal
     credo. Her description of Jean Latour's lonely journey in the
     beginning of <u>Death Comes for the Archbishop</u> is a fitting repre-
     sentation of her own lonely and individual journey through Amer-
     ican literature. A master of understatement, Cather selects
     only the essential detail for the most powerful evocation of the
     Southwest in literature.

34   MILTON, JOHN R. "From Artifact to Intuition in Great Plains
     Writing." <u>Prairie Schooner</u> 55 (Spring–Summer):131–40.
          Refers to <u>O Pioneers!</u> as illustrative of a process recog-
     nizable in western literature in which "things" change their
     function. An intuitive thought, or a philosophical idea, for
     example, grows out of observation of details of landscape.

35   MOYNE, ERNEST J. <u>Raising the Wind: The Legend of Lapland and</u>
     <u>Finland Wizards in Literature</u>. Edited by Wayne R. Kime.
     Newark: University of Delaware Press, pp. 193–94.
          A footnote to discussion about Lapland and Finland witches
     points out that Cather's Lena Lingard (<u>My Ántonia</u>) claims her
     mother may have been a Lapp, but her grandmother surely was. The
     supernatural powers attributed to Lapp women may have influenced
     some of Jim Burden's later comments.

36   MURPHY, JOHN J. "Cooper, Cather, and the Downward Path to
     Progress." <u>Prairie Schooner</u> 55 (Spring–Summer):168–84.
          Compares the prairie novels of Cather and Cooper and sees
     similar movement depicted in them. Both Cather and Cooper de-
     scribe heroic pioneering efforts in which the highly valued land
     is subverted by the encroachment of materialistic exploitation.
     Even the pioneer labor of early farmers gives way to settlement
     and town--and to the large-scale farming of the type engaged in
     by Nat Wheeler in <u>One of Ours</u>.

37   _____. "Euripides' <u>Hippolytus</u> and Cather's <u>A Lost Lady</u>."
     <u>American Literature</u> 53 (March):72–86.
          Explores the parallels between Euripides' Hippolytus and
     Niel Herbert, and between Phaedra and Marian Forrester, noting

that a celibate disdain for women and their sexuality similarly
afflicts both young men and contributes to the downfall of the
women whom they come to scorn. Cather uses the myth in giving
Marian qualities present in both Artemis and Aphrodite.

38   . "The Mesa Verde Story and Cather's 'Tom Outland's
    Story.'" Notes on Modern American Literature 5 (Spring):
    item 9.
       Discusses Cather's use of the actual story of the finding
and exploration of Mesa Verde, pointing out where Cather follows
the facts and where she does not.

39   . "'Presumptuous Girls' of Cather, Dreiser, and James."
    Platte Valley Review 9 (April):83-95.
       Compares Henry James's Isabel Archer and Theodore Dreiser's
Carrie Meeber with Cather's Thea Kronborg, all young women who,
under similar circumstances, experience self-expansion and
developing awareness. Cather combines Dreiser's "provincial
outlook and method" with James's "world vision, sensibilities
and method" in the creation of her heroine in The Song of the
Lark.

40 NAGEL, HAROLD G. "The Willa Cather Prairie." Nebraskaland
    59 (April):8-15.
       Combines photographs of the Willa Cather Prairie, a pre-
serve in Cather's honor south of Red Cloud, Nebraska, with dis-
course about the Cather Prairie and about Cather's undiminishing
love for the plants and other features of that landscape.

41 OLSON, PAUL A. "The Epic and Great Plains Literature:
    Rølvaag, Cather and Neihardt." Prairie Schooner 55 (Spring-
    Summer):263-85.
       Demonstrates how, in their use of the epic mode, Cather,
Ole Rølvaag, and John Neihardt displace the old conventions and
adapt their work to the heroic aspects of traditionally "non-
heroic" literary characters like women, peasants, and minorities.
Cather's use of the epic form is the most complex of the three
writers; she depends on the Aeneid in The Professor's House, but
also on the Georgics in My Ántonia.

42 PEARSON, CAROL, and POPE, KATHERINE. The Female Hero in Amer-
    ican and British Literature. New York: R.R. Bowker Co.,
    pp. 144, 149-51, 153-55 passim, 239.
       Points to Alexandra Bergson (O Pioneers!) as one of those
women who are liberated from the idea that life's fulfillment
lies in being taken care of by a man. Such women become responsible for their own lives. Like Dorinda Oakley in Barren Ground,
by Ellen Glasgow, Alexandra rejects sexual love when she rejects
finding fulfillment through romantic love with a virile male.
Both women express their passion in uniting with the land to
make it fertile. In O Pioneers! death and sexuality are ex-
plicitly linked.

43   PETERMAN, MICHAEL.   "'The Good Game': The Charm of Willa
      Cather's My Ántonia and W.O. Mitchell's Who Has Seen the
      Wind." Mosaic 14 (Spring):93–106.
          Although Who Has Seen the Wind is narrower in scope and
      harsher in approach than My Ántonia, both novels have a romantic
      outlook in which feeling is central. Both also celebrate endur-
      ing values, especially values inherent in a human relationship
      with the land.

44   PIGAGA, THOM, comp. "Bernice Slote: A Checklist of Published
      Writings." Prairie Schooner 55 (Spring-Summer):51–119.
          Reprints excerpts from Slote's writings about Cather, in-
      cluding four prefaces to works by Cather as well as a list of
      Slote's poetry and her essays about Cather and others. Also
      includes tributes to Slote, most of which acknowledge her excep-
      tional contribution to Cather studies. This entire issue of
      Prairie Schooner is, in the main, a tribute to Slote. Reprinted
      in part from 1962.19; 1966.15; 1973.62, 66; 1977.26.

45   _____. "Essays Written in Celebration of Bernice Slote."
      Prairie Schooner 55 (Spring-Summer):127–87.
          Contains, among other things in this special issue honoring
      a prominent Cather scholar, essays on Cather by Rosowski 1981.48;
      Murphy 1981.36; Fryer 1981.17; Comeau 1981.12; Greene 1981.23;
      and Olson 1981.41.

46   PRATT, ANNIS. Archetypal Patterns in Women's Fiction.
      Bloomington: Indiana University Press, pp. 18, 19, 22–24,
      78–79, 82–83, 126, 140.
          Cather's feminine heroes show her way of dealing with their
      natural eroticism. Cather has these women invest their eroticism
      in a mythic god of the green world, as Alexandra Bergson does,
      or in a superior man, as Lucy Gayheart does. Cather herself was
      ambivalent toward her female characters' erotic tendencies, for
      most of the polite world regarded such feelings as inappropriate
      for women. Thus, Cather "deflects her enthusiasm" for characters
      like Marian Forrester, and for her "sensual career women," by
      using another person, often a young man, to comment upon them.

47   ROSOWSKI, SUSAN J. "The Pattern of Willa Cather's Novels."
      Western American Literature 15 (February):243–63.
          Explores Cather's treatment of the emotional patterns of
      the second self in her novels, identifying the second self, the
      inner, creative self, in relation to the outer public self.
      Concentrates on O Pioneers!, The Song of the Lark, and The
      Professor's House as they reveal the various forms of growth or
      renewal disclosed by these patterns. The other novels are men-
      tioned as they depict characters seeking imaginative growth
      through second-self experience or substitutes for such growth.

48   _____. "Willa Cather--A Pioneer in Art: O Pioneers! and My
      Ántonia." Prairie Schooner 55 (Spring-Summer):141–54.
          Assesses Cather's way of describing the beauty of the Great
      Plains, heretofore not acknowledged as a suitable literary

setting, by a close examination of how Cather handles "the relation of subjects to objects" in O Pioneers! and My Ántonia.
Characteristically, a person begins by feeling alienated in
space, then moves into that space and feels unity with it, then
moves back out of that space but no longer feels alienated. In
My Ántonia, Ántonia is the "human intermediary" who assists Jim
Burden in this process. Through reversals of motion, through
imagery, and through spatial changes, Cather gives dramatic
emphasis to the beauty of the landscape.

49 _____. "Willa Cather's Women." Studies in American Fiction 9
(Autumn):261-75.
Although always concerned with human striving for permanent
values, Cather gradually focuses more and more on the narrower
question of what it is to be a woman in a society that seeks to
limit women to its conventional expectations or cultural myths.
Alexandra Bergson transcends these expectations in her own mystical union with the land, while Thea Kronborg, Ántonia Shimerda,
Marian Forrester, and Myra Henshawe defy them. In "Old Mrs.
Harris," however, Cather comes full circle and builds her story
around a woman who becomes exceptional by accepting her traditional role with exceptional personal strength.

50 SHOWALTER, SHIRLEY HERSHEY. "A Triumph of Comedy: Edith
Wharton, Ellen Glasgow, Willa Cather and a Professional
Coming-of-Age." Ph.D. dissertation, University of Texas at
Austin, 353 pp.
Views Cather, along with Wharton and Glasgow, as struggling
to succeed both as a professional and as a woman. Like Thea
Kronborg in The Song of the Lark, Cather protected herself
psychologically by concentrating her energies on her work. A
Lost Lady shows that Cather understood the sexual needs of women,
and Death Comes for the Archbishop indicates Cather's ultimate
triumph over conflicting desires. See Dissertation Abstracts
International 42 (1981):1223A.

51 SKAGGS, MERRILL MAGUIRE. "Willa Cather's Experimental Southern Novel." Mississippi Quarterly 35 (Winter 1981-82):3-14.
Explores the "experimental" qualities of Sapphira and the
Slave Girl, noting such things as her inversion of nearly all the
standard expectations of the southern novel, her insertion of a
number of episodes extraneous to the plot that loop back and
forth through the novel like the double-S in the Timber Ridge
road, and her narration of the story from the point of view of
the intruding author.

52 STROUT, CUSHING. The Veracious Imagination: Essays on American History, Literature, and Biography. Middletown, Conn.:
Wesleyan University Press, pp. 280-81.
Advocates the merger of psychology and biography in literary analysis, and argues that Leon Edel's analysis of The Professor's House (1954.3) is enhanced by his applying psychoanalytic methods to biographical data that otherwise could not
be seen in relation to Cather's fiction.

*53   SUZUE, AKIKO. "Willa Cather to Ellen Glasgow." In America bungaku no jiko keisei: 20 seiki America bungaku, I [Structures of American literature: Twentieth-century American literature, I]. Edited by Toshihiko Ogata. Kyoto: Yamaguchi, 548 pp.
        Listed in MLA International Bibliography (1981).

54   THACKER, ROBERT WILLIAM. "Landscape and Technique: The Background and Development of the North American Prairie Novel." Ph.D. dissertation, University of Manitoba.
        Treats the subject of artistic representation of the prairie beginning with early colonial landscape painters and travelers and ending with such prairie authors as Cather and Ole Rölvaag. Takes into account Canadian writers as well, arguing that the prairie novel as an art form reached its maturity in the blend of romanticism and realism found in the later prairie novels. See Dissertation Abstracts International 42 (1982):3604A.

55   WATERS, TRICIA. "Willa Cather Took Prose from Prairies." Heartland Grand Island (Nebr.) Sunday Independent, 21 June.
        Reports on a national seminar held in Hastings and Red Cloud, Nebraska for Cather scholars. Also provides biographical information and points out the need Cather had to leave the prairie before she could write about it.

56   WOODRESS, JAMES. "Willa Cather." In American Novelists, 1910-1945, pt. 1. Edited by James J. Martine. Dictionary of Literary Biography, edited by Matthew J. Bruccoli, C.E. Frazer Clark, Jr., and Richard Layman, vol. 9. Detroit: Gale Research Co., pp. 140-54.
        Provides factual details on Cather's life and work, then introduces and evaluates each of her books of fiction in turn. Cather is a writer whose novels and stories are firmly rooted in a sense of place--especially, but not exclusively, in Nebraska and the Southwest. She writes in an age of realism and naturalism, but she is essentially "a retrospective writer, a romantic." Her early portrayals of Nebraska are harsh and critical, but over the years she gained the perspective of distance and began to see positive values in midwestern prairie life.

1982

1   ADAMS, FREDERICK B., [Jr]. Foreword to Willa Cather: A Bibliography, by Joan Crane. Lincoln: University of Nebraska Press, pp. ix-xii.
        Describes precursors to the Crane bibliography (1982.19) and gives examples of the kinds of problems Crane solves for Cather scholars and researchers. For instance, Crane establishes the extent of Cather's involvement in the Georgine Milmine biography of Mary Baker Eddy.

2   BAILEY, JENNIFER. "The Dangers of Femininity in Willa
     Cather's Fiction." Journal of American Studies 16 (December):
     391-406.
         Argues that male writers have tended to idealize woman's
     role in accounts of frontier land settlement. They have por-
     trayed woman with her "femininity" making in the wilderness a
     garden that is a stronghold of cultural and moral values. But
     some women writers, and especially Willa Cather, have seen that
     this is a false feminine ideal, even a corrupt one, imposed on
     women by men. Cather shows the ideal woman as strong, individ-
     ual, uncorrupted by the requirements of the feminine ideal. Niel
     Herbert and Godfrey St. Peter are examples of men who have
     imposed feminine expectations on women and then blamed them for
     not living up to those expectations.

3   BAKER, BRUCE P[AUL]. "O Pioneers!: The Problem of Struc-
     ture." Great Plains Quarterly 2 (Fall):218-23.
         Reviews observations other critics have made about the
     structure of O Pioneers! and suggests further that the book is
     innovative in its unifying patterns of symbol and imagery. The
     main story is Alexandra's, but the love story of Emil and Marie
     interlocks with it. For example, language of sexual desire and
     procreation is used to describe Alexandra's relationship with
     the soil, but her comprehension, finally, of the love shared by
     Emil and Marie allows her to become at last a human being and not
     simply a mythic earth goddess. Thus, the thematic strands of
     youth and the land are united in an overriding theme of love.

4   BENNETT, JACK WASSON. "That Other America: A Comparative
     Study of American and Australian Literature." Ph.D. disser-
     tation, University of Oregon, 257 pp.
         Examines the work of three pairs of American and Australian
     writers in order to explore the "comparative roots and subsequent
     development of literary traditions" in the two countries. Cather
     is compared with Henry Handel Richardson, and both are treated as
     "post-frontier authors of the 1920's and 1930's." See Disserta-
     tion Abstracts International 43:1977A.

5   BENNETT, MILDRED R. "Avignon Today." Willa Cather Pioneer
     Memorial Newsletter 26, Literary issue, pp. 4-7.
         Describes a visit to Avignon, France, and the sites there
     that Cather had written about when she first saw them. Quotes
     some of Cather's reactions to places like the cathedral and the
     Papal Palace and gardens as Bennett attempts to see France as
     Cather would have seen it.

6   _____. "The Childhood Worlds of Willa Cather." Great Plains
     Quarterly 2 (Fall):204-9.
         Points to a myriad of details--people, events, places--in
     Cather's childhood that influenced and later became material for
     her art.

7 _____. "Willa Cather's Bodies for Ghosts." Western American
   Literature 17 (May):39-52.
         Describes in detail characters and types of events that
   recur in Cather's fiction, noting especially those in early stories ("ghosts") that reappear with variations ("bodies") in subsequent stories.

8 BERGERS, JOHN. "Catherland through the Artist's Eyes."
   Nebraskaland 60 (February):24-31.
         The text of Cather's books provides the inspiration for a
   lengthy series of paintings by John Blake Bergers. Several of
   these paintings, with titles and passages from the books, are
   reproduced in this article.

9 BOHLKE, L. BRENT. "Godfrey St. Peter and Eugène Delacroix:
   A Portrait of the Artist in The Professor's House?" Western
   American Literature 17 (May):21-38.
         Details numerous parallels in circumstance and attitude
   between Godfrey St. Peter and French artist Delacroix. Suggests
   that it may have been more than coincidence that in The Professor's House Cather alludes to St. Peter's desire to visit (with
   Tom Outland) the monument to Delacroix in Luxembourg Gardens.
   Delacroix is a prototype for St. Peter, whether Cather intended
   him to be or not.

10 _____. "Seeking Is Finding: Willa Cather and Religion."
   Ph.D. dissertation, University of Nebraska, 547 pp.
         Discovers in the work of Cather strong evidence of a con-
   tinuing religious quest, returned to--after a temporary depar-
   ture--with energy at the same time she returned to Nebraska in
   O Pioneers! One of Ours is the record of her struggle and questioning, but it becomes clear in The Professor's House and My
   Mortal Enemy that in Cather's view lapses in faith are accom-
   panied by unhappiness. Cather's last books, with the exception
   of Lucy Gayheart--an anomaly--all bear record of the importance
   she accorded to religious belief. And she herself was strongly
   identified with a religious faith for much of her life.

11 _____. "Willa Cather and the Life of Mary Baker Eddy."
   American Literature 54 (May):288-94.
         Argues on the basis of a letter Cather wrote to Edwin H.
   Anderson, director of the Carnegie Library in Pittsburgh, and
   then of the New York Public Library, that Cather was the prin-
   cipal writer of the Eddy biography attributed to Georgine
   Milmine. It should properly be included in the Cather canon.

12 BOUCHER, SANDY. "Catherland." In Heartwomen: An Urban
   Feminist's Odyssey Home. San Francisco: Harper & Row,
   pp. 117-40.
         A personal essay recounting one woman's visit to Cather's
   Nebraska, and especially the author's talk with some of the women
   who are preserving the Cather heritage in Red Cloud. Quotes
   extensively from an informal interview with Mildred Bennett in
   which Bennett talks about her research into Cather's life and the

obstacles she encountered in that research. Boucher concludes
that it has always been woman's task to preserve what is valuable. Women are society's "unofficial historians," making links
with women who went before them to guarantee continuity into the
future. That is what Mildred Bennett has done in establishing
the Cather foundation in Red Cloud.

13   BOURNE, RANDOLPH. "Morals and Art from the West." In
     Dictionary of Literary Biography Documentary Series. See
     Van Antwerp, 1982.73, pp. 72–74.
          Reprinted from 1918.1.

14   CAIN, KATHLEEN. "Cather Country." Bloomsbury Review 2
     (June–August):24–25.
          A mood piece describing the feelings produced by a visit to
     Red Cloud, Nebraska, the Willa Cather Pioneer Memorial Prairie,
     and other sites pertinent to Cather's work. Quotes from Cather
     and acclaims her writing as "sound," "powerful," and "true"
     enough to produce goose flesh on the arms of the reader.

15   CANBY, HENRY SEIDEL. "A Novel of the Soul." In Dictionary of
     Literary Biography Documentary Series. See Van Antwerp,
     1982.73, pp. 83–85.
          Review of The Professor's House. Reprint of 1925.8.

16   CARROLL, LATROBE. "Willa Sibert Cather." In Dictionary of
     Literary Biography Documentary Series. See Van Antwerp,
     1982.73, pp. 75–78.
          Reprinted from 1921.3.

17   COLLINS, ALEXANDRA. Review of Willa Cather's Imagination.
     English Studies in Canada 8 (March):108–17.
          Evaluates Stouck's book (1975.49), but makes numerous
     independent observations about Cather's fiction as well. Defines
     the tensions that pervade Cather's work and maintains that she
     was concerned with people's response to success. Observes, too,
     that many of Cather's male characters are unable to mature to an
     adult state, and hence go into retreat.

18   _____. "Who Shall Inherit the Earth? Ethel Wilson's Kinship
     with Wharton, Glasgow, Cather, and Ostenso." In The Ethel
     Wilson Symposium. Edited by Lorraine McMullen. Ottawa,
     Canada: University of Ottawa Press, pp. 61–72.
          Asserts that Wilson shares with Cather and others a concern
     for an encroaching urban culture and an ambivalent attitude
     toward a past that is relived through memory. Uses mainly
     O Pioneers! to make comparisons, declaring that Alexandra
     Bergson's shortcomings--her blindness, her underdeveloped con-
     sciousness, and her sometimes tragic lack of awareness of others
     --bring her troubles upon her.

19   CRANE, JOAN [ST. CLAIRE]. Willa Cather: A Bibliography.
      Lincoln: University of Nebraska Press, 440 pp.
         Provides a complete description of all known and assumed
      writings by Cather, recording such things as editions, printings,
      textual variants and errata, printing history, facts of publica-
      tion, binding material and paper, and current locations of edi-
      tion copies. The works of Cather are cataloged and grouped as
      (1) books (including collected works and works edited by Cather);
      (2) poems; (3) short fiction (including excerpted fiction in
      anthologies and novels first published in periodicals); (4) arti-
      cles, reviews, and essays in newspapers and periodicals; (5) for-
      eign language translations of novels and stories; (6) books
      printed in large type; (7) books printed in Braille; (8) books
      recorded for the blind; and (9) books adapted for film and
      theater.

20   CROUTHER, LOU-ANN. "Returning Home: Heroines as Rebuilders
      and Victims in American Fiction Written by Women." Ph.D.
      dissertation, Indiana University, 231 pp.
         Studies Ántonia Shimerda as one of six heroines in American
      fiction who leave home and then return. Treats the conflicts
      these heroines experience and explores their relationships with
      the community, their growth experienced during absence, and their
      ability to rebuild their lives. Such an ability depends largely
      on how well the heroines retain and develop their identities.
      See Dissertation Abstracts International 43:3593A.

21   DELL, FLOYD. "A Good Novel." In Dictionary of Literary
      Biography Documentary Series. See Van Antwerp, 1982.73,
      pp. 67-69.
         Reprinted from 1913.3.

22   DOUGLAS, ANN. "Willa Cather: A Problematic Ideal." In
      Women, the Arts, and the 1920s in Paris and New York."
      Edited by Kenneth W. Wheeler and Virginia Lee Lussier. New
      Brunswick: Transaction Books, pp. 14-19.
         An abridged text of 1974.15.

23   EDEL, LEON. "A Cave of One's Own." In Stuff of Sleep and
      Dreams: Experiments in Literary Psychology. New York:
      Harper & Row, pp. 216-40.
         A revised text of 1957.8. Reprinted: 1984.26.

24   EHRLICH, EUGENE, and CARRUTH, GORTON. The Oxford Illustrated
      Literary Guide to the United States. New York: Oxford Uni-
      versity Press, 478 pp., passim.
         Keys into a great many places where Cather lived and
      worked, and places she wrote about, from Greenwich Village to
      Gore, Virginia. The lengthiest treatment of Cather is in the
      Red Cloud, Nebraska, section. It notes Cather's use of the area
      and its people in her works, and describes activities of the
      Willa Cather Pioneer Memorial and Educational Foundation. It
      also points out sites of interest connected with Cather. See
      index for the multitude of pages relating to Cather.

25   FELD, ROSE C. "Restlessness Such as Ours Does Not Make for
     Beauty." In Dictionary of Literary Biography Documentary
     Series. See Van Antwerp, 1982.73, pp. 81–82.
          Reprinted from 1924.5.

26   FISHER, DOROTHY CANFIELD. Review of Youth and the Bright
     Medusa. In Dictionary of Literary Biography Documentary
     Series. See Van Antwerp, 1982.73, pp. 74–75.
          Reprint of 1921.5.

27   FOLSOM, JAMES K. Cather entry in Twentieth-Century Western
     Writers. Edited by James Vinson and D.L. Kirkpatrick.
     Detroit: Gale Research Co., pp. 150–52.
          After providing bibliography and a short biography, offers
     critical commentary on Cather's work, indicating that her farm
     novels are atypical of the genre; that is, they are traditional
     rather than radical and are not Populist in their sympathies.
     Cather's successful characters are those who put the past aside
     and place their faith in the future. Cather uses an agricultural
     metaphor to express this almost mystical faith, though she ab-
     stracts it into the "Garden of the Lord" in Death Comes for the
     Archbishop.

28   GRUMBACH, DORIS. "Heroes and Victims: Willa Cather's Mar-
     riage Theme." Quarterly Journal of the Library of Congress
     39 (Fall):242–49.
          Asserts, using A Lost Lady and My Mortal Enemy to prove the
     point, that in Cather's fiction marriages, even those begun with
     love and the best intentions, are doomed to fail. Better than
     the women they marry, Captain Forrester and Oswald Henshawe are
     heroic victims of marriages that destroy them and their wives.

29   H., F. "Willa Cather Talks of Work." In Dictionary of Lit-
     erary Biography Documentary Series. See Van Antwerp, 1982.73,
     pp. 69–71.
          Reprint of 1913.4.

30   HOWARD, MAUREEN. "City of Words." In Women, the Arts, and
     the 1920s in Paris and New York. See Douglas, 1982.22,
     pp. 42–48.
          Includes Cather among women writers who have a special
     sense of the city as "place." The city was a necessity for
     Cather, as it was for her most autobiographical heroine, Lucy
     Gayheart; but for the most part, she resisted its dazzle.

31   HOWARTH, WILLIAM. "The Country of Willa Cather." Photographs
     by Farrell Grehan. National Geographic 162 (July):70–93.
          Presents a personal description and response to Cather and
     to the areas on the American continent about which Cather wrote
     from firsthand experience--namely, Virginia, Nebraska, the South-
     west, and Grand Manan. Howarth visited these places and recorded
     his impressions, while Grehan photographed them. Several of the
     novels are described in relation to their particular landscapes.
     For Howarth, Cather always remains, somehow, elusive.

32   HUDSON, ROBERT V. The Writing Game: A Biography of Will
     Irwin. Ames: Iowa State University Press, pp. 57–58.
        Details the frustrations of Irwin's work at McClure's,
     mentioning his fears that Cather was after his job and his
     suspicions that she was having an affair with McClure.

33   JENSEN, MARVIN D., and SCHMIDT, OTIS RHEA. "Willa Cather:
     Historian of the Prairie and the Pioneer." Prairie/Plains
     Journal 3 (Winter-Spring):33–38.
        By portraying individuals and their personal struggles,
     Cather breathed life into the facts of pioneer prairie life in
     America, conveying in her art the paradox of change, and yet
     continuity, that marked the pioneer experiences about which she
     wrote.

34   KAUFMAN, ALAN. "Foreigners, Aliens, Mongrels: Literary
     Responses to American Immigration 1880–1920." Ph.D. disser-
     tation, Indiana University, 195 pp.
        Treats Cather as a writer whose work falls in the tradition
     of tolerance toward immigration to the United States, a tradition
     that dates back to the founding fathers and continues through
     Emerson and Whitman to William Dean Howells and Cather. These
     writers contributed to the national debate on immigration atti-
     tude and policy. See Dissertation Abstracts International 43:
     3596A.

35   KNOPF, ALFRED A. "Publishing Then and Now." In Dictionary of
     Literary Biography Documentary Series. See Van Antwerp,
     1982.73, pp. 102–4.
        Reprinted from 1964.13.

36   KRUTCH, JOSEPH WOOD. "The Lady as Artist." In Dictionary of
     Literary Biography Documentary Series. See Van Antwerp,
     1982.73, pp. 79–81.
        Review of A Lost Lady. Reprint of 1923.28.

37   _____. "The Modest Method of Willa Cather." In Dictionary of
     Literary Biography Documentary Series. See Van Antwerp,
     1982.73, pp. 85–86.
        Review of My Mortal Enemy. Reprinted from 1926.14.

38   _____. "The Pathos of Distance." In Dictionary of Literary
     Biography Documentary Series. See Van Antwerp, 1982.73,
     pp. 86–89.
        Review of Death Comes for the Archbishop. Reprint of
     1927.19.

39   KUBITSCHEK, MISSY DEHN. "St. Peter and the World All Before
     Him." Western American Literature 17 (May):13–20.
        Both the Blue Mesa and Hamilton are metaphorical Edens in
     The Professor's House, and both Godfrey St. Peter and Tom Outland
     deny the reality of evil. They are judgmental toward the imper-
     fections of their friends and loved ones. The basic movement of
     the book is toward their acceptance of the fact that they live

in flawed worlds. St. Peter finally relinquishes judgment and accepts connection with imperfect humanity.

40   LAMBERT, DEBORAH. "The Defeat of a Hero: Autonomy and Sexuality in My Ántonia." American Literature 53 (January): 76-90.
      Assumes the lesbianism of Cather and bases the argument of the essay on that premise. My Ántonia is a transitional novel for Cather, a novel in which, because of her fear of exposing her own sexuality and independence of conventional sexual roles, Cather shifts from presenting the strong, self-directed woman of O Pioneers! and The Song of the Lark. Instead, she presents the woman whose selfhood and sexuality are ultimately buried in the highly conventional and heightened role as the mother of sons ("Cuzak's Boys," not "Ántonia's Children"). Lambert blames the structural weaknesses of My Ántonia on Cather's supposed ambiguity regarding the lesbianism she refused to admit openly.

41   LICH, GLEN E. "Tom Outland: A Central Problem." Southwestern American Literature 8 (Fall):42-48.
      Tom Outland is the center, the ordering principle, of The Professor's House, just as the tower is the ordering principle in the cliff city. Tom, representing the lost ideal, is compared and contrasted with other major characters in the book. Cather, however, makes it clear that, like the cliff dwellers who had to go to the valley floor to grow crops for sustenance, Godfrey St. Peter has to leave the upper world of the ideal in order to survive in the less than ideal human realm.

42   LOVE, GLEN A. "The Cowboy in the Laboratory: Willa Cather's Hesitant Moderns." In The Westerner and the Modern Experience in the American Novel. Lewisburg, Pa.: Bucknell University Press; London and Toronto: Associated University Presses, pp. 107-69.
      Treats at length Cather and four other writers who are described as early moderns. Questions common assumptions about Cather's outlook and contends that she is forward as well as backward-looking. Many of her characters are progressive achievers in the modern world; they are "new Americans." Nearly all of her novels project the dual experience of the West and the westerner, the blend of primitive and progressive impulses. Alexander's Bridge is solidly in this pattern and in many ways foreshadows The Professor's House. Cather's heroic achievers are often those who achieve in science or machinery--the supposed enemies of the land--but they have also another kind of impulse that sets them above mere exploiters and followers, an impulse growing out of their "westernness." Tom Outland is the culminating figure of this group.

43   MENCKEN, H.L. Review of The Song of the Lark. In Dictionary of Literary Biography Documentary Series. See Van Antwerp, 1982.73, pp. 71-72.
      Reprint of 1916.2.

44   MOERS, ELLEN. "Landscape: Literary Metaphor for Female
      Sexuality." <u>Helicon Nine: The Journal of Women's Arts and</u>
      <u>Letters</u>, no. 7:52–61.
            An abridged text of 1976.18.

45   MONROE, WILLIAM FRANK. "A Persistence of Rhetoric: Willa
      Cather and Walker Percy in an Age of Alienism." Ph.D. dis-
      sertation, University of Chicago.
            Examines <u>The Professor's House</u> in a context of the various
      literary strategies of alienation, arguing that Cather recognizes
      the modern world as a waste land, but does not renounce it.
      Godfrey St. Peter experiences a "gnostic temptation," but he re-
      turns to his cultural and familial world. The "reticent style"
      Cather advocates in her theory about the unfurnished novel forces
      the reader into the story-making and world-making mode with St.
      Peter, and he is revealed as an unreliable narrator. Both Cather
      and Walker Percy, because they practice their rhetoric in a way
      that "deepens and depends on cultural identifications with man-
      kind," provide "constructive, beneficial, and needed alternatives
      to twentieth-century alienistic strategies."

46   MOSELEY, ANN. "The Pueblo Emergence Myth in Cather's <u>Death</u>
      <u>Comes for the Archbishop</u>." <u>Southwestern American Literature</u> 8
      (Fall):27–35.
            Observes in <u>Death Comes for the Archbishop</u> a thematic
      parallel with the "Pueblo Indian myth of creation, emergence, and
      migration" in which the mythic Pueblo Twins enable their people
      to rise to higher levels of spiritual being and harmony. This is
      done through unifying the basic duality of the cosmos into one
      whole and successfully seeking greater spiritual understanding.
      Bishops Latour and Vaillant are the counterparts of the Pueblo
      Twins.

47   MULLIGAN, HUGH A. "Tomorrow is Yesterday in Nebraska's
      Catherland." <u>Omaha Sunday World-Herald</u>, 20 June, sec. e,
      p. 1.
            Appraises the efforts of Red Cloud historians to restore
      various buildings in Cather's home town that she made familiar
      in her stories. Calis Red Cloud Cather's "magic looking glass."
      This article appeared in many newspapers under a variety of
      titles in the month of June. Some of them include the <u>Grand</u>
      <u>Island</u> (Nebr.) <u>Independent</u>, the <u>Lincoln Sunday Journal</u>, the
      <u>Honolulu Star-Bulletin</u>, the <u>Denver Post</u>, the <u>San Jose</u> (Calif.)
      <u>Mercury News</u>, the <u>Northwest Arkansas Morning News</u>, the <u>Indiana</u>
      <u>Post Tribune</u>, and the <u>Stars and Stripes</u> (Armed Forces periodi-
      cal) magazine section.

48   MUNN, DEBRA D. "A Probable Source for Glasgow's <u>Barren</u>
      <u>Ground</u>." <u>Markham Review</u> 11 (Winter):21–25.
            Even though Ellen Glasgow was probably jealous of Cather's
      literary success, it is quite possible that she was influenced by
      <u>O Pioneers!</u> in the creation of <u>Barren Ground</u>. The two books are
      similar in plot, character, and theme.

49   MURPHY, JOHN J. "One of Ours as American Naturalism." Great
      Plains Quarterly 2 (Fall):232-38.
            Argues that in some of its weaknesses--characterization
      violated by diatribe, overwritten passages--One of Ours resembles
      the work of some American naturalists. Here Cather renders
      Nebraska in more detail than in any other novel, but her descrip-
      tions are more prosaic and matter-of-fact. Furthermore, while
      Claude Wheeler is in Nebraska, he feels trapped by his environ-
      ment. Some sequences in the novel are romantically dreamlike,
      while others are horribly grotesque.

50   _____. "The Virginian and Ántonia Shimerda: Different Sides
      of the Western Coin." In Women and Western American Literature.
      Edited by Helen Winter Stauffer and Susan J. Rosowski. Troy,
      N.Y.: Whitston Publishing Co., pp. 162-78.
            Compares and contrasts Cather's treatment of the western
      "hero," in the person of Ántonia Shimerda, with Owen Wister's
      hero in The Virginian. The two characters have similarities of
      sensibility and experience, yet the West and the values Cather
      depicts are quite different from those of Wister. Ántonia is
      also a marked departure from the usual "prim and proper woman"
      who represents the conventional culture, a culture imaged in the
      Virginian's sweetheart, Molly Wood.

51   _____. "Willa Cather and Catholic Themes." Western American
      Literature 12 (May):53-60.
            In Cather's novels the Catholic Church serves to unite the
      sometimes conflicting realms of the world and the home because
      Cather understood the spiritual family system and the ideal of
      the priest inherent in Catholicism. She also understood the
      significance of Mary's role and the humanity of the priests she
      portrayed.

52   _____. "Willa Cather." In Fifty Western Writers: A Bio-
      Bibliographical Sourcebook. Edited by Fred Erisman and
      Richard W. Etulain. Westport, Conn.: Greenwood Press,
      pp. 51-62.
            Following the established format for the book, this essay
      first presents biographical data, then discusses Cather's prin-
      cipal themes as they are worked out in her fiction, and then
      finally provides a brief bibliographical essay and listing of
      primary and secondary sources. The predominant theme in Cather's
      fiction is "response to the western land," and her two positive
      treatments of that theme are O Pioneers! and Death Comes for the
      Archbishop. Her other works concerned with the western land show
      both the potential of the pioneer West and the failure to fulfill
      that potential, thus revealing a pessimistic response to the West.

53   "New Morning Nebraska Pioneers of '82." Vogue (London) 139
      (January):74-87.
            Features photographs taken of models in Red Cloud, Nebraska,
      showing the fashions of plains pioneers in Cather's time that
      still have currency in the present. Some of the photographs bear
      captions from Cather's works.

54 O'BRIEN, SHARON. "Mothers, Daughters, and the 'Art Neces-
    sity': Willa Cather and the Creative Process." In American
    Novelists Revisited: Essays in Feminist Criticism. Edited
    by Fritz Fleischmann. Boston: G.K. Hall & Co., pp. 265-98.
        Claims that Cather was "emotionally oriented toward women,"
    but she "camouflaged" these feelings by representing them only in
    male characters. These feelings are a reflection of her desire
    for love and nurturance from a mother figure, yet we are also
    aware that such an attachment to a mother threatens self-identity.
    Cather could not find her artist self until she got past that
    threat. Ultimately, we see her reconciliation with her mother
    as she worked toward it and finally achieved it in Sapphira and
    the Slave Girl.

55 PERRY, CONSTANCE MARIE. "Adolescence, Autonomy, and Vocation:
    Heroines of Künstlerromane by Modern American Woman." Ph.D.
    dissertation, Indiana University, 338 pp.
        Devotes a chapter to discussion of The Song of the Lark and
    Lucy Gayheart as examples of künstlerromane in modern American
    fiction by women. Asserts that in these works and others of the
    genre there is evidence of a literary tradition in which art pro-
    vides a woman with an escape from "the traps of female socializa-
    tion." See Dissertation Abstracts International 43:2669A.

56 PIACENTINO, EDWARD J. "Another Angle of Willa Cather's
    Artistic Prism: Impressionistic Character Portraiture in My
    Ántonia." Midamerica: The Yearbook of the Society for the
    Study of Midwestern Literature 9:53-64.
        In My Ántonia Cather's method is like that of the lyric
    poet; she evokes feeling through carefully selected imagery,
    especially in the delineation of character. Ántonia in particu-
    lar is portrayed through natural images, and so are Otto Fuchs
    and Anton Cuzak.

57 PLUNKETT, KEVIN MICHAEL. "The Symbol of the Frontier in
    Selected Novels of Willa Cather." Ph.D. dissertation,
    University of Rhode Island, 159 pp.
        Sees the frontier as having imaginative, more than histori-
    cal, significance for Cather, and outlines four phases of sym-
    bolic development of the frontier in her work. In the first, the
    individual identifies mystically with the land; in the second,
    the frontier is lost, but the idealist is still affected imagina-
    tively by it; in the third, the individual wishes to return to a
    "primitive oneness with nature"; and in the fourth, Cather finds
    peaceful resolution to the effects of change and loss by return-
    ing to the frontier. See Dissertation Abstracts International
    43:3597A-98A.

58 PONTRELLI, JEANNY ROSS. "The Archetypal Hero in Death Comes
    for the Archbishop." Heritage of the Great Plains 15
    (Spring):31-40.
        Compares Jean Latour to Aeneas and the knight of romance,
    then suggests that he finally achieves a blending of heart--

represented by Vaillant/Galahad--and intellect that allows him
to fulfill both the practical and spiritual aspects of his
mission.

59   QUIRK, TOM. "Fitzgerald and Cather: The Great Gatsby."
     American Literature 54 (December):574-91.
          Comments on F. Scott Fitzgerald's admiration for Cather and
     on the parallels in some of their work. Fitzgerald learned some-
     thing about the unfurnished novel from A Lost Lady and about the
     double self from "Paul's Case." But the strongest connection is
     between Alexander's Bridge and The Great Gatsby. In both novels
     the focus is on the desire for the vital self of a romantic past
     and the inevitable motion toward a crack-up and destruction.

60   "Recent Poetry." In Dictionary of Literary Biography Docu-
     mentary Series. See Van Antwerp, 1982.73, pp. 63-64.
          Review of April Twilights. Reprint of 1903.5.

61   Review of Alexander's Bridge. In Dictionary of Literary
     Biography Documentary Series. See Van Antwerp, 1982.73,
     p. 65.
          Reprint of 1912.10.

62   ROSOWSKI, SUSAN J. "Discovering Symbolic Meaning: Teaching
     with Willa Cather." English Journal 71 (December):14-17.
          The work of Cather provides an excellent bridge into lit-
     erature for students oriented to visual rather than printed
     media. Cather herself was a teacher and understood how to move
     observers of an unfamiliar or barren landscape (such as she found
     in Nebraska and young readers find on a printed page) to compre-
     hension through introducing objects into the language that
     gradually come to have symbolic significance.

63   _____. "Willa Cather's A Lost Lady: Art Versus the Closing
     Frontier." Great Plains Quarterly 2 (Fall):239-48.
          In A Lost Lady Cather simultaneously mourns the passing of
     the frontier and celebrates symbolic art for its expansive pos-
     sibilities, thereby creating a tension between loss and possi-
     bility that is felt in a great many aspects of the novel, includ-
     ing imagery and characterization.

64   SACKEN, JEANNEE PATRICIA. "'A Certain Slant of Light':
     Aesthetics of First-Person Narration, Readings of Gide's
     L'immoraliste and Cather's My Ántonia." Ph.D. dissertation,
     University of North Carolina at Chapel Hill, 269 pp.
          Studies My Ántonia and the aesthetics of the first-person
     narrator by employing two methods of analysis, one which looks at
     "first-person narration as a technique of fiction," and the other
     which explores the artistic value of the technique. See Disser-
     tation Abstracts International 43:266A.

65   SELTZER, SANDRA. "The Family in the Novels of Willa Cather."
     Ph.D. dissertation, St. John's University, 249 pp.
          Discusses recurring family themes in Cather's novels--the
     effect of the family on the individual, the outsider as nurturer,
     surrogate parent bonds within the family, and adult relation-
     ships--in connection with the development of the novels and
     Cather's own familial experiences. Concludes that Cather worked
     out her own conflicts through her writing. See Dissertation
     Abstracts International 43 (1982):1547A.

66   SKAGGS, MERRILL MAGUIRE. "Poe's Shadow on Alexander's Bridge."
     Mississippi Quarterly 35 (Fall):365-74.
          Cather admired Poe and wrote her first novel with Poe's
     principles in mind. She uses many of Poe's techniques, such as
     the device of doubling, and parallels can be traced between
     Alexander's Bridge and "The Fall of the House of Usher"--paral-
     lels of theme, conflict, phrase, and image.

67   SLOTE, BERNICE. "An Exploration of Cather's Early Writing."
     Great Plains Quarterly 2 (Fall):210-17.
          What has not been sufficiently seen or understood is the
     continuity between Cather's early writing--voluminous articles,
     columns, reviews, stories--and the body of her "public" work.
     They are linked, however, in tone and content, and by a layering
     of allusion from classical, French, Russian, and other litera-
     tures and myths. At the heart of her theme is the cyclical move-
     ment of history, the rise and fall of civilizations.

68   _____. "Willa Cather and Plains Culture." In Vision and
     Refuge: Essays on the Literature of the Great Plains. Edited
     by Virginia Faulkner, with Frederick C. Luebke. Lincoln:
     University of Nebraska Press for the Center for Great Plains
     Studies, pp. 93-105.
          Explores Cather's fictional uses of various aspects of
     plains culture, especially that culture's composition of diverse
     elements blended in historical processes.

69   SOUTHWICK, HELEN C. "Willa Cather's Early Career: Origins of
     a Legend." Western Pennsylvania Historical Magazine 65
     (April):85-98.
          Raises questions regarding commonly assumed notions about
     Cather, especially in her relationship with Isabelle McClung.
     Charges that many details that appear in Cather biographies were
     picked up from Elizabeth Moorhead Vermorcken (see 1950.20), who
     appears to have dramatized, romanticized, and exaggerated a
     large part of her reminiscences about Cather. Some of her
     "facts" are obviously in error, but later biographers have taken
     them at face value, and they too have been cited by still later
     commentators. The principal unsupported assumption questioned
     is Cather's alleged lesbianism.

70   STINEBACK, DAVID [C.]. "No Stone Unturned: Popular Versus Pro-
      fessional Evaluations of Willa Cather." Prospects 7:167-76.
          By and large, Cather's reviewers have given better assess-
      ments of her work than have scholars, who have made moralistic
      judgments of Cather and her work and slighted her artistic capa-
      bilities. Scholarship over the years has been politically,
      sociologically, or psychologically oriented, while reviews have
      maintained a spontaneity and flexibility that provide the most
      meaningful kind of evaluation of a writer like Cather.

71   STOUCK, DAVID. "Cather's Archbishop and Travel Writing."
      Western American Literature 17 (May):3-12.
          The rhetorical form of Death Comes for the Archbishop is
      actually travel writing, a form which places the book squarely in
      American narrative tradition. Cather uses Howlett's book, based
      on Bishop Machebeuf's letters about his travels and adventures
      in a strange new country, and her own travel experiences in the
      Southwest, for her materials. Inherent in travel writing are the
      digressive tales and experiences that characterize Death Comes
      for the Archbishop. The travel form also encompasses the book's
      religious vision in which the return from the journey is a return
      to an eternal home.

72   _____. "Marriage and Friendship in My Ántonia." Great Plains
      Quarterly 2 (Fall):224-31.
          Cather had a strong emotional attachment to Isabelle
      McClung and felt a distinct loss when Isabelle married in 1916,
      the year Cather began writing My Ántonia. That novel explores
      in breadth and depth the phenomena of marriage and friendship.
      These relationships in the novel, often following pastoral con-
      ventions, nearly always involve contrasting and complementary
      characters. Some of these relationships are highly fulfilling,
      while others are merely convenient. Cather believes that the
      essential ingredient for both the successful marriage and the
      satisfying friendship is a shared purpose.

73   VAN ANTWERP, MARGARET A., ed. Dictionary of Literary Biog-
      raphy Documentary Series: An Illustrated Chronicle. Vol. 1.
      Detroit: Gale Research Co., pp. 57-104.
          Supplements biographical data contained in 1981.56, provid-
      ing primary bibliography, plus a note on available biographies,
      bibliographies, and the location of archives containing Cather
      materials. This is a collection of pieces by and about Cather--
      her article on Stephen Crane, published letters, a variety of
      reviews of her books, interviews, and illustrations of various
      kinds, including manuscript pages carrying Cather's own correc-
      tions. Contains reprints of or from the following: 1903.5;
      1912.10; 1913.3-4; 1916.2; 1918.1; 1921.3, 5; 1922.36; 1923.28;
      1924.5; 1925.8; 1926.14; 1927.19; 1932.46; 1940.24; 1947.34;
      1964.13.

74   VEST, MIRA MEACHAM. "Willa Cather's Turkish Friend."
      American Collector, July, p. 29.
            Reveals that the Turkish doll Cather describes in O
      Pioneers! was an heirloom in Vest's family, the Cooks, and that
      it was a favorite of Cather's. The doll now resides at the Willa
      Cather Historical Center in Red Cloud, Nebraska.

75   WALSH, JEFFREY. American War Literature 1914 to Vietnam. New
      York: St. Martin's Press, pp. 81, 84, 89 passim.
            A look at the war fiction of writers like Cather and Edith
      Wharton presents a challenge to the "lost generation's" evalua-
      tion of itself. Claude Wheeler in Cather's One of Ours is dis-
      cussed as one who died before the disillusionment described in
      the fiction of the lost generation could set in.

76   WASHINGTON, IDA H. Dorothy Canfield Fisher: A Biography.
      Shelburne, Vt.: New England Press, p. 21.
            Speaks of Cather's lifelong friendship with Fisher and
      cites a 1949 letter from Fisher to Fraser Drew in which Fisher
      says that at a football game she gave Cather the idea to write a
      football story. In response, according to Fisher, Cather wrote
      "The Fear that Walks by Noonday," and it won a ten dollar prize
      which Cather split with Fisher. Cather gave permission for the
      story to be printed in a limited edition by a New York bookshop
      printer.

77   WASSERMAN, LORETTA. "The Lovely Storm: Sexual Initiation in
      Two Early Willa Cather Novels." Studies in the Novel 14
      (Winter):348–58.
            Disputes the view that Cather ran from fictional treatment
      of sexual experience and from sexuality in herself. Both The
      Song of the Lark and My Ántonia indicate that sexual experience--
      Thea Kronborg with Fred Ottenburg, Jim Burden with Lena Lingard
      in Lincoln--is an important step toward the full development of
      the artist and the person.

78   WATTS, EMILY STIPES. The Businessman in American Literature.
      Athens: University of Georgia Press, pp. 82–83.
            Uses Cather's "The Sculptor's Funeral" to illustrate the
      literati's view of the small-town businessman or financier in the
      1920s as one who was insensitive to the artist and narrowly
      prejudiced against anyone of independent spirit.

79   WEE, MORRIS OWEN. "Specks on the Horizon: Individuals and
      the Land in Canadian Prairie Fiction." South Dakota Review 19
      (Winter):18–31.
            Compares My Ántonia to W.O. Mitchell's Who Has Seen the
      Wind. Most Canadian prairie fiction does not treat human
      relationship with the land, generally taking the stance repre-
      sented by Jim Burden when on his arrival in Nebraska he feels
      obliterated by the landscape. But Who Has Seen the Wind is
      something of an exception, participating in Jim's later mood of
      unification--or at least spiritual connection--with the land.
      Both novels reflect the notion of the New Eden myth.

80   WEIXLMANN, JOE. American Short-Fiction Criticism and Scholar-
     ship, 1959-1977: A Checklist. Athens: Swallow Press/Ohio
     University Press, pp. 99-103.
          Lists Cather's short stories that have received critical
     attention and provides an index to the articles and books which
     discuss each particular story. This volume originated as an in-
     tended update of Thurston, 1960.14, but moved beyond it in scope.

81   WHITE, ROBERT J. "Willa Cather: More Dawns Than Sunsets."
     In A Feast of Favorite Authors. Dobbs Ferry, N.Y.: Cahill &
     Co., pp. 6-7.
          Literary catalog entry recommending four Cather novels.
     Observes beneath the flat surface of Cather's characters and
     style "hidden recesses of personality" and "complex artistry."
     There are echoes of Homer in her work; she is perhaps America's
     only singer of an heroic lost past. With Cather, however, the
     women are not simply wives of heroes, they are heroes. Reprinted
     in part: 1982.82.

82   _____. "Willa Cather: More Dawns Than Sunsets." Willa
     Cather Pioneer Memorial Newsletter 26 (Summer):15-16.
          Reprinted from 1982.81.

83   "Willa Cather, Novelist, Dies at Home Here." In Dictionary of
     Literary Biography Documentary Series. See Van Antwerp,
     1982.73, pp. 100-102.
          Reprint of 1947.34.

84   WILLIAMS, MICHAEL. "Willa Cather." In Dictionary of Literary
     Biography Documentary Series. See Van Antwerp, 1982.73,
     pp. 92, 94.
          Reprint of 1932.46.

85   WILSON, EDMUND. Review of One of Ours. In Dictionary of
     Literary Biography Documentary Series. See Van Antwerp,
     1982.73, pp. 78-79.
          Reprint of 1922.36.

86   WOODRESS, JAMES. "The Uses of Biography: The Case of Willa
     Cather." Great Plains Quarterly 2 (Fall):195-203.
          Discusses the problems of the biographer, and the particu-
     lar problems of the Cather biographer, and describes how the
     biographer can illuminate the imaginative processes of the writer.
     Cather is unusually biographical in her fiction, writing most
     often out of her own direct experience. Even a novel based on
     historical characters, like Death Comes for the Archbishop, is
     full of Cather herself. Cather's most autobiographical novel is
     The Professor's House, in which she projects her own midlife
     crisis at the peak of her success.

87   YARDLEY, JONATHAN. "The 22 Books of the Century." Washington
      Post, 1 February, sec. b, p. 1.
          Names Cather's Death Comes for the Archbishop as one of the
      twenty-two best works of fiction in America in the twentieth
      century.

88   YONGUE, PATRICIA LEE. "Marian Forrester and Moll Flanders:
      Fortunes and Misfortunes." In Women and Western American
      Literature. See Murphy, 1982.50, pp. 194-211.
          Compares the situations of Marian Forrester and Daniel
      Defoe's Moll Flanders, indicating that the latter can be a
      touchstone in helping the reader understand the dilemma of Marian
      Forrester who is similarly trapped between two generations and
      between the value systems of idealists and opportunists. Both
      characters exemplify woman's predicament—her socioeconomic
      bondage to those with power over her, whether they be men with
      idealistic expectations of her or men upon whom she is finan-
      cially dependent. Marian unconsciously grows to desire male
      attention—she shuns or scorns women—because she is helplessly
      dependent and must accept masculine guardianship if she is to
      survive.

89   ZABEL, MORTON DAUWEN. "The Tone of Time." In Dictionary of
      Literary Biography Documentary Series. See Van Antwerp,
      1982.73, pp. 99-100.
          Review of Sapphira and the Slave Girl. Reprint of 1940.24.

90   ZLOTNICK, JOAN. Portrait of an American City: The Novelists'
      New York. Interdisciplinary Urban Studies Series, edited by
      Raymond A. Mohl. Port Washington, N.Y.: Kennikat Press,
      National University Publications, pp. 98-102.
          Cather portrays New York City as a center for cultural and
      artistic pursuits. In The Song of the Lark, "Coming, Aphrodite!"
      and My Mortal Enemy, Cather evokes three different geographical
      settings within the city to show three different aspects of
      artistic life there.

91   ZWICK, RICHARD CHARLES. "The Agrarian Ethos in Willa Cather's
      Nebraska Stories and Novels: From Memory to Vision." Ph.D.
      dissertation, University of Nebraska, 223 pp.
          Uses Cather's early short stories, her Nebraska novels, and
      "Neighbour Rosicky" to portray the collective spirit of farm life
      and the agrarian ideology. The pioneer's or farmer's relation
      to the land is a spiritual one that ranges from the hostile to
      the supportive. Farm life represents an effort to find meaning
      and completeness. See Dissertation Abstracts International 43
      (1982):804A.

<u>1983</u>

*1   ABE, HIROSHI. "Willa Cather no Nijigen teki Sekai." In
      <u>Muraoka Isamu Sensei Kiju Kinen Ronbunshu: Eibungaku Shiron</u>
      [Willa Cather's world perspective. Essays written in honor of
      Professor Isamu Muraoka]. Tokyo: Kinseido, pp. 353-65.
          Listed in <u>MLA International Bibliography</u> advance printout
      for 1984.

2   ARNOLD, MARILYN. "Willa Cather." In <u>Critical Survey of Long</u>
      <u>Fiction</u>. Edited by Frank N. Magill. Vol. 2. LaCanada,
      Calif.: Salem Press, pp. 472-84.
          Provides preliminary encyclopedic information, then takes
      up most of Cather's novels in turn, discussing them as they
      exemplify her principal concern—the dual pulls of East and West,
      of civilization (or art) and the landscape, and the threat to
      both posed by the ethic of acquisitiveness in a money-centered
      society.

3   BOHLKE, L. BRENT. "Grace Church, Red Cloud—A 'True Story' of
      the Midwest." <u>Nebraska History</u> 64 (Winter):491-511; <u>Willa</u>
      <u>Cather Pioneer Memorial Newsletter</u>, Literary issue, nos. 1-2
      (1983):1-11.
          Traces the history of Grace Episcopal Church in Red Cloud,
      Nebraska, which is now one of the holdings of the Willa Cather
      Pioneer Memorial and Educational Foundation under the auspices of
      the Nebraska State Historical Society. Notes its relation to
      Cather's work, especially through its communicants Silas and Lyra
      Garber, who figure as models for the Forresters in <u>A Lost Lady</u>.

4   BUTTERFIELD, HERBIE. "Willa Cather." In <u>American Fiction:</u>
      <u>New Readings</u>. Edited by Richard Gray. London: Vision Press,
      pp. 133-49; Totowa, N.J.: Barnes & Noble.
          Combines plot summary with commentary on Cather's novels
      from <u>O Pioneers!</u> to <u>Sapphira and the Slave Girl</u>, and on the short
      stories in <u>Obscure Destinies</u>. Sees in Cather's work a multiple
      perspective issuing from her Southern Protestant background in
      Virginia, her experiences on the western frontier, and her regard
      for Catholicism's civilizing efforts in the new world. Cather
      was both a romanticist and a classicist, but she was neither
      realist nor fantasist. Hers was the greater art of "imaginative
      truth."

5   CHELL, CARA. "'No Myth Is Safely Broken': American Women and
      the Modernist Period." Ph.D. dissertation, Indiana University,
      pp. 116-88.
          In a chapter on Cather titled "'The Healthy Commonplace':
      Willa Cather and the Traditionalists," examines from a feminist
      perspective the myths that have been created about women by male
      writers in the modernist period. Devotes one chapter to explor-
      ing how Cather, as an apparent traditionalist, "capitalized on
      the image of the muse." Cather appears to subscribe to the
      agrarian myth in creating the character of Ántonia Shimerda, but

she unconsciously rejects that myth by showing the violence out
of which Ántonia sprang and the way in which she is used up and
then diminished as the book ends with "Cuzak's Boys."

6   CHERNY, ROBERT W.   "Willa Cather and the Populists." Great
     Plains Quarterly 3 (Fall):206-18.
         Insists that Cather's views on Populism have not been
     understood because they have not been related to the nature of
     Populism in Webster County, Nebraska, during her years there.
     Nearly all of Cather's associations, including those with Charles
     Gere, editor of the Nebraska State Journal and an ardent anti-
     Populist Republican, were with persons unsympathetic to Populism.
     An awareness of Cather's political references in her early news-
     paper columns and a perceptive reading of her fiction show her
     sympathies to be anti-Populist.

7   COMMIRE, ANNE, ed.   Something about the Author: Facts and
     Pictures about Authors and Illustrators of Books for Young
     People. Vol. 30. Detroit: Gale Research Co., pp. 75-83.
         Provides in a prescribed format biographical and biblio-
     graphical details, including information on reprints of Cather's
     works, books about Cather, and a representative sampling of
     criticism in journals. The bulk of the essay offers "sidelights"
     that focus on certain events in Cather's life. Acknowledges a
     debt to the Woodress biography (1970.33), but includes a great
     many quotations from a variety of sources that relate to dates
     cited and events being highlighted. The effect is a chronologi-
     cal overview of Cather's entire career, made personal through
     numerous quotations.

8   DITSKY, JOHN.   "'Listening with Supersensual Ear': Music in
     the Novels of Willa Cather." Journal of Narrative Technique
     13 (Autumn):154-63.
         Cather's works establish--even depend upon--a relationship
     between land and character and music. In this relationship
     Cather finds the impetus for narrative. Music, which vibrates
     from within her work, is most apparent and meaningful to the
     finely tuned ear.

9   DOANE, MARGARET.   "The Reliability of Godfrey St. Peter:
     Self-Knowledge and Isolation in The Professor's House."
     Southwestern American Literature 8 (Spring):21-25.
         Both Godfrey St. Peter and Tom Outland lack self-knowledge
     in the beginning, but they both come to realize that what they
     want and value most in life is isolation. Before they come to
     this knowledge, they unfairly blame others for their unhappiness.

10   _____.   "Willa Cather's Early References to Robert Browning."
     Studies in Browning and His Circle 11 (Spring):66-69.
         Cites numerous passages from Cather's literary commentary
     to make the point that Cather regarded Browning as something of
     an ultimate artist whose work could profitably serve as a standard
     of excellence against which other writing might be judged.

11   EDEL, LEON. "The Man in the Woman." New Republic 189
      (14 November):34-36.
         Review of the Robinson biography (1983.25) also offers
      Edel's view on Cather and her work. Asserts that Cather's sexual
      life "can be deduced" from her novels, even though she tried to
      cover it up. Claims that Cather sometimes thought or fantasized
      herself to be a man, and she overcame the frustration of her
      homosexuality by writing about fortitude and artistic careers
      rather than love. Not a born writer, she achieved artistically
      through ambition and discipline.

12   EPSTEIN, JOSEPH. "Willa Cather: Listing Toward Lesbos." New
      Criterion 2 (December):35-43.
         Questions the assumption made by some commentators, espe-
      cially Robinson (1983.25), that Cather was a lesbian, and sees
      little relevance in the issue to her work even if the assumption
      were true.

13   FENSTER, VALMAI KIRKHAM. Guide to American Literature.
      Littleton, Colo.: Libraries Unlimited, pp. 85-86.
         Lists Cather's published works and gives information about
      subsequent collections and edited texts. Also provides an
      evaluative discussion of selected biographical, critical, and
      bibliographical sources related to Cather study.

14   GELFANT, BLANCHE H. "The Forgotten Reaping-Hook: Sex in My
      Ántonia." In Fiction by American Women: Recent Views. Ed-
      ited by Winifred Farrant Bevilacqua. Port Washington, N.Y.:
      Associated Faculty Press, 1983, pp. 51-66, 150-51.
         Reprint of 1971.11.

15   GOODMAN, CHARLOTTE. "The Lost Brother, the Twin: Women
      Novelists and the Male-Female Double Bildungsroman." Novel:
      A Forum on Fiction 17 (Fall):28-43.
         Treats Cather's My Ántonia as one of five typical female
      bildungsromans which, unlike such novels that have males at their
      centers, focus on a double protagonist, male and female. By
      splitting the protagonist into female and male, Cather is able
      to dramatize how, in a society that defines gender roles rigidly,
      both male and female experience is seriously fragmented.

16   HUF, LINDA. "The Song of the Lark (1915): The Exception of
      Willa Cather." In A Portrait of the Artist As a Young Woman:
      The Writer As Heroine in American Literature. New York:
      Frederick Ungar Publishing Co., pp. 80-102, 168-70, 183-84.
         Revision of 1981.26. Argues that in Thea Kronborg Cather
      creates an artist very much like herself, devoted to art to the
      extent that men do not particularly interest her in a romantic
      way. Both writer and heroine live for their art. Thea's de-
      voted male associates are interested in her, in the main, as an
      artist rather than as a woman, and they help her realize her
      artistic destiny. At the same time, Cather takes pains to
      establish that Thea gives back to them as much as she takes.
      Also contains a selected bibliography of works by and about
      Cather.

17   JENSEN, MARVIN D.   "An Application of Bibliotherapy: Search
      for Meaning in the Writings of Willa Cather." Journal of
      Communication Therapy 2, no. 2:131-35.
           Argues that the reading of value-centered literature such
      as that produced by Cather can have therapeutic effects, and can
      assist a reader in the search for meaning as described by Viktor
      Frankl. That is, such reading can lead to freedom by teaching
      one to choose how to respond to circumstances. Several of
      Cather's books and stories are recommended, but "A Wagner
      Matinee" and My Mortal Enemy are given particular emphasis.

18   MANNING, MARGARET. "Novelist Willa Cather Held Out Against
      Onrushing Modernism." Omaha World-Herald, 17 July, p. 21.
           Attributed to the Boston Globe. Reviews The Song of the
      Lark on its reissue. Asserts that although Cather was not at all
      influenced by modern ideology, her work is strongly realistic.
      Commends Cather for her craftsmanship in depicting the western
      frontier, and ranks her alongside Hawthorne and James.

19   MINES, CYNTHIA. "Willa Cather's World." Kansas City Star,
      24 April, sec. h, p. 6.
           Reviews Cather's background as an artistic source for her
      novels, mentioning the restoration of her home in Red Cloud,
      Nebraska, and the founding of the Willa Cather Historical Center
      there.

20   MITGANG, HERBERT. "Spellbound in Santa Fe: Trailing Willa
      Cather." New York Times, 20 February, sec. 20, p. 16.
           Recommends reading Death Comes for the Archbishop as a
      substitute for the usual factual guidebooks in preparation for--
      or in reflection after--a visit to Santa Fe. Passages from the
      novel in which Cather makes Latour a unifying metaphor for her
      fictional portrayal of the Southwest are very much alive in
      today's Santa Fe.

21   MYERS, DWIGHT, and MYERS, CAROL. "The Fifty Most Popular New
      Mexico Books." New Mexico Magazine 61 (December):57-59.
           Reports the results of a poll taken "about a year ago" by
      the New Mexico Book League. A cross-section of New Mexico
      readers were asked to name their best-liked books. Nine hundred
      ten votes were cast, and Death Comes for the Archbishop came out
      as the number one favorite.

22   O'CONNELL, DOUG. "Willa Cather's Gore Home Inspired Last
      Novel." Winchester Star, 31 January, p. 13.
           Describes the area in Virginia where Cather spent her early
      childhood, recounting her experiences there and naming people who
      figured in her life. Also reports conversations with Cathers
      still residing in the vicinity.

23   PAOLI, RICHARD. "Red Cloud: A Novel Setting." San Francisco
      Sunday Examiner and Chronicle, 31 July, pp. 1, 11.
           Recounts a visit to the Red Cloud, Nebraska, area, comment-
      ing especially on Cather's use of the town and its people and

landmarks in her fiction. Suggests that Cather's later work in
other settings does not match the power of the portraits she
painted in her early Nebraska novels.

24 ROBINSON, PHYLLIS C. "Mr. McClure and Willa." American
    Heritage 34 (August-September):26-31.
       Adapted from Robinson's then forthcoming biography of
    Cather (1983.25). Focuses more on McClure than on Cather,
    delineating his nature and his conflicts with his staff at the
    time Cather arrived on the scene. Details some of Cather's expe-
    riences while at McClure's, stressing the mutual admiration that
    marked Cather's association with her boss.

25 _____. Willa: The Life of Willa Cather. New York: Doubleday
    & Co., 333 pp.
       In the mode of popular rather than academic biography, pre-
    sents a detailed and sometimes dramatized account--in which
    Cather's thoughts and conversations are imagined--of the years
    prior to the publication of Cather's novels. Less attention is
    given to the years of novel writing. Argues that some Cather
    stories contain hidden evidence of the bisexual "duality" of her
    nature, and that her narrative voice is typically androgynous.

26 ROSE, PHYLLIS. "Modernism: The Case of Willa Cather." In
    Modernism Reconsidered. Edited by Robert Kiely. Harvard
    English Studies, no. 11. Cambridge, Mass.: Harvard Univer-
    sity Press, pp. 123-45.
       Claims that Cather is clearly allied to modernism and is
    not the nostalgic traditionalist many have assumed her to be.
    Her methods most closely resemble the methods of modernist
    painters; she attempts both to simplify and enlarge. Much of
    what she creates assumes a grand scale, treated in a lyrical mode
    but partaking of the mythic and instinctual. Unlike some other
    modernists, she presents her characters from the outside, but her
    method is nevertheless a reaction against traditional kinds of
    characterization. Further, she seeks and achieves the aesthetic
    quality of anonymity, chiefly because she is clear and absolutely
    noneccentric. Death Comes for the Archbishop, in the way it
    blurs distinctions--between past and present, between the spir-
    itual and material--is a "surprising example in literature of the
    modern aesthetic in art."

27 SCHACH, PAUL. "Russian Wolves in Folktales and Literature of
    the Plains: A Question of Origins." Great Plains Quarterly 3
    (Spring):67-78.
       Explores possible folk sources for Cather's story of the
    wolves and the bridal party in My Ántonia, citing recorded German
    Russian tales that follow the essential plotline of Cather's
    version. Very legitimate possibilities are Robert Browning's
    "Ivan Ivanovitch" and Mela Meisner Lindsay's "Shukar Balan: The
    White Lamb." Both may have been based on the same source.

28   SCHUETT, FAYE. "Place, Memory, and the Double-Life: Expe-
     riencing Willa Cather's Novels." Ph.D. dissertation, Univer-
     sity of Tulsa, 200 pp.
          Distinguishes three groups into which Cather's novels fall
     and indicates that those novels are similar not only in theme,
     but also in the artistic method through which each theme is pre-
     sented. In the first group Cather creates similar stories about
     "experiences of place"; in the second group she writes stories
     that are alike in that they "imitate psychological experiences of
     memory"; and in the third group Cather explores surface and inte-
     rior antitheses in human relationships, in other words, "expe-
     riences of the double-life." See Dissertation Abstracts Inter-
     national 44:1089A.

29   SCHWIND, JEAN DENISE. "Pictorial Art in Willa Cather's Fic-
     tion." Ph.D. dissertation, University of Minnesota, 249 pp.
          Referring to Cather's own comments on her work, asserts
     that pictorial art formed a basis for the narrative structure of
     Cather's fiction. Seeing Cather's work this way enhances under-
     standing of its complexities beyond what the characters them-
     selves understand. See Dissertation Abstracts International 44
     (1984):3687A.

30   STEGNER, WALLACE, and ETULAIN, RICHARD W. Conversations with
     Wallace Stegner on Western History and Literature. Salt Lake
     City: University of Utah Press, pp. 123-24, 129, 133-34.
          Presents Stegner's responses to Etulain's questions.
     Stegner includes Cather with several other writers who share
     certain defining characteristics that make them western writers:
     a sense of spaciousness, a certain attitude and manner, and a
     particular kind of subject matter. Stegner considers Cather to
     be a good model for those who wish to write serious novels about
     the West. She knew her material, and her works about Nebraska
     are better than those set elsewhere. Shadows on the Rock, for
     example, lacks the energy of My Ántonia, which may be the best
     novel extant about growing up in the pioneer West.

31   STERNSHEIN, MARY KEMPER. "The Land of Nebraska and Ántonia
     Shimerda." Heritage of the Great Plains 16 (Spring):34-42.
          The picture of the changing land and changing weather
     parallels the development of Ántonia. Both are tamed, in a
     sense, but both retain something of their wild, free spirit. In
     the end, Ántonia truly becomes an earth mother; she and the land
     are synonymous.

32   TUSKA, JON, and PIEKARSKI, VICKI, eds. Encyclopedia of
     Frontier and Western Fiction. New York: McGraw-Hill Book
     Co., pp. 41-44.
          Combines biography with general commentary on Cather's
     books that are set in the West, indicating that her pioneer sto-
     ries, because the land is integral to them rather than simply a
     superficial setting, are true "regional" works. Death Comes for
     the Archbishop has qualities that last, but it is not an histori-
     cal novel.

33   WILSON, D. RAY. <u>Nebraska Historical Tour Guide</u>. Carpenters-
     ville, Ill.: Crossroads Communications, pp. 188-91.
        Outlines Cather's life and career, then describes features
     of "Catherland," particularly buildings associated with the Willa
     Cather Pioneer Memorial and Educational Foundation.

34   WOODRESS, JAMES. Cather entry in <u>American Writers Since 1900</u>.
     St. James Reference Guide to American Literature, edited by
     James Vinson and D.L. Kirkpatrick. Chicago: St. James Press,
     pp. 129-32.
        Reprint of 1979.43.

35   _____, ed. Introduction to the Variorum Edition of <u>The Troll
     Garden</u>. Lincoln: University of Nebraska Press, pp. xi-xxx.
        Comments on Cather's artistic development in the short
     story through brief references to some stories that precede those
     in <u>The Troll Garden</u>, then discusses each of the stories in the
     collection in relation to the troll garden theme alluded to in
     Cather's two epigraphs to the book. The central tensions in <u>The
     Troll Garden</u>, and in Cather's work generally, are the pulls to-
     ward East and West, civilization and primitivism.

                              <u>1984</u>

1   al-GHALITH, ASAD MOHAMMED. "The Function of Light Imagery in
     the Fiction of Willa Cather." Ph.D. dissertation, West
     Virginia University, 176 pp.
        Discusses Cather's use of light imagery in her twelve
     novels and in selected pieces of short fiction. Her method is
     similar to that of impressionist painters, and the images she
     draws evoke the emotional quality of her scenes. She also uses
     light imagery to reveal character and to emphasize theme. See
     <u>Dissertation Abstracts International</u> 45:1397A.

2   ARNOLD, MARILYN. "Cather's Last Three Stories: A Testament
     of Life and Endurance." <u>Great Plains Quarterly</u> 4 (Fall):
     238-44.
        Suggests that Cather's final stories, the three collected
     in <u>The Old Beauty and Others</u>, constitute a culmination of her
     lifelong struggle with two opposing inclinations--the urge to
     meet life head-on, and the urge to escape from its painful losses
     and changes. "The Old Beauty," with its condemnation of one who
     denies life and lives in the past; "The Best Years," with its
     glowing picture of life and love, and its stoic acceptance of
     change; and "Before Breakfast," with its triumph over doubt and
     its celebration of the human capacity to survive, are the final
     stages of a pattern that began early in Cather's career. <u>A Lost
     Lady</u>, which was anticipated by "The Way of the World" (1898),
     shows Cather's appreciation for Marian Forrester's determination
     to survive and thus serves as an important step in the evolution
     of that pattern.

3   _____. "Coming, Willa Cather!" Women's Studies 11:247-60.
     Argues that Cather's "Coming, Aphrodite!" effectively re-
futes the popular critical contention that she priggishly avoided
the subject of male and female sexuality. In this short story
Cather meets the subject head-on, creating in the two lovers, Don
Hedger and Eden Bower, the very symbols of the elemental and complementary sexual roles of man and woman. Further, in Eden's
ultimate rejection of Hedger, in favor of her career, a note of
authorial regret can be detected. In this story Cather may be
questioning the choice for art over more fundamental human
drives.

4   _____. Willa Cather's Short Fiction. Athens: Ohio Univer-
     sity Press, 213 pp.
     Introduces all of Cather's short stories in rough chrono-
logical order, relating them to her artistic development and her
other writings as well as providing interpretive commentary.
Insists that Cather's work is all of a piece, and that her short
fiction often serves to bind the whole together in terms of theme
and setting. The better known stories are given full discussion,
as are many others that have been virtually ignored by critics
in the past. Cather proves herself a master of the short story
as well as the novel.

5   BENNETT, MILDRED R., and ROSOWSKI, SUSAN J. "Willa Cather
     Today: An Introduction." Great Plains Quarterly 4 (Fall):
     211-12.
     Introduces the essays in this special Cather issue of Great
Plains Quarterly, all of which, in some form, were presented at
the second national seminar on Cather, held in Hastings and Red
Cloud, Nebraska, in 1983. The authors note that Cather was very
much associated with a particular place, but at the same time her
life was full of movement, journeys. The essays in the present
volume show the many paths taken by Cather studies today.

6   BETTS, GLYNNE ROBINSON. "At Home with America's Writers."
     Adventure Road 20 (November-December):18-21, 26.
     Cather is one of four writers whose homes are described,
particularly in terms of their influence on their gifted
occupants.

7   BLOOM, EDWARD A., and BLOOM, LILLIAN D. "Willa Cather and the
     Tradition." In Critical Essays on Willa Cather. See Murphy,
     1984.55, pp. 39-48.
     Reprinted from 1962.2.

8   BOHLING, BETH. "The Husband of My Ántonia." Western American
     Literature 19 (May):29-39.
     Compares the fictional characters, Anton Cuzak and Anton
Rosicky, with their real life prototype, John Pavelka, and concludes that Cather used actual details about Pavelka when it
suited her artistic purposes to do so. When it did not, she
invented whatever circumstances she needed to advance her stories.

9   BOHLKE, L. BRENT. "Willa Cather's Nebraska Priests and Death
     Comes for the Archbishop." Great Plains Quarterly 4 (Fall):
     264-69.
        In creating Fathers Jean Latour and Joseph Vaillant in
     Death Comes for the Archbishop, Cather used not only the lives of
     two French priests who served as missionaries in the New Mexico
     territory, but also the characters and experiences of her own
     Nebraska priests, George Allen Beecher and John Mallory Bates.
     Both of them traveled many miles in sparsely settled country to
     minister to their flocks, and Bishop Beecher built a cathedral.
     Cather herself was a "sacramentalist who saw the entire world as
     a possible vehicle for the action of God in his creation."

10   BOURNE, RANDOLPH. Review of My Ántonia. In Critical Essays
     on Willa Cather. See Murphy, 1984.55, pp. 145-46.
        Reprint of 1918.1.

11   BRANDE, DOROTHEA. Review of Lucy Gayheart. In Critical
     Essays on Willa Cather. See Murphy, 1984.55, pp. 282-84.
        Reprint of 1935.5.

12   BUCCO, MARTIN. Western American Literary Criticism. Boise
     State University Western Writers Series, no. 62. Boise,
     Idaho: Boise State University, 55 pp., passim.
        Mentions Cather throughout in connection with critical
     statements about her work by a variety of commentators. Also
     treats Cather as a critic on pp. 34-35, noting her youthful
     critical responses to such writers as Mark Twain and Frank
     Norris. Points particularly to the importance of her views about
     writers and writing in Willa Cather on Writing.

13   CANBY, HENRY SEIDEL. Review of Obscure Destinies. In Criti-
     cal Essays on Willa Cather. See Murphy, 1984.55, pp. 280-82.
        Reprint of 1932.8.

14   _____. Review of The Professor's House. In Critical Essays
     on Willa Cather. See Murphy, 1984.55, pp. 198-200.
        Reprint of 1925.8.

15   "Cather Scholar Disagrees with Lesbian Conclusion." Omaha
     World-Herald, 3 November, p. 4.
        Reports responses of two Cather scholars, Susan J. Rosowski
     and Mildred R. Bennett, to an article by O'Brien (1984.63) that
     assumes Cather's lesbianism largely on the basis of two admiring
     letters Cather wrote as a young woman to Louise Pound. Bennett
     sees them as letters of the school-girl crush variety with no
     significance beyond that, and Rosowski questions the automatic
     labeling of an emotional attachment to a woman as lesbian.

16   CHANG, L[OH-] C[HI]. "Willa Cather and China." Willa Cather
      Pioneer Memorial Newsletter 28, no. 1:1-4.
         Outlines the very basic similarities between the values of
      the Chinese people and the values Cather espouses in her work,
      stressing Cather's artistry and her universal appeal. Like the
      Chinese, Cather has a special feeling for the land, for the
      family unit, and for tradition; and her characters often practice
      a modest frugality typical of the Chinese. Furthermore, many of
      her characters could have been drawn right out of the Chinese
      countryside.

17   COMEAU, PAUL. "The Professor's House and Anatole France." In
      Critical Essays on Willa Cather. See Murphy, 1984.55,
      pp. 217-27.
         Explores the significance of Cather's several allusions in
      The Professor's House, both direct and indirect, to Anatole
      France. Concludes that although Cather's purpose varied from
      France's, the French novelist provided a model in Le mannequin
      d'osier that gave Cather an imaginative direction in pursuing her
      themes of betrayal and alienation.

18   COOPER, FREDERICK TABER. Review of O Pioneers! In Critical
      Essays on Willa Cather. See Murphy, 1984.55, pp. 112-13.
         Reprint of 1913.2.

19   COOPERMAN, STANLEY. "The War Lover: Claude." In Critical
      Essays on Willa Cather. See Murphy, 1984.55, pp. 169-76.
         Reprinted from 1967.7.

20   COUSINEAU, DIANE. "Division and Difference in A Lost Lady."
      Women's Studies 11:305-22.
         Treats the complexities inherent in Cather's choosing, in
      A Lost Lady, to portray a male narrator in his role as an ini-
      tiate into a patriarchal culture. In that culture he encounters
      a fascinating woman who both asserts her sexual difference from
      him and ambiguously allows herself to be identified through the
      masculine as merely its opposite. Explores this phenomenon
      largely through Freudian analysis of Cather's adherence to or
      contradiction of the various roles that figure in "the structure
      of family romance." Captain Forrester, for example, is the
      stable father figure for Niel Herbert, but he makes no allowances
      for the future and hence contributes to the crumbling of the
      social and sexual construct that his ideal has created.

21   CROSS, WILBUR. Review of Shadows on the Rock. In Critical
      Essays on Willa Cather. See Murphy, 1984.55, pp. 266-68.
         Reprint of 1931.15.

22   DICKINSON, JOAN YOUNGER. "Willa Cather and the Priest."
      Impact: Albuquerque Journal Magazine, 7 August, pp. 11-13.
         Compares Cather's Jean Latour in Death Comes for the Arch-
      bishop with her model, Bishop Lamy, and concludes that although
      Cather borrowed many things from the life of the actual priest

for her novel, in traits of personality Latour is more like
Cather herself than he is like Lamy.

23   DILLMAN, RICHARD. "Tom Outland, Emerson's American Scholar in
      The Professor's House." Midwest Quarterly 25 (Summer):375-85.
         Argues that Tom Outland closely approximates the character-
      istics of Emerson's ideal American scholar; he is self-reliant,
      unified, intelligent, perceptive, outgoing, and at home in
      nature. Being what he is, however, Tom cannot survive in a
      modern materialistic culture, and his inevitable death represents
      the tragic fall of America from the garden of Transcendentalism
      into pragmatism and materialism.

24   DOANE, MARGARET. "In Defense of Lillian St. Peter: Men's
      Perceptions of Women in The Professor's House." Western
      American Literature 18 (February):299-302.
         Observes that the male characters in The Professor's House
      typically make disparaging comments about women, and argues that
      the most damaging are those made by Godfrey St. Peter because he
      is the book's center of consciousness. His biases and insensi-
      tivities are often wrongly assumed to indicate a negative view of
      the women in the book, especially St. Peter's wife and daughters.

25   DRUCKER, LINDA. "Drama Redraws Cather Character." Lincoln
      Journal, 5 October.
         Describes the ways in which Albuquerque poet, playwright,
      professor, and museum curator, E.A. Mares, contrasted his view of
      the real Padre Martinez with Cather's portrayal of the New Mexico
      priest in Death Comes for the Archbishop. Mares made his point
      partly through a dramatization in which he reversed Cather's
      picture, representing Martinez as a devout, forward-looking
      visionary who tried to save his people and their artistic tradi-
      tions by bucking the destructive, uncomprehending decrees of
      French priest Lamy. Death Comes for the Archbishop, Mares
      claimed, is racist, with white Europeans at the top of the scale
      and New Mexico Indians at the bottom. Cather would not have
      dared to write it today.

26   EDEL, LEON. "A Cave of One's Own." In Critical Essays on
      Willa Cather. See Murphy, 1984.55, pp. 200-17.
         Reprint of 1982.23.

27   EICHORN, HARRY B[ERNARD]. "A Falling Out With Love: My
      Mortal Enemy." In Critical Essays on Willa Cather. See
      Murphy, 1984.55, pp. 230-43.
         Reprint of 1973.22.

28   FISHER, DOROTHY CANFIELD. Review of One of Ours. In Critical
      Essays on Willa Cather. See Murphy, 1984.55, pp. 165-68.
         Reprint of 1922.11.

29   _____. Review of Sapphira and the Slave Girl. In Critical
      Essays on Willa Cather. See Murphy, 1984.55, pp. 284-86.
         Reprint of 1940.7.

30 FORMAN, HENRY JAMES. Review of A Lost Lady. In Critical
    Essays on Willa Cather. See Murphy, 1984.55, pp. 177–78.
    Reprint of 1923.21.

31 GELFANT, BLANCHE H. "The Forgotten Reaping-Hook: Sex in My
    Ántonia." In Critical Essays on Willa Cather. See Murphy,
    1984.55, pp. 147–64.
    Reprint of 1971.11.

32 _____. "The Forgotten Reaping-Hook: Sex in My Ántonia." In
    Women Writing in America. See Gelfant, 1984.33, pp. 93–116,
    257–58.
    Reprint of 1971.11.

33 _____. Introduction to Women Writing in America: Voices in
    Collage. Hanover, N.H.: University Press of New England,
    pp. 1–9 passim.
         Introduction to a collection of Gelfant's essays describes
    the way in which women writers like Cather develop "narrative
    strategies" in order to conceal their sometimes nontraditional
    themes and manners in traditional guises. Cather is also men-
    tioned on numerous other pages (see index), some of which refer
    to the violence that erupts in her pages and her belief that
    desire lies at the core of art. The chapter on Ethel Wilson
    (pp. 164–65) speaks of Cather's interest in character and the
    fact that whatever her women characters do, they sense themselves
    to be a part of something significant and larger than they are.

34 _____. "'Lives' of Women Writers: Cather, Austin, Porter /
    and Willa, Mary, Katherine Anne." In Women Writing in
    America. See Gelfant, 1984.33, pp. 225–48 passim, 271–72
    passim.
         Considers what it is that biographers do when attempting
    to write the "lives" of artists. Notes especially the weaknesses
    in the Robinson biography (see 1983.25) of Cather and the "Willa"
    Robinson creates. Argues that the biographical character "Willa"
    may be someone quite different from the artist "Cather," who
    exists in her books. In part, "Willa" was shaped by role expec-
    tations in her society, but she nevertheless had the same freedom
    the male artist had to pursue her life and art and become
    "Cather." A great many women writers of her time did not have
    that freedom, though Austin and Porter did.

35 _____. "Movement and Melody: The Disembodiment of Lucy
    Gayheart." In Women Writing in America. See Gelfant,
    1984.33, pp. 117–43, 258–66.
         Urges a reassessment of Lucy Gayheart, suggesting that it
    offers important clues for understanding Cather's evolving feel-
    ings about life and art. In the novel Cather uses the trappings
    and characters of popular romance, heightening them into the
    abstract ideas and feelings of the romantic imagination--feelings
    that seem to be readily conveyed through music, but less easily
    evoked through words. In this way, Cather reveals her own strug-
    gle as an artist who has only words to express the inexpressible.

One could try to create art out of words, but one could not make it last. Cather had Lucy die physically in order to make her live in another sense: the creation of a living abstraction behind the writer's words is the only hope for immortality. But Cather was never sure that such a hope could be realized.

36 GEORGE, BENJAMIN. "The French-Canadian Connection: Willa Cather as Canadian Writer." In Critical Essays on Willa Cather. See Murphy, 1984.55, pp. 269–79.
    Reprint of 1976.7.

37 GIANNONE, RICHARD [JOHN]. "The Lyric Artist." In Critical Essays on Willa Cather. See Murphy, 1984.55, pp. 130–44.
    Reprinted from 1968.18.

38 GRIFFITHS, FREDERICK T. "The Woman Warrior: Willa Cather and One of Ours." Women's Studies 11:261–85.
    Declares that a close examination of One of Ours reveals a complexity beneath the surface that has not been seen or appreciated by critics to date. Explores a pervasive pattern of mirrors and reversals in the novel in which Cather uses the literary tradition of the war epic to establish a counterpoint between Claude's expectations of World War I and the war's actual realities. Central myths of the male warrior and the female nurturer are reversed in Cather's suggestion that Jeanne d'Arc is the heroic warrior image while the masculine image can be that of nurturer. The direction of the quest myth is also reversed, moving from new world to old.

39 GRUMBACH, DORIS. "A Study of the Small Room in The Professor's House." Women's Studies 11:327–45.
    Sees in the several small upstairs rooms that served as private sanctuaries for Cather over the years parallels to the upstairs study cherished by Godfrey St. Peter in his old house. Argues that St. Peter escapes to this room to get away from the demands of wife and family, demands that he comes to realize are foreign to his most essential self. That self is the person he was before he married, the person whose one great love was his student, Tom Outland. Like his earlier counterpart in the slight story, "The Professor's Commencement," St. Peter suffers deep depression in middle age. His brush with death reconciles him to the truth that one cannot be one's true self in this life if so being would mean living outside the social expectations and stringencies of heterosexual love, marriage, and family.

40 _____. "Willa Cather: An Introduction." Written as a part of Nickols, 1984[?].62, pp. 51, 53.
    Offers a general overview of Cather's life, indicating that her continuing popularity with American readers may lie in the shared appeal of her "reverence for the past," her "deep conservatism," and her romanticism. Furthermore, she "celebrated heroism among American women."

41   GWIN, MINROSE CLAYTON. "The Peculiar Sisterhood: Black and
      White Women of the Old South in American Literature." Ph.D.
      dissertation, University of Tennessee, 148 pp.
          Explores the violent "connection" between black and white
      women in two novels set in the nineteenth century, three set in
      the twentieth, and seven autobiographies of southern women.
      Sapphira Colbert's cruelty to her slave Nancy in Sapphira and the
      Slave Girl is examined as a case study of the evil use of power.
      See Dissertation Abstracts International 45:182A.

42   HAMNER, EUGÉNIE LAMBERT. "The Unknown, Well-Known Child in
      Cather's Last Novel." Women's Studies 11:347-57.
          Concludes, after exploring the question of the identity of
      the five-year-old child who narrates the epilogue of Sapphira and
      the Slave Girl, that the shift from the omnipresent narrative
      point of view to the child's point of view is an artistic fault
      that is nevertheless a happy event for the reader. Because the
      epilogue was born out of Cather's renewed memories of an impor-
      tant childhood event for her, the reader gains new insights into
      Cather and her development as a storyteller.

43   HELMICK, EVELYN THOMAS. "The Broken World: Medievalism in A
      Lost Lady." In Critical Essays on Willa Cather. See Murphy,
      1984.55, pp. 179-86.
          Reprint of 1975.24.

44   HUGHES, HOLLY. "Willa Cather's Enchanted Bluff." A "meet the
      author" introduction to a reprint of "The Enchanted Bluff."
      Literary Cavalcade 36 (April):6.
          Cather's roots are deep in the Nebraska landscape, and her
      chief interest is in the everyday flow of life. Her work is
      typified by the nostalgic qualities of "The Enchanted Bluff."

45   KATHE, BARBARA A. "The Influence of the Past: Metamorphosis
      in Willa Cather's Heroines." American Studies in Scandinavia
      16, no. 1:37-44.
          Holds that Cather's nostalgic attachment to the past caused
      her to transform her vibrant, human pioneer heroines into static,
      devitalized mythic figures. Sapphira Colbert is the culminating
      character in this process--cold, forbidding, devoid of sexual or
      emotional energy.

46   KEELER, CLINTON. "Narrative Without Accent: Willa Cather and
      Puvis de Chavannes." In Critical Essays on Willa Cather. See
      Murphy, 1984.55, pp. 251-57.
          Reprint of 1965.21.

47   KIMBEL, ELLEN. "The American Short Story: 1900-1920." In
      The American Short Story, 1900-1945: A Critical History.
      Edited by Philip Stevick. Boston: Twayne Publishers,
      pp. 34, 41-42, 51-59.
          Discusses the stories in The Troll Garden and Youth and
      the Bright Medusa, seeing in both groups Cather's repeated treat-
      ment of her favorite theme: the artist or person of special

gifts in conflict with, and thus in isolation from, an uncomprehending society. Concentrates mainly on "A Death in the Desert,"
"The Sculptor's Funeral," and "Paul's Case," arguing that the
earlier stories have a vitality and poignancy that is missing
from the later ones--perhaps because Cather was too close to the
artistic world when she wrote the later stories.

48   KRONENBERGER, LOUIS. Review of My Mortal Enemy. In Critical
     Essays on Willa Cather. See Murphy, 1984.55, pp. 228-30.
          Reprint of 1926.13.

49   McKEE, JAMES L. "Willa Cather: Narrative Beginnings in
     Lincoln." In Lincoln the Prairie Capital: An Illustrated
     History. Woodland Hills, Calif.: Windsor Publications,
     p. 75.
          Essentially a biography of Cather's career that emphasizes
     her Nebraska years, especially those spent in Lincoln.

50   MAXFIELD, JAMES F. "Strategies of Self-Deception in Willa
     Cather's Professor's House." Studies in the Novel 16
     (Spring):72-86.
          Argues that The Professor's House is not totally explained
     by the psychological interpretations of Leon Edel (see 1954.3).
     The principal source of Godfrey St. Peter's growing disillusion-
     ment and depression is the feeling that he has become subject to
     coercive circumstances which have robbed him of control over his
     own life. Essentially, his passion and energy shifted from his
     wife to his multivolume history of Spanish conquerors, and when
     it was completed he was left with a void in his life. Given his
     nature, it would be nearly impossible for him to take Augusta as
     his model, even though he seems ready to do so. She has spent
     her life in service to her fellow mortals; his values, on the
     other hand, celebrate romances of the imagination and individual
     solitude.

51   MENCKEN, H.L. Review of Alexander's Bridge. In Critical
     Essays on Willa Cather. See Murphy, 1984.55, pp. 96-97.
          Reprint of 1912.3.

52   MILLER, JAMES E., Jr. "Willa Cather Today." Great Plains
     Quarterly 4 (Fall):270-77.
          Points to several false starts in Cather criticism in
     recent years, then suggests some possibilities for interpretation
     of The Professor's House that have not been given the attention
     they deserve. One particularly rich area is the book's "remark-
     able ending," full of "intentional ambiguities."

53   MORROW, NANCY. "Willa Cather's A Lost Lady and the Nineteenth
     Century Novel of Adultery." Women's Studies 11:287-303.
          Observes that A Lost Lady has frequently been compared with
     Madame Bovary. It does indeed resemble, in some respects, the
     nineteenth-century novels of adultery that were especially popu-
     lar among European writers. A Lost Lady, however, differs from
     those novels particularly in its refusal to consider the moral

implications--for family and society--of Marian Forrester's
adultery. The principle that is foremost in A Lost Lady, as it
is in works like Anna Karenina and The Scarlet Letter, is an
artistic one, not a moral one.

54   MURPHY, JOHN J. "A Comprehensive View of Cather's O Pioneers!"
      In Critical Essays on Willa Cather. See Murphy, 1984.55,
      pp. 113-27.
           Observes O Pioneers! to be multidimensional, with Alexandra
      Bergson serving to unify the book through her creative power and
      eventual comprehensive vision. One dimension of the book devel-
      ops several aspects of the Genesis story--the Creation and the
      Fall, the account of Isaac, and the embodiment of Noah in Crazy
      Ivar. Beyond that, the novel is a clear presentation of domestic
      drama with its accompanying satirical portraits of Lou and Oscar
      Bergson and their families. Further, O Pioneers! examines the
      nature of four love relationships and develops the cosmic vision
      employed by Walt Whitman. Alexandra figures prominently in each
      of the novel's dimensions.

55   _____, ed. Critical Essays on Willa Cather. Critical Essays
      on American Literature, edited by James Nagel. Boston: G.K.
      Hall & Co., 318 pp.
           Provides a few original essays (see Comeau 1984.17; Murphy
      1984.54; Stouck 1984.87; Woodress 1984.94), plus a representative
      sampling of criticism on Cather's work, beginning with general
      estimates and then moving to essays and reviews of each of the
      novels and the last two story collections. Contains reprints of
      or from the following: 1912.3; 1913.2; 1915.5; 1918.1; 1922.11;
      1923.21; 1925.8; 1926.13; 1927.36; 1931.15; 1932.8; 1935.5;
      1940.7; 1948.21; 1952.11; 1960.9; 1962.2; 1965.21; 1967.7;
      1968.18; 1971.11; 1973.22, 71; 1974.79; 1975.24; 1976.7; 1977.26;
      1978.19, 21; 1982.23.

56   _____. "Nebraska Naturalism in Jamesian Frames." Great
      Plains Quarterly 4 (Fall):231-37.
           Detects in Cather's work the same kinds of materials being
      used by her contemporaries who wrote with a naturalistic bias,
      but sees her using them in the manner of Henry James and the
      impressionistic painters. In Cather, as in James, the materials
      are viewed through a detached observer with a highly developed
      consciousness, one who actually organizes the materials, creates
      the world he inhabits. My Ántonia is a good example of the
      reconciling nature of Cather's method, a method in which she
      introduces naturalistic violence and adventure--and a Words-
      worthian primitivism--by passing them through the refined sensi-
      bilities of a Jamesian consciousness.

57   _____. "Willa Cather and Religion: Highway to the World and
      Beyond." Literature and Belief 4:49-68.
           In early revolt-from-the-village fiction Cather is criti-
      cal of the Protestant ethic and revivalism, but there is
      change after One of Ours, and deep religious struggles charac-
      terize The Professor's House and My Mortal Enemy. Cather turns

toward the Catholic past in these crucial novels, which with
Death Comes for the Archbishop and Shadows on the Rock echo
Dante, the Grail legend, religious history, and scriptures.
Self-denial develops as a dominant Cather theme.

58   _____ . "Willa Cather's Archbishop: A Western and Classical
Perspective." In Critical Essays on Willa Cather. See
Murphy, 1984.55, pp. 258-65.
        Reprint of 1978.19.

59   _____ . "Willa Cather's Children of Grace." Willa Cather
Pioneer Memorial Newsletter 28 (Summer):13-15.
        Discusses three of Cather's short stories--"Jack-a-Boy,"
"The Joy of Nelly Deane," and "The Best Years"--as examples of
Cather's portrayal of "children of Grace" who create a redemptive
sense of family or community among their fellow mortals.

60   MURPHY, JOHN J., and SYNNOTT, KEVIN A. "The Recognition of
Willa Cather's Art." Introduction to Critical Essays on Willa
Cather. See Murphy, 1984.55, pp. 1-28.
        Provides a chronological review and evaluation of Cather
criticism over the years and then discusses the trends Cather
scholarship has taken, starting with the biographical studies
that began appearing after Cather's death. Emphasis has ranged
from psychological studies and considerations of Cather's concern
for values to studies of Classical influence.

61   NICHOLS, KATHLEEN L. "The Celibate Male in A Lost Lady: The
Unreliable Center of Consciousness." In Critical Essays on
Willa Cather. See Murphy, 1984.55, pp. 186-97.
        Reprint of 1978.21.

62   NICKOLS, THELMA. "The Canon of Willa Cather." In West Coast
Review of Books, [ca. 1984], pp. 50-51, 54, 59.
        Refers to the dramatic program about Cather on National
Public Radio, and characterizes Cather as a writer who incorporated her strong moral values and religious sense into her fiction. Lists all of the books that collect Cather stories, and in
addition provides an annotated listing of many of her lesser
known stories.

63   O'BRIEN, SHARON. "'The Thing Not Named': Willa Cather as a
Lesbian Writer." Signs: Journal of Women in Culture and
Society 9 (Summer):576-99.
        Assumes Cather's "lesbianism," that is, her emotional
attachment primarily to women, on the grounds of her letters as
a young woman to Louise Pound. Cather was reaching maturity at
a time when her culture, which had previously seen romantic
attachments between young women as normal, was beginning to regard such attachments as deviant. Thus, unlike Sarah Orne Jewett,
Cather was not free to "name" or write about such attachments.
Therefore, she masked them. Argues that criticism should begin
to recognize that Cather's lesbianism and her need to hide it

produced a tension between what is said and what is left unsaid
in her fiction. This gives a subtlety and a richness to her work
that would not otherwise be realized.

64   O'CONNOR, KAREN. "An American Pioneer." In Contributions of
     Women: Literature. Minneapolis: Dillon Press, pp. 29–49.
          Outlines for youthful readership Cather's life and career,
     but does not make critical comment on her work. Claims that
     Cather was extremely independent as a young woman, but that as
     she grew older she became increasingly averse to change.

65   O'CONNOR, MARGARET ANNE, ed. Introduction to special Cather
     issue of Women's Studies 11:219–21.
          Introduces each of the essays appearing in the volume and
     defines the purpose of the collection to be a consideration of
     the woman as artist, the effect of gender upon Cather's art, and
     the perception of her art by the male critical establishment.

66   PANNILL, LINDA. "Willa Cather's Artist-Heroines." Women's
     Studies 11:223–32.
          Argues that Cather resolved the conflict in herself between
     artist and woman by following in her own life the course she set
     for Thea Kronborg in The Song of the Lark. Thea detaches herself
     from conventional attitudes and role considerations and devotes
     herself wholly to art. In this way the woman artist remains a
     woman, but she is not like other women.

67   PERS, MONA. "Willa Cather and the Swedes." Great Plains
     Quarterly 4 (Fall):213–19.
          Describes Cather's critical reception in Sweden, noting
     that she is one of the American writers most frequently trans-
     lated into Swedish, but that like most other American writers
     before Sinclair Lewis was awarded the Nobel Prize, she was not
     accorded major attention. Cather was very interested in the
     Scandinavian market, and Swedish critics praised her for her
     artistic excellence.

68   PIACENTINO, EDWARD J. "Flower Imagery in a Willa Cather
     Novel." Platte Valley Review 12 (Spring):66–72.
          Points to many places in A Lost Lady where various kinds of
     flowers are associated with Marian Forrester. Through these
     floral images Cather is able to show Niel Herbert's initial
     idealistic attitude toward Marian, his later disillusionment, and
     his mature return to regard for her. Flower imagery is particu-
     larly well-suited to the circumstances of this novel because of
     the transitory nature of floral life and beauty.

69   POORE, CHARLES. Review of The Old Beauty and Others. In
     Critical Essays on Willa Cather. See Murphy, 1984.55,
     pp. 286–90.
          Reprint of 1948.21.

70   PORTER, KATHERINE ANNE. "Critical Reflections on Willa
      Cather." In Critical Essays on Willa Cather. See Murphy,
      1984.55, pp. 31-39.
          Reprint of 1952.11.

71   RANDALL, JOHN H., III. "Summary of Death Comes for the Arch-
      bishop: The Cathedral and the Stagecoach." In Critical
      Essays on Willa Cather. See Murphy, 1984.55, pp. 247-51.
          Reprinted from 1960.9.

72   Review of The Song of the Lark. In Critical Essays on Willa
      Cather. See Murphy, 1984.55, pp. 128-30.
          Reprint of 1915.5.

73   ROBINSON, DORIS. Women Novelists, 1891-1920: An Index to
      Biographical and Autobiographical Sources. New York: Garland
      Publishing, pp. 58-61.
          Provides primarily sources of biographical data on Cather,
      including a catalogue of standard reference works that contain
      Cather entries as well as biographical works that feature her.
      Also lists one autobiographical source, one bibliographical
      source, and seven sources of obituaries.

74   ROSOWSKI, SUSAN J. "Willa Cather: Living History." In
      Perspectives: Women in Nebraska History. Special issue of
      the Nebraska Department of Education and the Nebraska State
      Council for the Social Studies, edited by Susan Pierce. June,
      pp. 80-96.
          Discusses most of Cather's novels as illustrations of her
      response to history and thus to time. She regards history as
      most meaningful when it is a personal experience. For example,
      in O Pioneers!, My Ántonia, and Sapphira and the Slave Girl,
      objects and stories from the past are fused with the present to
      create for an individual a "personal sense of history." By con-
      trast, the past is separated from the present for characters in
      One of Ours, A Lost Lady, The Professor's House, and My Mortal
      Enemy. Ironically, Cather's novels most commonly called "his-
      torical novels," Death Comes for the Archbishop and Shadows on
      the Rock, are actually her least historical in the modern sense
      of that term because they portray characters who are unaffected,
      rather than affected, by social change. Characteristically,
      Cather sees history as something that people live.

75   _____. "Willa Cather's American Gothic: Sapphira and the
      Slave Girl." Great Plains Quarterly 4 (Fall):220-30.
          Suggests that in her last novel Cather actually creates an
      American Gothic using old world conventions but new world forms.
      Sapphira, at least until late in the novel, is the Gothic hero-
      villain, the master of the castle (the Mill House) who irration-
      ally plots the ruin of an innocent young woman. Using Sapphira
      and the Slave Girl as a "lens" through which to view Cather's
      other books, we can better see and understand "the threat of the
      irrational" that pervades Cather's writing, especially in charac-
      ters like the Wick Cutters in My Ántonia.

76   _____. "Willa Cather's Female Landscapes: The Song of the
    Lark and Lucy Gayheart." Women's Studies 11:233–46.
        Sees in The Song of the Lark and Lucy Gayheart a "relation-
    ship between gender and consciousness." In The Song of the Lark,
    however, Thea Kronborg's developing female imagination expands
    and asserts itself upon its world, while in Lucy Gayheart Lucy's
    desire for protective security, represented through a series of
    static, womblike images and through Lucy's desire for Clement
    Sebastian's security, encloses her female imagination and keeps
    it from expressing itself creatively. Lucy is prefigured by
    Nelly, heroine of an early story, "The Joy of Nelly Deane." Just
    as Lucy is attended and smothered into a constricting role by
    Sebastian, so is Nelly attended and smothered into a constricting
    role by the three old women (suggesting "the fates") who dote on
    her.

77   ROSOWSKI, SUSAN, and SLOTE, BERNICE. "Willa Cather's 1916
    Mesa Verde Essay: The Genesis of The Professor's House."
    Prairie Schooner 58 (Winter):81–92.
        Reprints a heretofore unknown essay written by Cather and
    published in 1916 in the Denver Times, suggesting that the essay,
    which recounts Cather's only visit to Mesa Verde, is the "real
    genesis" of The Professor's House. There are many parallels
    between the essay and the novel, and many transformations and
    refinements of earlier impressions and language. Furthermore,
    the conclusion of the essay, which treats Cather's "return to the
    present as a new beginning," suggests a less pessimistic inter-
    pretation of Godfrey St. Peter's return to society and family
    than is generally accorded it.

78   RYERSON, NED. "From the Tree House." Women's Studies 11:
    359–68.
        Reflects, in a personal memoir, on Ryerson's experience of
    finding intimacy in the isolation of a family cabin and the tree
    house he and his brother built there. Relates that experience to
    Ryerson's reading of Cather's stories about strong women like his
    mother for whom life was a search for intimacy as one struggled
    with the "dark knowledge" it held. Cather wrote of women who
    endured in spite of "the threatening forces of the class strug-
    gle, the loss of the past and a nostalgia for it, the ordinari-
    ness of small town and farming life, the hardships of prairie
    existence, and the presence of male brutality" that made intimacy
    difficult to achieve except in fleeting moments.

79   SALLQUIST, SYLVIA LEA. "The Image of the Hired Girl in
    Literature: The Great Plains 1860 to World War I." Great
    Plains Quarterly 4 (Summer):166–77.
        Seeks to discover who the midwestern hired girls were and
    why they hired out. Cites My Ántonia extensively because it, of
    all the works studied, contains the most detailed treatment of
    hired girls. Cather finds the uneducated girls to be much wiser
    than the town girls or than their younger siblings who have
    greater advantages. Cather's heroines lead spicy, exciting lives
    at odds with social norms, but because they possess heroic

qualities, Ántonia and the three Bohemian Marys later marry and rear large families, hardly the typical outcome for "fallen" women in nineteenth-century fiction.

80 SCHWIND, JEAN [DENISE]. "The 'Beautiful' War in One of Ours." Modern Fiction Studies 30 (Spring):53–72.
    Insists that One of Ours makes a clear separation between Claude's view of World War I and Cather's. Claude, lacking a "new world aesthetic," idealizes the war experience, while Cather, in her important final chapter, takes a very different view.

81 SHAW, PATRICK W. "My Ántonia: Emergence and Authorial Revelations." American Literature 56 (December):527–40.
    Traces the motif of submergence and emergence in My Ántonia as it applies to and explains what was happening to Jim Burden during the twenty-year hiatus in the novel. In that time he was moving toward a new concept of his relationship with Ántonia, toward a union that released him into the future because it transcended sexual concerns. In this union Cather is able to effect the two selves of her own nature which, after submergence in deference to social norms, are allowed emergence and transcendence in her art.

82 SLOTE, BERNICE. Introduction to Alexander's Bridge. In Critical Essays on Willa Cather. See Murphy, 1984.55, pp. 97–111.
    Reprint of 1977.26.

83 SMITH, CARL S. Chicago and the American Literary Imagination 1880–1920. Chicago: University of Chicago Press, pp. 53–56.
    Discusses Cather's The Song of the Lark as American literature's only major treatment of the dedicated woman artist in the city. Cather does not sentimentalize her depiction of the artist's struggle, nor does she suggest that art can address social concerns or redeem the city's essential sordidness. Rather art, which paradoxically can flourish only in the city, provides experiences through which the commercial city is transcended.

84 SMITH HAWKINS, ELAINE YVONNE. "Ideals and Imagination in the Novels of Willa Cather." Ph.D. dissertation, Stanford University, 255 pp.
    Traces the evolution of Cather's belief in ideals and her treatment of them. Observes that she made idealists the heroes of her early novels, but then she became interested in the nature of the imagination that constructs ideals. Cather became disillusioned in the 1920s, however, and produced a number of "dark" novels. Eventually, she worked through her despair and concluded that the impulse to strive for ideals endures; stories and memories preserve the striving imagination. See Dissertation Abstracts International 45:185A.

85   STINEBACK, DAVID [C.]. "The Case of Willa Cather." Canadian
     Review of American Studies 15 (Winter):385-95.
          Charges Cather critics in general, and a few in particular,
     with grossly misreading Cather. Critics have become so intent on
     calling her nostalgic and psychoanalyzing her that they have
     failed to see what she is really doing in her fiction. In fact,
     Cather's work does not dwell particularly on the past; rather,
     it concentrates on the complexity and mystery of human relation-
     ship. In roughly the first half of her career Cather focuses on
     heterosexual and inner self relationships; in the second half she
     explores with great skill and subtlety same-sex relationships.
     "Old Mrs. Harris" is discussed in some detail as an example of
     Cather's skill in handling such relationships, relationships in
     which communication is largely on an intuitive rather than an
     overt or sexually intimate level.

86   STOUCK, DAVID. Review of The Troll Garden. Great Plains
     Quarterly 4 (Fall):278.
          Review of the 1983 variorum edition of Cather's first col-
     lection of stories notes the importance of Cather's stories be-
     cause of their thematic ties to her novels and the insights they
     provide into the development of her art.

87   _____. "Willa Cather and the Impressionist Novel." In
     Critical Essays on Willa Cather. See Murphy, 1984.55,
     pp. 48-66.
          Considers Cather's artistic relationship with impressionist
     and symbolist painters and writers, especially the French writers
     Prosper Mérimée, Gustave Flaubert, Alphonse Daudet, and Stéphane
     Mallarmé. Cather shared with impressionists views about simpli-
     fication, selectivity, and the impersonality of the writer, and
     with the symbolists a belief in "the aesthetic power of sugges-
     tion." When Cather moves toward emotion indirectly through
     association and suggestion, she writes very well indeed, but when
     she tries to shape an idea out of emotion--as she does in The
     Professor's House and "The Old Beauty"--her art falters and
     appears contrived.

88   _____. "Willa Cather's Last Four Books." In Critical Essays
     on Willa Cather. See Murphy, 1984.55, pp. 290-304.
          Reprint of 1973.71.

89   STUART, HENRY LONGAN. Review of Death Comes for the Arch-
     bishop. In Critical Essays on Willa Cather. See Murphy,
     1984.55, pp. 244-47.
          Reprint of 1927.36.

90   TSIEN, JEAN. "Two Accounts of Willa Cather's Lecture at the
     University of Chicago in 1925." Willa Cather Pioneer Memorial
     Newsletter 28 (Spring):9-10.
          Provides commentary on and reprints accounts from the
     Chicago Daily Maroon (18 November 1925) and the Chicago Daily
     Tribune (21 November 1925) of a lecture titled "The Tendencies

of the Novel Today," delivered by Cather on 17 November 1925 at
the University of Chicago. Cather, expressing clearly modern
views about the need for flexibility in the novel form, argues
against the "machine-made novel" and suggests that the novel of
the future will be more concerned with a character's "emotional
pattern" than with what she calls "event pattern" (plot).

91   WARWICK, SUSAN JANE. "Telling Tales: Voice, Time and Image
      in the Fiction of Margaret Laurence and Willa Cather." Ph.D.
      dissertation, York University (Canada).
          Demonstrates that the central story in the work of both
      Cather and Laurence is the new land--the prairie Midwest--and its
      pioneers. Because both authors treat similar themes and sub-
      jects, this study focuses on how they produce meaning in their
      work. Part 1 analyzes narrative strategies, distinguishing be-
      tween the series of events as recorded in chronological order,
      and the disposition and articulation of the series in the text.
      Part 2 examines language, metaphor, and imagery, devoting a
      chapter each to the authors' use of garden, birds, house and
      landscape as symbols. See Dissertation Abstracts International
      44:3059A.

92   WEINER, ALAN R., and MEANS, SPENCER. Literary Criticism
      Index. Metuchen, N.J.: Scarecrow Press, pp. 107-8.
          Indexes the bibliographical sources that list criticism on
      every title in Cather's fiction for which there are bibliographic
      listings, including the short stories.

93   WELTY, EUDORA. "The House of Willa Cather." In Critical
      Essays on Willa Cather. See Murphy, 1984.55, pp. 66-81.
      Reprint of 1974.79.

94   WOODRESS, JAMES. "Cather and Her Friends." In Critical
      Essays on Willa Cather. See Murphy, 1984.55, pp. 81-95.
          Details Cather's relationships with women friends, explor-
      ing in some depth her close friendships with Isabelle McClung,
      Edith Lewis, and Elizabeth Sergeant. Also touches on her intel-
      lectual and literary friendships with Dorothy Canfield Fisher and
      Zoe Akins, and her lifelong Nebraska friendships with Carrie
      Miner Sherwood, Irene Miner Weisz, and Annie [Anna] Sadilek
      Pavelka. Argues that evidence simply does not exist, and prob-
      ably never did, to establish Cather's alleged lesbianism. What
      is certain is that Cather's closest emotional attachments were
      to women, at least partly because she felt that the artist was
      essentially married to her art and could not give herself fully
      to another companion.

95   WOODS, LUCIA. "Light and Shadow in the Cather World: A Per-
      sonal Essay." Great Plains Quarterly 4 (Fall):245-63.
          Presents several photographs and describes in personal
      terms how they came about and how they contribute to what Woods
      makes of her journey to the Southwest, Virginia, and Europe of
      Cather's experience. It is in their combination of the dark and

the light, but especially in their revelation of the dark, that
they disclose what is essential, both to the photographer and to
Cather.

96   WORK, JAMES C. "Cather's Confounded Conundrums in The Pro-
      fessor's House." Western American Literature 18 (February):
      303–12.
          Using The Professor's House for illustrative examples,
presents a tongue-in-cheek analysis of Cather's predisposition
toward allusion and symbolism. Serves at the same time as a
general spoof on academic writing for literary journals.

97   YONGUE, PATRICIA LEE. "The Professor's House and 'Rip Van
      Winkle.'" Western American Literature 18 (February):281–97.
          Draws parallels between Rip Van Winkle and both Godfrey St.
Peter and Tom Outland, contending that Cather has superimposed
the story of Rip Van Winkle over The Professor's House. All
three characters are confirmed in their "Americanness" in spite
of their efforts to escape from society. In terms of structure
and action as well as character, Cather's story recapitulates
Irving's.

                                    n.d.

1   BECKMAN, DON. "A Few Words about Willa Cather." Unidentified
      periodical clipping [post-1955] at Willa Cather Historical
      Center, Red Cloud, Nebraska.
          A highly negative, sarcastic response to Cather, charging
her with exploiting the town of Red Cloud which she thought
"stank." She made a "quick buck" off the townspeople, who did
not like her anyway, and then while they starved she lived
lavishly.

2   BOISSEVAIN, HEDY. "Mrs. Auld Recalls Early Life of Her
      Sister, Willa Cather." Unidentified periodical clipping
      [California? post-1947] at Willa Cather Historical Center,
      Red Cloud, Nebraska.
          Discloses aspects of Cather's youth as recalled by her
sister, Jessica Cather Auld, of Palo Alto, in a presentation
before a women's literary group. Mrs. Auld indicated that Cather
was educated largely by relatives and friends because she re-
belled against formal schooling. Before she left Virginia,
Cather loved to hear the mountain women tell stories, and she in
turn liked to tell them.

3   BUTCHER, FANNY. "Confessions." Unidentified periodical
      clipping [Chicago Tribune? late 1920s or 1930s?] at Willa
      Cather Historical Center, Red Cloud, Nebraska.
          Calls My Ántonia one of the best things an American woman
has done and attributes the fineness of Cather's work to her
fineness as a woman. Then prints a letter to Butcher from Cather
which addresses this question: what book would Cather probably

prefer to have written above all others? Cather's answer: <u>War
and Peace</u>, because she would like to have had that "torrent of
life and things pour through" her in the writing of it.

4   O'DONOGHUE, MICHAEL. Lessons on writing in unidentified,
     undated periodical clipping in Faulkner-Slote collection at
     University of Nebraska Library, Lincoln.
        Reports an ostensible conversation with "the great Willa
Cather" when O' Donoghue was a young, would-be writer. In
response to his pleas, Cather supposedly advised him to start
slowly by writing "short undemanding things." Cather is "quoted"
in O' Donoghue's language, but he confesses to having forgotten
most of the "wonderful and wise" things she told him.

Author Index

The following includes authors of items in this bibliography. Authors discussed in the entries appear in the Subject Index.

A., C., 1932.1
A-N, A., 1950.1
Abbott, Keene, 1921.1
Abe, Hiroshi, 1983.1
Adams, Frederick B., Jr., 1939.1;
 1940.1; 1982.1
Adams, J. Donald, 1935.1; 1940.2;
 1944.1; 1947.1-2; 1949.1;
 1951.1
Adams, Theodore Stanford, 1961.1;
 1973.1
Aichinger, Peter, 1975.1
Akins, Zoe, 1914.1; 1922.1
al-Ghalith, Asad Mohammed, 1984.1
Albertini, Virgil, 1979.1
Allen, David Arthur, 1972.1
Allen, Walter, 1964.1; 1969.1
Anderson, Carl L., 1957.1
Anderson, David D., 1972.2;
 1975.2
Anderson, June, 1959.1
Anderson, Quentin, 1965.1, 4
Andes, Cynthia J., 1972.3
Angoff, Charles, 1939.2
Arms, George W., 1947.3
Arnold, Marilyn, 1968.1;
 1975.3-4; 1978.1; 1981.1-2;
 1983.2; 1984.2-4
Arns, Karl, 1926.1
Arvin, Newton, 1931.1; 1935.2-3;
 1947.4
Ashley, Schuyler, 1925.1; 1926.2;
 1929.1-2; 1931.2
Atkinson, Brooks, 1961.2-4;
 1963.1-2
Attis, 1939.3

Auchard, John, comp., 1979.24
Auchincloss, Louis, 1961.5
Austin, Mary, 1932.2-3

B., E.A., 1920.2
Bailey, Helen Miller, 1964.2
Bailey, Jennifer, 1982.2
Baker, Bruce Paul, 1968.2-3;
 1982.3
Baker, Howard, 1941.1
Baker, Irving, 1968.4
Ballard, Doris, 1938.2; 1969.2
Ballotti, Geno, 1956.1
Ballou, Ellen B., 1970.1
Ballou, Robert O., 1927.1
Barba, Sharon Rose, 1973.3
Bardin, John Franklin, 1948.1
Barron, Rev. Mark, 1936.2
Bartlett, Alice Hunt, 1925.2
Bash, James Richard, 1954.1;
 1956.2; 1973.4
Bass, Eben, 1978.2
Bassett, T.D. Seymour, 1958.1
Basso, Hamilton, 1948.2
Bates, Arthur Dygert, 1931.3
Baum, Bernard, 1949.2
Beach, Joseph Warren, 1926.3;
 1932.4
Bean, Margaret, 1974.1
Beaton, Vera, 1927.2
Bechhofer [Roberts], Carl Eric,
 1921.2; 1923.1
Becker, May Lamberton, 1937.1
Beckman, Don [1], 1971.1
Beckman, Don [2], n.d.1
Beebe, Maurice, 1964.3

Beecher, George Allen, 1950.2
Beer, Thomas, 1925.3
Belfrage, Sixten, 1932.5
Bell, Martha S., 1959.2
Benét, Laura, 1925.4
Benet, Rosemary, 1940.3
Benet, Stephen Vincent, 1935.4;
    1940.3
Benet, William Rose, 1923.2
Benidt, Bruce, 1979.2
Bennett, J.Q., 1964.4
Bennett, Jack Wasson, 1982.4
Bennett, Mildred R., 1949.3;
    1951.2; 1957.2-3; 1959.3;
    1960.2; 1961.6; 1962.1;
    1964.5; 1965.2; 1968.5-6;
    1971.2; 1973.5-6; 1975.5-6;
    1977.1; 1979.3; 1982.5-7;
    1984.5
Bennett, S.M., 1974.2
Bennett, Sandra Margaret, 1976.1
Benson, Frederick R., 1973.7
Benson, Peter, 1981.3
Berg, Ruben Gustavson, 1925.5
Bergamo, Ralph, 1965.3
Bergers, John, 1982.8
Berkebile, John W., 1977.2
Berthoff, Warner, 1959.4-5;
    1971.3
Bessey, Mabel A., 1933.1
Bettman, Otto, 1956.4
Betts, Glynne Robinson, 1981.4;
    1984.6
Bianchini, Angela, 1958.2
Binsse, Harry Lorin, 1941.2
Birtwell, Lorna R.F., 1922.4;
    1948.3
Blackburn, William, 1950.3
Blake, Nelson Manfred, 1979.4
Blanck, Jacob, 1942.1
Blankenship, Russell, 1931.4
Blissett, William, 1963.3
Bloom, Edward A., and Bloom,
    Lillian D., 1949.4; 1950.4;
    1955.1; 1956.3; 1958.3;
    1962.2; 1967.1; 1974.3;
    1984.7
Bloom, Lillian D., 1977.3
Boas, Ralph Philip, 1933.2
Bogan, Louise, 1931.5; 1967.2
Bohling, Beth, 1984.8
Bohlke, Beverly, 1975.7
Bohlke, L. Brent, 1974.4; 1975.8;
    1977.4; 1982.9-11; 1983.3;
    1984.9

Boissevain, Hedy, n.d.2
Bolton, Sarah K., 1954.2
Bongartz, Roy, 1981.5
Bonham, Barbara, 1970.2
Booth, Alice, 1931.6
Bordner, Marsha Stanfield, 1979.5
Borgman, Paul, 1975.9
Boucher, Sandy, 1982.12
Bourne, Randolph, 1918.1; 1973.8;
    1982.13; 1984.10
Bowden, Edwin T., 1961.7
Bowman, Anthony, 1974.5
Boye, Alan, 1974.6
Boynton, Henry Walcott, 1915.1-2;
    1918.2; 1922.5; 1923.4-5
Boynton, Percy H., 1924.1-2;
    1931.7; 1936.3; 1940.4
Bradford, Curtis, 1955.2
Bradford, Gamaliel, 1922.6;
    1923.6
Bradley, Van Allen, 1969.3;
    1971.4
Brande, Dorothea, 1935.5; 1984.11
Breit, Harvey, 1949.5
Brennan, Joseph X., 1965.5
Brennan, Mary Elizabeth, 1948.4
Brenner, Sidney H., 1981.6
Brewster, Dorothy, 1934.1
Brickell, Herschel, 1925.6;
    1927.3
Bridges, Jean B., 1976.2
Brooks, Van Wyck, 1951.3; 1952.1;
    1953.1; 1956.4
Broun, Heywood, 1922.7-8; 1923.7
Brown, Edward Killoran, 1936.4;
    1946.1; 1950.5-6; 1953.2-3;
    1967.3
Brown, Marion Marsh, 1970.3;
    1973.9-10; 1980.1
Bruccoli, Matthew J., 1978.3
Brunauer, Dalma Hunyadi, 1975.10-
    11
Brunius, August, 1918.3
Brunk, Charlotte, 1973.11
Bruns, Friedrich, 1930.1
Bryan, George L., 1922.9
Bryden, Ronald, 1961.8
Bryfonski, Dedria, ed., 1978.4
Bucco, Martin, 1984.12
Buchan, A.M., 1953.4
Budz, Judith Kaufman, 1975.12
Bullett, Gerald, 1923.8
Bullock, Flora, 1949.6

Dahl, Curtis, 1955.3
Daiches, David, 1951.5; 1967.9
Danielson, Jeannette Crain, 1968.13
Daughaday, Charles H., 1967.10; 1969.8
Davenport, John, 1961.10
Davidson, Colleen Tighe, 1975.15
Davis, Robert Gorham, 1971.8
Dawson, Margaret Cheney, 1932.10
Dawson, N.P., 1919.1
Day, Bess Eileen, 1957.5
Dedmon, Emmett, 1948.8
Deegan, Dorothy Yost, 1951.6
Dell, Floyd, 1913.3; 1982.21
Demarest, David P., Jr., ed., 1976.5
Devoto, Bernard, 1944.3
Dickinson, Asa Don, 1925.10; 1928.1; 1931.16; 1937.6; 1948.9; 1953.6
Dickinson, Joan Younger, 1984.22
Dillman, Richard, 1984.23
Dinn, James M., 1972.5; 1973.16
Ditsky, John Michael, 1967.11; 1974.14; 1983.8
Doane, Gilbert H., 1927.8
Doane, Margaret, 1983.9-10; 1984.24
Dobie, J. Frank, 1952.5
Dodd, Lee Wilson, 1926.6; 1927.9
Dodd, Ora, 1973.17
Dolinin, Aleksandr, 1981.15
Donald, Miles, 1978.10
Donaldson, Scott, 1978.11
Dondore, Dorothy Anne, 1926.7
Donohue, John W., 1973.18
Dooley, Roger B., 1957.6
Doorly, M.H., 1920.4
Doughty, Howard N., Jr., 1949.9
Douglas, Ann, 1974.15; 1982.22
Draves, Rev. Cornelius J., 1973.19; 1975.16
Drew, Elizabeth A., 1926.8
Driftmier, David, 1978.12
Drucker, Linda, 1984.25
Drury, John, 1947.14
DuBois, Bessie, 1905.2
DuBose, La Rocque, 1955.4
Duchnes, Philip C., 1964.7
Duffy, Martha, 1973.20
Dunbar-Odom, Donna, 1979.7
Durham, Philip, 1957.7; 1972.6
Dyrud, David Lynn, 1979.8

Earnest, Ernest, 1966.2; 1970.7
Edel, Leon, 1954.3; 1956.5-6; 1957.8; 1960.4; 1965.8; 1966.3-4; 1967.12; 1971.9; 1973.21; 1974.16-17; 1982.23; 1983.11; 1984.26
Edgar, Pelham, 1934.2
Edgett, Edwin Francis, 1927.10
Edmiston, Susan, 1976.6
Edwards, John B., 1923.13
Edwards, Oliver, 1956.7
Edwards, Vincent, 1946.2
Eggan, Fred, 1929.21
Ehrlich, Eugene, 1982.24
Eichorn, Harry Bernard, 1968.14; 1973.22; 1984.27
Eifrig, Gail M., 1974.18
Eisinger, Chester E., 1963.5
Elgstrom, Anna Lenah, 1933.3; 1941.4
Eliasson, Torsten, 1981.16
Ellmann, Mary, 1968.15
Elmore, Wilbur Theodore, 1923.14-15
Emerson, O.B., 1960.14
Epstein, Joseph, 1983.12
Erisman, Fred, 1980.9-10
Escartin Nuñez, Emilio, 1973.23
Etulain, Richard W., 1972.7; (ed.) 1980.11; 1983.30
Evans, Ernestine, 1950.10

Fadiman, Clifton, 1932.11-12; 1940.6
Fairbanks Myers, Carol, 1979.9
Farrar, John, 1923.16-17
Farrelly, John, 1948.10
Faulkner, Virginia, 1965.2; 1974.69; 1979.10
Faverty, Frederic E., 1959.6-7
Fay, Eliot G., 1941.5
Feger, Lois, 1970.8
Feld, Rose C., 1924.5; 1982.25
Fenster, Valmai Kirkham, 1983.13
Ferguson, J.M., Jr., 1970.9
Fetty, Audrey Mae Shelley, 1973.24
Feuillerat, A., 1930.4
Fiegenbaum, Martha, 1929.4
Field, Flo, 1921.4
Field, Louise Maunsell, 1923.18; 1926.9

Greene, George William, 1956.11; 1957.10-11; 1981.23
Greenslet, Ferris, 1943.1
Gregory, Horace, 1931.18
Griffiths, Frederick T., 1984.38
Grimes, George, 1935.11; 1940.8
Gross, Barry, 1977.8; 1981.24
Grover, Dorys Crow, 1977.9
Grumbach, Doris, 1982.28; 1984.39-40
Gubar, Susan, 1981.25
Guiterman, Arthur, 1915.8
Gunsky, Frederic R., 1940.9
Gurko, Leo, 1947.19
Gwin, Minrose Clayton, 1984.41

H., C.L., 1918.4
H., F., 1913.4; 1966.8; 1982.29
Haas, Jakob, 1935.12
Hackett, Francis, 1921.7
Hafer, John Williams, 1975.21
Haines, Helen E., 1925.15; 1942.4
Halac, Dennis, 1976.9
Hale, Edward Everett, Jr., 1915.9; 1932.14; 1941.6
Hall, Mourdant, 1925.16
Halleck, Reuben Post, 1934.4
Haller, Evelyn H., 1978.14
Hamada, Masajiro, 1941.7
Hamaya, Mieko, 1962.8
Hamilton, Clayton, 1939.5
Hamner, Eugénie Lambert, 1976.10; 1984.42
Handlan Campbell, Bertha, 1949.11
Handy, Yvonne, 1940.10
Haney, John Louis, 1923.25
Hansen, Harry, 1925.17; 1926.11
Harper, Howard, 1967.14
Harper, Marion, 1966.9
Harper, Moses, 1925.18
Harris, Celia, 1913.5; 1972.9
Harris, Richard Casey, 1974.25; 1978.15
Harris, William E., 1931.19
Hart, Clive, 1972.10
Hart, James D., ed., 1965.16
Hartman, Carl, 1960.14
Hartwick, Harry, 1934.5; 1936.18
Harvey, Alice G., 1930.5; 1934.6; 1964.10
Harvey, Margaret, 1915.10
Haskell, Henry C., 1965.17; 1971.12; 1973.26; 1975.22

Hass, Victor P., 1948.11; 1949.12; 1967.15; 1973.27
Hatcher, Harland, 1935.13
Havighurst, Walter, 1949.13; 1950.13; 1953.9
Hawkins, Ethel Wallace, 1925.19; 1931.20; 1935.14
Hawthorne, Hazel, 1932.15
Hawthorne, Hildegarde, 1922.14
Haycraft, Howard, ed., 1942.6
Hazard, Lucy Lockwood, 1927.16
Hearne, Laura Guthrie, 1964.11
Heilbrun, Carolyn G., 1979.15
Heiney, Donald, 1958.7
Heller, Shirley H., 1975.23
Hellman, Geoffrey T., 1948.12
Helmick, Evelyn Thomas, 1968.19; 1975.24; 1976.11; 1984.43
Hemingway, Ernest, 1952.7
Henderson, Harry B., III, 1974.26
Hendrick, George, 1961.14; 1970.10
Herman, Dick, 1974.27
Herron, Ima Honaker, 1939.6
Hertz, Henri, 1925.20
Herzberg, Max J., ed., 1962.9
Heyeck, Robin, 1979.16
Hicks, Granville, 1931.21; 1933.7-8; 1967.16
Hiers, John T., 1980.16
Hilfer, Anthony Channell, 1963.10; 1969.10
Hillegas, C.K., 1962.10
Hinman, Eleanor, 1921.8
Hinz, Evelyn J., 1972.11
Hinz, John P., 1949.14-15; 1950.14-15; 1953.10; 1977.10
Hockett, Ethel M., 1915.11; 1966.10
Hoffman, A.C., 1979.17
Hoffman, C.G., 1979.17
Hoffman, Frederick J., 1951.7; 1955.5; 1962.11
Holman, C. Hugh, 1979.18
Homer, Sidney, 1926.12
Horgan, Paul, 1961.15; 1974.28; 1976.12
Hough, Lynn Harold, 1934.7
Howard, John Tasker, 1935.15
Howard, Leon, 1960.7
Howard, Maureen, 1977.11 (ed.); 1982.30
Howard, Patsy C., comp., 1973.28

Myers, Rawley, 1972.20
Myers, Walter L., 1932.28

N., M., 1927.24
Nagel, Harold G., 1981.40
Nance, William L., 1975.34
Nankin, Frances, 1980.32
Narita, Shigehisa, 1941.15
Nestlbichler, Paul, 1944.6
Nevius, Blake, comp., 1970.19
Newbranch, Harvey, 1921.16
Newman, Frances, 1927.25
Nicholas, Sister Mary, 1934.9
Nichols, Kathleen L., 1978.21;
     1984.61
Nickols, Thelma, 1984.62
Nishikawa, Masami, 1949.18
Nolte, William H., ed., 1964.18
Norton, Sybil, 1952.4
Nourse, Joan T., 1964.19
Nyquist, Edna, 1965.27

O--DH, 1920.10
O'Brien, Edward J., 1923.37
O'Brien, Sharon, 1975.35-36;
     1976.21; 1978.22; 1979.32;
     1982.54; 1984.63
O'Connell, Doug, 1983.22
O'Connor, Frank, 1956.18
O'Connor, Karen, 1984.64
O'Connor, Margaret Anne, 1971.20;
     1974.51; 1984.65
O'Donoghue, Michael, n.d.5
Odožilík, Otakar, 1958.12
O'Flaherty, Terrence, 1978.23;
     1980.33-34
Ohashi, Kensaburo, ed., 1980.35
Okita, Hagime, 1961.22
Oldfield, Barney, 1971.21
Olsen, Tillie, 1978.24
Olson, Lawrence, 1973.43
Olson, Paul A., 1981.41
Omori, Mamoru, 1962.14; 1976.22
Orvis, Mary Burchard, 1948.19
Osborne, E.W., 1923.38
Österling, Anders, 1938.7;
     1957.18
Overing, Robert, 1973.44
Overton, Grant, 1918.7;
     1928.11-12; 1929.15

P., R.H., 1935.29
Pannill, Linda Susanne, 1975.37;
     1984.66

Paoli, Richard, 1983.23
Paris, Rosemary, 1950.21
Parker, Jeraldine [Jeri],
     1973.46; 1975.38
Parks, B.K., 1979.33
Parrington, Vernon Louis,
     1927.27; 1930.9
Paterson, Isabel, 1926.21;
     1936.13
Pattee, Fred Lewis, 1930.10
Payne, William Morton, 1903.4
Pearce, Thomas Matthews, 1938.6;
     1940.15; 1979.34
Pearson, Carol, 1981.42
Pearson, Edmund Lester, 1920.11-
     12
Pearson, Norman Holmes, 1949.19;
     1953.18
Peattie, Elia W., 1895.1;
     1896.1; 1918.8; 1923.39
Peden, William, 1948.20
Pelantova, Artemis, 1927.28;
     1932.31; 1935.30
Perry, Constance Marie, 1982.55
Pers, Mona, 1974.52; 1975.39;
     1976.23-24; 1984.67
Pertinax, 1922.26
Peterman, Michael, 1981.43
Peterson, Glenda, 1967.42;
     1969.13
Peyre, Henri, 1947.25
Pfund, Harry W., 1955.9
Phelps, William Lyon, 1928.13;
     1932.32
Phillips, R. LeClerc, 1928.14
Piacentino, Edward J., 1979.35;
     1982.56; 1984.68
Piechowske, Marjorie Pauline,
     1978.25
Piekarski, Vicki, ed., 1983.32
Pigaga, Thom, comp., 1981.44-45
Pike, Rafford, 1904.1
Piper, Henry Dan, 1965.28;
     1971.22
Placide, Sister M. See
     Karczewska, Irene
Plomer, William, 1935.31
Plunkett, Kevin Michael, 1982.57
Pogel, Nancy H., 1977.19
Poli, Bernard, 1972.21
Polk, Noel, 1973.47
Ponsonby, Marion, 1922.27
Pontrelli, Jeanny Ross, 1982.58

Salo, Alice Bell, 1980.39
Salter, Christopher L., 1977.24
Sato, Hiroko, 1961.27; 1974.61-
   62; (ed.) 1975.54; 1978.29
Savery, Gilbert, 1967.45; 1971.25
Schach, Paul, 1983.27
Scheideman, J.W., 1973.56
Scherman, David Edward, 1951.10;
   1952.15-16
Schloss, George, 1950.23; 1967.46
Schmidt, Otis Rhea, 1980.19;
   1982.33
Schmittlein, Albert Edward,
   1962.16
Schneider, Sister Lucy, 1967.47-
   48; 1968.29-31; 1970.22;
   1973.57-59; 1974.63; 1975.45
Scholes, Robert E., 1962.17;
   1975.46
Schroeter, James, 1959.16;
   1965.31; 1967.49-50
Schuett, Faye, 1983.28
Schwartz, Narda Lacey, 1977.25
Schwarz, Heino, 1934.11
Schweider, Nancy, 1965.32
Schwind, Jean Denise, 1983.29;
   1984.80
Scott, C.A. Dawson, 1924.15
Scott, John Charles, 1980.40
Scott, Wilbur S., 1947.27
Sedgewick, Ellery, 1937.13
Seibel, George, 1903.10; 1947.28;
   1948.24; 1949.26; 1967.51
Seidel, Alison P., 1978.30
Seldes, Gilbert, 1922.30
Sell, Henry Blackman, 1919.8
Sellars, Richard West, 1973.60
Seltzer, Sandra, 1982.65
Sennwald, Andre, 1934.12
Sergeant, Elizabeth Shepley,
   1925.34; 1926.27-28; 1927.35;
   1931.43; 1940.19; 1953.19-20;
   1967.52
Sewell, C.S., 1925.35
Seymour-Smith, Martin, 1973.61;
   1976.28
Shaw, John Mackay, 1967.53
Shaw, Patrick W., 1984.81
Shelton, Frank Wilsey, 1971.26;
   1976.29-30
Sherman, Caroline, 1951.11
Sherman, Stuart P., 1925.36;
   1926.29

Sherwood, Margaret, 1912.11
Shiga, Masaru, 1947.29
Shively, James R., 1948.25;
   1950.24
Showalter, Shirley Hershey,
   1981.50
Shults, Donald, 1974.64
Shuster, George N., 1934.13
Simons, W.J., 1937.14
Simonson, Harold P., 1970.23
Skaggs, Merrill Maguire, 1981.51;
   1982.66
Slocum, John, 1935.37
Slote, Bernice, 1962.18; 1964.21;
   1966.15-16; 1967.54; 1969.15-
   17; 1970.24; 1973.62-66;
   1974.65-69; 1975.47; 1977.26;
   1979.37; 1982.67-68; 1984.77,
   82
Small, Harold, 1931.44
Smith, Anneliese H., 1971.27;
   1978.31
Smith, Carl S., 1984.83
Smith, David, 1973.67
Smith, Dorothy J., 1970.25
Smith, Eleanor M., 1956.22
Smith, R.D. Hilton, 1929.21
Smith, Rebecca W., 1938.6;
   1942.8; 1946.5
Smith, Thelma M., 1955.13
Smith Hawkins, Elaine Yvonne,
   1984.84
Snell, George, 1947.30
Snyder, Richard C., 1980.3
Soskin, William, 1931.45;
   1936.16
Southwick, Helen C., 1982.69
Speckner, Rev. Killian, 1955.14
Stafford, Jean, 1973.68
Stagg, Hunter, 1922.31
Stallings, Frank L., Jr., 1972.26
Stalnaker, John M., 1929.22
Star, Louis M., 1979.27
Steensma, Robert C., 1968.32
Stegner, Wallace, 1965.33;
   1969.18-19; 1983.30
Stern, Gwynneth, 1969.20; 1969.21
Sternshein, Mary Kemper, 1983.31
Stevens, Holly, ed., 1966.17
Stevenson, Anne, 1977.27
Stevenson, David L., 1958.14
Stewart, David H., 1966.18
Stewart, Grace B., 1979.38-39

Van Doren, Dorothy, 1931.50
Van Doren, Irita, 1932.43
Van Doren, Mark, 1923.48;
   1925.38; 1939.7
Van Dyke, Henry, 1929.25
Van Ghent, Dorothy, 1964.25;
   1974.77; 1977.30
Van Vleck, Charlotte, 1980.46
Vargo, Edward P., 1973.77
Vest, Mira Meacham, 1973.78;
   1982.74
Vierneisel, Karen Helene, 1977.31
Vigil, Ralph H., 1975.50
Vocădlo, Otakar, 1934.14
Voss, Arthur, 1973.79

W., C.R., 1923.49
Wagenknecht, Edward, 1929.26;
   1950.25; 1952.18; 1953.23;
   1957.22
Wager, Willis, 1968.34
Wagner, Linda W., 1977.32-33
Walbridge, Earle F., 1936.20;
   1953.24; 1956.23
Waldman, Milton, 1925.39;
   1933.19; 1934.15
Walker, Don D., 1966.21
Walpole, Hugh, 1922.35; 1923.50
Walsh, Jeffrey, 1982.75
Walters, Raymond, Jr., 1965.35
Walton, Eda Lou, 1933.20
Walton, Edith H., 1935.39
Ward, Alfred Charles, 1932.44
Ward, Christopher, 1923.51-52
Warwick, Susan Jane, 1984.91
Washington, Ida H., 1982.76
Wasserman, Loretta, 1982.77
Waters, Tricia, 1981.55
Watkins, Floyd C., 1977.34-35;
   1980.16
Watts, Emily Stipes, 1977.36;
   1982.78
Weales, Gerald, 1972.34
Weaver, Dorothy, 1976.33
Weber, Carl J., 1947.31
Wee, Morris Owen, 1982.79
Weeks, Edward, 1932.45; 1941.19
Weigel, John A., 1958.16
Weiner, Alan R., 1984.92
Weixlmann, Joe, 1982.80
Wellborn, Grace Pleasant, 1963.19
Wellman, Paul I., 1937.17
Wells, Nancy, 1973.80

Welty, Eudora, 1974.78-80;
   1978.33; 1980.47; 1984.93
Wermuth, Paul C., 1958.17
West, Paul, 1963.20
West, Rebecca, 1927.40; 1928.19;
   1967.59
Westbrook, Max, 1980.48
Westbrook, Perry D., 1951.14;
   1979.42
Whaley, Elizabeth Gates, 1974.81
Wheelock, John F., 1926.32
Whicher, George F., 1951.15
Whipple, Leon, 1931.51
Whipple, Thomas King, 1923.53;
   1928.20; 1943.3; 1967.60
White, Barbara A., 1977.37
White, George Leroy, Jr.,
   1937.18; 1942.9
White, Harold N., 1955.15
White, Robert J., 1982.81;
   1982.82
White, William, 1951.16; 1957.23;
   1958.18; 1965.36
Whitman, William, III, 1927.41
Whitney, Blair, 1975.51
Whittington, Curtis Calvin, Jr.,
   1965.37; 1968.35; 1972.35
Wild, Barbara, 1978.34
Williams, Blanche Colton, 1920.17
Williams, Cecil Brown, 1962.21
Williams, Michael, 1927.44;
   1928.21; 1931.54; 1932.46;
   1940.23; 1941.21; 1982.84
Williams, Orlo, 1920.18
Williams, Stanley Thomas,
   1926.34; 1933.25; 1953.25;
   1955.16
Williamson, Edward, 1923.55
Wilson, Benjamin Harrison, Jr.,
   1965.38
Wilson, D. Ray, 1983.33
Wilson, Edmund, 1922.36; 1924.16;
   1926.35; 1952.19-20;
   1956.24; 1967.62; 1982.85
Wilson, Harold S., 1970.32
Wilson, J. Harold, 1933.1
Wilson, James Southall, 1931.55;
   1935.41
Winner, Viola Hopkins, 1974.82
Winsten, Archer, 1932.47-48
Witham, W. Tasker, 1947.37
Wittke, Carl, 1946.6
Woltemath, Glenda, 1966.22-23

Subject Index

The following are subjects discussed in entries in the bibliography. They include titles of books and stories, names of persons referred to, fictional characters, themes in Cather's works, etc.

"Accomplished Desires," 1980.45
Adams, Frederick B., Jr., 1964.7
Adams, Henry, 1961.10; 1974.26; 1977.40; 1979.13
Aeneas, Aeneid, 1961.16; 1968.19; 1978.19; 1981.41; 1982.58. See also Epic
Aestheticism, 1962.16
Agape, 1966.1
Agrarian mode, myth, ideology, 1956.15; 1958.7; 1979.1, 35; 1982.91; 1983.5
Akins, Zoe, 1984.94
Alcott, Louisa May, 1979.32
Alexander's Bridge
-Cather's explanation of, 1912.2; 1977.26
-criticism of, 1950.14; 1952.8; 1961.16; 1980.49; 1982.42, 59, 66
-introduction to, 1977.26; 1984.82
-Japanese criticism of, 1961.27
-mentioned, 1915.1; 1921.2, 12; 1925.36; 1926.21; 1928.18; 1930.9, 11; 1931.5; 1934.10; 1936.14; 1947.34; 1948.18; 1953.2, 24; 1962.20; 1975.52
-reviews of, 1912.3-11; 1982.61; 1984.51
Alienation, exile, 1948.18; 1966.14; 1971.26; 1973.62; 1976.12; 1981.48; 1982.45; 1984.17. See also Isolation
All the King's Men, 1968.35

Allegory, 1949.4, 8; 1960.10; 1963.6; 1972.31; 1975.24; 1976.3; 1978.14, 38
Allusion, 1964.9; 1974.68, 85; 1982.67; 1984.96. See also Biblical allusion
Alter ego. See Double self
America and American literature, Cather's work in relation to, 1913.16; 1920.2; 1922.3, 12; 1941.3; 1947.4, 22; 1949.8; 1971.29; 1976.8
America in Cather's fiction, 1920.2; 1924.5; 1941.13; 1950.13; 1956.15; 1961.18; 1974.85; 1975.25; 1978.10. See also Cather, as American writer
American "Eve," 1973.35
"American Scholar, The," 1984.23
"Ancient mariner," 1974.29
Anderson, Edwin H., 1982.11
Anderson, Sherwood, 1922.2; 1926.3; 1929.22; 1939.6; 1956.18; 1974.82; 1976.16; 1977.24; 1978.10, 17
Androgynous
-ideal, 1979.6
-narrative voice, 1983.25
-woman character, 1980.15; 1983.25
Angelou, Maya, 1981.13
Anglo-Saxons, Americans, Cather's portrayal of, 1936.4; 1977.34; 1981.20

Bates, John Mallory, 1984.9
"Beast in the Jungle, The,"
    1975.10
Beatty, Jerome, Jr., 1959.9
Beaumont, Guy, 1970.31
Beautiful, beauty in Willa
    Cather's works, 1915.9;
    1918.1, 8; 1922.6, 14;
    1923.20, 22, 26, 35; 1924.5;
    1926.33; 1927.8, 19, 26;
    1929.26; 1932.32, 46;
    1936.14; 1937.1, 12; 1938.5;
    1948.16; 1960.6; 1968.37;
    1972.20; 1975.18
Beecher, George Allen, 1984.9
"Before Breakfast," 1948.2, 5,
    17, 20-21; 1984.2
Bellini, Vincenzo, 1965.14;
    1973.22; 1975.11
Bennett, Mildred R., 1951.12;
    1979.2; 1982.12
Bergers, John Blake, 1982.8
Bernhardt, Sarah, 1976.2
Best Short Stories of Sarah Orne
    Jewett, The, Cather's
    preface to, 1925.17
"Best Years, The"
-criticism of, 1968.7; 1973.59;
    1984.2, 59
-mentioned, 1948.5, 11, 13, 16,
    20-21
Bible, Cather's use of, 1978.9,
    13; 1980.14; 1984.54
Biblical allusions, parallels,
    1973.24; 1978.13, 34
Bibliographies, full length, of
    Cather's works, 1975.27;
    1982.19
Bibliography and Criticism,
    sources of, 1922.20; 1927.42;
    1928.6-7; 1929.12, 27;
    1933.21; 1936.18; 1939.1;
    1940.14, 21; 1941.20;
    1942.1, 6; 1944.5; 1947.21;
    1948.15; 1954.7; 1956.13;
    1959.10; 1960.1, 14; 1961.14;
    1967.49; 1968.9; 1969.7, 15,
    17; 1970.6, 10, 16, 19, 28;
    1972.7, 12, 18; 1973.7, 28,
    49; 1974.32, 38, 45, 54-55,
    67, 82-83, 86; 1975.27, 29;
    1976.20; 1977.5, 15, 25, 37;
    1978.4, 30; 1979.9-10, 24-25,
    30, 43; 1980.31, 35; 1981.14,

19; 1982.1, 19, 25, 52, 73,
    80; 1983.7, 13, 16; 1984.55,
    73, 92
Bildungsroman(e), American. See
    Genre
Biographical sketches of Cather,
    sources of biographical
    information, 1915.4, 20;
    1918.7; 1920.5; 1921.10;
    1922.20; 1925.2; 1927.42;
    1928.12; 1929.5, 27; 1930.8;
    1931.5, 22, 27; 1933.10;
    1934.4, 10; 1936.8, 17;
    1937.6; 1939.1; 1940.14, 21;
    1941.20; 1942.1, 6; 1944.5;
    1946.2; 1947.10, 22, 33-34;
    1948.6, 9, 15; 1954.2, 4;
    1958.7; 1959.14; 1960.4;
    1961.5; 1962.3; 1964.2, 19;
    1965.2; 1967.31; 1969.13;
    1970.11, 28; 1971.9; 1972.19,
    23; 1973.7, 17, 50, 54,
    66-67; 1974.17, 82-83;
    1975.18, 23, 38, 42; 1977.5,
    20, 29; 1978.4, 8, 30;
    1979.9, 33, 43; 1980.46;
    1981.4, 31, 55-56; 1982.25,
    52, 73; 1983.7, 24, 33;
    1984.40, 49
Biographies of Cather, full
    length, 1930.11; 1951.2;
    1953.2, 13, 20; 1958.4;
    1970.2-3, 33; 1980.1, 3;
    1983.25
-assumptions of questioned,
    1982.69; 1983.12; 1984.3
-reviews of, 1953.5, 8, 11-12,
    18, 22-23; 1958.4; 1960.8;
    1976.13
Biography in Cather's work,
    1927.8, 14, 38; 1931.11, 19;
    1933.10; 1940.20; 1954.3;
    1966.3; 1971.23; 1981.52;
    1982.86
Blacks portrayed as individuals,
    1940.6, 9, 18
Blake, Forrester, 1964.17
Blithedale Romance, The, 1975.33
Bogan, Louise, 1975.13
Bohemian elements in Cather's
    fiction, 1972.3; 1978.11
"Bohemian Girl, The"
-editorial announcement of,
    1912.1

(Cather, Willa)
--understatement, 1928.12;
    1974.64; 1981.33
--"unfurnished," 1953.10;
    1972.29; 1982.59
-as "almost a radical," 1924.7
-as American writer, 1933.4;
    1936.18; 1941.3; 1950.3;
    1951.11; 1955.6; 1956.6;
    1961.8; 1962.2; 1963.5;
    1964.18; 1967.38; 1972.14;
    1973.2, 66, 76; 1974.5, 23;
    1977.17; 1980.31. See also
    America
--influence on American litera-
    ture, writers, 1913.12;
    1964.15; 1965.9, 28; 1971.22;
    1982.48, 59
-as aristocrat, 1941.21; 1951.7;
    1963.5; 1966.11; 1973.84;
    1980.49
-as artist. See Artist; Cather,
    critical assessment of
-as biographer. See Biography in
    Cather's work
-as catastrophic writer, 1974.26
-as Christian novelist, 1941.2;
    1947.16; 1963.6
-as classic, classicist. See
    Classicism
-as conservationist, preserva-
    tionist, 1947.8; 1979.20;
    1984.40
-as conservative writer, 1932.17;
    1959.14; 1963.5; 1984.40
-as drama critic, 1895.1; 1920.5,
    16; 1949.6; 1971.21; 1972.34
-as early modern, 1982.42
-as escapist. See Escapism
-as essayist, 1949.6; 1960.3.
    See also reviews of Cather's
    essays and essay collections
-as genteel writer, 1947.25;
    1961.8
-as historian. See History
-as historical novelist. See
    History
-as holistic writer, 1974.26
-as humanist, 1931.30; 1966.21;
    1978.11
-as individualist, 1931.1, 5
-as intellectual, 1955.15;
    1958.8; 1973.52; 1977.39
-as linguist, 1901.1

-as literary critic, 1895.1;
    1921.3; 1927.42; 1928.1;
    1946.3; 1949.6; 1956.14;
    1959.16; 1964.21; 1966.15;
    1971.15; 1972.34; 1974.3;
    1975.35; 1984.12. See also
    collections of Cather's
    critical writings and reviews
    of them
-as literary genius, 1913.3;
    1922.23; 1923.34; 1937.1;
    1948.16
-as masquerader, 1965.1
-as midwesterner, 1975.51. See
    also Midwest
-as member of American Academy
    of Arts and Letters, 1938.1
-as modernist. See Modernism
-as music critic, 1920.16
-as Nebraska writer, 1967.19.
    See also Nebraska
-as newspaper woman, journalist,
    editor, 1895.1; 1903.6;
    1915.12; 1921.24; 1925.28;
    1927.7; 1930.15; 1947.34;
    1950.15; 1953.2; 1955.15;
    1957.17; 1965.2; 1966.15;
    1968.8; 1969.16; 1970.6, 32;
    1971.7, 30; 1972.34; 1973.65;
    1977.2; 1981.3; 1982.66.
    See also reviews of The
    World and the Parish
-as novelist, 1927.41; 1929.12,
    15; 1931.23; 1932.17;
    1933.19; 1938.5; 1946.3;
    1947.17, 22, 36; 1956.14;
    1973.61; 1980.38
-as Pittsburgher, 1959.3, 17.
    See also Pittsburgh
-as poet, 1923.2, 47; 1925.2;
    1929.9; 1931.38, 42; 1934.4;
    1946.3; 1962.18; 1967.53;
    1977.27, 36. See also
    reviews of April Twilights
--as epic writer, 1923.48;
    1965.20. See also Epic mode
-as post-frontier author, 1982.4
-as primitive. See Primitivism
-as psychologist. See Psychology
-as realist. See Realism, dis-
    cussions of individual works
-as regionalist. See Regionalism

(Characters)
-development of, 1912.9, 11;
   1913.9; 1915.3; 1918.3;
   1920.7; 1922.11, 15, 24;
   1923.3, 30; 1924.9; 1925.1,
   31; 1926.8, 20, 24; 1927.12;
   1932.31, 44; 1933.14;
   1935.14, 24, 27; 1965.22, 28
-female, 1913.7; 1939.2; 1947.1;
   1948.1; 1949.1; 1951.6;
   1968.15, 21; 1973.3; 1975.15;
   1976.8, 20; 1977.40; 1979.15;
   1980.20; 1981.25, 46;
   1982.81; 1984.33. See also
   Women in Cather's fiction
-incomplete, weak, 1926.6, 12-13
-male, 1949.1; 1974.48; 1979.15;
   1982.17. See also Man
-models for, 1951.2; 1953.24;
   1954.4; 1958.4-5; 1961.15,
   28; 1963.9; 1974.30; 1975.48;
   1976.9; 1983.3; 1984.8-9
-romantic, 1923.21. See also
   Romance
-sculptural, poetic quality,
   1932.1
-stock, 1924.8; 1927.25; 1940.6,
   9, 18, 20; 1950.21
-Swedish. See Swedish characters
-unrealistic, 1925.23, 30
Characters in Cather's fiction.
   See also titles of works in
   which characters appear
-Alexander, Bartley, 1925.36;
   1926.21; 1977.26. See also
   reviews of Alexander's Bridge
-Auclair, Cécile, 1974.63
-Augusta, 1951.6; 1978.18;
   1984.50
-Aunt Georgiana, 1974.30
-Aunt Tillie (Thea Kronborg's),
   1951.6; 1981.10
-Bergson, Alexandra, 1919.6;
   1925.36; 1930.6; 1931.12;
   1937.18; 1951.6; 1961.27;
   1965.1, 7, 12; 1968.21, 28,
   31; 1972.24; 1975.8, 20,
   35-36; 1977.20; 1978.11, 28;
   1979.19; 1980.18, 31;
   1981.42, 46, 49; 1982.3, 18;
   1984.54. See also reviews of
   O Pioneers!
-Bergson, Emil, 1961.5; 1965.7,
   12; 1974.48; 1982.3

-Birdseye, Nellie, 1926.2, 13;
   1965.14; 1973.1, 22; 1975.11,
   26; 1978.20, 27
-Blake, Rachel, 1967.20
-Blinker, 1974.63
-Bower, Eden, 1984.3
-Burden, Jim, 1924.1; 1926.11;
   1946.4; 1958.11; 1961.20;
   1962.17, 20; 1965.33;
   1967.5; 1968.35; 1969.11;
   1970.8, 23; 1971.11;
   1972.32; 1973.55; 1974.41,
   48, 70; 1975.33; 1976.2, 11,
   17; 1978.15, 26; 1979.6, 18,
   23; 1980.31; 1981.20, 35, 48;
   1982.77; 1984.81
-Chabanel, Father, 1974.48
-Charron, Pierre, 1974.63
-Cleric, Gaston, 1962.6
-Colbert, Henry, 1967.20; 1981.9
-Colbert, Sapphira, 1940.9;
   1961.5; 1984.41, 45, 75.
   See also reviews of Sapphira
   and the Slave Girl
-Cutter, Wick and Mrs., 1978.14;
   1984.75
-Cuzak, Anton, 1982.56; 1984.8
-d'Arnault, Blind, 1961.28;
   1964.8
-Deane, Nelly, 1984.76
-Dillon, R.E., 1932.8, 45
-Doctor Archie, 1915.7
-Doña Isabella, 1967.55
-Ellinger, Frank, 1923.3; 1931.37
-Ericson, Nils, 1937.18
-Eusabio, 1975.7
-Ferguesson, James, 1973.59
-Ferguesson, Lesley, 1973.59
-Ferguesson, Mrs., 1973.59
-Forrester, Daniel (Captain),
   1923.21; 1926.19; 1934.1;
   1942.5; 1969.18; 1972.38;
   1975.10, 24; 1976.10;
   1977.23; 1978.21, 31;
   1982.28; 1984.20
-Forrester, Marian, 1923.21, 41;
   1924.1, 4, 9, 12; 1925.36,
   38; 1926.19; 1927.20;
   1928.11; 1929.15; 1931.12,
   37, 49; 1934.1; 1940.9, 22;
   1948.26; 1955.11; 1961.23;
   1968.15, 22; 1972.38;
   1974.29; 1975.10, 24, 35;
   1977.23, 28; 1978.31; 1980.1;

(Death Comes for the Archbishop)
-Padre Martinez, controversy over
   Cather's portrayal of,
   1971.28; 1973.38; 1975.48,
   50; 1984.25
-Reviews of, 1927.1-6, 8-10, 12,
   14-15, 17, 19, 22, 25-26,
   30, 32-34, 36-41, 43-44;
   1928.8; 1932.32; 1933.11;
   1938.7; 1959.6; 1967.27;
   1982.38; 1984.89
"Death in the Desert, A,"
   1905.1-2; 1920.7
"Death in the Woods, A," 1976.16
"Dedicatory," 1964.26
Deerslayer, The, 1961.7
Defoe, Daniel, 1925.17; 1982.88
Delacroix, Eugène, 1982.9
Description, Cather's use of
-in fiction, 1912.8-9; 1913.6;
   1915.17; 1918.11; 1919.1;
   1923.49; 1930.5; 1931.47, 50;
   1934.2; 1935.41
-in poetry, 1903.4
Desert, 1974.66. See also
   Southwest; New Mexico
Detail, Cather's use of, 1915.14,
   18; 1916.2; 1922.16; 1925.9;
   1941.19
Determinism. See Naturalism
Dialogue, 1950.1; 1974.64
"Diamond Mine, The," 1921.4-5;
   1926.3; 1937.5
Dickens, Charles, 1971.12
Diction, 1912.10; 1915.16;
   1920.15; 1926.6; 1930.8;
   1960.2; 1974.64; 1977.14
Dionysian elements in Cather's
   fiction, 1952.8; 1979.31
Divine Comedy, The, 1966.18
Dos Passos, John, 1922.22;
   1961.8
"Double Birthday," 1973.74;
   1976.5
Double protagonist: male,
   female, 1983.15
Double self (other), dual
   persona, 1964.3; 1965.1;
   1968.1; 1969.21; 1973.62;
   1974.19; 1975.14; 1977.26;
   1980.18; 1981.29, 47;
   1982.59; 1983.28-29; 1984.81

Drama in Cather's works, 1912.9;
   1913.15; 1920.9; 1923.47;
   1926.8; 1933.20; 1939.7
Dreiser, Theodore, 1929.22;
   1932.36; 1957.1; 1971.26;
   1981.39
Drew, Fraser, 1982.76
Duality, dualism, doubling,
   1966.15; 1968.1; 1969.21;
   1976.26; 1981.29; 1982.46,
   66; 1983.2, 25

Early Stories of Willa Cather
-introduction to, 1957.2
-review of, 1957.6, 9, 22;
   1967.14
Early writing. See Writing
Earth, earth mother, goddess in
   Cather's work, 1972.24;
   1975.23; 1976.11; 1977.11;
   1978.15; 1982.3; 1983.31
East, East-West conflict,
   1966.12; 1973.25; 1974.13;
   1976.12; 1983.2, 35. See
   also West
"Easter Rabbit," 1968.4
Eclogues, 1974.56, 73
Ecstasy, 1975.8
Eddy, Mary Baker
-Cather's work on biography of,
   1939.1; 1963.14; 1971.13;
   1974.60; 1982.1, 11
-parallels with Cather, 1971.13
Edel, Leon, 1977.29; 1981.52
Eden. See Myth
Education, Cather's contribution
   to, view of, 1967.19;
   1973.76
Edwards, Alice, 1955.17
"El Dorado: A Kansas
   Recessional," 1901.2
"Eleanor's House," 1981.2
Elegaic elements in Cather's
   work, 1927.19; 1937.7;
   1942.5; 1947.38; 1948.18;
   1949.7; 1951.3; 1961.18;
   1962.18; 1978.6. See also
   Past; Nostalgia
Elemental. See Primitive
Eliot, T.S., 1949.2; 1958.15;
   1962.2; 1975.47; 1977.36
Ellis, Havelock, 1927.19

Horgan, Paul, 1964.17; 1975.22; 1976.9; 1981.21; 1984.22, 25
Horney, Karen, 1975.53
Houghton Mifflin, 1970.1
House Made of Dawn, 1980.37
House of Mirth, 1924.15
Housman, A.E., 1932.13; 1947.31; 1951.16; 1957.23; 1958.9, 18; 1965.36
Howe, Edgar Watson, 1979.1
Howells, William Dean, 1956.19; 1965.38; 1970.4; 1978.25
Howlett, William Joseph, 1955.1; 1982.71
Huckleberry Finn, 1959.4; 1961.7; 1966.6; 1970.29; 1973.81
Hugo, Victor Marie, 1972.21
Human relations. See Relationships
Humanism, 1932.8; 1973.36
Humanism, New, 1947.37
Humanity, human spirit, 1923.47; 1944.1, 3; 1966.21
Humor, 1916.2; 1947.28; 1972.11

Ibsen, Henryk, 1976.30
Ideal, idealism, idealist, 1923.18; 1927.22; 1932.19; 1934.8; 1937.16; 1949.4; 1955.15; 1957.20; 1958.3; 1960.9; 1962.2; 1965.16; 1966.15; 1968.1; 1969.5; 1970.23; 1971.16; 1972.21, 31-32; 1973.36; 1974.48, 54; 1975.25; 1976.3, 12, 29; 1978.2; 1979.45; 1982.2, 41, 88; 1984.84
Idyl(1)s, 1931.33; 1935.6; 1951.3
Images, imagery, 1927.26; 1951.3; 1952.6; 1959.8; 1960.9; 1962.4, 19; 1967.5; 1968.2; 1970.8; 1972.5, 11, 21; 1974.20; 1975.21; 1976.30; 1977.7, 36; 1978.34; 1979.35; 1981.48; 1982.3, 56, 63; 1984.38, 76. See also Symbol
-corn, 1977.19
-cricket, 1980.37
-family, 1976.29. See also Family
-flower, 1984.68
-light, and dark, 1984.1, 95

-plow, 1974.41; 1979.18; 1980.37
-religious. See Religion
-rock, 1976.29. See also Symbol
-water, 1977.1
-window, 1976.24
Imagination, 1905.9; 1908.1; 1920.14; 1922.15; 1923.53; 1927.14, 32; 1932.46; 1934.14; 1937.4; 1975.49; 1984.84
"Imaginative prose," 1927.13
Imitation, 1915.11; 1921.16
Immigrant, immigrants in Cather's experience and writing, 1913.4-5, 15; 1918.3; 1921.2-3; 1923.54; 1927.27; 1930.5, 13, 16; 1931.7; 1933.4; 1937.4; 1946.4, 6; 1947.32; 1949.11; 1951.14; 1952.15; 1954.4; 1958.5; 1959.13; 1960.15; 1962.3; 1965.2, 24; 1970.23; 1971.25; 1972.15; 1973.54; 1974.4; 1975.12; 1977.35; 1979.1, 8; 1980.13; 1981.20; 1982.34. See also Frontier; Pioneers; and discussions of Cather's stories and novels about immigrants, especially O Pioneers! and My Ántonia
Immigration, 1982.34
Immoraliste, L', 1982.64
Impressionism, 1972.35; 1982.56; 1984.1, 56, 87
Indian, 1980.37
Indian in the Southwest, Cather's portrayal of, 1927.12; 1940.15; 1947.13; 1953.25; 1956.1; 1961.12; 1966.7; 1973.56; 1975.7; 1976.32; 1977.34
Individualism, individuality, 1943.3; 1956.11; 1968.12; 1971.2, 16; 1974.34; 1975.47; 1976.13, 32; 1980.17, 19; 1981.29
Inductive approach to study of human behavior, 1980.19
Industrialism, 1933.7-8; 1973.46
Innocence, 1973.35; 1978.7
Inset narratives, 1970.8; 1971.11; 1972.35
Integration, 1968.1

Lady, The, 1965.9
Lagerlöf, Selma, 1939.4; 1947.32
Lamy, Jean Bautista, 1961.15;
    1976.9; 1980.40; 1981.21;
    1984.22, 25
Lamy of Santa Fe, 1975.22;
    1976.9; 1981.21
Land, landscape, Cather's treat-
    ment of and human relation-
    ship to, 1913.7, 12; 1918.2;
    1919.5; 1921.3; 1923.24, 33;
    1924.16; 1925.34; 1927.2, 16;
    1931.25; 1932.7; 1935.12;
    1936.4; 1937.16; 1938.7;
    1940.19; 1947.20; 1949.4;
    1950.22; 1951.7; 1955.9;
    1956.15; 1963.15; 1965.12,
    24; 1966.21, 25; 1968.3;
    1970.4; 1972.1, 22, 26;
    1973.4, 25, 84; 1974.4, 14,
    75, 79; 1975.36, 38;
    1976.14, 18; 1977.6, 19, 35;
    1978.5, 10; 1979.1-2, 19, 21;
    1981.1, 34, 42-43, 48;
    1982.3, 52, 57, 79, 91;
    1983.2, 8, 31; 1984.16, 76
Land-Nostalgia, 1967.11
Land-Philosophy, 1967.47-48;
    1968.29-31; 1970.22;
    1973.57-59; 1975.45
Landscape and the Looking Glass,
    The: Willa Cather's Search
    for Value, 1960.9
-response to, 1961.3; 1965.21
Language, 1912.6; 1915.11;
    1932.46; 1933.16; 1949.11,
    20; 1972.11. See also
    Diction; Style; etc.
Latin American criticism, 1949.10
Laurence, Margaret, 1971.29;
    1984.91
Lawrence, D.H., 1923.10; 1927.40
Legend, 1975.28; 1977.34;
    1978.27; 1981.35
Lesbianism, bisexuality,
    attachment to women, Cather's
    alleged, 1970.27; 1975.44;
    1982.40, 54, 69; 1983.11-12,
    25; 1984.15, 63, 94
Letters, Cather's. See also
    Cather
-published, 1927.7, 23; 1931.10;
    1933.21; 1947.16, 31;
    1961.3; 1968.5; 1973.81;
    1982.73; n.d.3

-unpublished, 1949.26; 1958.1;
    1971.4; 1974.51; 1979.34;
    1980.23, 49; 1984.15, 63
Lewis, Edith, 1956.17; 1973.9;
    1984.94
Lewis, Sinclair, 1921.17, 22;
    1922.9, 27-28, 33; 1923.56;
    1929.22; 1930.3, 7; 1931.29;
    1932.36; 1939.6; 1957.1;
    1958.13; 1961.2, 8; 1962.2;
    1963.10; 1964.1; 1971.7, 26;
    1975.46; 1978.10, 17;
    1984.67
Library edition of Cather's
    works, 1937.11; 1938.4;
    1960.8
Life of the Right Reverend
    Joseph P. Machebeuf, The,
    1955.1
Life, sense of in Cather's
    fiction, 1915.11; 1921.8,
    21; 1923.24; 1935.5; 1966.15
Lindsay, Mela Meisner, 1983.27
Lindsay, Vachel, 1979.12
London, Jack, 1932.7
Loneliness. See also Isolation
-atmosphere of, 1974.36
-of the artist, 1956.18
Longfellow, Henry W., 1938.4
"Lost generation," 1982.75
Lost Girl, The, 1923.10
Lost Lady, A
-Cather's comments about, 1925.27
-criticism of, 1927.20; 1928.11;
    1934.1; 1936.11; 1947.12;
    1948.26; 1961.17, 19; 1962.7;
    1964.1; 1965.5; 1968.22;
    1969.18; 1972.14, 29, 38;
    1974.18, 56, 68; 1975.10,
    21, 24, 33-34; 1976.10;
    1977.23; 1978.15, 31;
    1979.18, 26, 43; 1980.49;
    1981.7, 11, 32, 37, 50;
    1982.28, 63, 88; 1984.2, 20,
    53, 68
-film review of, 1925.16, 35;
    1934.12
-introduction to, 1961.23; 1980.2
-Japanese criticism of, 1967.18;
    1974.29
-mentioned, 1923.5; 1924.4, 7,
    9, 12; 1925.5, 8; 1926.8,
    13, 19, 22, 25, 31; 1927.16,

398

(Lost Lady, A)
    19; 1928.5, 9, 12, 14, 20;
    1929.3, 9; 1930.6, 8-9, 11;
    1931.49; 1932.37, 44;
    1933.14; 1936.14; 1937.5, 9,
    41; 1947.9, 11, 30, 33;
    1948.13; 1949.7-8; 1951.13;
    1952.4; 1953.24; 1955.11;
    1956.7; 1960.3; 1961.26;
    1963.10; 1965.9; 1973.41;
    1977.11, 38; 1980.38;
    1982.59; 1984.74
-reviews of, 1923.3, 5, 7, 9-10,
    12-13, 16-18, 21-23, 28-31,
    38, 41, 44-45, 49, 55;
    1924.1, 3, 8, 10, 15-16;
    1925.9; 1931.37; 1932.25;
    1962.10; 1967.25, 62;
    1973.11, 20, 68; 1974.45;
    1982.36; 1984.30
-Swedish mention of, 1925.5
Love, 1973.22; 1975.9, 26, 32,
    35-36; 1979.36; 1981.42;
    1982.3; 1983.11; 1984.39.
    See also Theme
Lucy Gayheart
-criticism of, 1936.11; 1962.7;
    1972.19; 1973.70; 1980.30;
    1981.12; 1982.55; 1984.35,
    76
-Japanese criticism of, 1981.27
-Japanese edition, 1949.28
-mentioned, 1937.5; 1942.4;
    1956.11; 1964.25; 1982.10
-reviews of, 1935.1, 3-11, 14,
    16-21, 23, 25-29, 31, 33-34,
    36-40; 1956.7; 1980.17;
    1981.46; 1984.11
Lyrical, lyricism, 1903.11;
    1923.2; 1932.43; 1933.24;
    1939.7; 1983.26

McClung, Isabelle, McClung
    family, 1932.13; 1959.3;
    1966.12; 1980.3; 1982.69,
    72; 1984.94
McClure, S.S., 1939.1; 1963.14;
    1964.4; 1970.26, 32;
    1973.82; 1982.32; 1983.24
McClure's Magazine, 1911.1;
    1973.82; 1982.32; 1983.24
McCullers, Carson, 1979.11
"Macon Prairie," 1923.19

Machebeuf, Father Joseph,
    1931.44; 1955.1
Madame Bovary, 1975.35; 1979.36;
    1984.53
Magee, Christopher, 1970.32
Main Street, 1975.46
Mallarmé, Stéphane, 1984.87
Man, male, men, masculine,
    1949.1; 1974.44; 1975.53;
    1976.28; 1977.16; 1978.21,
    31; 1979.6, 32; 1981.25, 42,
    46; 1982.2, 88; 1984.20, 24,
    38, 78. See also Narrators
-protagonists, 1979.15
Manfred, Frederick, 1971.17
Mannequin d'osier, Le, 1941.5;
    1960.5; 1980.39; 1984.17
Manuscript corrections, 1982.73
Marble Faun, The, 1975.33
Mares, E.A., 1984.25
Marriage, 1971.11; 1972.24;
    1975.31; 1976.15, 17;
    1982.28, 72; 1984.39, 94.
    See also Theme
Martin, St. Thérèse, compared to
    Cather, 1973.18; 1975.8
"Mary Gloster, The," 1948.21
Masochism, 1975.53
Masters, Edgar Lee, 1939.6;
    1978.17
Materialism, commercialism,
    1923.34, 45; 1935.13;
    1943.3; 1947.24; 1950.4, 22;
    1952.6; 1962.2, 6; 1963.19;
    1966.11, 14; 1968.37; 1969.6;
    1971.16; 1972.17; 1973.4, 39;
    1976.33; 1979.12; 1981.1;
    1983.2; 1984.23
Matriarchy, 1977.31
Maupassant, Guy de, 1905.1, 8
Media programs on Cather,
    1978.23, 35; 1980.33; 1984.62
Medievalism, 1975.24; 1978.14
Melville, Herman, 1949.5, 21;
    1962.2
Memory, 1948.10; 1949.13; 1952.3;
    1961.9, 20; 1965.2; 1966.15;
    1967.5; 1969.12; 1974.58;
    1980.31; 1983.28
Mencken, H.L., 1921.14, 17;
    1926.17; 1957.21; 1964.18;
    1967.17; 1968.23; 1973.56

Menuhin, Yehudi, 1955.7;
    1977.17; 1980.6, 26
Mérimée, Prosper, 1984.87
Mesa ideal, 1976.29. See also
    discussions of The Profes-
    sor's House
Mesa Verde, 1952.2; 1957.15;
    1973.9; 1981.38; 1984.77
Metaphor, 1982.27
Mexican, 1961.12; 1963.18;
    1966.7; 1977.34
Middle age, 1925.4, 11; 1935.36;
    1979.26; 1980.17; 1981.30;
    1982.86; 1984.39
Midland, The, 1975.41
Midwest, Middle West, Middlewest,
    1918.12; 1935.9, 12; 1937.3;
    1949.30; 1950.22; 1959.8;
    1973.51; 1974.10; 1975.46;
    1977.19
Milmine, Georgine, 1971.13;
    1974.60; 1982.1, 11
Miner, Mrs. J.L., 1921.20
Ministers, priests, Cather's
    portrayal of criticized,
    1923.14; 1973.38
Miracles of Perception: The Art
    of Willa Cather, 1980.6
Misérables, Les, 1972.21
"Miss Tempy's Watcher's," 1973.13
Mitchell, W.O., 1981.43
Moby Dick, 1949.5
Mode. See also each mode by name
-agrarian, 1979.35
-allegorical, 1976.3
-epic, 1975.49; 1981.10, 41
-lyrical, 1983.26
-pastoral, 1975.49
-satirical, 1975.49; 1981.10
Modernism, modern life, modern
    art, 1923.4; 1928.4, 9;
    1931.42; 1937.14; 1948.21;
    1962.7; 1967.21; 1973.33;
    1975.18; 1980.25; 1981.10;
    1983.18, 26
Modjeska, Helena, 1973.14
Moers, Ellen, 1977.29
Moll Flanders, 1982.88
Momaday, N. Scott, 1980.37
Mood, 1905.9; 1927.19; 1933.25;
    1938.3; 1940.7; 1966.25;
    1974.52

Morals, moral realism, moral
    vision, morality, 1923.10;
    1934.8; 1940.5; 1949.4, 21;
    1952.13; 1960.6; 1970.18;
    1972.30; 1975.9; 1984.53,
    62. See also Values
Morris, Wright, 1967.37
Mother figure in Cather's
    fiction, 1973.37; 1974.70;
    1976.18; 1979.6; 1980.45
Motif. See also Theme
-fall of man, 1975.33
-homosexuality, 1975.43
-nature, death, 1975.34
Music, in Cather's life and
    fiction, 1915.6; 1918.11;
    1931.42; 1935.6; 1938.8;
    1949.28; 1952.6; 1957.13;
    1964.8-9; 1965.5, 10-14;
    1966.7; 1968.18; 1970.14;
    1971.1; 1973.16; 1976.19;
    1983.8. See also titles of
    works that treat musicians
-in poetry, 1903.2, 5
Music in Willa Cather's Fiction,
    1968.18
Mutability, 1969.21; 1975.36;
    1977.23
My Ántonia
-bibliography of criticism,
    1974.55
-Cather's comments on, 1921.8,
    20; 1924.5
-Cliff's Notes, 1962.10
-criticism of, 1947.3, 27;
    1954.10; 1955.3; 1956.15;
    1958.11-12; 1959.13; 1961.7,
    16, 20; 1962.7, 17; 1964.1,
    8, 21; 1965.4, 27, 33;
    1966.19; 1968.22, 35;
    1969.1, 12; 1970.8, 12, 23,
    25, 29-30; 1971.11, 29;
    1972.14, 19, 26-27, 32-33;
    1973.17, 31, 39, 55, 60-61;
    1974.2, 10, 18, 56, 70-71;
    1975.21, 23, 31-32; 1976.11,
    14, 17; 1977.5, 16, 35;
    1978.5, 11, 14-15, 26;
    1979.6, 18, 23, 29, 42-43;
    1980.9-10; 1981.20, 29, 32,
    41, 43, 48-49; 1982.20, 40,
    50, 56, 64, 72, 77, 79;
    1983.15; 1984.8, 74, 79

Travel writing, 1982.71
"Treasure of Far Island, The,"
  1964.26
Troll Garden, The
-criticism of, 1953.7; 1963.3;
  1984.47
-introduction to, 1983.35
-mentioned, 1923.37; 1930.9;
  1931.5
-reviews of, 1905.1-9; 1906.1;
  1908.1; 1984.86
True, truth, 1913.3; 1927.32;
  1931.36; 1932.28; 1961.19;
  1974.46
Turgenev, Ivan, 1948.1; 1974.4
Turner, Frederick Jackson,
  1961.20; 1974.13
Twain, Mark. See Clemens,
  Samuel L.
"Two Friends," 1932.6, 8-10, 16,
  25, 35, 42; 1974.52

Ukranian criticism, 1972.15
"Uncle Valentine," 1973.74
Uncle Valentine and Other Stories
-introduction to, 1973.62
-mentioned, 1973.27
-reviews of, 1973.12, 27, 32,
  52, 70, 74; 1974.11, 57
Understanding, 1927.32; 1948.4
Undset, Sigrid, 1939.4; 1947.32
Unity, 1923.43; 1925.15, 26;
  1944.4
Universality of Cather's art,
  1936.14; 1940.10; 1944.1;
  1957.7; 1968.3; 1971.2;
  1972.11; 1974.28; 1979.22
Urban frontier, 1978.25
Urban life, urbanization,
  1973.61-62

Valkyr, 1913.17
Values, 1932.47; 1934.5; 1936.6;
  1940.10; 1942.5; 1948.1;
  1951.13; 1955.5; 1956.11,
  22; 1957.11; 1958.6; 1960.4,
  12; 1961.7; 1962.2, 12;
  1963.19; 1965.11; 1966.2, 12;
  1967.11; 1968.3, 37; 1969.6;
  1970.30; 1972.21, 33;
  1973.19, 59; 1974.38, 86;
  1975.18, 25, 45; 1976.5, 10,

33; 1978.18, 28, 35; 1979.7,
  36; 1981.10, 43; 1982.2, 50,
  88; 1983.17; 1984.62
-Cather's search for, 1957.20;
  1960.9; 1975.9
-for the artist, 1977.17
-moral and religious, 1934.8;
  1949.8
-rural over city, 1931.9;
  1979.35
-spiritual, 1932.31; 1934.14;
  1949.8; 1955.16; 1981.31
Van Geyzel, Leonard C., 1966.17
Varieties of Religious
  Experience, The, 1975.14
Vermorcken, Elizabeth Moorhead,
  1982.69
Vibert, Jehan George, 1978.36
Victorian, 1973.10; 1979.32
Vigil, Ralph H., 1975.48
Villains, Anglo-American,
  1979.29
Violence, 1967.37; 1970.8
Virgil, Vergil, Virgilian
-influence on Cather, 1932.12;
  1955.3; 1961.16; 1973.31;
  1974.73
-Eclogues, 1974.56, 73
-Georgics, The, 1955.3; 1974.56;
  1981.41
Virginia, 1903.6; 1930.16;
  1933.4; 1940.2, 8, 19, 23;
  1953.2; 1958.17; 1964.1;
  1971.17; 1973.67; 1979.3;
  1982.31; 1983.4, 22; n.d.2.
  See also reviews of
  Sapphira and the Slave Girl
Virginian, The, 1978.19; 1982.50
Vision, 1923.47; 1968.1
-pastoral, 1979.20
-Walt Whitman's cosmic, 1984.54
Vitality, human, 1980.2
"Voice," sound, oral qualities
  in Cather's fiction, 1974.24

Wagenknecht, Edward, 1953.23
"Wagner Matinee, A," 1938.8;
  1971.1, 16; 1974.30; 1975.13;
  1976.12; 1983.17
-Polish criticism of, 1971.16
Wagner, Wagnerian influence in
  Cather's fiction, 1963.3;
  1970.14; 1976.26

DATE DUE